AMERICA
AND THE MEDITERRANEAN WORLD
1776-1882

America and the Mediterranean World

1776-1882

BY JAMES A. FIELD, JR.

Princeton University Press

Princeton, New Jersey

1969

For Lila

Preface

This book is perhaps most simply described as an essay on some of the interstices in the history of America's relationship with the outer world.

The investigation began a good many years ago, when I happened on the fact that in the 1830's, after the catastrophe at Navarino, the rebuilding of the Ottoman Navy was carried on under the direction of an American naval constructor. Coming at a time when Turkey was again under pressure and was receiving important (and presumably unprecedented) American aid, the discovery had a certain topical interest and led to a first inquiry into the surrounding circumstances. From this investigation there developed a broadened curiosity about the possible interconnections of a number of generally known but little regarded episodes of American activity along the borders of nineteenth-century Europe, and about what these might signify for American attitudes toward the transatlantic world.

As the study progressed, these transatlantic goings-on, the unknown or forgotten as well as the remembered, seemed to sort themselves into four principal categories. The first of these was concerned with efforts to foster a profitable and mutually beneficial foreign trade. The second, closely allied, centered on naval matters, and on the peacetime employment of the Navy as an instrument of policy. The third concerned the origins and vigorous growth of an overseas missionary movement dedicated to bringing the light to those who dwelt in darkness. The fourth, related in greater or lesser degree to all the others, involved the workings of a kind of secularized missionary spirit, as shown in a variety of efforts (again with the assumption of mutual benefit) on behalf of freedom, the self-determination of peoples, and the modernization of traditional societies. All these subjects have a fairly obvious relation to the role of America and the Americans in the world; none, at least in the transatlantic context, seems to have received much attention in histories of American foreign relations.

There is, of course, a general agreement that maritime commerce was of vital importance to the young republic. The painful exclusion from the British West Indies, no less than the words of Washington and Jefferson, proves the point; the traditional emphasis on the China trade confirms it. But if the voyage of the *Empress of China* and the discoveries of Robert Gray are the important mileposts, leading by way of the West Coast fur trade and continental expansion to ultimate involvement in Asia, whatever led the pacifistic, antinaval, anticommercial Jeffersonians to war with Barbary? What was the importance to the Republican party of unhindered access to the Mediterranean? Was the Tripolitan War the wrong war in the wrong place at the wrong time, or did it pay off? What were, in fact, the consequences of the struggle?

One might perhaps argue from the history of subsequent naval operations—the conquest of California, the opening of Japan, the Battle of Manila Bay—that war with Tripoli was just a small aberration, and that transatlantic activity was quickly abandoned in favor of more appropriate policies. Yet the middle of the nineteenth century found the U.S. Navy accomplishing the first scientific survey of (of all places) the Dead Sea, and ferrying Hungarian revolutionaries westward from Turkey. In 1904, when Perdicaris was captured by the Moroccan bandit Raisuli, the administration of Theodore Roosevelt had four battleships and eight cruisers in the Mediterranean. Where did these vessels come from? How were they available when needed? What conceivable purpose, to anticipate for a moment, moved an isolated and westering United States to keep a squadron in the Mediterranean? How, with no territorial holdings in the area, was it possible to support and maintain a naval force at such a distance?

Once more the search for answers turns up new questions. The investigator of commercial and naval activity in the Mediterranean shortly discovers the existence, from an early date, of a sizable American missionary effort. But here again details are hard to come by: more even than the history of maritime trade and peacetime Navy, missionary history has been neglected. The domestic historian may remember Marcus Whitman and perhaps the Cherokee cases; those looking outward, noting the missionary successes in Hawaii and Peter Parker's large ideas about Formosa, may presume a natural connection with "imperialism," the annexation of the Philippines, and the origins of the China Lobby. But this is scarcely helpful in explaining the existence of Robert College, or Wilson's unwillingness to go to war with Turkey in 1917, or American concern for the starving Armenians. Nor does it go far to answer some larger questions. Why, with so much to do at home, did nineteenth-century Americans feel compelled to labor so energetically for the evangelization of the world? Why have their twentieth-century descendants persisted so diligently in efforts, paralleled by no other nation, for its improvement?

From a consideration of the commercial, naval, and evangelical questions, one is drawn back to the Sultan's naval constructor. Was he a unique instance of the early export of American techniques, or were there others? Why did the Sultan go beyond the more readily available Europeans to employ an American? Why, at a later date, should the Viceroy of Egypt have staffed his army with American officers? Given the important role of the military in underdeveloped countries, what was the significance of these contributions to the welfare of Turks and Egyptians? Were there other techniques, political or scientific, which seemed transferable from the most rapidly developing of underdeveloped countries to other societies seeking to modernize themselves?

So the trail led backward and forward until what had first seemed isolated and unrelated events came to appear parts of a connected history. A network of activities began to manifest itself, possessed (as Dr. Johnson would have it) of intersections as well as interstices. But this development merely raised the further problem of how to reconcile this transatlantic past with the authorized American version of escape from Europe, westward expansion, and advance into the Far East. Was it possible to discover an intellectual framework that would accommodate both the traditional story and the forgotten history without doing too much violence to either? Would such a framework, if discoverable, turn out to be merely a latter-day construct, or could it be shown to represent the views of contemporaries?

It will be apparent to the reader of these pages that I think that such a framework does exist, that it was pretty fully articulated in the first generation of independence, and that it is still in large measure subscribed to. The passage of time has, of course, brought geographical and other shifts of emphasis and has altered the meanings of some of the formulations. On various occasions the pressure of events has produced an uncomfortable realization that the theory, presumably so elegantly unified, in fact contains hidden contradictions. But in remarkable degree, it seems to me, American doctrine concerning the country's proper role in the world is still the doctrine of the American Enlightenment.

This is not, of course, to say that nothing has changed since 1776, but merely to suggest that such change as has occurred has been less in the area of theory than in that of structure and implementation. In this context two principal developments may be noted. The first, paralleling the course of events in the domestic sphere, is the shift of functions from the private to the public sector, the increasing politicization of foreign affairs, which has seen the transformation of privateer into naval officer, of missionary into Peace Corps functionary, and of private merchant into governmental lending authority. The second and more difficult adjustment, still by no means comfortably resolved, concerns the accommodation of great and ever-growing national power to an inherited body of doctrine that sees power as the enemy. These developments, of course, have been most evident in the twentieth century, but their roots can be discerned within the time span covered by this book.

Whether and to what extent these views are persuasive, the reader must judge. But of one thing the author can be reasonably certain: that a net so widely cast will have more than its own share of interstices. I should perhaps take this chance to say that the viewpoint of the book is American, and that while I have been at pains not to do injustice to Greek or Turk or Arab, my main concern has been with American actions and American aims. Still, it seems hardly probable that an essay of this sort can avoid being subject to correction and improvement, and I shall be very grateful if those detecting errors will point them out to me.

One area, it may as well be said, in which accuracy (or at least agreement) is impossible is that of the spelling of proper names, whether of persons or of places. Place names, in the modern world, are writ in water, a fact of which the replacement of Constantinople by Istanbul affords a prime example. But in a region of such cultural and linguistic complexity as the Near East, and in a time of increasingly precise and specialized scholarship, the troubles are compounded. Should Arabic be transliterated after the French fashion? Or in the English manner? Or in the style of the modern specialist? Is it to be Mehmed, or Mohammed, or Mehemet, or Muhammad? Assouan or Aswan? Tewfik or Tawfiq? In dealing with this intractable problem I have modernized in a few arbitrary instances, as in substituting Urmia for the missionary mouthful Oroomiah. But in general I have followed old-fashioned usage and have kept the names as they appear in the sources: the missionaries labor at Constantinople, the Egyptians invade Abyssinia. Insofar as it can be rationalized, this procedure rests on two assumptions: that the older names are more likely to be recognizable to the general reader than are the modern versions; and that in Egypt, where the issue is perhaps most difficult, the old transliterations (Mehemet Ali, Assouan) provide a secondary gain in their indication of the extent of nineteenth-century French cultural penetration.

Over the years that I have been working on these matters I have acquired many obligations. I am grateful to colleagues and students who have listened to, or read, or criticized successive versions. Still more fundamental, perhaps, is my debt to those who assisted me with research problems and who typed and retyped the manuscript. I owe special thanks to the late Edward Meade Earle, who pioneered in the study of American Near Eastern activity and who very generously passed on to me his accumulated notes. Howard Williams of the Swarthmore College Library has been most helpful in the pursuit and capture of elusive source material. I have profited from the skills and kindnesses of the staffs of the National Archives and of the libraries of Harvard College, the U.S. Naval War College, the University of Pennsylvania, and the Crozer Theological Seminary. I wish to thank the American Board of Commissioners for Foreign Missions (now merged in the United Church Board for World Ministries) for the privilege of working in and quoting from their archives, and the Organization of American Historians for permission to abstract from an article of mine published in the *Mississippi Valley Historical Review*. Without the opportunities for uninterrupted research provided by the generous leave policy of Swarthmore College, the project could hardly have been undertaken; its progress has been greatly assisted by grants from the Fund for the Advancement of Education, the Social Science Research Council, and the American Council of Learned Societies.

JAMES A. FIELD, JR.

Swarthmore, Pennsylvania

Contents

MAPS

AMERICA
AND THE MEDITERRANEAN WORLD
1776-1882

This great american revolution, this recent political phaenomenon of a new sovereignty arising among the sovereign powers of the earth, will be attended to and contemplated by all nations. Navigation will carry the american flag around the globe itself; and display the thirteen stripes and new constellation at *bengal* and *canton*, on the *indus* and *ganges*, on the *whang-ho* and the *yang-tse-kiang*; and with commerce will import the wisdom and literature of the east. That prophecy of *Daniel* is now literally fulfilled— *ishotatu rabbim vetrabbeh hadaugnt*—there shall be an universal travelling *too and fro, and knowledge shall be increased.* This knowledge will be brought home and treasured up in america: and being here digested and carried to the highest perfection, may reblaze back from america to europe, asia, and africa, and illumine the world with truth and liberty.

Ezra Stiles, *The United States Elevated to Glory and Honor,* 1783

CHAPTER I

Novus Ordo Seclorum

1. The Back of the Great Seal

ON 20 JUNE 1782, three months to the day after the fall of Lord North's government, the Congress of the United States approved the design for a seal which had been placed before it by its secretary, Charles Thomson. It had taken as long to settle upon a design as it had to win the war: the committee to prepare the seal had been set up by congressional resolution late in the afternoon of the Fourth of July, 1776. Yet if this delay might have seemed excessive, the passage of time had at least confirmed the usefulness of the enterprise, and had given meaning to the Virgilian mottoes, "Annuit Coeptis" and "Novus Ordo Seclorum," which appeared, the latter in American-ized orthography, at top and bottom of the reverse.

Describing the proposed reverse of the seal, with its uncompleted thirteen-tiered pyramid of states surmounted by the eye of Provi-dence, Thomson observed that "the date underneath it is that of the Declaration of Independence, and the words under it signify the beginning of the new American Æra, which commences from that date."[1] From his wording it remains unclear whether the adjective "American" is to be construed as geographically limiting or as broadly descriptive. Much of American history is implicit in this question, and the history of American history appears to favor the former view. But this attitude would seem to do less than justice to the American genius for generalizing from American experience. In any event there is impressive evidence that to many of Thom-son's contemporaries the larger reading was the true one.

The new order of ages, as befitted a creation of the eighteenth century, was founded on a theory of politics as simple, elegant, and universal as Newton's laws. It was based upon the self-evident truths stated in the Declaration of Independence, the document which John Quincy Adams rightly described as "the fountain of all our

---

[1] Gaillard Hunt, *The History of the Seal of the United States* (Washington, D.C., 1909). Those unfamiliar with the reverse of the seal will find it conveniently repro-duced on the back of the dollar bill.

3

municipal institutions."² All men, says the Declaration, are created equal and endowed with certain unalienable rights; it is to secure these rights that governments are instituted among men. From this statement, then a scientific fact and still an article of faith, flows all the rest. Insofar as the statement is true, or can be made to become so, it applies not merely to the inhabitants of British North America but to men everywhere.

If all men are created equal, if they are endowed with unalienable rights, and if the purpose of government is less to govern than to secure those rights, there follow two political conclusions of primary importance. The first is that all peoples have the right of self-determination, of defense against the enemy without, which entitles them if they so desire to assume a separate and equal station among the nations of the earth. The exercise of this right made the American Revolution. The second conclusion, which defends against the enemy within, is the idea of minimum government. "Government," said Paine, "like dress, is the badge of lost innocence." The Americans, a virtuous people, have consequently always been political nudists, and the Declaration marked the beginning of the first consistent effort in history to make government wither away. The revolution which gave America her separate and equal station was directed not merely against government from without but against too much government; too much government by the states under the Articles of Confederation brought forth the Constitution with its manifold restrictions on state powers; fear of too much government under the new dispensation led to the adoption of the Bill of Rights. That government should be government by consent, and that the less there is of it the better, these too are ideas not subject to the restriction of national frontiers.

The American Revolution was, in essence, a war in favor of the theory and against the practice of the eighteenth century. Although it was the Americans who first attempted to act upon the great ideas of the Enlightenment, and although the Declaration is the most striking single statement of this philosophy, the underlying preconceptions were the common coin of advanced European thought. The philosophy which throughout the century had concerned itself on one side of the Channel with the rights of man and on the other with the opportunities of Englishmen was a philosophy of the ris-

² To R. C. Anderson, 27 May 1823, W. C. Ford (ed.), *Writings of John Quincy Adams* (New York, 1913-17), VII, 460.

ing bourgeoisie, and while its central focus was on the internal regulation of states, its assumptions regarding the nature of man had important consequences for foreign affairs. Rationalist and libertarian in domestic matters, it was also by implication internationalist, in its emphasis on the free individual and the common attributes of humanity, in its belief in the natural order, and in its opposition to the artificial structures of government which both oppressed and divided mankind. Inevitably, in view of its origins, this philosophy was strongly economic in motivation, which is to say that it was deeply concerned with commerce, and in this sense, again, international or antinational in bias.

The views of the radical European thinkers as to the proper nature of the relations between states were of course well known to Americans of the revolutionary generation, whose independence, indeed, was both cause and consequence of crises in transatlantic affairs. In France, the forcing-house of eighteenth-century thought, the development of this subject had proceeded along two main lines. On the one hand were the Physiocrats, to whom economics was all: only bring about unhindered exchange of goods, only establish free trade, and the artificialities of international intercourse would disappear. Mutual benefits would lead to mutual prosperity, would end the antagonisms of states and bring about the reign of peace. Contrasted with these were the thinkers of a more political inclination such as Condorcet and Rousseau, the one advocating in the interest of peace an increased popular control over foreign relations, the other wishing to gain that end through a second social contract which would remove the nations from their state of nature and lead to world federation. Similar if less generalized ideas had developed in England, where pamphleteers had attacked first the Hanoverian entanglement and then the policy of continental alliances, and had argued that a trading nation should hold aloof from all particular connections and "avoid all Treaties except such as tend toward promoting Commerce or Manufactures." Throughout this body of thought in both countries ran a thread of hostility to the diplomatic and military apparatus of the great mercantilist states, and to their system of alliances, wars, and balances of power. Internal perfection and external peace, not power, were the goals. The ideal government lay not in Paris or London or Madrid, but rather in Venice or Holland, in states, that is to say, which followed their rational and calculable commercial interests, and so prospered peacefully.

5

The close correspondence between this kind of thinking on international affairs and the progress of the American experiment is clear enough. As the British by their Act of Settlement had guarded against the threat of continental involvement presented by the Hanoverian connection, so the Americans severed their relation with the British crown and thus, presumably, the link with Europe's wars. Having exercised their right of self-determination, the thirteen colonies did in fact remove themselves from the state of nature by federalizing. A measure of popular control over foreign relations was provided, under the Constitution, by the division of responsibility for diplomatic and military matters between an elected executive and an elected legislative. To the advanced thinkers of Europe a removal of commercial barriers and an increase of commercial intercourse seemed highly desirable; to the new nation an expanded commerce was a matter of life and death and a forward commercial policy unavoidable.[3]

Yet if the broad lines of American practice inevitably followed European precepts, the origins of the new society were in certain respects unique. It had a definite starting point in time: it was born on a Fourth of July, in the latter part of the eighteenth century. The circumstances of its birth were such as to force the thinking of the era deep into the national subconscious; this thinking was validated by the most conclusive of proofs, that of musket and ball. By 1782 an uncompromising theory of politics, universally applicable, had been married to the stubborn fact of military success. The cause of all mankind had produced its sacred texts, its propaganda, and its apostles, and had been sanctified by the blood of martyrs. All this gave to the new nation an origin more akin to those of the great missionary religions than to those of other nations, whose beginnings were lost in the distant past.

The parallel was not unnoticed by contemporaries. In a poem of 1778 celebrating *The Prospect of Peace* which arose with the conclusion of the French Alliance, Joel Barlow compared America's

[3] Felix Gilbert, "The English Background of American Isolationism in the Eighteenth Century," 1 *William and Mary Quarterly*, 138-60; *idem*, "The 'New Diplomacy' of the Eighteenth Century," 4 *World Politics*, 1-38; *idem*, *To the Farewell Address* (Princeton, 1961). J. F. Rippy and Angie Debo, "The Historical Background of the American Policy of Isolation," 9 *Smith College Studies in History*, 71-165; P. A. Varg, *Foreign Policies of the Founding Fathers* (Michigan State, 1963), pp. 1-10.

new birth of freedom to the star seen over Bethlehem, and looked forward to the second coming:

> So eastern kings shall view th'unclouded day
> Rise in the West and streak its golden way:
> *That* signal spoke a Saviour's humble birth,
> *This* speaks his long and glorious reign on earth![4]

One quite natural result of all this was the growth of an American hagiography and the apotheosis of the revolutionary generation. Another was the development of an enduring confidence in the universal applicability of the fathers' counsel. Americans, someone has said, talk with their nation's founders as if they were still alive. The first years of independence witnessed the development of a body of doctrine which would persist from the period of primitive origination into very different times and circumstances and would provide, for both domestic aspiration and the conduct of foreign affairs, the frame of reference within which subsequent generations of Americans would maneuver in response to the recurrent crises of human existence.

2. *The Prospects of Futurity*

The views of the revolutionary generation have of course been given their due share of attention by later ages, but this attention has been increasingly concentrated on the utterances of the makers of governmental policy. Since the War for Independence was among other things a first step in a continuing effort to escape from the stream of European history, and was followed by neutrality in the French Revolution, by abrogation of the French Alliance, and by efforts to settle problems of neutral rights by novel methods of peaceful coercion, the conclusions which flow from this political approach have inevitably an isolationist bias. As the aim in constitution-making was to insulate the citizen from the enemy within, the power of the state, so in foreign policy it was to insulate him from the threat posed by the great monarchies of Europe. Political isolationism was thus the external counterpart of the Bill of Rights, seeking to limit the capabilities of governments in the interest of the liberties of individuals. This attempt at insulation, it should be noted,

[4] Joel Barlow, *The Prospect of Peace: A Poetical Composition Delivered in Yale College, at the Public Examination of the Candidates for the Degree of Bachelor of Arts; July 23, 1778* (New Haven, 1778).

was functional rather than geographical in nature, aiming at protection from the arbitrary exercise of European power rather than at separation from Europeans.

But in so undergoverned and underadministered a country, where many of what were elsewhere considered powers of government were reserved to the people, the political texts tell only a part of the story. They do, it is true, point the way toward the desired mixture of national political disentanglement and individual commercial forwardness: to Paine the fact that Europe was America's market for trade made partial connections with particular European countries undesirable; to Washington the great rule of conduct was to extend commercial relations with foreign nations while avoiding political involvement; in the same breath Jefferson called for commerce with all and entangling alliances with none. Clearly, secession from the European political system did not involve secession from the human race. Nevertheless, the revolution of 1776 had gone far beyond the mere gaining of political independence and creation of a successor government: as the inscription on the seal proclaimed, it had inaugurated a new era. In this new dispensation the limitation of the powers of government opened up new areas for individual activity, abroad as well as at home, and minimized the distinction between foreign and domestic affairs. In such circumstances the anticipated relationships between Americans and their fellow men across the seas, if politically negligible, had other far-reaching implications. For evidence as to the nature of these hoped-for relationships one must go beyond the speeches and writings of the statesmen to a consideration of the literary sources of the day.

It was a Scot, not an American, who observed that if he could make a nation's songs he cared not who made her laws, but the Scots, too, had been concerned with problems of alien rule. Sermons as well as songs were important in late-eighteenth-century America, and while the politicians were busy with war-making and constitution-making and lawmaking, poets and preachers were working out the ecumenical meanings of the American experience and charting the course of the "new American Æra." Freer to aspire than those in responsible official position, they could lift their eyes above the day-to-day struggle for survival and discern the mission of America,

> The task, for angels great, in early youth
> To lead whole nations in the walks of truth,

Shed the bright beams of knowledge on the mind,
For social compact harmonize mankind.[5]

The destiny of America, it appeared, was to lead the way into the future peaceful world of free individuals and federalized states by political innovation, the expansion of commerce, and scientific development.

Just as European believers in the idea of progress, rejecting what had gone before, came to concern themselves increasingly with the prospects of their posterity, so Americans, rebelling against Europe, looked forward to the ages yet to come. Since the history of the past was but that of the crimes and follies of mankind, the history of the future took on increasing meaning. Such anticipations received literary expression as early as 1771 in *The Rising Glory of America*, an epic poem composed by two members of the graduating class of Princeton, Philip Freneau and Hugh Henry Brackenridge. Twelve years later, with revolution accomplished and peace approaching, Ezra Stiles, the president of Yale, embraced the theme in a notable election sermon entitled *The United States Elevated to Glory and Honor*.

Looking back at the development of the American settlements, and in particular at the epochal events of recent years, Stiles saw the present condition of "God's American Israel" as the fulfillment of the vision of Noah and the realization of Deuteronomy 26:19: "to make thee high above all nations which he hath made, in praise, and in name, and in honour; and that thou mayest be an holy people unto the Lord thy God." Looking to the future, he foresaw a population growing to fill the continent, and a society based on liberty, a wide diffusion of property, a purified Christianity, and a democratical polity. On this continent the arts, transplanted from Europe and Asia, would flourish in greater perfection and with augmented luster; from it ships would circle the globe, bringing back the riches of the Indies and "illuminating the world with TRUTH and LIBERTY." Here, in America, lay the future. The world would never be the same again.[6]

This was the authentic American dream. But Stiles was of the older generation, and it was three younger sons of Yale—Timothy

---

[5] Joel Barlow, *The Vision of Columbus, A Poem in Nine Books* (Hartford, 1787), p. 204.

[6] Ezra Stiles, *The United States Elevated to Glory and Honor* (New Haven, 1783), pp. 7, 69.

Dwight of the class of 1769, David Humphreys of the class of 1771, and Joel Barlow of the class of 1778—who were to become pre-eminent among the patriotic visionaries of the first years of independence. All had begun to write before Stiles spoke: as a chaplain in the revolutionary army Dwight had already embodied the vision in his song "Columbia," as had Barlow in his Yale commencement poem on *The Prospect of Peace* and Humphreys in his "Poem on the Happiness of America." And as the years went by, in work after work illumined by their belief that the American Revolution had ushered in a new golden age, the three set forth their hopes for the future of their country and of the world.

Although deeply concerned with the creation of a national literature, these Connecticut Wits were no closet scholars. Counting as they did among their activities the study of divinity and service in the Revolution, commercial ventures and diplomatic missions, the administration of a college, speculation in western lands, and travel throughout the Western world, they came close to epitomizing the experience of their generation. After serving in the Revolution as Washington's military secretary, Humphreys lived out a useful life as diplomat, and as pioneer in efforts to improve American agricultural and industrial techniques. Following a distinguished career in the ministry, Dwight expired in the odor of sanctity as president of Yale, while Barlow, after a notable life on three continents, died on the frozen plains of Poland while on a diplomatic mission for the Madison administration. Like their lives, their politics were diverse; for Humphreys became a firm Federalist and Dwight a fierce one, while Barlow developed into an equally radical democrat. But despite all differences, much remained common to their thought and to their aspirations for their country's future. And if the thinking of such very worldly philosophers seems visionary, it is but the greater testimony to the power of the vision.[7]

So far as the fundamental nature of the "new American Æra" was concerned, it seemed most easily understood when contrasted with all that had gone before. It was of course possible to give credit to the European philosophers who had created the intellectual climate of freedom:

> In Europe's realms a school of sages trace
> The expanding dawn that waits the Reasoning Race; ...

[7] Leon Howard, *The Connecticut Wits* (Chicago, 1943).

> Of these the first, the Gallic sages stand,
> And urge their king to lift an aiding hand.[8]

"Great Louis" himself could be described as an apostle of self-determination, and praised for espousing "the liberal, universal cause," but the end result of both Gallic thought and Gallic action was to bring into existence a society almost wholly different from that which gave it birth: new as opposed to old, American as opposed to European, commercial not military, virile not decadent, free not slave.

> Mark modern Europe with her feudal codes,
> Serfs, villains, vassals, nobles, kings, and gods,
> All slaves of different grades . . . .
> Too much of Europe, here transplanted o'er
> Nursed feudal feelings on your tented shore,
> Brought sable serfs from Afric.[9]

And again,

> Ah then, thou favor'd land, thyself revere!
> Look not to Europe for examples just
> Of order, manners, customs, doctrines, laws, . . .
> Thrice wretched lands! where wealth and splendour glow,
> And want, and misery, in dire contrast show; . . .
> There, in sad realms of desolating war,
> Fell Despotism ascends his iron car . . . .
> One wide Aceldama the region lies, . . .
> See this glad world remote from every foe,
> From Europe's mischiefs, and from Europe's woe! . . .
> Here Truth, and Virtue, doom'd no more to roam,
> Pilgrims in eastern climes, shall find their home; . . .
> See the wide realm in equal shares possess'd!
> How few the rich, or poor! How many bless'd![10]

The trouble with Europe, quite simply, was that it had a past. History, as Barlow and the others read it, taught that the Ages of

---

[8] Joel Barlow, *The Columbiad, A Poem* (Philadelphia, 1807), vii, lines 13-14, 33-34.

[9] Barlow, *Columbiad*, viii, lines 377-79, 383-85.

[10] Timothy Dwight, *Greenfield Hill* (New York, 1794), i, lines 233-35; vii, lines 177-78, 287-88, 299, 87-88, 77-78, 126-27. Speaking on the Fourth of July, 1821, J. Q. Adams referred to "that Aceldama, the European world." W. H. Seward, *Life and Public Services of John Quincy Adams* (Auburn, N.Y., 1849), p. 132.

Hierarchy and Chivalry had imposed on that unhappy continent a feudal system and a state church, the one intended to establish order but perverted into a system for the control of power by the idle, the other the most powerful engine of state for the debasement of human nature. These survivals of a Gothic age had successfully perpetuated "the aristocratical principle, that men must be governed by fraud," so that although natural enmity did not exist and no popular offensive war had been waged since the conquest of the Sabines, wars remained an effective part of the machinery for the subjection of the individual. It was the triumph of America to have removed these shackles of tyranny and superstition. The disappearance of "Fell Despotism," the ending of the slavery of degree, the abolition of the established church, would free "the Reasoning Race" and bring science and genius westward to a new and better home. In contrast to the violent history of Europe,

> A new creation waits the western shore,
> And reason triumphs o'er the pride of power.

If the trouble with Europe was history, in America history would have another chance.[11]

This removal of the historic restraints on the individual was fundamental. To an age that subscribed to the psychology of Locke and that saw causal connection between elevated foliage and the neck of the amiable giraffe, environment was all. Society itself was the cause of all crimes; the perfectibility of man was a truth of practical and universal importance; the individual was perfectible by education, and "nations are educated like individual infants. They are what they are taught to be."

To Barlow the whole art of politics lay in the substitution of moral for physical force. Evils could be abolished and men restrained from injuring each other by the elimination of the forms through which oppression had historically worked. Institutionally, this presupposed governments founded on the equality of the individual and on free elections. The primary object of such a government was to provide an environment suitable to individual development: by frugality to maintain allegiance and avoid the oppressive engine of the public debt, by improvement of land and water communications to unite dispersed settlements in common enterprise, and by education to ful-

---

[11] Joel Barlow, *Advice to the Privileged Orders* (London and Paris, 1792-93), I, 21-24, 48, 58, 69-70; II, 90-91; *The Prospect of Peace*.

fill the freeman's "right of being taught the management of the power to which he is born." So much would vindicate internal liberty; more was undesirable. As to the precise form that political institutions were to take, this was a matter to be decided by the people immediately concerned: "If the Algerines or the Hindoos were to shake off the yoke of despotism, and adopt ideas of equal liberty, they would that moment be in a condition to frame a better government for themselves, than could be framed for them by the most learned statesmen in the world."

If such an emphasis on self-determination seemed to promise fragmentation, and ran counter to the observable historic tendency toward the development of larger political units, a solution was at hand. This was the principle of federalism, which provided the answer to the administration of vast areas while maintaining the necessary close local connection between the people and their governments. In this, as in the fundamental matter of local government, the American experience lit the way, and when revolution next broke out Barlow urged the French to subdivide their land and federate with the other revolutionary republics in a United States of Europe. For nations, as for individuals, absolute independence was a chimera, but federalizing would make for equity within and for security without. Only with the world organized as a league of peoples would the plans for perpetual peace ever work.

> Each land shall imitate, each nation join
> The well-based brotherhood, the league divine,
> Extend its empire with the circling sun,
> And band the peopled globe beneath its federal zone.[12]

Such, in the realm of politics, were the simple universal answers which America offered to the world:

> Based on its rock of Right your empire lies,
> On walls of wisdom let the fabric rise;
> Preserve your principles, their force unfold,
> Let nations prove them and let kings behold.
> EQUALITY, your first firm-grounded stand;
> Then FREE ELECTION; then your FEDERAL BAND;

[12] Joel Barlow, *A Letter to the National Convention of France* (New York, [1793]), pp. 20, 31-53, 55, 58-62; *Letters from Paris* (London, 1800), pp. 41-44, 48-50; *Oration Delivered at Washington, July Fourth, 1809* (Washington, 1809), pp. 6, 9-10; *Columbiad*, IX, lines 701-4.

> This holy Triad should forever shine
> The great compendium of all rights divine, . . .
> Till men shall wonder (in these codes inured)
> How wars were made, how tyrants were endured.[13]

This would perhaps take time, yet even Dwight thought it possible that kings would some day "esteem it more desirable to tread the pleasing, beneficial walks of science and justice, than to sacrifice thousands of lives, and millions of treasure, to secure the possession of islands or deserts, designed by Providence as an inheritance for serpents and owls." During the Revolution the successes of Hyder Ali against the British in India had seemed encouraging, while Barlow, at a later date, observing with pleasure that the "honest and industrious" French mobs were working out the answers to the problems that history had inflicted on their country, foresaw further improvement as those "formerly dukes and marquisses are now exalted to farmers, manufacturers, and merchants." Belief in the inevitability of progress was strong, whether in the lay terms of the rationalists or the chiliastic ones of the divines. "It is the tendency of human affairs," wrote Dwight, "to be constantly progressing towards what may be termed natural perfection," and he saw in the American Revolution, which had produced the first consenting government and a society without an established church and friendly to genius, an event directly related to the coming millennium. "Could stupid heathens, or hardened Jews, sit silent and unmoved, under such mighty interpositions as those, by which Providence hath distinguished this land?"[14]

Mighty the interpositions surely were; local in significance they certainly were not. Neither believers in reason nor believers in God could conceive of the American Revolution as a revolution for one country only. "America," wrote Humphreys, "after having been concealed for so many ages from the rest of the world, was probably discovered, in the maturity of time, to become the theater for displaying the illustrious designs of Providence, in its dispensations to the human race."

> All former empires rose, the work of guilt,
> On conquest, blood, or usurpation built:

[13] Barlow, *Columbiad*, viii, lines 395-406.
[14] [Timothy Dwight], *A Sermon, preached at Northampton, on the twenty-eighth of November, 1781* (Hartford, n.d.); Barlow, *Advice*, i, 8n., 47.

> But we, taught wisdom by their woes and crimes,
> Fraught with their lore, and born to better times;
> Our constitutions formed on freedom's base,
> Which all the blessings of all lands embrace;
> Embrace humanity's extended cause,
> A world our empire, for a world our laws.[15]

The commencement of the "new American Æra" had thus brought a new birth of freedom, and a society founded upon the self-evident truths. A political framework designed to secure the unalienable rights had been erected on freedom's base. "Annuit Coeptis" had been written across the top of the seal in acknowledgment of the mighty interpositions: "He has favored our undertaking." But the dispensation intended for the human race encompassed only the thirteen states, and under the favoring eye of Providence the federal pyramid remained incomplete. Doubtless the tendency of human affairs to progress toward natural perfection had been demonstrated, but there was still some distance to go. It was fortunate that a chief mechanism for this progress had also been provided by the Deity. This mechanism was an expanded commerce.

Timothy Dwight, who did not consider himself a rationalist, thought that the increase of commercial intercourse would expand the mind, lessen prejudice, confer reciprocal benefits, and bring about improved ideas of civil polity. Barlow, who welcomed the label, held that a perfect liberty of commerce was an indubitable right of man. "It has long been the opinion of the Author," he wrote, "that such a state of peace and happiness as is foretold in scripture and commonly called the millennial period, may rationally be expected to be introduced without a miracle." The civilizing of the world was a matter of three principal stages: the population of its various parts, the development of mutual knowledge on the part of the various nations, and the increase of their "imaginary wants . . . in order to inspire a passion for commerce." The progress of discovery indicated that the second stage was nearing completion, and with the opening of the third would come an accelerated progress toward natural perfection: "The spirit of commerce is happily calculated by the Author of wisdom to open an amicable intercourse between all countries, to soften the horrors of war, to enlarge the field of science and specula-

---

[15] David Humphreys, "Poem on the Future Glory of America," *Miscellaneous Works* (New York, 1804), p. 47; "Poem on the Happiness of America," *ibid.*, p. 30.

tion, and to assimilate the manners, feelings, and languages of all nations."[16]

Here was the Physiocratic view of commerce raised to a higher American power, by necessity as well as by inclination. Commercial restriction had been a principal cause of revolutionary agitation. The opening of the ports and the decision for independence had been in large measure forced upon the colonists by the economic paralysis of the winter of 1775-76: only as "Free and Independent States," able to establish commerce and contract alliances, could the colonies hope to acquire the means of resistance. And while independence could be won by war and confirmed by treaty, survival required the speedy development of new relationships with the outer world to replace those lost on departure from the British Empire.

This was more easily said than done, for although philosophers might celebrate the sovereign virtues of commerce, kings were not yet philosophers and the European world still ran on reason of state. Some Americans cherished, with Humphreys, the hope that the costs of independence would be but slight and formal:

> Albion! Columbia! soon forget the past! . . .
> Let those be friends whom kindred blood allies,
> With language, laws', religion's holiest ties!
> Yes, mighty Albion! scorning low intrigues,
> With young Columbia form commercial leagues.[17]

To some in England—to Pitt and Shelburne, Adam Smith and Francis Baring—such views seemed reasonable, but in the end more traditional counsels prevailed. Trade with Britain and her possessions could be had only on British terms, and the West Indies remained closed to American shipping. With other nations, too, commercial treaties came but slowly: the forays of Algerine corsairs inhibited the Mediterranean trade, and with the outbreak of war in Europe in 1793 the Age of Commerce, with its rational institutions as worked out in America, was brought into violent contact with the European powers, survivals of the Ages of Chivalry and Hierarchy. It seemed, indeed, that before commerce could reorder the world in the interests of peace the world had somehow to be reordered in the interests of commerce.

---

[16] [Dwight], *Sermon preached at Northampton*; Barlow, *Letters from Paris*, 1, 9-10; *Vision*, pp. 242-43n.

[17] Humphreys, "Poem on Happiness," *Works*, p. 40.

During the Revolution the prospect of the Armed Neutrality had offered hope:

> Europe's pacific powers their counsels join
> The laws of trade to settle and define.
> The imperial Moscovite around him draws
> Each Baltic state to join the righteous cause;
> Whose arm'd Neutrality the way prepares
> To check the ravages of future wars;
> Till by degree the wasting sword shall cease,
> And commerce lead to universal peace.[18]

But the attempt of 1794 to revive this institution proved abortive in the face of British determination and spreading conflict. The "imperial Moscovite" and the Baltic powers soon had troubles enough of their own, and other means seemed needed to vindicate the "liberal main."

Two obvious, if opposing, courses presented themselves. To Humphreys, who felt that "a defense on the water is our most natural, most necessary, and most efficacious defense," and who as diplomat found himself preoccupied with the problem of the Barbary pirates, naval construction and a campaign to free the Mediterranean seemed the answer.

> Where lives the nation, fraught with such resource,
> Such vast materials for a naval force?
> Where grow so rife, the iron, masts, and spars,
> The hemp, the timber, and the daring tars?

With the pirates out of the way the navy would still remain, a useful weapon for the maintenance of neutral rights:

> Then should far other pirates rove the main,
> To plunder urg'd by sateless lust of gain;
> Rise, fathers of our councils! trade protect,
> Make warring pow'rs our neutral rights respect;
> To vengeance rous'd by many a corsair-crime,
> Resume in wrath an attitude sublime;

---

[18] Barlow, *Columbiad*, VII, lines 101-8. See also his *Poem, Spoken at Yale College, September 12, 1781* (Hartford, 1781); *Vision*, p. 183.

And make, as far as heav'ns dread thunder rolls,
Our naval thunder shake the sea-girt poles.[19]

But Barlow, in France, seeing in a navy the "terrible scourge of maritime nations . . .[and] the ruin of every nation that has hitherto adopted it," had other views. Opposed to entering so suicidal a competition, he urged economic reprisal against the European powers by sequestration of debts, together with a thoroughgoing reformation of international law in the interests of the trading neutrals to "vindicate our commercial liberty." America should take the lead in the creation of an international "unarmed neutrality" with authority to inflict commercial punishment for commercial violence and to maintain, by collective economic sanctions, the freedom of the seas.[20]

The world is no respecter of logic, and both of these courses were adopted by the United States. On the one hand a navy was created; on the other the reform of international law in the interests of the trading neutral became historic American policy. That this apparently fundamental opposition was thus subject to compromise derives from the common presuppositions of the two proposals: both contemplated international rather than unilateral action; both were based on the fundamental assumption that the interests of the inhabitants of the United States were in harmony with the interests of mankind. It was to be a rationalist, not a mercantilist, navy. Its purpose was not to command the seas but to free them. "It is time," wrote Humphreys, the navalist, that "the ocean should be made what heaven intended it, an open highway for all mankind."[21]

In such an intellectual climate, where the abiding realities are the individual and mankind and where commerce is the mediator, the lines between domestic and foreign policy and between private and public action are blurred. As believers in minimum government, the founders were necessarily isolationist in matters concerning the intercourse of states. On the level of the individual, however, and in matters concerning trade, they were fiercely internationalist. America, wrote Barlow, "ought not to have any other political intercourse abroad, but what relates to commerce," but this was a large "but." Reluctant even in the face of dire necessity to conclude a political alliance with France, the Congress had nonetheless been eager

---

[19] Humphreys, "Thoughts on the Necessity of Maintaining a Navy," *Works*, p. 85; "Poem on Happiness," *ibid.*, p. 41; "Future Glory," *ibid.*, p. 61.
[20] Barlow, *Letters from Paris*, pp. 10-15, 23-24, 85-92, 101-16.
[21] Humphreys, "Thoughts on a Navy," *Works*, p. 88.

to expand commercial relations by treaty. This attitude, made plain in the Plan of 1776 for commercial treaties with foreign powers, was spelled out in the Treaty of Amity and Commerce with France, which John Quincy Adams later described as "the corner stone for all our subsequent transactions of intercourse with foreign nations."[22]

Commerce was thus not only the key to the advancement of civilization: in more immediate terms it was essential to the survival of the American experiment. Since the cause of humanity and the national future were both at stake, the propagation of commerce was doubly the duty of Americans. "Awake, Columbians," wrote Humphreys, concluding his "Poem on the Future Glory of the United States,"

> Progressive splendors spread o'er evr'y clime!
> Till your blest offspring, countless as the stars,
> In open ocean quench the torch of wars:
> With God-like aim, in one firm union bind
> The common good and int'rest of mankind;
> Unbar the gates of commerce for their race,
> And build the gen'ral peace on freedom's broadest base.

If this was the aspiration of a visionary, it was the aspiration of one who was also soldier, diplomat, and man of affairs, and other practical men dreamed the same dream. The commissioners of 1785, appointed to negotiate a treaty of commerce with Prussia, saw themselves acting to unite the nations in a peaceful world by the "total emancipation of commerce."[23]

Thus far, in its concern with individual freedom, a peaceful world, and the importance of commerce, the American vision was at one with the stream of advanced European thought. Yet there were variations of emphasis. The *philosophes* had concerned themselves principally with the internal perfection of the state; having perfected theirs but finding themselves still economically dependent on the outer world, the Americans placed greater stress on commercial expansion and international order. Equally a result of local conditions was another aspect of the American Enlightenment: the peculiar importance given to the advancement and application of science as a prime means for improving the condition of man.

---

[22] Barlow, *Letters from Paris*, p. 10; Adams to R. C. Anderson, *Writings*, VII, 460; Gilbert, "New Diplomacy," p. 28.

[23] Humphreys, "Future Glory," *Works*, p. 65; Gilbert, "New Diplomacy," p. 31.

A comparison of two leading figures of the age should make this difference clear: as between Voltaire and Franklin there could be little question who was the American. Europeans, for more than a century, had been widely preoccupied with problems of natural philosophy, and this concern had been reflected in the colonies with sufficiently solid results to permit pride in the accomplishments of Franklin, Rittenhouse, Bushnell, and others. But whereas the great European successes had been in theoretical science and in the extension of the new scientific method to political thinking, Americans hungered for the scientific end products which could be employed in social amelioration. The fear that social progress would suffer had led Barlow to regret the effects of the Revolution on "Neglected Science," while Dwight looked forward to the development of new arts and sciences by American genius. On the outposts of Western civilization, where the Americans were engaged in subduing a trackless wilderness, the abstract concerns of European philosophers had been transmuted into a strong preoccupation with better methods for doing the work of the world. The pursuit of happiness cried out for mechanization, for new tools, new weapons, new methods of transportation, and their development presupposed the advancement of

> Knowledge, the wise Republic's standing force,
> Subjecting all things, with resistless course; . . .
> See strong invention engines strange devise,
> And ope the mysteries of earth, seas, and skies.

Only let education be provided for science as well as for virtue. Then Franklin and the others would prove but forerunners, and

> . . . crowds, around them, join the glorious strife,
> And ease the load that lies on human life.[24]

Married to a contempt for the lessons of history and to a firm environmentalism, this belief in the omnipotence of applied knowledge early brought forth the American confidence that problems apparently insoluble in human terms could be resolved by reformulation with mechanic aids. This, in a sense, was what had already been done politically through the process of constitution-writing, but the atti-

[24] Barlow, *Prospect of Peace*; *Poem, Spoken at Yale College*. [Dwight], *Sermon preached at Northampton*; *Greenfield Hill*, VII, lines 403-4, 409-10, 435-36.

tude went beyond politics. Thus Humphreys could envisage West Indian slavery falling victim to the exploitation of the sugar maple,

> ...the dulcet tree
> Whose substituted sweets one slave may free.

And Barlow, late in life, despairing of ever eliminating British control of the seas by law or treaty, saw in the submarine invented by Fulton a device that "carried in itself the eventual destruction of naval tyranny," and urged a vigorous development program upon his government.[25]

In no area was the importance of the application of science to society greater than in the field of transportation. The question of internal improvements, indeed, formed the domestic counterpart to that reformation of international law which would make the open ocean a highway for mankind. To Barlow, roads, bridges, and canals were not only of commercial and economic importance, but "ought likewise to be regarded in a moral and political light." When urging his French friends to establish a United States of Europe, he postulated a general government whose powers were limited to the conduct of external relations and to such defined common causes as roads, canals, and commerce. In his vision of the future, he saw as specific items in that progress "which draws for mutual succour man to man," canals which would cut the isthmuses of Suez and Panama, and would link the Hudson with the Ohio and Lake Superior with the Mackenzie. Dwight too foresaw the days when

> ...public bliss, from public hands, shall flow,
> And patriot works from patriot feelings grow.
> See Appian ways across the New World run! ...
> See long canals on earth's great convex bend!
> Join unknown realms, and distant oceans blend.[26]

In America, at least, the importance of improving communications so as to foster commerce and cement the federal structure was indisputable. Inevitably, the surprising omission from the Federal Constitution of any specific power so to contribute to public

[25] Humphreys, "Poem on Industry," *Works*, p. 99; Barlow, *Oration*, pp. 13-14; Adrienne Koch, *Power, Morals, and the Founding Fathers* (Ithaca, N.Y., 1961), pp. 128-31.

[26] Barlow, *Oration*, p. 7; *Letters from Paris*, pp. 49-50; *Vision*, pp. 246-47; *Columbiad*, x, lines 203-38. Dwight, *Greenfield Hill*, vii, lines 351-53, 355-56.

bliss gave rise to one of the most enduring constitutional contro-
versies in American history. But the poets were wiser than the politicians, and if the frame of government was deficient in this regard, a full appreciation of the importance of technology to the
advancement of society shone clearly in contemporary thought. Barlow had dedicated the *Columbiad*, the epic by which he hoped to
be remembered, to Robert Fulton, and one can perhaps say that
the most meaningful unwritten work in the history of American
literature was one which they projected jointly: "The Canal: a
Poem on the Application of Physical Science to Political Economy
in Four Books."[27]

As with America's political innovations and the expansion of commerce, the promise of applied science was universal. What America
developed, humanity would share. The ingenuity so important to
progress at home would help expand commercial contacts abroad,
and the export of new techniques would further stimulate the mutually beneficent influence of expanding trade. So Humphreys, in
his "Poem on the Happiness of America," would

> Bid from the shore a philanthropic band,
> The torch of science glowing in their hand,
> O'er trackless waves extend their daring toils,
> To find and bless a thousand peopled isles.
> Not lur'd to blood by domination's lust,
> The pride of conquest, or of gold the thirst;
> Not armed by impious zeal with burning brands,
> To scatter flames and ruin round their strands;
> Bid them to wilder'd men new lights impart,
> Heav'n's noblest gifts, with every useful art.[28]

Such were the universal implications of the "new American Æra."
Since man was perfectible and environment was all, the rationalist
word that had been made flesh in America proclaimed itself to all
nations. History, as a later product of the Enlightenment was to
observe, was bunk; the dead hand of the past had been exorcised and
the future was in the hands of the present. Education, both of men
and of nations, could make all new, and America was to be educator
to the world. Individual equality and free election, the foundation
stones of her society, ensured the rights of man and guaranteed both

---

[27] Howard, *Connecticut Wits*, p. 307.
[28] Humphreys, "Poem on Happiness," *Works*, p. 42.

local self-determination and a government which would be servant, not master. The federal principle provided the means to the harmonious cooperation of numerous sovereignties and permitted indefinite growth. Expanding commerce would foster amicable intercourse; advancing science would lighten the burdens of mankind. As the great Secretary of State was later to point out, the Declaration of Independence and the Treaty of Commerce with France, the bases of domestic and foreign policy, were "parts of one and the same system."[29] America neither stopped at the water's edge nor pointed solely west.

Many and various were the means by which the gospel would be spread. Kings, as Dwight hoped, might profit by the example and learn to tread the paths of progress. Commerce would assimilate the nations. Neighboring colonies of the Old World powers would find themselves subject to the magnetic American example of liberty, frugality, and happiness. Distant realms would receive the glad tidings as future generations of Americans

> In freedom's cause unconquerably bold, . . .
> Brave the dread powers, that eastern monarchs boast,
> Explore all climes, enlighten every coast;
> Till arts and laws, in one great system bind,
> By leagues of peace, the labours of mankind.[30]

Westward expansion and the establishment of the transcontinental republic would speed the work of the Western world,

> . . . by heaven designed,
> Th' example bright, to renovate mankind.
> Soon shall thy sons across the mainland roam;
> And claim, on far Pacific shores, their home;
> Their rule, religion, manners, arts, convey,
> And spread their freedom to the Asian sea . . . .
> Then to new climes the bliss shall trace its way,
> And Tartar deserts hail the rising day;
> From the long torpor startled China wake;
> Her chains of misery rous'd Peruvia break;
> Man link to man, with bosom bosom twine;
> And one great bond the house of Adam join.

[29] Adams to R. C. Anderson, *Writings*, VII, 460.
[30] [Dwight], *Sermon preached at Northampton*. Barlow, *Letters from Paris*, pp. 66, 79-80; *Vision*, p. 146.

For Europe, as compared with startled China, the hopes were less immediately sanguine. On that small continent, covered with the detritus of the Ages of Chivalry and Hierarchy, were powerful and dangerous monarchies certain to resist all change.

> Yet there, even there, Columbia's bliss shall spring,
> Rous'd from dull sleep, astonished Europe sing, ...
> Thus, thro' all climes, shall Freedom's bliss extend,
> The world renew, and death, and bondage, end.

The American vision ends only with a federal world and a liberated humanity, as

> The mask of priesthood and the mace of kings,
> Lie trampled in the dust.[31]

3. America and the Outer World

How far did the posture which Americans actually assumed toward the outer world conform to this body of doctrine?

From the time of the Treaty of Amity and Commerce with France the foreign policy of the government was a commercial one, the fundamental question of independence alone excepted. Commercial treaties with other countries were eagerly sought, following the liberal most-favored-nation principles laid down in the Plan of 1776, and if in Europe these were forthcoming only from the smaller nations, this fact merely confirmed the belief that the great states were managed in the interests of the rulers rather than the ruled. Territorial expansion itself was in great part a function of commerce: the Mississippi question, which led to the purchase of an empire to gain a riverbank, was fundamentally a question of exports and not of land; as the acquisition of New Orleans freed the mouth of the Mississippi, so that of the Floridas opened the exit from the Gulf; the line of the Oregon settlement and the boundary of the Mexican cession were in large measure determined by the geography of the Pacific coast, the location of Pacific harbors, and the promise of Pacific Ocean commerce.

Beyond all this there was at once begun a vigorous effort to generate commerce with the lesser-known parts of the world. In this effort to explore all climes and try all ports, nothing was heard of the

[31] Dwight, *Greenfield Hill*, II, lines 705-10, 735-40; VII, lines 303-4, 311-12. Barlow, *Columbiad*, x, lines 600-601.

concept of the two spheres, a concept which in any event was more a reflection of contemporary cartographic techniques than of convictions about the nature of the world. More accurately, the earth was conceived of as comprising four principal parts—Europe, Asia, Africa, and America—of which the first, unhappily, had succeeded in extending its dominion in various degrees over the others.[32] But this was a dominion which Americans were in no way inclined to concede, least of all in matters of commerce. As American shipping circled the globe, the government moved with it in the establishment of pioneering treaty arrangements, in Barbary and Turkey, in Muscat and Siam, and ultimately to the openings of Japan and Korea.

In practice, therefore, as well as in theory, foreign intercourse remained in large measure an affair of individuals, and the development both of policy and of its instruments conformed to this fact. Ministers, not ambassadors, and as few of these as possible, were dispatched abroad, while emphasis was laid on the expansion of consular representation. The Army was developed as a frontier police and as an engineering force, designed to protect and improve the national estate. The Navy, abjuring the role of makeweight of Europe in America as well as the European rank of admiral, evolved into an institution for the protection of commerce and for the advancement of science through hydrographic work and exploration.

The corollary to the forward commercial policy, and the necessary consequence of a government divested in theory and devoid in practice of the coercive apparatus of the great mercantilist states, was a policy of no political entanglement. This meant, among other things, a policy of no war; for as all but War Hawks, to whom the conquest of Canada was a mere matter of marching, were fully aware, war with great powers was the greatest entanglement of all. So periods of increasing European pressure brought more active efforts at disengagement, as in Jay's Treaty, in the liquidation of the French Alliance, or in Clay's attempts to create an inter-American system as

---

[32] Early-nineteenth-century atlases conventionally showed the world in a stereographic or "globular" projection, with hemispheres dividing at 20°W and 160°E; Mercator worlds, although growing in popularity as the century wore on, were long subordinated to the hemispheric presentation. See, e.g., *Carey's General Atlas* (Philadelphia, 1796); A. Arrowsmith and Lewis, *New and Elegant General Atlas* (Boston, 1805); John Pinkerton, *A Modern Atlas* (Philadelphia, 1818); H. S. Tanner, *A New Universal Atlas* (Philadelphia, 1836). Political reality, as opposed to cartographic convention, emerges in the four-part world described by Hamilton in *Federalist* xi.

counterpoise to the Holy Alliance. So also, when a generation of European warfare made it seem that commerce might prove more the great entangler than the great pacifier, efforts to solve the problem remained chiefly in the commercial realm: economic measures of embargo and nonintercourse and, these failing, commercial warfare carried out both by the Navy of the government and by the citizen's navy, the privateers. Not even when faced with the phenomenon of popular revolution would the government adopt a forward policy. Well-wisher to the freedom of all peoples from the time of Hyder Ali's revolt in India, the United States remained, despite a near approach to a more positive policy in 1823, "vindicator only of her own."[33]

With the ending of the great European wars the government returned to its original task of opening the doors for individual enterprise and of securing for its citizens that liberty of commerce which was one of the indisputable rights of man. The American ship of state remained a merchantman, the need for commercial links and for the earnings of the merchant marine remained undiminished, and the forty-five years that followed the Treaty of Ghent witnessed the great age of American shipping. With the ships went individuals, seeking out new trade, selling their technical skills to all in whom "imaginary wants" existed or could be created, as volunteers striking blows for freedom on all continents, and as missionaries carrying the gospel and the healing arts.

It is, of course, always dangerous to impose a structure on the past, but a summary view of the American attitude toward the world may perhaps be hazarded: hope that the dangerous power of the European monarchies might be contained, and in time eroded, by the spread of enlightened ideas and of popular revolution; popular sympathy for and individual assistance to those desirous of throwing off or of resisting the imposition of alien control; efforts to integrate into the liberating network of commerce those non-European societies which, having escaped the heritage of barbarism and religion, were presumed to be more amenable to the counsels of pure reason. The government was to hold back, the individual to go forward, but the responsibility of both was to lead, by example and precept, toward the better world.

[33] J. Q. Adams, Fourth of July Oration, 1821, in Seward, *Life*, p. 132; Gilbert, *Farewell Address*, pp. 68, 71.

CHAPTER II

To the Shores of Tripoli

1. The Commerce of the Mediterranean

THE WORLD on which the Americans looked out from their scattered coastal settlements gave little evidence of justifying the optimism of the patriotic visionaries. Alone of all its civilizations, that of Europe, against which they had just revolted, had harnessed the energy requisite to outward expansion, and although this process had just received its first setback, it was still sufficiently impressive. To the north the new nation was bordered by the territories of the King of England; westward across the Mississippi and southward from the Floridas to the deserts of Patagonia the continent was subject to the King of Spain. If the new American Æra had in fact commenced, it was not to be proven by the American map.

Yet while the powers of the Old World were still dominant in the New, and controlled in addition the Indian subcontinent and many of the isles of the sea, much of the globe remained untouched, hostile or indifferent to the progress of Western civilization. From the Sahara to the Cape, interior Africa remained a mystery. The vast Pacific had just begun to yield its secrets to the explorations of Captain Cook. In the Orient, beyond the Spice Islands, China still slept in satisfied isolation. Except for the Dutch peephole at Nagasaki, Japan was unknown territory. Although the maritime powers of Europe had subjected the Americas from Hudson's Bay to Cape Horn, Europe herself remained small, compressed by the Moslem conquests of centuries before. The Balkans were still the property of the Turkish sultan; the Mediterranean remained a frontier between two civilizations. From the Atlantic to the Isthmus of Suez, the African shore lay in the hands of Moslem potentates, formally if doubtfully subordinate to the Sultan at Constantinople.

If one looked at this world in terms of Barlow's concept of the progress of civilization, it appeared indeed to fit his description. Although its parts were populated, the development of mutual knowledge remained incomplete, while the third stage, the increase of man's imaginary wants in order to develop a passion for trade, had been only very imperfectly begun. In much of Europe these wants were restricted and directed as a matter of state policy; in much of the rest of the world they did not exist. For Americans, vitally concerned with trade, the problem was to find others of like mind who could be persuaded to adopt the enlightened policies which would contribute to the advancement of commerce. Such had been the aim of the Congress from the spring of 1776.

Experience, however, had been disappointing. Commercial treaties could be negotiated, but the facts of economic life proved resistant to political manipulation. Factors quite other than the Acts of Trade had made Britain at once the source of manufactured goods and the prime market for exports, and her West Indies the pivot of the indirect trades. Yet these were the important relationships, as the Congress and Americans in general well knew, and many besides Humphreys had nourished the pleasant prospect that Albion and Columbia would form commercial leagues.

There was, it was true, some sympathy for such ideas in the mother country, where Adam Smith had declared his independence of the old mercantile system in the same year that the colonists had announced theirs. But his suggestion of nondiscrimination, as embodied in the bills of his pupil Pitt, failed in Parliament. There the influence of British shipowners was strong, and there the important literary influence was less that of *The Wealth of Nations* than of the mercantilist Lord Sheffield, whose *Observations on the Commerce of the American States*, published in the year of the Peace of Paris, argued firmly against relaxation of the Navigation Laws while demonstrating the inability of the disunited Confederation to retaliate effectively.

The war fought against a king for "cutting off our Trade with all parts of the world" had consequently resulted in even further restrictions. Not only did victory end the old relationship with the British Empire, and, most painfully, that with the British West Indies; with it also ended French commercial favor and Spanish commercial lenience. So far as the great powers were concerned, the Americans found themselves facing a closed mercantile world. Since these powers appeared determined to remain the prisoners of their antique and erroneous practices, other trading opportunities had to be developed. Of these, three seemed promising.

The first possibility was to bypass the mercantilist powers on the north, and to enter the Baltic: along this sea were small commercial states, European by geography but not by policy, and at its end lay Russia, that vast and distant nation whose ruler had shown her enlightenment in the Armed Neutrality. A second was to reach past Europe's southern flank: here in colonial times there had existed a sizable commerce, here too were small trading states, and here the sea led onward to a great non-European empire presided over by the fascinating figure of the Grand Turk. Finally, there were prospects in the Orient trade. Of these three possibilities the commerce of the Mediterranean, for the moment, held the most interest, but it too was subject to the costs of independence, for the Barbary powers controlled the southern shore.

With the princes of Barbary the powers of Europe entertained a curious relationship. The decline of crusading ardor had been followed by a transformation of the ancient hostility between Cross and Crescent into a businesslike relationship of piracy, ransom, and tribute. By piracy and ransom the rulers of Barbary maintained themselves; by ransom and tribute the major powers manipulated the corsairs to their own ends. For those who set the level of tribute, "great fallen pow'rs,"

> . . . whose mean policy for them equips,
> To plague mankind the predatory ships—

the pirates provided a useful check on competing merchant marines.[1] For England, France, and Spain the corsairs made little difficulty, but it was otherwise with smaller states: Dutch, Scandinavians, and Austrians all were tributaries, and in 1782 the Republic of Venice, despite victory in war, was constrained to fee these relics of the gorgeous East to the tune of 40,000 sequins. Colonial shipping had early suffered from the pirates, and the Algerines had captured a Harvard man as early as the seventeenth century. But by the eighteenth century the regularization of British relations with Barbary had made for plain sailing, and the colonists had developed a considerable trade with both shores of the Mediterranean: codfish and barrel staves to Catholic, wine-drinking Europe, codfish and wheat to Moslem Barbary. This favorable situation ended with the Revolution, when the British, by withdrawing their protection, enlisted the corsairs in the war against their colonies. Early in the struggle the Mediterranean trade was abandoned, and efforts were begun to

[1] Humphreys, "Future Glory," *Works*, p. 54.

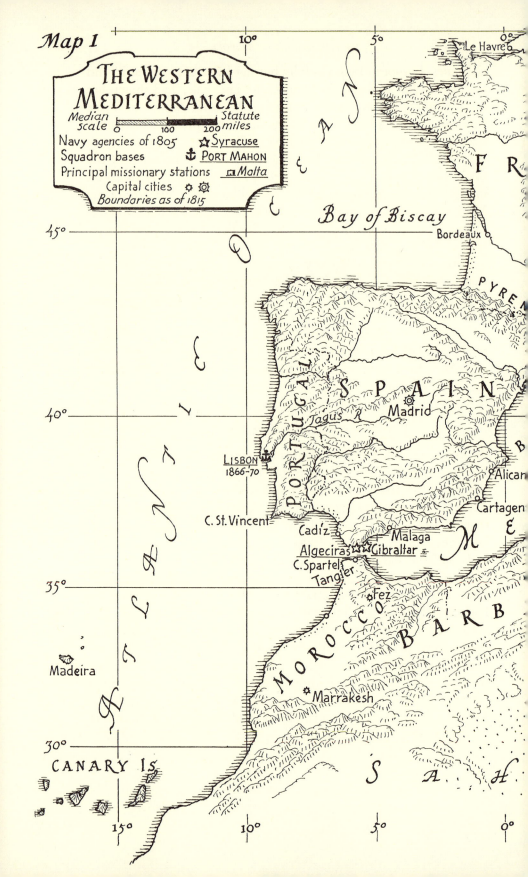

Map 1

THE WESTERN MEDITERRANEAN

Median scale
0   100   200 Statute miles

Navy agencies of 1805 ☆ Syracuse
Squadron bases ⚓ PORT MAHON
Principal missionary stations ⌷ Malta
Capital cities ✿ ✪
Boundaries as of 1815

FR

Le Havre

Bay of Biscay

Bordeaux

45°

PYREN

SPAIN

Tagus R.   Madrid

40°

LISBON
1866-70

Alican

Cartagen

C. St. Vincent

Cadíz   Malaga

Algeciras ☆ ☆ Gibraltar

C. Spartel

Tangier

35°

Fez

MOROCCO   BARB

Madeira

Marrakesh

30°

CANARY Is.

S A H

15°   10°   5°   0°

PORTUGAL

ATLANTIC

FR A N C E

10°   5°   0°

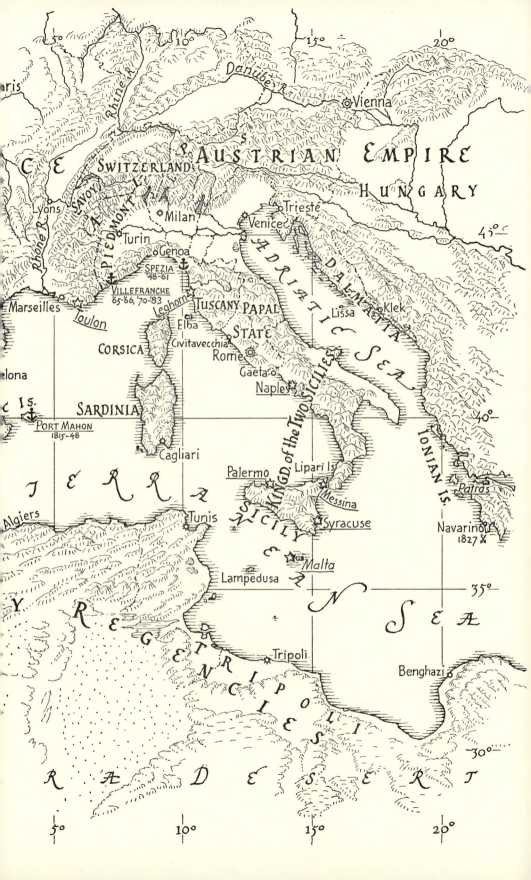

obtain from others the protection once provided by the mother country.[2]

These efforts were not notably successful. The attempt to extract a guarantee of protection from France got only an assurance of good offices. The best that could be obtained from the Dutch was a promise to support American negotiations. That good offices and diplomatic support were not the same as protection was speedily demonstrated when American shipping returned to the Mediterranean: in March of 1783 American vessels bound homeward from Marseilles were pursued by Algerine corsairs.

Report of the incident was made to the peace commissioners at Paris, but an attempt to write a promise of British protection into the peace treaty was unsuccessful. Here, as in the question of reciprocity, Lord Sheffield barred the way. "It is not probable," he wrote in his *Observations*, "the American States will have a very free trade in the Mediterranean; it will not be the interest of any of the great maritime powers to protect them there from the Barbary States. . . . The Americans cannot protect themselves from the latter; they cannot pretend to a navy." The argument had indisputable immediate validity, but in the long run it accomplished things foreign to Sheffield's hopes. If, as has been said, his responsibility for Britain's commercial pressure on her former colonies made him one of the prime movers of the American Constitution, his views on the utility of the Barbary auxiliaries also made him, at long remove, a progenitor of the United States Navy.

This Navy, however, was far in the future. The immediate problem was the opening of the Mediterranean. Having failed to gain European protection, the Congress responded to an overture from Sidi Mohamet, Emperor of Morocco and the most progressive and least piratical of the Barbary potentates. In May 1784 a commission composed of Franklin, Adams, and Jefferson was established, with David Humphreys as secretary, to negotiate treaties of amity and commerce with the four states of Barbary; in the following year the expenditure of $80,000 was authorized. Efforts to gain French diplomatic support for the Moroccan negotiations proved labor lost, but a different climate developed at Madrid, where interest in the Mississippi question gave rise to an attitude of extreme cooperation. Al-

---

[2] *American State Papers, Foreign Relations*, I, 104. On Barbary diplomacy: R. W. Irwin, *The Diplomatic Relations of the United States with the Barbary Powers* (Chapel Hill, N.C., 1931); G. W. Allen, *Our Navy and the Barbary Corsairs* (Boston, 1905).

though the American negotiators went "armed only with Innocence and the Olive Branch," Spanish aid and Moroccan affability resulted in the Treaty of 1787, binding for fifty years and surprisingly favorable in its terms. How far this fortunate result was due to the Emperor's complaisance, and how far to the "King's preacher," who expatiated to Sidi Mohamet on the close correspondence of the Moroccan and American forms of religion, remains uncertain. The King of Spain got a vote of thanks from Congress, but not the closure of the Mississippi. The religious factor would reappear in subsequent negotiations with Moslem potentates. Most significant, perhaps, as regards the future, and certainly most surprising to Europeans, was the fact that the Americans had refused to pay tribute and had got away with it.

The Moroccan treaty, ratified by the Congress of the Confederation while the convention at Philadelphia was designing the machinery that would replace it, was the sole accomplishment of the old government in Barbary diplomacy. On commerce its effects were very limited. For the protection of shipping inside the Mediterranean it promised only a hope of mediation: there treaties were needed with Algiers, strongest of the regencies at sea, and with Tunis and Tripoli. But negotiations with these powers had been abortive, and the cries of American prisoners testified to the diplomatic weakness of the Confederation.

The captures had taken place during the summer of 1785. While the commission created to treat with the Barbary states was still in the process of organization, the Algerines found themselves momentarily at peace with Spain and Portugal, and so with unhindered access to the Atlantic. Urged on by the British consul at Algiers, they made a foray into the Western Ocean, picked up a Boston schooner off Cape St. Vincent and a Philadelphia ship off Lisbon, and supplied a major theme for the poet of navalism:

> See what dark prospect interrupts our joy!
> What arm presumptuous dares our trade annoy?
> Great God! The rovers who infest thy waves
> Have seiz'd our ships, and made our freemen slaves.[3]

Renewed hostilities with Portugal soon bottled the pirates up again, but twenty-one Americans were now enslaved in Algiers, and American shipping within the Mediterranean was dependent on convoy by

[3] Humphreys, "Future Glory," *Works*, p. 51.

Dutch or Spanish cruisers. Attempts at ransom by Adams and Jefferson met with failure. Although the Dey of Algiers professed admiration for General Washington and was reported, Moslem doctrine notwithstanding, to have requested his portrait, the $4,200 the Americans were authorized to expend compared unfavorably with the Algerine asking price of $59,496. Nor were negotiations with Tripoli more successful. Conversations in London between Adams and the Tripolitan envoy Abdurrahman led only to an equally impossible proposal: perpetual peace for 30,000 guineas, or term insurance at 12,500 a year.

Lack of funds made it impossible to ransom the captives or to purchase peace, or even to better the lot of those enslaved in Algiers. But although the impotence of the Congress of the Confederation obliged its citizens to languish in slavery, its European representatives could hardly be charged with inaction or indifference. To Adams in London there was "nothing to be done in Europe of half the importance" of the Tripolitan treaty; in Paris, Jefferson had shown himself both forceful and imaginative in his search for a solution. Yet the reactions of the two envoys were different, and the difference had significance for the future.

To John Adams, whose belief in universal truths was wearing thin under the trials of European experience, it seemed sensible to pay up. The realistic New Englander, the advocate of the expansion of commerce whose administration was to see the establishment of the Navy Department and a naval war with France, felt that the price was not unreasonable and that those who thought it more manly to fight showed "more spirit than prudence." Doubtful that the Congress would ever adopt a forceful policy, Adams felt it the part of wisdom "to negotiate and pay the necessary sum without loss of time." How the Congress that could not produce a navy could produce the money, and whether a perpetual peace with Barbary would be any more perpetual than those made and broken by the Christian nations of Europe, he did not perhaps sufficiently consider.

The views of Jefferson were different. Wishing to fight for national honor and the furtherance of trade, the peaceful agrarian urged the speedy creation of a navy. With less faith than Adams in the pledged word of pirates, he discounted the prospect of perpetual peace and observed that the duration of a treaty "would depend on their idea of our power . . . and on the life of the particular dey." In reply to Adams, he argued that a fleet of 150 guns would be less expensive than tribute; that justice, honor, and "the respect of Europe" argued against payment; that a navy "will arm the federal head with the safest of all the instruments of coercion over its delinquent members"; that purchase of peace, if decided on, should not be delayed, but that "I should prefer the obtaining it by war." Although willing to fight alone, he felt that Portugal and Naples would be impelled in their own interests to make common cause. If this were so, others perhaps would join. In these spirited and progressive views he was joined by the secretary of the commission:

> Hark! thro' the vales the clarion breathes afar,
> The thrilling accents of piratic war.
> Nations attend! --- arise thou wak'ning age!
> Combin'd Humanity! --- arise in rage ---
> To blot that scandal, be thy flag unfurl'd ---
> To conquest sail --- thou congregated world![4]

Thinking along these lines, Jefferson worked out a plan for policing the Mediterranean in cooperation with the small European states. By contributing designated quotas of ships, those at war with the Barbary powers would keep a naval force controlled by an international committee in constant cruise along the African coast. Portugal had already indicated interest in such a proposal; inquiry brought favorable responses from Naples, Venice, Malta, Denmark, and Sweden; the project was cleared with the French. But the frigate which the United States was to contribute existed neither in actuality nor in prospect, the Congress declined to participate, and not for the last time a scheme of collective security, American in origin but deprived of American participation, came to nought.[5]

Except for the Moroccan treaty the failure was thus complete. Solution of the Barbary problem was to await the coming of a new government. But although it was perhaps not evident at the time, the efforts of Adams and Jefferson to open the Mediterranean to their country's commerce had at least demonstrated one of the abiding realities of American history. The practical men, the realists, are willing to make deals. It is the ideologues, even the peaceful ones, who will fight.

The Moroccan success and the Algerine and Tripolitan failures were followed by a lapse in negotiations. Only after the financial

---

[4] Humphreys, *Poem on Industry* (Philadelphia, 1794), p. 21.
[5] Irwin, *Diplomatic Relations*, pp. 40-50; Allen, *Barbary Corsairs*, pp. 32-41.

question, so insoluble under the Articles of Confederation, had been faced, and in good measure conquered by Hamiltonian funding, could these ancient problems be attended to. But in the last days of 1790 the Congress received two reports, one on the state of the Algerine captives and one on the importance of the Mediterranean trade, from the pen of Thomas Jefferson, now secretary of state. Observing that "our navigation . . . into the Mediterranean, has not been resumed at all since the peace," Jefferson enclosed information on Algerine naval strength, commended the use of force, and recurred to his earlier proposal of an organized international effort.[6] Together with a report from the Secretary of War on the cost of a naval establishment, these comments led to a Senate recommendation for the creation of a naval force, as soon as finances would permit, as the only way to protect Mediterranean commerce. This time would be long in coming, but already the finances did admit of attempts to treat and to ransom. In February 1791 the Senate, presided over by John Adams and impressed by the importance of the Mediterranean question, resolved that it would consent to expenditures of up to $100,000 annually for peace with the regencies and of $40,000 for ransom. On 1 June John Paul Jones was named peace commissioner and consul at Algiers.

But the ill luck which had so long beset these efforts continued. Both Jones and his successor died before reaching Algiers. Not until September 1793 did David Humphreys, the third appointee, commence his journey to the capital of the Dey, only to learn at Gibraltar of a truce between Portugal and Algiers which again gave the pirates access to the Atlantic. In early October, seven or eight Algerine cruisers passed the straits; with his maritime prospects looking up, the Dey refused to receive the American emissary; sailing beyond the Pillars of Hercules the Algerines captured eleven American ships with over a hundred seamen.

Coming at a time of increasing pressure on American shipping everywhere, these seizures had profound effects. War in Europe had broken out in February 1793, and in June a British order-in-council had directed the Royal Navy to bring in all neutral ships carrying provisions to French ports. This was bad enough, but a second order-in-council, promulgated in November and calling for detention of all ships found trading with French colonies, resulted, early in 1794, in the Caribbean captures of over 250 American vessels. As the truce

[6] *ASP, FR,* I, 100-105.

between Portugal and the Dey, which had let the corsairs out into the Atlantic, had been negotiated by the British consul at Algiers, it seemed only too probable that it was but another part of the deep-laid British design, in the tradition of Lord Sheffield, to destroy American commerce. Although disavowed in London, the supposition was given color by reports from Portugal, where the government seemed as surprised as any at the truce, and from a prisoner at Algiers who reported that the Consul had advised the pirates on where best to cruise in the search for American shipping.

News of the truce and of the loss of ships to the Algerines reached America in January 1794, to be followed in March by reports of the Caribbean captures and of British activity among the northwest Indians. The result was a major Anglo-American crisis, which the Washington administration dealt with in the only possible way: force against the weak, negotiations with the strong. In March, after a spirited debate, the Congress authorized the procurement of six frigates for use against Algiers. In April, Chief Justice Jay sailed for London in a last effort to avert a war with the mistress of the seas. Although the fifth article of Jay's instructions, echoing the collective security ideas of the Continental Congress and of Jefferson's Mediterranean project, contemplated alliance with other neutrals in the event of failure at London, the prospect of such action was remote. The government depended for survival upon its revenues, and these on the import duties which war would destroy. A settlement was essential.

Step by step the crisis was surmounted. In England, Jay got a treaty which at least prevented war. Portugal, meanwhile, had refused to ratify the truce negotiated by the British consul, had resumed hostilities with Algiers, and had cleared the Atlantic approaches. In July 1794 Edmund Randolph, who had succeeded Jefferson as secretary of state, placed $800,000 at Humphreys' disposal for the purchase of peace and for ransom. Furious at Great Britain for not enforcing the Portuguese truce, the Dey became more amenable. Negotiations in the autumn of 1795 in which James Leander Cathcart, one of the American captives, acted for the Dey, trimmed the asking price from more than $2,000,000, two 35-gun frigates, and a guarantee of future presents, to a cash payment of $642,500 plus an annual tribute of $21,600 in naval stores. Such a treaty might have seemed a sufficient contribution to the welfare of the Algerine ruler, but more was to come. War in Europe made money scarce, and while Humphreys scoured the continent for specie, his colleague Barlow collected some trinkets in France and hastened to Algiers. There he found affairs in crisis, and only by the promise of an additional gift of a 36-gun frigate did it seem possible to salve the Dey. Ultimately the required amount of money was scraped together, and in June 1796 the Wits obtained the freedom of the captives.

At long last, now that the government could tax, diplomacy was possible. By the first year of the Adams administration the United States had negotiated treaties with all of the Barbary powers. With Morocco relations remained agreeable: in 1795, on the accession of a new emperor, the required renewal of the treaty was accomplished without difficulty. But Tunis and Tripoli proved more refractory. Aspiring to emulate the Algerines, the Bey of Tunis seized an American schooner in June of 1796, and Tripolitan corsairs brought in two ships in September. In November, negotiations with the Pasha of Tripoli conducted by Richard O'Brien, a former Algerine captive, produced a treaty at the modest price of $56,000. But the Bey held out for more and got it: $107,000 in August of the next year.

So peace of a sort, if not of the creditable sort sought by Jefferson, came to American relations with Barbary. The Mediterranean had been opened to the healing ministrations of commerce. But even if the peace was peace by purchase, it was justifiable on the ground that sound national policy calls for but one war at a time; for the deterioration in relations with France, which was shortly to lead to an outbreak of fighting at sea, had already begun.

2. *All Federalists, All Republicans*

The years which saw the states of Barbary brought into treaty relations with the United States were also the first years under the new Constitution, and the years of Federalist control of American policy. In this period the new government had accomplished many things: most importantly, in a world dominated by great warring powers, it had survived. But while the question of survival had necessarily taken precedence over all else, progress had also been made in Mediterranean commercial matters. Unable to resort to force, the Federalists had necessarily passed over the Jeffersonian remedy of resistance in favor of the Adamsite solution of tribute, yet the solution had not been cheap. By January 1793 the treaty with Algiers alone had obligated the country to the extent of almost a million dollars and had elicited for the first time, in Scandinavian strictures on this inflation of the treaty market, foreign complaint about American extravagance abroad. But that this procedure had proven possible, and on so substantial a scale, was impressive testimony to the soundness of the country and to the taxing power of the new government.

The long effort on behalf of Mediterranean commerce had not only tested the new government; it had also raised, for the first time, concrete questions about American relations with non-European societies. Although no final answer had emerged by the time the treaties provided a breathing space, the problems had at least been presented and some of their dimensions seen. Before the new Æra could begin in sleeping China and Peruvia, some settlement had to be reached with Barbary.

If any one thing was plain it was that the nations of Barbary, like any others, deserved and in some ways commanded respect. When Royall Tyler, whose play *The Contrast* had already shown his understanding of the differences between Old and New Worlds, turned his hand to the Algerine theme, his fictional captive saw this clearly. To Dr. Updike Underhill the Algerine system of justice was admirable, and many aspects of Moslem religion and society contrasted favorably with conditions in Europe; piracy, certainly, was reprehensible, but its existence was in large degree the result of unenlightened European policy. To Barlow, as well, despite his difficulties in negotiation, the pirates' maritime "principles of public law [were] more rational, and approaching nearer to civilization, than those of Europe." Like all peoples, those of Barbary enjoyed the sacred right of self-determination: if only the Algerines would adopt ideas of equal liberty they would be better able to frame a government for themselves than would the wisest of outsiders.[7]

There had, of course, been debate as to how ideas of equal liberty should be inculcated. Humphreys had called eloquently for the use of naval force:

> Give me the music of the sounding axe—
> Let the keen adze the stubborn live oak wound—
> And anvils shrill, with stronger strokes resound.
> Give me the music, where the dock equips,

[7] [Royall Tyler], *The Algerine Captive; or, the Life and Adventures of Dr. Updike Underhill* (Walpole, N.H., 1797). Barlow, *Letters from Paris*, p. 107; *Letter to the National Convention*, p. 20.

With batt'ries black and strong, the battle-ships,
To whose broad decks, the hast'ning crouds repair,
And shouts, and drums, and cannon, rend the air.
  Blow ye the trumpet! - sound - oh, sound th'alarms—
To arms—to arms—brave Citizens! to arms ---[8]

Jefferson, too, had been an advocate of the cannon's mouth, and Barlow's fervent hope that "there are persons now living who will see the day when not a cannon shall be allowed to be carried to sea, at least on the Atlantic, and the European seas," carried at least an implication that powder and ball might prove a civilizing agency on the maritime as on the western frontier.[9] But this was to overlook the possibilities of redemption by trade, now dawning as a result of successful negotiations. The last years of the century had seen a steady increase of American commerce with the Mediterranean, and in 1799 some eighty ships were reported passing eastward through the straits.

Peace and prosperity now made possible that increased representation in Barbary that President Washington had earlier urged. But the nature of this representation was affected by the purposeful de-emphasis of diplomacy which stemmed from the individual and commercial nature of American policy and from its felt difference from that of Europe. Some in America had proposed that even commercial treaties should be made only with extra-European states; others, hoping that the need for a diplomacy would be but temporary, had combined both foreign and domestic responsibilities in the Department of State; to many the American way seemed to call for the fewest possible permanent diplomatic representatives, and these of as low a grade as possible. These attitudes, indeed, had early been made plain to the Moroccans by the first Secretary of State: "The emperor has intimated that he expects an Ambassador from us. Let him understand that this may be the custom of the old world, but it is not ours: that we never send an ambassador to any nation."[10]

Consuls, however, were another matter, and with their installation in all the regencies the effort at commercial conversion of the pirates was begun. Sound doctrine on the importance of the develop-

---

[8] Humphreys, *Poem on Industry* (1794), p. 20.

[9] Barlow, *Letters from Paris*, p. 26.

[10] Rippy and Debo, "Historical Background of Isolation," pp. 126, 150-51; Gilbert, *Farewell Address*, pp. 70, 73; *ASP, FR*, i, 288-89.

ment of trade was evidenced in Secretary of State Pickering's instruction to William Eaton, consul-designate at Tunis: the "great commerce" of that place, properly developed, offered the "best encouragement to the attempt" to reclaim the regency from its predatory habits. "If ever the states of Barbary lay aside their practice of depredating on the commerce of Christian nations it will probably be owing to an extension of their own commerce, which may convince them where their true interest lies by the greater advantage derived from trade." In pursuit of the civilizing goal, Eaton, who himself saw his mission as the start of a great commercial expansion, was directed to gather all possible information on prices, commodities, and methods of trade. As for Pickering, his own actions make it impossible to question the sincerity of his belief in the advantages to be derived from commerce: the frigate *Crescent*, promised to Algiers by Barlow and duly built by the naval constructor at Portsmouth, sailed in January 1798, commanded by one nephew of the Secretary of State and insured and victualed by another.[11]

Indeed, for a time it seemed that Barlow's promise would prove only the first step toward making the United States the arsenal of piracy. In June 1797 the Dey had asked the United States to build and equip him two more cruisers, this time at his expense. Adams supported the request, the Congress advanced funds, and when Eaton sailed for Tunis in December 1798 he sailed in company with the 22-gun brig *Hassan Bashaw* and two armed schooners. "These corsairs," wrote Richard O'Brien, ex-Algerine captive and outward-bound consul general for Barbary, "is the finest ever built in this country and preferable to any ever built by any nation in Europe—will sail faster than any vessels, that ever was in the Mediterranean."[12]

Jefferson, while secretary of state, had clearly seen the danger of providing the rulers of Barbary with this sort of producer's goods; as President he continued in this belief, and in 1803 would exasperate the Dey by an effort to commute a promise of naval stores to money payment. But Jefferson was out of office when the treaties were made and the negotiators, for what seemed sufficient reasons, adopted the opposite course. Not only the annual tribute to Algiers but much of the purchase price of the Tripolitan and Tunisian treaties was to be paid in kind; an article in the treaty with Tunis called for a continu-

---

[11] L. D. White, *The Federalists* (New York, 1948), p. 282.

[12] Office of Naval Records and Library, *Naval Documents Related to the United States Wars with the Barbary Powers* (Washington, D.C., 1939-44), I, 223.

ing supply of gunpowder in return for the courtesy of salutes; the renegotiation of the Moroccan treaty involved gifts of fieldpieces, small arms, and powder. Humphreys' "philanthropic band" had already set sail, but the illumination it took to " 'wildered men" was, for the moment, concerned largely with military and naval science.

That the rulers of Barbary were interested was not surprising: the first concern of any government, piratical or other, is its self-preservation, and if the necessary tools cannot be found at home they must be obtained abroad. But the Americans' willingness to provide these armaments, and the disproportionate share allocated to Algiers, made for continual and competitive demands. Already the excellence of American naval architecture was becoming known abroad: as Adams proudly reported to Congress, "the Dey of Algiers has manifested a predilection for American built vessels"; and this excellence, together with future developments in arms manufacture, was to make the United States, throughout the century, an important supplier of the instruments of self-determination to countries which could not fabricate their own. But the annoyance of continued bickering with dey, bey, and pasha and the humiliation inherent in the position of tributary had their consequences, and later efforts by the Dey of Algiers to strengthen his navy with American help were evaded. One lesson, at least, was learned in Barbary: not for long would arms aid be extended to potentially hostile powers, and never again as open tribute.

So far as the future was concerned, the most important consequence of Federalist grappling with the Mediterranean problem was the establishment of the United States Navy. The Act of March 1794, passed at the peak of the crisis with Britain, had authorized the procurement of six frigates, but with the proviso, forced by a determined opposition, that building should cease in the event of peace with Algiers. None of these vessels had been completed by the time of the Algerine treaty, and the Senate debate on that document was accompanied by vigorous congressional dispute as to the disposition of the ships under construction. In April 1796 a compromise bill was passed which permitted completion of three of the six frigates, and the following year saw the launching of *United States, Constitution,* and *Constellation.* Two years later the French crisis brought a rapid expansion: three more frigates were authorized, together with the conversion of available merchant ships; a permanent Marine Corps was established; the Navy was removed from the care of the

Secretary of War to the jurisdiction of a separate department. In 1799 appropriations were made for construction of ships of the line and for purchase of timber and timberlands; this act the lame-duck Adams administration interpreted, by judicious broad construction, as authority to purchase and develop sites for navy yards, and so to create a sizable shore establishment.[13]

Although the Act of 1794 had been specifically directed against Algiers, the Federalists never employed the Navy against the powers of Barbary. Operations against the French were carried on in the western Atlantic, the Caribbean, and the Indian Ocean; in 1800, owing to this major preoccupation, a proposal by Sweden and Denmark for combined action against the pirates was declined. In the last months of the Adams administration the possibility of a Mediterranean cruise again came under consideration, but the reaction that followed settlement with France brought naval retrenchment. By congressional enactment more than half the ships were ordered disposed of, the number of officers and enlisted personnel was greatly cut down, and reduction to a limited peace establishment was in process when the administration of Thomas Jefferson came to power.

Jeffersonian scripture can be quoted to the advantage of many views, and it is perhaps unnecessary to be too concerned with what this many-sided man really thought about the linked problems of maritime trade and maritime force. While in France he had vigorously urged creation of a navy and the chastisement of the pirates of Barbary. As secretary of state he had effectively organized the diplomatic and consular service, urged commercial expansion as the means of increasing the happiness and improving the condition of mankind, and had emphasized "our determination to prefer war in all cases to tribute under any form and to any people whatever."[14] During the period of extreme Federalist dominance he seems to have altered these views. The question, in any event, is of doubtful importance, for the leader of the party which came to power in the election of 1800 was no free agent, but was bound by the limitations of the practical politician.

Of his party it has been said that it "was pledged by every line of

[13] Harold and Margaret Sprout, *The Rise of American Naval Power* (Princeton, 1944); Marshall Smelser, *The Congress Founds the Navy, 1787-1798* (Notre Dame, 1959); White, *Federalists*, pp. 156-63.

[14] *ASP, FR*, 1, 288-89, 303. J. H. Macleod, "Jefferson and the Navy: A Defense," 8 *Huntington Library Quarterly*, 153-84, is an important article.

its history not to create a navy,"[15] but this is perhaps a little strong. Not all Republicans had opposed the naval bills in Congress. But if not all Republicans opposed, the opponents were indeed Republicans, and their opposition, worked out in the debates on the Constitution and on the naval bills, rested on three consistent lines of argument. A navy would unwisely aggrandize the general government and would threaten domestic liberty. A navy would inevitably become a vested interest, paid for by the agrarian groups but benefiting only the mercantile sections of the community. A navy would increase the danger of foreign involvement, whether by tempting other nations to attack or by leading an American government into hazardous foreign ventures.

Much of the fear of the Navy as an instrument of oppression was doubtless the result of the character of the administration in power. The function of an opposition is, after all, to oppose on first principles steps which seem unwise at the moment, and as the Federalists became more and more northern in tone, more and more anti-French in policy, and more and more subversive of domestic liberties, it was easy to believe that the naval armament was planned with malice domestic. But these fears proved groundless, and in time objections were to arise from a new source when Jefferson, who had pointed out in 1786 that a navy was the safest of instruments of coercion, began twenty years later to coerce in a good Republican way by using it to enforce the Embargo.

It might, of course, be argued that the Navy itself was Federalist, and such presumably was the inclination of the majority of its officers, but theirs was a Middle State Federalism, not the intransigent New England variety, and their outlook tended to be national rather than sectional. The men of Massachusetts preferred privateering; with a few notable exceptions, such as Preble and Hull, the Navy's officer corps was drawn almost entirely from states south of the Hudson River, principally from Pennsylvania and Maryland, importantly from Virginia and Delaware.[16] So, too, the history of the votes

---

[15] Henry Adams, *History of the United States in the Administrations of Jefferson and Madison* (New York, 1889-91), VI, 162.

[16] Office of Naval Records and Library, *Naval Documents Related to the Quasi-War between the United States and France* (Washington, 1935-38), VII, 135-36, 315-61. This was to prove a lasting state of affairs: C. O. Paullin, "Naval Administration under Secretaries of the Navy Smith, Hamilton, and Jones," 32 *U.S. Naval Institute Proceedings*, 1302, 1320; *American State Papers, Naval Affairs*, III, 158-62; *ibid.*, IV, 295-97.

on the naval bills showed a division of interest rather than of section or of party. New England representatives had backed the Federalist program, but not all New Englanders of maritime leanings were Federalist: Jacob Crowninshield of Salem, one of the great merchants of the day, was an uncompromising Jeffersonian. Nor had New England been alone in supporting the creation of a navy. Representatives from Pennsylvania and New Jersey had been prominent in the cause; C. C. Pinckney of South Carolina, so instrumental in the Republican victory of 1800, had been an early naval partisan; Maryland had voted overwhelmingly both for the creation of a navy and for its enlargement during the French imbroglio.

More could perhaps be said for the contention that a navy, once established, would become a powerful interest which could never, or but with the greatest difficulty, be uprooted. Fully aware of the implications of their building program, the Federalists had wisely federalized the Navy, and had spaced the contracts for the frigates and the sites of the navy yards to cover the coast from Portsmouth to Norfolk. The frigates had been designed by a Pennsylvania shipbuilder. Pennsylvania and Maryland not only built and manned ships but were important sources of naval ordnance and naval administrators. From these Middle States came not only votes and support for the Navy but votes and support for Jefferson: Samuel Smith, Baltimore shipowner, congressman, and a power in the Republican party both locally and through his sister's marriage to a Nicholas of Virginia, had gone down the line in support of the Act of 1794, of the proposal to continue building after peace with Algiers, and of the plan to construct ships of the line. When Thomas Fitz-Simons of Philadelphia, a Federalist congressman who had brought in the report on the frigates in 1794, was defeated in the election of that year, his anti-Federalist replacement turned out to have similar mercantile and naval concerns. Most prosperous, most active, fastest growing of the nation's cities, favored with hinterlands as well as harbors, Philadelphia and Baltimore well understood the interrelationship of agriculture and commerce; through their exports of wheat and flour they were interested in the Mediterranean, and so in the creation of a naval force. Fluctuating as they did politically, Pennsylvania and Maryland were necessarily of concern to an administration that proposed to remain in power by showing that all were Republicans and all Federalists. Not only on the coast of Barbary was the question of naval stores important to a government that desired to maintain itself.

The Navy of 1801 was, after all, not an abstraction. It was a living organism made up of officers and seamen, clerks and contractors, shipbuilders and artisans, all of them real people whatever their party affiliations, with interests, votes, influence, and connections. Lieutenant David Porter's father-in-law was a minor power in Pennsylvania politics. The eldest son of Dr. Benjamin Rush was a lieutenant. Captain John Rodgers' sister was married to William Pinkney of Maryland, a leader of the bar and a moderate Federalist who was to perform important services for the new Republican administration. The father of Midshipmen Thomas and James Macdonough had long been politically active in Delaware. Charles W. Goldsborough, chief clerk of the Navy Department, was a cousin of the Governor of Maryland. Indeed, in this matter of tribal connections the crowning example was that of Albert Gallatin himself, long a leader of the Republican party, long an opponent of the Navy, and now about to become secretary of the treasury. Gallatin was no pacifist, and in later life was to advocate naval adventures at which others would stand aghast; but he had consistently opposed the Federalist naval program both on financial grounds and as temptation to embroilment, and so great was his preoccupation with reduction of the public debt that in 1801 his views on the Navy could only be described as appropriate to the country of his birth. Yet while most men have in-law problems, his were remarkable: Mrs. Gallatin's father, prominent in Burrite political circles in New York, had commanded the revolutionary navy; her uncle was the second-ranking captain on the active list; and while one cousin, Joseph Hopper Nicholson, was about to become one of the Republican leaders in the House, she had seven others serving in the Navy.[17]

Whatever the feelings of the agrarians who had called so loudly for withdrawal from the seas and for the election of Jefferson, their views were to prove of little account. Like all doctrinaires, these found themselves left behind once the revolution was completed and administration was the order of the day. Upland Republicans might

[17] C. B. Davenport and M. T. Scudder, *Naval Officers, Their Heredity and Development* (Washington, 1919), pp. 38, 120-21, 180; L. H. Butterfield (ed.), *Letters of Benjamin Rush* (Princeton, 1951), II, 814; C. O. Paullin, *Commodore John Rodgers* (Cleveland, 1910), p. 18; L. D. White, *The Jeffersonians* (New York, 1959), p. 281; H. Adams, *History of the U.S.*, I, 251-52, 261, 268; J. F. Cooper, *History of the Navy of the United States of America* (Philadelphia, 1839), I, 226.

urge the hiring of Europeans to convoy American shipping, but they reckoned without Jefferson's pride in his country and his desire to have her set an example to the world. Gallatin's fiscal program received official support, and the budget promised a severe paring of expenditures, but this was all. A motion for a committee to consider the abolition of the Navy got nowhere; despite the importance of the Army to the frontier and of the frontier to the party, it was the Army that suffered most. The administration would indeed withhold the commissions of the midnight justices, but despite violent complaints about their illegality, no attack was made on the midnight navy yards.

It remained to be seen whether the Navy would prove a temptation to foreign ventures. Here the Federalists, despite the troubles with France, had kept the original end in view. In January 1800, Pickering had written to William Eaton at Tunis that a cruise to the Mediterranean was contemplated in the event of a settlement with the French; in July, John Marshall had confirmed the fact in a letter to John Quincy Adams. Such news was calculated to please both consuls and naval officers. Eaton, most belligerent of the former, frustrated in his efforts to develop "the great commerce of Tunis," had long urged force; he had improved his idle hours in military and topographical study of the regencies, and by early 1801 was asking for a frigate and a thousand marines with which to seize and destroy the Bey's arsenal. William Bainbridge, after being forced to carry Algerine tribute to Constantinople in the U.S.S. *George Washington*, had formally expressed the hope that he would never again be sent "to Algiers with *tribute* except it be from the *mouth of a cannon.*"[18] In October 1800 a demand from the Pasha of Tripoli for a new treaty and increased tribute had reached the State Department, and as the inauguration of the new Republican administration approached, the prospect of peace in Europe promised both the liberation of commerce from great-power oppression and the possibility of dealing with Barbary in accordance with Jefferson's earlier aspirations.

Somewhat surprisingly, perhaps, no purge of operating personnel

---

[18] A discouraged Eaton wrote in June 1799 that the Congress should "wrest the *quiver of arrows* from the left talon of the eagle . . . and substitute a *fiddle* bow or a *segar* in *lieu.*" L. B. Wright and J. H. Macleod, *The First Americans in North Africa* (Princeton, 1945), p. 47. [Charles Prentiss], *The Life of the Late Gen. William Eaton* (Brookfield, Mass., 1813); H.A.S. Dearborn, *The Life of William Bainbridge, Esq.*, ed. James Barnes (Princeton, 1931).

was made by the incoming Republicans. In Africa the same consuls remained at their posts. At the Navy Department the Federalist chief clerk and the Federalist accountant remained in office. A radical reduction of officer strength was called for by the Act of 3 March, but in its administration it was not "the Politics of the Party" but "Merit & services & a due proportion for each state" which governed.[19] The celebrated William Marbury would for good and sufficient reasons find himself out of his job as Navy Agent for the city of Washington, but so little did politics affect the Navy List that Midshipman Timothy Pickering, Jr. was among those retained on active duty. The views of the implementers of policy were consequently not in doubt. Those of the President and of his Secretary of the Navy remained to be ascertained.

It did not prove easy to find a Secretary. Men of consequence were reluctant to take office merely to preside over the liquidation of the Navy, and the first four candidates declined the compliment. As the end of March approached and the Federalist incumbent grew tired of waiting, Jefferson found a locum tenens in General Samuel Smith of Maryland, Republican politician and Republican shipowner, who had vigorously supported the Federalist naval program and whose firm of Smith and Buchanan, one of the leading commercial houses of Baltimore, was deeply interested in the Mediterranean trade. Although Smith had been one of those originally approached for the office of Secretary, and had declined because he preferred to retain his seat in Congress, he now expressed willingness to assume the duties until a successor could be found. This did not prove possible until July, when the successor turned out to be the General's brother Robert, the leading admiralty lawyer of the day.[20]

Promising though it must have seemed to those who wanted action, and discouraging to pure agrarians, the presence of Baltimore maritime interests at the head of the Navy Department merely reflected previous decisions. Less than two weeks after the inauguration, and ten days before Samuel Smith assumed responsibility for the Department, the President decided to send a squadron to the Mediterranean, and warning orders went out before the end of March.

[19] *Naval Documents: Quasi-War with France*, VII, 186, 195.
[20] H. Adams, *History of the U.S.*, I, 220ff.; White, *The Jeffersonians*, pp. 270-71; G. E. Davies, "Robert Smith and the Navy," 14 *Maryland Historical Magazine*, 305-22. For a family so long prominent in business and politics, the Smiths have been surprisingly neglected by historians.

On 2 June 1801 Commodore Richard Dale, who had been John Paul Jones' first lieutenant on the *Bon Homme Richard*, sailed from Norfolk with three frigates and a schooner; should any of the Barbary powers have declared war against the United States, he was to "protect our commerce and chastise their insolence; by sinking, burning, or destroying their ships & Vessels" wherever found.[21] Thus war was begun, or at least accepted. Jefferson had returned to his original view that tribute was "money thrown away." Gallatin's fiscal reforms were placed in jeopardy before they had been begun. And with the passing of time the administration of the strict constructionist agrarian was to find itself obliged to commit ever-increasing forces to a police action fought in the interests of commerce, in distant waters, and without the sanction of a congressional declaration of war.

3. War with Barbary

On 1 July 1801 Dale reached Gibraltar with his squadron. There he learned that Tripoli had declared war, and there by fortunate chance he encountered the two largest Tripolitan cruisers, the *Meshuda* (ex-*Betsy* of Boston) and a 16-gun Swedish-built brig, commanded by the Scottish renegade who served as the Pasha's admiral. Leaving one frigate to blockade the corsairs, Dale entered the Mediterranean, where during the summer he employed his limited forces as best he could in showing the flag, convoying American shipping, and maintaining an intermittent blockade of Tripoli. One engagement took place a month later, when *Enterprise* defeated a Tripolitan polacca, and there was a brush with some gunboats off Tripoli in September, but Dale's force was inadequate for sustained offensive action. With winter coming on, one frigate was left in the central Mediterranean with orders to cruise off Tunis and Tripoli, and the other ships were ordered home.[22]

In America the fact of war had by this time made its mark. In his message of December 1801 Jefferson asked the Congress to consider "measures of offense also," and the Act of 6 February gave him full discretion in employment of the Navy. Seamen were now enlisted for a two-year term, and a relieving squadron of five frigates and a

[21] *Naval Documents: Barbary Powers*, I, 423-69, 486.
[22] An excellent short treatment of the Tripolitan War is in R. C. Anderson, *Naval Wars in the Levant* (Princeton, 1952); see also Allen, *Barbary Corsairs*, and Wright and Macleod, *First Americans in North Africa*.

schooner was assembled; commanded by Commodore Richard V. Morris, the new force reached Gibraltar in May 1802. In June the frigate *Constellation* arrived off Tripoli to resume the blockade, but difficulties with Morocco and pointless cruises about the western basin delayed the balance of the force. Although orders to lay his whole squadron before Tripoli reached Morris in July 1802, this was not accomplished until the following May, by which time his sole accomplishment had been the capture of *Meshuda*, which the Tripolitans had finally extricated from Gibraltar. After five weeks off Tripoli, the Commodore resumed his desultory cruising; by September 1803 he had returned to Gibraltar, where he received orders to sail for home.

To neither of the participants had the war brought much satisfaction. The Tripolitans had lost some ships and had been inconvenienced by blockade. The Jeffersonians found their prestige involved in a struggle against an enemy difficult to punish and their economical plans mortgaged to naval war. A quick victory would have contributed to the rising glory of America and to the expansion of commerce, and would have satisfied the Smiths as being a settlement and the Randolphs, perhaps, by its speed. But stalemate promised serious strains on party unity. At Tripoli, on returning from his encounter with *Enterprise*, the commander of the polacca had been mounted backwards on a jackass, paraded through the streets with the entrails of a sheep around his neck, and bastinadoed, *pour encourager les autres*. Such methods were not in vogue at Washington, but following a court of investigation which reported Morris "censurable for his inactive and dilatory conduct," the President revoked his commission. The penalty was perhaps deserved, although the manner of proceeding was unfortunately arbitrary; but even this was understandable when dealing with one who was nephew not only to a British general but to so fierce a Federalist as Gouverneur Morris.

Morris had proven himself inadequate, but it should be recognized that his was no simple task. Four thousand miles from home, and in an area again beset by major war, the American squadron had to deal with the Pasha of Tripoli while at the same time keeping watch on the other restless rulers of a fifteen-hundred-mile stretch of African coast. Indeed, it is difficult to think that the administration had seriously considered the logistical problems inherent in such a venture, in which maintenance, base facilities, and supply all posed new problems. Slowly, however, the lessons were learned and the difficulties overcome, and if victory did not come quickly it nevertheless proved possible to maintain and reinforce the squadron in the Mediterranean. That Robert Smith and Goldsborough, pressed as they were between Gallatin and the Pasha, were able to do so much, must be reckoned a considerable accomplishment. The Federalists, reputed to possess a near monopoly of the country's administrative skills, had never attempted anything like this. They had voted the ships, they had purchased the navy yards, they had defended their commerce against the French. But the complexities of conducting a transoceanic campaign had been left to their successors, and for these it was a matter of learning by doing.

When Morris sailed for home in September 1803 the first units of Edward Preble's relieving squadron were already moving into the Mediterranean. Although in gunnery strength Commodore Preble's force was inferior to its predecessor, its more flexible composition was evidence that the lessons of the war were being applied. The Jeffersonians had inherited a frigate navy, but for inshore blockade and pursuit of Tripolitan gunboats, lighter ships were needed. The Congress had appropriated funds in February, and by November two brigs and two schooners had reached the Mediterranean.

More important even than the new ships was the new man: in contrast to his predecessor, Preble was a fighter. Like Morris he was greeted on arrival by threats of war from Morocco. Unlike him, he at once sent two ships forward to Tripoli while staging, with the help of two of the homeward-bound frigates, a show of force that quieted things at Tangier. By November the Commodore was approaching Tripoli, when he received the shattering news that one of his two frigates had been lost: seeking to deliver his tribute from the cannon's mouth, Bainbridge had run *Philadelphia* up on an uncharted reef while in hot pursuit of a vessel entering the harbor. Efforts to free the ship proved vain, and the Pasha acquired more prisoners than the Dey of Algiers had ever had, as well as a potent accretion of force, for within the space of a few days an onshore wind enabled the Tripolitans to refloat *Philadelphia*, stop her leaks, and bring her into port.[23]

In the face of disaster and worsening winter weather, Preble dis-

---

[23] Lorenzo Sabine, "Life of Edward Preble," in Jared Sparks (ed.), *Library of American Biography, Second Series* (Boston, 1847), XII; A. S. Mackenzie, *Life of Stephen Decatur* (Boston, 1846).

played a notable activity. The flag was shown in all the ports of Barbary. Storeships were brought forward in convoy from Gibraltar. In February, Stephen Decatur and a crew of volunteers entered the harbor of Tripoli and under the guns of the fort succeeded in destroying *Philadelphia* without the loss of a man. This done, the blockade was strengthened, and by summer of 1804 the Pasha could see from his palace windows one frigate, three brigs, three schooners, six gunboats, and two mortar-boats, flying the colors of the distant republic. Still declining to negotiate on reasonable terms, he saw first his gunboats, then his forts, and finally his town subjected to bombardment.

This crescendo of action terminated, most regrettably, in Preble's relief. His early requests for reinforcement had run up against the fiscal requirements of the Louisiana Purchase, and had elicited from Gallatin the opinion that the Commodore had already twice the strength he needed. But the loss of *Philadelphia* brought a complete about-face, and the force assembled and dispatched by Secretary Smith in the spring and summer of 1804 was very impressive: five frigates, three brigs, three schooners, ten new gunboats, and two bomb vessels. Since, in these circumstances, it proved impossible to find enough captains junior to Preble to keep him on the job, the command of the squadron, by now comprising almost the entire United States Navy, was entrusted to Commodore Samuel Barron. Barron, unfortunately, was no Preble, but he was accompanied by a remarkable man who was eager to close with the enemy, and who was certain he knew just how.

As early as 1801 William Eaton, the American consul at Tunis, had advanced the plan of espousing the cause of Hamet Caramanli, the exiled Pasha of Tripoli, against his usurping brother, and of revolutionizing the country so as to install a ruler beholden to the United States and amenable to rational influences. Hamet had proven agreeable, if vacillating, but Commodore Morris had been unhelpful. The result was that while Preble was in the Mediterranean, Eaton had been back in Washington, pressing his plan upon Congress and administration. To Eaton the cabinet, with the single exception of Robert Smith, seemed both pusillanimous and ineffective, but again the decision was made at the top. Exasperated both at the duration of his own little war between elephant and whale and at a growing defeatism among American representatives abroad, Jefferson seems to have felt that the proposition was worth a small investment. Eaton was placed on the Navy Department payroll, and carefully qualified instructions were sent to Barron, authorizing him, if it seemed expedient, to cooperate with the exiled Pasha. But Madison had qualms about the propriety of such interference with Tripolitan self-determination; his instructions to Colonel Tobias Lear, consul general for the Barbary regencies, were consequently still more qualified, and it was Lear who was to conduct the negotiations with Tripoli.

The voyage out apparently enabled Eaton to convince the Commodore, for on arrival in the Mediterranean he was ordered to Egypt to seek out the pretender. In November 1804 he reached Alexandria, where he found the country in a state of more than usual turmoil. Despite the embarrassment of finding Hamet among the rebels against Ottoman authority, Eaton secured his ends. The cooperation of the Turkish viceroy was gained by flattery and by touching upon "the affinity of principle between the Islam and American religion"; the pretender was granted a safe-conduct and brought back to Cairo. On 23 February 1805 a fourteen-point convention was signed between the United States of America and "his Highness Hamet Caramanly, Bashaw of Tripoli," which established perpetual peace between the two governments while providing for the exchange of prisoners in case of war, and which recognized William Eaton as commander in chief of all land forces to be used against the common enemy. The Yankee bargain was completed with a provision which departed somewhat from the theoretical American attitude toward the outer world, and which pledged Hamet to reimburse American expenditures in restoring him to his rightful position from tribute paid to Tripoli by Sweden, Denmark, and the Batavian Republic.

Eaton and his subordinates had in the meantime been recruiting, and in March the self-appointed General led his force out into the Western Desert: one lieutenant, a sergeant, six other enlisted Marines, one midshipman, and a collection of Greeks, Levantines, and Arabs to a total of some four hundred men. With this crew he proposed to march the five hundred miles to Derna, a journey which no Christian had accomplished in all the centuries since the Moslem conquest. With this crew, despite the tergiversation and noncooperation of his prince, threats of mutiny by the native auxiliaries, and extreme shortages of food and water, he did. The shores of Tripoli were reached somehow, and on 29 March Eaton addressed the inhabitants in a proclamation which stressed the orthodoxy of the American religion and extended the American promises of peace, extensive trade, and prosperity to those who rallied to Hamet's cause. In April, with the help of gunfire from ships of Barron's squadron, Derna was taken by storm.[24]

The tide of war had turned. To continuing blockade and further captures had been added the fact that the Americans and the pretender now held the second city of Tripoli. "A deep impression" had been made upon the Pasha. But Barron was sick and Lear was weak: rightly willing to discuss conditions of peace, they wrongly concluded that an immediate settlement justified the abandonment of Hamet's cause and the ransoming of the crew of *Philadelphia*. Captain John Rodgers, so much of a fighter that he offered to raise the ransom money from the officers of the squadron if only the war could go on, had maintained the blockade while Barron lay sick ashore; but formal command was only turned over to him along with orders to negotiate.

So peace was made, the ransom paid, the prisoners released, and Eaton and Hamet evacuated from Derna, greatly to the fury of the former at being undercut by timorous superiors. Some satisfaction was afforded, however, to those of Eaton's persuasion, by Rodgers' handling of a renewed threat of war from Tunis. With an overwhelming American squadron anchored in his harbor the Bey, offered a quick choice between war and negotiation, opted for peace. The talks were transferred to the United States and Suliman Mellimelli, "a distinguished Tunisian soldier and statesman," was embarked with his suite in *Congress* for the voyage to the New World.

Peace, as the Jeffersonians now discovered, has her own difficulties, and speedily becomes a party matter even when war does not. The deeds of the Navy and of William Eaton had gripped the popular imagination, and the contrast between his wrongs at the hands of Barron and Lear and his reception by his compatriots led the hero to injudicious utterances. The upshot was that the Federalists, now seeing no substitute for victory, seized upon him and the unfortunate Hamet as sticks with which to beat the administration. Only after months of wrangling was the Tripolitan treaty ratified.

Nor did the presence in Washington of the distinguished Tunisian soldier and statesman ease Jefferson's lot. The Oriental splendor of

---

[24] Eaton's proclamation, which well repays study, is printed in *Naval Documents: Barbary Powers*, v, 467-70.

this first Moslem emissary to the Republic of the West drew crowds to the hotel that the State Department had rented for him, and where his loneliness was eased by governmental provision, through broad construction of the necessary and proper clause, of "Georgia, a Greek." While negotiations continued and the Ambassador proceeded on a grand tour, his retinue, freed from the pressures and austerity of Tunisian life, got drunk, quarreled, and deserted to the land of freedom and plenty. His departure in September 1806 left much unresolved, but the Navy still cruised the Mediterranean and in the next year the Bey compromised all his demands for $10,000 cash.[25]

The administration of Thomas Jefferson had been successful in meeting the requirements of money and effort imposed by the Tripolitan War. The experience, nevertheless, had left its mark. The Navy had perhaps not proven to be the "syphon" that Barlow had anticipated, but the 1802 budget of less than a million dollars had risen by 1805 to almost a million and a half, while the need for reinforcement following the loss of *Philadelphia* had obliged Gallatin to resort to the device of a special "Mediterranean Fund," supported by special levies. At no time had it proven possible to conform to the legal limits on naval personnel: those of the Act of 1801 were simply ignored, while the Act of 1806 was evaded by the expedient, worthy of "constructionists," of not counting personnel in the Mediterranean.

The logistic problem of supporting a squadron at such a distance had resulted in the development of a sizable administrative structure. Although storeships followed both Dale and Morris to the Mediterranean, and although a supply depot was early established at Gibraltar, it had originally been assumed that the squadron would maintain itself largely by local purchase. Credits on which commanding officers could draw were set up by way of London with a Baltimore firm at Leghorn and a French firm at Toulon; together with the consul at Gibraltar, these fiscal agencies were designated Navy Agents, with responsibilities in disbursing and in the purchase, custody, and issue of stores. But resumption of war in Europe ended the usefulness of Toulon, limited that of Gibraltar and Malta, and increased the requirements for supply from home, while the remote-

---

[25] C. O. Paullin, *Diplomatic Negotiations of American Naval Officers, 1778-1883* (Baltimore, 1912), p. 104; L. B. Wright and J. H. Macleod, "Mellimelli," 20 *Virginia Quarterly Review*, 555-65; Irving Brant, *James Madison, Secretary of State* (New York, 1953), p. 306.

ness of Gibraltar from the operating area brought orders to advance the depot.

This forward strategy, and the necessity of local procurement of small craft and supplies, led to a further proliferation of Navy Agents. In 1803 Preble established agencies at Malta, Syracuse, Naples, Messina, and Palermo; at Syracuse, which developed into the principal base, a considerable shore establishment grew up; and during the climactic campaign of 1804-5 additional agencies were created at Algeciras, Alexandria, and Cairo. Although effective enough, these improvisations in the logistic sphere proved costly, and in Washington the Secretary and the Chief Clerk continually bemoaned the extravagance of commanding officers. Following the settlements with Tripoli and Tunis, the facilities at Syracuse were given up and the number of agencies reduced, but the United States nevertheless retained an impressive network of commercial and naval representatives in the Mediterranean. The State Department had consuls at Lisbon, Cadiz, Gibraltar, Malaga, Alicante, Port Mahon, Leghorn, and Messina, and at Algiers, Tunis, and Tripoli; Navy Agents were maintained at Syracuse, Leghorn, Naples, and Malta.

Such an administrative structure inevitably tends to take on a life of its own, and it is to the credit of Smith and Goldsborough that they kept the ends rather than the instruments of policy in view. There was, of course, no intention of withdrawing again to the western shore of the Atlantic. To keep the peace with Barbary, to train up young officers, to testify to the rising glory of the young republic in this show window of the European world, the permanent Mediterranean Squadron long desired by Jefferson and Humphreys was to be maintained. But the wastefulness of the extemporized wartime structure had to be remedied: to follow up the policy of "Occonomy . . . without an improper parcimony" laid down at the start of the administration by General Smith, the oversized central Mediterranean establishment had to be cut down and the lines of communication strengthened. In 1806 and 1807 new arrangements were worked out: Navy Agents would be appointed for Madeira and Cadiz in the Atlantic approaches, and for Malaga; all Mediterranean activities were to be consolidated in a single place of deposit and under a single agent at Port Mahon, Minorca. This agency was confided to Dr. John Bullus, former surgeon of the Washington Navy Yard. Boarding the relieving flagship of the Mediterranean Squadron, the U.S.S. *Chesapeake*, Bullus sailed from Norfolk for the

Mediterranean on 22 June 1807. Off Cape Henry the frigate encountered H.M.S. *Leopard*.[26]

The national fury which followed the *Chesapeake-Leopard* affair only emphasized the fact that continued war in Europe, with its concomitant belligerent pressure on American commerce, had again made relations with the great powers the paramount concern. The country was back in the situation of 1794 and the Jeffersonians, having implemented Federalist intentions of using force against the weak, now followed Federalist example in resorting to negotiations with the strong. William Pinkney, Maryland lawyer and brother-in-law of Captain Rodgers, was dispatched to England to attempt a settlement. By late summer all ships of the Mediterranean Squadron had been hastily brought home. Although in subsequent years naval vessels on European business from time to time looked into the Mediterranean, no force could be maintained there. From the summer of 1807 until the Treaty of Ghent, American shipping in these waters was on its own.

Predictably enough, the embroilment of the United States with Britain was soon followed by renewed activity on the part of the rulers of Barbary. Angered by delayed receipt of tribute, the Dey of Algiers sent out a raider which captured three American ships, one of which, however, was retaken by her complement and the prize crew spiritedly thrown overboard. Payment of the arrears by Tobias Lear gained the release of the captured vessels, although a further sum was exacted by the Algerine ruler as compensation for his missing mariners. Two days later trouble came again: encouraged by Britain, the new incumbent increased an arrearage by appeal to the more rapidly revolving Moslem calendar, and, after forcing Lear to pay up, expelled him and ordered out the corsairs. But this was 1812: the Royal Navy had swept the board and only a single American ship could be found. War with Britain, in its turn, was followed by trouble with Tunis and Tripoli, whose rulers, disregarding their treaties with the United States, permitted the British to retake prizes sent in by American privateers.

Deprived, while the War of 1812 was in progress, of the chance to prey on American shipping, the Algerines undertook hostilities with

---

[26] *Naval Documents: Barbary Powers* contains much scattered information on logistic problems. See, in particular, the orders to squadron commanders: I, 468; II, 99-100; III, *passim*; IV, 133-35. For the structure as of May 1806, VI, 438; for the intended rationalization, VI, 505, 524-25.

Sweden and carried out a raid on the Spanish coast in which they kidnapped a number of inhabitants and committed impressive outrages. But chastisement, when it came, came not from Spain but from afar. For all his antinaval record, Madison was not slow to move. Less than a week after the Senate consented to the Treaty of Ghent, he asked the Congress for authority to proceed against Algiers. In May 1815 Decatur sailed for the Mediterranean, to be followed by Bainbridge in July, and the impressive force with which they were entrusted pointedly included not only the first American ship of the line to show the flag abroad but also the frigate *Macedonian* and the sloop *Épervier*, both captured from the British and recommissioned in the United States Navy. Within four days of Decatur's arrival the fighting was over: the Algerine admiral was dead, and two ships and five hundred prisoners were in American hands. Proceeding to Algiers, the Commodore presented the Dey with a treaty of a "liberal and enlightened" nature, which was accepted on 30 June, less than six weeks from the time the squadron left New York and but fifteen days after its passage of the straits. To adequate force there had now been joined a decisive commander: the boat came off with the signed treaty just as Decatur had signaled a general chase and was getting his squadron underway in pursuit of an Algerine cruiser that had appeared in the offing.

Tunis and Tripoli were soon dealt with on the same sound system. By the time Bainbridge arrived in August, all outstanding issues had been settled; nevertheless the appearance of this second armament had a salutary moral effect and diminished any inclinations to second thoughts. In October the greater part of the squadrons sailed for home, leaving two frigates and two brigs to watch over American interests in the Mediterranean. For all practical purposes American troubles with Barbary were over. To some this might have seemed the end of the story. In reality it was only the beginning.

4. *The Navy of the Enlightenment*

Late in life, in retrospective mood, John Adams offered Thomas Jefferson the title of father of the American Navy. This distinction, so contrary to Federalist scripture and to later historical interpretation, the Sage of Monticello gracefully accepted. Whatever the truth of the matter, this exchange of views between the realist and the ideologist who forty years before had wrestled with the problem of

Mediterranean commerce seems peculiarly appropriate. Although it was Adams who first employed the Navy in the defense of trade, it was Jefferson who had first urged such action, and the Jeffersonian offensive in the central Mediterranean marked the start of the effort to carry the American message into regions hitherto untouched by the light of rational institutions. Even if there was not, one might say there ought to have been some close connection between the advocacy of an ideology which knows no national boundaries and the creation of so important an instrument of distant policy. And perhaps there was: alone among American presidents, Jefferson enjoys the distinction of having spent more money on the Navy than on the Army.[27]

By 1815 the success of this first American crusade had been assured, with implications which were far-reaching. Long before, Humphreys had seen the pirates of Barbary as the first obstacle to be overcome in the progress toward the better world:

> See a new æra of this globe begun
> And circling years in brighter orbits run;
> See the fair dawn of universal peace,
> When hell-born discord through the world shall cease!
> Commence the task assign'd by heaven's decree,
> From pirate rage to vindicate the sea!

The task had now been commenced, and the effects, upon both the American reputation abroad and American confidence at home, were considerable. "The unexpected appearance of a squadron from the new world in the Mediterranean," reported Humphreys, "and the consequent decided measures . . . astonished the regents of Barbary . . . [and] operated powerfully in placing the character of the United States in a more advantageous point of view."[28] An Italian writer noted that many in Europe would like to see the American republic, as the nation which had shown the Old World powers "how subjects should be defended," as a nation "daily rising in splendor, glory, and prosperity," and as a commercial competitor with Great Britain, acquire a port in the Mediterranean. Praise for the conduct of the campaign against Tripoli came from such diverse author-

[27] L. J. Cappon (ed.), *The Adams-Jefferson Letters* (Chapel Hill, N.C., 1959), II, 582-84; U.S. Bureau of the Census, *Historical Statistics of the United States, Colonial Times to 1957* (Washington, D.C., 1960), p. 719; Macleod, "Jefferson and the Navy."

[28] Humphreys, "Poem on Happiness," *Works*, p. 41; "Remarks on the war between the United States and Tripoli," *ibid.*, p. 73.

ities in the fields of faith and works as the Pope and Admiral Nelson: the latter saw future trouble for the Royal Navy in the skillful handling of Dale's ships, and considered the burning of *Philadelphia* "the most bold and daring act of the age"; the former observed that Preble, "with a small force and in a short space of time, has done more for the cause of Christianity than the most powerful nations of Christendom have done for ages." Under the impact of the American example, however, the "most powerful nations" were beginning to stir. A year after Decatur and Bainbridge had settled with Algiers, Lord Exmouth appeared before the town with a fleet which included six ships of the line, only to pay a heavy ransom for the release of captives. In this episode there were pleasant ironies which moved one American officer to observe that the conduct of the Dey had been "as honorable to him as his Lordship's was disgraceful to the British." But the government of the Prince Regent had profited by the example of the Americans, and Exmouth was ordered back to do better.[29]

Even more important than the luster shed upon the American name abroad was the contribution of the Barbary wars to the feeling of American nationality and patriotism. "Ours be the toil, the danger, glory ours," Humphreys had written, expressing an attitude shared by the consuls and naval officers in the Mediterranean. "It must be mortifying to some of the neighboring European powers," wrote the American consul at Tripoli, "to see that the Barbary states have been taught their first lessons of humiliation from the Western World." Vigorous and successful action abroad led to increased national feeling at home. The deeds of Preble seized the popular imagination. Eaton, on his return, was hailed as the new Alexander, the new Cambyses, "the IV or Modern Africanus." "The midnight death of Somers was told in every farmhouse; the hand to hand struggles of Decatur against thrice his numbers inflamed the imagination of schoolboys."[30] In the thirties, when Jared Sparks published his "Library of American Biography," the only post-revolutionary lives which he included were those of Preble, Decatur, and Eaton; and if Preble was bound in the same volume as William Penn, the

[29] Filippo Pananti, *Narrative of a Residence in Algiers* (London, 1818), p. 400; *Naval Documents: Barbary Powers*, v, 42; Allen, *Barbary Corsairs*, pp. 173, 214; O. H. Perry to John Rodgers, Area 4 File, Naval Records Collection, National Archives.

[30] Humphreys, "Future Glory," *Works*, p. 55; Paullin, *Diplomatic Negotiations*, p. 105; H. Adams, *History of the U.S.*, ii, 436.

fact served merely to emphasize the identity of their ultimate goals. The impact of war in the Mediterranean was thus considerable, and was shortly to be reinforced by the naval feats of 1812. When to all this were added the connections between American Navy and American literature visible in the writings of Irving and Cooper and Willis and in the naval services of Pinkney and Paulding and Kennedy, it seemed unlikely that the efforts off the shores of Tripoli would be soon forgotten.

Yet while the Barbary wars had fostered the growth of nationalism, it was nationalism with a difference, harnessed and directed by those same universal theories and American facts that had directed the war itself. Jefferson, it may be said, had fought a rationalist's campaign. Constitutional scruples had arisen at the start in the question of how far a commander could go in repelling attack, lacking the sanction of congressional declaration of war. When the vigor of Preble's blockade had seemed to infringe upon the rights of neutrals, he had been ordered to modify his practices. Madison had worried lest Eaton's use of the pretender Hamet infringe upon Tripolitan rights of self-determination. So little was the artificial apparatus of the state obtruded into the affair, and so far were Old World procedures eschewed, that no diplomatic effort was made to obtain port facilities for the squadron. It seems simply to have been assumed that Dale would be permitted to base at Gibraltar. The extensive cooperation of the British at Malta excited gratification but not surprise. In the later stages of the war, armaments and crews were obtained from the Kingdom of Naples, and Syracuse became the principal base, yet not a single communication had passed between the two governments by the time peace came with Tripoli.

The conduct of the war with Tripoli, moreover, well illustrates the differential American approach to the problems of European great-power diplomacy and to those of the extra-European consular world. Although fought on the frontier of Europe by a squadron based on European ports, the war was carried on in almost complete isolation from the course of American relations with the European powers. Although the threat of France in New Orleans led Jefferson, in April 1802, to contemplate marriage with the British fleet and nation, it did not move him to redeploy his own frigates: throughout that spring and summer the ships of Morris' squadron were moving to the Mediterranean, away from the scene of impending crisis and into waters adjacent to the potential enemy. That the problem of New Orleans, like that of Tripoli, was fundamentally one of maritime commerce was sufficiently well symbolized when General Smith moved the two million dollar appropriation bill, but there the resemblance ended. Vindication of the seas from pirate rage was a part of the forward commercial policy; difficulties with the great powers called for other solutions. Nine days after deciding to relieve Morris for insufficient fighting spirit, the President was writing, apropos the Louisiana problem, that "peace is our passion," and a similar dualism was evident in relations with Great Britain. The embroilment of the two countries over questions of neutral rights and impressment was of no apparent relevance to the campaign in Barbary: the Navy in the Mediterranean operated from British bases and was financed through London bankers; the navy agencies at Messina and Malta were held by British merchants and that at Alexandria by a British firm. Proud though they were of their accomplishments, and jealous of their prestige, the Americans conducted their police action less as nationalists than as the self-appointed agents of the international commercial society.

Granted the assumptions of the period regarding the solidarity of mankind and the artificiality of states, this was in no way unnatural. Fact, in these matters, approximated theory in the world of the early nineteenth century, and individuals moved in osmotic fashion from nation to nation as from calling to calling. The Tripolitan admiral had been born a Scot; Joel Barlow became a citizen of France and John Paul Jones an admiral in the Russian service. In 1821, when the Pasha of Egypt dispatched an expedition against the tribesmen of the Upper Nile, his topgi bashi or artillery commander, Mahommed Effendi, was a former Harvard divinity student by the name of George Bethune English; with him marched Khalil Aga of New York and the Swiss-American Achmed Aga.[31] Just as eighteenth-century philosophy saw no sharp distinction of nationality or race, so eighteenth-century ship design drew no sharp line between merchantman, privateer, and warship, and no sharp line separated merchant and consul, sea captain and naval officer. Barlow in France and Eaton at Tunis combined profitable speculative ventures with diplomatic activity. The Baltimore firm of DeButts and Purviance, later Degen, Purviance, and Company, was the Navy's Mediterranean fiscal agent: a DeButts had served in the Navy during the

---

[31] G. B. English, *Narrative of the Expedition to Dongola and Sennaar* (Boston, 1823).

French war, a Purviance was consul general at London, a Degen became Navy Agent and consul at Naples. Bainbridge and Rodgers made trading voyages in times of slack naval activity. Preble's brother was engaged in commercial ventures in Europe and had hopes of becoming the first consul at Constantinople. While warring with the Pasha, the great Commodore yet found time to investigate and report on commercial possibilities for American traders, and his aims and accomplishments were succinctly described on the gold medal voted him by the Congress:

EDWARDO PREBLE DUCI STRENUO COMITIA AMERICANA
VINDICI COMMERCII AMERICANI ANTE TRIPOLI
MDCCCIV

This inscription, indeed, reflected the aims that had governed the Navy from its birth. Its ships might be the best in the world, but their number was small: the six frigates of 1794 were no force with which to go adventuring in big-power politics. Thinkers of a European cast like Hamilton and Gouverneur Morris had argued that a few ships of the line would make their country the arbiter of Europe in America, but none was seriously considered until the French affair, and none built until the War of 1812. Robert Smith understood the meaning of command of the sea as well as Mahan, but it was the freedom of the seas that was the American goal, quite apart from any limitations on American capabilities.[32]

Intended as a police force to keep the oceans clear for legitimate commerce, the Navy was projected for use against Algiers, was employed against the French, was sent against Tripoli. There was no intention of using it against the mistress of the seas. Thus both Madison and Hamilton opposed it in 1794 on the ground that it might lead to collision with Britain. As the War of 1812 approached, the Navy was weakened rather than reinforced, and when war came philosophy and necessity alike called for attacking the ships of the British merchants in preference to those of the British Admiralty. After 1814 there was projected a systematic program of naval expansion, paralleling the growth of commercial opportunity, but a police force the Navy remained until late in the century. Its squadrons were deployed around the globe, in the Mediterranean, in the West

[32] *Federalist*, xi; *ASP, FR*, 1, 408-9; *Naval Documents: Barbary Powers*, vi, 280-82; G. H. Preble, *Genealogical Sketch of the First Three Generations of Prebles in America* (Boston, 1868).

Indies, in the Pacific, in China seas, showing the flag of freedom and protecting a modern and progressive commerce against the activities of those who preferred the more primitive economic process of piracy. In simplest terms the Navy, like its parent nation, was a creature of the American Enlightenment.

With regard to such rational aims almost all could be Republicans, almost all Federalists, as the Navy coalition in Congress in 1809 and the party breakup after 1815 made clear. Observers who in 1801 expected a change in the attitude of government toward the problems of maritime commerce were disappointed, and no less so in 1829, when the Age of Reason gave way to the Age of Jackson. The Middle State Navy well represented the middle state of mind, and the old antinaval Republicans soon found themselves relegated to the dust heap of history. A grandson and namesake of Melancton Smith, who had violently opposed a navy, would in time retire as rear admiral; a descendant of the fiercely agrarian Senator Maclay would in time write a three-volume naval history unmarred by critical views. The Democrats, more ideologically committed than their opponents, would become the party of naval as of territorial expansion, the vigorous amphibious exponents of the new Æra.

The design and employment of the Navy as an instrument of policy thus conformed to fundamental American theory. Equally, the experience gained in the Mediterranean confirmed American preconceptions about the nature of the outer world. It was in Europe that danger lay, in the three great states of England, France, and Spain, all with warlike histories and with oppressive monarchical governments and religious establishments. To these "iron despotisms," wrote Charles Pinckney from Madrid, "We are such an Eyesore, that I am convinced there is not one which does not wish us sunk in the Sea."[33] From them help was welcome if forthcoming in the cause of progress, but they were not dependable. Early French support in the Mediterranean had been followed by anti-American intrigue in Naples and Egypt and by a gift of armaments to Tripoli. Early British employment of the Algerines as allies gave way to courteous assistance at Gibraltar and Malta and Cairo, and this in turn to difficulties over impressment. Spain had been helpful in Moroccan negotiations and had at one time given convoy to American shipping, but in 1804 she was supplying carpenters to build gunboats for the Pasha and in 1805 the capture of one of Barron's storeships

[33] *Naval Documents: Barbary Powers*, v, 183-84.

by a Spanish privateer and the breakdown of negotiations over Florida brought the Mediterranean Squadron to war alert. Clearly one could not look "to Europe for examples just." The great powers operated on the inconstant basis of expediency rather than on the immutable lines of principle. Trade with them was desirable, indeed essential, but it seemed unlikely that they would soon modify their historic practice of permanent commercial warfare punctuated by military shock. There could be no common cause.

Europe was dangerous, and all agreed on no involvement in its broils. But Europe, in a sense, was more a functional than a geographical concept: "Europe" was the great imperial powers who were always broiling. With the smaller trading states, as both theory and experience showed, there could be postulated a real community of interest. Less powerful at sea, less addicted to war, seeking to prosper rather than to dominate, more concerned with man and less with the state, they offered a more eligible entanglement. Neither in the Armed Neutrality nor in Jefferson's plan for armed belligerency had this been formalized, but commercial treaties had been negotiated and the history of the Mediterranean venture shows a continuing cooperation: the convoys provided by Portuguese and Dutch, the helpfulness in negotiation of the Swedish consul at Algiers and of the Danish consul at Tripoli, cooperation with the Swedish Admiral Cederström in the blockade of Tripoli, the loan of gunboats by the Kingdom of Naples.

And however defined, Europe was geographically limited. The seas that washed her shores led onward to other regions whose inhabitants, free from the oppressive legacy of the European past, might profitably be recruited into the civilizing world of trade. Here, too, theory seemed to have been confirmed by experience. From the head of the Baltic the vast territories of Russia reached southward to the Black Sea; it was "the imperial Moscovite" who had organized the Armed Neutrality "to check the ravages of future wars," and Russian intervention at Constantinople on behalf of the imprisoned crew of *Philadelphia* had led Preble to make special concessions to Russian vessels in his administration of the blockade of Tripoli. At the far end of the Mediterranean lay the empire of the Ottoman sultan, ostensible overlord of the regents of Barbary, custodian of the riches of the Levant, and guardian of the entrance to the Black Sea, and here again the prospect was promising. Bainbridge, bringing tribute from Algiers, had been flatteringly received; in Egypt, Eaton had been given helpful assistance by the Ottoman authorities. Consuls and naval officers had repeatedly urged the commercial and political desirability of a treaty of amity and commerce with the Grand Signior, while diplomatic reports from St. Petersburg, information from merchants in the Levant, and the observations of the Navy in the Mediterranean uniformly indicated a receptive attitude on the part of the Ottoman government.

In the Levant, moreover, the praiseworthy religious principles which Dr. Underhill had noted in Algiers held sway. There the religious affinities emphasized by the Moroccan "King's preacher" and by Madison and Eaton could be presumed to operate. Like American Protestantism, Islam was culture as well as religion: iconoclastic, individualistic, commercially minded, founded upon a Book. The central emphasis on the priesthood of all believers and the absence of any hierarchy placed Americans and Moslems in common opposition to the priest-ridden faiths of Europe, and called to mind the ancient view that the Protestant heresy was but that of Mohammed revived. So far as the future was concerned, this too augured well.

So the prospects for the new American Æra were not wholly unpromising, and already an important discovery had been made: not only were the material products of America—the rum, the grain, the fish—in wide demand, but there was an eager market for American skills. John Paul Jones had been called to command the Russian Black Sea fleet. Robert Fulton was doing weapons research in France. American naval architecture had excited the avarice of the Barbary rulers and the admiration of all. At Algiers the administrative abilities of the captive Cathcart had made him secretary to the Dey; at Tripoli the skills of the *Philadelphia* prisoners had been put to use, most notably in the service of Dr. Cowdery, the ship's surgeon, as physician to the Pasha.

The dawning of the great century of Western influence on the outer world found the United States in a peculiarly favorable position. Its maritime genius and its abstinence from Europe's wars made it a useful neutral carrier; its forward commercial policy made its services available; its remoteness and its policy of noninterference made its help acceptable. If the techniques first exported seemed largely military, this reflected not only American excellence in the design and manufacture of armaments but also the fact that rulers maintain themselves, and peoples their freedom, by force of arms.

With the liberal principles of commerce that America advocated came the technology that would make them work: the instruments of political self-determination were the corollaries of commercial interdependence.

The liberal commercial principles remained the key to the new age. In the belief that if only commerce were freed "the greatest mass possible would then be produced of those things which contribute to human life and human happiness; the numbers of mankind would be increased, and their condition bettered," Jefferson had worked to open both the Mediterranean and the Mississippi.[34] Sharing this basic viewpoint, Pickering had defined the true interest of the states of Barbary. In this spirit Eaton, on the outskirts of Derna, had promised the Tripolitans "perpetual peace and a free and extended commerce." Once these lessons had been taught and the corsairs curbed, the way lay open to the Levant. The task assigned by Heaven's decree had been begun. The first step in the spread of the American way had been taken.

[34] *ASP, FR,* I, 103.

CHAPTER III

The Missionary Impulse

1. The New England Religion

THE WAR with Tripoli, then, was not fought merely out of resentment of injury: unlike some other wars, it may be said to have been prosecuted with the welfare of both parties in mind. As was suggested by Pickering's instructions to Eaton and by the latter's proclamation to the inhabitants of Tripoli, the attempt to convert the Barbary states to liberal principles and an appreciation of the virtues of legitimate trade could at least be rationalized as an effort to make them see their own best interests. Given this pedagogical content, the campaign in the Mediterranean can be looked upon as a first missionary effort in spreading the principles of the new American Æra. Nor was it to be the last such effort: for much of the nineteenth century, Americans would work to open the world to the beneficent influence of commerce.

But the products of America could be exported in a variety of forms. In addition to the wheat and fish and rum, and to the liberal commercial doctrines which accompanied them across the sea, there was also the American religion. To many members of the revolutionary and post-revolutionary generations, this religion was a matter of deep concern. For Timothy Dwight it constituted the focus of his career, from chaplain in the Revolution to president of Yale. For David Humphreys other matters took precedence, yet after singing of freedom and commerce, of naval expansion and the improvement of the mechanic arts, Humphreys could spur his Pegasus still higher:

> To cure the pangs that nerve-torne nations feel,
> A bleeding world with better balm to heal;
> Come, emanation from the King of Kings,
> Religion! come, with healing on thy wings! ...
> Remit thy influence mild through every clime!
> Wide as existence, durable as time,
> Make earth's far corners feel thy sacred flame,
> And man adore th' UNUTTERABLE NAME![1]

---

[1] Humphreys, "Future Glory," *Works*, pp. 64-65.

No more than the new order of ages was the New England religion for one country only; like the gospel of commerce, this gospel had universal applicability. Equally, the requirements of its propagation soon called for action overseas.

In theory, at least, the missionary element in American history dates back to the time of the first settlements. Among the purposes of the Virginia Company was that of "propagating the Christian Religion to such people as yet live in Darkness." The charter of the Massachusetts Bay Company declared the inciting of the natives to the "Christian fayth" to be the "principall ende" of the enterprise. Yet however natural this attitude to seventeenth-century colonizers, and however sincere the efforts of such apostles to the Indians as John Eliot, the problem of survival came first. Although Cotton Mather and Samuel Sewall briefly entertained hopes of evangelizing the Mexicans, it was only with the religious revivals of the eighteenth century that the seeds were sown of that missionary enterprise that flowered in the nineteenth.[2]

The nineteenth century was to distinguish itself in all forms of humanitarian endeavor. In such an atmosphere the old New England Calvinist, cheerfully able to contemplate his own election and the damnation of his less deserving neighbors, would have seemed much out of place. Yet despite this inheritance it was the Congregationalists of New England who were to contribute most vigorously and effectively to the development of the American concern for human welfare. The latter half of the eighteenth century had brought forth, in the development of the New England theology, a new Protestantism which emphasized the individual rather than the system, and which led to a release of energy much like that of the Reformation of the sixteenth century. Underlying the revolutionary agitation and the growth of American patriotic aspiration, and helping to provide the energy that led American merchants across the oceans and the American Navy to Tripoli, were changes in American religious thought; and these same changes lay at the base of American nineteenth-century reforming efforts, whether at home or beyond the seas. That such developments took place is indicative of the vigor of New England religious thinking, but the seeming paradoxes involved require a brief examination of the underlying theological considerations.

[2] Harry Bernstein, *Origins of Inter-American Interest* (Philadelphia, 1945), pp. 66-69.

A hundred years after the first colonial foundations, the old Calvinism of New England had become a stultifying affair. The zeal that had freed Holland, changed England, and settled Massachusetts had vanished. Life had outpaced theology, and the effects were manifest in declining church membership, the Half-Way Covenant, and an unconverted ministry. But all this was ended by the new formulations propounded by Jonathan Edwards, developed by Joseph Bellamy, and systematized by Samuel Hopkins, which infused a new American content into the old Calvinist structure. By succeeding in a new synthesis, which reaffirmed the sovereignty of God while at the same time emphasizing human freedom, the Edwardeans made religion and morality one, and accomplished the paradox of releasing, through justification by faith, tremendous energy for good works. From a religion of despair, Calvinism was transmuted into one of hope.[3]

In the Edwardean system an infinitely good God, the moral governor of the world, loved His children and acted for their welfare. But the children, in their turn, bore great responsibility. For while predestination remained, one of the decrees by which God established His divine plan provided for that freedom of the will through which the others were to be realized. Thus the New Divinity repudiated the paralyzing doctrine of inability in ways favorable to preaching and the winning of souls. Sinners might still suffer in the hands of an angry God, but it was not necessary to be a sinner. The alternative of life or death was up to the individual; the regenerate soul, seeing the perfection of God, could choose conversion. With the choice now left to the individual, the proportion of elect to damned rose rapidly; even, perhaps, as Samuel Hopkins suggested, to a ratio of thousands to one. Still further hope was held out by the enlarged meaning of the Atonement, for no longer had Christ died merely for the elect. His sufferings were "sufficient to expiate for the sins of the whole world. . . . Therefore the gospel is ordained to be preached to the whole world, to all nations, to every human creature."[4]

This emphasis on the freedom of the will and on the ability to choose salvation had powerful consequences. A premium was placed

[3] F. H. Foster, *Genetic History of the New England Theology* (Chicago, 1907); Alan Heimert, *Religion and the American Mind* (Cambridge, Mass., 1966).

[4] Foster, *Genetic History*, pp. 167-86; *Works of Samuel Hopkins* (Boston, 1852), I, 365.

upon the evangelical approach, revivalism was encouraged, church membership increased, missionary interest revived. The stress placed on piety and on the experience of conversion, transcending creedal boundaries, had unifying and nationalizing consequences for the inhabitants of the thirteen colonies. The balancing of theocentricity by ethnocentricity had individualistic and democratic implications of importance for the revolutionary movement. Since virtue was defined as love of being in general and since sainthood called for zeal and activism, the implications ran beyond revolutionary agitation to include all kinds of reform that would renew the individual. In the furtherance of such reforms the use of human endeavor was now more than acceptable: it was imperative.[5]

Excepting only, perhaps, Edwards himself, the individual most influential in the change of the New England Calvinists from pharisaical exclusiveness to apostolic fervor and from passivity to self-sacrificing service was the Reverend Samuel Hopkins. Born in 1721, of a Sunday, and consequently intended by his father for the ministry, Hopkins' career as preacher and theologian spanned two colonial wars, the Revolution, and the establishment of the new government, and extended into the administration of Thomas Jefferson. As a member of the class of 1741 at Yale, Hopkins came to maturity in the period of the Great Awakening; having been aroused in his last year in college by the preaching of Whitefield and Jonathan Edwards and by personal acquaintance with David Brainerd, a missionary to the Indians, he immediately undertook the study of divinity with Edwards at Northampton. Two years later he was ordained pastor of a newly organized congregation at Great Barrington, on the western frontier of Massachusetts, where he labored with varying success until dismissed in 1769.

Such an ending to a quarter-century of effort must have seemed unpromising, but his second pastorate was to last still longer. In 1770 he accepted a call to the First Congregational Church at Newport, where, except for the period of British occupation, he remained until his death in 1803. Two more contrasting parishes it would be difficult to imagine, but together they embodied the American experience. Deep in the western forest, recently settled, sparsely populated, and exposed to the northern Indian tribes, Great Barring-

[5] Heimert, *American Mind*, pp. 12-18, 112, 131-33, 308-13.

ton was still a missionary field. Of prosperous and worldly Newport, looking outward to the seven seas, the same might have seemed true to this stern thinker, but if so it was in a wholly different sense.[6]

It has been said that Hopkins' *System of Doctrines*, which he published in 1793, provided the first closely articulated scheme of New England theology. He himself felt that he had made "some improvement" upon the teachings of Jonathan Edwards. In any event his system, a fusion of the zeal of the Great Awakening, the metaphysic inculcated at Yale and reinforced through friendship and study with Edwards, and the experiences of seventy years, came rapidly to have great influence.

To Hopkins and to his followers, the Hopkinsians or "Consistent Calvinists," love of God and submission to His will were in no way dependent on the question of one's own election. Quite the contrary, the Christian should rejoice only in submission to the sovereign will, whatever its effect on him, being both willing and indeed eager to suffer perdition "if the greatest good of the universe and the manifestation of the divine perfections should so require." The essence of true religion was disinterested benevolence, benevolence to being in general, the desire of true Christians that God's kingdom "may be promoted and come to perfection, so as to comprise the greatest possible happiness and glory of the universe." There was to be no thought of self: rejoicing even in his own destruction, if "necessary for the glory of God and the greatest good of the whole," the disinterested Christian would say, "I have no condition to make; let God be glorified, and let his kingdom be most happy and glorious, whatever becomes of me."

But the glory of God, to the Old Calvinists a matter of individual concern and future promise, had been modernized by the vision which equated it with the happiness of men. Since God's design in creating the world was the greatest good, and since true Christianity consisted in disinterested "benevolence to being in general," it followed that the chief duty of man was to work to ensure the highest degree of happiness to the greatest possible number. Number and world were literally construed by Hopkins: "The doctrine that Christ

[6] For Hopkins' life, see the memoir by the Rev. Edwards A. Park in *Works of Hopkins*, I, 9-266; F. B. Dexter, *Biographical Sketches of the Graduates of Yale College, First Series* (New York, 1855); R. D. Birdsall, "Ezra Stiles versus the New Divinity Men," 17 *American Quarterly*, 248-58.

died for the elect only, found no mercy at his hands. He taught that Christ suffered equally for all mankind."[7]

So the New Divinity brought forth not only a notable release of energy but a new ethicizing of religion. It encouraged the revivalism of Edwards and his followers; it made Yale the mother of colleges and Hopkins the father of foreign missions. But these changes, far from being isolated phenomena, had much in common with developments in other spheres, and in this lay their great strength. The government of a loving God on the best of all possible plans implied a faith in predestined progress. The Congregational polity bore strong resemblance to the American ideal of a world of self-determination and small government. The individualism of the conversion experience had correspondences with both revolutionary agitation and subsequent reform movements, while the obligation to disinterested benevolence became the source of the persistent American propensity to the performance of good works. Firmly though some of the New England divines would have reprobated the thought, the new theology carried more than a touch of Jeffersonianism in its emphasis on the individual and in its confidence in progress. Much, indeed, is to be said for the suggestion that the American Enlightenment was in large measure a translation into secular terms of the aspirations of the Great Awakening.[8]

These aspirations, in any case, were those of the new American Æra, and had little to do with the religion of the Old Lights. The universe was moving toward the greatest happiness of all; no longer was it impious of man to aid in the working out of the great design. If unrighteousness, oppression, and cruelty were to be taken away, it would only be by the spread of universal benevolence in the form of Christian love. But since "divine revelation is of service to men no further than it is attended to and understood," the spread of Christianity among the unregenerate depended upon the work of men.[9]

The Hopkinsian contribution to Calvinist thought brought it, one may say, to a point where only external missionary work could have provided an adequate outlook for the energies of the believers. Disinterested benevolence, the obligation to work in God's service

---

[7] Park, "Memoir," *Works of Hopkins*, I, 179, 211, 237; Hopkins, "System of Doctrines," *ibid.*, I, 382-95; "Dialogue between a Calvinist and a semi-Calvinist," *ibid.*, III, 156-57.

[8] Heimert, *American Mind*, p. 538.

[9] Hopkins, "System of Doctrines," *Works*, I, 398; "An Inquiry into the Nature of True Holiness," *ibid.*, III, 261.

for the happiness of others, inevitably brought to mind the disparity of condition between the elect living in New England and those who dwelt in outer darkness. Christ had said, "If any man will come after me, let him deny himself, and take up his cross, and follow me." The idea that for the glory of God man should labor joyfully and without thought of recompense to increase the sum total of the world's happiness was perhaps the greatest contribution of the Consistent Calvinists. Such altruism can make Christian martyrs. It made, in America, a notable missionary movement.

2. *Evangelism and the Millennium*

If one overlooks the somewhat theoretical preoccupation of Cotton Mather and Samuel Sewall with the possibilities of missionary work in Mexico, it was Samuel Hopkins who first conceived the idea of sending American evangelists to foreign lands. The proposal followed naturally from his thought, from the implications of Consistent Calvinism and disinterested benevolence, and from the experiences of his long career.

"His patriotism," Hopkins' biographer tells us, "fitted him to be a theologian, and his theology made him a patriot."[10] But neither patriotism nor theology was narrow in outlook: both the universal spirit of his religion and the experiences of his life made parochialism impossible. French and Indians in the forest, the wide mercantile horizons of pre-revolutionary Newport, the passage of European armies during the Revolution all tended to inculcate a world view, while the contrast, in his two congregations, between Stockbridge Indian and Newport merchant spanned the entire history of man.

Inevitably, the patriot and friend of liberty who had worked for the salvation and education of the Indians was impressed by the large slave population of Newport. Inevitably, too, he saw the slaves not just as servants, but as representatives of yet another aboriginal culture, untouched by gospel light except through the unchristian institution of bondage. With a strong faith in his religion and in his country, unable to perceive any difference in logic between the liberty contended for by the colonists and the liberty denied the slave, Hopkins quite naturally became a champion of the abolition of slavery and of the Christianizing and civilizing of Africa.

The plan, which Hopkins put forward in cooperation with Ezra

---

[10] Park, "Memoir," *Works of Hopkins*, I, 43.

Stiles in 1773, was to colonize the Dark Continent with American Negroes, aided temporarily by white missionaries. Funds were raised to support the enterprise, and two converted and willing Negroes were put to the study of divinity with Dr. Witherspoon at Princeton. But by the time the candidates were ready to go, the state of public unrest prevented. Although Hopkins still felt that "while we are struggling for our civil and religious liberties, it will be peculiarly becoming and laudable to exert ourselves to procure the same blessings for others," the war made action impossible, and the scheme met with no success in his lifetime. Only in 1825 was a Negro church, led by two of his now aged pupils, constituted in Boston and embarked for Liberia on the brig *Vine*. But the seed had by that time borne other fruit in a missionary effort extending far beyond Africa.[11]

Despite the dislocations of war and postwar years, the Edwardean emphasis on activist zeal and the Hopkinsian concern for disinterested benevolence survived. Stimulated by this revivified Congregationalism, by the vigorous efforts of the Baptists, by a generation of Methodist camp meetings, and by the heady effects of independence, there came, at the century's end, another awakening. For many, it is true, the Great Revival began in a period of darkness and despair, in which the very foundations of religion and good government seemed threatened. But if it was, in its origins, a defensive reaction to infidelity, Jacobinism, and European intrigue, it soon became, at least for the bolder spirits, a counteroffensive.

At first the emphasis was internal. Vigorous efforts were made to bring about a return to true principles of religion and morality, and to resist such liberal phenomena as Unitarianism and Universalism. New colleges sprang up to provide an educated ministry: Bowdoin, Middlebury, Union, and Williams were all established in the century's final decade. In Connecticut, Massachusetts, and Rhode Island, missionary societies were founded by activists of the Edwardean-Hopkinsian persuasion, a missionary press developed, and a revived missionary effort was directed toward the frontier settlements and toward such Indians as remained conveniently accessible. For the moment this investment in the weapons of spiritual warfare was out of proportion to the available tasks. The Indians remained un-

[11] *Ibid.*, I, 44-46, 115-56; Hopkins, "Dialogue Concerning the Slavery of the Africans," *ibid.*, II, 547-88; Ezra Stiles and Samuel Hopkins, *To the Public* (Newport, 1776); F. B. Dexter (ed.), *The Literary Diary of Ezra Stiles* (New York, 1901), I, 363-64.

responsive; work on the frontier was generally of an interim nature. But one thing these new developments did ensure: that organizations and techniques—"means," in the language of the day—would be available when the American churches suddenly took the world for their province.[12]

This startling enlargement of the American missionary horizon was the product of a variety of causes. The latter part of the eighteenth century had been a notable age of exploration: the voyages of Captain Cook and the African travels of James Bruce and Mungo Park, reported in both secular and missionary press, had called attention to distant lands and to the sad condition of their pagan inhabitants. To this new knowledge, patriotism and religion combined to suggest the response: in his election sermon of 1783 Ezra Stiles had looked forward to the time when "the babel confusion of contradicting missionaries" would be ended, and had confidently foreseen that an "unexpected wonder, and a great honor to the united states" would come with American success in "christianizing the heathen, in which romanists and foreign protestants have very much failed." Yet the work of "foreign protestants," successful or no, was itself important to the commencement of the American effort. In England a new missionary age was dawning, stimulated in part by the activities of English explorers, and just as Portuguese voyages to the Orient had been followed by the missionary ventures of Matthew Ricci and Francis Xavier, so news of the new discoveries brought forth the Protestant evangelizers. These English actions elicited an American response.[13]

Theological independence for the Americans was, after all, a matter of slow development rather than an event of the year 1776, and the enduring relationships of the Atlantic community were reflected in the missionary sphere. Jonathan Edwards had written an influential life of David Brainerd; through a reading of this book William Carey, England's great pioneer missionary to India, had found his calling; Carey's own writings exercised a powerful influence on the American churches. The very existence of the English missionary movement, with its promise of the conversion of the

---

[12] O. W. Elsbree, *The Rise of the Missionary Spirit in America, 1790-1815* (Williamsport, Pa., 1928); C. J. Phillips, "Protestant America and the Pagan World" (unpublished doctoral dissertation, Harvard University, 1954).

[13] Elsbree, *Missionary Spirit*, pp. 102-3; Stiles, *The United States Elevated to Glory and Honor*, pp. 57, 69.

heathen, was heartening to American believers. Observing that since the foundation in England of the first modern missionary society a "whole concourse of missionary and Bible societies have come into existence," a Boston minister pointed out that "the most distinguished writers on the prophecies, though differing in other respects, have been constrained to agree . . . that in 1792, a new era opened to the world."

The first response of the American brethren to the organization of English foreign missionary societies was consequently one of attempted cooperation and mutual assistance. But cooperation proved impossible, owing to administrative difficulties and to the tensions that developed between the two countries as the War of 1812 approached. If this was a setback, there was nevertheless enough religious vitality and self-confidence among the Americans to permit it to be overcome. When the American missionary movement turned outward, to bring about the salvation of the heathen, the conversion of the Jews, and the speedy fulfillment of prophecy, it did so on its own.[14]

However logically it followed from what had gone before, the decision of these early-nineteenth-century Americans to undertake the evangelization of the world must seem a little breathtaking. Citizens of a country but newly independent at the cost of an exhausting war, and of one still subject to foreign pressure and internal disaffection, they undertook the task without benefit of state support, depending solely on their own resources and on their burning zeal. The shift in aim of the evangelizers, from Indian tribe to the great globe itself, betokens an extraordinary confidence in the cause.

Such confidence and optimism were needed, given the magnitude of the task confronting those who undertook Christ's Great Commission, going into all the world to teach the gospel. An estimate of 1803 concluded that of a world population of 800,000,000, some 500,000,000 were pagans and another 250,000,000 either Mohammedans, Jews, or Papists. Only some 50,000,000 could be classed as Protestants, and these, of course, were far from united in determined support of the goal. Yet a bare thirteen years later the board of the most important American missionary organization would formally resolve that the energies of Christendom, wisely directed

[14] Elsbree, *Missionary Spirit*, pp. 18, 47-48, 84, 112, 130; Phillips, "America and the Pagan World," p. 33.

and attended with the blessing of the Spirit, might send the gospel over the world within a quarter of a century.[15]

American missionary ardor had outrun its domestic opportunities. American confidence was high. The explorers and divines of the mother country were showing the way. But despite these favorable circumstances it may be doubted that a handful of American believers would have attempted the evangelization of the world without the existence of one added factor: the apocalyptic fervor derived from the conviction that the millennium was at hand. This conviction, at that time, was very real.

The belief that the end of the world was imminent and the Kingdom of Heaven nigh had been strong in the early Christian church. Medieval man had been preoccupied with the problem of the last judgment. The Reformation brought a vigorous revival of millennial ideas among the Protestant sects, together with a new antipapal bias which anticipated for the Church of Rome that destruction earlier predicted for the Roman Empire. In this form millennial thinking accompanied the Puritans to New England, to become a favorite subject for speculation and for sermons and to produce, as its principal literary monument, the 224 annotated stanzas of Michael Wigglesworth's *Day of Doom*. Together with the body of doctrine, the site of the impending event was also Americanized: Cotton Mather and Samuel Sewall thought that Mexico City would become the New Jerusalem; more provincial in outlook, the citizens of seventeenth-century New Haven expected Christ to return in person to dwell among them.[16]

The eschatology of the first generations of colonists, like that of the early Christians, was premillennial: to Mathers and Wigglesworths a cataclysmic second coming would precede the thousand years of Christ's reign on earth. But the eighteenth century brought radical change, with the development of the idea that the Kingdom of Heaven might be realized by gradual means through the conversion of the world to Christianity, and that Christ's coming would follow rather than precede the thousand years of peace. Like the reenergizing of Calvinism, of which, in fact, it formed a vital part, this change owed much to Jonathan Edwards, who advanced the idea

[15] Elsbree, *Missionary Spirit*, p. 143; *Memorial Volume of the First Fifty Years of the American Board of Commissioners for Foreign Missions* (Boston, 1861), p. 130.

[16] I. V. Brown, "Watchers for the Second Coming," 39 *Mississippi Valley Historical Review*, 441-58.

of a golden age within history which would prepare the way for Christ's return. So encouraged by the Great Awakening that he felt it possible that the millennium had already begun at Northampton, Edwards put forward these thoughts in a series of sermons which he published before mid-century. Taken up and popularized by his followers, the millennial hope became a central feature of the American Protestant tradition, and indeed of American thinking generally.

However surprising it may seem, given the scientific bias of the age, that so powerful and acute a mind should hold these views, Edwards was in good company. Although the new science had raised problems as to the physics of the day of wrath, it had not diminished the interest of the scientists in the end of the world: in his later years Isaac Newton devoted himself to the study of the crucial prophetic texts of Daniel and of Revelation; toward the end of the eighteenth century the scientist Joseph Priestley saw in the outbreak of the French Revolution signs of an imminent second coming. For educated Americans, moreover, the Edwardean gradualist view of the millennium, with its supporting parables of the leaven and of the mustard seed, fitted well with the atmosphere and energy of the times. For much of the nineteenth century this millennial view remained a respectable belief, held by college presidents and learned divines, and a driving force behind American reforming efforts. So well, indeed, did it accord with the aspirations of the post-revolutionary generation that its religious aspects are not easily disentangled from its secular ones.[17]

The latter, in point of fact, also enjoyed a respectable ancestry. The promise of an untouched hemisphere had been an intoxicating one, and the early exploration and settlement of America had been marked not only by a healthy greed but by a considerable utopianism. In the first half of the eighteenth century the philanthropist George Berkeley, disgusted at his age and clime and hoping for something better from the New World, had seen the westward course of empire leading to the consummation of history in America: "Time's noblest offspring is the last." With the Revolution, the two branches of millennial thinking coalesced in the patriotic concept of the new American Æra. Grandson of Jonathan Edwards and

[17] Brown, "Watchers"; Heimert, *American Mind*, pp. 59-61, 66, 345-46; Perry Miller, "The End of the World," 8 *William and Mary Quarterly* (3rd series), 171-91. D. E. Smith, "Millennarian Scholarship in America," 17 *American Quarterly*, 534-49, touches on some of the important ramifications of the millennial viewpoint.

a Berkleyan scholar during his undergraduate days at Yale, Timothy Dwight gracefully echoed his benefactor's lines in his poem "Columbia." Joel Barlow, who thought that the millennial period could "rationally be expected to be introduced without a miracle," saw the Revolution as signaling the Saviour's "reign on earth." Although Humphreys' "Poem on the Future Glory of America" was largely concerned with the facts of Barbary piracy, it was nonetheless set in the millennial framework and looked forward to "the consummation of all things" and the coming of "heav'n's perennial year."[18]

While patriots, fired by the success of the Revolution, were employing the millennial rhetoric to proclaim the imminent golden age, the course of history was strengthening the confidence of the divines that the last days were near. Accomplishments in exploration and discovery were suggestive of the prophet Daniel's description of "the time of the end"—"Many shall run to and fro, and knowledge shall be increased"—which would bring the deliverance of the Jews and the conversion of the world. Wars and revolutions, the spread of Jacobinism, and the rise of Bonaparte all seemed to presage the imminence of the events promised by the prophets of Israel and the author of Revelation. If the phraseology of prophecy was sometimes cloudy, great assistance in its interpretation could be derived from the contemporary chiliastic writings of George Stanley Faber, a young English clergyman. Reprinted in America and widely drawn upon, Faber's works provided the key that would relate the happenings of the present to the visions of the past. For two decades following the commencement of the Great Revival, the imminent millennium was both a staple of American sermonizing and a stimulus to American action.[19]

Interpreting the times with the aid of Revelation 16, Timothy Dwight, now president of Yale, showed how John had foreseen the rise of deism and the coming of the *philosophes*, while the *Connecticut Evangelical Magazine* saw in Paul's Second Epistle to Timothy a description of the Age of Reason. Considered in the light of history and prophecy, the course of the European wars seemed

[18] M. C. Tyler, *Three Men of Letters* (New York, 1895), pp. 20-27, 55; Barlow, *Prospect of Peace*; Humphreys, "Future Glory," *Works*, pp. 50-51, 65.

[19] Elsbree, *Missionary Spirit*, p. 122. The title of Faber's book, *A Dissertation on the Prophecies, that have been fulfilled, are now fulfilling, or that will hereafter be fulfilled, relative to the Great Period of 1260 Years; the Papal and Mohammedan Apostasies; the Tyrannical Reign of Antichrist, or the Infidel Power; and the Restoration of the Jews* (London, 1807), sufficiently describes the tenor of its 773 pages.

to indicate that "the great pillars of the Papal and Mahometan impostures are now tottering to their fall." Belief in the imminent conversion and restoration of the Jews, the importance of which was demonstrated by numerous passages of Scripture, was now widespread. In Boston and New York it resulted in the formation of organizations dedicated to speeding the day, while in New Haven action reached the level of eccentricity as the Reverend David Austin expended his substance in the construction of houses, wharves, and magazines for the Jews whom he believed would foregather there on their way to the Holy Land to await the Messiah.

Still, if Napoleon could be considered as the eighth king of Revelation 17:11, and if his concordat with the Pope fulfilled the prediction of the healing of the wound of the beast in Revelation 13:12, it remained to establish the chronology of coming events. As to this, the holy writings were, to the uninitiated, somewhat vague, but as the Millerite delusion of the 1840's was to prove, a millennium with a date has greater impact than one obscured by the mists of an impenetrable future. Fortunately, it may be said, there was on the question of timing a general agreement that the span described by John in Revelation—the holy city being trod underfoot for forty and two months, and the thousand two hundred and threescore days clothed in sackcloth, as well as Daniel's "time, times, and an half" until "all these things shall be finished"—meant that the reign of Antichrist would endure for 1,260 years. To most, Antichrist was the Pope of Rome, although some preferred to substitute for him, or to include as his eastern coadjutor, the Sultan of Turkey. In any event it remained to fix the starting point of the reign in order to project its end, and the contention that in A.D. 606 the Pope first rose to the dignity of universal ruler and "became a beast in the highest and most proper sense" was bolstered by the belief that the Turkish Empire had arisen in the same year.[20]

Eighteen sixty-six was thus the foreordained time, and if, to skeptical moderns, such certitude seems surprising, the absence of ambiguity at least testifies to sincerity of belief. Such belief, moreover, accentuating as it did that sense of expectation that had pervaded American evangelical thought since the time of Edwards, could hardly avoid having operative consequences. The commencement of the millennium was but a half-century or so away, and while few of the confident interpreters of prophecy could hope to see the day,

[20] Elsbree, *Missionary Spirit*, pp. 124-35.

their children certainly would. The result was to give both a new urgency and a new sense of obligation to Christ's Great Commission—"Go ye into all the world, and preach the gospel to every creature"—and a heartening promise of predestined success in the task. For those capable of disinterested benevolence, the call to labor on behalf of humanity and the coming kingdom was extraordinarily compelling.

The kingdom for which these Americans were to labor had a very American tone. Both in theology and in politics, by the beginning of the nineteenth century, it seemed to many that the mainstream of history had shifted to the New World. In this the divines had perhaps led the way, with Mather's suggestion that Mexico City would prove to be the New Jerusalem, and with Edwards' sense that the millennium had begun at Northampton. But similar claims concerning the affairs of this world had by now been made by the propagandists of the Revolution, by the designers of the Great Seal, and by the patriotic poets. By the turn of the century, evangelical theology and democratic politics had become inextricably mixed, as shown by suggestions that the election of 1800 was the natural outgrowth of both the Great Awakening and the Revolution, or that the inauguration of Jefferson signaled the prelude to the millennium and the democratization of all the world's governments. Although conversion remained central to the New Divinity, the mixture of democratic and scientific ideas with which the Work of Redemption was surrounded made it almost interchangeable with the work of America. The vision of the millennium toward which this work was aimed differed little from the *Vision of Columbus*, or from that of Joel Barlow.[21]

We may contemplate the millennium through the eyes of Samuel Hopkins. For Hopkins, as for many of his contemporaries, the attraction of this future state was immense. If anywhere, it is in his writings on this subject that grandeur and realism are evident in the work of the "prosaic divine." As Channing, who loved the man while rejecting his doctrine, observed, "The Millennium was more than a belief to him. It had the freshness of visible things. He was at home in it. His book on the subject has an air of reality, as if written from observation."[22]

The promise, then, was not only of a new heaven but of a new

[21] Heimert, *American Mind*, pp. 537-38, 540-44.
[22] Park, "Memoir," *Works of Hopkins*, I, 208.

earth. It was the vision of the frontier farming preacher, hindered by the requirements of living from the furtherance of his thought:

> They will then have every desirable advantage and opportunity to get knowledge. . . . They will all have sufficient leisure to pursue and acquire learning of every kind, that will be beneficial to themselves and to society . . . and great advances will be made in all arts and sciences, and in every useful branch of knowledge, which tends to promote the spiritual and eternal good of men, or their convenience and comfort in this life.

It was the vision of a man who knew the New England soil:

> And at that time, the art of husbandry will be greatly advanced, and men will have skill to cultivate and manure the earth in a much better and more easy way than ever before; so that the same land will then produce much more than it does now . . . and that which is now esteemed barren, and not capable of producing any thing by cultivation, will then yield much more for the sustenance of man and beast than that which is most productive now. . . .

It was the vision of the Yankee mechanic:

> There will also, doubtless, be great improvement and advances made in all those mechanic arts, by which the earth will be subdued and cultivated, and all the necessary and convenient articles of life, such as utensils, clothing, buildings, etc., will be formed and made in a better manner, and with much less labor than they now are. There may be inventions and arts of this kind which are beyond our present conception. And if they could be now known by anyone, and he could tell what they will be, they would be thought by most to be utterly incredible and impossible. . . .

> When all those things are considered . . . it will appear evident that in the days of the millennium there will be a fulness and plenty . . . to render all much more easy and comfortable in their worldly circumstances and enjoyments. . . . It will not be necessary for each one to labor more than two or three hours in a day, and not more than will conduce to the health and vigor of the body; and the rest of their time they will be disposed to spend in reading and conversation, and in all those exercises which are necessary and proper in order to improve their minds and make

progress in knowledge, [and it seems almost an afterthought] especially in the knowledge of divinity.[23]

Yet while the millennium offered answers to the problems of American life, its blessings were by no means limited to America:

Then shall all the world be united in one amiable society. All nations, in all parts of the world, on every side of the globe, shall then be knit together in sweet harmony. . . . and the art of navigation, which is now applied so much to favour men's covetousness and pride, and is used so much by wicked debauched men, shall then be consecrated to God, and applied to holy uses.[24]

Such were the promises of the new American divinity. Almost two centuries later, such promises still move men.

3. The Outward Thrust

The Edwardean synthesis, with its emphasis on the individual conversion experience, on the greatest happiness for all, and on the importance of activist zeal, introduced a new note of responsibility and energy into American life. The imperative to work for the general good was strengthened by Hopkinsian Consistent Calvinism and disinterested benevolence. As this concern for others came to be institutionalized by the foundation of missionary organizations, new geographical knowledge and the search for commercial opportunity strengthened the outward look. As the prophecies of old were reinforced by the signs of the times, the sense of urgency and anticipation increased. By the first decade of the new century almost everything was in readiness for an effort to evangelize those dwelling in outer darkness. All that was needed were the volunteers.

These, too, were products of the vigor and the ferment of the time. The Great Revival had reemphasized the need for an educated ministry. The last decade of the century had brought the foundation of four new colleges, of which two, Williams and Union, were presided over by Edwardeans. Yet progress was not without its difficulties: the divisions between Old Calvinists and Hopkinsians made for trouble within the Congregational fold, while the advance of atheism and free thought, locally disguised as Unitarianism and Universalism, endangered the very foundations of orthodoxy. In

[23] Hopkins, "Treatise on the Millennium," *Works*, ii, 274-75, 285-87.
[24] Edwards, "Work of Redemption," quoted in Heimert, *American Mind*, p. 99.

1803 the election of the liberal Henry Ware to the Hollis Professor-ship of Divinity in Harvard College revealed the magnitude of the threat.

The violent dispute which followed need not detain us here. Suffice it to say that the accession to this professorship of one doubtful both of the Trinity and of the total depravity of man meant that Har-vard was lost to the orthodox. The need for a new foundation was plain. Under the leadership of the Reverend Jedidiah Morse of Charlestown, father of American geography and of the inventor of the telegraph, the answer was found in the establishment of a new theological seminary at Andover, Massachusetts. Skillful strategy on the part of Morse and his followers and the immediacy of the need secured the cooperation of the Hopkinsians, who had been planning a seminary of their own. And on one point, at least, the reuniting factions presented a united front, for Morse, somewhat surprisingly for an Old Calvinist if not for a geographer, was him-self an ardent proponent of missionary endeavor and a millennialist who anticipated the fall of both Pope and Sultan in 1866.[25]

In the autumn of 1808 the Andover "Theological Institution" opened its doors. The sermon, on this auspicious occasion, was preached by Timothy Dwight. To this sturdy patriot, the state of the world appeared encouraging. The founding of a new establishment to teach the doctrines of the Reformation, of primitive Christianity, and of early New England was itself an inspiring sign, and the pres-ent era offered added inducements to the preaching of the Ameri-can truth. "The ancient establishments, civil, literary, and religious, of the Old World are, to a great extent, crumbling into ruins. The throne of the *Romish* hierarch is shaken. . . . The tottering mosque of Mahommedism announces its own approaching fall." From the four corners of the earth could be heard a Macedonian cry; soon the Jews would hasten to the land of their fathers and the heathen "*cast their idols to the moles and to the bats.*" In view of the imminence of the millennium the response of the present generation was crucial.[26]

The attitude of the elders was clear, if perhaps a little theoretical. The young remained to be heard from. But at Andover, as is so often the case, the students were ahead of their teachers, and it was from

[25] Elsbree, *Missionary Spirit*, pp. 93-99.
[26] Timothy Dwight, *A Sermon preached at the opening of the Theological Institution in Andover; and at the ordination of Rev. Eliphalet Pearson, LL.D.* (Boston, 1808).

the students that action was to come. By 1810 the seminary had enrolled seven young men whose efforts were to bring into being the
first important American missionary organizations, the American
Board of Commissioners for Foreign Missions and the American
Baptist Missionary Union.

Four of the seven—Samuel J. Mills, James Richards, Gordon Hall,
and Luther Rice—were graduates of Williams College of the class
of 1809; Adoniram Judson had graduated first in the class of 1807
at Brown; Samuel Nott was an alumnus of Union College and
Samuel Newell of Harvard. All were in one way or another to work
for the conversion of the world; five were to become the first missionaries to leave the United States for foreign shores, and the zeal with
which they consecrated their lives is evidenced in the circumstances
of their deaths. Mills, the leader in the enterprise, was first to go,
dying in 1818 of a fever off the coast of Africa, where he had been
in the service of the American Colonization Society. Three years later,
after work in Calcutta, Mauritius, and Ceylon, Newell fell victim to
the cholera, acquired while ministering to the sick of Bombay. In
1822 Richards died in Ceylon, where he had labored both as missionary and physician. After thirteen years in India, Hall succumbed
to cholera when he interrupted a preaching tour in the interior to
assist in combating an epidemic. In 1850, his health shattered by
thirty-seven years of work in Burma, Judson died aboard ship, three
days out of Moulmein on the sea voyage which it had been hoped
would restore him.[27]

The impulse to carry the light to the heathen seems to have come
first to Samuel Mills, son of a Hopkinsian divine, who as a child
was said to have been consecrated by his mother to service to God
as a missionary. In 1806, in his freshman year at Williams, Mills and
some fellow students were engaged in prayer and meditation when
a thunderstorm drove them to refuge in the lee of a haystack. The
site of the haystack is now marked by a monument, for it was there,
while waiting for the sky to clear, that Mills proposed to his comrades
that they carry the gospel across the seas. The result was the formation of an undergraduate secret society dedicated to this purpose, the
constitution and records of which Mills and Richards subsequently

[27] For biographical sketches of the early missionaries (and much information on
all aspects of the missionary effort): Harvey Newcomb, *A Cyclopedia of Missions*
(New York, 1855), E. M. Bliss, *The Encyclopaedia of Missions* (New York, 1891),
and H. O. Dwight et al., *The Encyclopedia of Missions* (New York, 1904).

took with them to Andover. There the number of interested spirits was augmented, and there in 1810 Mills and his colleagues appealed to their elders to be sent to foreign lands. Their request was transmitted to the General Association of Massachusetts, then in session; the establishment of the American Board of Commissioners for Foreign Missions was approved in June and the Board itself constituted in September.

Since the magnitude of the task made it seem the part of wisdom to approach the London Missionary Society on the possibilities of joint action, Adoniram Judson was dispatched to England on this errand. But cooperation proved impossible, and in January 1812, despite both the impending Unitarian schism and the financial distress of the times, the Board decided to pledge its support of the enterprise, "trusting that, as it seemed clearly the will of God that those men should go, by His aid and the use of proper means, the requisite funds would be obtained." By great efforts the sum of $6,000 was collected, and on 6 February 1812 Judson, Hall, Newell, Nott, and Rice were ordained at Salem. Before the month was out Judson and Newell, with their wives, had sailed from Salem for Calcutta, while the others had taken ship at Philadelphia for the same destination.[28]

The month which witnessed the departure of the first missionaries also brought an important step in the organization of the movement. Finding itself the beneficiary of funds and charged with their management, the Board felt the need for incorporation, and on 12 February petitioned the Massachusetts legislature for a charter. The response was at first discouraging. To the decline of evangelical feeling in the Boston area and to the distractions of imminent war were added problems of party conflict. Ridicule of the missionary idea by Benjamin Crowninshield, Salem merchant and future secretary of the navy, whose arguments gained weight from his experience in the India trade, led to failure of the bill, and a second attempt also encountered difficulties. But perseverance had its reward and in June the act of incorporation finally passed.

At the same time that it was acquiring legal identity, the Board, originally conceived of as an enterprise of Massachusetts and Connecticut Congregationalists, was being broadened. The suggestion in 1811 that the Presbyterian General Assembly might wish to estab-

---

[28] Phillips, "America and the Pagan World," pp. 20-31; Elsbree, *Missionary Spirit*, pp. 99-100, 111; *Memorial Volume of ABCFM*, pp. 41-49.

lish a cooperating organization for the evangelization of the heathen elicited a statement of preference for a single directing body, together with an offer of aid. In the next year eight Presbyterians from New York, New Jersey, and Pennsylvania were added to the Board, while the Congregational representation was expanded by the appointment of members from Rhode Island, New Hampshire, and Vermont. In 1813 the Episcopalian John Jay was co-opted, and a representative added from the Associate Reformed Church. A scant three years after the General Association of Massachusetts had responded to the pleas of the young men of Andover, the Board had become a "national" institution.

The composition—one might better say the weight—of the Board of 1813, the group later looked back upon as the founders, is indicative of the strength and nature of the missionary appeal. Eighteen of its twenty-six members were college graduates: eight from Yale; two each from Dartmouth, Harvard, Columbia, and the College of New Jersey; one each from Brown and Pennsylvania. Of eleven ministers of the gospel, five presided over the colleges of Yale, Bowdoin, Middlebury, Union, and New Jersey, while two were professors of divinity. Most prominent of the representatives of the world of letters were Timothy Dwight, oldest of the members, president of Yale, and patriot; and Jedidiah Morse, Calvinist controversialist and mover in the foundation of the Andover seminary, whose concern for the Word was matched only by his interest in far places. The sphere of politics provided the governors of Connecticut and Rhode Island; John Jay, diplomat, former chief justice, and former governor of New York; Elias Boudinot, signer of the Declaration, sometime member of the Congress and director of the mint, and future organizer and first president of the American Bible Society; and John Langdon, delegate to the Constitutional Convention, senator, and late governor of New Hampshire. From the world of affairs came William Bartlet of Newburyport, William Phillips of Boston, and Robert Ralston of Philadelphia, three of the richest merchants of America.[29]

National and nonsectarian though it was, the American Board did not long stand alone. In wholly unanticipated fashion, its own first effort led to the establishment of a rival body. Although interest in missionary work had been increasing among the Baptists of Amer-

---

[29] *Memorial Volume of ABCFM*, pp. 19-20, 71-82, 104-25.

ica, owing to the efforts of William Carey and other English brethren, no attempt had been made at organized activity. Suddenly, however, the Baptists found themselves faced with an appeal for support from Adoniram Judson and Luther Rice, who, from the study of Scripture while surrounded by watery vastnesses on their passage to India, had changed their views on the subject and mode of baptism, and who, barely arrived, had resigned their commissions from the American Board. The result of this defection was the organization of the American Baptist Missionary Union and the undertaking by this sect of active operations overseas. In 1819 the Methodists took up the challenge, to be followed by other denominations as the century wore on, while from its founding in 1816 the work of all groups was increasingly aided by the American Bible Society.[30]

The purpose was the evangelization of the heathen. The article of export was the Word. But the packaging was done in America and the theologians, like Hopkins, were patriots. Although the American gospel was still that of the Protestant God, not yet fully transmuted into that of capitalism, the visible evidences of grace were what gave weight to the teaching. Just as the astronomical knowledge of Father Ricci, centuries before, had gained him access to the court of Peking, so now the useful and mechanic arts, so central to the American millennium, would prove helpful to his American successors.

These arts, indeed, had already been employed in attempts to convert the American Indian, and although some efforts had foundered on account of the cost of school and industrial equipment, it was the equipment that had had the strongest appeal. Nor was this practical outlook on missionary work the sole property of those on the receiving end. The implications for worldly happiness of the Hopkinsian doctrine of disinterested benevolence powerfully affected the evangelists themselves. "It seems impossible," said the Reverend Leonard Woods of Andover, who had preached at the ordination of the first five missionaries in 1812, "that any man who considers the Christian religion a blessing should not desire its universal diffusion. ... Think of the difference between the inhabitants of New England, and the people in those countries where pagan influence prevails. To what is all the difference owing, but to the Christian religion?"[31]

Inevitably, the missionary facet of early American life had much

---

[30] Elsbree, *Missionary Spirit*, pp. 113-21; histories of the various societies in Bliss, *Encyclopaedia of Missions.*

[31] Elsbree, *Missionary Spirit*, pp. 54, 57, 142; Park, "Memoir," *Works of Hopkins,* I, 144.

in common with the other projections of American influence overseas. Commercial and naval policy, Hopkinsian divinity, and missionary endeavor can all be seen as aspects of the American Enlightenment. All had an internationalist bias, all aspired to a better future, all were concerned with man whoever and wherever he might be and paid little heed to race or allegiance. A commercial policy aimed at reducing artificial barriers to the free and rational flow of trade, a Navy created in this interest and conceived less as an instrument of war than as one of policy, and a religious enterprise with the humanitarian and civilizing emphasis of Hopkinsianism all share these common elements.

In all the seaports were important. America, as the nineteenth century opened, was a maritime civilization, and its urban centers were windows on the outer world. There, in the seaport towns, were to be found the influential divines: Samuel Hopkins at Newport, his brother Daniel at Salem, Jedidiah Morse at Charlestown. There merchant marine and Navy linked the Western world with far places, and permitted traffic in both visible and invisible commodities: one of the founders of the American Board had been Navy Agent at Portsmouth and had declined the secretaryship of the Navy; another was collector of the port of New London. There also, in the profits of trade, were the means which would further the work, and in its prospects a motive for their consecration. These prospects, indeed, had been an integral part of Hopkins' own vision of the Africans' future: "if they were brought to embrace Christianity, and to be civilized, it would put a stop to the slave trade and make them happy. And it would open a door for trade which would be for the temporal interest of both Americans and Africans."[32]

The merchants rose to the challenge. Among those who contributed most heavily to the new theological foundation at Andover was John Norris, East India merchant and parishioner of Hopkins' brother Daniel, to whom "the missionary idea was practically synonymous with Hopkinsian disinterested benevolence," and whose initial gift of $10,000 was the result of his belief that the new school would advance the missionary cause. Still larger gifts came from Moses Brown and William Bartlet, merchants of Newburyport where Hopkins had preached during his revolutionary exile, who were persuaded that "missionary work and the seminary are the same." William Phillips of Boston, kin to the founders of the acad-

[32] *Ibid.*, I, 146, 153.

emies at Andover and Exeter and inheritor of a large mercantile fortune, was a contributor to the theological school, a president of the American Bible Society, and one of the original incorporators of the American Board.

Nor were the Baptists immune to maritime influence. Although the years since the Awakening had brought a rapid growth in rural, southern, and frontier areas, they still retained substantial strength in southern New England and in the Middle States. At the organizing convention of the American Baptist Missionary Union in 1814, the leading members were from the seaport cities. An honorary member of the convention was the Presbyterian Robert Ralston of Philadelphia, a successful East India merchant who had aided English missionary efforts, founded the Philadelphia Bible Society, and had been one of the Presbyterian members added to the American Board in 1812. Other members of the Baptist convention had also acquired an unparochial world view: prominent among the clerical members were the Reverend William Staughton, born and brought up in England, and the Reverend Stephen Gano, whose early career as a privateersman had involved shipwreck, marooning, and imprisonment.[33]

In direction of effort, as well, the missionary crusade came to resemble the naval and commercial aspects of American overseas policy: the Old World was largely bypassed. The highly organized and governed states of Europe had proven too much for the United States to deal with, whether in questions of restrictive commercial policy or of battle fleets. Whatever the preferences of their captive citizens, the governments remained unresponsive to the individualistic bias of American commercial policy. Trade, with them, could be had only on terms set by the chancelleries for reasons of state.

Such reasons did not argue in favor of the New England theology as a desirable import item. Although Edwards had hoped that America, having become the Old World's source of gold and silver, would also become its source of spiritual treasure, the Erastianism of its states and the monolithic organization of the Catholic Church posed mighty obstacles, in Europe and in Latin America as well, to efforts to reach and convert the individual. Evangelization was therefore directed toward the Indies, the Levant, and the Isles of the Sea. Although the American Board explored a considerable part of South America in 1823-26, no action followed; only in mid-

[33] Elsbree, *Missionary Spirit*, pp. 96-98, 105-7, 112, 117, 150.

century, with the foundation of the American and Foreign Christian Union, was some slight effort expended on the redemption of "those who were in the bondage of Roman Catholicism." In theory, no doubt, the Pope was the preferred Antichrist, but in practice the missionaries contended with the Sultan.

Their campaign, in the beginning at least, they waged alone, relying for their protection on God and not on government. All agreed that individual salvation was not properly of governmental concern; a sectarian expeditionary force could hardly expect support from the secular arm in a nation dedicated to minimum government and religious freedom. Sympathy the authorities might give: Madison, while at the State Department, had asked his consul at Canton to extend good offices to an English missionary; but it was not a policy matter.[34]

With time this would change. Repeating the history of Christianity itself, the missionary effort would become institutionalized, would acquire property, would become a vested interest. Webster, when secretary of state, would act in defense of threatened missionary property, and by the end of the century the missionary interest had become a principal focus of gunboat diplomacy. All this, however, was far in the nationalistic future. The beginning was a manifestation of that individualistic internationalism implicit in the doctrine of the rights of man, in the idea of progress, and in the New Divinity. Jefferson's view that the free flow of trade would maximize "those things which contribute to human life and human happiness" was complemented by Hopkins' confidence that the spread of New England's civilizing Christianity would promote commerce, "unite mankind," and bring about "the most happy state of public society that can be enjoyed on earth."[35]

4. To the Levant

The first missionary efforts, the venture to India and its offshoots in Burma and Ceylon, were directed toward "pagans." But the American Board had large ideas. Although created and chartered to propagate the gospel in "heathen lands," the Board rejected all geographical restriction on its labors. By interpreting "heathen lands" to mean unevangelized communities wherever found, it

---

[34] *Memorial Volume of ABCFM*, p. 80; Bliss, *Encyclopaedia of Missions*, "American and Foreign Christian Union"; Elsbree, *Missionary Spirit*, p. 107.
[35] *ASP, FR*, I, 303; Hopkins, "System of Doctrines," *Works*, I, 398.

brought within its purview not only the Indian tribes of the United States but also the Moslems, the "more benighted parts of the Roman Catholic world," and the "nominal Christians of Western Asia." Such loose construction of its charter was of particular importance with regard to the Near East, where territory under Moslem rule, extending from Egypt and Palestine to Armenia and Persia, contained many thousands of nominal Christians in a state of deplorable ignorance and degradation. To hope for the conversion of Mohammedans without the exemplification of a true Christianity seemed vain; the Oriental Churches had lost "nearly all the essential principles of the Gospel"; a wise plan of attack upon the Moslem world called for the preliminary purification of Near Eastern Christianity. In 1818, therefore, it was resolved to commence a mission to western Asia, and in September of that year two young graduates of Middlebury College and of the Andover seminary, Pliny Fisk and Levi Parsons, were appointed to this work. After a year of preparation and fund-raising at home, Fisk and Parsons sailed from Boston for Smyrna in November 1819.

Their instructions were very general. Their task,

> ... for angels great, in early youth,
> To lead whole nations in the walks of truth,

was very large. They were to look upon their mission as "a part of an extended and continually extending system of benevolent action for the recovery of the world to God, to virtue, and to happiness." From the heights of the Holy Land and of Zion they were to look out on the widespread desolations that presented themselves on every side to Christian sensibility. "The two grand inquiries ever present to your minds will be, WHAT GOOD CAN BE DONE? and BY WHAT MEANS? What can be done for Jews? What for Pagans? What for Mohammedans? What for Christians? What for the people in Palestine? What for those in Egypt, in Syria, in Persia, in Armenia, in other countries to which your inquiries may be extended?" Thus the New World commenced to pay its debt to the cradle of Christianity. Early in 1820 the ship *Sally Ann* reached Smyrna, where Fisk and Parsons were welcomed by an international trading community which included English, Dutch, and Swiss, as well as some Philadelphia merchants and Boston loyalist exiles.

This first invasion of the Levant was to last but two years. After repairing to the celebrated college at Scio for a summer's study of modern Greek, the two missionaries proceeded to spy out the land, and in November made an exploratory tour of some three hundred miles, visiting the places where once had stood and flourished the Seven Churches of Asia. After exploration came action. While Fisk returned to Smyrna to prosecute his studies, Parsons moved onward to Jerusalem, where he arrived in February 1821, bearing the Scriptures in nine languages and five thousand religious tracts, the first Protestant missionary to enter the city with the intention of making it a permanent field. So American missions to Bible lands, "like their apostolic predecessors," were begun in the Holy City, and so commenced "that strange undertaking to carry the Gospel to the people living heedless in the land where it was first proclaimed."[36]

Parsons' labors in Jerusalem were brief. The revolt of the Greeks against Turkish rule had brought increasing disorder throughout Ottoman dominions. At Smyrna frequent outbreaks of violence forced Fisk to live much in retirement, and as the terror spread to the Greek population of Jerusalem, Parsons was obliged to abandon his post. Returning to Smyrna, his health enfeebled, he rejoined his companion, and in early 1822 the two embarked for Alexandria in the hope that the benefits worked by a change of climate would permit a return to Jerusalem in the spring. But the disease grew worse, and in February, aged barely 30, Parsons died.

The blood of martyrs is the seed of the church. The intimate association of Parsons' name with the scenes of the Saviour's life had made him something of a personage at home, and his death was widely lamented. In America the Board bestirred itself to provide a replacement, but for the moment the Jerusalem mission was abandoned. Although Fisk had intended to proceed alone to the Holy City, the continuing disturbances in Palestine made it seem prudent to repair to Malta, where another laborer was momentarily expected. The voyage was made interesting, if not encouraging, by the presence as fellow passenger of the American renegade George B. English, bound homeward from service in the Egyptian Army, whom Fisk labored in vain to reconvert. But the arrival was more cheering. Reaching Malta in April 1822, Fisk found the Reverend Daniel

[36] *Memorial Volume of ABCFM*, pp. 79-80, 229-31; Rufus Anderson, *History of the Missions of the American Board of Commissioners for Foreign Missions to the Oriental Churches* (Boston, 1872), i, viii-x, i, 9-13; Alvin Bond, *Memoir of the Rev. Pliny Fisk, A.M.* (Boston, 1828); Dwight, *Encyclopedia of Missions*, "Levi Parsons." Julius Richter, *History of Protestant Missions in the Near East* (New York, 1910) is the standard secondary work.

Temple and his wife, recently arrived from Boston with a printing press for the use of the missionaries in the Mediterranean.

Eastern outpost of Protestant rule, safe from turmoil under British control, Malta was also an important stopping place for shipping bound for the Levant. For a decade the island was to remain the most important missionary station in the Mediterranean, site of the press, refuge in time of trouble. Here, while recruiting his spirits, Fisk gained a new helper. Although the responsibilities of the press prevented Temple from journeying eastward, news had been received that the Reverend Jonas King, graduate of Williams and of the Andover Seminary and professor-elect of Oriental languages at Amherst, was studying in Paris. Invited by Fisk to join him, King volunteered for a three-year term with the American Board and, without awaiting an answer, started at once for Malta. There the two Americans were joined by the celebrated and difficult Joseph Wolff, and in January 1823 all three set out for Jerusalem by way of Egypt and the desert.[37]

During their stay in Egypt the missionaries visited Alexandria and Cairo and made a three-hundred-mile ascent of the Nile to the ancient city of Thebes, preaching as they went. Observing the stupendous ruins of Luxor and Karnak, fallen "as all human glory will soon fade and wither," Fisk remarked with good democratic spirit that the "proud monarchs, and their abject slaves, now sleep in the dust, and their spirits receive their just reward from Him who is no respecter of persons," and with Hopkinsian zeal that "there is a Temple, whose columns shall never fall, . . . whose worship shall never cease, and whose inhabitants shall never die." As they moved about the country the missionaries disputed with rabbis and Catholic monks, with Coptic priests, a Persian sufi, and the "President" of the Pasha's college. In some places they found that their preaching excited "a high degree of fanaticism," but the concern

[37] Bond, *Memoir of Fisk*; Anderson, *Oriental Churches*, I, 13-16; D. H. Temple, *Life and Letters of Rev. Daniel Temple* (Boston, 1855); [Mrs. F.E.H. Haines], *Jonas King: Missionary to Syria and Greece* (New York, 1879); biographical sketches in Bliss, *Encyclopaedia of Missions*. One of the remarkable migratory figures of the nineteenth century, Joseph Wolff was born the son of a Bavarian rabbi, successively embraced Catholicism and Anglicanism, traveled widely in the East, married a daughter of the Earl of Oxford, was ordained deacon by the Bishop of New Jersey and priest subsequent to his return to England, and spent his last years in charge of a Somersetshire parish; animadversions on his character are scattered throughout the correspondence in Archives of the American Board of Commissioners for Foreign Missions, ABC 16.9, Vol. 1 (Houghton Library, Harvard University).

which this engendered was diminished by the helpful support of two English consuls. In the course of their journey the Americans were able to "communicate religious truths in several languages," and to distribute 900 Bibles and some 3,700 tracts, while a meeting with the Prince of the Druses, a Christian descendant of the Prophet temporarily in exile, led to an invitation to visit on Mount Lebanon.

Early in April the three engaged a guide and thirteen camels to carry themselves, their food and water, and their books, and set forth on "course E.N.E." to cross the desert to the Promised Land. The journey was a hot one and the caravan was quarrelsome, but the missionaries' spirits remained high. Singing and discoursing they proceeded onward, passing through Gaza, where blind Samson slew the Philistines, and after an eighteen-day journey entered the Holy City. Three and a half years after leaving America, and after many detours and much effort, Fisk found himself at last upon the Mount on which his Saviour died. Here, from their rooms in the Greek convent, the missionaries could walk out to Bethlehem and Calvary; here they visited the fields where David tended his flocks and the cave where Jeremiah wrote the Lamentations, and descended to Jericho and the Dead Sea. Surrounded, as Fisk wrote, by dangers, trembling at every step, cast down by the desolations of a Jerusalem where three-quarters of the inhabitants denied the divinity of the Lord and the atoning efficacy of his death, they redoubled their efforts to teach all comers and to distribute the Word. But difficulties ensued, the hot and sickly season was approaching, and much territory remained unexplored. Late in June, after two months in Jerusalem, Fisk and King set out northward by way of Jaffa, Tyre, and Sidon for the previously unvisited city of Beirut, capital of the Turkish province of Syria.

Topographically an eastern Naples, Beirut lies on rising ground at the edge of a large bay. With a population of perhaps five thousand at the time the Americans arrived, it was the "great emporium" of Syria and a port where the steady movement of shipping offered good communications with the outer world. To the south the plain abounded with olive and fruit trees; to the eastward the terraced vine-clad slopes of Mount Lebanon, with its remaining cedars, rose upward to an altitude of ten thousand feet. Snow-crowned for much of the year, the mountain offered an eligible retreat for the hot months, as well as opportunities for missionary labor among two interesting groups: the Druses, who professed what appeared to be a peculiar variant of Mohammedanism; and the Maronites, descendants of an ancient Christian sect which, subsequent to the fifteenth century, had reunited with the Church of Rome. Other opportunities existed in the cities of Damascus, Tripoli, Sidon, and Tyre, and on the island of Cyprus, all within two or three days' journey and hence easily supplied with books and tracts. To Fisk these advantages, together with the presence of a friendly British consul, argued strongly for Beirut as a possible missionary station. Summer visits to Mount Lebanon and to Tripoli made him think the region a hopeful field. In October he left the city to return to Jerusalem, but within a month others had occupied his place.[38]

Two new workers, Isaac Bird and William Goodell, had arrived at Malta in early 1823, accompanied by their wives. After nine months devoted to the study of Italian, useful as lingua franca in much of the Levant, they had again taken ship, to reach Beirut in November. Such were the continuing troubles in Palestine that Fisk and King advised them to make the city their headquarters. The apparent advantages of the site made the advice compelling, and with this decision the first Protestant mission in Syria was begun. Again the first step was language study, and while Bird concentrated on Arabic, the vernacular of the Maronites and Syrian Catholics, Goodell devoted himself to Turkish written in the Armenian alphabet, the so-called Armeno-Turkish, the language of most of the Armenians of the Ottoman Empire.[39]

The year 1824 brought two milestones in the history of the missionary effort. In Beirut the wives of the missionaries opened a class for six Arab children. In Palestine there developed the first persecution. Of far less importance over the long run, the latter event gave rise to immediate problems. The arrival of the Americans in Palestine and Syria and the visits of a number of British missionaries had thoroughly alarmed the papal church. So, at least, the Americans thought, when they reported letters from Rome of January 1824 which urged the Catholic and Maronite authorities to take every measure against the Protestants. Shortly the two Antichrists were

[38] Bond, *Memoir of Fisk*; Anderson, *Oriental Churches*, I, 16-20; Richter, *History of Missions*, pp. 185-86.

[39] A. L. Tibawi, *American Interests in Syria, 1800-1901* (Oxford, 1966), pp. 22-25. Bird is sketched in Bliss, *Encyclopaedia of Missions*; on Goodell, see E.D.G. Prime, *Forty Years in the Turkish Empire* (New York, 1876), one of the best of the missionary biographies, and William Goodell, *The Old and the New; or the Changes of Thirty Years in the East* (New York, 1853).

linked in cooperation, with the issuance of a firman by the Sultan, "influenced, as it would appear, by Rome," which forbade the distribution of Christian Scripture.

Little attended to by the generality of the pashas, this firman nevertheless gave some added weight to Christian complaints. In Jerusalem, where Bird had joined Fisk, the two were arrested in February while selling Scripture to Armenian pilgrims. Their rooms were searched; some papers were seized; shortly they found themselves haled before Moslem judges and charged, on the evidence of a copy of Genesis, with distributing books neither Mohammedan, Jewish, nor Christian. From this plight, however, they were extricated by the vigorous action of the British consul at Jaffa; shortly, for whatever reason, the Governor of Jerusalem was removed. Already assistance had been given the Americans by British agents, in Egypt and in travel along the Syrian coast. Now there had been positive intervention. Nor was this the last time the American missionaries in the Levant would benefit from English diplomatic support.

Again, with the hot season, the missionaries retired upon Beirut. From that base journeys were made throughout the summer to Damascus and Aleppo, to Antioch, Latakia, and Tripoli, to preach and to distribute tracts. By now their activities were known, and news of their coming ran before them in rumors that they purchased converts or engaged in devil worship. But despite these complications and the hardships of road and lodging, of beating sun and drenching rains, they persevered. In the spring of 1825 another visit was made to Jerusalem, but the arrival of the Pasha of Damascus, collecting tribute with his army, led to such disorder that the effort was again cut short.

King's three-year term of service had now expired, and in August 1825 he sailed for home. A heavier blow was soon to follow, for in October Pliny Fisk, the first arrival, died at Beirut after an illness of two weeks. In his nearly six years in the Levant, Fisk had explored Egypt, Palestine, and Syria and had reputedly fitted himself to preach in four languages; his loss seemed irreparable. All the Beirut consulates half-masted their flags and a numerous procession followed the body to the grave, but most affecting to his brethren were the weeping Arabs, who asked who now would tell them of God's Word. For the Palestine mission, at least, no answer was readily apparent; the state of continuing tumult in the Holy Land and the lack of personnel made it necessary to abandon this station.[40]

By 1826, then, both pioneers were dead, and the Jerusalem mission appeared a failure. In all the Levant, only Goodell and Bird remained at Beirut. Although Eli Smith, a young graduate of Yale and Andover, would reach Syria early in the next year, his visit was for the purpose of language study, and his primary responsibility was the administration of the press at Malta. Amid these discouragements the two Americans at Beirut continued their efforts in preaching, teaching, and the study of tongues, transcribing "useful works" into the local languages, and trusting in God. Some twenty hopefully pious individuals could now be counted up—Armenians, Maronites, and Greeks—who had been convinced of the errors of their churches; two Armenian "bishops" had been converted; and there had been the bittersweet experience of the first native martyr, Asaad Shidiak, who for embracing the antipapal truth had been brought before the Maronite patriarch, bastinadoed, loaded with chains, and cast into the prison from which only death would release him.

Such persecution, together with orders from the Patriarch that the missionaries be avoided "as a putrid member, and as hellish dragons" and his excommunication of all who should associate with the "Bible men," could perhaps be accepted as normal hazards for those who sought to spread the word of God. But the increasingly chaotic situation in Syria placed insuperable obstacles in the way. In 1826 a Greek raid on Beirut plundered the houses outside the walls, and the Bedouin, sent down by the Pasha of Acre to repel the attackers, plundered within. In the spring of 1827 the city was visited by the plague. In October the destruction of the Turkish fleet at Navarino was followed by the departure of the European ambassadors from Constantinople and of the British consul from Beirut.

With no source of protection, with a breakdown in trade which made funds impossible to obtain, with war apparently imminent, and with no visits from British or American warships, the times seemed hopeless. In May 1828, accompanied by the two Armenian "bishops" who had joined their church, the Americans boarded an Austrian ship and retired, as Fisk had done five years before, to Malta. The sadness of the occasion was somewhat mitigated by the

---

[40] Bond, *Memoir of Fisk*; Anderson, *Oriental Churches*, I, 20-31, 42-44; Tibawi, *American Interests*, pp. 26-36.

number who came to say farewell and to ask divine protection for the travelers, "comforting evidence that, whatever may be the impression we have left on the general population, there are *some* hearts in Syria, which are sincerely attached to us."[41]

Retreats are never heartening, and retreat had now been forced. But if the accomplishments of eight and a half years' devotion seemed meager, the enterprise had been unprecedented and a beginning had at least been made. This beginning should not be underestimated: amid a strange and hostile civilization, preaching had been begun. As in the time of the primitive church, the effort to carry the word of God through the ethnic chaos of the Levant required the gift of tongues, and posterity can marvel at the linguistic accomplishments of these young apostles, the products of New England farms and New England colleges. Pliny Fisk, before his death, was said to have preached in French, Italian, Greek, and Arabic; at Malta, Daniel Temple had held services in Italian; Bird had made himself fluent in Arabic and was writing a series of controversial letters in that language which would reach a printed total of 535 pages; Goodell was mastering both Turkish and Armenian, and before his death would complete the translation of the entire Bible into Armeno-Turkish.

For the press at Malta, where all the missionaries had now gathered, the parallel requirement was the gift of types. The first fonts, for work in Italian and in modern Greek, had been ordered from Paris when the enterprise began; returning from Syria in the winter of 1826-27, Jonas King obtained funds from interested and pious friends in Paris and London for the purchase of Armenian and Arabic type. In the decade that the establishment remained at Malta, equipment was obtained which permitted printing in English, Armenian, Greco-Turkish, Arabic, Italian, modern Greek, and Armeno-Turkish.

Although Temple had seen in Malta a second Wittenberg, destined by Providence to promote the Reformation of the nineteenth century, the results at first were small. The enterprise had been begun under the misapprehension that "a considerable taste for reading and reflection existed in the Levant," and in the hope that this situation might be exploited by the distribution of Scripture and tracts. But work proceeded slowly, owing in part to the lack

[41] ABC 16.5, Vol. 1: Goodell, Smith, and Bird, Report of 18 June 1828; Anderson, *Oriental Churches*, 1, 45-51; Tibawi, *American Interests*, pp. 35-50.

of a competent printer, and the choice of material for publication was, at the outset, somewhat less than ideal.

For the first few years the emphasis was on Italian and Greek: the first tract in Italian was printed in August 1822, and by 1827 the output in this language amounted to more than 55,000 copies of 43 publications, to a total of 1,700,000 pages. Although a Greek *Pilgrim's Progress* was printed in 1824, the bulk of the material was made up of such tracts as Legh Richmond's *The Dairyman's Daughter* and Hannah More's *The Shepherd of Salisbury Plain*, and looking back in later years the Secretary of the American Board felt some doubt as to whether these "publications were well suited to the apprehension of the Oriental mind." In December 1826, however, Fisk's appeal for "a missionary printer, an able, faithful, pious man," was answered. The arrival of Homan Hallock, a competent journeyman, and the acquisition of two more presses increased the efficiency of the enterprise, while the decision of 1829 to make the furnishing of books for elementary schools a leading object opened a new area for service and an almost limitless market. By 1830 *The Dairyman's Daughter* and *Serious Thoughts on Eternity* had given way to the lives of the prophets, history books, *The Child's Arithmetic*, and *Peter Parley's Geography with lithographed maps*, while Hallock's letters to the Board were carrying repeated requests for a steam-powered press. In 1831 the output in modern Greek reached 78,000 copies of 14 works totaling nearly 5,000,000 pages; a single primer, the *Alphabetarion*, had had a run of 27,000 copies. By this time, too, a beginning had been made in Arabic, while in Armeno-Turkish a notable accomplishment had been completed. On reaching Malta from Beirut, William Goodell had started a translation of the New Testament into Armeno-Turkish, working from the original Greek with the assistance of one of the converted Armenian bishops. Printing had been begun early in 1830, and the last sheets were run off in January 1831.[42]

The Malta press and the short-lived school at Beirut were the two most important seeds yet planted. The central importance of God's

[42] On the language problem, see Josiah Brewer, *A Residence at Constantinople* (New Haven, 1830), pp. 197-99. On the Malta press, W. J. Burke, "The American Mission Press at Malta," 41 *N.Y. Public Library Bulletin*, 526-29; ABC 16.5, Vol. 1: Hallock to Anderson, 10 September 1829; ABC 16.9, Vol. 1: same to same, *passim*; Temple, *Life and Letters*, pp. 11-29; Tibawi, *American Interests*, pp. 51-57. The modern reader of *The Dairyman's Daughter*, that most popular of nineteenth-century tracts, can only agree with the Secretary as to its remarkable unsuitability.

written Word to the evangelists, the fact that theirs was a scriptural religion, made a literate audience imperative. Since the population of the Levant did not in fact evince much taste for reading and reflection, this audience had to be created. Before the gospel candle could be lit, the candle of education had to burn in the wilderness, and for these graduates of New England colleges its lighting would prove a congenial task. Already the school at Beirut had testified to a thirst for learning: the enrollment of six Arab children with which it began in 1824 had by year's end grown to fifty; two years later the average attendance was three hundred; in the next year it had doubled again. Shortly the printing establishment would respond to the same need, with the switch in emphasis from tracts for adults to primers for abecedarians. Education and the press are powerful engines; in the years to come they would interact to produce more and higher schools. By the century's end a network of American colleges would cover the Levant, their graduates would be prominent in every walk of life, and their influence in teaching the arts of the West, in creating discontent, and in perpetuating and strengthening the various and dissident linguistic groups of the enfeebled Ottoman Empire would have become immeasurable. The Americans had set out across the world to teach the word of God; quite without intention, as T. E. Lawrence was to observe, they taught revolution.[43]

Nor was the traffic in words a one-way traffic only: in this literary commerce imports balanced exports. While God's word, in gospel and tract, flowed eastward to the heathen and the depraved, the words of the American workers flowed back across the Western Ocean to the constituency which had sent them forth. At home, these communications excited the deepest interest.

Next, perhaps, to that of their own country, the geography of the Holy Land was most familiar to Bible-reading Americans, and indeed there were visible similarities: as the *Encyclopaedia of Missions* would later point out, the Promised Land was about the size of New England, while the two halves of Palestine, east and west of Jordan, were of the size of New Hampshire and Vermont and "very similarly situated."[44] Concerning this region, site of events familiar from childhood and essential to salvation, fresh news was flowing in.

Americans had traversed the country of the Seven Churches of

[43] T. E. Lawrence, *Seven Pillars of Wisdom* (New York, 1935), p. 45.
[44] Bliss, *Encyclopaedia of Missions*, II, 373.

Asia; they had visited Egypt, where Pharaoh had oppressed the Jews, and had crossed the desert into the Promised Land. Americans had visited Jaffa, where Noah had built his Ark of gopher wood and where Jonah had been spewed up out of the whale's belly. New England feet had trod the ground of Jerusalem, visited the Holy Sepulcher, climbed the Mount of Olives. The reports of the travels of Parsons and Fisk, the journals of Jonas King, with their "singularly dramatic interest," were eagerly read as they appeared in the *Missionary Herald,* and brought forth, in increased donations, the sinews of spiritual war.[45]

[45] Anderson, *Oriental Churches,* i, 18.

CHAPTER IV

Turkey Trade and Greek Revolt, 1815-1826

1. The Mediterranean Naval Base

AMONG the reasons adduced by the missionaries for their withdrawal from Beirut in 1828 had been the lack of visits from American men-of-war; although they had written to the squadron commander to tell him of their plight, the letter had been sent in ignorance of his whereabouts and with no real confidence that it would reach him. But while the lack of American trade with Syria and the pressure of duty elsewhere had indeed prevented visits to that coast, the United States still maintained an active force within the Mediterranean Sea. On the island of Minorca, six hundred miles to the west of Malta, the Navy had established its own Mediterranean base. In 1825 a growing concern with the Levant led to reinforcement of the squadron, and in the year the missionaries retired upon Malta it reached a new peak strength of seven ships. An advance to the eastward was in preparation.

As far back as 1796 President Washington had urged a permanent protecting force for America's Mediterranean commerce; at the end of the Tripolitan War, Jefferson had written that the United States would "ever" be obliged to keep a squadron in that sea. In 1815, therefore, when Decatur and Bainbridge sailed for home after their chastisement of Algiers, they left behind them five ships under the command of Commodore John Shaw. The decision to leave this force "to watch the conduct of the Barbary Powers, particularly that of Algiers" was logical enough, but while it answered certain obvious questions about the security of American commerce, it also raised the question of a base.

During the wars with Barbary the Navy had benefited from the interested friendship of the Kingdom of Naples and from British hospitality at Malta and Gibraltar. But a permanent peacetime force was something yet again. The problem, indeed, had been faced by the Jefferson administration, once peace had been made with Tripoli, and a base had been selected in accordance with the advice of the celebrated Andrea Doria:

Junio, Julio, Agosta y Puerto Mahon
Los mejores puertos del Mediterranea son.

The merits of this fourth harbor, located at the southeastern corner of the Spanish island of Minorca, had long been emphasized to the government at Washington. Commodore Dale had urged the desirability of a consulate at Port Mahon, and among the appointments to the expanded Mediterranean establishment of Tripolitan War days had been that of John Martin Baker, a recently naturalized citizen who had long lived in Mediterranean lands, as consul for the Balearic Islands. In 1803 Baker had strongly advocated basing the squadron at Mahon rather than Gibraltar. In 1805 he returned to the same subject, sending copies of a "perspective view" of the harbor to both President and Secretary of State; his arguments and those of the naval officers had led to the attempted rationalization of 1807, which had been frustrated by the *Chesapeake-Leopard* affair. But the plan had not been dropped, and on a visit to Washington in the autumn of 1807 Baker gained, or thought he gained, the promise of the appointment as Navy Agent for Port Mahon, "then decided, as our Naval Mediterranean rendezvous."

Baker never got his agency, but in time he did get his squadron. In 1815, following the treaty of peace with Algiers, Stephen Decatur asked the Spanish for warehouse facilities and exemption from the quarantine regulations at Cartagena and Mahon. Again diplomatic preparation had been neglected, and the request was denied by a somewhat startled Spanish government, apparently out of considerations of neutrality vis-à-vis the Dey. An October request from Commodore Shaw for permission to occupy warehouses and establish a hospital at Algeciras raised the question of whether such an American lodgment might not develop into another Gibraltar, and a month later this too was turned down. But by that time the squadron was comfortably in possession of Port Mahon.

Having been refused the use of Cartagena, Mahon, and Algeciras, Shaw had proceeded on a cruise of inspection of alternative ports. At Malaga, in October, he happened upon Consul Baker, whose persuasive powers, reinforced by the approach of winter weather, had their effect. The Consul was embarked on board the flagship *United States*, and on 5 November the squadron entered Doria's fourth harbor, where it anchored for the winter, inaugurating a relationship between Mahonese and Americans which was to last for more than a generation.[1]

At Port Mahon the Americans were courteously received by the Governor, and Shaw and Baker were able to gain the "temporary admission of those facilities required for the squadron and the national advantage." Permission to land stores and provisions was granted, part of the lazaretto was turned over to be used as squadron hospital, and the Port-Admiral promised the use of the arsenal and all assistance. When funds were for the moment lacking they were obligingly advanced by a Mahonese merchant, G. T. Ladico, a man of many parts who had been consul of the Ottoman Empire, consul of the "Republic of Venisse, when she existed," and acting consul in Baker's absence, and who in 1820 would begin a fourteen-year term as American consul at Port Mahon.

Despite the hospitality shown by the Governor, the problems normally incident to the basing of military forces on foreign soil soon developed. The Captain General of the Balearic Islands had his doubts about the arrangement, while a worried Spanish government saw in the presence of the American squadron a need to reinforce the island's garrison. In appreciation for the facilities provided him, Shaw had assisted his hosts in the refit of a Spanish warship and had lent some seamen to help sail her to Cartagena. But the hulk foundered en route, giving rise to Spanish suspicions of foul play, and the resulting tension was not diminished by the famous riot at the "Jackass Tavern," in which 125 Americans engaged some 300 of the Mahonese soldiery, with the loss of one midshipman.

Upon his arrival in November the Commodore had desired to unload stores and provisions so as to facilitate ships' work, and had received the Governor's permission to deposit these items duty-free. In January, however, the local customs officer had refused to release the goods without payment of duty, and Shaw's protest was productive only of multiplied correspondence between Spanish agencies. By March, exasperation was such that the commanding officer of the U.S.S. *Java* was spiritedly hoping for war, while the issue had finally reached the diplomatic level in a forceful protest to the Spanish government from the American secretary of legation, Thom-

---

[1] Despatches, Port Mahon: 1803-16, *passim,* and especially Baker to Sec. of State, 7 March, 11 March, 28 November 1803; 28 August 1805; 16 July 1806; 28 December 1814; 5 October 1815; 1 January 1816 (Records of the Department of State, National Archives). J. M. Baker, *View of the Commerce of the Mediterranean* (Washington, 1819), pp. 105, 111.

as L. L. Brent. Asking not only the immediate release of the stores, but also the issuance of orders which would give the squadron free use of the port, dockyard, and hospital facilities, and the privilege, "conformable to reason," of duty-free deposit, Brent concluded with the observation "that as the american Nation feel very sensibly any want of attention to their favorite Navy, not only the Government but each individual is filled with gratitude for any attentions that may be shewn it."[2]

The result of this effort was a royal order, refusing the free use of arsenal and hospital but permitting the Americans to rent warehouses and to use the hospital if they paid for it. The decision with regard to the impounded stores does not appear in the records, but by this time America's "favorite Navy" had already procured their release under threat of bombardment, with the result that a renewed request for the privilege of deposit was haughtily declined.

For some time the problem of a base remained unresolved. In July 1816 Commodore Isaac Chauncey came out in the ship of the line *Washington*, bringing with him, on a special mission to the Kingdom of the Two Sicilies, the Maryland lawyer and diplomat William Pinkney. Although Pinkney's primary purpose was to obtain compensation for Neapolitan spoliations of American shipping in 1809, he was also instructed to ask permission for the squadron to resort to Sicilian ports, and Chauncey had hopes of using Messina or Syracuse for the deposit of stores. At Pinkney's suggestion of a show of force, the Commodore concentrated the squadron at Naples; with memories of American action at Tripoli and Algiers still green, the gathering caused a certain excitement. The Neapolitans were reported to have reinforced their garrison and manned their batteries; in Europe there developed a fear that the King, unable to pay, was about to cede Lampedusa or one of the Lipari Islands or Syracuse to the United States. But more than two months of negotiation proved fruitless, and neither compensation nor depot was obtained. Rejoicing that no cession had been made, a

---

[2] Despatches, Mahon: Baker to Sec. of State, 1 January 1816; Ladico to Sec. of State, 10 December 1809, 19 December 1833. Area 4 File: O. H. Perry to John Rodgers, March 1816; Shaw to Sec. of Navy, 8 August 1816 (Naval Records Collection, National Archives). S. F. Holbrook, *Threescore Years* (Boston, 1857), pp. 124-32, 184-87. Mahon Papers (Library of Congress Facsimiles: Archivo Historico Nacional, Seccion Estrada, Legajo 5558, Expediente 1), pp. 78-84. F. J. Grund, *The Americans in their Moral, Social, and Political Relations* (London, 1837), ii, 340, notes that "of all the institutions of the United States the navy is the most national and popular."

London paper observed that while "the Americans are certainly a rising people, . . . it is rather premature, we think, for them to begin the re-action of colonizing Europe."[3]

Despite the difficulties of the previous year, the squadron spent the winter of 1816-17 at Port Mahon. But nothing had been permanently settled. Weak and threatened by revolt, the Spanish government was disinclined to make concessions; relations between America and Spain were touchy; and there seems, indeed, little obvious reason why the Spanish should have obliged their most troublesome neighbor in the New World with a grant of military facilities in the Old. The questions of the Venezuelan revolutionary Miranda and of the navigation of the Mississippi were by now history, but the cession of Louisiana was still unrecognized by Spain, the Florida problem remained acute, and in 1817 the arrival of a Russian squadron at Cadiz would inaugurate the preparations for a "Great Expedition" to recover Spain's revolted American colonies. That these issues were all of a piece is apparent from the Spanish filing system: correspondence about Port Mahon is in the same box as papers relating to the recovery of Louisiana, the American invasion of West Florida, and American activity in revolutionizing Spanish colonies.

Four years went by while Washington and Madrid haggled over the Floridas and the Louisiana boundary. The principal deposit of stores remained at Gibraltar in custody of the Navy Agent for the Mediterranean; the vessels of the squadron rendezvoused there, at Malta and Naples, and at other Mediterranean ports. But except for a period of crisis following Jackson's invasion of East Florida, which saw the squadron brought to war alert, intermittent use also continued to be made of Port Mahon. With the relaxation of tension which followed the signing of the Adams-Onís Treaty came an attempt to expand this usage and to develop this harbor, hitherto an occasional winter anchorage and rendezvous, into a full-fledged naval base.

Early in 1820 the squadron visited the port. In the summer there developed some difficulties with the British at Gibraltar; in August the brig *Spark* called at Mahon to inquire if use could be made of the navy yard in case of need. The local authorities were agreeable,

---

[3] H. R. Marraro, *Diplomatic Relations between the United States and the Kingdom of the Two Sicilies* (New York, 1951), I, 112-17; P. C. Perrotta, *The Claims of the United States against the Kingdom of Naples* (Washington, 1926), pp. 29-37.

and soon Commodore Bainbridge was writing the President of the Navy Board to point out that if only Spanish duties were less onerous, Port Mahon would be by far the best location, both as fleet rendezvous and as depot for stores. In January 1821 he raised the question with the legation at Madrid, and in February, citing "the late happy arrangement of all past differences between the two Countries," Brent twice urged the Spanish government to grant the privilege of a duty-free deposit at Mahon. This time the King consented, and the grant was made for a period of six months, with the possibility of renewal.

The American response to this temporary concession was remarkably vigorous. The naval hospital long maintained at Pisa was deactivated in favor of facilities at Mahon; orders were issued to move the spare spars, anchors, and other gear forward from Gibraltar; and before the year was out four storeships had arrived from the United States bringing additional supplies. Such wholehearted action, one might suppose, would make it difficult for the Spanish to change their minds, and perhaps it did: at the end of the six months the American request for renewal was answered by the statement that the question would be considered, and for the moment the privilege remained in effect. But again events upon the larger scene made themselves felt: in March 1822 President Monroe proposed to Congress the recognition of the new states of Latin America; in an immediate protest the Spanish minister at Washington emphasized, among other evidences of American perfidy and ingratitude, the privileges which Spain had granted the American Navy; in May the pending request for extension of the privilege of deposit was refused by the King and the duties were reimposed.[4]

Again the storeships unloaded at Gibraltar; again the squadron found itself without a home. But again, with the passing of time, tensions diminished. In 1823, despite complaints from the French, two American warships were repaired at Port Mahon. In 1825, at the request of Commodore John Rodgers, the royal assent was given for the establishment of an American naval depot and for duty-free deposit of food and other squadron supplies. With this decision

---

[4] Area 4 File: Stewart to Sec. of Navy, 15 August 1818; Bainbridge to Rodgers, 27 October 1820; Jones to Sec. of Navy, 26 November 1821; Jones to Rodgers, 4 December 1821. Mahon Papers, pp. 186-91, 209-15, 222-85. Despatches, Mahon: Ladico to Sec. of State, 5 February 1822. *ASP, FR,* IV, 845.

America acquired her first overseas naval base: the Navy's occupation of Mahon would continue for almost twenty years.[5]

Originally chosen both for its safety and its strategic location—there was no better place from which to keep a watch on Barbary—Port Mahon was also an extremely attractive spot. To Rodgers the harbor was unquestionably the finest he had ever seen. Beyond the entrance, "as narrow, proportionately, as the neck is to a flask of champagne," the little arm of the sea widened into a sheltered basin at the foot of the town. To starboard, as a ship moved up the passage, could be seen the lazaretto, next to that of Marseilles the finest in Europe, with Hospital Island a little further on. On the larboard hand, the entering sailor passed the village of Georgetown, built during the British occupation, with its deserted stone barracks and its friendly inhabitants who "extend their hospitality even beyond that line where virtue should pause." Then the great mansion built by Lord Collingwood, and then the town, clean, scrubbed, and whitewashed, and the navy yard, itself located on a small island, with the warehouses and other facilities built by the British. Here ships could anchor in water deep enough for the heaviest three-decker, with the quay a hundred yards ahead and green fields a hundred yards astern. Here, behind the drawbridge, the American naval storekeeper was in charge; here United States Marines did sentry-go; and here the artificers—smiths, carpenters, sailmakers, and ropemakers—did their work.

For the officers of the squadron a winter at Mahon could be very agreeable. Many took lodgings ashore, where the opera house provided entertainment and where walks and rides across country and duck-shooting on the lake vied with drinking and gambling as favorite amusements. So great, indeed, was the lure of the monte table that in time there developed an annual influx of gamblers and sharpers from the Spanish mainland. But there were other pursuits, including the literary: in 1835 a *Journal of a Cruize in the U.S. Ship* Delaware, *74, in the Mediterranean,* written by two members of the crew, appeared under the imprint of "Mahon: Widow Serra & Son."

[5] Despatches, Spain: Forsyth to Sec. of State, 24 February 1823; Nelson to Sec. of State, 14 May 1825; Rich to Sec. of State, 22 August 1825; Everett to Sec. of State, 8 September 1825. Despatches, Mahon: Rich to Sec. of State, 1 March 1845. Area 4 File: Francisco de Zea Bermudez to Rich, 20 August 1825. Mahon Papers, pp. 291-94, 424-26.

For foremast hands, in those days of infrequent liberty, the island situation permitted a relaxation of restraints, and indulgence in those simple and unexceptionable activities which the chaplains described as "all kinds of dissipations." From time to time the pleasure of fighting with members of the garrison or the police was indulged in; frequently, the Consul reported, costs had to be paid for "damage often caused by them breaking doors and walls of the Jale when confined." But except for the proverbially lazy Mahon soldiers, the inhabitants were uniformly kind, friendly, and hard-working.

They were also poor: to one American chaplain it seemed that the island was populated entirely by priests and beggars. Whether this poverty was to be attributed to the ignorance and frivolity of a people brought up in the Catholic faith, or, as one bluejacket opined, to the destructive results of a cruel and tyrannical despotism, it indubitably existed, and its existence gave virtue to the presence of the Americans. More than a third of the 45,000 islanders lived at Mahon; many more, after the French seizure of Algiers in 1830, returned there; increasingly the authorities came to realize that the annual circulation of some $150,000 by the 2,000 or more officers and men of the American squadron constituted an immensely valuable economic resource. In 1832 a request for further concessions in the matter of dutiable goods, coupled with a threat to seek another rendezvous, received a favorable answer in what was, for the Spanish government, an astonishingly short space of time.

Snug harbors are important to seafaring men, the winter gales outside were fierce, and as year after year some thousands of Americans wintered at Port Mahon the place became the Navy's spiritual home: sailing the far Pacific in the U.S.S. *Neversink*, Melville's White Jacket found prestige, proverbial wisdom, and standards of judgment set in terms of the Mediterranean and of Mahon. Looking back in later life, Admiral John Dahlgren observed that "the continued intercourse of nearly half a century has begotten the feeling of the kindliest character between the townspeople and the Americans." As another writer remarked, "Mahon is like a Mediterranean home, and becomes absolutely endeared to the officers; every little cove and nook and bosky hillside are full of pleasant associations; and to many, the joy of a return to Mahon, with its quiet comforts and familiar places, is so great that the prospect of an active autumn cruise is scarcely agreeable."

Home it was to the sailor, and some never left it. In the English

111

graveyard, a scant mile from the anchorage, there is a collection of "modest monuments to American officers and seamen."[6]

Through the years the squadron remained busy at its tasks of protecting commerce, making the country "advantageously known to foreign nations," transporting consuls and diplomats, supporting negotiations, and showing the flag. Some further pressure had to be exerted upon the refractory Dey of Algiers in 1816 and again in 1822, and visits to all the ports of Barbary remained an annual task. The Neapolitan claims issue, which Pinkney had failed to resolve, remained unsettled. But although President Monroe, in his annual message of 1819, had predicted that a strong Mediterranean Squadron would remain a necessity, the passing years brought increasing security to the western basin and the strength of the force declined. In 1822 and 1823 the squadron under Commodore Jacob Jones, smaller, as the Secretary of the Navy reported, than ever before, consisted only of the frigate *Constitution*, the sloop of war *Ontario*, and the schooner *Nonesuch*; in 1824 the frigate was relieved by a second sloop.[7]

So far as the original reason for a naval presence in the Mediterranean went, it could be written down as a mission accomplished: peace prevailed with Barbary. In 1824, nevertheless, the Monroe administration decided to strengthen the squadron. Behind this action lay a variety of reasons, of which the possible hazard to commerce from a threatened war between Britain and Algiers was the one publicly avowed. Pursuant to the decision, the ship of the line *North Carolina* was ordered to the Mediterranean together with *Constitution*, and command of the strengthened force was entrusted to Commodore Rodgers, president of the Board of Navy Commissioners and senior officer of the Navy.[8]

At Naples, where a second attempt to collect the American claims was about to be made, news of the augmentation of the squadron caused alarm. But as things turned out the western basin remained

[6] Mahon Papers, pp. 296-306. Despatches, Mahon: Ladico to Sec. of State, 9 October 1833. Of works of naval reminiscence, perhaps the most useful for Mahon and for squadron life in general are: [Walter Colton], *Ship and Shore* (New York, 1835); [R. F. Gould], *Life of Gould, an ex-man-of-war's-man* (Clairmont, N.H., 1867); Harry Gringo (pseud. for H. A. Wise), *Scampavias from Gibel Tarik to Stamboul* (New York, 1857); F. S. Schroeder, *Shores of the Mediterranean* (New York, 1846).

[7] References to the Algerine problem are scattered through the Area 4 File. Squadron strength and composition from Secretary of the Navy, *Annual Reports*.

[8] Paullin, *Rodgers*, pp. 327-28.

comparatively peaceful, while the Levant became a cockpit of international rivalry. Into the eastern Mediterranean, where Venetian and Ottoman fleets had long contended and where the Russians had appeared in the eighteenth century, the Western powers had been projected by the Napoleonic wars. Into this region American commerce had penetrated, expanding vigorously once peace was gained with Barbary. In this region an American missionary effort had begun. The revolt of the Greeks against their Turkish overlords, difficulties between the Pasha of Egypt and the Sultan of Turkey, the Russian advance toward Constantinople, and the involvement of England and France all made for a situation of extreme delicacy. Levantine problems had been of concern to Commodore Bainbridge in 1820, and had a prominent place in the reasons which brought the reinforcement of the squadron and the appointment of Rodgers to the Mediterranean command. Increasingly, from the middle twenties, affairs in the eastern basin would excite American interest.

2. *The Commerce of the Black Sea*

Direct American commerce with the Levant, forbidden the colonists by the Acts of Trade, had begun soon after the Revolution: in 1785 Smyrna raisins were on sale in Boston. Although early records are scanty, there is evidence that an American ship had visited Constantinople by 1786; one was at Smyrna in 1797; one at Alexandria in 1800. But the Barbary pirates lay across the path, and in the early years the trade grew slowly: not until 1800 was Turkey mentioned in Treasury Department import-export statistics, and then but as a part of "China and East Indies, generally"; only in 1803 did "Turkey, Levant, and Egypt" attain the dignity of a separate listing.

As the opportunities opened to neutral flags by the Napoleonic wars led to a great expansion of American shipping, so victory over Tripoli was followed by increased activity in the Levant. After landing Eaton in Egypt, Isaac Hull had been ordered to convoy American merchantmen from Alexandria and from Smyrna. The records for 1805 show five American vessels calling at the latter port. In 1807 there was a sizable movement of American shipping to Gallipoli for oil, wheat, and cotton. Two years later some twenty American ships were recorded as visiting Smyrna, with which a regular trade had been developed by the shipmasters of Philadelphia and

Baltimore; in 1812, despite increasing tension with England, a dozen American vessels reached Smyrna before news of war was received. The import from "Turkey, Levant, and Egypt" of goods dutiable on an *ad valorem* basis, principally opium for the China trade, quadrupled between 1806 and 1812, while the amount of figs and raisins brought in increased by astronomical proportions. As imports rose so did exports, while at the same time American ships gained a sizable slice of the lucrative carrying trade between England and the Levant.

Although the War of 1812 interrupted the Smyrna trade, revival was rapid: in 1816-17 the import total approached the prewar record. And while the twenties were to prove a dull period for foreign commerce in general, that with the Levant enjoyed a steady growth, with but minor setbacks from the depression of 1819-20 and the Russo-Turkish War of 1828-29. Steadily, as the decade wore on, the import of figs and raisins increased and the acceptance of Turkey opium expanded, until by 1828 almost the entire crop was being taken by the Americans. Steadily, too, the proportion of colonial goods taken on the outward voyage declined in favor of such processed items as cottons, worked metal, and rum. Since the rum, so gratifying to the Near Easterners and so disturbing to the American missionaries, was produced in New England, and since most of the opium was ultimately destined for the New England-controlled China trade, these developments led to a shift in the American base of the commerce. In the early years the traffic had been conducted almost entirely by Philadelphia and Baltimore ships; in 1830, of thirty American vessels calling at Smyrna, thirteen were from Boston and seven from other Massachusetts ports, and the trade had become "a leading Boston interest."[9]

Throughout this period the United States had no diplomatic relations with the Ottoman Empire. Trade there was in increasing measure, and one can perhaps postulate some spiritual affinity: in 1800, when the Grand Signior first set eyes upon the Stars and Stripes, he deduced a similarity between American and Ottoman character,

---

[9] S. E. Morison, "Forcing the Dardanelles in 1810," 1 *New England Quarterly*, 208-25. The most extensive account of early contacts is W. L. Wright, Jr., "American Relations with Turkey to 1831" (unpublished doctoral dissertation, Princeton University, 1928); Chaps. 4 and 6 deal with the Smyrna trade. For commercial information: *ASP, C & N*; Adam Seybert, *Statistical Annals* (Philadelphia, 1818); Timothy Pitkin, *Statistical View of the Commerce of the United States of America* (New Haven, 1835).

for there were "*Stars* in the United States flag . . .[and] that of Turkey was one of the heavenly bodies"; by 1812 four American merchantmen had borne the name *Grand Turk*. But although the American government had intermittently considered the desirability of a treaty of amity and commerce, effective action was long delayed.

The first such thoughts had been stimulated by the post-revolutionary need to develop a Mediterranean commerce. Although the precise relationship between the Sultan and the North African regencies was obscure, it had seemed possible that a treaty with Constantinople would prove prerequisite to peace with Barbary; the Ottoman Empire had consequently been listed among those countries with which Adams and Jefferson were authorized to negotiate. Adams himself looked favorably on the idea, thinking that a minister to Constantinople would be well received and that "our Commerce and Naval Stores would be there an object." Barlow and a number of others involved in Barbary negotiations thought a Turkish treaty desirable in the interests of commerce. But the French were discouraging, and a decade passed and Adams reached the presidency before any serious effort was commenced.

In 1797 the idea was broached anew to Rufus King, minister to London, by an English merchant from the Levant. After discussion with the Turkish ambassador to Great Britain, King passed the suggestion to the administration at home, and a year later returned to the proposal. Early in 1799 Secretary of State Pickering took up the idea, and William Loughton Smith, chargé d'affaires in Portugal, was nominated for the mission. But although Adams favored the venture and Smith was eager to go, the time was out of joint. Politics at home and complications abroad combined to frustrate the enterprise; Smith never received his commission and the effort lapsed.

Although American action was not forthcoming in the early years, American talk appears to have laid some groundwork for the future. In his conversations at London, Rufus King so impressed the representative of the Sultan that his successor arrived from Constantinople in full awareness of the "country of diamonds and gold." A more important result of this propaganda, if such it was, was the reception accorded Bainbridge in 1800, on his arrival at Constantinople bearing tribute—a mixed bag including 100 blackamoors, 4 lions, 4 tigers, 150 sheep, and 12 parrots—to the Sultan from the Dey of Algiers.

The emissaries of the Dey were inhospitably received: when they presented a letter from their sovereign the Turk received it with "great rage, first spat, and then stamped upon it." But except for a brief attempt at extortion by the Foreign Minister or Reis Effendi, Bainbridge was treated with great consideration. None had heard of the United States, but the idea of the "New World" was understood; the good order of the *George Washington* and her crew excited the admiration of the Turks; the Capudan Pasha accorded the Americans the honor of his personal protection. This honor was significant, for the office of capudan pasha, in which were cumulated the responsibilities of secretary of the navy, grand admiral, and governor of strategic coastal districts and of the Aegean Islands, was of great importance in the thalassic Ottoman Empire, and the incumbent at this time was Hussein Kutchuck, creator of the modern Ottoman Navy, foster brother of the Sultan, and power behind the throne. Relations with Hussein were facilitated by the fact that his secretary had known Franklin in Paris; like the other officers of the Porte, and more than most, he evinced "much solicitude . . . that an ambassador should be sent from the United States to Constantinople." In an interview with Bainbridge shortly before the American's departure, Hussein set the pattern for thirty years of diplomacy by formally expressing "a very great desire" that a minister be sent to make a treaty.[10]

The seed fell on stony ground. Although Bainbridge reported the moment ripe for a commencement of negotiations, Smith's mission was not revived. Tripoli, for the moment, took precedence over Turkey, and in any case the new Jefferson administration was guided by its theoretical preference for commercial rather than diplomatic connections. Following the by now traditional procedure of appointing consuls without prior diplomatic preparation, Jefferson in 1802 nominated William Stewart, a Philadelphia merchant, to fill this office at Smyrna. The nomination was approved and 1803 found Stewart at his post, but a system which had worked successfully with Christian nations proved ineffective in the special Turkish situation. Relations between European countries and the Ottoman Empire were founded in the treaty provisions for extraterritorial juris-

[10] Wright, "Relations with Turkey," pp. 3-41; H.A.S. Dearborn, *A Memoir on the Commerce and Navigation of the Black Sea* (Boston, 1819); *idem, Life of Bainbridge*; Thomas Harris, *Life and Services of Commodore William Bainbridge* (Philadelphia, 1837); E. D. Clark, *Travels in Various Countries* (London, 1817), III, 78-79; Adolphus Slade, *Record of Travels in Turkey, Greece, &c.* (Philadelphia, 1833), I, 63.

diction, the so-called capitulations; lacking the recognition of the central government, Stewart was unable to exercise the most important prerogatives of Western consuls. After reporting on the prospects of a growing Smyrna commerce and appointing a British merchant as "pro-consul" to process the papers of American ships, Stewart returned to Philadelphia. Five years later the appointment of a Baltimorean to the Smyrna post proved equally ineffective.

Yet the Turks continued willing. While war with Tripoli was still in progress, Commodore Barron was apprised by the American consul general at St. Petersburg of the Ottoman disposition to encourage intercourse with the United States. Expounding, in January 1805, the commercial benefit that would follow admission to the Black Sea, the American consul at Leghorn reported assurances from an "unquestionable source" in Constantinople that an accredited agent would easily obtain a treaty. In October of the same year Captain John Rodgers advised the Secretary of the Navy that the time seemed propitious for extending commercial relations to Turkey, and emphasized both the "immense importance" of the Black Sea trade and his confidence that the Porte would enter a commercial arrangement. In 1810 a Boston sea captain managed to pass the straits and visit Odessa; reporting on his reception at Constantinople, he observed that the new Capudan Pasha "invariably expatiated" on the Sultan's desire for a treaty; in the next year high Turkish officials repeatedly expressed their displeasure that no embassy had yet been sent to the Porte. But troubles with England and France preoccupied the United States, and neither these advances nor the representations of interested Boston merchants produced the desired consequences. A later capudan pasha was to succeed where his predecessors had failed, but for the moment the American trade with Smyrna continued, as before, under the protection of the British Levant Company.

The British, naturally enough, were complaisant for British reasons: what one protects one tends to control. However helpful to American merchants in the short run, this situation contained real possibilities of trouble, which fructified in 1811 when the withdrawal of British protection led to doubled duties on American goods. The same year, however, had seen the founding by David Offley, a Philadelphia Quaker, of the first American commercial house at Smyrna. When the duties were doubled, Offley refused to pay them; when one of his ships was seized, he proceeded on his own responsibility to Constantinople, where, by a combination of bribery and brass, he secured what amounted to a private treaty guaranteeing most-fa-vored-nation treatment to Americans. This wholly private and un-authorized negotiation well exemplifies the individualistic Ameri-can world view, and this Americanism showed in Offley's other acts. Rather than resorting to the shelter of a European flag, he placed himself under Ottoman protection, with the result that for fifteen years the Americans alone, among Westerners in Turkey, held the status of "Sultan's guests." The compliment, it may be presumed, was not lost upon the Turks.

War delayed the benefits of this accomplishment, but with the re-vival of trade after 1815 Offley became in fact what he later became in name, an American commercial agent. Although other American firms now settled themselves at Smyrna, his establishment re-mained dominant, handling two-thirds of the American arrivals be-tween 1811 and 1820. Equally important, Offley in these years gained the friendship of Husrev, the new capudan pasha and the most durable member of the progressive and Westernizing faction at Con-stantinople. Born a slave, illiterate throughout his life, this Turkish Talleyrand survived intrigue, poison, and the bowstring to hold high office for nearly half a century: Pasha of Egypt before Mehemet Ali, he lived to approve the declaration of the Crimean War. Like his predecessors, Husrev was predisposed from the necessities of his office to the mariners from the New World, and under his "powerful protection American trade prospered for fifteen years."[11]

In these years after the Treaty of Ghent this growth of commerce brought new pressures for a Turkish treaty. In October 1816 the cap-tain of a ship belonging to the Baltimore firm of Smith and Bu-chanan wrote home from Smyrna urging negotiations. Although Robert Smith no longer held office, Samuel Smith was now a sena-tor, still a merchant, and still influential. After discussing the matter with President-elect Monroe, Smith dispatched a secret agent to Constantinople, to receive in due course a report that a negotiator would be welcomed and that the presentation to Turkey of one of the new steamboats would be helpful. This information he forwarded

[11] Wright, "Relations with Turkey," pp. 45-67; Morison, "Forcing the Darda-nelles"; *Naval Documents: Barbary Powers*, v, 211, 285, 295; vi, 299; M. M. Noah, *Travels in England, France, Spain, and the Barbary States* (New York and London, 1819), p. xxxvii. Husrev appears in contemporary sources variously as Hussereff, Hosrew, Khosrew, Usref; the *Encyclopaedia of Islam* gives Khusraw.

to the administration at Washington, where the Department of State was now headed by a New Englander, John Quincy Adams, who was fully sensible of the commercial basis of American policy, and who while in Russia in 1810 had urged a treaty to open the Black Sea trade to American shipping.

Others were also interested in the matter. In 1819 Henry Preble, brother of the great Commodore and a connection of Joel Barlow, became concerned. Consul at Palermo and a merchant long active abroad, Preble interested himself in the Turkish problem in the hope that if a treaty were negotiated he could obtain either the consulate at Constantinople or that at Odessa. Although unsuccessful in an attempt to persuade Commodore Jacob Jones to support his efforts with a warship, Preble proceeded to the Levant, and after visiting Smyrna, Constantinople, and Odessa forwarded a long report of commercial interest to the government at Washington. At home, in the same year, two books called attention to these possibilities, as Mordecai Noah, a former consul at Tunis, expounded both the value of the Odessa trade and Turkish eagerness for diplomatic relations, and as Henry A. S. Dearborn, collector of the port of Boston and shortly to be elected to Congress, published a compendium of information on *The Commerce of the Black Sea* coupled with a vigorous plea for government action. All this had its result in 1820 when John Quincy Adams dispatched a New York gentleman, Luther Bradish, on a secret mission to sound out the Porte. And simultaneously a new American interest in Turkish dominions was manifesting itself, with the arrival of Pliny Fisk and Levi Parsons at Smyrna.

While the missionaries commenced their explorations and while Bradish prepared for his mission, Commodore Bainbridge was ordered out to command the Mediterranean Squadron. Twenty years after his first visit to the capital of the Grand Turk, Bainbridge was instructed to gather information on the Levant trade, and if possible to pay another visit to Constantinople. In April 1820, with Bradish as passenger, the Commodore sailed from Hampton Roads in the newly commissioned ship of the line *Columbus*; on 21 July he wrote from Syracuse to Baron Stroganoff, the Russian ambassador to the Porte, inquiring if the flagship and another vessel would be permitted to pass the Dardanelles; in September, no reply having been received, he sent Bradish to Smyrna in the brig *Spark*, together with his secretary, Charles Folsom, to whom was assigned the task of collecting commercial intelligence.

The arrival of *Spark* at Smyrna on 12 October 1820 marked the first presence of an American warship at the commercial metropolis of the Levant. There, in conversation with members of the trading community, Folsom succeeded in gathering the desired information. When a communication from Stroganoff indicated that passage of the straits would not be possible, Bradish proceeded alone to Constantinople, where he was courteously received by both Russian ambassador and Turkish government. The previously rumored Turkish desire for a treaty was substantiated in conversations with the Reis Effendi; possible complications from a presumed Russian link were averted when Bradish, like Offley before him, proclaimed himself under the protection not of the Russians but of the Porte.

In the course of the talks, the Turks again intimated that a gift of ships would be an acceptable *quid pro quo* for commercial concessions; passed on by Bradish to acquaintances in New York, this proposal in time gave rise to an attempt to sell the *Robert Fulton,* a successful but unprofitable steamship, to the government for presentation to the Sultan. But the suggestion was not pressed, and Bradish, reporting on his mission, stated that while British opposition was to be expected, the anticipated benefits from American participation in the Black Sea carrying trade would lead the Russians to support the negotiation. If the talks were kept secret and the use of intermediaries avoided, it appeared that a treaty could be had for 350,000 piasters, 50,000 of which were "to preserve Halet Effendi's opinion the same as at present."

That particular problem shortly ceased to be of importance, for Halet fell from grace and was strangled. But more important ones arose with the outbreak of the Greek War for Independence. This event was to have profound influence on important factors of the treaty problem: on American public opinion, making it violently anti-Turk; on Turkish hopes for an American treaty, making them stronger; and on British efforts to hinder the negotiations, limiting their effectiveness. For the moment, however, the cabinet at Washington decided to suspend the talks. In February 1821 Bradish departed Constantinople, leaving affairs in the hands of his interpreter, and for two years intercourse lapsed. Trade with Smyrna continued to grow; in 1823, in response to another Turkish initiative, Adams would send another envoy. But for the moment the attention of all parties was focused on Greece.[12]

[12] Wright, "Relations with Turkey," pp. 78-93; Noah, *Travels*, p. xxvii; Dearborn,

3. The Greek War for Independence

In America, news of the Greek revolt touched the mystic chords of memory. As early as 1785 Jefferson had written of his hope that Greece might once again be free, and that he might "see the language of Homer and Demosthenes flow with purity, from the lips of a free and ingenious people."[13] And in a country which gave its rulers a classical education, whose politicians disputed under classical pseudonyms, which built in the classical style, and which named its towns for the cities of antiquity, many had similar feelings. In the fifty years since their own revolution the Americans had seen their example emulated first by the French, then by the Spanish colonies to the southward, and now by the heirs to the ancients. Little wonder that this mixture of classicism and the Spirit of '76 had heady effects, that the reappearance of wily Odysseus in the mountains of Greece was greeted by applause, that a sixth American Athens sprouted in Tennessee, or that a town in Michigan was named for Ypsilanti, the president of the Greek legislative assembly. Byron was not needed here.

In Greece, where the revolt broke out in the spring of 1821, the American example was well known. Esteeming America "nearer" than the nations on their frontiers, trusting that in imitating America they would be imitating their own ancestors, the Senate of Calamata in May appealed to the land where "Liberty has fixed her abode," and called upon the "fellow-citizens of Penn, of Washington, and of Franklin" to aid the cause of Greek freedom. By autumn this appeal had reached the United States, and was being widely reprinted and distributed. In the next year popular excitement began to grow, accelerated by the Greek Declaration of Independence and by Greek adoption of a democratic constitution. But the "Greek fever" in its most contagious form was the result of an article by Edward Everett,

---

Commerce of the Black Sea; Preble, *Genealogical Sketch*, pp. 269-70; C. F. Adams (ed.), *Memoirs of J. Q. Adams* (Philadelphia, 1874-77), v, 197-98. Instructions, Turkey: M. J. Jaussand to J. Q. Adams, 3 May 1818; Navoni to Henry Clay, 24 January 1828. Much of the correspondence relating to the Bradish and later missions is in 22C 1S *HED* 250. Useful published accounts of the negotiations are in C. O. Paullin, *Diplomatic Negotiations* and D. H. Miller, *Treaties and Other International Acts of the United States of America* (Washington, 1931-37).

[13] J. P. Boyd (ed.), *The Papers of Thomas Jefferson* (Princeton, 1960-), viii, 418. The sentiment was a recurring one: *ibid.*, xii, 128, 161.

professor of Greek at Harvard, in the October 1823 issue of the *North American Review*.[14]

This article, which began as a review of "Coray's Aristotle," became in short order a paean to the Greeks, an anathema directed at the Turks, and a call to action. Although he had traveled in Greece and should have known better, Everett ignored the fact of a war of reciprocal massacre to describe the struggle as one "between cruel and barbarous masters, and a people whose hard-earned wealth is devoted to the collection of libraries," between barbarous Turk and a "Christian, civilized, enterprising, industrious people." Urging his readers to give aid to the Greeks, he called upon President Monroe to follow the precedent established during the South American revolutions and to dispatch a commission of investigation. "Should they report, as they must . . . the circumstances we have enumerated, then let the independence of Greece be acknowledged . . . and a minister sent." Appealing for volunteers to join the fight and emphasizing, on the analogy of America's own revolution, the importance of sending supplies and arms, Everett defined in familiar terms his country's mission. The call of the Senate of Calamata "must bring home to the mind of the least reflecting American, the great and glorious part which this country is to act, in the political regeneration of the world. . . . In the great Lancastrian school of the nations, liberty is the lesson, which we are appointed to teach."[15]

Some volunteers did go, but not many. George Jarvis of New York, first on the scene, rose in this war of bushwhackers to the rank of lieutenant general. Recently graduated from the Harvard Medical School, desirous of adventure and self-improvement, and disappointed in love, Dr. Samuel Gridley Howe left Boston for Greece, where he became surgeon general of the navy and accomplished prodigies in relief work. James Williams, a Baltimore Negro who had sailed with Decatur to Algiers, performed heroically as helms-

---

[14] On the Greek revolt and its American repercussions: E. M. Earle, "American Interest in the Greek Cause," 33 *American Historical Review*, 44-63, and "Early American Policy Concerning Ottoman Minorities," 62 *Political Science Quarterly*, 337-67; M. A. Cline, *American Attitude Toward the Greek War of Independence, 1821-1828* (Atlanta, 1930); H. J. Booras, *Hellenic Independence and America's Contribution to the Cause* (Rutland, Vt., 1934); S. A. Larrabee, *Hellas Observed* (New York, 1957); Merle Curti, *American Philanthropy Abroad* (New Brunswick, 1963), pp. 22-40.

[15] 17 *North American Review*, 389-424. It was Everett's hope that he would be the commissioner, thus ensuring the fulfillment of his own prophecy: *Memoirs of J. Q. Adams*, VI, 173, 227.

man and adequately as cook. There were a few others. But this handful compared poorly in number with either the foreign volunteers
in the American Revolution or the European volunteers in Greece:
on the tablet erected at Nauplia in memory of the 263 philhellenes
who died for the independence of Greece appears the name of only
one American, a Lieutenant Washington, and he, said Howe, was
"an unprincipled, dissipated fellow" and a "disgrace to the
country."[16]

The campaign for funds was more successful. Newspaper articles,
public meetings, and resolves passed by college undergraduates and
state legislatures so heated the public mind that $32,000 had been re-
mitted by May 1824, and more was coming in. By the end of the
year the sum raised by the New York committee alone was reported
in the London *Morning Chronicle* as approaching that collected in
18 months' effort in the United Kingdom, while Howe estimated
the total American contribution at $80,000. Only in Boston did re-
sistance to the propaganda and fund-raising campaign appear, and
there only in the persons of those merchants with interests in the
Smyrna trade.

But if collection went well, administration of the funds was not all
that could have been desired. Forwarded to London, where they
were presented to the Greek representatives by Richard Rush, the
American minister, the monies were rapidly dissipated. And an attempt to procure war materials in the United States had a somewhat
similar outcome.[17]

In Greece, as elsewhere in the Mediterranean, the excellence of
American naval architecture was known. In November 1824 the
London Greeks approached Rush on the question of procuring a
naval armament from the government of the United States. While
observing that the American government could itself provide neither
warships nor personnel, Rush nevertheless undertook to put the
Greeks in touch with private American shipbuilders through the
agency of the American consul at London. But the contract which
was subsequently made for the construction of two frigates proved
costly, as the London committee found itself fleeced by New York

[16] Raoul de Malherbe, *L'Orient, 1718-1845* (Paris, 1846), II, 719; L. E. Richards
(ed.), *Letters and Journals of Samuel Gridley Howe, the Servant of Humanity*
(Boston, 1906-9), I, 100, 102; J. P. Miller, *The Condition of Greece in 1827 and
1828* (New York, 1828), p. 160.

[17] S. G. Howe, *Historical Sketch of the Greek Revolution* (New York, 1828);
Morison, "Forcing the Dardanelles."

commission merchants, who looked upon Greek money as "a fund on which rapacity might securely prey." Promised for October 1825, the frigates were not completed until well into the next year, and then at a greatly inflated cost. One had to be sold to the United States Navy, in which, as the U.S.S. *Hudson*, she had a brief and undistinguished career; the second, the *Hellas*, purchased at double the estimated price, did not reach Nauplia until December 1826. Still, the ship was a fine one, an oversized frigate mounting sixty-four guns, and Dr. Howe and others were astonished by "her size, beauty, and strength." Employed as flagship of the Greek Navy by the British Admiral Cochrane, *Hellas* performed useful service until she was blown up in 1831 during an internal revolt in Greece.[18]

Whatever the limits of the material contributions of the American philhellenes, their enthusiasm had none, and so vocal a movement inevitably had its effects in American life. Although Greek revival had preceded Greek revolt, the influence of the latter on the arts was not negligible, producing as it did Halleck's "Marco Bozzaris," a number of poems by Bryant, and such plays as John Howard Payne's *Ali Pacha* and Mordecai Noah's *Grecian Captive*, the last performed in 1822 at the height of the excitement with a cast which included a live elephant and a camel, a philhellene American officer, and a Turk named "Nadir." And finally, of course, after a lapse of twenty years, there came that most famous example of nineteenth-century nudity, Hiram Powers' "Greek Slave."

There was also an impact on politics. As early as December 1822 President Monroe had publicly rejoiced at "the reappearance of [the Greek] people in their original character," and had expressed a "strong hope" that they would "recover their independence." In 1823 Madison suggested including a statement on behalf of the Greeks in the contemplated Anglo-American declaration concerning Latin America. Lafayette had already written from France to urge the use of American warships against the Ottoman Navy to "insure the liberties of that classic country," while Gallatin, forgetful of his earlier views, twice urged employment of the Mediterranean Squadron against the Turks. For a time, indeed, Monroe himself gave serious thought to recognizing Greek independence in his fa-

---

[18] On the Greek frigates, see 1 *American Quarterly Review*, 254-86 and Edward Everett's review article, "Greece and the Greek Frigates," 25 *North American Review*, 33-62; Anderson, *Naval Wars in the Levant*, pp. 510-18, 544-49.

mous message of December 1823. From this, however, he was dissuaded by his Secretary of State, who had a double motive. Not only did Adams wish "to make an American cause, and adhere inflexibly to that," but he had given hostages. Once again, in response to Turkish initiative, he had an agent at Constantinople.[19]

It proved possible to control the President, and the message, in its final form, expressed only "ardent wishes" for Greek success. But the Congress, as always, posed the harder problem. Petitions were flooding in, information was called for from the executive on "the condition and future prospects" of the Hellenes, and January 1824 brought a long debate on a resolution, introduced by Webster and strongly supported by Clay, which proposed the appointment of "an Agent or Commissioner to Greece." With all his eloquence Webster urged his countrymen to take a stand. The character of the times and America's "active commercial spirit" had necessarily connected us with other nations; we could not hold aloof. The great political question of the age was that between absolute and regulated governments; in its support of the Ottoman Empire, as elsewhere, the Holy Alliance challenged both liberal principles and the principle of nationality. On the occasion of the Greek Revolution the United States should range themselves against the doctrines of the Allied Powers. "Our place is on the side of free institutions."

Eloquently though it was supported, the resolution failed of passage. The opposition, led by John Randolph of Virginia and Joel Poinsett of South Carolina, mustered strong support from New England and the Middle States, as well as from the south. Assisted from behind the scenes by John Quincy Adams, the opponents emphasized what Clay referred to as a "miserable invoice of figs and opium," the property interests in the Smyrna trade. Figures were produced by the Secretary of the Treasury to show that this had averaged a million dollars a year for 1820-22, and had since continued to rise. The danger of incurring reprisals by a "crusade on behalf of republican principles" was stressed, as was the tradition, so recently reemphasized by the President, of noninterference in "European" affairs. But the opposition's central point was less that of the two spheres than that of the two policies, and the inherent limitations on the role of the American government. Popular senti-

[19] J. D. Richardson (ed.), *Compilation of the Messages and Papers of the Presidents, 1789-1897* (Washington, 1899), II, 193, 217; Gaillard Hunt (ed.), *Writings of Madison* (New York, 1900-10), IX, 157-60; *Memoirs of J. Q. Adams*, VI, 173, 197-99, 204.

ment was one thing, government policy another. Individuals might cheer and aid the Greeks, but the government was bound to use its treaty-making power in the interest of industry and commerce. Together with the maintenance of a navy and an army to redress injury, this marked, in foreign affairs, the limit of its authority.

As is so often the case in American political quarrels, everybody won. On the one hand the "traditional" policy of nonentanglement won out in the voting and the attitude of government remained, as Adams had earlier described it to the London Greeks, one of sympathetic observation and strict neutrality. At the same time, however, a due regard for public opinion ensured that ceremonial good wishes for the Greek cause would continue to issue forth in presidential messages to Congress. There was virtue in this at home, where all but the interested Smyrna traders were wholeheartedly on the side of the rebels. There was also, perhaps, some virtue in it abroad. A pamphlet translation of Webster's great speech had a wide circulation in Greece; in 1827 the Greek government thanked the United States for extending "a helping hand towards the Old World" and encouraging its march to freedom and civilization; to at least one later Greek historian the message of Monroe, despite its restrained phrasing, marked "a great date in the history of Greek independence," from its indication of American concern with and resentment of injuries inflicted upon the liberties of peoples.[20]

One further and surprising consequence ensued. What Secretary Adams had reprobated, President Adams did, and in the autumn of 1825 an agent was sent to Greece. Appropriately enough this emissary, William C. Somerville, sailed in the U.S.S. *Brandywine* in company with Lafayette, then voyaging homeward from his triumphal visit to the United States. Sensibly, the mission was a secret one: ostensibly departing as chargé d'affaires for Sweden, Somerville was instructed that this appointment would terminate upon his arrival in Europe, at which time he should proceed without delay to Greece, express the deep interest of the United States in the "existing contest," investigate the capacity of the country to sustain its independence, assist American commerce, and on application provide advice, information, and good offices. Surprisingly, the secret was well kept, and indeed appears to have lasted out the century. But

[20] Earle, "Ottoman Minorities"; *Annals of Congress*, 18C, 1S, 1, 1084-1214; Richardson, *Messages and Papers*, 11, 259-60, 309, 384; *Writings and Speeches of Daniel Webster* (Boston, 1903), v, 61-93.

Somerville died in France before reaching his destination, and the mission was not renewed.[21]

For the philhellenes this was perhaps just as well. As often in such matters, distance made the heart grow fonder, and familiarity with Greece tended to disenchant. "All came expecting to find the Peloponnesus filled with Plutarch's men; and all returned thinking the inhabitants of Newgate more moral." Dr. Howe had been reasonably frank about the behavior of the people for whom he worked; among the missionaries William Goodell and others had reservations; the Smyrna merchants had even more positive views.

The merchants, indeed, thought poorly both of Greeks and of the philhellene activity in America. Writing from Smyrna in 1824, David Offley reported that news of American assistance to the Greek cause had led to considerable uneasiness about the safety of the $200,000 worth of American property at Smyrna and to inquiries as to the wisdom of placing it under the protection of a foreign consul. In other circles the knowledge of American philhellene feeling had lent interest to the reinforcement of the Mediterranean Squadron and the arrival of Rodgers, and in September 1825 an extraordinary rumor ran through Europe to the effect that the American fleet had bombarded Constantinople and Smyrna and had landed troops in Greece. But in fact the Navy was neutral on the other side.[22]

In the Archipelago, piracy had become a leading Greek occupation. A Boston brig had been plundered off Scio in the spring of 1825, and President Adams, while noting in his diary that "all the commanders of our armed vessels in the Mediterranean, have great abhorrence and contempt for the Greeks," had commented more tactfully in his annual message that although the pirates were "wearing the Greek flag," they "were without real authority." In the next year two more ships were victimized, and the Secretary of the Navy reported that "piracies of the worst kind are daily increasing"; more vessels were attacked in 1827. These events imposed upon the Medi-

[21] Earle, "Ottoman Minorities"; *Memoirs of J. Q. Adams*, vi, 400; vii, 48-49. Special Missions: Sec. of State to Somerville, 6 September 1825 (Records of the Department of State, National Archives).

[22] T. S. Perry (ed.), *Life and Letters of Francis Lieber* (Boston, 1882), p. 34; Richards, *Letters of S. G. Howe*, pp. 89-91; Goodell, *The Old and the New*, pp. 51, 69-73. Despatches, Smyrna: Offley to Sec. of State, 17 March 1824. Lafayette to Clay, 25 November 1825, Calvin Colton (ed.), *Works of Henry Clay* (New York, 1904), vi, 246. Edouard Driault and Michel Lhéritier, *Histoire diplomatique de la Grèce de 1821 à nos jours* (Paris, 1925-26), i, 288-89.

terranean Squadron the task of running a regular convoy system between Malta and Smyrna, with repercussions both abroad and at home. In the autumn of 1827 the sloop *Warren* and the schooner *Porpoise* destroyed a number of piratical vessels and, in reprisal for attacks on American shipping, put a landing force ashore to burn the town of Mykonos. In Washington, in early 1828, the Senate Finance Committee, with Samuel Smith as its interested chairman, raised questions as to the need for further reinforcement of the already strengthened squadron.[23]

So the two policies of popular concern with freedom and government support of commerce pursued their separate ways. At home, financial aid to Greece and philhellene activity in general declined markedly in 1825, but in the latter part of the next year the campaign began again. The discouragement resulting from Ottoman successes in the Morea and from the Greek frigate affair was forgotten; increasingly it seemed probable that the powers would intervene on the side of the rebels. New appeals were launched by Everett, who had exchanged his chair of Greek at Harvard for a seat in the Congress at Washington, and by Matthew Carey in Philadelphia. Although a move for a congressional relief appropriation failed, money and goods again poured in: "a Widow gave 1 barrel of Indian meal and 25 chemises," individual donations as high as $100 were recorded, churches took up collections, benefit balls were held. Something over $100,000 appears to have been realized, and in the spring of 1827 a number of ships bearing relief supplies set sail for the Aegean. In the next year Howe returned temporarily to America and made a swing around the circuit which brought in another $59,000, the equivalent of a couple of shiploads of supplies.

With this revived effort there was also set an important precedent for American relief activity, and one which was to outlast the century. No longer were the funds entrusted to the doubtful mercies of the London Greek committee, or the supplies to the Greek government. Somewhat to the disgruntlement of the latter, arrangements were made for the clothes and provisions to be distributed under American supervision, and the supervisors were instructed to supply noncombatants only.[24]

[23] *Memoirs of J. Q. Adams*, VII, 463; Richardson, *Messages and Papers*, II, 309; R. W. Neeser, *Statistical and Chronological History of the U.S. Navy, 1775-1907* (New York, 1909), II, 60-61, 312-13; *ASP, NA*, III, 175-77.

[24] Earle, "American Interest"; Cline, *American Attitude*, pp. 120-29, 139-47, 199; Miller, *Condition of Greece*, pp. 282-84.

In Greece, 1827 proved to be the decisive year. The intervention of the European powers, the destruction of the Ottoman fleet at Navarino, and the approach of war between Russia and Turkey assured the Hellenes their freedom. Although relief remained a major problem, it now seemed possible to build for the future, and now the missionary groups spurred to the aid of Greece: "only the prevalence of a pure Christianity is needed to give her again the high relative position which she once held."

In point of fact American philhellenism, never wholly a matter of classical echoes, had from the start contained a sizable infusion of the struggle of Cross against Crescent and of Bible Christianity against the Turkish Antichrist. Luther Bradish had proclaimed the war in Greece a struggle between the "deformity of Islamism and the religion we profess." In a sermon of 1824 the Reverend Sereno Dwight, son of Timothy, had looked upon Greek independence as the possible key to the liberation of Christian minorities from Turkish bondage and the evangelization of western Asia. "Missionaries loaded with books will feel their way into the farthest retreats of Mohammedan darkness. In Egypt, Arabia, and Persia, in Chaldea and Tartary, the tidings of salvation will be proclaimed." And indeed the missionaries had already been busy around the periphery.[25]

At Malta, in 1823, when an influx of refugees had followed the massacre at Scio, Fisk and Temple had persuaded the American Board to undertake the education of some Greek boys in America. The first of these were sent to the mission school at Cornwall, Connecticut, founded seven years before as a consequence of the interesting arrival of some young Hawaiians in the United States. But the Greek youths, outnumbered by Pacific islanders, Cherokees, and Choctaws, were not entirely happy at Cornwall, and the later comers, to the total of about a dozen, were educated in the Edwardean climates of Amherst and Yale. This enterprise in international education proved beneficial to the United States, for it produced a number of missionary interpreters, a consul, a colonel, a naval captain, the inventor of the stenotype, and Evangelinus Apostolides Sophocles, for forty years a teacher of Greek at Harvard. But by the same token it seemed less than wholly profitable to Greece, and as the denationalizing effects of education in America became apparent,

---

[25] Newcomb, *Cyclopedia of Missions*, p. 371; S. G. Howe, *A Voice from Greece* (Boston, 1828?), p. 16; S. E. Dwight, *The Greek Revolution* (Boston, 1824), pp. 27-28.

the Cornwall school was closed and the policy changed to one of educating in the country of origin.[26]

As the success of the Greeks in their war for independence appeared increasingly probable, the missionary effort increased. Arriving in the East as representatives of the Female Society of Boston and Vicinity for Promoting Christianity among the Jews, Josiah Brewer and Elnathan Gridley found their clientele unresponsive; while the latter turned to work among the Greeks of Smyrna, the former, after a visit to Constantinople and travel in Asia Minor, opened a Greek school at Syra. Resigning his professorship at Amherst and declining one at Yale, Jonas King in 1828 accepted a commission from the Ladies' Greek Committee of New York to bring out and distribute a shipload of relief supplies; this mission completed, he stayed on to set up a female school on Tenos, to marry a Greek girl from Smyrna, and to rejoin the service of the American Board. In the next year the American Episcopalians appeared on the scene: although a missionary organization had been founded in 1820, no missionaries had as yet been sent abroad, but in early 1829 the Reverend John J. Robertson arrived in Greece to investigate the opportunities of redeeming a sister church from its corruptions of the gospel. In 1830, following a visit to the United States, Josiah Brewer returned to the Mediterranean under the auspices of the Ladies Greek Association of New Haven to found a new school at Smyrna.[27]

Such, indeed, was the interest at home that in the autumn of 1828 the American Board had ordered out its assistant secretary, Rufus Anderson, to survey the scene. Highly intelligent, thoughtful and judicious, and of forceful personality—the missionary educator Cyrus Hamlin, who did not always agree with him, called him "a man of great power"—Anderson was to become perhaps the most important single individual in America's nineteenth-century foreign missionary movement. Having assumed the post of assistant secretary

---

[26] ABCFM *Annual Report, 1826*; *Memorial Volume of ABCFM*, pp. 329-32; Anderson, *Oriental Churches*, I, 143; Booras, *Hellenic Independence*, pp. 193-97.

[27] Brewer, *Residence at Constantinople*; ABC 17.1, Vol. 1: King to Anderson, 3 September 1829; Anderson, *Oriental Churches*, I, 141-44; Bliss, *Encyclopaedia of Missions*, I, 398; P. E. Shaw, *American Contacts with the Eastern Churches, 1820-1870* (Chicago, 1937), pp. 15-22. Although Brewer's work at Smyrna is noted in various travelers' accounts, the prior severance of his connection with the American Board has deprived him of notice in the works of Rufus Anderson and the *Encyclopaedia of Missions*. He is perhaps best remembered for his connection with the Supreme Court: as brother-in-law of Stephen J. Field, who spent two years with him in the Levant, and as father of David Josiah Brewer, born at Smyrna in 1837.

in 1824, after graduation from Bowdoin and Andover, Anderson succeeded as secretary in 1832, and so to the chief executive position of the American Board. In this post, in which he continued for thirty-four years, he became the architect of the Board's efforts, and after his retirement its historian. Secretaries of state might come and go, but from the reign of Andrew Jackson to the administration of Andrew Johnson the foreign office of the New England religion enjoyed a devoted continuity of administration. By ceaseless correspondence and by journeys to the Mediterranean, to India and Ceylon, and to the Sandwich Islands, Anderson deployed and directed his little bands in Asia, Africa, and the Isles of the Sea in the effort to place, through the medium of Hopkinsian benevolence, the impress of the New England religion on peoples around the world.

Anderson's instructions, for his Mediterranean visit of 1829, were largely concerned with Greece, and called for a broad inquiry into the condition of that country, the state of its morals, and its interest in education, to permit an assessment of the possibilities for missionary work. The prospect, it soon appeared, did not lack difficulties. The Greeks at Malta showed no gratitude for the education of their children and were resistant to conversion; missionaries in the Ionian Islands found their work hindered by the British protecting power; conditions in mainland Greece were chaotic. Yet the Board had had an encouraging correspondence with the Greek government, and when in the course of his tour Anderson met the President, Count Capo d'Istria, he was well received. Clearly, it seemed, the renovation of Greece would be a ticklish task, but the disinterested nature of American aid had already made the "American name" the best passport, while the Greek desire for schools and schoolbooks provided a lever. At Malta, Anderson's report led to the decision to concentrate the work of the press on schoolbooks; at home his recommendations with regard to education were accepted and the export of workers began in earnest.[28]

In the autumn of 1830, while the Turks still held the Acropolis,

[28] Cyrus Hamlin, *My Life and Times* (Boston and Chicago, 1893), p. 414. There is a brief sketch of Anderson in *Apppleton's Cyclopaedia of American Biography*, but he is not noticed in the *DAB*, nor is there a biography; the archives of the American Board and the collection of his published works form his monument. His Mediterranean tour of 1828-29 is reported in his letters (ABC 16.5, Vol. 1) and in his *Observations upon the Peloponnesus and Greek Islands* (Boston, 1830); a review of the book by Edward Everett is in 34 *North American Review*, 1-23.

Jonas King visited Athens and purchased a residence. In the next year, preceding the Greek government to its intended capital and endowed by the Greek School Committee of New York with "3,456 slates and 74,000 pencils," he founded an evangelical school and a theological class. On Tenos, in 1830, the Episcopalian Robertson had been joined by the Reverend John Henry Hill; in the next year both advanced to Athens, where they set up a short-lived press and a school which was to endure. Soon an American visitor would report upon these enlightened philanthropic labors, and upon the happy fact that the "works of the divine Plato, are now for the 1st time being printed by men from the new world, in his own city." In the years that followed, the personnel of the American Board was reinforced, new stations were opened at Argos and on Cyprus, and new schools were established, while sizable subventions from the American Bible Society assisted the good work. In December 1836 a third force entered the contest, as two representatives of the American Baptist Missionary Union arrived to educate Patras. Although there remained a sufficiency of obstacles, stemming from resurgent Greek nationalism and the opposition of the hierarchy, there were at least some grounds for optimism. And for two new developments—the institution of Bible study in the public schools and an appreciation of the usefulness of female education—the Americans could rightly claim that credit was due to them alone.[29]

Such, then, was American aid to revolutionary Greece. In what it gave—sympathy both popular and presidential, volunteers, money, supplies and supervised relief, and missionaries to carry the Word—it established what would long remain a pattern. A pattern was also set in what was withheld, and if Everett was right in his belief that liberty was the lesson we were "appointed to teach," the work had nevertheless to be done by private enterprise. The congressman who had limited the range of governmental activity to the negotiation of commercial treaties and the resentment of injury had seen his views borne out. Injuries from Greek pirates had been resented by the Mediterranean Squadron; in the absence of commercial opportunity no treaty was made with Greece until 1837 and then only on Greek initiative, and no representative sent until 1868. Viewing

[29] ABC 17, Vol. 1: King to Anderson, 3 May 1831. Despatches, Turkey: Porter to Sec. of State, 30 October 1832. Newcomb, *Cyclopedia of Missions*, pp. 371-76; Shaw, *Eastern Churches*, pp. 15-22; W. P. Strickland, *History of the American Bible Society* (New York, 1849), pp. 263-84.

its functions in this limited way, protected from enthusiasm by the Newtonian checks and balances, and guided by perhaps more realistic considerations than those which moved the excitable philhellenes, the government refused to become entangled. For this it was to be rewarded in 1862, when the Sultan forbade the use of Turkish ports to Confederate raiders: "Do you realize," said Seward, "that Turkey is the only country upon the face of the earth which officially has supported the American Government in these our trials?"[30] Indeed, this neutrality was to have an even earlier reward, in the long-sought treaty of commerce with Turkey.

4. A Diplomacy Altogether Commercial

Under the protection of the Mediterranean Squadron the Smyrna trade had continued to prosper throughout the Greek War for Independence. Despite the incursions of Greek pirates, the import-export statistics for "Turkey, Levant, and Egypt" remained high and the possibilities of the Black Sea trade alluring. The negotiations with Turkey, broken off in 1821 with the departure of Luther Bradish from Constantinople, were consequently reopened in 1823, to be continued, although unsuccessfully, by John Quincy Adams until his retirement from the White House.

Again the initiative came from the Turks. Early in 1823 soundings were made through Bradish's translator, whom he had authorized to solicit further information from the Porte. In Washington the receipt of this news found a suitable agent at hand in the person of George B. English, that remarkable individual who had progressed from a study of divinity at Harvard through doubt to an acceptance of Islam, and from the editing of a country newspaper through the Marine Corps to become an Egyptian general of artillery. Leaving Egypt in 1822, English had sailed to Malta on the same ship that carried Pliny Fisk, defying all efforts at reconversion, and had thence returned to the United States to attach himself to John Quincy Adams. Dispatched by Adams in April 1823 to investigate the chances of successful negotiation, English reached Constantinople in November. There, while the Greek fever was raging at home, he cultivated the acquaintance of useful Turkish officials: "Among my neighbors," he reported, "I pass for an American mus-

---

[30] Quoted in L. J. Gordon, *American Relations with Turkey, 1830-1930* (Philadelphia, 1932), p. 12.

sulman who has come from a far distant country to visit the Capital of Islam." In December, with the return of the Capudan Pasha from a cruise against the Greek rebels, serious conversations were begun.

In these talks the participants conducted themselves as befitted their national backgrounds. English emphasized the religious equality of Moslem and Christian in the United States and the high character of the Americans resident in the Levant. Husrev blamed Bradish's lack of success on the intrigues of a European ambassador. To frustrate such activity in the future, the Turk suggested a meeting at sea between himself and the commander of the Mediterranean Squadron, at which he would receive the American proposals for direct transmission to the Sultan. Reporting, upon his return to Washington, that the Capudan Pasha "had been for several years the avowed and acknowledged patron of the American nation at the Porte," English urged this plan upon the government, while from Offley at Smyrna came dispatches reemphasizing the need for a treaty.[31]

The facts of Greek piracy and the fear of war between Britain and Algiers had already led to the decision to strengthen the squadron. The appointment to this enlarged command had fallen upon Commodore Rodgers, who had first gone to sea on a ship owned by the Baltimore Smiths, and who twenty years earlier had advocated the negotiation of a treaty with Turkey which would open the Black Sea. To the recommendations of English and Offley were now added petitions from Boston merchants, and in December, as his flagship *North Carolina* was preparing for sea, Rodgers received secret instructions to endeavor "to ascertain in what manner a treaty of commerce founded upon principles of reciprocity, and by which access to the navigation of the Black Sea should be secured . . . may be obtained." English was to go along as interpreter.

By August 1825 Rodgers was at Smyrna with *North Carolina*, the frigate *Constitution*, and two sloops of war. His reception by the Pasha was a flattering one and the courtesies were returned by squadron personnel, who helped put down a threatened conflagration. Although Husrev was busy with the siege of Missolonghi, and the attempt to rendezvous with the Ottoman fleet proved unsuccess-

---

[31] Instructions, Turkey: Adams to English, 2 April 1823; English to Adams, 23 November 1823, 27 December 1823, 8 February 1824 (Records of the Department of State, National Archives). *Memoirs of J. Q. Adams*, vi, 320, 414; Wright, "Relations with Turkey," pp. 94-99.

ful, Ottoman good will continued to be manifest. David Offley was informed "how much pleasure" Husrev would derive from a meeting with Rodgers, and reported "considerable disappointment" at Constantinople from the fact that a minister to the Porte had not been sent out with the Commodore.

Eleven months went by, but at last, in July 1826, the meeting at sea was consummated when the American squadron and the Turkish fleet rendezvoused first at Tenedos and then at Mytilene. On both sides the friendliest dispositions were shown: gifts were exchanged, salutes were fired, and when Rodgers left the Turkish flagship the personal flag of the Sultan was broken at the main, an honor which had "never been conferred on the flag of any European Nation." Turkish requests for useful naval information were gratified; the impression made by the American ships and ship-handling was emphasized by the grounding of a Turkish frigate. Husrev himself proved most accommodating, and indicated that treaty negotiations would be successful, but that "owing to the recent changes . . . at Constantinople"—a euphemism for the destruction of the janissaries which had taken place only the month before—there might be some delay.[32]

Delay, however, was prolonged. The autumn passed, the new year came, and still Rodgers heard nothing from the Capudan Pasha. This silence the Commodore attributed to British diligence at Constantinople in ensuring Turkish awareness of American aid to revolutionary Greece, and he may well have been right: Offley had earlier noted some Turkish difficulty in comprehending the dual nature of American policy and in making the distinction, so clear to Americans, between acts of citizens and acts of government. More probably the delay stemmed from difficulties within the Ottoman government and from the rise to power of Pertew Effendi, "last of the Turks," a poet and politician of pronounced anti-Western attitude. Quite possibly the pressing problems of the Greek war, now complicated by Egyptian and European intervention, provided a sufficient explanation. Yet while temporarily a hindrance to negotiation, the sea of troubles which beset the Turks worked ultimately

---

[32] Instructions, Turkey: Adams to Rodgers, 7 February 1825; Rodgers to Clay, 19 July 1826. Despatches, Turkey: Rodgers to Clay, 14 October 1825, 25 December 1825; Offley to Clay, 28 November 1825; Offley to Rodgers, 30 November 1825. *Memoirs of J. Q. Adams*, VI, 358, 442-47; [George Jones], *Sketches of Naval Life* (New Haven, 1829), I, 156-59, 185-89; Paullin, *Rodgers*, pp. 340-51; Wright, "Relations with Turkey," pp. 108-23.

to make the American treaty still more desirable, while the consolidation of American attitudes toward the outer world ensured that a negotiation would continue to be sought.[33]

The efforts of half a century for the expansion of commerce had had their effect. Begun by the Continental Congress, reemphasized in Washington's Great Rule and in Jefferson's tenure as secretary of state, continued by successive administrations, the American attack on the discriminatory commercial practices of the great powers had gained a considerable success. As well as abroad, the consequences of this success were visible at home: by the 1820's the commercial nature of American policy had become an unquestioned assumption. The belief in the beneficence of trade, earlier made eloquent by the Wits, was soon to be found in the mouths of foremast hands: on seeing the great Liverpool docks, Melville's young Redburn would be moved to observe, in words reminiscent of Barlow, Humphreys, and Dwight, how "under the beneficent sway of the Genius of Commerce, all climes and countries embrace; and yardarm touches yard-arm in brotherly love."[34]

Nor did the concepts of the new Æra lack continuing official sanction. The differences between America and "thrice-wretched Europe" had been stressed by the patriotic poets—"one wide Aceldama," Dwight had called that region—and John Quincy Adams, in his celebrated Fourth of July oration of 1821, had not been backward in echoing the contrast between the happy republic and "that Aceldama, the European world." Two years later the Secretary of State provided a definitive description of American policy when, in the interval between United States recognition of the newly independent Latin American nations and Canning's proposal for joint Anglo-American action, he drew up the instructions for Caesar Rodney and Richard C. Anderson, the first envoys to the sister republics to the southward. To Adams the occasion appeared momentous: the emancipation of the South American continent, following the example of the United States, opened great prospects to the whole race of man and ranked among the most important events of modern history. Appropriately, the lengthy and eloquent papers that he produced are

---

[33] Instructions, Turkey: Rodgers to Clay, 14 February 1827. *Memoirs of J. Q. Adams*, vi, 414; Wright, "Relations with Turkey," pp. 126-27.

[34] V. G. Setser, *The Commercial Reciprocity Policy of the United States, 1774-1829* (Philadelphia, 1937); Herman Melville, *Redburn*, Chap. xxxiii.

of fundamental importance for their exposition of the essence of American policy.

This, in foreign affairs, was based upon the statement of commercial principles in the Preamble to the Treaty of Amity and Commerce with France of 1778, "and as the declaration of independence was the foundation of all our municipal institutions, the preamble . . . laid the corner stone for all our subsequent transactions of intercourse with foreign nations." At home America stood for that "*Civil, political, commercial* and *religious* liberty" which derived directly from the unalienable rights of human nature; externally, "*commerce* and *navigation,* and not . . . empire . . . are the principles upon which *our* confederated republic is founded." On the adoption of these and the rejection of European practices depended the great future: where Humphreys had called for the diffusion of the American religion, "Wide as existence, durable as time," Adams— was it another echo?—looked forward to the spread of those "principles of politics and morals new and distasteful to the thrones and dominations of the elder world, but coextensive with the globe and lasting as the changes of time."[35]

That these views commanded widespread acceptance was shown in 1826 with the publication of Theodore Lyman, Jr.'s *The Diplomacy of the United States,* the first historical treatment of the subject and a work sufficiently well received as to require reissue in an enlarged version within two years. In this work the author, although a strong political opponent of Adams, observed that "the whole system of this republic" was reducible to three or four general commercial propositions, and that "our diplomacy may be termed, altogether, of a commercial character." By 1834 the expositions of both statesman and historian had been drawn on by Jonathan Elliot for the preface to his *American Diplomatic Code,* in which, with copious quotations from Adams' letter to Anderson and from the "clear and forcible writer" of the diplomatic history, he defined the foreign policy of the United States. Elliot's publication was a serviceable one, embracing as it did "a collection of Treaties and Conventions. . . . With an abstract of important judicial decisions, on points connected with Our Foreign Relations. Also, a concise diplomatic manual. . . . Useful for Public ministers and consuls, and for all others

[35] Adams to Caesar Rodney, 17 May 1823; to R. C. Anderson, 27 May 1823; *Writings of J. Q. Adams,* VII, 424-86.

having official or commercial intercourse with foreign nations." Its adoption by both State and Navy departments, and its employment for a generation by ministers, consuls, and naval officers, transformed these concepts into operating doctrine for American officials overseas.[36]

Nor was there any overturning of the ancient attitudes with the rustication of Adams and the arrival of Jackson at the seat of power. Louis McLane, diplomat, secretary of the treasury, and secretary of state, had begun life as a midshipman; the *History* of George Bancroft, Jacksonian politician and future secretary of the navy, perpetuated the optimism of Jonathan Edwards and the patriotism of Joel Barlow. The General's first administration saw the commencement of the great boom in American maritime activity—in the 1830's alone the tonnage in foreign trade rose by 30 percent—and in forwarding and stimulating this remarkable development the Jacksonians were by no means passive. Both in naval and in commercial policy expansion was the order of the day, and this expansion was along traditional lines.

The opening, at long last, of the West Indies trade, and the conclusion of numerous commercial treaties with both European nations and far places, was accompanied by an active supporting naval policy. Beginning in 1831, increased naval expenditures brought an increase in tonnage, guns, and personnel. No diminution could be discerned in the appreciation of the importance of the Mediterranean. To that stout westerner Thomas Hart Benton the consummation of the Turkish treaty and the settlement of the long-standing Neapolitan claims controversy ranked among the "most remarkable" successes of an administration with an unequaled record in foreign affairs. To the Secretary of the Navy the "large interest engaged in mercantile adventures" in the Mediterranean required the presence of the strongest and most efficient squadron, and in 1833 a ship of the line was again sent out. But American commerce was now worldwide, and in 1835, noting that the force at his disposal was inadequate to protect the country's expanding trade, the Secretary asked for more ships.[37]

---

[36] Theodore Lyman, Jr., *The Diplomacy of the United States* (Boston, 1828), pp. 464, 495; Jonathan Elliot, *The American Diplomatic Code* (Washington, 1834), pp. ix-xi.

[37] Heimert, *American Mind*, pp. 66, 194, 551; *Historical Statistics of the U.S.*, p. 445; T. H. Benton, *Thirty Years' View* (New York, 1864), 1, 604-8; Secretary of the Navy, *Annual Reports*; Sprout, *Rise of American Naval Power*, pp. 106-80.

Less even than that of Jefferson does it seem possible to make the administration of the Hero of New Orleans a narrowly agrarian one. To open new areas of the world to trade, Edmund Roberts was sent on two missions to the Far East, and although he died before reaching Japan, he did gain treaties with Siam and Muscat. To avenge an attack on an American merchant ship, the frigate *Potomac* was sent to Quallah Battoo; to support the American whaling fleet, *Lexington* was ordered to the Falkland Islands; for the first time an American warship circled the globe. Plans were laid and preparations made for the Navy's exploring expedition, which sailed in 1838 for a four-year investigation of the Pacific vastnesses. In his farewell address the General called for further enlargement of the Navy, both as the country's natural means of defense and as the protector of its "rich and flourishing commerce on distant seas." What can, perhaps, be said is that the Jacksonian period marks a moment of transition: since commerce had been pretty well liberated throughout the Atlantic world, attention was beginning to shift outward to new areas.

In none of this, whether in the expositions of the great Secretary of State, or of the historian, or of the editor, or in the actions of the Jacksonians, is much to be seen of the principles of Mr. Monroe. No mention of the famous message of 1823 is to be found in Lyman's history or in Elliot's *Diplomatic Code*. As late as 1849, when Seward, subsequently a notable defender of the hemisphere against European incursion, published his biography of John Quincy Adams, he saw no need to refer to the message in the chapter on Adams' tenure at the State Department. In time, indeed, these principles would be assembled by posterity from their widely dispersed location in the message of 1823 for use in analogous situations. But to contemporaries they were of small import, too specific, too localized, and too defensive to serve as guides. Most simply, perhaps, they were too political. What mattered, and what were of widespread applicability, were the commercial generalities.

Equally absent from Adams' papers, from the books of Lyman and Elliot, and from the activities of the Jacksonians, is the related defensive concept of the two spheres. The idea, certainly, had come into existence in the centuries since Columbus' voyage, and was implicit in the very term "New World." Released from the cares of office and relaxing in theoretical speculation, Jefferson in the twenties began to toy with it, and to talk of a "meridian of partition." Doubtless, too, the notion had been fortified by the revolutions in the

Americas as well as by contemporary use of the "globular" or hemispheric projection for world maps.[38] But so political a concept could be of only secondary or emergency importance to a nation whose diplomacy was "altogether, of a commercial character," and the idea was, in any case, as European as it was American, useful as a defense against republican contagion as well as against the aggressions of the colonial powers. Buffon had postulated the biological degeneracy of the Americas; the dividing line had been emphasized in the writings of the Abbé de Pradt; Canning had proposed joint action to forestall the Holy Alliance.

The two spheres, moreover, were not equally homogeneous. The Americas might stretch from pole to pole, but Europe certainly did not; in contrast to "this sphere," the unhappy continent was generally denominated "that quarter." Nor was Europe itself unitary: within it were to be found those small and rational states—Sweden, Holland, Portugal—with whom cooperation rather than conflict was normally to be expected; at its farthest edge lay the largest of "Europe's pacific powers," ruled over by "the imperial Moscovite." Baltic contacts with this vast region—distant, undeveloped, potentially vastly productive, and lacking its own merchant marine—had proven profitable, and had led both to the desire for access to the Black Sea and to a confidence in diplomatic support founded in the experiences of the Armed Neutrality and the War of 1812.

Finally, navigation is by Mercator projection, and Mercator shows no hemispheres. Certainly there was no intention of conceding to the powers of Europe the commercial dominance of outer areas which Adams had described as being, like the United States, "essentially extra-European" in policy. Both of the countries to which the Secretary of State referred lay along the frontiers of Europe. One of them was the Ottoman Empire.[39]

[38] See Chap. I, note 32.
[39] Adams to Henry Middleton, 5 July 1820, *Writings of J. Q. Adams*, VII, 49-50.

CHAPTER V

The Turkish Treaty and After,
1827-1845

1. The Treaty Made

GIVEN the American passion for commerce, the delays which affected the making of the Turkish treaty appear at first sight surprising. Despite friendly overtures from Constantinople dating from Bainbridge's visit and equally ancient suggestions from American merchants and naval officers, official action waited until the 1820 mission of Luther Bradish. And while Bradish's visit to Constantinople was followed within five years by the efforts of English and Rodgers, these emissaries also lacked authority to treat and were limited by their instructions to inquiry as to possibilities and methods.

This diffidence on the part of the American government and the secrecy with which the exploratory efforts were clothed seem to have been due both to philhellenic fervor at home and to fear of great-power intrigue. Founded on the philosophical opposition of New Order and Old World and reinforced by a Mediterranean experience reaching back to the British-made peace between Portugal and Algiers, this distrust was in no way diminished by repeated Turkish references to European machinations. If, at this distance in time, the American reaction seems exaggerated, it nevertheless reflected a basically sound appreciation of the conflict between the apostles of commerce and the disciples of power.

As well as delaying the commencement of negotiations, these preoccupations inhibited comprehension of the problems of those with whom it was proposed to negotiate. It seems quite clear that the Americans little understood the situation in Turkey. There the Sultan Mahmud II, who had come to power "amid scenes of carnage and terror rarely equalled even in Constantinople," was attempting the superhuman task of controlling and defending his far-flung dominions while at the same time forcing through a cultural revolution along Western lines. In such a situation the needs of Mahmud and his ministers transcended the profits realizable from a simple increase in the exchange of goods: the latter goal placed great premium on the arts of the West; the former on those specific instruments which contribute to military and naval power.[1]

For the Ottoman Empire in the nineteenth century, defense meant defense against Russia and was principally a matter of armies. But for the control of Mahmud's thalassic realm the key question was the naval one, and the maintenance of this crescent-shaped structure, which embraced the eastern half of the Mediterranean and all its islands, depended on control of the sea. Quite unlike its American counterpart, the Turkish fleet was less an instrument for the protection of commerce than one for maintaining the integrity of the realm. This situation, emphasized by the position of Mehemet Ali in Egypt, was reemphasized by the Greek revolt: recovery of the Archipelago and of the Morea were naval problems, presented at a time when Mahmud's resources were dangerously weakened by the defection of the Greek sailors who had traditionally manned the Turkish ships.

Help from without had previously been available. The graving dock at Constantinople was the work of a Swedish engineer, and French naval architects had built many of the Sultan's ships. But France was now philhellene and worse: she had espoused the cause of Mehemet Ali, whose province she increasingly regarded as the eastern outpost of Gallic culture, and the contumacious Pasha of Egypt was building himself a navy at Marseilles. It might seem that Britain, the strongest sea power, would have provided an obvious alternative, but the British had long supplied admirals and artisans to the Czar of Russia, the Sultan's hereditary enemy; the British were also philhellene; and a British admiral and a British general were directing insurgent forces in Greece. The British government, it is true, had realized the importance of maintaining Turkish control of the straits, but the chosen method was that of the St. Petersburg Protocol and the Treaty of London: to restrain the Russians by joining them, and to prevent a Russo-Turkish war by a settlement of the Greek question. And although the Treaty of London was, as Adams said, "a triple alliance against one of the parties to it," this cure by amputation was not calculated to endear Great Britain

[1] Harold Temperley, *England and the Near East: The Crimea* (London, 1936), p. 5. On the general problem of modernization: H.A.R. Gibb and Harold Bowen, *Islamic Society and the West* (London, 1950-57); Bernard Lewis, *The Emergence of Modern Turkey* (London, 1961); *idem*, *The Middle East and the West* (Bloomington, Indiana, 1964); R. H. Davison, *Reform in the Ottoman Empire* (Princeton, 1963).

to the Porte. In need of naval assistance but faced by a hostile Europe, Mahmud and Husrev had to turn elsewhere. This they had previously attempted. That they were still able to do so was due, in the last analysis, to the existence of a disengaged, extra-European maritime nation, and to the "miserable invoice of figs and opium."[2]

The Greek situation reached its crisis in September 1827, with the landing of Egyptian reinforcements in the Morea. There an attempt by Admiral Codrington, commander of the combined British, French, and Russian squadrons, to impose an armistice on the contending parties, led through confusion and misunderstanding to a naval battle at Navarino. In this battle, on 20 October, the Turkish and Egyptian fleets were almost totally destroyed.

As the cannonade at Navarino echoed around the world, the response again illustrated that division of sentiment between statesmen and people so apparent throughout the Greek revolt. To Metternich it was a "frightful catastrophe"; to Wellington an "untoward incident"; to Calhoun an event pregnant with "consequences, which the most segacious cannot anticipate." Other circles, however, evinced more pleasure. Byron was dead but Victor Hugo issued a statement on his behalf; the town of Algoma, Wisconsin, got its Navarino Street; and in Cherry Valley, New York, the citizens turned out and celebrated by collecting another $150 for the Greeks.[3] In time Navarino could be seen as marking, within the Mediterranean, the first step in the territorial expansion of Europe at the expense of the neighboring Islamic culture. Even while the statesmen were wringing their hands and the people were ringing the bells, the battle appeared to have decided the question of Greek independence. Less obvious, perhaps, but equally incontestable, was its effect on the American negotiations for a Turkish treaty.

At Smyrna, where news of the battle arrived on the evening of the 27th, there was "great consternation and alarm among the Franks." To Offley the affair appeared the most "treacherous transaction" since Copenhagen. Fearing for the safety of their goods and persons, many Western merchants moved bag and baggage aboard

---

[2] Adolphus Slade, *Turkey, Greece, and Malta* (London, 1837), ii, 16n., 351; L.P.B. d'Aubignosc, *La Turquie nouvelle* (Paris, 1839), i, 95; ii, 76; Georges Douin, *Les premières frégates de Mohamed Aly* (Cairo, 1926); [J. Q. Adams], 3 *American Annual Register*, 288.

[3] Anderson, *Naval Wars in the Levant*, pp. 512-35; "Correspondence of John C. Calhoun," *American Historical Association Annual Report, 1899,* ii, 258; Victor Hugo, "Navarin" (1827); Booras, *Hellenic Independence*, p. 218.

Map 2

15° 20° 25°

Vienna

AUSTRIAN EMPIRE
HUNGARY
RUM

Danube

Milan

Po R.

Venice
Trieste

DALMATIA

45°

Genoa

SPEZIA
1848-61

VILLEFRANCHE
1865-66
1870-83

Leghorn
TUSCANY

Elba
CORSICA
Civitavecchia

PAPAL

STATE

Rome

Klek

Lissa

Danube

Bu

BULGA

Sofia

Samokov

Philippopolis

RUMELI

Adr

MACEDONIA

Salonica

Teñed

Gaeta
Naples

SARDINIA

40°

Cagliari

KINGD. of the TWO SICILIES

Lipari
Is.

Palermo

Messina

SICILY

Syracuse

IONIAN SEA

IONIAN IS.

NEGROPONT

Scio

GREECE

Patras

MOREA

Argos

Athens

My

Navarino
1827

Melos

M
E
D

Tunis

TUNIS

35°

Lampedusa

Malta

SMITH & DWIGHT 1830

CRET

T
E
R
R
A
N
E
A

FISK-KING 1822-'23

Tripoli

VIDAL '74

Benghazi

Derna
Bomba

VIDAL '74

Tobruk

Si

CYRENAICA

TRIPOLI

30°

SAHAR

D

THE
EASTERN MEDITERRANEAN
and the NEAR EAST

Median scale 0   300 Statute miles

Navy Agencies of 1805   ☆ Syracuse
Squadron Bases   ⚓ SPEZIA
Principal Missionary Stations 🏛 Athens
Missionary Stations with Colleges 🏛 BEIRUT
Capitals ✳ ◉   Boundaries as of 1815

25°

10° 15° 20° 25°

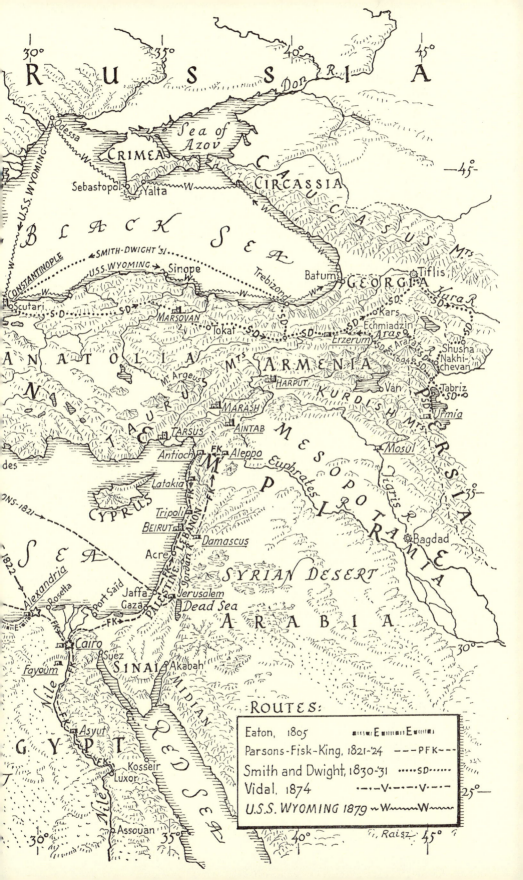

ship, while the commanders of European warships shifted their vessels "close in shore, so as to command the Turkish town." But Captain Patterson of the U.S.S. *Constitution* ostentatiously made no move, not wishing it thought that he anticipated danger to American citizens or property, and his course "was immediately remarked by the government," to whom it "gave much satisfaction."[4]

It may be presumed that it gave much satisfaction in Constantinople as well, for on 11 November David Offley received an express from Husrev, no longer capudan pasha but now advanced to the post of seraskier, or minister of war. In a "particularly friendly and complimentary letter," Husrev invited Offley to come at once to Constantinople, "as the moment was favorable for the termination of a commercial treaty between the Porte and the Government of the United States." Once more the initiative had been taken by the Turks.

The starry flag still beckoned to the Crescent. Disengagement had paid off. Not only was the United States wholly unconnected with the Allied Powers, but it appears that the belief in the essential difference between European and American systems was as firmly held in Constantinople as in the United States. Although the British had attempted to impress the Porte with the extent of American aid to Greece, the Turks, far from resenting American philhellenism, were reported to feel a "grateful sense of their friendly disposition towards the Musselmans," and some who had heard of the Greek frigate chose to believe that it had been intended for the Sultan and captured on the way to Constantinople. At that capital, moreover, the views of the Moroccan "King's preacher" seem to have prevailed, in a feeling that the Americans, if not Moslem, were at least something better than Christian. And finally, they built good ships. The Reis Effendi was said to have told an English merchant that "however you may act towards us the Americans will be our good friends; and an American ship, you very well know, is worth two of yours of the same size."

Enraged by Navarino, Mahmud had summoned the faithful to a jihad, and in December 1827 the ambassadors of the European allies left Constantinople. But the American negotiations still continued. In January 1828 the dragoman Navoni, whom Bradish had

[4] *ASP, NA*, III, 139; Wright, "Relations with Turkey," p. 131; Charles MacFarlane, *Constantinople in 1828* (London, 1829), pp. 123-25; [Jones], *Sketches of Naval Life*, II, 186-89.

employed on his visit to Constantinople, informed the Secretary of State that the Porte rejoiced in the rupture of diplomatic relations with England, which removed the surveillance which that power had previously exercised over the project of the American treaty. In the next month the Boston brig *Delos* was permitted to pass the Dardanelles, an event which led David Offley to appoint an agent for American commercial affairs at the capital.

But while the Americans looked only for a treaty of commerce and navigation, the Turks were interested in more. Pertew, now reis effendi, minced no words, but suggested that commercial concessions be accompanied by a formal alliance. Informed by Navoni that this proposal had small chance of acceptance, Pertew then pointed out that the circumstances in which the Porte found itself obliged it to seek political as well as commercial advantage. Wishing to repair as speedily as possible the losses sustained at Navarino, it at least wanted to know if it could procure the needed vessels in the United States.

Similar information reached Washington from Offley at Smyrna, who reported that the Sultan, hoping that "if a treaty of friendship existed . . . they would be allowed to have vessels of war built in the United States so as to replace those destroyed at Navarino," had ordered the Reis Effendi to conclude a treaty. For all of his anti-Western feelings, Pertew could no longer resist. In February he forwarded a formal proposal to Offley.[5]

At home the resurgent Greek fever had convinced Adams that negotiations were politically impossible. But by the time Offley's information arrived he was willing to try, although concerned about the difficulty of preserving secrecy. News that the Boston brig had passed the Dardanelles raised his hopes; the absence from the capital of Henry Clay left negotiations in his hands. With the need for caution reemphasized by fears of European obstruction at Constantinople and of philhellenist outcry at home, all papers were marked "secret and confidential"—an unusual proceeding in those days—and all were drafted by the President himself. In the Mediterranean the command of the squadron, now increased to seven ships, had passed from Rodgers to Commodore William M. Crane.

[5] Instructions, Turkey: Offley to Clay, 26 November 1827. Despatches, Turkey: Navoni to Clay, 24 January 1828; Offley to Clay, 17 February 1828. [Jones], *Sketches of Naval Life*, ii, 192; H.A.V. Post, *A Visit to Greece and Constantinople in the Year 1827-8* (New York, 1830), pp. 310-11; Wright, "Relations with Turkey," pp. 132-48.

In July 1828 Adams appointed Crane and Offley as commissioners to negotiate a treaty of commerce and navigation which would admit American shipping to the Black Sea, but with the caution, stemming from Pertew's remarks, that no provision could be accepted which might compromise the neutral status of the United States. By November the Commodore had received his orders and had reached Smyrna, where he remained while Offley proceeded to Constantinople.

There the situation was still deteriorating, and the need for ships was even more acute. Russia had declared war in April, and the weakened Turkish fleet was unable to contest the control of the Black Sea. Assisted by French constructors, the Pasha of Egypt was rapidly making good his own losses at Navarino and, no longer content with frigates, had begun to build ships of the line. But little understanding was evinced by the American negotiator, who limited his argument to the praise of commerce. In reply, and with some apparent reason, Pertew pointed out that the Americans would profit most from a reciprocal commercial treaty, and suggested that in return for the privilege of navigating the Black Sea "the United States would not hesitate to present to the Porte a certain number of vessels of war." Observing that such a purchase of friendship was inconsistent with the dignity of his country, and perhaps influenced by memories of the tribute earlier paid the Barbary powers, Offley rejected the suggestion, while conceding that the Porte might be allowed to build in the United States at its own expense. For a time negotiations lapsed; again old Husrev interceded and talks were resumed; reluctantly the question of warships was abandoned. But in the end the discussion broke down on the question of tariffs, and in March 1829, blaming his failure upon British intrigue, Offley returned empty-handed to Smyrna.[6]

By the time the news reached Washington the administration had changed, and John Quincy Adams, lamenting in his final message to Congress the "state, perhaps too much prolonged, of coldness and alienation" between America and the Ottoman Porte, had given way to the warrior from the West. Shortly, Jackson's acting secretary of

[6] *Memoirs of J. Q. Adams*, VII, 463; VIII, 6, 60. Instructions, Turkey: Adams to Offley, 21 July 1828; Adams to Crane, 22 July 1828. Despatches, Turkey: Crane to Adams, 7 December 1828; Offley to Crane, 10 December 1828, 15 December 1828, 10 January 1829, 17 February 1829; Offley to Adams, 31 January 1829. Wright, "Relations with Turkey," pp. 140-58.

state came out to Meridian Hill to consult with the ex-President and to report that the Turks, after first asking for two ships of the line, had ultimately come down to $50,000 in cash, more than twice the amount Crane had been authorized to spend. But although Adams, fearing that opportunity would once again be lost, urged closing at this price if it could still be done, the American taxpayer was saved this expenditure by the Czar of Russia. With the coming of summer his armies renewed the campaign and advanced rapidly on both European and Asiatic fronts. From Constantinople, where American merchant ships continued to be cordially received, overtures continued to issue; in August, with the fall of Adrianople impending, Offley wrote President Jackson to point out the favorable opportunities for negotiation which were likely to follow the conclusion of peace between Turkey and Russia, the more so if Russian good offices could be employed. This was to prove a fruitful suggestion.[7]

In September 1829 the Jackson administration appointed a new commission, in which Offley was joined by Commodore James Biddle, the new Mediterranean commander, and by Charles Rhind of New York, self-described as "one of the oldest American merchants trading to the Levant." The instructions to the commissioners were modified to permit them to compromise temporarily on the most-favored-nation tariff provision; no compromise, however, was permitted regarding the "neutral obligations of the United States." On 20 October, after talks with the Russian minister to Washington, Rhind sailed from New York "under a feigned name" to join his colleagues. On 28 November he reached Gibraltar, where he learned that the war between Russia and Turkey had ended two months before.

Autumn brought not only an end to the war and the appointment of new American negotiators; it also saw a new definition of Russian policy. Before news of the Treaty of Adrianople had reached St. Petersburg the Czar had decided, in view of increasing English and French concern with the Eastern question, to change from a policy of Turkish partition to one of support of the status quo. Desirous also of good relations with the United States, the second great-

[7] Richardson, *Messages and Papers*, II, 407; *Memoirs of J. Q. Adams*, VIII, 110, 117, 146, 151. Despatches, Turkey: Offley to Jackson, 21 March 1829, 9 August 1829; Offley to Clay, 8 July 1829. Confidence in the possibility of Russian support was widespread: Willard Phillips, review of Dearborn's *Commerce of the Black Sea*, 10 *North American Review*, 170, 179; [J. Q. Adams], 3 *American Annual Register*, 341-43, 397-98, 425; *Niles' Weekly Register*, 27 November 1830.

est carrying nation, to counterbalance the maritime power of England, he instructed Count Orlov, his negotiator at Constantinople, to assist the American commissioners in their effort.

Rhind, who had been selected to do the actual negotiating, reached Constantinople on 8 February 1830, and at once waited on the Reis Effendi. Negotiations began in classic form. Like a true Turk, Pertew began by proposing special duties and presents for the officers of the Porte; like a true American, Rhind replied with abstractions, stressing the value of the friendship of his distant and disinterested country and the contrast between the purely commercial character of American policy and the "chicanery and diplomatic intrigues" of Europe. These arguments failing, Rhind consulted with Orlov, who volunteered his assistance. Within a week Pertew was deposed and replaced by the more compliant Mohammed Hamid, and in March the talks were resumed. Shortly, the Sultan ordered Hamid to agree to the American proposals; but intrigues, British and domestic, supervened. The usual appeal was made to Husrev and hope was restored; Rhind resisted a proposal of differential duties, and threatened to appeal for Russian support; on 7 April the Sultan again commanded his ministers to close. This time, at long last, they did, and a month later the treaty was signed.[8]

With the establishment of diplomatic and consular relations, most-favored-nation treatment, and the promise of admission to the Black Sea, the Americans had gained their essential objectives. For a moment, indeed, it was rumored in Levantine circles that they had also acquired the island of Crete. But the Porte had also accomplished its aims, for Rhind had accepted a "separate and secret article" which permitted the Turks to build warships and procure ship timber in the United States with the assistance of the United States government. To the other diplomats at Constantinople this article remained no secret, but the successful outcome of the negotiations did come as something of a surprise. "Thus," wrote the chaplain of the British embassy, "while we of the old world were destroying the fleet of

---

[8] Instructions, Turkey: Van Buren to Biddle, Offley, and Rhind, 12 September 1829. Despatches, Turkey: Rhind to Van Buren, 14 October 1829, 20 October 1829, 28 November 1829; Rhind to Jackson, 10 May 1830. B. P. Thomas, *Russo-American Relations, 1815-1867* (Baltimore, 1930), p. 70; F. A. Golder, *Guide to Materials for American History in Russian Archives* (Washington, 1917), pp. 54-56, 88; *Memoirs of J. Q. Adams*, viii, 71; *Reminiscences of James A. Hamilton* (New York, 1869), pp. 143-45; Wright, "Relations with Turkey," pp. 164-90.

our ancient allies at Navarino, those new-comers had supplied them with a new one."[9]

The first consequence of the "separate and secret article" was a violent quarrel between Rhind and his separate commissioners. Summoned to Constantinople to sign the treaty, and apprised of that provision only following their arrival, Offley and Biddle strongly disapproved its inclusion and signed only under protest. Rhind himself defended the article by declaring it "a *perfect nullity*," although "necessary to show the Sultan that *something* had been granted for the concessions he had made"; and further, somewhat inconsistently, by arguing that if the President declined to accept it the fact would make no difference to the Turks. This last, at least, was far from the truth. The article was rejected by the Senate, in part out of consideration for Russia, and the result was deep Turkish dissatisfaction. But oddly enough, as things turned out, the Turks ended up with more than they had asked.

The treaty of commerce, less the separate and secret article, passed the Senate on 1 February 1831. In April, Jackson appointed Commodore David Porter chargé d'affaires at Constantinople. Although the selection seems to have been made for personal reasons, it was, under the prevailing circumstances, a peculiarly felicitous one; for Porter, hero of the war with Tripoli and of the War of 1812, former member of the Board of Navy Commissioners and former commander in chief of the Mexican Navy, was as competent a naval adviser as could be found. As America's first naval expansionist, moreover, who as early as 1815 had suggested the opening of Japan, he was not one to be backward in furthering American influence in foreign parts. But his nomination was a blow to Charles Rhind, who had himself hoped for appointment as first envoy to the Sublime Porte.[10]

Rhind had returned to the United States in the previous November. Failing in his effort to win appointment as chargé, he then

[9] Despatches, Turkey: Rhind to Van Buren, 25 May 1830. Robert Walsh, *A Residence at Constantinople* (London, 1836), II, 342. For the text of the treaty, see Miller, *Treaties*, III, 541-57.

[10] Despatches, Turkey: Rhind to Van Buren, 1 June 1830. Miller, *Treaties*, III, 562-85; *Reminiscences of J. A. Hamilton*, p. 203; D. D. Porter, *Memoir of Commodore David Porter* (Albany, 1875), pp. 394-96; A. B. Cole, "Captain David Porter's Proposed Expedition to the Pacific and Japan, 1815," 9 *Pacific Historical Review*, 61-65.

vainly endeavored to be selected to carry the ratified treaty and instructions to Porter, who was already in Europe. Despite Senate rejection of the secret article Rhind also persevered, whether from a sense of obligation to the Turks or with an eye to personal profit, in an attempt to fulfill the spirit of the engagement. In this he was encouraged by the fact that his friend Henry Eckford had a warship for sale.

One of the leading shipbuilders of the day, Eckford had been largely responsible for winning the naval race on the Great Lakes in the War of 1812. For some years thereafter he had served as naval constructor; he had designed, among other vessels, the U.S.S. *Ohio*, finest of all American ships of the line, and had also done work for the navies of Latin America. After suffering reverses he had recently built the 26-gun corvette *United States*, apparently as a speculation, although rumor had it that the vessel was intended for Russia. But it is at least possible that the intended destination was Turkey: the link between New York shipbuilders and New York diplomatic agents was close, and Eckford had been one of the owners of the steamship *Robert Fulton* when the attempt was made, on information from Luther Bradish, to palm it off on the government as a present for the Turks.

On 16 April 1831, one day after Porter's appointment as chargé, Rhind wrote the Secretary of State that Eckford had "some idea" of taking his corvette to Constantinople, and suggested that the bearer of the treaty and instructions take passage on her. Again he was disappointed: the papers were confided to William B. Hodgson of the State Department, who sailed in late April on the U.S.S. *John Adams*. Undaunted, the New Yorkers prepared to follow along. A letter of recommendation for Eckford, written by the President of the United States "in his individual capacity," was procured, and the Secretary of State appended to Porter's instructions a notice of the shipbuilder's intended visit to Constantinople.

Commanded by George C. DeKay, a grandson-in-law of Eckford and a former commodore in the Argentine Navy, the *United States* sailed in June. As passengers she carried the shipbuilder; the captain's brother, Dr. James E. DeKay; and the moving spirit, Charles Rhind. After a fast passage they reached the Dardanelles on 3 August, where they found the U.S.S. *John Adams*, with Porter aboard, awaiting the south wind that would permit the passage of the straits.[11]

Naval constructor, naval adviser, and the treaty which would admit American shipping to the Black Sea thus arrived together at the capital of the Grand Turk. But the missionaries had beaten them all. While Rhind was negotiating with the Turks, two missionary explorers had passed through Constantinople; while ratification of the treaty was in progress they had explored Anatolia, had entered Persia, had sailed the Black Sea. Instructions from the American Board to establish a station at Constantinople had reached the Mediterranean in the month of Porter's appointment as chargé, and these instructions had already been carried out.

2. The Exploration of Armenia

Drawn to the Mediterranean by the magnet of the Holy Land, the American missionaries in the course of their first decade had thoroughly explored its eastern shores. With Parsons, Fisk had traversed the country of the Seven Churches of Asia; with King he had ascended the Nile; with their other colleagues these pioneers had on various occasions covered the greater part of Syria and Palestine. But the Greek struggle for independence had brought a change in direction, and between 1827 and 1829 Rufus Anderson, with King, Smith, and others, had ventured through the Ionian and Aegean islands and into the Morea, while on the African shore Isaac Bird had visited Tunis and Tripoli. From these travels a considerable fund of information had been derived concerning the religious and moral condition of the various Christian churches—Coptic, Maronite, and Greek —of the countries along the Mediterranean's eastern rim.

But to the northward, Constantinople and Asia Minor had been little explored. Pliny Fisk had sojourned briefly at Smyrna. On his homeward voyage in 1826 Jonas King had visited Constantinople. As a missionary to the Jews, Josiah Brewer in 1827 had made a somewhat profitless stay at the capital. In the same year Elnathan Gridley had penetrated into Cappadocia, but his ascent of Mount Argeus,

[11] Despatches, Turkey: Rhind to Van Buren, 16 April 1831. Instructions, Turkey: Van Buren to Porter, 22 April 1831. *Reminiscences of J. A. Hamilton*, pp. 203-6; Miller, *Treaties*, III, 584; [David Porter], *Constantinople and its Environs* (New York, 1835), I, 13. On Eckford: P. DeK. Wheelock, "Henry Eckford," 7 *American Neptune*, 177-95; Henry Howe, *Memoirs of the Most Eminent American Mechanics* (New York, 1842), pp. 211-16; *Niles' Register*, 18 June 1831; H. I. Chappelle, *History of the American Sailing Navy* (New York, 1949).

in an attempt to test the affirmation of Strabo that both the Black Sea and the Mediterranean were visible from its summit, had cost him his life.

Concerning the condition of the more easterly Christian sects, then, little was yet known. With the Armenians, most numerous of these, some limited contact had been gained in Syria; but Armenia itself remained unexplored, while with regard to Georgians, Nestorians, and Chaldeans almost total ignorance prevailed. To investigate the condition of the Armenians in their own country and to ascertain what the churches of America could do for this people, scattered and oppressed by a history of wars and persecutions, the American Board in 1829 resolved upon another exploring expedition. To carry out this lengthy and hazardous journey into the unknown the Board selected Eli Smith, by now an experienced traveler to whose familiarity with Arabic was added some competence in Turkish, and the newly appointed Harrison Gray Otis Dwight.[12]

Dwight reached Malta with the instructions in late February 1830, and another month found the travelers at Smyrna. There, after fruitless efforts to acquire information on interior Asia Minor, the two engaged post horses and a Tatar, rode northward to the Sea of Marmora, and crossed over to Constantinople. In a month's stay at the capital they benefited from the politeness of Charles Rhind, then negotiating the Turkish treaty, who gained them the opportunity to preach to English residents and who facilitated the procurement of firmans for travel in Turkey and passports for entrance into Russia. In their investigation of the political, moral, and religious aspects of the Armenian community, Smith and Dwight called upon the Patriarch and visited the Armenian Academy and its famous teacher, Gregory Peshtimaljian, the Erasmus of his nation. The Patriarch received them affably; at the academy it appeared that in some categories, at least, knowledge was wholly up to date, for the location of Andover was precisely known.[13]

The western border of Armenia, that landlocked mountainous territory at the junction of three empires, lies some six hundred miles east of Constantinople. An approach to this region by way of the

---

[12] Brewer, *Residence at Constantinople*, pp. 50, 214n., 246-47; Anderson, *Oriental Churches*, I, 79, 142; Eli Smith, *Researches in Armenia* (Boston and New York, 1833), I, iii-iv.

[13] Smith, *Researches*, I, 44, 53-54, 64-66, 71. ABC 16.9, Vol. 1: Smith to Anderson, 1 June 1830.

Black Sea had been considered but rejected, since the prevailing northerly winds of summer threatened too great delay; equally, however, travel by caravan was too slow. So again a Tatar was engaged and post horses arranged for. To lighten their baggage the missionaries exchanged their trunks for saddlebags and their mattresses for carpets with coverlets of painted canvas. For warmth they procured Turkish pelisses lined with Caucasian fox, and for eating, copper mess kits and a coffee mill. A circular piece of leather with a chain run through rings in its circumference would both carry food and serve as a table. All could be carried on one extra horse. Early on the morning of 21 May the two crossed by boat to Scutari to start out on their errand into the wilderness.

So these pioneers of the Lord set off into the unknown: Eli Smith of Northford, Connecticut, twenty-nine years old, graduate of Yale and of the Andover seminary and veteran of four years in the Levant; H.G.O. Dwight, born in northern Massachusetts and brought up in upstate New York, twenty-seven years of age, graduate of Hamilton and Andover and only five months from home. To their friends they would have been hardly recognizable. For their "own snug dress" they had substituted the loose robes of the Turk, and for the European hat the turban; their feet were encased in the enormous stockings and boots of the Tatar; there were pistols on their saddle-bows. It was a stirring moment as they prepared to mount; as Smith wrote,

> . . . a moment of sadness. How many must be our fatigues, anxieties, perhaps sicknesses, before seeing again the face of a countryman and a friend! Could we even expect that both would escape with life the perils from sickly climates and pestilence, in the wilderness, in the city and in the sea, among robbers and false brethren, that awaited us? I had commenced the enterprise with a strong presentiment of never surviving to revisit my friends. . . . In my companion, a similar feeling was enhanced by unacquaintance with the country and its people, and greater freshness and intimacy of attachment to friends left behind. But neither of us did it lead to a moment's despondency or wavering of resolution, for we doubted not that Providence had led us into the path we were pursuing, nor that our object was worth all that we were risking for it.

Thus hoping and fearing, but sustained by Hopkinsian zeal, they set off eastward at ten o'clock in the morning in "a slight shower of rain."[14]

Along the road through Anatolia, flat lands with large flocks of grazing sheep alternated with stretches of mountain and unbroken forest. At times the excellent soil reminded the Americans of that of upstate New York, but its uncultivated state and the filthy villages, flea-bitten posthouses, and arrogant Turks led them to wonder at the ways of Providence in entrusting so rich a soil to so blighting a government and so indolent a people. After ten days' hard riding the travelers reached their first sizable city, Tokat in Armenia Minor, where Henry Martyn, pioneer British missionary to India and Persia, lay buried; here they stayed for three days to study the Armenian community and its schools. Then upward into the Armenian highland, where mountains grew higher and ravines deeper, and where the first nomads—black-tented Kurds—were seen. As the advance continued, there appeared signs of increasing disorganization, the consequence of the Russian invasion of the previous summer. No horses could be obtained, but only oxcarts, and with frequent and tedious changes of cattle this humiliating mode of conveyance took the Americans up the headwaters of the "noble Euphrates" and into the plain of Erzerum. In the approaches to this city, reputed to have been founded by a grandson of Noah, the missionaries overtook the rearguard of the Russian Army, assembling for its withdrawal, and bewailed the "false and scandalous specimen of Christianity" exhibited to Moslems by the drunken and dancing soldiers. On 13 June horses were again obtained, and at midday, twenty-three days and nearly eight hundred miles from Constantinople, Smith and Dwight entered Erzerum.[15]

High in the mountains, at an altitude of six thousand feet and with a cold and inhospitable climate, Erzerum was a provincial capital, the site of an Armenian diocese, and the largest city of Turkish Armenia. But the prospects of useful investigation had been frustrated by the impact of war: the Armenian population was leaving with the Russian conquerors. So eastward again, past the battlefields of the recent war and through poverty-stricken regions where an illiterate

[14] Smith, *Researches*, I, 73-74.

[15] *Ibid.*, I, 122-23. Martyn's career had been inspired by the example of William Carey, and, as in the case of Carey himself, by a reading of Jonathan Edwards' *Life of Brainerd*. Richter, *History of Missions*, pp. 93-94; Bliss, *Encyclopaedia of Missions*, II, 36-37.

population lived in underground houses and worshiped in underground churches presided over by ignorant priests. In this high country, night temperatures near freezing chilled sleepers in the open air, but even the cold seemed preferable to the verminous dwellings and fetid stables which had been the travelers' usual lot. At Kars, a hundred miles onward, whence the Turkish population had fled before the invader and whence the Armenians were preparing to depart, a helpful Russian commander provided army post horses and a Cossack guide; thus aided, the Americans reached the Russian frontier on 3 July. Some days were spent in quarantine, and more in penetrating the mountains, but on the 21st the road led steeply down into the valley of the River Kura, anciently the Cyrus, and on the next day the travelers entered Tiflis, capital of Georgia.

The population of this crowded city, administrative center for the Caucasus and Transcaucasia, was predominantly Armenian, and its merchant and mechanic classes wholly so. Its location, midway between Black and Caspian seas, gave it considerable commercial importance and still greater commercial promise. In this commerce, if only indirectly, America was already a participant, for on their first visit to a caravanserai the missionaries discovered a hogshead of New England rum. Granted that the Georgians were to be counted among the hardest drinkers in the world, it was still shocking to find one's own countrymen placing love of gain above love of souls. "What a harbinger, thought we, have our countrymen sent before their missionaries! What a reproof to the Christians of America, that, in finding fields of labor for their missionaries, they should allow themselves to be anticipated by her merchants, in finding a market for their poisons!"[16]

Already a generation under Russian control, Tiflis seemed partly Europeanized. But while public order had been improved, the level of learning had not: an educational reform movement among the Armenians had been destroyed and the Georgians were vegetating in happy ignorance. In morals the situation was no better: "Infamous as the Georgians have always been known to be for chastity, it must be confessed that they have deteriorated. The devotees of lust have multiplied." Nor did this people, whose welfare was one of the Americans' stated concerns, offer a suitable mission field. Having long suffered under Persian rule, the Georgians had been conquered simultaneously by Russian emperor and by Russian Church; the replace-

[16] Smith, *Researches*, I, 215-16.

ment of their Catholicos by a Russian bishop excluded "the hope of their becoming a field for missionary effort, destroyed our interest, and discouraged us from prosecuting our inquiries concerning them."[17]

After a two-week stay at Tiflis, the brethren set out for Shusha, in the mountains of Russian Armenia, where they hoped to wait out the hot weather and recruit their strength before venturing on into Persia. The journey down the unpopulated valley of the Kura was made painful by a hot dry wind "surcharged with noxious vapors" and by clouds of mosquitoes rising from the irrigation ditches; before the trip was half done both Smith and Dwight had burning fevers and could scarcely travel; from their arrival at Shusha in mid-August until their departure on 1 November they remained housebound. Yet the move had proven doubly fortunate. For seven years some emissaries of the Basle Missionary Society had been laboring at Shusha, and the Americans were received with great hospitality. In that summer the cholera was moving from Persia into Europe; during their stay some thousands of deaths took place at Tiflis and a reported seventy thousand in the surrounding region, but Shusha remained untouched.[18]

By November their health was restored, and with winter approaching it was time to move onward to Persia. Although the caravan route led south from Shusha to Tabriz, Smith and Dwight proceeded by a circuitous and untraveled way, so as to visit Echmiadzin and beard the Armenian catholicos in his lair. The track, more difficult than any yet attempted, led over the mountains through a nine-thousand-foot pass. Here, in remotest Armenia, a night was spent at the monastery of Dater, where hospitality was combined with ignorance and irreligion but where the bishop, surprisingly, had not only heard of America but knew something of its history. On 4 November, after some days of threatening weather, drizzling rain turned to driving snow; movement across the steep ridges became impossible and the travelers found themselves isolated in a small village, where zero temperatures were compensated for by the kindness of the impoverished inhabitants. On the 9th, the storm having ceased, the missionaries descended into the valley of the "rapid and furious Araxes" to reach Nakhichevan. But the passage had taken its toll: fever had returned.

[17] *Ibid.*, I, 211, 245.

[18] *Ibid.*, I, 276ff.; Richter, *History of Missions*, pp. 97-103; Bliss, *Encyclopaedia of Missions*, I, 140.

Since it was at Nakhichevan that Noah resided after descending from the Ark, the city is the oldest in the world. From this second cradle of the human race Smith and Dwight turned to the northwest, to ascend the valley of the Araxes to Erivan and Echmiadzin. Although the territory up to the river had been annexed by Russia at the close of the recent Persian war, the contrast with the region to the north remained apparent: travel was now measured in fursakhs, not hours; many Persian Armenians had moved north to settle here; manners were more polished, if less sincere. Throughout the journey up the valley the great cone of Ararat—still, as the Armenians believed, the resting place of the Ark—towered to the southward, a stimulus to Biblical discussion.

Erivan was reached on 18 November, and on the next day the Americans entered the miniature walled city of Echmiadzin, for almost four centuries the ecclesiastical capital of the Armenians. Although the travelers bore letters from Armenian bishops, their reception at first was cool. But in time the atmosphere improved, and before their departure the missionaries had assisted at the feast of the sacrifice of the Catholicos, indulged in theological discussion with his secretary, met the governor of the province, and dined on trout from Lake Sevan. On 23 November they started back downstream toward Nakhichevan and Tabriz.

In Persia, beyond the Araxes, the weather continued cold and rainy, and Smith's illness recurred with increasing virulence. When both riding and walking proved impossible, a halt was made at a small Moslem village, where, in the corner of a miserable stable and among a primitive and hostile people, he lay unconscious for the space of two days. But fortunately help was at hand. At Tabriz, residence of the Persian prince royal, the English had established an embassy, and a letter from Dwight brought instant response. The embassy physician rode out eighty miles to meet them, a horse-borne litter was provided, and with this providential assistance the missionaries gained the city, to be lodged and cared for by the English with unexampled kindness.

After seven months of travel across fifteen hundred miles of country, repose was needed. At Tabriz, in company with their English friends, the Americans remained from December to March. Capital of Azerbaijan and an important commercial center, this city of mud walls, canals, and fruit trees had a population of some sixty thousand. Centrally located between the Indus, the Persian Gulf, Constantinople, and Russian marts, Tabriz traded with all, but the greater traffic moved by northern routes, east to the Caspian and west to Trebizond. Yet despite its size and commercial importance, Tabriz held little of missionary interest. Persian civility, it is true, contrasted with the rougher manners of the Anatolian Turks, as did Persian willingness to engage in religious discussion and to accept European innovation. But the Persians were only incidental objects of the inquiry, while the Armenians of Azerbaijan, ruled by unprincipled wine-bibbing priests, appeared of low moral character, notable for their dishonesty and ingratitude and addicted to concubinage. One bishop of good private character the Americans did find, but although expert in canonical doctrines and ceremonies, he, like all his compatriots, proved wholly ignorant of evangelical ideas.

Yet while prospects at Tabriz were barren, opportunity lay nearby. A principal object of the journey had been to visit the Nestorians, a people greatly distinguished in former ages for Christian missionary zeal and enterprise. For although Nestorius, patriarch of Constantinople, had been excommunicated and banished by the Council of Ephesus in 431, his cause had survived in the East, to become dominant in Persia and spread eastward as far as China. This period of greatness had been ended by the Mongol conquests: the church had been all but destroyed, and its surviving membership of some seventy thousand souls was now concentrated in the mountains of Kurdestan and on the headwaters of the Tigris. Still fewer in number were the Chaldeans or Papal Syrians, a schismatic seventeenth-century offshoot of the Nestorian Church, who accepted the supremacy of the Pope. Isolated in these distant fastnesses, Nestorians and Chaldeans had been forgotten by the outer world, and even the English at Tabriz were ignorant of their doctrines and character. Only a chance mention in a magazine, at the time the instructions for Smith and Dwight were being prepared, had led Rufus Anderson to include the Nestorians among the objects of the enterprise.[19]

In their approach to these sects, Smith and Dwight had originally intended to circle south about the Kurdish mountains, penetrate into upper Mesopotamia, and thence regain the Mediterranean by way of Syria. But the lack of any practicable route between Tabriz and Mesopotamia and the danger from the warlike Kurds forbade, and the investigations were consequently limited to the neighbor-

---

[19] Smith, *Researches*, II, 175; Anderson, *Oriental Churches*, I, 85.

hood of Lake Urmia, a hundred miles to the west of Tabriz, in eastern Kurdistan.

March 1831 was devoted to this enterprise. Leaving Tabriz, the missionaries advanced through scattered communities of Jews and Chaldeans, reached the western side of the great salt lake, and toured the plain of Urmia, while avoiding the town itself on account of the plague. Doctrinal discussion with a bishop, Mar Yohannan, and with other clergy showed the Nestorians possessed of a liberal attitude toward other sects, a gratifying antipapalism, and an encouraging distaste for the ancient clerical police system of auricular confession. But there was also a notable degree of ignorance: the art of printing was unknown, and although an ancient manuscript New Testament was discovered, preserved with veneration in a box, no complete Bible could be found.

With the visit to the Nestorians, the missionaries had completed their task. On 9 April, therefore, after a few more days at Tabriz, Smith and Dwight set out on their return. The journey through the northern mountains of Kurdistan promised to be hazardous, owing to the danger of robbers and wolves, and the guide was fearful. But the nomads were rarely encountered, few wolves were seen, and the principal difficulties were those presented by uncivil hosts, shortage of food and forage, sloughs of mud resulting from the spring thaw, and a snowstorm in a high pass which forced temporary abandonment of the baggage. In due course the Turkish border was crossed, and on 23 April the Americans reached Erzerum.

Impoverished though it had seemed when contrasted with Constantinople, Erzerum from the Persian side appeared solid, spacious, and comparatively Europeanized, but the Armenian exodus of the previous year had left it a city with little life. Passing on to the westward and retracing their earlier path for a hundred miles, Smith and Dwight then turned north along the road followed by Xenophon and his Ten Thousand, and after traversing rivers and chasms of awful grandeur they at last, like those earlier wayfarers, sighted the sea. Four weeks after leaving Tabriz they reached the city of Trebizond, principal seaport of the Black Sea's southern shore and the only port at which European vessels touched with regularity.

Behind them lay some 2,500 miles of travel, a journey as long as Xenophon's. To both had come a violent recurrence of the fever. In these circumstances Smith and Dwight were happy to embark on an Illyrian ship, which after a stormy and unpleasant voyage deposited them at Constantinople on 25 May, just over a year from the day of their departure. Here, for the first time since that date, they received communications from friends at home and colleagues at Malta; here, shortly, they reembarked, and after touching at Smyrna reached Malta on 2 July, to end an absence of fifteen and a half months. "The Lord had delivered us from all our fears. The forebodings of misgiving nature or of wavering faith had not been realized. In the midst of pestilence, among barbarous people, and in inhospitable countries, the 'angel of the Lord had encamped around about us for our deliverance,' and we were brought back again in peace."[20]

Throughout their anabasis the two travelers had observed and meditated on the customs of these antique lands, and on what good could be done their inhabitants by the churches of America. Inevitably, in their researches, they saw through New England eyes. But while the New England standard of judgment was always there, the overt comparison was rarely made, and New England herself was not without blemish: if the intemperance of the peoples of the Near East was everywhere regrettable, and the spectacle of drunken Russians shameful, still more so was the export of New England rum.

Everywhere in the journey dishonesty and chicanery had proven major obstacles: if the Armenians, with their dominant love of money, cheated less than the Greeks, still they cheated plenty, while in Persia both Armenians and Moslems were extraordinarily deceitful. Everywhere there existed a general immorality, and a prevalence of both natural and unnatural vice. As a final obstacle to letting in the light, there was the activity of the Church of Rome: although in fact Catholic missionary activity in these regions had been long declining, the New Englanders saw the sentinels of the Mother of Harlots everywhere.[21] Yet nothing in the picture led to discouragement. If at times Smith was saddened by the abominations he encountered, he was never patronizing and he never drew back. The darker the prospect, the greater the need for action. Ignorance, not intent, was at the bottom of it all. Men were what they were taught to be. The need was to drive away the darkness.

This attitude was reflected in the missionaries' great concern with education. At Constantinople the famous school of Peshtimaljian

<hr/>

[20] Smith, *Researches*, II, 329.
[21] On the Catholic menace: *Ibid.*, I, 129, 252-55, 321; II, 62, 92, 191.

lacked modern pedagogical improvements, and instruction was confined to the ancient Armenian tongue; at Tiflis the academy founded a generation earlier had greatly degenerated. Yet these were the only Armenian schools worth mentioning. In many areas no schools at all were to be found, while the monasteries were seats of ignorance, making no attempt to enlighten their nation.

To the self-perpetuating consequences of ignorance and to the absence of any desire for education was to be added the lack of printed materials. For the more than two million Armenians, the Americans' prime concern, there were only the five presses of Vienna, Constantinople, Moscow, Astrakhan, and Tiflis; the press at Echmiadzin, once active, had been idle for twenty years, while at Shusha the efforts of the German missionaries had been throttled by Russian censorship. Nowhere did there exist a newspaper in the Armenian language.

Nor was the situation better with the other nationalities visited by Smith and Dwight. Among the Georgians, educational opportunity was negligible. Despite some evident fondness for learning, Chaldeans and Nestorians were grossly ignorant. Only in Persia, where the mosques maintained schools in the interests both of religion and of business, was there an appreciable amount of literacy. Everywhere and among all sects there existed a strong prejudice against female education, which indeed was almost nonexistent.[22]

But whatever the obstacles, the cause remained, and the deeply affecting spiritual condition of all these peoples called upon the Americans to labor for their conversion. Most compelling, perhaps, were the requirements of the nominal Christians, who were "in a perishing state," hurrying blindfold to perdition. Deluded by the objectionable theatrical pantomime of the Mass, all were lacking in Biblical religion, while the Armenians were additionally subject to the horrid practice of auricular confession, so conducive to immorality. For all, the central question was that of salvation, which to members of the Oriental Churches was gained not by grace, nor even by works, but simply by ceremonies.

So the challenge cried out to be taken up and the researches in Armenia brought forth recommendations for the churches of America. In Armenia Minor, Tokat offered the best site for a mission sta-

[22] On printing: *Ibid.*, I, 297, 318. On education in general: I, 65, 210, 219, 243, 249; II, 13, 34, 81, 164, 190, 220, 240, 246. On the education of females: I, 243, 288, 293-94, 314; II, 165, 220.

tion. Although the needs of Russian Armenia were great, the attitude of the government and the experience of the Shusha Germans suggested insuperable obstacles; here the most eligible course was to assist the existing effort with money and with books. At Erzerum the Armenian exodus had made a mission station purposeless. Trebizond, however, was strategically located in relation to all of Armenia, could serve as an advanced base for an effort among the Nestorians of Persia, and offered a promising site for work among Greeks and Armenians.

But it was the Nestorians who presented the most interesting prospect of all. At Tabriz the Armenian population was small, dispersed, and degraded, while the Moslem population was theologically inaccessible. But Urmia, where religious improvement and instruction were badly needed, offered great promise. The Nestorians were liberal and friendly in their attitudes, and the climate was reputed fine. The British ambassador would befriend and protect the missionaries; quite possibly the Persian prince royal would patronize an effort for the improvement of his Christian population. Certainly it would be a distant and a lonely post, but communications would be facilitated by the British diplomatic express, while necessary supplies could be sent in through Trebizond, a mere five hundred caravan miles away. Weighing up the advantages and disadvantages, Eli Smith grew eloquent in his hope of helping to restore a true Christianity to this oldest of Christian sects.

So for at least some of the territory visited, it seemed possible that the requirements could be met and the people saved. If the Russian government prevented access to the Georgians and Armenians within its borders, the curious structure of the Ottoman Empire made its Christian peoples accessible to workers from outside. This, indeed, was the great tactical advantage offered by work in Turkey, in contrast to the Barbary regencies where no Christian communities existed to provide an opening. In Persia, too, despite the distance and the intervening inhospitable country, the Nestorians offered opportunity. Only from other Christians was opposition to be expected, and while the Papists were indefatigably hostile, the Oriental Churches were not. For those who would obey their Lord's command there was work to do. Good in itself, this work among Christians had the further virtue of giving entry to the heart of the enemy's country; a purification of Oriental Christianity would be a city set on a hill to the Mohammedans. If the difficulties were great, so was the promise: if our countrymen "shrink not from our duty to the world, she will glide safely into the haven of millennial rest."[23]

Already, indeed, the challenge had been taken up. At Malta, in February 1829, at the time the exploring tour was being planned, it had also been tentatively decided to send William Goodell to Constantinople as soon as the political situation would permit. Before leaving Constantinople for the east, Smith and Dwight had earnestly recommended the formation of a station at the capital of the Grand Turk. Their letter had been received at Malta in July 1830, and while the explorers continued onward into Armenia and Persia, communications were crisscrossing the Atlantic. In April 1831, as Hodgson was preparing to sail from the United States with the ratified Turkish treaty, William Goodell's orders to advance reached Malta. On 21 May he sailed on the Boston brig *Banian*. The passage was a stormy one, but the discovery of three Jesuits among his fellow passengers opened an opportunity for disputation which eased the pains of passage. On 5 June, as Smith and Dwight were descending the Hellespont, the *Banian* was lying off the Dardanelles awaiting a change of wind. On the 9th Goodell reached Constantinople.[24]

3. Aid to Turkey

Turkish ratification of the Treaty of 1830 was gained only with some difficulty. The government of the Sultan was both disappointed by American rejection of the secret article and irritated at being sent an emissary with the lowly rank of chargé d'affaires. But while Porter was powerless in the second problem, his instructions went far to counteract the former difficulty: pointing out that the contemplated shipbuilding would prove advantageous to the United States, they directed the Chargé to render his good offices "whenever the Sublime Porte may wish to construct Ships of War in the United States . . . thus securing to the Sublime Porte all the advantages contemplated by it from the article in question." Pursuant to this Jacksonian nullification of Senate action, the Commodore attempted to calm Turkish resentment by offering to try to obtain a small steamboat to tow the Sultan's barge, and by signing "as an *Equivalent* for the aforesaid rejected Separate Article" a paper, "binding on the

[23] On missionary possibilities: *Ibid.*, I, 101, 327; II, 263, 325-29.

[24] ABC 16.9, Vol. I: Smith and Dwight to Evarts, 15 May 1830; Goodell to Evarts, 21 July 1830, 31 May 1831, 11 June 1831; Goodell to Anderson, 21 July 1831, 5 August 1831. Anderson, *Oriental Churches*, I, 77, 79, 93.

part of my successors," in which he undertook to advise at any time on methods of obtaining ship timber and ships of war from the United States.[25]

By the time these conversations had taken place, all the Americans were in close contact. In early August a great fire at Pera had burned out Goodell's house and had forced him to remove temporarily to Buyuk Deré, eight miles up the Bosporus. There for a time he shared lodgings with Eckford, Rhind, and the others who had come out on the *United States*, while Commodore Porter took a house nearby; in October the missionary moved in to spend the winter with the Chargé d'Affaires. Mollified by Porter's "Equivalent," the Turks in their turn now ratified, and the negotiations of thirty years were over. A treaty sought for reasons of commerce had been gained for reasons of state, and the disparate interests of figs and opium, the gospel mission, and the great powers had led to what amounted, in fact if not in form, to an American naval mission to Turkey.[26]

Since the time of Bainbridge's visit the excellence of American warship design had been repeatedly borne in upon the Turks. With the arrival of the Americans this impression was again renewed, and such was Mahmud's admiration of *John Adams* that he sent a constructor on board to take her lines. Some difficulty, indeed, was caused by the simultaneous arrival of Porter and Eckford, for the Turks at first assumed the *United States* to be a present from the American government. With time, however, the more conventional gifts of jeweled knickknacks were provided and the customs of private enterprise explained. Soon the corvette was sold for hard cash and Eckford, after building a fast dispatch boat which gained the Sultan's favor, was installed at the arsenal as naval constructor, with "high pay and perquisites." By October 1832 he had begun the construction of a ship of the line, a frame of live oak for a second had been ordered from New York, and a crew of American ship carpenters had sailed from New York for Constantinople. Although Eckford died suddenly in November of "inflammation of the bowels," and went home in a cask of wine, Porter succeeded "by a little management" in keeping the building program under Ameri-

---

[25] Instructions, Turkey: Sec. of State to Porter, 15 April 1831. Despatches, Turkey: Navoni to Sec. of State, 26 April 1831; Porter to Sec. of State, 26 September 1831, 23 October 1831. Miller, *Treaties*, III, 585-87.

[26] ABC 16.9, Vol. 1: Goodell to Anderson, 15 August 1831, 16 August 1831, 5 November 1831, 19 June 1832.

can control. In December he was able to report that Eckford's foreman, Foster Rhodes, was carrying on "under my personal council and advice."[27]

So, under American supervision, the rebuilding of the Ottoman Navy was begun. This work was urgently necessary, for the years that followed Navarino were years of continuing crisis. Only with the greatest effort did Mahmud succeed in destroying Ali, the rebellious Lion of Janina. The Greek revolt could not be suppressed. It proved impossible to put down the Pasha of Egypt, whose invasion of Syria in 1832 culminated in a great Turkish defeat at Koniah. With the Egyptian armies approaching the Bosporus and with his own levies in flight, Mahmud "embraced the serpent" and accepted the aid of the ancestral enemy: the Treaty of Unkiar Skelessi, which marked the zenith of Russian influence at Constantinople, was signed in the house of Husrev, previously the most anti-Russian of ministers.

With Russian support, the Egyptians were turned back from the capital. But with all Syria remaining in the grasp of the Egyptian pasha, whose own navy continued to grow, the need to strengthen the armed forces became more urgent than ever. Deeply interested in the work, Mahmud gave it his full support, and his relations with Porter became increasingly intimate. The Commodore, for his part, developed a liking for the Turks, who "treated him with great distinction and kindness," and "esteemed them for their apparent honesty, for they would not lie like Europeans, nor steal like Mexicans." Relations between the Sultan and Rhodes were also cordial: Mahmud conferred upon his naval constructor "snuffboxes, rings, stars, pins, and chains, all set in diamonds of great size and purest water," and went so far as to offer him a pashalic.

With such harmony at the highest levels and with the help of two able capudans pasha—Halil, adopted son of Husrev and son-in-law of the Sultan, and Tahir, who had won his third tail at Navarino—progress was rapid. And while Porter and Rhodes attended to materiel, the no less important problem of personnel training received the attention of the missionary. In addition to establishing Lancaster-

[27] Despatches, Turkey: Porter to Sec. of State, 11 August 1831, 17 August 1831, 12 April 1832, ? October 1832, 18 November 1832, 16 December 1832. [Porter], *Constantinople*, II, 7-8; Walter Colton, *A Visit to Constantinople and Athens* (New York, 1836), pp. 48, 104; Porter, *Memoir of David Porter*, p. 413; Wheelock, "Eckford." On 15 September 1832 *Niles' Register* reported the departure of American ship carpenters for Constantinople.

ian schools for the Greek and Armenian Christians of Constantinople, Mr. Goodell in 1833 set up "two Turkish schools of the same
kind . . . at the desire of the Sultan," where army officers were taught
writing, ciphering, and topographical and military drafting. For
these schools he prepared the necessary books and instruments; to
them he presented "a planetarium, and celestial and terrestrial
globes." By the next year the two schools had become seven, with
more than two thousand students, and the missionaries were busy
compiling a Turkish geography at the request of the Sultan's
advisers.[28]

The flattering position which the Americans so quickly gained
was reemphasized in the treatment of their visiting compatriots.
In 1832 Captain George C. Read of the U.S.S. *Constellation* visited
the capital with his wife; although Porter's rank did not entitle him
to be received by the Sultan, the Chargé and naval officer were nevertheless summoned, together with Eckford, to an interview, and given
an unprecedented invitation to visit the new palace. In the autumn
of 1833 Commodore Daniel T. Patterson paid a month's visit to
Constantinople in his flagship the U.S.S. *United States*; although
no frigate of any nation had previously been permitted to pass the
straits unless carrying a minister or ambassador, the firman was
granted unconditionally and the reception was cordial in the extreme.
All the higher officers of government vied to honor the Americans,
and the Sultan gave an audience to Porter, Patterson, and the flag
captain. In company with Mr. and Mrs. Goodell, the two commodores inspected the Turkish military schools which the missionaries were assisting. With patriotic pride the Chargé reported that
"it is a matter of much surprise among the different Legations, why
so much respect should be shown to an American Commodore when
it was not shown to Russian, to English, and to French Admirals."
This respect, indeed, extended even to private citizens, and when
Dr. Valentine Mott, a distinguished New York surgeon, visited Con-

[28] Despatches, Turkey: Porter to Sec. of State, 25 October 1834. [Porter], *Constantinople*, II, 311-12; Porter, *Memoir of David Porter*, pp. 403-5, 412-13. ABC 16.9,
Vol. I: Goodell to Anderson, 13 August 1833, 2 October 1833, 3 March 1835, 18 May 1835; Goodell to Temple, 27 August 1833; Goodell to Schauffler,
27 August 1833. [J. E. DeKay], *Sketches of Turkey in 1831 and 1832* (New York,
1833), pp. 138-40; Valentine Mott, *Travels in Europe and the East* (New York,
1842), pp. 407-8, 438; [J. L. Stephens], *Incidents of Travel in Greece, Turkey, Russia, and Poland* (New York, 1845), I, 223-29; Henry Wikoff, *The Reminiscences
of an Idler* (New York, 1880), pp. 284-85.

stantinople with his family, he received favors previously granted no private individual and so extensive as to give rise to the rumor that he had operated upon the Sultan.[29]

Such attentions dramatized the esteem in which the Americans were held, and the visits of Read and Patterson emphasized the naval link. But it was not only at sea that American instruments of self-determination were found useful. Within a few weeks of his arrival Porter had interested the Seraskier with a description of a new type of rifle used in the United States Army; by the autumn of 1832 a number of Hall's rifles had been received and distributed to the Sultan and his principal officers. Soon reports were circulating that Turkish uniforms and gear were being remodeled to conform to the American pattern; by the summer of 1834 the Sultan had some troops in training "as sharpshooters according to the American discipline," and had outfitted his guard of honor with American dragoon's caps. In the next year John W. Cochran of Boston, the inventor of a new type of cannon, came to Constantinople and entered the Sultan's employ. This event Porter hoped would induce the Sultan to "call to his aid the genius of Americans for mechanical inventions, which is so much wanting here." To further this hope he instructed his dragoman to inform the Turkish officials "that there is no part of the world so famous for men of ingenuity and useful mechanical Talents, as the United States of America, and that whenever H. H. the Sultan may wish persons of that description to execute any of his views connected with manufactures of any kind, or with the operations by Steam," the Chargé would "take pleasure in making known his wishes to persons . . . capable of executing them." In 1838 there developed a somewhat exotic manifestation of this ingenuity with the arrival of two Americans, recommended by the Turkish embassy at London, with a newly invented machine "for projecting balls without powder."[30]

Nevertheless the navy remained central. At the great arsenal at Constantinople, Foster Rhodes and his American assistants pressed

[29] Despatches, Turkey: Porter to Sec. of State, 17 September 1832, 25 March 1833, 24 October 1833, 22 November 1833; Brown to Porter, 15 July 1838. ABC 16.9, Vol. 1: Goodell to Anderson, 8 October 1832, 3 March 1834. Mott, *Travels*, p. 426; S. D. Gross, *Memoir of Valentine Mott* (New York and Philadelphia, 1868), p. 36.

[30] Despatches, Turkey: Porter to Sec. of State, 27 September 1831, 17 September 1832, 3 February 1835, 7 February 1835, 9 March 1835, 11 March 1835, 12 March 1835, 5 April 1835, 10 June 1835; Porter to J. Asker, 12 March 1835; Brown to Porter, 15 July 1838, 25 September 1838.

on with the building program. When material ordered from America was delayed in shipment, Porter interceded with a personal letter to President Jackson. A number of warships had already been completed when, in the summer of 1837, Rhodes staged a dramatic spectacle by launching, in the presence of the Sultan and a great crowd and within the space of one hour, two cutters, a frigate, and a brig. The date had been chosen by the astrologers. Four sheep were sacrificed to make the event auspicious and prayers were said by the Grand Mufti, when, in the words of the Turkish *Gazette*, "the said vessels—filled with victory—one after another with ease and excellence, descended upon the face of the sea." By the next year Rhodes had completed a new steamship, which by its superiority in speed and towing power excited great envy among English and Austrians and led to attempts to undermine the constructor's position with the Sultan.

The steamship was perhaps not the only cause of such envy. Concerned by the Russian threat, Palmerston had begun to press for the introduction of British personnel into the Turkish forces. But the Porte refused these offers, while at the same time requesting the loan of American officers for the Turkish fleet. None, it appeared, could be made available, although permission was granted the Mediterranean Squadron to embark Turkish officers for instruction. Nevertheless, the predilection for Americans continued, and a former United States naval officer, arriving at Constantinople in search of employment, was avidly seized upon and placed in command of a frigate.

With this American help some very considerable progress was made in rebuilding the Ottoman Navy. Both in new construction and in the reactivation of ships in ordinary, Foster Rhodes accomplished significant results. From the four ships of the line and the two or three frigates that remained after Navarino, Mahmud's fleet had been built up by 1838 to eleven ships of the line and ten or a dozen frigates, thus gaining parity with the Russian Black Sea fleet and keeping pace with Mehemet Ali's building program. The effort had resulted in a somewhat increased control over Tunis, and had given rise to hopes that even the Pasha of Egypt might be restrained. In America, too, satisfaction was evinced at the increase both of American influence and of American trade, and in 1839 Congress raised Porter's status from the rank of chargé d'affaires to that of minister resident.[31]

Yet however successful, the naval program was but a part of the larger Westernizing problem which faced Mahmud, and which placed great strains upon the fabric of Ottoman society. Some things, indeed, the Sultan had accomplished: he had destroyed the janissaries, he had cut down the power of the provincial pashas, he had effected administrative reforms and created a new model army. Islamic law had been reinterpreted to permit measures of quarantine against the plague, a larger degree of toleration had been granted the non-Moslem subjects of the empire, and foreign instructors in considerable number had been employed to teach the practical arts of the West. All this, for a time, had augured well: four years after his arrival Porter had noted "Very great . . . improvement in the nation in every respect," and had added that "the more I see of the character of the Sultan, his untiring devotion to his duties as a Sovereign and steady perseverance in reform and socialization, the more I see to admire in him. Should his life be spared the Turks will ere long cease to be 'a peculiar people.' "[32]

But such a program inevitably aroused fierce opposition. A far milder Westernizing effort had cost Mahmud's predecessor Selim his throne and his life. On all sides there arose resistance to the introduction of infidel ways, a reaction facilitated by the Sultan's tendency to take Western forms for Western facts, and to insist on such superficial but irritating changes as reforms in dress or the appearance in public of the women of the seraglio. Some of these goings-on were ridiculous enough, as when the Sultan's physician, the hakim bashé, giving a feast for his lord and master, approximated his experience at ambassadorial receptions by collecting "together all the dancing-boys, one half of whom were dressed in the Frank male dress, and the other half in the Frank female dress," and having them dance the "*contre* dance, cotillions and waltzes, before the Sultan." Even worse, perhaps, was the taste for strong drink, which distinguished members of the Westernizing faction and proved a

[31] Despatches, Turkey: Porter to Jackson, 24 April 1835; Porter to Sec. of State, 13 May 1835, 19 May 1835, 23 May 1835, 10 September 1835, 11 January 1837, 3 August 1837, 9 August 1837, 22 August 1837, 9 September 1837, 1 March 1838, 1 May 1838; G. A. Porter to Porter, 7 May 1836. Instructions, Turkey: Sec. of State to Porter, 16 May 1837. Temperley, *The Crimea*, pp. 404-5.

[32] Despatches, Turkey: Porter to Sec. of State, 25 July 1835. [Porter], *Constantinople*, ii, 315-19.

further scandal to the orthodox: after one party Commodore Porter noted that "the Hakim Bachi was so far gone that they had to carry him to his boat," and after another that the Turks "all got fuddled and danced."

With time the opposition grew formidable. Provincial pashas rose against the "Giaour Sultan"; fires were set at Constantinople by dissident elements; rebellion was threatened and the reactionaries prospered in palace intrigue. Too late, Mahmud attempted to restore solidarity by public celebration of the ancient ways, including such radical measures as the festive open-air circumcision of the heir to the throne, along with some four thousand other striplings. Even the Christian authorities protested a toleration which gave Protestant missionaries access to their charges; the importance of the Armenian community gave their complaints a weight which was not diminished by explicit Russian interest, and the objectors had to be appeased by measures against the representatives of the American Board.[33]

With peace, which was not granted him, the Sultan might have succeeded in his Sisyphean task; as it was, the immediate effects of his reforms were debilitating to an empire beset by both internal and external difficulties. Most pressing of the external problems in the years after Unkiar Skelessi was the continued Egyptian occupation of Syria, which had led to six years of urgent effort to strengthen the army and navy. In the new ships built under American direction and in the new formations added to the army, these years had their reward; but they also had their cost. Worn down by the stress of his labors, the Sultan had himself taken heavily to drink, and by 1839 he was a dying man. As the end approached, the desire to punish Mehemet Ali became an obsession. The Ottoman Army was ordered across the Euphrates, and despite the efforts of the European powers, war was declared in June. With the hand of death upon him Mahmud boarded his flagship and harangued his officers, and on the 9th the rebuilt fleet sailed from the Bosporus "with such a thunder of artillery as had never before shaken Constantinople."

On 24 June the Turkish Army was routed at Nezib. One week later, but before news of the disaster had reached the capital, the great

---

[33] [Porter], *Constantinople*, II, 6; [DeKay], *Sketches*, pp. 255-62. ABC 16.9, Vol. 1: Goodell to Anderson, 5 November 1831; ABC 16.7.1, Vol. 3: Goodell to Anderson, 24 June 1839. Goodell, *The Old and the New*, pp. 78-80; Hamlin, *My Life and Times*, pp. 196-99; Anderson, *Oriental Churches*, I, 115-18.

Sultan died, attended, by a remarkable irony, by the same doctor who at Missolonghi had watched over the deathbed of the greatest of philhellenes. As yet the fleet had not left the Dardanelles, and Husrev, now grand vizier, at once ordered its return to Constantinople. But he reckoned without the new capudan pasha, Achmet Fevzi, who had risen by virtue of his face and form from stroke oar in the Sultan's caïque to this position of greater maritime power. Knowing his protector dead and fearing loss of his job or worse, Achmet weighed anchor; on the pretext that the government had sold out to the Russians, he took the fleet to Alexandria and there delivered it up to Mehemet Ali. Within a month Turkey had lost her army, her Sultan, and her fleet.[34]

Although the new Sultan, the sixteen-year-old Abdul Medjid, inherited a government dominated by the Westernizing faction, this dominance was brief and the reactionaries soon returned to power. More important, however, than the nature of Abdul's government was his acquisition of new friends, and the fact that Constantinople was now a principal focus of great-power diplomacy. British policy, in particular, had been influenced by a growing concern for the short route to India. Whether this route would go by way of Euphrates and Persian Gulf, or by Suez and the Red Sea, remained for the moment unsettled, although the explorations of Captain Chesney perhaps suggested a preference for the former; in any case both routes were menaced. To the northward the Russian wars with Persia and Turkey had cast a shadow, and with Unkiar Skelessi and the arrival of the Russians at Constantinople the threat was clear. Southward, the danger lay in an Egypt increasingly controlled by France and with an army and navy officered by Frenchmen, whose Pasha, not content with the occupation of Syria, was extending his sway across the Arabian peninsula to the Persian Gulf.

The pressures created by these developments were released by the Ottoman disasters of 1839. With Britain now fully committed to the support of the Turk, the intervention of the powers resulted, after a year of maneuvering, in an ultimatum to the Pasha of Egypt, whose refusal to retire from his Syrian conquests was followed by British seizure of Beirut and by Syrian revolt against Egyptian rule. With the capture of Acre by the British, the Egyptian armies withdrew

---

[34] Juchereau de St. Denys, *Histoire de l'empire ottoman* (Paris, 1844), IV, 134-39, 184-85, 198-203, 219; Cyrus Hamlin, *Among the Turks* (New York, 1878), p. 29; Edouard Driault, *L'Égypte et l'Europe* (Cairo, 1930-31), I, 133-42, 149-65.

homeward. Shortly the Turkish fleet was returned to Constantinople. In 1841 the Straits Convention, signed by the European powers, undid the provisions of Unkiar Skelessi and made the ancient
peacetime closure of the straits to foreign ships of war "a part of
European public law." But this was hardly of concern to Americans,
and the ships of the United States Navy continued to enter.

The second Syrian War left Great Britain firmly established at
Constantinople. The wishes of Palmerston were gratified, British
personnel were posted to important positions in the Ottoman Navy,
and the result was a decline in American influence. The personal
relationship which Porter had enjoyed with Mahmud and which
had led the Chargé, desirous of doing something for the Sultan, to
order rocking horses from America for presentation to the little
princes, was not renewed with Abdul Medjid. When Foster Rhodes
quarreled with the naval authorities, his resignation was cheerfully
accepted and he returned to the United States.[35]

Whatever its feelings in the matter, the Porte was unable to resist
this British pressure, and the American government was not designed
to do so. Consistent with American theory, the initiative in Levantine affairs had always come from outside the government: from
merchants, from shipbuilders, and from representatives overseas. Although friendly, the government at Washington was properly
passive, limited in both power and inclination.

Yet there was no sudden break. Inevitably the Turks preferred
not to commit themselves too wholeheartedly to a single interested
benefactor; the initiative of American entrepreneurs remained
lively; the American representatives at Constantinople hewed to the
same old line. When Commodore Porter died in 1843, his place
was taken by Dabney Smith Carr of Maryland, an individual well
qualified by both heredity and experience to continue the American
policy of spreading the blessings of civilization through the expansion of commerce. A relation of Thomas Jefferson by blood, a connection by marriage, and the son of his onetime private secretary,
Carr was also nephew to Samuel Smith; he had begun life as a clerk
for Smith and Buchanan and had served for fourteen years as naval
officer of the port of Baltimore. And a further assurance of continuity of policy existed in the person of John Porter Brown, nephew to

---

[35] Porter, *Memoir of David Porter*, p. 415. Despatches, Turkey: Porter to Sec. of
State, 21 October 1835, 10 February 1840. Charles MacFarlane, *Turkey and its Destiny* (London, 1850), II, 349-50; *Niles' Register*, 20 June 1840.

the Commodore and uniquely qualified by training and experience, who, while his nominal superiors came and went, would remain as dragoman, secretary of legation, and interim acting minister until his death in 1872.

So the connection continued, and Carr's efforts to expand commerce by impressing the Turks with "the difference between the open, straight-forward, and above-board character of our diplomacy, which 'asks nothing but what is right and submits to nothing that is wrong,' and the dark, tortuous, selfish character of that of the European Governments," bore at least some fruit. Although Foster Rhodes had departed, his brother-in-law, John Reeves, stayed on at the arsenal for three more years to build the *Essiri Jadid*, the first steam frigate in the Ottoman Navy. In 1845 the Turks for the first time acquired a representative in the United States, with the installation of a consul at Boston. Two years earlier a Maine shipbuilder had brought out the steamboat *Bangor* in the hope of operating between Constantinople and Salonica; desirous of establishing its own Ottoman-flag service, the Porte denied permission, but *Bangor* and her crew were taken on by the Ottoman Steam Navigation Company and the ship was placed on the Constantinople-Beirut run under the name of *Yanee Dunia* or *New World*. In 1846 a second steamer arrived, her way smoothed by instructions from the State Department, to ply between Constantinople, Smyrna, and Syria. In equally useful if more personal ways, American technology continued its spread when a Dr. Hitchcock of Boston sent out "a set of teeth made by himself, a specimen of the Dental Art unsurpassed," together with a small treatise on the care of the teeth, for conveyance by the American minister to the Sultan. And of course the missionary effort continued to grow.[36]

[36] Despatches, Turkey: Porter to Sec. of State, 12 January 1843; Brown to Sec. of State, 24 May 1843, 7 February 1846; Carr to Sec. of State, 16 February 1844, 27 September 1844, 17 January 1845, 16 June 1845. Instructions, Turkey: Sec. of State to Carr, 15 June 1844. *Niles' Register*, 4 February 1843, 22 July 1843, 23 August 1845. MacFarlane, *Turkey*, II, 350-51.

CHAPTER VI

Missions and Commerce, 1832-1845

1. Missionary Expansion

IF THE Jacksonians are rarely thought of as deeply concerned with commerce and the Navy, or the General's administration as marking the start of the boom years of the merchant marine, still less frequently is the period remembered as a great age of foreign missions. Yet such it was. In the twenties the income of the American Board had risen from $57,000 to $85,000, an increase of about 50 percent. But in the next decade the figure tripled, to stabilize in the forties at about a quarter of a million dollars a year. In rate of growth this expanding budget surpassed that of the expanding Navy, and indeed that of the federal government as a whole, while within the missionary total the funds allocated to the Near East grew still more rapidly. Despite the lingering effects of the Panic of 1837, the money available for the Levant in 1841 was five times the amount of ten years before.[1]

The actual sum—about $76,000—available in 1841 for the missions to the Oriental Churches may seem comparatively small. It cost, after all, something over $80,000 to keep a frigate in the Mediterranean for a year. But in an era when a missionary family in the Levant could be supported for less than $1,000 a year, such prosperity on the part of the Board could be quickly translated into visible results. The period between the Turkish treaty and the outbreak of the Mexican War witnessed a rapid expansion of the Near Eastern missionary structure as work was pressed in Greece, the Syrian enter-

[1] Income figures from ABCFM *Annual Reports*. The first three American foreign missionary societies were founded between 1810 and 1819, the next four between 1835 and 1837: Bliss, *Encyclopaedia of Missions*, II, 578-79. Commenting, on 21 September 1839, on the expanding funds available for missionary enterprise, *Niles' Register* echoed the views of Hopkins, Barlow, and Jefferson: "It should be remembered that these contributions may be and undoubtedly are wise even on the score of secular policy. They tried to do away with war, that most expensive of all national enterprises; to furnish the materials and rouse the spirit of commerce, and to multiply the sources of human happiness." Grund, *The Americans*, I, 351-65, discusses the unparalleled willingness of Jacksonian America to tax itself for the "moral and religious improvement of humanity."

prise was renewed, and stations were opened among the Armenians of Turkey and the Nestorians of Persia.

Like almost all the Board's Near Eastern efforts, the Constantinople mission, founded by William Goodell, was concerned not with the Moslem community but with the Christian churches. Although willing to do good in any way, and happy to assist in the improvement of the Sultan's military schools, Goodell had as his first objective the welfare of the Armenians of Constantinople. But this work was delayed by the fire which destroyed his house and which, by forcing him to move from Pera to Buyuk Deré, translated him from the Armenian community into the midst of the Greeks. Undaunted by the catastrophe, Goodell turned at once to the assistance of his new neighbors, establishing, with financial support from American merchants at Smyrna, a number of Lancasterian schools and providing others with information on modern educational techniques. His efforts at once excited interest. Opposition from the Greek patriarch and the Ulema subsided in the face of the publicly expressed approval of the Seraskier; at one school Commodore Porter undertook the support of a number of charity students; visits from the Russian and Spanish ambassadors and from other inquisitive dignitaries helped to spread the news. By the summer of 1832 Goodell was actively assisting a score of Greek schools with a total enrollment of some two thousand children.[2]

Despite this fortuitous involvement with the Hellenic community, the Armenians were not forgotten. More than this, they were for the moment accessible. Even before the arrival of the Americans, it seemed, the educational reforms of Peshtimaljian had prepared the Armenian mind for the receipt of truth. In the summer of 1832 the Goodells were joined by H.G.O. Dwight and his family; heartened by the Armenian interest in evangelical matters, the two missionaries turned to concentrate upon this group, studying the language and preparing spelling cards, books, and other educational materials. As word of the Americans' activities spread through the Armenian community, some graduates of the school of Peshtimaljian called and were put to work. In the autumn of 1834 a small Armenian high school was opened, supervised first by a Greek refugee from Scio

[2] On the history of the Constantinople mission: Archives of the American Board, ABC 16.9 and ABC 16.7.1; Despatches, Turkey; Prime, *Forty Years*; Anderson, *Oriental Churches*, which has a roster of missionaries, II, 492-96; Richter, *History of Missions*; Leon Arpee, *The Armenian Awakening* (Chicago and London, 1909).

who had been educated in the United States, and subsequently by one of the Armenians. Soon progress exceeded all expectations, relations with the Armenians became ever closer, and with American financial assistance, the moral support of the Russian and Spanish ambassadors, and the backing of the Seraskier, the enterprise seemed to promise well.

With its foothold secure, the American Board now pressed its advance. In December 1833 Daniel Temple and the printer Homan Hallock moved the mission press forward from Malta to Smyrna; in the next year the Arabic section was transferred to Beirut. From America the Board was sending forth reinforcements for the Armenian mission: in 1834 three couples arrived and in 1835 two more. Three missionaries were by this time laboring at Constantinople; two had taken up their station at Brusa beyond the Sea of Marmora, a site selected by Goodell after a visit in company with Commodore Porter in 1832; another, after assistance from the Commodore had obtained the needed firman, had established himself at Trebizond, far to the eastward, where he was to receive a companion in the following year.

All this was promising, and reinforcements were certainly needed, yet on occasion the good work advanced without human intervention. Among those places where Goodell had distributed tracts on his journey of 1832 around the Sea of Marmora had been the town of Nicomedea. Six years later, when Dwight visited the place, he found two Armenian priests who had been converted by reading *The Dairyman's Daughter*, some sixteen individuals who were seriously and intelligently conversant with gospel truth, and a developed spirit of inquiry among the populace.

Steadily, in these years, the press at Smyrna increased its output. Soon the Armenian pupils at Constantinople would be reciting a translation of Young's *Night Thoughts* and singing the hymns of Watts in Armenian verse. Although Goodell was conducting weekly meetings in Turkish for Bible study and prayer, and although Dwight had begun to preach in Armenian, these purely evangelical activities remained subordinate to the fostering of education, whether for Turks, Armenians, or Greeks. The rapid success of this effort, conducted by so few in so strange an environment and for so short a time, was certainly remarkable. By 1836 thirty Greek and eight Turkish Lancasterian schools had been started by the Constantinople mission. Three years later, when the thirst of the Armenians for both religious and secular knowledge seemed to require the establishment of a boarding school, the Reverend Cyrus Hamlin, a graduate of Bowdoin College, was sent out to assume this responsibility. And not only had new educational techniques been introduced and new schools founded, but that peculiarly American heresy, the belief that females also deserve education, had made its appearance with the establishment of schools for girls at both Smyrna and Constantinople. By 1835 Mr. Goodell could report that the mission had never been more prosperous.[3]

To the south, in Syria, a similar optimism had developed. Interrupted in 1828 by the troubles that followed Navarino, the Syrian mission had been resumed even before Goodell reached the capital. In May 1830, as Smith and Dwight were heading eastward from Constantinople into distant Armenia, Isaac Bird and George B. Whiting sailed from Malta for Beirut, accompanied by the two Armenian ecclesiastics who had earlier followed Goodell and Bird into exile. On their arrival the Americans were warmly welcomed by the English consul and by their former native friends. With the Greek community of Beirut cordial relations were resumed; not so, however, with the Maronite clergy. Here the impact of Isaac Bird's weighty 535-page reply to the Maronite bishop's attack on Jonas King had produced a lasting grudge, and this group, in communion with Rome, forbade its flock all contact with the Bible men.

In Syria the first years of resumed activity were complicated by plague, cholera, and the conquest of the province by the armies of Mehemet Ali. One "outrage" took place in the summer of 1833, when Isaac Bird and his servant were roughed up by a battalion of Egyptian infantry, but strong protests from Commodore Porter and the American consular agent at Alexandria and the support of Captain Sir John Franklin of H.M.S. *Rainbow* had rapid effect. Great pains were taken by the Egyptians to identify and punish the offenders, and for the duration of the Egyptian occupation the relations between the missionaries and the authorities remained generally cordial.[4]

With its transfer from Smyrna to Beirut in 1834, the Arabic section

[3] On schools: ABC 16.9, *passim*, and especially Goodell to Anderson, 19 June 1832, 13 June 1836, and the "Tabular View" of the mission, 1 March 1836. Hamlin, *Life and Times*, pp. 205-76; Richter, *History of Missions*, pp. 107, 110-11.

[4] Despatches, Turkey: Porter to Sec. of State, 9 September 1833, 25 November 1833, 7 January 1834, 6 May 1834. On the Syrian mission: Anderson, *Oriental Churches*; Richter, *History of Missions*; Tibawi, *American Interests*.

of the press came under the supervision of Eli Smith, who had returned from the United States in the preceding year after the publication of his *Researches in Armenia*. To make the output palatable to the intended audience, great pains were taken to improve the Arabic type. A manuscript collection of the best available calligraphy was assembled by Smith, the punches were cut by the ingenious Hallock and the type cast at Leipzig, and so great was the success that the products of the Beirut press set the standard for Arabic typography for many years. In quantity, too, and in diversity, the output was impressive: in 1836, 381,000 Arabic pages were printed; six years later the figure had reached 1,708,000, and spelling cards, hymnbook, and *The Dairyman's Daughter* had been joined by the Sermon on the Mount, an arithmetic, tracts on the cholera and on temperance, and the Westminster Catechism.

Such items as the spelling cards and the arithmetic were in urgent demand, for the educational effort which Goodell and Bird had begun before the Battle of Navarino had been promptly resumed. No sooner had the mission been reopened than ten young men appeared asking to learn English; rapidly accommodated in their desire, they were given lessons in geography and astronomy as well. Somewhat remarkably, a girls' school conducted by the ladies of the mission drew a few Moslem children. A high school, opened in 1835, was expanded into a boarding school in the following year despite a grievous shortage of books and supplies. As the curriculum grew and as attendance increased there came a pressing need for personnel, and, like that at Constantinople, the Syrian mission received reinforcements from home.[5]

In addition to their printing and teaching, their preaching and their distribution of tracts, the members of the Syrian mission continued the work of exploration begun by Pliny Fisk. Instructed by the American Board to investigate the country east of Jordan, Smith and Dr. Asa Dodge advanced inland to Damascus, worked southward through the almost wholly unknown territory of the Hauran, on into the homeland of the Bull of Bashan, and then back by way of the Anti-Lebanon. Useful for the pursuit of their primary task of evangelism, these explorations and the accumulated experience of

[5] Bliss, *Encyclopaedia of Missions*, I, 92; Anderson, *Oriental Churches*, I, 228, 233; II, 514-15; Thomas Laurie, *The Ely Volume, or, The Contributions of our Foreign Missions to Science and Human Well-Being* (Boston, 1881), p. 427; Richter, *History of Missions*, pp. 189-91; Tibawi, *American Interests*, pp. 71-72, 81-82.

the American missionaries led also to important contributions to knowledge.

Although scholarly interest in Bible lands had been long developing, and although the early nineteenth century had brought such notable explorers as Burckhardt, the discoverer of Petra, it was the Americans who revolutionized the study of Palestinian archaeology. In 1838 the Reverend Edward Robinson, a leading American biblical scholar, reached the Levant and put himself under the guidance of Eli Smith. Four years of study in Germany had given Robinson the best technical training of his time; Smith, the experienced and traveled missionary, knew Arabic, the Arabs, and the country. One result of their collaboration was the development of a standardized system for the romanization of Arabic names; the second, which followed their travels from Cairo through Sinai to Jerusalem, the Dead Sea, and the Valley of the Jordan, was Robinson's *Biblical Researches in Palestine, Mount Sinai and Arabia*. Published in 1841, and hailed as surpassing "the total of all previous contributions to Palestinian geography from the time of Eusebius and Jerome," this work provided the firm foundation for subsequent nineteenth-century investigation.

Yet, however creditable the accomplishment in printing, education, and exploration, something seemed lacking. Despite the work of the schools and the circulation of very large numbers of tracts and of portions of Scripture, no material change could be observed in the character and condition of the Syrian people which could be attributed to the mission in their midst. Conversions, too, were negligible in number, and since none had been reported outside those of individuals in personal contact with the missionaries, some questions arose as to the value of circulating tracts.

This discouragement, however, was relieved by opening prospects for the spread of truth among the Druses, a warlike, nominally Moslem population dwelling in the mountains of Lebanon and in the Hauran to the southward. In 1835 the attendance of two Druses at Beirut gospel readings induced the missionaries to advance upon this people, and to open schools and begin preaching in their villages on Mount Lebanon. Larger and larger grew the audiences, only to have their sincerity become suspect when the threat of conscription into the Egyptian Army produced a flood of applications for baptism and the presumably protected status of Christian. But preaching continued, although the wholesale petitioners were turned away, and two apparently sincere converts and their families were baptized. Against the persecution that at once ensued the converts stood fast, and intervention by the European consuls secured their release from prison. By 1838 an increasing number of Druses was again resorting to the missionaries for instruction, and grounds for hopefulness were once again discerned.[6]

Five hundred miles to the northeast, on the far side of Mesopotamia, another mission also had reason to be hopeful. There, beyond the Kurdish mountains, the explorations of Smith and Dwight had borne fruit in a mission to the Nestorians. In 1833 the Reverend Justin Perkins, a tutor at Amherst College, had been appointed to the task, and in September of the same year sailed with his wife for Malta. The voyage was a rough one, made rougher by the fearful profanity of American seamen, but once past Malta the Perkinses were heartened by the growing Americanization of the eastern Mediterranean. Their ship was under charter to a Greek whose brother had been an Amherst classmate; its captain possessed a *Life of Franklin* and admired the American form of government. At Syra, most populous and important city of Greece, they visited the school founded by Josiah Brewer; on their arrival at Constantinople they were met by Goodell and Dwight.[7]

At the capital, five months were spent in the study of Turkish, in awaiting the subsidence of political difficulties in Persia and the arrival of the summer season for crossing the mountains, and in the vain anticipation of promised colleagues. In May 1834 the Perkinses sailed for Trebizond on an English-owned ex-Baltimore slaver, and in June set out inland over the mountains. With snow still on the heights, it was a cold journey to Erzerum; beyond that city reports of Kurdish robbers led to an unfortunate detour through Russian territory, where suspicious and boorish officials stripped the travelers of all their baggage. By the time they entered Persia they had covered some five hundred miles on horseback, Perkins was suffering from the strains of travel, and his pregnant wife was seriously ill. But again, as in the case of Smith and Dwight, the English

[6] Anderson, *Oriental Churches*, I, 235-44; Robinson, *Biblical Researches* (London, 1841); W. F. Albright, *The Archaeology of Palestine* (Harmondsworth, England, 1949), p. 25; Tibawi, *American Interests*, pp. 77-78.

[7] On the Persian mission: Anderson, *Oriental Churches*; Richter, *History of Missions*; Justin Perkins, *A Residence of Eight Years in Persia* (Andover, 1843), and the review article, 57 *North American Review*, 156-84; Thomas Laurie, *Dr. Grant and the Mountain Nestorians* (Boston, 1853).

in Tabriz came to the rescue. A horse litter was provided, in which Mrs. Perkins completed the last stages of the journey; and although three days after her arrival she gave birth to a daughter, and lay for a time at death's door, both mother and child survived.

At civilized Tabriz the Perkinses found themselves among the "French of Asia," surrounded by a population which seemed, to New England eyes, to be principally characterized by politeness, deceptiveness, hospitality, and sin. Nor was the condition of the people improved by the hogsheads of New England rum which arrived regularly by caravan. But if man seemed vile, the white plaster and rich carpets of the Persian dwellings, the caged birds and iced sherbets, and the bewitching none-too-modest Persian beauties afforded an approximation of paradise, if not of the New England kind. Residence among the Nestorians at Urmia waited on the arrival of an associate, but at the earliest opportunity Perkins visited his future station. All whom he met received him gladly, from sophisticated Persian prince to Nestorian patriarch, rapturous at the thought of scripture and school books printed in the language of his people. Mar Yohannan, the bishop who had befriended Smith and Dwight, volunteered to come to Tabriz as teacher of Syriac in exchange for lessons in English; the offer was accepted; and with excursions, investigations, and mutual instruction, the months passed rapidly until the arrival of Perkins' colleagues in the autumn of 1835.

Like the other early missions, that to the Nestorians of Persia was fortunate in its personalities. To Perkins himself, a sufficiently remarkable man who was to labor in the field for thirty-six years, were now joined the Reverend James L. Merrick and Dr. Asahel Grant. Sent out originally as missionary to the Moslems of Persia, and versed in Persian, Arabic, Hebrew, and Turkish, as well as the more usual tongues, Merrick would become the author of the first life of Mohammed published in America as well as of a work on astronomy. Grant, the second medical missionary to reach the Near East, was an individual of presence, decision, and courage, eminently fitted for an adventurous life: as a member of the English embassy remarked, "a good soldier was spoiled when that man became a missionary." His young wife Judith, twenty-one when she reached Tabriz and twenty-five when she died, joined to a shining personality a remarkable degree of learning, for she could read her testament in the original Greek, and learned Syriac by way of a Latin lexicon. The presence of the physician, in the early days of the mission, was of the greatest advantage, for Grant's skills gave him access to all religious sects, while his growing fame brought patients from afar and ran before him on his travels, keeping him safe from harm.[8]

In November 1835 the missionaries advanced from Tabriz to Urmia, birthplace of Zoroaster and principal settlement of the Nestorian country. Set on rising ground between the lake and the Kurdish Mountains, whose spurs run down to enclose it in an eastward-facing amphitheater, the city enjoyed a dramatic location. In it, and on the surrounding plain, dwelt perhaps a quarter of the surviving Nestorians, suave and peaceable in comparison with their wild brothers of the mountains. At Urmia the Americans were hospitably received; as they commenced their work on school cards, and on the translation of testament and hymns, their hopes were high that this once-noted missionary church could be reawakened and its dry bones made to live.

At Constantinople, observing the passage of missionary families on their way to Persia, Commodore Porter remarked that they were "generally men of liberal education and well-cultivated minds," and foresaw that by their gospel work, their establishment of free schools, and their "historical and scientific researches, these countries, and mankind in general, will be much enlightened, and that the United States in particular will derive . . . both honor and benefit."[9] In the matter of schools, at least, he was immediately proved correct, for success attended the educational effort. In January 1836 the first Lancasterian school in central Asia was opened at Urmia, and such was the response that to prevent destructive jealousy it became necessary to provide for the Moslem population as well. Study and the revival of scriptural knowledge proceeded apace, aided by the arrival from America of an electrical machine and other philosophical apparatus helpful in kindling a desire for knowledge and improvement. Within the space of two years a female boarding school was begun.

The introduction of printing presented more complications, for the first press sent out from Boston proved too heavy to be brought

[8] Anderson, *Oriental Churches*, I, 173, 176, 222, 324; Bliss, *Encyclopaedia of Missions*, I, 394-95; II, 64; Perkins, *Residence*, pp. 368-70; Laurie, *Dr. Grant and the Mountain Nestorians*; D. H. Finnie, *Pioneers East* (Cambridge, Mass., 1967), pp. 214-24.

[9] Despatches, Turkey: Porter to Sec. of State, 6 August 1835.

in over the mountains. Undiscouraged, the American Board arranged for the casting of a special press, designed for easy disassembly, which arrived in the autumn of 1840 accompanied by a printer, Edwin Breath of Illinois. The event was heartening to those at Urmia, for inroads by Jesuits had been noticed, and one of the first works to be struck off was *Twenty-Two Plain Reasons for not Being a Roman Catholic*. But this menace soon subsided, and there followed the usual output of tracts, schoolbooks, and portions of the Gospel. By 1843 printing in Syriac exceeded half a million pages a year.

Isolated in distant Persia, and with the nearest representative of their government more than six weeks away, the members of the Nestorian mission relied heavily on the protection of the British. But relations between Britain and Persia were uneasy, and in the fall of 1838 difficulties on the Afghanistan border were followed by the arrival of a British expedition at Bushire, and this by the departure of the embassy. Apprehensive of the future, Perkins and Grant proceeded to Tabriz to seek the protection of the Russian representative, but in fact no troubles developed. The friendship of both the local population and the Persian government was manifested in numerous ways, and difficulties with a local magnate were followed by royal intervention on the side of the missionaries and the unsolicited issuance of a firman endorsing and encouraging their labors. Such success on the plain of Urmia seemed to call for expansion of the effort to include the mountain Nestorians. In 1839 Dr. Grant made a winter circuit of Kurdistan, visited Mosul on the upper Tigris, and then, protected only by his reputation, penetrated into the mountains to call upon the Nestorian patriarch.

So the decade of the thirties saw the representatives of the American Board established across a thousand-mile strip of territory, from Greece on the west to Persia on the east, and from Constantinople southward to Syria and Palestine. The result of this invasion of some of the oldest of cultures by the representatives of the newest had been the appearance, wherever a Christian community seemed accessible, of centers of American Protestant evangelism. With these had come the accomplishments in missionary exploration, the expanded output of the missionary press, the growing educational structure, the increasing funds and personnel. All this, of course, was but means toward the end of conversion, and conversions had admittedly been few. But some had taken place, and more were confidently expected. Surely, it seemed, there was reason to feel that the favorite missionary parable of the mustard seed—least of all seeds when sown, but when grown the greatest of herbs—was being borne out.

Yet in retrospect it seems that the missionaries only imperfectly understood the nature of their sowing. Protestants the evangelists surely were, but they were also Americans, and at every station, in addition to the gospel message, the message of America was set forth. For those who had eyes to see, the mission provided a continuous demonstration of the American approach to life on earth, as well as to life everlasting. However hard to measure accurately, the effect upon this audience of novel concepts of the dignity of labor, the status of women, the values of literacy, the virtues of honesty, and the importance of technology should certainly not be underestimated.

Most important, perhaps, of all the American contributions was one implicit in the belief that progress toward the millennium could be acceptably accomplished by the use of human means. This was the idea of change. In a static society, where the community was governed by tradition and the individual was saved not by his own effort but by the intercession of his priests, the idea that change was possible—that education would change the child, conversion the individual, and science the environment—had revolutionary implications. For those few in contact with the West at Smyrna and at Constantinople, some inklings of this message had earlier been apparent. But it was only with the arrival of the Americans that the word was made flesh and dwelt among the people, in Greece and Syria, in Anatolia and in distant Persia.

2. *God and Trade*

The years that followed the Turkish treaty had brought American involvement in Ottoman naval matters and a great expansion of the missionary effort, with its associated work in printing and education. But these were unintended consequences of an interest in the Levant which had stemmed from other factors. The lure of the Smyrna trade and the commercial bias of American foreign policy had occasioned the original involvement. The desire for broadened opportunity from the establishment of most-favored-nation arrangements, together with high hopes for the commerce of the Black Sea, had motivated the long negotiation.

Yet the commercial consequences of the Treaty of 1830 had not been great. Compared to the contemporary treaty with Austria, negotiated by the Adams administration and perfected by the Jacksonians, which had generated a considerable traffic with Trieste on the Adriatic, the Turkish treaty had done little. Except at ports already frequented by American ships, the Ottoman Empire seemed barren of opportunity. In 1834, commercial curiosity and rumors of piracy took the frigate *United States* to Salonica, but although the captain's report expatiated on the delightful scenery, the town itself appeared wretched, impoverished, and unpromising.[10] Nor did the commerce of the Black Sea develop in anticipated fashion.

Although a number of American vessels entered the Black Sea in the year following Porter's arrival at Constantinople, this traffic soon diminished: in 1836 the arrival of single American ship with cargo for Odessa was the occasion of a special dispatch from Constantinople. Among the presumed advantages of Black Sea navigation, as advocated by General Dearborn and others, had been its promise, in contrast to the Baltic, of ice-free access to Russian ports. Ice-free it was, but there were other difficulties: the prevailing northerly winds and southward-setting current made passage of the straits difficult for sailing vessels, and the resultant delays were more serious for the American merchant marine with its comparatively high costs than for its local competitors. Additionally, there existed a serious man-made obstacle in the shape of the Tariff of Abominations of 1828, whose exorbitant duties on raw wool greatly complicated the problem of return cargoes.

Already, it is true, American influence and American techniques were beginning to penetrate Russia. In the thirties, travelers in the Crimea were surprised to find, in the second-ranking official of that province, an ex-sailing master of the U.S.S. *Wasp*, born in Philadelphia, who had commanded a Russian frigate and entered Paris with the Russian armies, who read Irving and Cooper, and whose daughter played "Hail, Columbia!" on the piano for his guests. In the next decade, Whistler's father would set forth to construct the Moscow-St. Petersburg railroad and to build the Cronstadt naval base. In time some of the American artisans who had worked for Eckford and Rhodes at the Constantinople arsenal would move northward across the Black Sea. But despite all this, the Odessa trade never matched the original vision.[11]

[10] Area 4 File: Porter to Ballard, 1 July 1834; Ballard to Patterson, 5 October 1834.
[11] Despatches, Turkey: Porter to Sec. of State, 13 June 1832, 5 December 1834; G. A. Porter to Porter, 5 September 1836. [Stephens], *Incidents of Travel in Greece*, I, 264-67.

As well as northward to Odessa, the Black Sea led eastward to Trebizond, gateway to the commerce of Persia. As early as 1832, Commodore Porter had taken note of Persian possibilities, had quizzed H.G.O. Dwight on his travels, and had forwarded to Washington a lengthy memorandum on Persian trade and the facilities at Trebizond which he had secured from the missionary. But his offer to investigate these matters on the spot brought no response from Washington, and in any case the American tariff structure restricted opportunity. So long as the rates on wool remained high the question of a return cargo appeared insoluble, and American trade with Persia was limited to an indirect commerce in rum carried on by foreign-flag shipping.[12]

Greece also was unproductive. Although free, that nation had signally failed to fulfill the hopes of its American friends for a reappearance of "those liberal institutions of which [that] country furnished the earliest examples." In place of liberal institutions there had developed piracy at sea and turmoil on land, amid which the concrete American contributions proved short-lived. In August 1831, in the course of a revolt against Capo d'Istria, the frigate *Hellas*, largest unit of the Greek Navy, was blown up by her crew to prevent capture; at Corinth the hospital built by Samuel Gridley Howe was destroyed; only in 1832, when the Hellenes were presented by their great-power benefactors with a Bavarian prince and a Bavarian xenocracy, was order restored. American relief work had been of indubitable value, and American aid had founded a "tradition" of Greek-American friendship. But with the passing of time and the continuing commercial stagnation, philhellene interest disappeared.[13]

Despite the nonexistence of trade, the American government had been optimistic enough to appoint a consul. But in the absence of diplomatic relations he was not received, and Jeffersonian views put forward by Commodore Elliott in explanation of the American preference for consular as opposed to diplomatic representation failed to carry conviction. Only in 1837 was the treaty which the philhellenes had earlier so insistently demanded finally signed, and then only as a result of Greek initiative. And while ratification of the treaty was followed by Greek acceptance of an American consul,

[12] Despatches, Turkey: Porter to Sec. of State, 18 June 1832, 6 August 1835. Perkins, *Residence*, p. 225.

[13] J. Q. Adams, Message to Congress, 4 December 1827, in Richardson, *Messages and Papers*, II, 384; [J. Q. Adams], 5 *American Annual Register*, 431; Anderson, *Naval Wars in the Levant*, p. 549; Mott, *Travels*, p. 274.

more than a generation was to pass before an American diplomatic representative was sent to Athens.[14]

In its contrast with the prosperity of Near Eastern missions, this absence of any noteworthy expansion of commerce raises the question of how far, if at all, trade follows the tract. The relationship has, of course, been argued at various times, by both supporters and opponents of the effort to evangelize the world. As far back as the eighteenth century, Samuel Hopkins had urged, as part of his argument for an African mission, that the conversion and civilization of the Africans "would open a door for trade which would be for the temporal interest of both Americans and Africans." As the nineteenth century wore on, some of the missionaries in the Levant and elsewhere came to feel that the civilizing influence of Christianity was a prime factor in that increase of imaginary wants which Barlow had seen as prerequisite to the "passion for commerce." The spread of European habits of dress was hailed as an index of advancing taste and civilization; note was taken of the fact that in Turkey "those who do not read the Bible live on in their gloomy and comfortless abodes," while "chairs and tables, books and book-cases, Yankee clocks and glass windows, mark the homes of Bible-readers." By the end of the century, missionary organizations would be adducing commercial statistics as arguments for popular support and government protection, arguments which in later years their critics would diligently turn back upon them.[15]

To the extent that the missionaries were agents of innovation, the argument from the Yankee clock commands acceptance. Some of this cultural diffusion was accidental, as when the produce of Isaac

[14] Despatches, Turkey: G. A. Porter to Sec. of State, 5 July 1836. Miller, *Treaties*, IV, 107-24.

[15] On the general question of cultural transmission as seen by nineteenth-century missionaries, see Thomas Laurie, *The Ely Volume*, which deals *inter alia* with the relation of missions to geography, archaeology, ethnography, literature, music, education, medical science, and "national regeneration." On the specific question of trade, see the article "Commerce and Missions" in Bliss, *Encyclopaedia of Missions*; Gustav Warneck, *Modern Missions and Culture* (Edinburgh, 1883); and above all the three volumes of J. S. Dennis, *Christian Missions and Social Progress* (New York, 1898-1906). These works lend themselves to excruciating quotation: " 'The first call of a convert from heathenism is for clean clothes and a better house.' Clean clothing is suggestive of a long list of textiles, and a better house implies the importation of a vast cargo of industrial products. Races that accept Christianity almost invariably increase their imports." Yet however dated their approach, these sources also provide extremely suggestive accounts of the impact of one civilization on another.

Bird's garden, harvested after he was driven from northern Lebanon, so pleased his former neighbors as to make the potato, within a few years, a staple of the local diet. Some of it was purposeful, as in that emphasis on literacy which led these visitors from overseas to capture the educational leadership of the Near East, and to conduct a very large portion of the printing and publishing of the region. But there were also occasions when even purposeful efforts did not succeed.

William Goodell once suggested that if pious American merchants and mechanics could be sent to Constantinople, they would be productive of good and would prosper as well; the regrettable fact that all foreign artisans in Persia were both European and papist led Justin Perkins to reflect on "the good result to Zion as well as to the temporal interests of Persia, were their places to be occupied by pious, energetic, American mechanics!" Here, once again, was the idea of Humphreys' "philanthropic band," but all such proposals for organized effort foundered on the rock of Rufus Anderson's conviction that conversion, not civilization, was the Board's proper concern.[16]

Again, however, a qualification must be made. Anderson could determine policy, but Boston was far away, and for missionary, no less than for naval officer and diplomat, distance afforded opportunity for initiative. The Board might eschew the civilizing effort but many of its emissaries, products of rural New England in an age of self-sufficiency, themselves qualified as "pious mechanics," and their individual attributes colored their activities. Wishing, as he reported, "to do anything I could for the development of neglected resources," Cyrus Hamlin journeyed from Constantinople to Macedonia to assay the output of a newly opened mine. When the request of the Constantinople mission for philosophical apparatus for the schools was gratified by the arrival of a telescope and an excellent "Electrical Machine," they promptly wrote off for an air pump, a globe, and a magic lantern. The critical Armenian bishop who, after inspecting one of the schools, equated chemistry and Protestantism, was not, it would seem, too wide of the mark.

None of this, however, quite bears upon the commercial question. Unquestionably the missionaries were agents of innovation, but there is an important distinction between the introduction of Western

[16] Bliss, *Encyclopaedia of Missions*, ii, 35; ABC 16.9, Vol. i, Goodell to Anderson, 18 April 1833; Perkins, *Residence*, p. 431; Rufus Anderson, *Foreign Missions: Their Relations and Claims* (New York, 1869), pp. 94-108.

ways and the promotion of American commerce. Although merchants provided much of the support for the Andover seminary and the missionary organizations, not all merchants were favorable to such activities: Benjamin Crowninshield, after all, had opposed the chartering of the American Board. If some missionaries rejoiced in the spread of chairs and tables and Yankee clocks, no rejoicing was produced by the trade in New England rum, and the highest praise was still reserved for him who was "no mere industrial and civilizing missionary," but who touched the heart with grace. Be he missionary or merchant, a man inevitably carries his cultural baggage with him, but missionary and merchant have different imperatives and may travel to different destinations.[17]

Of this particular truth a striking example may be seen in Zanzibar. There, in the early years, Yankee traders acquired a near monopoly of foreign trade; in 1833 the United States negotiated with its ruler that worthy's first commercial treaty; three years later an American consulate was opened. So successful was the exchange of American cottons for ivory and cloves that *merikani* became the generic East African term for cotton goods and blankets; on his arrival in 1841 the first British consul was perturbed to find the Sultan's palace decorated with prints of American naval victories in the War of 1812. But although the representatives of the American Board had rounded the Cape of Good Hope as early as 1834 to begin work among the Zulus, no attempt was ever made to advance to Zanzibar.[18]

In like manner, in the Mediterranean, Bible and tract did not invariably follow trade, nor commerce the missionary. The Holy Land, original goal of Fisk and Parsons, imported little and exported less. In the decade of the thirties Beirut enjoyed a considerable expansion of mercantile activity, but little of this was American. Although both Greece and Persia were targets of missionary endeavor, and although the "benefit" which Porter had anticipated from the Persian mission was a commercial one, neither country developed much attraction for American traders. As the years went by it was Constantinople, the political capital of the Ottoman Empire, which became the center

[17] Hamlin, *Among the Turks*, p. 156. ABC 16.5, Vol. 2: Goodell to Schauffler, 6 December 1834; ABC 16.9, Vol. 1: Goodell to Anderson, 27 January 1835, 8 July 1835, 30 November 1835; ABC 16.7.1, Vol. 3: Mission Journal, 12 February 1839. Perkins, *Residence*, pp. 295-97, 505; Dwight, *Encyclopedia of Missions*, p. 419.

[18] Robert Coupland, *East Africa and its Invaders* (Oxford, 1938), pp. 361-81, 477; Bliss, *Encyclopaedia of Missions*, I, 16; II, 534, 538-42.

of the missionary web, while Smyrna, principal mart of the Levant, remained a subordinate station.

So the development of trade remained the responsibility of the American merchant and sea captain, of the American government's commercial diplomacy, and of the Navy of the Enlightenment. And while the Turkish treaty had not lived up to expectations, there remained one further Mediterranean possibility. Eight hundred sea miles from Constantinople, at the southeastern corner of the Mediterranean, the domain of the insubordinate Pasha of Egypt attracted interest. Here General Eaton had recruited his forces for the march on Tripoli; intermittently, since the beginning of the century, American ships had visited Alexandria; there was a story that in the twenties Mehemet Ali had bought two warships in America. Since that time Egypt's shortage of important resources, notably timber, had been reemphasized by the struggle with the Sultan over Syria, and the Pasha had an agent in America shopping for naval stores.

In January 1832, five months after his arrival at Constantinople, Commodore Porter had appointed an English merchant, John Gliddon, to the post of American consular agent at Alexandria. Soon Gliddon was proving his value by intervening in the Bird outrage and by working dutifully to foster commercial relations with the United States. These, indeed, were reportedly desired by His Highness, whose wishes seemed worthy of investigation, "particularly in reference to the wants of his Navy." In April the U.S.S. *Concord* stopped by at Alexandria, and when her commanding officer, Matthew C. Perry, called on the Viceroy, he was most hospitably received.

In fact, however, with the possible exception of naval stores and equipment, commercial prospects were dubious. In 1833 a long dispatch from Gliddon pointed out that the similarity of Egyptian and American exports left small basis for an exchange of goods. Yet Mehemet Ali's stature was increasing, and his conquest of Syria had given him control of the important seaport of Beirut and of its hinterland. In January 1833, in the crisis following the battle of Koniah, Porter called upon Commodore Patterson to bring the squadron eastward, and Patterson, in the Egyptian victory, saw opportunity for both his country and himself. Writing to the Secretary of State, Patterson reported Mehemet Ali to be both independent of the Sultan and desirous of a commercial treaty, and expressed the hope that he would be entrusted with the Egyptian negotiations as his predecessors had been in the case of Turkey.[19]

Unquestionably the Viceroy appeared friendly. Visits of the squadron had been well received, as had the appointment of the consular agent. The Egyptians had been assiduous in redressing the outrage committed by their troops upon the person of Isaac Bird. In the summer of 1834, when logistic problems delayed Patterson's projected second visit to Alexandria, Mehemet Ali was reported to be anxiously awaiting his return and his son to have favorably contrasted the American Navy with that of the British. But although the Jackson administration, solicitous of the needs of commerce, responded to the proffered opportunity, the Commodore's wish did not come true. As in the Turkish negotiations, it was decided to send a secret agent on a preliminary visit of investigation prior to commencing formal talks. This mission was delegated to William B. Hodgson.

Hodgson was America's first language officer. In 1826 he had been posted to Algiers by John Quincy Adams as a first step toward the development, within the structure of the federal government, of a fund of competence in exotic tongues. At Algiers he had prosecuted his studies to good purpose, and had acquired an expertise which in due time made him a contributor to the *Proceedings* of the American Philosophical Society and the author of a book on the region. Like other Americans abroad, he had at times had large ideas: in 1828, during a moment of difficulty with the Dey, he had recurred to the Tripolitan strategy of William Eaton, and had urged that the United States, in the event of rupture, should arm and incite the Berbers and Moors of the countryside against their urban ruler. Having returned from Algiers to America, Hodgson had carried the ratified Turkish treaty to Constantinople and brought back the Turkish copy, and then, appointed dragoman, had again proceeded to the capital of the Grand Turk.

At Constantinople his career was an unhappy one. Bright, young, and brash, he soon overreached himself with Porter, and after a

---

[19] Despatches, Turkey: Hodgson to Sec. of State, 2 March 1835; Porter to Sec. of State, 12 January 1832, 9 April 1832, 8 May 1832, 1 January 1833, 24 October 1833; Patterson to Sec. of State, 19 June 1833. Patterson's Eastern cruise in the ship of the line *Delaware* was reported as having done much for American prestige in Egypt and the Levant: [J. L. Stephens], *Incidents of Travel in Egypt, Arabia Petraea, and the Holy Land* (New York, 1851), I, 33; 48 *North American Review*, 191.

vigorous quarrel found himself excluded from legation business and with no option but to prosecute his solitary language studies. In October 1833 his moans were answered by the Department with the issuance of instructions to proceed secretly to Egypt, investigate its commerce, and ascertain whether the Pasha was in fact desirous and competent of entering commercial arrangements.[20]

Of the desire there seemed little question. In the course of a month's visit to Alexandria, in September 1834, the secret agent was received twice by the Pasha and twice by his Minister of Foreign Affairs, both of whom emphasized their hope for a more intimate commercial connection with the United States. Despite the similarity of exports, some opportunities did exist: the newly introduced opium crop of Egypt was increasing, the Pasha's maritime ambitions had already resulted in the purchase of American naval stores, and suitably mixed cargoes promised to turn a profit. The extension of Egyptian dominion, which now stretched from the Taurus Mountains to the Upper Nile, promised an important future, which indeed was emphasized by the contemporary advance of Egyptian forces upon Mocha, Yemen, and the Hejaz. As for the question of sovereignty, although it seemed "probable that Mehemet Ali will be the Henry 8th of Egypt, and by rejecting the temporal and spiritual authority of the Sultan, establish an independent state," the approval of the Porte remained for the moment necessary to dealings with foreign nations. Subject to such approval, it seemed desirable to establish a consulate general at Alexandria. Given the Pasha's need for support against his overlord, such a step might lead to future commercial benefits.[21]

Although establishment of a consulate general had to wait, Gliddon soon found himself upgraded from consular agent to consul; in 1837 his son, vice-consul at Cairo, crossed the Atlantic to purchase cotton ginning and other machinery for Mehemet Ali, and to provide the State Department with further information of Egyptian affairs. Naval diplomacy meanwhile continued active, and when Commodore Jesse D. Elliott relieved Patterson as squadron com-

---

[20] *Memoirs of J. Q. Adams*, VII, 106-7; VIII, 170-71, 227. Area 4 File: Hodgson to Sec. of State, ? 1828. Despatches, Turkey (Vol. 6): June 1831-March 1835, *passim*. Instructions, Turkey: 10 October 1833. Finnie, *Pioneers East*, pp. 89-93; H. M. Wriston, *Executive Agents in American Foreign Relations* (Baltimore, 1929), pp. 556-58, 707-8.

[21] Despatches, Turkey (Vol. 6): Hodgson to Sec. of State, 25 August 1834, 28 September 1834, 2 March 1835.

mander he followed in the tradition of his predecessors. On a visit in 1836 Elliott procured a firman which guaranteed to Americans most-favored-nation treatment in Egyptian-controlled Syria, and discussed with Mehemet Ali the missionary desire for a cemetery at Jerusalem; in his report he noted the Pasha's evident wish to have the post at Alexandria raised to the status of consulate general. On a second visit, in 1837, Elliott encouraged the Egyptians with the expression of his confidence that, as a result of his representations to Washington, such an elevation would soon take place.[22]

This visit of 1837 was a somewhat special one, for it took place in the course of a commercial reconnaissance of the entire eastern Mediterranean. In the previous autumn the Jackson administration had moved to repair its breach with France by the appointment of a new minister. The choice had fallen upon Lewis Cass, secretary of war and former governor of Michigan Territory, whose appointment to Paris carried with it the additional responsibility of a commercial and political fact-finding tour through Egypt, Syria, Turkey, Greece, and the islands of the Aegean. "There are," Cass wrote to Commodore Elliott, "considerations connected with our intercourse with those regions which render such a measure important." In April 1837 the Minister left Paris to embark on the flagship *Constitution* for a cruise which would last until October.

First came a trip through Italy and an audience with the Pope; then Greece, where Cass met the King and Queen and visited Corinth and Marathon. The ruins of antiquity provoked reflection, but the scenery was not unequaled: as *Constitution* traversed the Archipelago on her way to the Troad and Constantinople, Cass was forcibly reminded of the islands of upper Lake Michigan and Lake Huron, which he had formerly known so well. Plague at the Turkish capital cut the visit short and prevented a reception of the Sultan on board Old Ironsides, but an agreeable interview was had with the Capudan Pasha. Heading southward, the travelers passed by way of Smyrna, Rhodes, and Cyprus to Jaffa and to Beirut. From Jaffa visits were made to the Holy Places; in Syria, minister and commodore proceeded on an extended camping trip, making themselves known by hoisting the flag "wherever we encamped, in the remotest deserts and among the wildest tribes." Here many attentions were received from the Governor of Damascus; here they

[22] Despatches, Turkey: Elliott to Porter, 20 October 1836; Porter to Sec. of State, 11 October 1837. Finnie, *Pioneers East*, p. 153.

called on Lady Hester Stanhope, the niece of William Pitt, who for almost a quarter-century had lived in eccentric feudal splendor among the Druses of the Lebanon. After a September visit to Egypt, where Cass and Elliott talked with Mehemet Ali and with Ibrahim, his heir, *Constitution* headed westward for Port Mahon.

The trip had been great fun. In addition to the visits to contemporary rulers and antique sites, it had permitted some early American souveniring. In Turkey Elliott had managed to procure "four Colossal granite Balls" of the type formerly fired by the cannon guarding the Dardanelles, together with "two marble sarcophagi, with antique devices of remote antiquity," which he was confident would "be appreciated by the antiquaries and the learned of our country;" for his more practical compatriots, concerned with improving the breed, he had also acquired some pure-blooded Arabian horses. On his departure from the flagship, Cass thanked the Commodore for a successful cruise on which valuable information had been gathered, and Elliott expressed the hope that "we shall be able to make a report . . . which will prove an essential service to the political and commercial interests of the country."[23]

Whether or not they did remains obscure, but in any case no treaty with Egypt eventuated, nor did much commerce develop with that country. The intervention of the powers in the second Syrian War was followed, in 1841, by a clarification of the Viceroy's role in foreign affairs which postponed for a generation the emergence of a would-be Egyptian Henry VIII. After a visit to Alexandria in 1843, the commanding officer of *Congress* reported negligible American trade, owing both to the similarity of exports and to declining Egyptian manufactures, the result of the Pasha's pernicious interposition of despotic monopolies between producer and purchaser. Although American visitors were invariably well received, and visits from the squadron appreciated, the principal conclusion seemed to be that Mehemet Ali's considerable fleet might make him "very troublesome to commerce when desirous."[24]

[23] Area 4 File: Sec. of Navy to Elliott, 1 October 1836; Cass to Elliott, 1 October 1836; Elliott to Sec. of Navy, 23 November 1837. Instructions, France: Sec. of State to Cass, 4 October 1836. Despatches, France: Cass to Sec. of State, 1 April 1837. Captains' Letters: Elliott to Sec. of Navy, 22 July 1837, 25 October 1837, 10 November 1837 (Naval Records Collection, National Archives). A. C. McLaughlin, *Lewis Cass* (Boston, 1899), p. 172.

[24] Letters from the Commanding Officer, Mediterranean Squadron: Morris to Sec. of Navy, 9 November 1843 (Naval Records Collection, National Archives).

One further naval effort to forward the Levant trade took place in the years before the Mexican War. Disappointment in the Black Sea trade had been followed by a steady diminution in the number of American ships arriving at Constantinople: of 6,286 vessels which passed the Dardanelles in 1843, only 2 were American. So discouraging a situation called for a remedy, and led, in the following year, to the attempt of the Tyler administration to send a man-of-war into the Black Sea on a tour of commercial exploration.

In January 1844 orders were issued to Commander Henry Henry to sail from the United States in *Plymouth* and proceed independently to the Black Sea. There he was to visit the principal ports of the far shore, from Odessa to Trebizond, to ascertain where the installation of consuls seemed desirable, and to collect and bring home samples of seeds, plants, and useful domestic animals. Again the procedure was informal and liaison with the State Department imperfect: at Constantinople, Dabney Carr learned of the impending voyage only through private correspondence, on the strength of which he applied for a firman to pass *Plymouth* through the Dardanelles. Despite the provisions of the Treaty of London of 1840 and of the Straits Convention of 1841, which closed the Dardanelles to foreign warships in time of peace, the firman was obtained without difficulty, as had been that for the brig of war *Truxton*, sent out the previous summer to return the body of Commodore Porter to the United States. But admission to the Black Sea was something else again, and here the Minister was doubtful.

His fears were justified. Not only had preparation been neglected, but the Navy Department's choice of agent had been unfortunate. Inflated by the independent nature of his mission, Henry began by taking high tone with the squadron commander and emphasizing his intimacy with the heads of government at home; on his arrival at Constantinople he quarreled with the American minister and proved himself loud and boisterous in conversation and rude and inhospitable to the Turks who visited his ship. Although Carr, from the first, had thought it impossible for *Plymouth* to enter the Black Sea, he regretted this irrational restriction upon freedom of navigation: "I hope the time is not distant when the civilized maritime powers—the U.S. taking the lead, will say to this people, and all others, that no such obstructions will be allowed on the great highways of nations." But Henry's behavior was certainly not conducive to this end, and the only interpretation the Minister could place on the officer's conduct was to see it as a conscious effort to frustrate the mission which had been assigned to him.[25]

So American trade with the Levant remained, to all intents and purposes, a Smyrna trade. But it also continued prosperous, stable throughout the thirties and forties and expanding considerably in the fifties. Rum and cotton cloth were carried in, along with large quantities of foreign produce; opium, fruits, and nuts were carried out. Behind its whitewhashed warehouses the city of Smyrna, the emporium of Asia Minor, where Arab met Frank and camel met ship, and where turban, robe, and beard confronted hat, short coat, and shorn chin, remained attractive and important. Set in a mountain amphitheater at the end of a thirty-four-mile gulf, this "most modernized, walkable, Mohammedan town under the banner of the Crescent" looked down upon a harbor which might at any time contain a score of foreign warships and more than a hundred merchant vessels.

For sea captains a visit offered profit; for naval officers it promised pleasure, and naval visits followed a regular drill. The Pasha, in blue frock coat ornamented with gold lace, would be received aboard and edified by exercises at the guns; the American missionary would come aboard to hold services. These things accomplished, it was time to go ashore, to visit the fruit market, whose grapes, oranges, figs, and pomegranates had a "richness of flavor unknown to other climes"; to observe the women of the Armenian quarter, with "their rounded voluptuous forms, . . . sipping spoonfuls of sweet-meats, like veritable houris"; to walk on the Marina or visit the Casino with its ballroom, billiard rooms, and card rooms, and its reading room stocked with all the gazettes and reviews of Europe. In this mercantile society, whose houses flew the flags of most of the nations of the Western world and whose members, responsible only to their own consuls, lived together in cordial equality, America was most honorably and hospitably represented. Few could forget their visits to the Offleys' villa, with flowers and shade and dancing, "sweet music, ices, champagne, and milk punch."[26]

[25] Record of Confidential Letters: Sec. of Navy to Henry, 18 January 1844, 22 January 1844, 11 March 1844; Sec. of Navy to Smith, 22 January 1844 (Naval Records Collection, National Archives). Despatches, Turkey: Carr to Sec. of State, 17 July 1844, 27 September 1844. Squadron Letters: Smith to Sec. of Navy, 31 October 1844.

[26] Gordon, *American Relations with Turkey*, p. 46; [Colton], *Ship and Shore*, pp. 290-92; [Gould], *Life of Gould*, pp. 145-54; Gringo, *Scampavias*, pp. 335-47;

3. The Missionary Balance Sheet

The years after 1830 had seemed to augur well for the missions to the Oriental Churches. But optimism was to prove premature, as the winds of change now blowing through the Ottoman Empire and the pressures exerted from without combined to make the future difficult for both Turk and foreigner. As the Greek revolt had earlier interrupted the work of Goodell and Bird at Beirut, so anti-Western reaction at Constantinople and the contest with Egypt for the control of Syria now impinged upon the expanded missionary effort. In Turkey, in Syria, and even in Persia, the American missionaries saw their work affected by the strains of reform, the death of Mahmud, and the second Syrian War.

Beginning in 1837 the Constantinople mission found itself facing a period of financial stringency, the consequence of depression at home; two years later, in the final months of Mahmud's reign, a "severe persecution" developed at Constantinople. Already the Greeks had become less hospitable to the efforts of the evangelists, and anathemas had been directed by their bishops against the Americans. Now, in addition, tensions developing within the Armenian community reacted upon the missionary effort. A conservative group of artisans, which numbered the imperial architects among its members, gained the Sultan's ear. Shortly the tolerant and friendly Armenian patriarch was deposed. Soon the missionaries found their schools in decline, their literature banned, and their friends kidnapped, imprisoned, or exiled from the capital. At the outstations of Brusa and Trebizond persecution also developed; the Russian ambassador gave evidences of hostility; efforts to obtain the expulsion of the missionaries appeared to be underway.

But the crisis was surmounted by an apparent intervention of Divine Providence. The victory of the Egyptians at Nezib, the death of Mahmud, and the accession of Abdul Medjid were followed by European efforts—most notably on the part of Protestant Great Britain—to rescue the Ottoman Empire. At the Porte the reformers temporarily regained control, the hostile Greek patriarch was ousted from his post, and among the Armenians the reforming faction returned to power. Shortly the government of the new Sultan produced the Hatt-i Sherif of Gulhané, a notable rescript which, along

---

J. W. Revere, *Keel and Saddle* (Boston, 1872), pp. 35-36; N. P. Willis, *Summer Cruise in the Mediterranean* (Auburn and Rochester, N.Y., 1853), pp. 391-92.

with numerous concessions to progress, promised the equal protection of life, liberty, and property to members of whatever creed.
"God blew," said Cyrus Hamlin, and his enemies were scattered,
and while the promises of the Hatt were hardly matched by the
performance, this document, which first announced "to the people
the true object of government," appeared to be a milestone in the
awakening of "the slumbering East."[27]

With the crisis past, the schools for Armenians were reopened
and the output of missionary printing again increased; soon it was
noticed that attendance at meetings was growing rapidly and that
conversions were on the rise. But difficulties now developed from a
wholly new and unexpected quarter. Already the Congregationalists
at Constantinople had been irritated by traveling American Episcopalians who had limited their activities to sight-seeing and criticism; with the arrival of an Episcopal missionary, the Reverend
Horatio Southgate, this exasperation increased.

The conduct of this individual, who after training at Andover had
turned to the Episcopal Church, showed once again that the heretic
is worse than the infidel. Appointed to investigate the Near East,
Southgate had traveled extensively in Turkey and Persia in the years
between 1836 and 1838, and had published a narrative of his explorations. In 1840, after ordination to the priesthood, he returned to
Constantinople as a missionary. Disapproving of the evangelical
approach of his former brethren, Southgate allied himself with the
Armenian hierarchy, supported the Patriarch in his persecutions,
and engaged in pamphlet warfare with the missionaries of the Board.
On a second return to America in 1844 he acquired the impressive
title of Missionary Bishop in the Dominions and Dependencies of
the Sultan of Turkey. But although Southgate's activities seemed for
a time so distressing as to lead the Prudential Committee of the
American Board to pass a resolution of censure, in the end they
proved more nuisance than threat, and the progress of evangelical
truth continued. To a query from the Armenian patriarch as to how
long the missionaries proposed to sojourn in Turkey, Goodell had
once replied that they would stay until there were so many good
schools that theirs were no longer attended, and so much good
preaching that none came to hear them preach. For the moment

---

[27] ABC 16.7.1, Vol. 3: Mission Journal, 1839-40. Goodell, *The Old and the New*,
pp. 78-80; Hamlin, *Among the Turks*, pp. 37-56; Anderson, *Oriental Churches*, I,
104-22; Arpee, *Armenian Awakening*, pp. 95-103.

such a time appeared in sight, and in 1844 he wrote that if the next decade went as well as the last, there would be no need for the Americans to remain.[28]

For Justin Perkins and his colleagues in Persia the Turkish crisis had also posed problems. The Armenian persecutions at Trebizond and at Erzerum threatened their line of communications with the outer world; an effort to bring the mountain Nestorians within their field of operations fell victim to the disorder which followed the Syrian War. Attempting to enter the mountains from the west in the summer of 1839, Dr. Grant was caught up in the backwash of defeated Turkish forces from the battle of Nezib and narrowly escaped with his life. For a time, the effort was continued, and in 1841 reinforcements arrived from America to establish a station at Mosul on the upper Tigris. But endemic border warfare made for continued disorder, and 1843 brought a great massacre of Christians as Turks and Kurds combined to fall upon the Nestorians. Less and less did it seem possible to carry on constructive work in this region, and when to social chaos was added the death of Dr. Grant from typhoid and the announced intention of American Episcopalians to establish a station, the mission to the mountain Nestorians was discontinued.

East of the Kurdish Mountains, however, the Urmia mission continued to enjoy success. Returning temporarily to the United States in 1841, Justin Perkins brought with him the Nestorian Bishop Yohannan; delayed by storms, their arrival at New York fortuitously coincided with the annual meeting of the American Board, at which the entrance of the Nestorian bishop, with long black beard and exotic robes, created a sensation. So dramatic a trophy stimulated sectarian jealousy, and an Episcopalian attempt to capture Yohannan afforded the visitor from the East opportunity to read his American friends a lesson on brotherly love. On his return to Persia in 1843 Perkins was accompanied by Fidelia Fiske, a former student and teacher at Mount Holyoke, who was to perform remarkable work in furthering female education. Momentarily, a resurgence of papal aggression and the removal of British protection led to fear for the future and induced Perkins to journey to Teheran to defend

[28] ABC 16.7.1, Vol. 3: Goodell to Anderson, 7 March 1844, 17 April 1844, 17 May 1844. Phillips, "Pagan World," pp. 158-61; Shaw, *Eastern Churches*, pp. 35-70; K. W. Cameron, "The Manuscripts of Horatio Southgate," 42 *American Church Monthly*, 155-73.

his mission. But no defense proved necessary. The Jesuits were expelled by the Shah, a Christian governor was appointed for the Nestorians, and in 1846 the awakening of numerous converts and a real old-fashioned revival heartened the Americans by showing that the word of God worked similarly the world over.[29]

In Syria, during the period of Egyptian rule, routine work had continued to go forward, punctuated by routine adventure. Responding in 1839 to reports of the illness of Hester Stanhope, the missionary William M. Thomson accompanied the British consul to her mountain fastness, where, finding her dead and her body abandoned by her retainers, they buried her at midnight by the light of torches. In this province, in contrast to Constantinople, there had been no persecution; but the decision of the powers in 1840 to restore the governance of the Porte, and the reluctance of Mehemet Ali to accept this decision, made the region again the seat of war. At Beirut, missionary operations were suspended, and while a number of the Americans retired to Jerusalem, others were removed to safety in Cyprus by the U.S.S. *Cyane*. Anxious for the fate of the missionary establishment, the Reverend Samuel Wolcott returned with the attacking British squadron, to witness the heavy bombardment that preceded the landing and to accompany the assault force into the city. For a time it seemed that much might have been lost, but although the American consul's house had been battered by gunfire and spoiled by the Egyptians and although the missionary gardens had been ploughed by cannonballs and the mission walls breached, the library, the philosophical apparatus, and the press remained unharmed.

Upon their reassembly in 1841 the members of the Syrian mission faced new problems. French discontent with the Syrian settlement now resulted in the arrival of heavily subsidized Jesuits, bent upon another kind of conquest. In apparent alliance with these, the Maronite patriarch petitioned the Porte to expel the Americans, while in Lebanon a war developed between Druses and Maronites which would continue intermittently for years, and which in the autumn of 1841 forced the missionaries to abandon their mountain residences and retire to Beirut.[30]

---

[29] Anderson, *Oriental Churches*, I, 198-223, 315-33; Laurie, *Dr. Grant and the Mountain Nestorians*. On Fidelia Fiske: Thomas Laurie, *Woman and her Saviour in Persia* (Boston, 1863).

[30] Anderson, *Oriental Churches*, I, 236-60; Phillips, "Pagan World," p. 157. Despatches, Turkey: Porter to Sec. of State, 12 August 1840, 2 October 1840, 16 May 1841, 16 October 1841, 27 November 1841.

So in Syria, as in Turkey and Persia, life brought troubles enough; yet on balance all three of these missions could be considered going concerns. In 1844 Rufus Anderson again visited the Mediterranean, and the contrast with the situation of fifteen years before, when all American missionaries had been huddled up in Malta, was certainly a striking one. But any recapitulation, as of the mid-forties, would have had to set off against these considerable successes some equally obvious failures.

The decision to approach the Mohammedans by way of the Christian sects which dwelt among them, in effect a decision not to approach them at all, had proven abundantly justified. In the exception that proved the rule, James L. Merrick, sent to minister to the Moslems of Persia, had enjoyed great personal success and total evangelical failure. Far from tottering to its fall, as the millennial expectation had it, Islam appeared an impressive structure, impervious, invulnerable. In 1842, after seven years of unrewarded effort, Merrick was transferred to the Nestorian mission, and soon afterward returned to the United States.[31]

With the Jews the story was much the same. The early venture of Josiah Brewer had accomplished nothing, and not until 1832 was the mission renewed. But in that year there arrived at Constantinople the Reverend William G. Schauffler, born in Stuttgart, brought up in Odessa, and educated at Andover through the agency of Jonas King. Another of the Board's astounding linguists, Schauffler ultimately was to be credited with speaking ten languages and reading twenty, but his work among the Jews of Constantinople met with small response. In 1846 the mission was discontinued, and Schauffler's lifework came to center on Bible translation. Already he had completed a Hebrew-Spanish version of the Old Testament, published in 1842. Now he devoted himself to the translation of the entire Bible into Turkish, a task which he completed in 1873.[32]

In Palestine, the original goal, the cause had also suffered defeat. Only in 1834, nine years after the death of Pliny Fisk, was the Jerusalem station reoccupied by the Reverend William M. Thomson, the Reverend George B. Whiting, and Dr. Asa Dodge, the first medical missionary to the Levant. Greeted first by an earthquake and then by a rebellion against Egyptian rule, in which their house became

---

[31] Anderson, *Oriental Churches*, I, 324; Bliss, *Encyclopaedia of Missions*, II, 64; Phillips, "Pagan World," pp. 147-48; Finnie, *Pioneers East*, pp. 221-24.

[32] Anderson, *Oriental Churches*, II, 150-60; Bliss, *Encyclopaedia of Missions*, II, 313-14; Richter, *History of Missions*, pp. 397, 401.

the scene of violent fighting, the party was bereaved within a year by the deaths of Mrs. Thomson and Dr. Dodge. Despite harassment by the authorities the mission was reinforced and schools were opened, but the population proved unresponsive, and illness struck again. In 1843 the Board made the difficult decision to suspend work at the birthplace of Christianity, and in the following year the visit of Rufus Anderson to the Mediterranean brought the execution of this resolve.[33]

Most disappointing of all, to the evangelically as well as to the commercially minded, was the situation of Greece. On hearing of Navarino, Jonas King had confided to his diary, "I shed tears of joy. . . . The road of the east will open up to freedom and true religion, and I must return to the field." Return he did, and for perhaps a decade the road lay open. His movement to Athens, and that of the Episcopalians Hill and Robertson, marked the beginning of an expanding effort. In 1833 Elias Riggs, a graduate of Amherst College and "a thorough scholar," arrived with his wife, and by 1837 the American Board had five missionary couples in Greece. In 1836 the first Baptists arrived, with more to follow. At Constantinople, Goodell and his colleagues found themselves deeply involved with the Greek population and with the improvement of Greek schools. Printing in modern Greek grew rapidly: in 1843 more than a million and a half pages issued from the Smyrna press, while the Greek monthly *Magazine of Useful Knowledge,* edited by Daniel Temple, gained a surprisingly large circulation.[34]

But Greek nationalism, so praiseworthy when directed against the foreign tyrant, was now regrettably turned against the missionaries: what had earlier appeared to resemble the Spirit of '76 now seemed merely a generalized xenophobia. Byzantine rather than classic memories dominated the Greek mind; the "Great Idea" which formed the new rallying point looked less to the re-creation of the age of Pericles than to the recovery of Constantinople. Evangelical efforts, moreover, faced a special barrier, for orthodoxy and nationality had been so long equated under Turkish rule that disloyalty to church was, to the Greeks, the same as disloyalty to country. Conversions, consequently, were few: the Baptists, whose "native con-

---

[33] Anderson, *Oriental Churches,* I, 34-39; Richter, *History of Missions,* pp. 235-36; Tibawi, *American Interests,* pp. 73-74, 101, 105.

[34] Shaw, *Eastern Churches,* p. 75; Anderson, *Oriental Churches,* I, 146-63; II, 504-6; Newcomb, *Cyclopedia of Missions,* pp. 372-77; William Gammell, *A History of American Baptist Missions* (Boston, 1849), pp. 300-304.

verts have in no period numbered more than seven," claimed none-theless to be "the most numerous Protestant communion in Greece."

Armed with the weapons of nationalism and xenophobia, and jealous of its prerogatives, the Greek hierarchy stood firm, and indeed soon assumed the offensive. In his first year at Athens, Jonas King had counted 170 pupils in his school, but by 1838 both his school and that at Argos had been closed down; with the exception of Athens, all stations of the American Board had been abandoned by 1841. Overt hostility to the Americans appeared: Hill, the Episcopalian, was accused of immoral practices and threatened with expulsion, while the mobbing of a Baptist on grounds of enmity to St. Spiridion led to riot and loss of life. Casting up accounts on his visit of 1844, Rufus Anderson observed that twenty-seven ordained missionaries of various denominations had labored in this field; more than ten thousand Greeks had attended mission schools in Greece and Turkey, and a considerable number had been educated in America; two hundred thousand New Testaments and a million books and tracts had been supplied the Greek community. Yet not ten persons could be pointed out as "truly converted to God."

In this situation all denominations decided to cut their losses. In 1845 the Baptist station at Patras was closed and the single remaining Baptist missionary moved to the Piraeus, to labor fruitlessly for another decade. For the Episcopalians, only John Henry Hill stayed on, maintaining his school at Athens. Except for Jonas King, bound both by love of his God and by love of his wife to the country of his adoption, all emissaries of the American Board were transferred. As the Board's historian was later to observe, a "deplorable change had come over the Greeks . . . since the freedom of Greece from Turkish rule"; all efforts had come to naught; "the good seed [had been] thus sown, though not often on good ground."[35]

But Jonas King remained. Lacking diplomatic support, on but distant terms with his Episcopalian compatriot, he labored on in isolation, a foreign Luther in a strange land. Tireless in spreading God's word, preaching every Sunday in his house to all who would come to hear, he soon found himself the center of a storm.

The trouble, as once before in Greece, broke out over a young girl called Helen, when marital problems led her English husband to

[35] ABC 17.1, Vol. 1: King to Anderson, 30 May 1831; Vol. 2: King, Riggs, and Benjamin to Anderson, 7 November 1837. Newcomb, *Cyclopedia of Missions*, pp. 135, 378; *Memorial Volume of ABCFM*, pp. 356-57; Anderson, *Oriental Churches*, I, 161-62.

seek consolation from King. In reply to this slight upon her reputation the lady and her family accused husband and minister of urging Protestant dogma upon her, and, upon her refusal to recant, of performing upon her person acts too shameful to mention publicly. Shortly the Greek press at Smyrna, at Athens, and elsewhere was publishing these horrid accusations, and charging the missionary with impiety against the Virgin Mary. "It seems," wrote King as the excitement spread, "as if Satan were let loose upon me with great rage," and his published reply, which quoted the early Greek fathers against the practice of Mariolatry, served but to increase the abuse. Undaunted, the missionary expanded his attack in "A little duodecimo Vol." of theological argumentation: "I have been drawn into the stadium, & must run—& I hope in God so to run, that I may win the prize."

But valiantly though he ran, superstition and bigotry continued to "growl from their dark den." In the summer of 1845 King was excommunicated by the Greek synod and his prosecution was demanded of the government. By autumn his house had been raided, he had been examined by a judge, and a second excommunication had issued from the Great Church at Constantinople. In January he was assailed on the street. Shortly, his case was adjudged criminal and remanded to Syra for trial, a step followed by a rash of inflammatory publications and by rumors of an assassination conspiracy. But when King and his Greek lawyers reached Syra, their steamer was greeted by so great a mob that the authorities forbade the defendant to land, and the trial was postponed.

Another year had passed in preaching and in planning a new school when again King was cited for trial. Again public opinion became heated, this time by the publication of articles on "The Orgies" in which the American and his followers allegedly indulged. All this pressure was stoutly resisted by the missionary, as were the urgings of government officials that he cease preaching, even within his house. But a request from the Greek monarch, relayed by the Swedish minister, that he leave the country for a time seemed unanswerable; and in the summer of 1847, accompanied by more accusations in the press, Jonas King departed for western Europe.[36]

[36] ABC 16.7.1, Vol. 2: King to Anderson, 1844-46, *passim*, and especially 25 January 1845, 10 February 1845, 10 June 1845; ABC 17.1, Vol. 3: King to Anderson, 1846-47, *passim*, and especially 25 August 1847, 27 August 1847.

4. The Mediterranean Squadron

For the squadron in the Mediterranean, as the activities of Patterson, Elliott, and Henry Henry showed, the expansion of commerce remained a live issue. Not so, however, the problem of its protection. The stabilization of Europe in the generation following the Congress of Vienna had been accompanied by a stabilization of the Mediterranean, and although the squadron was maintained at a strength of five or six ships through the first Jackson administration and reinforced in 1833 by the addition of a ship of the line, its activity was limited to peaceful cruising. Except for some very minor and intermittent outbreaks in the Gulf of Salonica, Greek piracy had ended. The Egyptian pasha's navy might excite momentary apprehension, but in fact he never used it against shipping. Algiers was now French, and while one could sympathize on grounds of self-determination with the resistance movement of Abd el Kader, which limited French control to the area within cannon-shot of seaport towns, at least the Algerines no longer sailed the sea.

With the remaining princes of Barbary few problems developed. In Tripoli, in 1832, the Pasha found himself embroiled both with Great Britain and with his subjects; when in the ensuing confusion the American consul felt himself aggrieved and struck his flag, the Tripolitan chief minister called upon Commodore Patterson to judge the dispute, promising in advance to accept the Commodore's decision. In Morocco, a quarrel over consular jurisdiction led to a street scuffle, a mob which the American consul described as "anxious to trace a few Sarracen hieroglyphs on my belly," and a call for naval support; in 1842 another Moroccan "outrage" required the summoning of naval units and a prolonged negotiation. But not all of the outrages were Moroccan, for one of the American consuls attempted the assassination of his successor, and the latter subsequently became deranged by drink. At Tunis, by contrast, throughout the long-continued consulship of the estimable Dr. Samuel D. Heap, a former naval surgeon and a brother-in-law of Commodore Porter, all went peacefully, and even in his absence nothing worse developed than an argument over consular housing, which was satisfactorily settled on orders from the Porte.[37]

There were also minor brushes with the states of Europe. In 1831 dynastic war in Portugal called squadron units to the Atlantic; in

[37] Area 4 File: *passim.* Despatches, Barbary Powers: *passim.*

the next year a blockade of Madeira, established by one of the contending factions, was broken by *Constellation* on grounds of insufficient effectiveness and partial administration. The year 1832 also brought the third and ultimately successful attempt to collect the long-standing Neapolitan claims. In January, John Nelson arrived at Naples to begin the negotiation, and by March he was exasperatedly urging naval coercion. In July the appearance of *Brandywine* and *Constitution* made the King commence defensive preparations, but the departure of Old Ironsides was followed by further procrastination. In September, however, Commodore Patterson arrived in *United States* with instructions for Nelson to request his passports if settlement was further delayed, and by 2 October four American warships were anchored off the city. On the 8th, agreement was finally reached, much to the gratification of the Commodore, who reported that it was "admitted by Mr. Nelson that the appearance of the Squadron in this bay had had great effect in producing so favorable a result."[38]

In the case of France, the tension which followed the Jacksonian quarrel over claims was prolonged by the armed search and seizure, at Smyrna, of the American brig *Banian* by a party from a French warship. With American recognition of the Republic of Texas, the squadron was alerted for a possible breach with Mexico and the appearance in the Mediterranean of Mexican letters of marque. From time to time Anglo-American friction produced alarms. In April 1839 newspaper reports of the Maine boundary troubles and the absence of news from home led Isaac Hull to sortie briefly to the Atlantic; in 1841 apparent British preparations for war brought warnings of imminent conflict from the legation at London. Giving his men a fighting speech, Hull got under way from Port Mahon and prepared for action; but the crisis passed quickly, and its only consequence was the unauthorized return of *Brandywine* to the United States, an exercise in initiative which produced a Senate debate and a court-martial for her commanding officer. Four years later, Polk's assertion of American rights in Oregon had Mediterranean echoes, as Commodore Joseph Smith set up special arrangements for speedy communication with the American minister at Paris. But all these affairs blew over rapidly, and none occupies more space in the dispatches than the difficult problem of transporting to

---

[38] Secretary of the Navy, *Annual Report, 1832*; Perrotta, *Claims*, pp. 52-71; Marraro, *Two Sicilies*, I, 286-87.

America the marble statuary made by Luigi Persico for the Capitol at Washington.[39]

Quite accurately, then, the Secretary of the Navy could report in 1838 that "some of the causes which originally dictated the policy of employing a portion of our navy in the Mediterranean have in a great measure ceased." In the orders to squadron commanders the references to Barbary were now merely historical, and the instructions enjoined active cruising, the assertion of America's just rights and the avoidance of encroachment upon the rights of others, the preservation of friendly relations with all, and the procurement, as opportunity offered, of new plants and seeds to aid the agricultural interests of the country. Nevertheless, as the Secretary continued, "it is believed that as a school of discipline under experienced officers, as a means of exhibiting a portion of our naval force in contact and comparison with that of the principal maritime states of Europe, and for the purpose of affording countenance and protection to our commerce a perseverance in this policy will equally contribute to the good of the service and the honor of the U.S."[40] And by now there existed a branch of American commerce, unheard of when the original policy was formed, which was beginning to advance its own claims to "countenance and protection." This was the subsidized commerce in invisible exports carried on by the missionary bodies.

The responsibility for the protection of this commerce had developed slowly. The call for help from Beirut in 1828 had gone unanswered by the squadron; five years later, the attack on Isaac Bird had been redressed by Mehemet Ali after protests from the consular agent Gliddon. In 1834, however, Commodore Patterson paid a first visit to Beirut with *Delaware* and *Shark*, and continuing reports on the "dreadful state of Syria" led Porter to attempt to divert the frigate *United States* for a second visit to that port. In the next year, an effort by Egyptian soldiers to oust the Palestine mission from its habitation in Jerusalem pointed up the difficulty of providing protection from Constantinople in areas under Egyptian control and emphasized the importance of Elliott's Egyptian negotia-

[39] Despatches, Turkey: G. A. Porter to Porter, 12 October 1836; G. A. Porter to Sec. of State, 21 February 1837. Despatches, France: Cass to Sec. of State, 5 March 1837. Captains' Letters: Hull to Sec. of Navy, 14 April 1839, 18 April 1839, 22 April 1839. G. W. Allen (ed.), *Papers of Isaac Hull* (Boston, 1929), pp. 296-319. Squadron Letters: Smith to Sec. of Navy, 4 May 1845.

[40] Secretary of the Navy, *Annual Report, 1838*. Squadron Letters: Morris to Sec. of Navy, 29 April 1843.

tions. It also produced a flood of missionary correspondence, much of which was ultimately forwarded by Porter to the State Department, and some of which was vigorous in tone. His blood boiling at the behavior of the Syrian pasha, Eli Smith called for strong and severe measures: "They ought to know that we are a powerful nation. And there is no other way to teach them this but to make them *feel* it."

Through the ensuing five years of minor anarchy, the question of the Syrian missionaries revolved primarily about the need for a consulate, established in 1835 only to be abolished four years later. To Porter this step, which forced the Americans to turn to British protection, seemed both regrettable and humiliating, a view which he emphasized by appointing an unpaid consular agent at Beirut and by calling upon Commodore Hull for naval support. The call proved opportune and the September arrival of *Cyane* permitted the removal of mission personnel from Beirut prior to the British bombardment.

In Lebanon, in 1845, the resumption of warfare between Druses and Maronites produced new calls for help. In April, Minister Carr asked for a summer visit to Syria by the largest available force; in June, when news of anti-Christian outbreaks reached Commodore Smith, *Plymouth* was ordered east. Commander Henry's orders directed him to give all legal protection to Christians of whatever nationality and to take American citizens on board if necessary, but by the time he reached Beirut the bloody conflict was over. Having preserved their neutrality, the missionaries continued influential with both parties to the conflict, but the arrival of *Plymouth* was nonetheless welcome. A letter of thanks, signed by ten members of the Syrian mission, stated that "the presence of one of our noble ships of war has always had a happy influence, both upon the Turkish authorities, and upon the people generally," and earnestly solicited the repetition of such visits as often as the exigencies of the service would permit. In the future they were to be repeated frequently.[41]

Throughout these years, despite the importance of events in the east, the Navy continued to base at Port Mahon. Porter, shortly after his arrival at Constantinople, had urged advancing the rendezvous to one of the Greek islands, perhaps Melos, and had sug-

[41] Despatches, Turkey: Porter to Sec. of State, 5 August 1834, 2 September 1835, 9 June 1840, 14 July 1840. Squadron Letters: Smith to Sec. of Navy, 19 April 1845, 11 September 1845.

gested that the squadron be instructed to avoid the agreeable ports of Europe and concentrate its efforts in the Levant. In 1844 Dabney Carr again stressed the importance of showing the flag in the east rather than "hugging around Port Mahon," and observed, much in the tone of Eli Smith, that "nothing has so good an effect here as the exhibition of *power*." But notwithstanding the pressures from these interested parties, the depot remained at Minorca, far to the westward.

This was not, be it said, from lack of opportunity. As far back as 1825 it had been rumored that Rodgers had acquired the island of Paros from the Greeks. In 1836, when reporting an offer by a former governor of Salonica to sell the United States some islands off Negropont which contained a suitable fleet anchorage, Commodore Porter noted that since his arrival in the East he had received repeated overtures for the sale of islands, Cyprus included, which he had uniformly discouraged on principled anticolonial grounds.[42]

At Port Mahon the relations between the representatives of the Great Republic and those of the decadent Spanish monarchy traveled a reasonably even road. The privilege of deposit gained by Rodgers in 1825 was renewed two years later, and although difficulties over customs regulations recurred from time to time, all such arguments were settled in favor of the Americans, and with one exception settled perfunctorily.

Protesting, in December 1836, the imposition of new duties, the American chargé at Madrid threatened the departure of the squadron in the event the situation was not rectified. Shaken by civil conflict and confused by constitutional change, the cumbersome Spanish bureaucracy addressed itself to the question only to discover the archives incomplete and the history of the American occupation of Port Mahon obscure. In May, having received no answer, the American legation pressed for a reply, and its statement that another power had proposed another place of rendezvous finally stimulated the Office of State to produce a résumé of past history and an estimate of American intentions.

The memorandum opened with some gratuitous observations on the commercial nature of American foreign policy, founded as it was on reciprocal treaties which worked only to the benefit of the

---

[42] Despatches, Turkey: Porter to Sec. of State, 26 December 1831, 20 April 1836; Carr to Sec. of Navy, 16 July 1844. Wright, "Relations with Turkey," p. 117; Paullin, *Rodgers*, p. 340.

United States. Lacking the pretext of Algerine piracy for the maintenance of their Mediterranean fleet, the Americans now alleged their use of the Minorcan depot to be of benefit to the islanders. Yet if reason to indulge such people was lacking, the American suggestion of an alternative raised the scent of danger: to the belief that the United States had been secretly negotiating with the Moroccan emperor for the purchase of a coastal port, the Spanish joined the facts that a new Moroccan treaty was indeed being negotiated and that Commodore Porter, on leave from Constantinople, was traveling in the western Mediterranean. Perhaps the government of the Union desired a Spanish denial of Mahon to justify its seizure of an enclave on the Barbary coast. But such a base, in proximity to the straits, might well be dangerous. Better, then, to forestall the Americans by continuing the Mahon deposit, for which, in any case, some favors might be asked in return. And so it was decided, and the information communicated to the American legation a year after the question had been raised.[43]

The late thirties and early forties saw Mahon at the zenith of its glory. At no other Mediterranean port could "more pleasure be extracted per square foot." The casino was flourishing and the dances at the arsenal were famous throughout the Mediterranean. An Italian opera company had imported a prima donna who had sung in New York and New Orleans. New riding horses had been brought in, tenpin alleys had been set up to cater to the visitors, and the multiplied grog shops were becoming Americanized, as shown by the case of the proprietress Iñes Abraham, "vulgarly known as Riley." But not all this pleasure commended itself to the authorities at home. A Navy Department order of 1839, which forbade marriage to local girls, was followed in 1842 by a proposal for the systematic interchange of ships between Mediterranean and Brazil stations, so that those "dangerous connections and fatal habits, so often formed amid seductions of luxurious ports, will be avoided."

There were also more serious problems. Moments of tension with the European powers emphasized Minorca's potentially dangerous isolation. With mail service intermittent and with Toulon, Gibraltar, and Malta all the strongholds of potential enemies, "the first indication of hostilities," as one officer wrote, "might have been the

[43] Mahon Papers, pp. 308-11, 316-19, 324-77, 409, 412-13. C. K. Webster, "British Mediation between France and the United States in 1834-6," 42 *English Historical Review*, 75.

summons of a hostile fleet." Elliott, at the time of the 1836 dispute, had been willing enough to shift his base, either outside the straits to Lisbon or forward to Italy; Isaac Hull had feared blockade. To this strategic problem was added the recurrence of civil war in Spain, which affected the discipline of the island garrison and brought violence and disorder ashore. In 1837 such disorder had led the squadron to winter elsewhere. In 1842, following the assassination of the sailing master of *Congress*, Commodore Charles W. Morgan took his ships to Genoa, and early in the next year received orders to find another rendezvous and to transfer the squadron's stores.[44]

For the moment, however, no better location offered itself. The orders were countermanded, and soon affairs across the Atlantic took charge. In March 1845, in response to the American annexation of Texas, Mexico broke off relations with the United States; the consequent diversion to the Gulf of the scheduled April reinforcement left the Mediterranean Squadron with only *Cumberland* and *Plymouth*. In June, Commodore Smith received orders to detach the latter to Sloat's Pacific command; in August, as General Taylor was advancing into Texas, *Cumberland* was ordered home. Smith received these instructions on 20 September. Reaching Port Mahon five days later, he loaded all stores, broke up the hospital, paid the bills, and on 1 October put to sea, heading for the Western Ocean.[45]

[44] E. S. Maclay, *Reminiscences of the Old Navy* (New York, 1898), pp. 39-41; Schroeder, *Shores of the Mediterranean*, II, 296-97; Albert Gleaves, *Life and Letters of Stephen B. Luce* (New York, 1925), p. 15; W. F. Lynch, *Narrative of the United States' Expedition to the River Jordan and the Dead Sea* (Philadelphia, 1849), pp. 30-31. Area 4 File: *passim*. Squadron Letters: Morgan to Sec. of Navy, 3 October 1842, 10 November 1842.

[45] Confidential Letters: Sec. of Navy to Smith, 29 April 1845, 13 May 1845, 14 August 1845. Squadron Letters: Smith to Sec. of Navy, 8 November 1845.

CHAPTER VII

The Extension of the Area of Freedom, 1847-1859

1. The Revolutions of 1848

IN THE main plaza of Mexico City the clatter of hooves ceased, the bugles sounded, and the Stars and Stripes rose slowly over the halls of the Montezumas. Oregon and California had already been secured, and all that remained was for a treaty to confirm and a swarming population of gold-seekers to guarantee that the vision of Timothy Dwight had been fulfilled. The spread of freedom had reached the Asian sea.

Well before this date, and in Europe and Latin America as well as to the westward, the new order of ages had shown its vigor. The existence and continued growth of an independent United States had altered the world's strategic pattern and had modified forms of government, concepts of empire, and doctrines of political economy. A successful example of popular government proved in action what had previously rested only on the assertions of theorists, and remained a standing inspiration to generous minds and an exasperation to legitimists. Convinced of the importance of the great experiment, Europeans of all persuasions had been much preoccupied with the study of American institutions: as one patriot observed, even Schmidt-Phiseldek, a defender of the Holy Alliance and so "no bigotted republican," had begun one of his books by "remarking that the fourth of July, 1776, was the commencement of a new era in the history of the world."[1]

To the patriotic citizens of the several states, subsequent history had fully substantiated the promises of the new Æra and the fundamental soundness of its premises. Extending westward, the federal system was about to embrace the state of California, 2,500 miles from the Atlantic. The expansion of a civilizing commerce had continued apace, aided by the successes of the American reciprocity policy and by European abstention from destructive wars. With this

[1] [A. H. Everett], *America* (Philadelphia, 1827), pp. 69-70.

expansion had come that of the merchant marine, which with the stimulus of newly acquired West Coast harbors and the discovery of California gold was about to enter its moment of fastest growth and greatest glory. Treaty relations existed with "startled China"; soon an American naval officer would accomplish the opening of Japan. The march of science and invention had continued: as Dwight had foreseen, canals and Appian Ways now crossed the New World's convex; "engines strange" had been devised. Soon the international reputation won by American ingenuity was to be confirmed at the Crystal Palace Exhibition. Admittedly the evangelization of the world was incomplete, but an impressive effort was underway and the sun never set on the American missionary. Some heathen, at least, had cast their idols to the moles and bats; new forces were undermining the throne of the Turkish sultan; shortly the Pope would find his own in danger as his people rose to demand a liberal government. It was a moment of triumph.

At home, triumph would soon enough be followed by disaster: far from freeing the slave, technology had riveted his fetters. For the moment, nevertheless, the tragic depth of the sectional fissure could go unnoticed, and Americans could still look outward. Throughout Europe the echoes of Concord Bridge continued to reverberate, as legitimacy gave ground to nationality and mercantilism to free trade. The year of the Treaty of Guadalupe Hidalgo saw the Continent shaken by risings on behalf of rational institutions, nationality, and the rights of man. Along the shores of the Old World these and subsequent portentous events would present new problems, new opportunities, and new hazards to the uncommitted and independent emissaries of the New.

The landing at Vera Cruz had taken place in March 1847. In June, the capture of Tabasco marked the end of the naval offensive in the Gulf of Mexico. Now that strength was available for use elsewhere, reports of Mexican privateering in the Mediterranean acted to hasten the intended reestablishment of an American presence in that sea. In late July, as Scott's forces were advancing on Mexico City, the U.S.S. *Princeton*, Captain Frederick Engle, sailed for Gibraltar, where she arrived on 5 September. By October two more ships were on station; in December Commodore George C. Read arrived from the African coast in the frigate *United States* to command the reconstituted Mediterranean Squadron.

As the first screw-propelled warship in the world, and the first to burn anthracite, *Princeton* was well calculated to renew the ancient respect for American naval architecture; in 1845 a plan to send her on a bragging cruise of European ports had fallen victim to the course of events in Mexico. Instructed to show the flag as rapidly and in as many ports as possible, Engle vigorously complied; everywhere the reception of this smokeless wonder was all that could be desired. By January 1848 a cruise of the Archipelago and the Adriatic had been completed, and *Princeton* was anchored in the harbor at Malta, when reports of revolution in Sicily were received.[2]

Sailing promptly, Engle reached Messina on 23 January, to find the city prepared for revolution but awaiting the outcome of events at Palermo. Efforts to maintain the peace were at once begun in cooperation with the consular body and the captain of a British warship; despite bombardment of the town by royal forces holding the forts and royal ships in harbor, these efforts by mid-February produced a temporary armistice. Sympathetic to the popular cause, although taking the greatest pains to maintain neutrality, Engle reported that the people were determined not to be tricked and that he expected fighting. On Washington's birthday the fighting broke out, and the revolutionaries, after seizing a fort, celebrated the occasion by saluting the American flag. On the 23rd Engle reported that he had enjoyed a splendid view of "the best conducted and most united revolution imaginable."[3]

The uprising in Sicily was but the first of many insurrections which for the next year and a half convulsed the Continent, and which suggested, at least momentarily, that Columbia's bliss had reached Europe as well as the Asian sea. In Paris an outbreak, also occurring on Washington's birthday, toppled the reign of Louis Philippe; four days later a provisional government was proclaimed. Spreading eastward across Europe, the report of this great event led, in the space of a few months, to revolutions in Germany, Italy, and Hungary.

Across the Atlantic, the news of these developments, with its suggestion of the imminent downfall of all monarchy, produced great outbursts of enthusiasm and a wave of the meetings, toasts, and flag-raisings prescribed by republican ritual. Of this American enthusi-

[2] Confidential Letters: Sec. of Navy to Smith, 29 April 1845; Sec. of Navy to Engle, 20 July 1847; Sec. of Navy to Read, 20 August 1847. Squadron Letters: Engle to Sec. of Navy, 7 August 1847, 5 September 1847, 10 January 1848, 20 January 1848.

[3] Squadron Letters: Engle to Sec. of Navy, 23 January 1848, 9 February 1848, 16 February 1848, 23 February 1848.

asm one sizable ingredient was the conviction that once again the seeds of 1776 were sprouting, and that the Europeans were proceeding on the American plan. Nor was this conviction wholly unfounded: at Milan the difficulties began with a boycott purposefully patterned on the Boston Tea Party; in Venice the republican leader consciously aspired to emulate the great Washington. Yet however gratifying the events of 1848, they raised again the basic question: revolution in one country only or world revolution? For individuals, as earlier in Greece, the question posed no great difficulties. At least one American fought on the Paris barricades, and two sons of Dr. Valentine Mott joined the revolutionary forces in Italy. But for the officers of government the problem remained more difficult.

In Paris, on 26 February, Richard Rush was waited on by Major Guillaume Tell Poussin, both revolutionary French officer and naturalized American citizen, and called upon for a testimonial of republican solidarity. Less restrained than Engle, the American minister hesitated but two days. On the 28th, alone of all the foreign representatives at Paris, Rush proceeded in full diplomatic dress to the Hôtel de Ville and there, in a scene reminiscent of the action of James Monroe in an earlier revolution, felicitated the members of the new regime. This step in due course received the approval of the American government; in due course Major Poussin was appointed minister to the United States; in April the Congress congratulated the French people on their adoption of republican forms. But in other countries, where revolutionary success was less clear-cut, the question of recognition was to present difficulties.[4]

Nor did these problems confront only the diplomats. The Navy was also involved. As individuals, the American officers were moved by the advance of freedom: seeing in the European outbreaks a divine punishment of the nations, one officer looked forward to the happy world "when the whole worthless tribe of kings, with all their myrmidons, will be swept from their places and made to bear a part in the toils and sufferings of the great human family." As professionals, however, the naval officers found their responsibilities increased by the upheavals. In Italy, where the turmoil continued

---

[4] Richard Rush, *Occasional Productions* (Philadelphia, 1860), pp. 364-68, 373-74, 413, 425; Priscilla Robertson, *Revolutions of 1848* (New York, 1960), pp. 338, 390. To some in America the outbreaks of 1848 seemed the obvious consequences of the voyage of the *Mayflower*, the American birth of freedom, and the work of the Anglo-Saxon race for the elevation of mankind. Hollis Read, *The Hand of God in History* (Hartford, 1851), pp. 366-82.

for more than a year, the protection of American commerce at Genoa, Leghorn, and Sicilian ports, and at Austrian Trieste, became a matter of importance, while at most of these places American citizens were also resident. But the performance of duty was complicated by the common republicanism: as the commanding officer of *Jamestown* wrote, whenever the flag of freedom had appeared "where liberal opinions have been struggling with despotic rule it has been greeted with pleasure by the liberal party and its presence has afforded them encouragement to contend more obstinately with their oppressors."[5]

Although at times presenting complications, this cordiality was at the moment the more interesting for a very practical reason: the American squadron required a new base. The French occupation of Algiers and the coming of steam had made the Spanish hold upon the Balearic Islands increasingly tenuous. As early as 1837, Commodore Elliott had warned that the French might acquire Minorca. In 1840 France had threatened to seize the islands in the event of war; in 1843, following a Spanish refusal of coaling facilities at Port Mahon, the French formally protested the privileged position of the American Mediterranean Squadron. Two years later Spain promised to regularize the situation, and in 1846 took advantage of American preoccupation with the Mexican War to terminate the grant of facilities.

On his arrival in the Mediterranean, Commodore Read had nevertheless proceeded directly to Port Mahon, where he remained until early February 1848. There he occupied himself with voyage repairs, with the liquidation of the former base, with logistic planning, now complicated by the problem of coal, and with the schedule for future operations. Encouraged by, and himself encouraging, the exertions of the inhabitants to obtain a renewal of the American deposit, Read raised the issue with the legation at Madrid. Since exclusion was the result of "improper representations of French agents," and since the inhabitants desired the return of the squadron, he hoped that something could be done. For the immediate future, as he reported to the Department, he planned to send two of his three ships on a summer cruise to the Levant; with an eye on affairs

[5] Lynch, *Expedition to the Dead Sea*, p. 322. Squadron Letters: Mercer to Sec. of Navy, 14 September 1849.

in Sicily he observed that the course of Mediterranean political events lent great interest to his command.[6]

So it did, and when *United States* reached Genoa in early March, Read found a situation which forced complete revision of his cruising plans. Yet not all the effects were adverse, for here in Piedmont, where Alfieri had earlier hymned *America Liberata* and had dedicated a play to Washington, unsettlement favored the Republic of the West. As the agitation had developed, the American minister had been ostentatiously cheered in public; bending before the storm, the King had promulgated a constitution; now a liberal government held power and liberal feelings ran high. A request to the new government for permission to deposit squadron stores at Spezia was immediately approved, and on the most liberal terms: no duties would be levied; the use of a public building at the lazaretto would be provided without charge. But March also brought the revolution to Berlin and Milan, and as disorder spread throughout Europe the Commodore wrote home for reinforcements. Anxious to increase the force in European waters, the Department at once took steps to comply.

In Sicily, in contrast to Piedmont, there had come not reform but revolution. On the mainland the authority of the Bourbons still prevailed, but by late April, when Read reached Palermo, the revolutionaries controlled the island and Neapolitan authority was limited to the beleaguered garrison at Messina. Despite pressure from resident Americans, the Commodore refrained from saluting the revolutionary flag, but the solidarity of free men and the desire for outside backing brought radical action from the Sicilians. Having alluded in conversation with the Governor of Syracuse to the squadron's new logistic facilities at Spezia, Read tentatively raised the possibility of similar arrangements in Sicily; within a few days he received the startling news that the Sicilian legislature had conferred base rights upon the United States. The offer was tempting: the harbor of Syracuse, one of the best in the world, possessed excellent facilities, a milder climate than Spezia, and a far more central location. But the uncertain prospects of the revolution caused Read to hesitate, an attitude in which the Department concurred, instructing him to preserve a strict neutrality and to delay tactfully any

[6] Secretary of the Navy, *Annual Report, 1846*. Mahon Papers, pp. 530-37. Confidential Letters: Sec. of Navy to Read, 30 March 1848, 1 June 1848, 10 July 1848. Squadron Letters: Read to Sec. of Navy, 31 December 1847, 1 January 1848, 13 January 1848, 7 February 1848.

acceptance of the generous offer until the Sicilian government should be sufficiently established to warrant recognition.[7]

For a time it seemed that the Sicilians would maintain their freedom. In July the assembly offered the crown to a son of the Piedmontese king. From Palermo the American consul reported that British and French warships had saluted the Sicilian flag, and that he himself had officially recognized the government. But by September British policy had changed, a Neapolitan expedition had landed, and the Consul's act, disavowed by the government at Washington, had led to harassment of squadron units visiting the seat of reaction at Naples.

Read, in the meantime, had been wavering between the actuality of Spezia, the desirability of Syracuse, and the possible availability of facilities at Porto Ferraio on the island of Elba. In July the arrival of the storeship *Supply* forced a decision for Spezia, but this too brought danger of involvement, for Piedmont was now at war with Austria. Since in addition to the squadron stores the port of Spezia held a million dollars worth of American property, and the harbor a number of American merchant ships, Read concentrated his forces there.

The Piedmontese declaration of war on Austria, in answer to appeals from revolutionary Milan, drew support from all Italy. But early success was followed by overwhelming defeat in late July, and within two weeks the Austrians had driven the Italian Army from Lombardy. With an Austrian invasion apparently imminent, and with rumors of French intervention, there came outbreaks in Tuscany which led Read to proceed to Leghorn with *United States* and *Princeton*. There, in early August, assistance was provided the Tuscan government by the detention of a vessel loaded with arms until the authorities were ready to receive it. But in mid-October, when further outbreaks brought a second visit, Read found that revolution had taken place, that the Grand Duke had fled, and that when the provisional government had taken office amid the plaudits of the populace the only foreign flag displayed had been that of the United States.[8]

[7] Despatches, Sardinia: Wickliffe to Sec. of State, 8 November 1847; Niles to Sec. of State, 16 June 1848, 2 July 1848. Squadron Letters: Read to Sec. of Navy, 29 March 1848, 20 May 1848, 9 June 1848, 20 June 1848. Confidential Letters: Sec. of Navy to Read, 24 July 1848. H. R. Marraro, "Spezia: An American Naval Base, 1848-68," 7 *Military Affairs*, 202-8.

[8] Squadron Letters: Read to Sec. of Navy, 20 June 1848, 22 July 1848, 29 July

In the north the war with Austria had been halted by an August armistice. In the south the Neapolitans were preparing the reconquest of Sicily. Elsewhere on the Italian checkerboard complications continued. Venice still held out, and while a Venetian request to Nathaniel Niles, the American minister to Piedmont, for a warship to break the Austrian blockade had been evaded, *Taney* and *Princeton* had visited the city and it was rumored that salutes had been exchanged and an American consul installed. At Vienna, a report that an American warship had supplied the Venetian rebels excited apprehension; warned that the Austrian Navy would sink the next such ship, William Stiles, the American chargé, jauntily replied that they were welcome to do so if they could catch her. Hearing at Leghorn of the outbreak of radical insurrection in the Papal States, Engle considered taking *Princeton* to Civitavecchia "to receive the Pope, if [he] should desire to take refuge on board a ship of war." But the belief that *Princeton* drew too much water to enter that port forced him "to relinquish his laudable and humane intention," and Pius fled instead to Neapolitan territory.[9]

Winter brought comparative calm, but by early 1849 all Italy was again in ferment: as one officer wrote, "in fact we are all seated upon a volcanoe." In February the killing of an American citizen and interference with American shipping led to the dispatch of *Jamestown* to Palermo; on his arrival Commander Mercer saluted the revolutionary authorities and was rewarded, upon landing, with "loud huzzahs for the Americans and death to the King of Naples," and "with vivas of an immense crowd of Sicilian democrats." All this could only increase his sympathy with the cause of Sicilian freedom, and as his sympathy grew so did his optimism. But alas, Palermo fell in May, and the next call upon the squadron for service in the south was for a ship to support American damage claims against the royal government at Naples.[10]

1848, 10 August 1848, 1 September 1848, 27 September 1848, 14 October 1848. Confidential Letters: Sec. of Navy to Read, 28 October 1848.

[9] Despatches, Sardinia: Niles to Sec. of State, 27 September 1848. Squadron Letters: Read to Sec. of Navy, 1 September 1848, 27 September 1848, 17 February 1849. Robertson, *Revolutions of 1848*, p. 393. Some Americans saw in the flight of the Pope the fulfillment of prophecy; others urged that he be invited to the United States. H. R. Marraro, *American Opinion on the Unification of Italy* (New York, 1932), pp. 55-58.

[10] Squadron Letters: Bolton to Sec. of Navy, 18 February 1849; Engle to Sec. of Navy, 28 February 1849; Mercer to Sec. of Navy, 24 March 1849; Gwinn to Sec. of Navy, 20 May 1849.

In January 1849 Commodore Read returned to the United States. Two months later, the death of Read's relief and the movement of *Constitution* to the Levant again left Engle senior officer in the western basin. Felicitating himself on the policy of strict neutrality, which had kept for America "the respect of both parties, which neither England nor France can boast," he had written to the Department that "the great point to be observed is the law laid down by Mr. Monroe, 'we will not meddle in your affairs, nor shall you in ours.'" But his troubles were not yet over. A letter from Niles at Turin warned of an imminent renewal of hostilities, and on 12 March Piedmont denounced the armistice. On the 31st Engle reported that Austrian victory had been followed by abdication of the Piedmontese king and by disorder throughout the kingdom, and that the Genoese, outraged by the course of events, would in all probability declare a republic. Shortly the citizens of that city did create a provisional government, headed by General Giuseppe Avezzana, who after fighting for freedom in Spain and Mexico had become a citizen of the United States, and who had left his family and business in New York to strike a blow for the liberty of his native land. But the Austrians arrived, the Genoese were suppressed, and the revolutionary leaders were forced to flee. For these fugitives from resurgent reaction, ships flying the flag of freedom offered a very eligible refuge: by mid-April *Princeton* had reached Leghorn with General Avezzana and a number of the other principals on board, while *Allegheny*, anchored nearby, sheltered another defeated general.[11]

Only in Tuscany, Venice, and Rome did the revolution still survive. But the first two were threatened by Austrian armies, and on 24 April a French expedition, bent on suppressing the Roman Republic and restoring the Pope, landed at Civitavecchia. An appeal from the American consul at Leghorn, reporting anarchy at his post and the French landing to the southward, found the greater part of the squadron at Spezia, with Captain John Gwinn, now returned from the East with *Constitution*, the senior officer present. Ordering *Taney* and *Princeton* to Civitavecchia to protect the American colony at Rome, Gwinn at once sailed for Leghorn, accompanied by *Allegheny*. With these movements his force was fully committed.

[11] Squadron Letters: Engle to Sec. of Navy, 27 March 1849, 31 March 1849, 7 April 1849, 17 April 1849. Despatches, Sardinia: Niles to Sec. of State, 22 February 1849, 14 April 1849.

Reports of piracy in the Archipelago and calls from Piedmont, Constantinople, and Alexandria could no more be answered than could the suggestion of Niles at Turin that a ship in Venetian waters "would certainly give a moral strength to the struggling cause of freedom and independence without subjecting us to the charge of illegal interference." On 8 May, reporting his movements, Gwinn observed that if things did not quiet down he would need more ships.

Already the refugee problem had developed at Genoa; at Leghorn, with the Austrian attack on the city, it reappeared in aggravated form. With a party of officers and seamen Gwinn garrisoned the United States consulate, where he found, at the last, "everyone who had been prominent in the city" flying for safety to the American flag. Ashore, the Stars and Stripes sheltered three hundred fugitives, including the Bishop of Leghorn and a number of priests; an American merchant ship at the mole was crowded with men, women, and children, as was *Allegheny*, while *Constitution*, anchored further out, also had some prominent revolutionaries aboard. Despite the plentiful possibilities for trouble, things worked out surprisingly well: hearing indirectly that the Austrian general preferred not to find people he would have to shoot, Gwinn openly sent the refugees to Corsica in *Allegheny*, with passports issued by the French and American consuls.[12]

At Civitavecchia, in the meantime, Engle had gone ashore from *Princeton*, passed through the French lines, and entered Rome. There a considerable American colony had assisted at the stirring events of the previous months. Feeling that "this cause is OURS, of all others," its most vocal member, Margaret Fuller Ossoli, had worked in the hospitals and, while conceding that her government could not interfere, had repeatedly urged American individuals to help by contributions of cannon or money. On his arrival at Rome, where General Avezzana, now minister of war of the Roman Republic, had revived resistance by bringing Garibaldi into the city, Engle reaped the reward of his earlier actions: anxious "to return the attentions which I had shown him at Genoa," Avezzana proved helpful in providing horses and passes for the evacuation of American ladies. But the issue of the siege was not long in doubt. By the time *Princeton* sailed, on 19 May, the French had 25,000 men ashore,

---

[12] Despatches, Sardinia: Niles to Sec. of State, 22 February 1849. Squadron Letters: Gwinn to Sec. of Navy, 8 May 1849, 14 May 1849, 20 May 1849.

and although the American squadron was no longer involved, other Americans were. As the French advanced on Rome, the American consul assisted the flight of numerous republican leaders by the issuance of passports; by autumn the rumor was current throughout Italy that Garibaldi had made his escape through Spezia with the help of American papers.[13]

A year of European turmoil, with its constant temptation to involvement on the side of freedom, had raised important questions for the American government and for its representatives. No serious difficulties had arisen over the shelter given refugees, although the large number of passports issued by American consuls was for some years to remain a minor nuisance. But recognition was another matter. Richard Rush had gambled and won, but the action of the consul at Palermo had been disavowed by the government. Concern in Washington over these matters had led to consultation between the State and Navy departments and to the issue, in October 1848, of orders to the squadron to observe a strict impartiality between contending parties and to leave the recognition of new governments up to the authorities at home. Pursuant to these instructions, Engle had reprimanded the commanding officer of *Jamestown* for saluting the revolutionary government of Sicily. Against this criticism Commander Mercer had defended himself with precedents from an earlier Portuguese revolution, but the reproof had nevertheless been effective: in the last days of Sicilian resistance, while energetic in keeping Americans safe from harm, he refused requests for shelter from both the commander and the chief of staff of the revolutionary army.

In July 1849, with the arrival of Commodore Charles W. Morgan, the new policy was spelled out in cruising orders to Captain Gwinn. The Monrovian distinction between Europe and the outer world was emphasized: on the African coast, in the Archipelago, and in the Levant there was to be a forward policy, and pirates, freebooters, and slavers would be seized and turned over to the proper authorities; on the Continent, by contrast, although American interests were to be protected, all interposition between contending parties was forbidden, no individuals were to be given passage between

[13] M. F. Ossoli, *At Home and Abroad* (Boston, 1856), pp. 248-49, 361-98, 410-21; Henry James, *William Wetmore Story and His Friends* (Boston, 1903), I, 133-57. Squadron Letters: Engle to Gwinn, 13 May 1849, 24 May 1849; Morgan to Sec. of Navy, 24 September 1849. The father of Franklin Roosevelt is reputed to have campaigned briefly with Garibaldi in 1848-49.

places at war or in revolt, and neutrality was to be strictly preserved.[14]

No sooner were the orders issued than they were violated. Under pressure from the Chargé d'Affaires at Naples, Gwinn took *Constitution* to Gaeta, where, with the republicans in the interior still resisting the French, he received on board and entertained with full honors the Pope, with his attending cardinals, and the King of Naples. So outraged was the Commodore, on hearing of the twenty-one-gun salutes given these heads of reaction, that he recommended the immediate transfer of *Constitution* to the Brazil station; and for some time echoes of this cannonade ran about the capitals of Europe in puzzling rumors of the American attitude toward European affairs and of American support for the status quo.

The status quo, in any case, was winning. The Sicilians were put down and Venice fell to the Austrians. In Hungary the revolutionaries were defeated. In France, in place of the federal system urged by Rush, there developed a conservative resurgence under Louis Napoleon. By October 1849 the revolutionary complications were over and a new cause of tension had developed when diplomatic relations with France were broken as result of the behavior of the French minister to the United States, the same Guillaume Tell Poussin who had worked with Rush to gain American recognition. Alert to the situation, Morgan in the Mediterranean was keeping his squadron concentrated and in readiness for a sortie into the Atlantic. But his reports urged the Department to feel no apprehension for his safety unless a greater power than France should intervene, and his expressions of hope that the squadron could be strengthened were motivated not by the threat of France but by the incalculable moral effects which resulted from the showing of the American flag in the Mediterranean.[15]

For the United States Navy the complications of 1848 were not limited to the Mediterranean. On the northern shore of the European peninsula there also developed possibilities of involvement, as the German revolutionary movement excited enthusiasm both in America and in Americans on the spot. The American minister to

[14] Confidential Letters: Sec. of Navy to Read, 28 October 1848; Sec. of Navy to Morgan, 31 May 1849. Squadron Letters: Mercer to Sec. of Navy, 1 June 1849; Morgan to Gwinn, 25 July 1849.

[15] Squadron Letters: Morgan to Sec. of Navy, 4 September 1849, 29 September 1849, 29 October 1849, 15 November 1849. Beckles Willson, *America's Ambassadors to France, 1777-1927* (London, 1928), pp. 234-35; Henry Blumenthal, *A Reappraisal of Franco-American Relations, 1830-1871* (Chapel Hill, N.C., 1959), pp. 12, 77-79.

Prussia had early requested the dispatch of a warship, and in October 1848 the U. S. S. *St. Lawrence*, Captain Hiram S. Paulding, dropped anchor at Bremerhaven. This visit was interpreted by the Germans as evidence of fraternal republican feeling, and the ship's officers received an enthusiastic welcome ashore. Before the month was out there came a request from the Frankfurt Assembly for an American naval officer to serve as admiral of the proposed new German Navy, and an expression of a desire to purchase warships in the United States.

Although a Piedmontese attempt to buy arms in America had been earlier discountenanced by the government, the German request for an American admiral was sympathetically received. Secretary of State Buchanan, Secretary of the Treasury Walker, Secretary of the Navy Mason, and Attorney General Toucey all supported the idea. But Polk doubted the constitutionality of compliance, and Captain Paulding's dispatches from Germany were pessimistic as to the prospect of liberal success. Some limited response seemed nevertheless desirable, so in December 1848 Commodore Foxhall A. Parker was placed on leave and sent to Germany to investigate.

There the first thrust of reform had ended and the drift to confusion had begun. Conferences with the King, with officials at Frankfurt, and with the German Naval Board showed small prospect of effective action. The German Navy had but the barest existence even on paper, and no preparations had been made to resist a threatened Danish blockade. Although the plans of the Frankfurt Assembly called for the acquisition of some forty ships and the employment of an equivalent number of American naval officers, Parker saw little chance of creditable service and doubted that any of his countrymen would accept.

Once again the United States had led the nations in the recognition of a new government, and the receipt of Parker's report in early 1849 coincided with the arrival of a minister plenipotentiary from the new Germany. Among the first of the Minister's official acts was a request for the assignment of an American naval officer to select, fit out, and command a steam frigate for the German Navy. Again the request was partly met: the German was provided with information on naval organization and administration, and Commodore Matthew C. Perry was detailed to assist him. With Perry's advice, the mail packet *United States* was purchased; under his supervision and with the assistance of the Brooklyn Navy Yard the ship was fitted out, her upper deck removed, and two 10-inch and four 8-inch guns installed.

But the period of cooperation was brief. In March 1849, as the delegates at Frankfurt were painfully completing their constitution, a change of government at Washington put an end to the policy of limited aid. With the ideologists of expansion out of office and the more conservative Whigs in power, the orders to Perry and to the navy yard were revoked, and, following a Danish protest, the German minister was advised that the *United States* could not sail unless bond were given not to use her against Denmark.

Despite all difficulties, sail she did. Bond was given, and on 30 May the ship set forth, commanded by an American merchant skipper and carrying a former captain of the Revenue Service and three junior naval officers who had been recruited for service in the German Navy. After hanging up for six hours on South Nantucket Shoal, the *United States* completed her crossing, to reach England in mid-June and Bremerhaven in mid-August, where she was rechristened *Hansa*.

Little came of the enterprise. Although the National Assembly had planned for forty ships, the navy of the Germanic Confederation never acquired more than a dozen. Although they had hoped for an American admiral, the Germans were forced to settle for a compatriot with some experience in the American merchant marine and in the Greek Navy. Some slight evidence of official American interest continued, and in the summers of 1849 and 1850 *St. Lawrence* was again sent to cruise the Baltic. But the American officers drifted away, and when, after three years of inactivity, the navy of the Germanic Confederation was dissolved in 1852, only two of them were still in service.[16]

2. Kossuth and Koszta

In notable contrast to the nations of western Europe, Turkey in 1848 had remained quiet. In August of that year the American minister justified an eight-months' silence with the observation that noth-

---

[16] Despatches, Sardinia: Niles to Sec. of State, 25 August 1848. J. G. Gazley, *American Opinion of German Unification* (New York, 1926), pp. 22-25; A. J. May, *Contemporary American Opinion of Mid-Century Revolutions in Central Europe* (Philadelphia, 1927), pp. 16-32; G. W. Allen (ed.), *Papers of F. G. Dallas* (New York, 1917), pp. 58-94, 150-61; M. M. Quaife (ed.), *Diary of James K. Polk* (Chicago, 1910), III, 47, 56, 169-71; D. W. Knox, *History of the United States Navy* (New York, 1948), pp. 181-82.

ing had been happening in his territory, and that he assumed there had been plenty of correspondence from distracted Europe. But by the summer of 1849 the backwash of revolution had come to affect the Ottoman Empire.

Beyond the Balkan frontier, the events of 1848 had shaken the Habsburg realms. Under the leadership of Louis Kossuth, Protestant as well as patriot, the Hungarians had won a grant of self-government. But the effective suppression of revolutionary agitation at Vienna, and success in Italy and in putting down the Czechs emboldened the reactionary party. Early in 1849 Austrian armies invaded Hungary.

Hungarian resistance to alien rule, reminiscent of the American and Greek revolutions, excited sympathy in the United States; the proclamation of a Hungarian republic did more. Chary though the Whigs had been of assisting the German Navy, the appeal of this issue to popular feeling gave it irresistible force. In June 1849, on the suggestion of a Hungarian resident in New York, powers of an unprecedented nature were issued to a roving diplomat, A. Dudley Mann, who was instructed to proceed to the scene of action and, at his discretion, to recognize the new Hungarian government and negotiate a treaty of amity and commerce. Analogous in many respects to the earlier instructions to Somerville at the time of the Greek revolution, these were yet different in two important ways: they were vastly broader, and they leaked.[17]

At Constantinople, as at home, events in Hungary excited American sympathy and American hopes. In August, John Porter Brown reported the continued success of Hungarian arms and the arrival of Count Andrassy as envoy to the Sublime Porte. But liberal optimism was to be disappointed. Mann never reached Hungary, the Czar intervened against the revolutionaries, and Brown's dispatch was penned on the very day that a defeated Kossuth and his surviving colleagues fled across the border into Turkey. All resistance had ended, and while in Hungary the Habsburg authorities busied themselves with barbarous reprisals, the Sultan found himself pressed by both Russia and Austria for the surrender of the refugees.

Failure of the cause served only to stimulate American support. From Paris, on 22 September, a group of sixteen Americans forwarded to the legation at Constantinople an expression of their

---

[17] Gazley, *German Unification*, pp. 55-59; M. E. Curti, "Austria and the United States, 1848-1852," 11 *Smith College Studies in History*, 152-67.

concern. Included among the signers of this letter were George N. Sanders, who a year earlier had helped at the barricades and had received an ovation at the Hôtel de Ville; Thaddeus P. Mott, a son of the famous surgeon, fresh from the campaign in Sicily; and Samuel Colt, the inventor of the revolver. Strongly praising the Sultan's action in receiving the Hungarians, the Americans compared Kossuth to Washington and emphasized his right to sanctuary. Observing that the defense of republican refugees was "peculiarly the task of an American minister," they urged the legation to go to any length in offering the fugitives the shelter of our fleet and in supporting the Sultan "with every possible assurance that if he is attacked, the U.S. will have the power to sustain him, and will do it."

At the Ottoman capital, Carr had received his recall, his successor had not arrived, and Brown, ever forward in the cause of freedom, was in charge. Already he had made contact with the Hungarians and had provided them with passports: when Count Andrassy left Constantinople for England in November he traveled as Herbert Neuman, a native of Switzerland en route to the United States. Already, too, Brown had attempted to stiffen the Turks in their defense of the refugees, an effort in which he was assisted by newspaper reports, perhaps inspired from Paris, that the United States was prepared to commit the Mediterranean Squadron. Soon Samuel Colt arrived from Paris, to encourage the Chargé's efforts and to attempt to advance his own. Presented to the Seraskier and assured that the Sultan had been deeply touched by the Paris letter, Colt profited to the extent of an order for five thousand revolvers and the present of a snuffbox set with diamonds. In January 1850, reporting on the internment of Kossuth and his party and on the Hungarians' desire to visit Europe and the United States, Brown suggested to the Department that he be authorized to intercede privately for the freedom of "the noblest, yet the most unfortunate Patriot of his Times."[18]

At home, in the meantime, excitement had developed in a fashion reminiscent of the 1820's, and the old philhellene faces and rhetoric were again in evidence. The return from Italy of General Avezzana and of Garibaldi had stirred the people, and when Congress met in December the growing resentment of Austrian atrocities brought forth resolutions for the suspension of diplomatic relations. Amid the rising clamor the government, in January 1850, instructed George

[18] Despatches, Turkey: Brown to Sec. of State, 17 August 1849, 19 December 1849, 15 January 1850.

P. Marsh, the new minister to Turkey, to intercede on behalf of the Hungarian refugees and to offer them passage to America in a national ship and "a retreat under the American flag."

At Constantinople, Brown had already worked to limit the Hungarians' term of internment, and had supported his arguments at the Porte with extracts from presidential remarks and congressional speeches. In correspondence with Kossuth he had expounded, in elevated tones and on his own initiative, the desires of "the Country of Washington [to have] the Honor and Glory of receiving a Kossuth." Arriving at his post in February 1850 in the steam frigate *Mississippi*, Marsh held the ship in the Bosporus for some weeks in the hope that the Hungarians might be embarked. But the Porte, unable to obtain Austrian and Russian consent to the release of the refugees, felt obliged to retain the principal revolutionaries for a period of perhaps a year.[19]

Stimulated by the arrival of fugitives from European tyranny, by the publication of Mann's reports, and by President Taylor's statement that recognition of Hungary would assuredly have been forthcoming had the revolution been successful, American enthusiasm had lasted out the summer. In September, information on the condition of the refugees in Turkey, derived from dispatches from Constantinople, was communicated to the Congress. Neither the activity abroad nor the excitement at home eased relations with the Austrian Empire. At Turin the American chargé was told by the Austrian envoy that the American squadron "had become, if not designed so to be, the receptacle of fugitives from justice & that its presence might therefore be regarded as offensive to the countries bordering on that sea." At Washington the Austrian representative, the Chevalier Hülseman, submitted a bitter protest against American unneutrality. The result was Webster's famous letter, based on a draft by the former philhellene Edward Everett, which defended the Mann mission, expounded American affection for republican forms, and animadverted on the inferior patch of ground presided over by the Habsburg dynasty.

The hurrahs that greeted the publication of the Webster-Hülseman correspondence brought the Hungarian patriot again to the fore.

[19] Marraro, *American Opinion*, pp. 165-69. Instructions, Turkey: Sec. of State to Marsh, 12 January 1850. Despatches, Turkey: Brown to Sec. of State, 18 February 1850; Marsh to Sec. of State, 14 March 1850, 25 March 1850. In the course of this visit *Mississippi* passed the Bosporus, to become the first American warship to enter the Black Sea. Squadron Letters: Long to Sec. of Navy, 10 March 1850.

In February 1851, Senator Foote of Mississippi introduced a joint resolution to encourage the President to bring Kossuth to America in a naval ship. The moment found John Porter Brown in the United States on a special mission; six days later, in reply to a query from Webster, he summarized the Turkish aspects of the situation and urged that *Mississippi* be ordered back to Constantinople. While the joint resolution awaited House action, Webster, in an eloquent dispatch, instructed Marsh to renew the effort to obtain the freedom of Kossuth, and advised him that the government would provide a national ship to remove the Hungarians from the gloomy continent of Europe. On 4 April, after further prodding by Brown, orders went out from the Navy Department to the squadron commander.[20]

With Brown in the United States and with Marsh, the new minister, absent on a visit to Egypt, the conduct of the Constantinople legation had devolved on Henry A. Homes, for fifteen years a member of the Armenian mission, who had recently assumed the post of assistant dragoman. In January 1851, Homes had given passports for America to 270 Poles. In February, reporting diminished Austrian resistance to the liberation of the refugees, he suggested that a visit to Smyrna by an American naval vessel might bring the release of the Hungarians. By early April he had private information from Brown that *Mississippi* would be ordered in his direction; before Webster's instructions arrived he had so informed Commodore Morgan, had requested a firman for the ship to pass the Dardanelles, and was in correspondence with Kossuth.

The popular excitement in the United States, the statements of the President and other politicians, and the intervention of the government on behalf of the Hungarian Washington had echoed throughout Europe. Soon Webster's instructions became general knowledge. All this resulted in a heavy commitment of American prestige to the effort to bring Kossuth to the New World. Yet there were problems. In April, Homes reported his suspicion that the Hungarians, wishing to maintain contact with European revolutionary movements, would prefer to go to England or France; in May he suggested that their stated eagerness to visit the United States might be merely a ruse to shorten their captivity. Writing to Commodore Morgan, he

---

[20] Gazley, *German Unification*, pp. 59-60; May, *Mid-Century Revolutions*, pp. 53-73. Despatches, Sardinia: Kinney to Sec. of State, 21 December 1850. Despatches, Turkey: Brown to Sec. of State, 23 February 1851, 1 April 1851. Confidential Letters: Sec. of Navy to Morgan, 4 April 1851.

expressed fears that should *Mississippi* be delayed, either the Turks would embark the refugees upon an English steamer or Austria and Russia would bring renewed pressure on the Porte to deprive "the cause of liberty of the prestige that would be gained for it by the transportation of these rebels in the public vessels of our Republic." On his return to Constantinople in late July, Brown warned the State Department of British competition for the possession of Kossuth, and of his expectation that a British steamer would arrive with an invitation to take refuge in England.[21]

This obstacle, at least, did not develop, and on 30 August *Mississippi* reached Constantinople. On 6 September, Marsh advised Captain Long of the release of the Hungarians and of arrangements for their embarkation; in view of Kossuth's patent desire to visit England, he urged the greatest speed of movement to the United States. Next day the frigate dropped down the Dardanelles to receive, on the 10th, a total of fifty-five refugees, brought down by Turkish steamer under the escort of the dragoman Homes.

Like other great men, revolutionary heroes are often easier to deal with in contemplation than in action, and the need for speedy movement of this touchy cargo was quickly confirmed. The intent of the government at Washington had been to receive the Hungarians as immigrants to the land of the free, but the revolutionaries themselves had other ideas. At Smyrna, where the arrival of the frigate caused a considerable commotion, three of the passengers left the ship; as *Mississippi* steamed westward through the Mediterranean it quickly became apparent that the planning for the next spring's revolutions called for a meeting between Kossuth and Mazzini and for other preparatory measures. Arriving at Spezia to coal, the ship was at once surrounded by boats bearing bands of music and crowded with admirers, whose calls for the Magyar hero were gratified by an inflammatory speech. For three days Kossuth engaged in acerbic correspondence with Commodore Morgan, complaining of his treatment and insisting upon a visit to England before proceeding to America. As tension on board the warship grew, as excitement among the people increased, and as the Piedmontese government became increasingly concerned, *Mississippi* broke off her half-completed coaling and sailed for Marseilles.

[21] Despatches, Turkey: Homes to Sec. of State, 18 February 1851, 5 April 1851, 25 April 1851, 5 May 1851; Brown to Sec. of State, 24 July 1851, 25 August 1851. Squadron Letters: Morgan to Sec. of Navy, 29 April 1851, 28 May 1851, 15 July 1851.

At Marseilles things grew worse. Such was the excitement produced by the presence of Kossuth that the authorities revoked his permission to land. At the anchorage the revolutionary dialogue continued as conventions of boats surrounded the ship, their passengers bringing garlands and singing the Marseillaise, while Kossuth replied with oratory. In the city, great public demonstrations developed; on board ship, the increasingly contentious Hungarians accused Captain Long of being a worse jailer than the Turks. But at last coaling was completed and the voyage resumed. And although Kossuth and his family did debark at Gibraltar for a trip to England, the ordeal of *Mississippi*'s crew continued until 10 November, when the frigate finally reached New York and discharged the remainder of the refugees.[22]

The release of the Hungarians, the arrival of *Mississippi*, and the impending appearance of Kossuth brought further excitement to the American scene. Questions as to the proper reception of the illustrious Magyar were raised by President Fillmore in his message to Congress, and a formal reception was voted by that body. On his arrival by British packet at New York Kossuth received a wild welcome, and there followed two weeks of entertainment at the national capital. This period was enlivened by a dinner at which Webster, stimulated by champagne, called for Hungarian independence, and looked forward with anticipation to seeing "our American model upon the Lower Danube and on the mountains of Hungary," an effusion which resulted in another protest from the Austrian chargé and that individual's temporary retirement from the country.

Leaving the seat of government, Kossuth next proceeded on a grand tour of the United States, west to St. Louis, downstream to New Orleans, east to Atlanta and Charleston, and north again to New England and New York. The tour was certainly interesting, and indeed, in many respects, a triumph. But despite the Kossuth beards and Kossuth hats, despite the jewelry contributed by emotional females and the vogue for Hungarian music and dances, enthusiasm was neither unanimous nor limitless. The presence of the revolutionary had again posed the question of American intervention on behalf of freedom overseas, and many were having second thoughts.

[22] Squadron Letters: Morgan to Sec. of Navy, 25 September 1851, 7 October 1851. Despatches, Sardinia: Kinney to Sec. of State, 27 September 1851.

Kossuth, at least, had been consistent. In a letter to Homes, written during his Anatolian internment, he had added to an emotional recital of his wrongs a long discussion of American abstention. Sensible while the nation was young, this policy was no longer necessary now it had become a giant. Should the United States still wish to uphold the cause of freedom it would be impossible, "even if she should desire it, not to put a weight into the balance where the destinies of the Old World and its civilizations are to be weighed; it will scarcely be possible not to give anything more to the sufferings of nations than sentiments of sympathy, commiseration to the fallen, and 'a salaam to oppressed humanity' as your Jefferson said." His actions while a passenger in *Mississippi*, his behavior in England, and his speeches in the United States had followed in this vein. But his attempt to commit the President to an official expression of concern was turned aside; Webster on the whole behaved discreetly; no progress was made with Clay. The Congress was divided on the issues and the tour made clear the existence of wide regional differences of attitude. In the South, where freedom had a double meaning, the reception tended to be cool. In the North, and especially in New England, it was warm indeed, yet even there tension developed when Kossuth declined to commit himself on the domestic institution of slavery. Throughout the American visit, the clearer the appeal for involvement the clearer was the negative reaction. As in the debate over intervention in Greece a generation earlier, so at mid-century: the United States would sympathize; it would not intervene. Well-wisher to the liberty of all, America remained as John Quincy Adams had described her, vindicator only of her own.[23]

That she would indeed vindicate her own was forcefully demonstrated, a year after the departure of Kossuth, in the case of another refugee. Hungarian by birth and a participant in his country's revolution, Martin Koszta had proceeded by way of England to the United States, had declared his intention of becoming an American citizen, and had subsequently returned to the Levant. At Smyrna, on 21 June 1853, Koszta was seized by armed men while walking

---

[23] Gazley, *German Unification*, pp. 60-70; May, *Mid-Century Revolutions*, pp. 86-114. Despatches, Turkey: Homes to Sec. of State, 5 June 1851. The Barbary wars, as well as the revolutions of 1848, had their echoes in the slavery controversy: in *Uncle Tom's Cabin* (1852), Chapter xvii, Mrs. Stowe explicitly compared the escaping slave, George Harris, to "a Hungarian youth"; in "Derne" (1850), Whittier equated enslavement in Tripoli with enslavement in the United States, and Eaton with the abolitionists.

on the quay; thrown into the harbor, where a boat lay in waiting, he shortly found himself a prisoner on board the Austrian brig of war *Hussar* and the center of a growing storm. The European population of the town was enraged by the seizure: officers from the Austrian brig were set upon, and Edward S. Offley, third of his family to hold the post of American consul, was called upon to intervene. On the next day, by fortunate chance, the United States sloop of war *St. Louis* entered port. Advised of what had passed, Commander Duncan N. Ingraham visited the Austrian ship to inquire into Koszta's status. On the 24th, Offley wrote to Constantinople for instructions in the case.

There, in the absence of the Minister, John Porter Brown learned of the outrage on 26 June, and at once began to act. Redress was not to be expected from the Porte: seventeen years earlier, in the case of the *Banian*, protests against the French seizure had drawn only the reply that the Turks did not feel answerable for the behavior of Europeans within their jurisdiction. On the 27th, therefore, Brown wrote two letters, one to Offley at Smyrna, approving Koszta's claim to protection and asking the continuation of efforts on his behalf, and the second to the Austrian internuncio, demanding the Hungarian's release. The reply of the Austrian, dated the 27th and contending that the seizure was legal under existing treaties, was not received until the 29th, a delay which Brown thought intended to cover the transmission of orders to Smyrna to embark Koszta on the Austrian steamer for Trieste. But the scheme, if such it was, miscarried.

At Smyrna, having learned of the plan to ship Koszta out, Commander Ingraham asked the Austrian commander to defer action until word from Constantinople was received, and emphasized his request by shifting his anchorage to a position close to the brig and the waiting mail steamer. News of this action, reported to the capital, brought a protest from the Austrian internuncio on 3 July. But events at Smyrna had by that time outrun discussion.

On the 28th, Brown had sent Ingraham a copy of his protest to the Internuncio, together with a dispatch in which he reported general indignation at the brutal conduct of the Austrians, regretted that Koszta had not been taken out of the Austrian brig, stated that such action would have "much pleased" the Porte, and suggested that Ingraham take Koszta and let the governments argue the case. This forceful stand was backed up by a letter from a traveling navalist congressman, Caleb Lyon of New York, which urged Ingraham not to miss the chance "to acquit yourself nobly and do honor to our Country. . . . The eyes of nations are upon the little St. Louis and her Commander. For Godsake and the sake of humanity stand for the right." Although both Ingraham and Offley entertained doubts about Koszta's right to protection, these effusions did the trick.

Early on the morning of 2 July, Ingraham again went aboard *Hussar*, to present her commander with the choice of releasing the Hungarian or having him taken by force: "An answer to this demand, will be returned by four O'clock p.m." While both ships cleared for action, Offley proceeded to the Austrian consulate, where, after acrimonious debate, it was agreed to place Koszta in the custody of the French consul general pending a settlement between the Austrian and American governments. To "show his spite to the last," the Austrian consul landed the prisoner in chains, but the Frenchman had them immediately struck off. In the town the excitement "was very great. An immense concourse of people were present on his landing, and Vive l'Amérique and our gallant officers who saved Costa from Austrian barbarity was in the mouths of all present, and the heartfelt thanks of all the European Population has been given to our Country on this occasion."

Civis Americanus had been rescued, the flag had been vindicated, and that in the face of superior force. In addition to *Hussar*, the Austrians had a schooner of war and three armed Lloyd's steamers in port, and Ingraham had been outgunned twenty-six to eighteen. Despite his triumph, the naval officer remained a little uncertain as to the propriety of his action: "And now," he wrote to Marsh at Constantinople, "you Gentlemen of the pen must uphold my act as it was done in accordance with Mr. Brown's instructions backed by Mr. Lyon's advice." But only the Austrians were angry. On his return to Constantinople, Marsh supported Ingraham in a long and carefully argued dispatch. Apprised of the affair, the squadron commander, Commodore Silas H. Stringham, gave his entire approval, regretting only that Koszta had not been received on board *St. Louis*. At home, amid cheers from the press and from politicians, both State and Navy departments gave their endorsement. The Porte protested the original seizure to the Austrian government. Every independent newspaper on the Continent was said to have supported the American action, as did the British, who had had their Don

Pacifico: a year later Ingraham received the gift of a chronometer subscribed for by "thousands of the working classes of England."

All summer the unfortunate Hungarian remained in the custody of the French consul general. At Constantinople a compromise settlement was worked out with the Austrians, only to be rejected by Koszta with the support of Consul Offley. There followed an acrid correspondence between Offley and Marsh; the Frenchman began to tire of his boarder. But in due time a solution was reached, and on 14 October Koszta sailed for America on the bark *Sultana* and disappeared from the pages of history.[24]

3. Young America

For none of the Americans in the Mediterranean, private citizens, diplomats, missionaries, or naval personnel, had the years since 1847 lacked excitement. Returning from the Mexican War, the Mediterranean Squadron had found itself at once embroiled in the revolutionary outbreaks of 1848-49. These had been followed by a minor and not wholly edifying dispute with Tunis, settled by a naval visit and by pressure brought to bear through Constantinople. Beset by these complications, Commodore Read had appealed for reinforcements, and the Department had moved to comply. By the end of 1849 Commodore Morgan had under his command the flagship *Independence*, a ship of the line razeed to a two-decker and the largest "frigate" in the world, together with three other frigates, a steamer, a sloop, and a storeship. This force, the new Whig Secretary proudly reported, "is believed to be larger and more efficient than at any previous period in our history, with the exception, perhaps, of the years 1804 and 1805, during the Tripolitan War."[25]

The principal employment of the expanded squadron was in connection with a claims dispute with Portugal which required a visit to Lisbon in the summer of 1850, first to lend weight to an American ultimatum and then, in the face of continuing Portuguese procrastination, to take off the American chargé. But the next year

[24] Despatches, Turkey: Brown to Sec. of State, 28 June 1853, 5 July 1853, 27 July 1853; Marsh to Sec. of State, 7 July 1853, 4 August 1853, 17 August 1853, 14 September 1853, 3 October 1853, 20 October 1853. Squadron Letters: Stringham to Sec. of Navy, 29 July 1853, 2 August 1853, 28 October 1854. Confidential Letters: Sec. of Navy to Ingraham, 19 August 1853; Sec. of Navy to Stringham, 26 August 1853.

[25] Squadron Letters: Read to Sec. of Navy, 1 April 1848; Morgan to Sec. of Navy, 9 August 1849. Despatches, Turkey: Brown to Sec. of State, 25 July 1849, 12 August 1849. Secretary of the Navy, *Annual Report, 1849.*

brought a redeployment. The Cushing Treaty with China, the problem of the new West Coast possessions, and the impending expedition to Japan required a westward movement of naval force, and for the remainder of the fifties the principal concentrations were in Western Hemisphere and Far Eastern waters. But size is not everything. Although no longer a clear-cut frontier between two civilizations, the Mediterranean remained a focus of world diplomacy and the show window of the world's navies; although the squadron's strength was diminished, its command remained the prized reward. A not inconsiderable amount of persuasion was required to induce Commodore Perry to abandon his chance at this assignment for the unlikely prospect of commanding an expedition to attempt the opening of Japan.[26]

Through the fifties the squadron continued to base at Spezia on the Gulf of Genoa. Early in 1852, intimations reached Washington that the Piedmontese government would itself require these facilities; apprised of this possibility while preparing to sail for the Mediterranean, Commodore Stringham asked the legation at Madrid to raise again the question of a depot at Port Mahon or Cartagena. In Spain, where the strategic importance of the Balearic Islands had been recently emphasized by visits from both French and British squadrons, the inquiry occasioned another flurry, and ultimately there came the refusal of a deposit at either place. But the answer required six months, and by that time Piedmontese plans had changed. Five years later the squadron's Spezia warehouses were in fact taken over by the Italians, but the town, averse to the departure of the Americans, provided others, and the depot was continued.[27]

The reduction in squadron strength was matched by no similar reduction in activity. In the years before the guns opened on Fort Sumter, the affairs of Kossuth and Koszta, the Crimean War with its attendant crises, violence and disorder in Syria, war between Italy and Austria, and the unification of the Italian peninsula combined to provide a busy time for ministers and commodores alike. And in these years, moreover, there begins to be heard a new tone in the conduct of American foreign relations: no longer is official con-

---

[26] Squadron Letters: Morgan to Sec. of Navy, 25 June 1850, 16 July 1850. Paullin, *Diplomatic Negotiations*, pp. 251-52.

[27] Squadron Letters: Stringham to Sec. of Navy, 21 September 1852, 31 October 1852; Breese to Sec. of Navy, 9 January 1857, 19 January 1857, 29 January 1857. Mahon Papers, pp. 538-627. Marraro, "Spezia."

tact with the outer world conceived of solely within the framework of the expansion of commerce. Where previous American conflicts had concerned the defense of liberty and the resentment of injury, the war with Mexico had shown the possibilities of the use of power in extending the "area of freedom." Reflected in the triumphantly enlarged Mediterranean Squadron of 1849-50, this understanding was also evidenced in a certain politicizing of thought with regard to foreign problems that was not confined to affairs in Cuba and Nicaragua.

In 1824 General Lafayette had made a triumphant return visit to the United States. Since that time a whole series of visitors—Mar Yohannan, General Avezzana, Garibaldi—had drawn American attention to the march of liberty and progress abroad. The European revolutions, the response of Richard Rush at Paris, the problem of refugees, and the agitation over the liberation of Kossuth had focused this attention, while with the arrival of the Hungarian the question of intervention was injected into politics. In the aftermath of the Mexican War the interventionist argument, based on the increased power of the United States, had a certain plausibility, and while the ultimate decision was adverse, not all preferred the passive part. Remembering his great days in the isles of Greece, Samuel Gridley Howe was willing to accept war in a righteous cause, and by the early fifties a number of Young Americans, sensible of the ancient concern for the linked blessings of commerce and freedom, were prepared to set aside the second half of Washington's Great Rule.

Although the term had enjoyed some earlier use in the press, the program, or at least the ethos, of the Young American movement was first articulated by a southerner, Edwin DeLeon, in a speech at South Carolina College in 1845. Seeing in Young America the incarnation of freedom in the full flush of exulting manhood, unrestrainable by the worn-out powers of the Old World, DeLeon called for increased national feeling as the prerequisite to greatness and glory. Such heightened feeling, together with a somewhat vague desire for action, seems to have been the essence of the doctrine, which in its early years was largely focused on Texas and Oregon. Nourished by the heady triumphs of the war with Mexico and broadened and generalized by the European revolutions of 1848, the Young American attitude reappeared in the debates on the Hungarian revolution. And while some, like William H. Seward, dwelt in traditional terms on the commercial benefits to be anticipated from the establishment of republicanism in Hungary, the newer note was struck by Robert Field Stockton, Democratic senator from New Jersey. Stockton had served with Rodgers in 1812 and later as Hull's flag captain; he had helped design the revolutionary *Princeton* and had been her first commanding officer; he had carried the resolution of annexation out to Texas and had presided over the conquest of California. Now, in the Senate, he urged the use of force on behalf of other republics.[28]

In time, of course, Seward's expansionism would have its chance, but for the moment the movement for an energetic policy was a Young American and Young Democratic one, coalescing about the presidential candidacy of Stephen A. Douglas and led by such energetic southerners as Pierre Soulé and Robert J. Walker. Its name it derived from Mazzinian precedents in Europe, whether by way of the newspapers or by way of DeLeon; its organ was the *Democratic Review*, edited by that same George N. Sanders who had fought on the Paris barricades and had signed the Paris letter to the legation at Constantinople. In the first six months of 1852, the months preceding the meeting of the Democratic convention, Sanders' deep concern with the linked expansion of commerce, liberal institutions, and the Navy formed the burden of the contents of the magazine.

As to earlier generations, so to Sanders, the freedom of commerce was a positive right of mankind, and one with which no government other than a democratic republic could properly interfere. From this there derived the imperative of an American opening of Japan, as well as a heavy emphasis upon the commercial importance of the Levant. The failure of the United States to act in 1848 in the defense of European freedom was criticized; the American obligation to return the favors of Lafayette and Rochambeau was proclaimed; Russian despotism was assailed, and the position of the Ottoman Empire, to which "Europe must gaze for the rise of freedom's cause," endorsed. Calls for governmental reform and for the cleansing broom were accompanied by a heavy attack upon that "fogyism" in the diplomatic service and in the Navy which so fettered the re-

[28] Edwin DeLeon, *The Position and Duties of "Young America"* (Columbia, S.C., 1845). M. E. Curti, "Young America," 32 *American Historical Review*, 34-55; S. F. Riepma, "'Young America': A Study in American Nationalism before the Civil War" (unpublished doctoral dissertation, Western Reserve University, 1939).

public's freedom of action. At one point the program ascended into verse, and while the stanzas of "Young America!" were markedly inferior to the poetry of the Wits, its ultimate aims were much the same.[29]

Ancient and respectable as were these ideas, and stemming from the early days of the republic, the context of mid-century was different and the tone was subtly altered. Where Barlow and Humphreys tended to envision an osmotic spread of Columbia's bliss, the Young Americans called for deeds. DeLeon's speech had emphasized the exulting manhood of the young giant of the West; with talk of stalwart arms and iron hands dealing blows to caitiff kings, the poet of "Young America!" emphasized the virtue of action. But the sectional struggle at home and the approach of the presidential election inhibited support, and Pierce, not Douglas, obtained the nomination.

Although the Young Americans were now relegated to the fringes of politics, their maneuvers and the Democratic victory at the polls caused some concern abroad. There were reports that American arms were being supplied to European revolutionaries; it was whispered that filibustering expeditions were preparing for the Adriatic. Early in 1853, one of the exiled Hungarians was urging the administration to support a new rising in Milan, to side with Turkey against Austria, and to enhance American prestige by the purchase of naval bases at Klek on the Dalmatian coast and at Thera in the Cyclades. The appointment of A. Dudley Mann, erstwhile envoy to revolutionary Hungary, as assistant secretary of state, the rumor that Stockton was to become secretary of the navy, and the known sympathy of Attorney General Cushing with the schemes of Young America added to European worries. Nor did the rapid rise in American naval expenditures which marked the decade of the fifties, or the rumors emanating from Washington that the United States was negotiating for an island in the Archipelago, tend to assuage these fears.

The concern was unnecessary. In America matters of more pressing importance were developing. Mrs. Stowe had published a book, the Nebraska Bill was before the Congress, and shortly Cuba would take the center of the scene. But while the Young America movement now dwindled away at home, the Young American ideology remained evident abroad. In the first months of the Pierce adminis-

---

[29] 30 *Democratic Review*, 319-32, 401-25; 31 *ibid.*, 33-43, 86-87, 160-66.

tration George Sanders enjoyed a brief, conspiratorial tour as American consul in London, in the course of which his house became a resort of the revolutionary international. Edwin DeLeon, who had started it all, became consul general at Alexandria, whence he was soon reporting on the possibility of acquiring a Greek island for use as a naval base. The position of chargé d'affaires at The Hague went to August Belmont, who had gained riches as a banker in New York and respectability through marriage to a daughter of Commodore Perry; appointed in part as a result of Sanders' influence, Belmont espoused a navalist program and was soon writing from his post that both the responsibilities and the security of the United States called for the use of force in support of the republicans of Europe.[30]

This increasingly political approach to the outer world, with its enlarged preoccupation with power, was neither confined to a few appointees of the Pierce administration nor wholly concerned with the subversion of monarchical Europe. When wars in the Crimea and against Austria added to the prestige of Napoleon III, worried American diplomats warned Washington of the Emperor's hatred of republican institutions and of the danger that he might intervene in the New World as the champion of a reactionary Catholicism. In their dealings with the Turks and in the course of efforts to negotiate a Persian treaty, both Whig and Democratic ministers at Constantinople stressed the possibilities of war and the desirability of potential allies. Clearly the question posed by Kossuth from his Anatolian exile and debated by Americans both at home and abroad, of whether the newly powerful United States should not "put a weight into the balance," was a real one. And while the new answer of the Young Americans never quite moved from words to action, there were tremblings on the brink. European wars and revolutions offered continual temptation to embroilment; the flag of freedom remained an inspiration to the oppressed. In 1859 the Circassians, victims of thirty years of Russian expansion, appealed to the American Congress for assistance in the defense of their liberties.[31]

At Constantinople, as the Crimean War approached, America's stand on the side of freedom continued to be made manifest by John

[30] Curti, "Young America"; Riepma, " 'Young America,' " pp. 269-324. Despatches, Alexandria: DeLeon to Sec. of State, 6 July 1854. Instructions, Alexandria: Sec. of State to DeLeon, 19 September 1854.

[31] Despatches, Turkey: Williams to Sec. of State, 8 June 1859, 9 July 1859, 13 September 1859.

Porter Brown. Having earlier attempted to stiffen the Turkish stand on Kossuth, and having forced the issue with the Austrians in the case of Koszta, he now pressed the Porte to hold fast against the overbearing Russians; informing the Turks that his government was not indifferent to abuse of right and that the Sultan would "possess its friendly sympathies," he urged them to resist "the offensive conduct of the Russian ambassador." To the State Department, at the same time, Brown pointed out that Turkey, on the outskirts of Europe, was exposed to the pressures of the great absolutisms. Arguing that "the Government of the U.S. cannot be indifferent to infractions of those Principles of National Right," he urged joining with other liberal and constitutional governments in supporting the Ottoman Empire.

In June 1853, amid the deepening crisis, Commodore Stringham visited Constantinople in his flagship *Cumberland*. On his arrival Brown arranged an audience with the Sultan, at which the squadron commander delivered some remarks in praise of Turkish modernizing and "calculated to impress H.M. with the belief that he possessed the sympathies of the Government and People of the U.S." A few days later, in another long dispatch, Brown emphasized the progress of Turkish reform, which placed the Sultan's government "among the more liberal and constitutional" of the world, and stressed the fact that the cause of Turkey was the cause of all mankind; should the war expand and England become involved in the support of civil and religious liberty, surely the United States also "has a 'Destiny' assigned her by an overruling Providence" which "will not permit her to remain a *silent* Spectator of the struggle."[32]

In October Turkey declared war on Russia. In February 1854, as Anglo-French intervention appeared imminent, the U.S.S. *Saranac* reached Constantinople bringing the new American minister, Carroll Spence. There they found *Levant*, stationed in the Bosporus since the previous autumn, and on the 9th, accompanied by the two commanding officers, Spence called officially upon the Sultan. Emphasizing the beneficent effects of the spirit of progress in their two countries, the American minister went on to affirm the universal desire of the American people for the preservation of the empire which had "so often afforded an asylum to the exiled friends of Liberty," and to express his own hopes that the conflict with the

[32] Despatches, Turkey: Brown to Sec. of State, 10 March 1853, 25 May 1853, 20 June 1853, 25 June 1853.

Czar would develop in accordance with the Sultan's "most sanguine expectations."

In Turkey, at least, this desire and these hopes were shared by American diplomats, naval officers, and missionaries alike. For these last, indeed, Czarist aims with regard to the Holy Places at Jerusalem and the Orthodox Church in Turkey presented a serious threat, and reports were circulating that the Russians, if successful, would expel the Protestant missionaries from the Sultan's dominions. But in the United States the situation was otherwise, and the divergence of opinion between those at home and those in the field is illustrative of the decentralized pressures which affected the making of foreign policy before the telegraph linked the capitals of the world. In America the traditional Anglophobia was strengthened by the tradition of Russian friendship. Numerous congressmen were Russophile and the press was loudly so. Whatever the views of the evangelicals, the Episcopalians, in communion with the Orthodox Church, saw the struggle as one of Cross against Crescent, while for the State Department, another war between Britain and a continental power threatened to raise old questions of freedom of the seas. Although no exception had been taken to Turcophile sentiments in Brown's dispatches or to Stringham's remarks, Spence's report of his audience elicited a reprimand. But the Minister stoutly defended himself, arguing that expansion of the Russian Empire was expansion of the area of despotism and that a triumph of the Greek Orthodox Church would mean the destruction of all other Christian sects in Turkey.[33]

War in the Crimea, in contrast to the events of 1848, drew attention to the east, and so reinforced a tendency discernible since the first excitement about Kossuth. At intervals, it is true, the squadron did move westward. In 1854, revolutionary activity in Spain required visits to Iberian ports; in 1856, tension with Great Britain over Crimean War recruiting and the dismissal of the British minister induced Flag Officer Samuel Breese to sortie his force into the Atlantic. But these events ran counter to the trend. More and more the focus of diplomatic activity and of squadron operations shifted to the Levant; increasingly, attention was concentrated upon the Archipelago, upon the capital of the Grand Turk, and upon the waters of the Black Sea. These, however, were not reached. Both Stringham in 1854 and Breese in 1855 had hopes of passing the Bosporus and

---

[33] Despatches, Turkey: Spence to Sec. of State, 25 February 1854, 29 April 1854.

visiting the theater of operations, but the former was prevented from doing so by Turkish uneasiness resulting from rumors of Russo-American alliance and the latter by engine-room troubles on *Saranac*.[34]

Still, the East remained the center of concern. Whatever the problems of western Europe, in the Mediterranean the tides of change all related to the advance of the European frontier. East and south of this frontier lay societies under pressure and in need of help; in their contacts with these societies Europeans and Americans revealed their contrasting attitudes toward the non-Western world. Not only was the Levant the area of America's greatest missionary commitment; it was also an area in which America's secular contributions seemed likely to have great leverage. In the exertion of this leverage, whether technological or political, the role of the United States Navy remained important, and the eastward deployment of the Mediterranean Squadron did but reflect this fact.

4. Trade, Technology, and Naval Aid

Through the years of political excitement provided by the Mexican War and the European revolutions, men's wants continued to occasion the exchange of goods. Among Americans the Barlovian passion for trade remained lively, the growth of commerce and the spread of technology were still equated with the advance of freedom, and the promotion of commercial opportunity remained the keystone of national policy. No change in tone could be discerned in instructions to diplomats, consular officials, and naval officers, which inevitably adjured them to report on commercial conditions and to work to expand commercial intercourse. Briefly, however, and despite these basic continuities, expansion at home had repercussions overseas, in matters of trade as well as in questions of revolutions and of refugees.

From the time of Ezra Stiles and Timothy Dwight, the prospect of expansion to the Pacific coast, with its promise of engrossing the commerce of the Orient, had glittered in the American imagination. A history of increasing private and governmental interest had culminated in the war with Mexico, in which the strategy of the Polk administration, both diplomatic and military, had been governed by the location of Pacific harbors. Yet even in 1848 there re-

[34] Squadron Letters: Stringham to Sec. of Navy, 10 September 1854; Breese to Sec. of Navy, 5 January 1856.

mained a good deal of the theoretical in these aspirations: the Oregon sea-otter trade was dead, the California hide trade had diminished, and the overland distance between the eastern metropolis and the Pacific coast, whether measured in time or in money, was very great. Suddenly, however, hopes were renewed, as the acquisition of these distant provinces emphasized the need for improved communications, and as the discovery of California gold provided an extraordinary stimulus.

Already there had been some talk of railroads. But with the existing rail system still short of the Mississippi, the West Coast would remain for twenty years most easily accessible by sea. The burden consequently fell upon the merchant marine, and with dramatic results. In 1849 the number of ships clearing the East Coast for California, in previous years a mere handful, rose to 775. Since the passage to California came within the American coastal trade monopoly, the new demand not only stimulated shipbuilding but also forced the withdrawal of tonnage from other routes. In September 1849 a naval officer reported the eastern Mediterranean barren of American merchant ships; in 1850 the commanding officer of *Cumberland* was greeted at Trieste by consular complaints that the demand for California shipping had reduced arrivals at that port.[35]

The greatly increased pressure for access to the Pacific which developed with the conquest of California focused attention on the Central American isthmus. From this attention there resulted, in addition to the activities of diplomats and filibusters, some proposals reminiscent of an earlier time. Before going out to Italy, Nathaniel Niles had formulated a plan for an international commission to develop and administer an isthmian canal with equal opportunity for weak and strong nations. This plan, which he caused to be published in 1849, would have pleased Joel Barlow: together with its emphasis on commerce as the great pacifier, it combined the sacred and secular American missions. The project "so favorable to the rapid extension of Christian civilization throughout the eastern hemisphere, and the opening of so many new and prolific sources of private wealth and general public prosperity, would, in no small degree, serve to divert the excited and distempered popular mind of Europe from the pursuit of those visionary and impracticable po-

---

[35] J.G.B. Hutchins, *The American Maritime Industries and Public Policy, 1789-1914* (Cambridge, 1941), pp. 266-68. Squadron Letters: Mercer to Sec. of Navy, 14 September 1849; Morgan to Sec. of Navy, 1 November 1850.

litical theories, so dangerous to the whole fabric of society, now so prevalent in this part of the world."[36]

But the American shipbuilding industry soon began to catch up with the new demands, and in any event the older trades survived. Despite the impact of revolutions in Europe and gold rush in America, a sizable American commerce continued with the Mediterranean. In the west, American vessels passed the straits to steer for the southern shore of France, for Genoa and Leghorn, and for Sicilian ports. East of the narrows the deliveries of American cotton to Trieste continued to grow, while at Beirut and Jaffa the beginnings of a traffic in olive oil and wool were visible. In various quarters hopes arose that changes in the British navigation laws would facilitate the development of trade with Egypt. With the Crimean War there grew up a considerable commerce with Constantinople, which city by 1855 was seeing the weekly arrival of an American ship bringing rum, sugar, and flour for the armies and a problem of distressed seamen for the diplomats. And finally, the old Smyrna trade remained vigorous, with import-export figures for the decade of the fifties which consistently exceeded those of earlier years.[37]

Both politically and economically the Mediterranean remained in flux. With Europe increasing in vigor and with the Ottoman Empire declining, great changes were in prospect. Like the earlier Syrian Wars, the war in the Crimea assisted the penetration of the Near East by the powers of western Europe. As steamship lines crisscrossed the Mediterranean, the navigation of the Levant became subject first to the Austrians, then to the French, and finally to the British. No longer a clear-cut frontier between civilizations, the Mediterranean was becoming a European lake, and this change in the conditions which had drawn the first Americans would affect the activities of their descendants. Yet if some of the early romantic and speculative appeal was gone, the Levant trade still continued profitable, certain American commodities remained in great demand, and on other counts the United States retained a position in the Near East. The growth of the missionary effort went on apace; the Mediterranean Squadron still cruised the inland sea; American ships still

[36] Despatches, Sardinia: Niles to Sec. of State, 3 June 1849; *National Intelligencer*, 3 August 1849.

[37] J. S. Homans, Jr., *An Historical and Statistical Account of the Foreign Commerce of the United States* (New York, 1857). Despatches, Turkey: Spence to Sec. of State, 5 January 1855; Brown to Sec. of State, 10 October 1854, 9 June 1855.

commanded respect, as did American diplomats and the American policy of detachment.

At Constantinople American representation remained of a high order. Dabney Carr had been raised in the old Jeffersonian school. High-tariff Whig though he was, George P. Marsh had hopes for a great expansion of the Turkey trade and for an increased acceptance of American agricultural and mechanical products. His successor Carroll Spence, bred to commerce as the Maryland son of a hero of the war with Tripoli, saw Constantinople as a promising market for American cottons. The last of the antebellum ministers, James Williams, later to become one of the Confederacy's ablest European agents, laid stress on his country's historic policy of commerce promotion and was hopeful of greatly improving trade. And throughout these years, as ministers came and went, John Porter Brown remained at the Constantinople legation, providing a continuity compounded of old-fashioned patriotism and unsurpassed expert knowledge.

So the commercial link remained, if subtly modified, and so, for that matter, did the activities of the "philanthropic band" in spreading science and technology. Impressed by Mehemet Ali's success in growing cotton in the Nile Valley, the Turkish government in early 1846 formally requested the United States to nominate a planter "to introduce, into [the Sultan's] dominions, the culture of cotton." Despite the fact that it had a war on its hands, the State Department was quick to comply. Engaged to take charge of the Sultan's model farm, Dr. James B. Davis of South Carolina sailed for Turkey in August, followed shortly by his family and by four Negro field hands. Soon J. Lawrence Smith, who had done important work in agricultural chemistry, set forth on the same errand; finding himself in disagreement with Davis over procedural matters, Smith was on the verge of returning home when he was engaged by the Porte as a mining engineer and began a three-year stint investigating the mineral resources of Anatolia and serving as chemist in the imperial ironworks.[38]

The task of the foreign innovator is a delicate one, and success is

[38] Despatches, Turkey: Brown to Sec. of State, 5 January 1846, 22 May 1846, 18 June 1846. Instructions, Turkey: Sec. of State to Brown, 26 March 1846, 14 May 1846, 18 August 1846. J. B. Moore (ed.), *Works of James Buchanan* (Philadelphia, 1909), VI, 400-402, 433-34; VII, 62-63, 236-37. J. Lawrence Smith, *Original Researches in Mineralogy and Chemistry* (Louisville, Ky., 1884), pp. x, xxvii; MacFarlane, *Turkey*, I, 59-63.

often limited. Although Carr had reported in enthusiastic Jeffersonian terms on the Sultan's desire "to draw the principles of the resuscitation of his country from the only pure and healthful source —its *Agriculture*," and had urged the government to present the Turks with implements, machinery, and seeds, difficult problems arose. Dr. Davis' efforts to grow cotton came to nothing, and his attempts to prevent frauds on the government embroiled him with the Armenian bureaucracy. Having lost an eye and with his family sick, with promises unredeemed and his salary in arrears, he gave up after two years and sailed for home. Smith's mining work was more successful: he made some finds of coal, chrome, and emery; he discovered some new mineral substances, one of which he tactfully called "medjidite" after the new Sultan; he had "heaped upon him decorations and costly presents." But he too had troubles with the bureaucracy. His discoveries were not followed up and his movements were restricted, and when his contract expired in 1850 he returned to the United States.[39]

As well as the teachers, there were the salesmen, for whom life was sometimes simpler: that it is easier to sell a device than to inculcate a technique was shown in the visit of Samuel Colt. As early as 1839 an attempt had been made by one of Samuel F. B. Morse's representatives to interest the centralizing Sultan in that most centralizing of inventions, the telegraph. The machine failed to work, and the traveling man drowned in the Danube while en route to Vienna for parts; but in 1847 a successful demonstration was given by Smith, aided by one of the missionaries and by John Porter Brown. Yet while the Sultan was pleased, and sent Morse the inevitable diamond-studded trinket, the pashas, for obvious reasons, united in opposition to the invention, and the telegraph reached Turkey only with the Crimean War.[40]

However unsuccessful in business terms, this demonstration by the scientist, the missionary, and the government official well illustrates the web of American activity in the Levant, and a circular digression

[39] Despatches, Turkey: Carr to Sec. of State, 6 June 1847, 24 October 1848, 14 December 1848, 4 February 1849; Brown to Sec. of State, 14 January 1850. Smith, *Original Researches*, pp. x, xvii, xxix-xxxi; MacFarlane, *Turkey*, I, 62-63; II, 209, 629-39.
[40] Smith, *Original Researches*, p. xxix; M. W. Lawrence, *Light on the Dark River* (Boston, 1854), p. 140; Hamlin, *Among the Turks*, pp. 185-94; S. I. Prime, *Life of S.F.B. Morse* (New York, 1875), p. 411. Despatches, Turkey: Carr to Sec. of State, 24 October 1848.

may serve to emphasize the point. As has been noted, Luther Bradish and Charles Rhind had ties with the New York shipping group, and with Henry Eckford in particular. Eckford had been a naval constructor in the years that Commodore Porter was serving on the Naval Board. At the Constantinople legation, Porter was succeeded by a nephew of that Samuel Smith who, both as merchant and as politician, had played a prominent role in the Navy's first penetration of the Mediterranean and in initiating negotiations for the treaty which brought the Commodore to Constantinople. Porter's own nephew, John Porter Brown, was one of those demonstrating Morse's invention; two other nephews and a brother-in-law held Mediterranean consular posts. The inventor's father, the Reverend Jedidiah Morse, had been one of the founders of the American Board of Commissioners for Foreign Missions; his biographer's brother was both son-in-law and biographer to William Goodell, the missionary. The first missionary explorers at Constantinople had been assisted by Rhind; in later years the entire missionary effort benefited from the subventions of the American Bible Society, of which Luther Bradish, long a supporter, became president in the last year of his life.

Yet to put it this way may do injustice to the naval link, and the enduring impression made by the presence in the Mediterranean of a squadron from the extra-European world. Despite, or perhaps because of, the vigorous policy of Palmerston, the Navy's influence remained important long after the support of Turkey had become a principle of British diplomacy. In 1846 the Capudan Pasha had proposed to send three Turks to America to study naval architecture, and had revived an earlier proposal to place Turkish officers on American warships for training. The visit of *Jamestown* to Constantinople in the autumn of 1849 and the presence of *Mississippi* throughout the following March had kept the American Navy in view. The Capudan Pasha had told Captain Long that the Turkish government was a maritime government, and Marsh, reporting on the visit, had commented that "it is only through our navy, that we can make any direct impression upon the East."

In May 1850, two months after *Mississippi's* departure, Marsh advised the Department, in a dispatch of considerable interest, of his belief that closer Turkish acquaintance with American power and American mechanic skills would effectively promote commercial intercourse, create a demand for the products of industry, and establish relations "which, in the event of a collision between us and any of the Powers of Continental Europe, might be of the most essential service." Since the Turks, despite British opposition, appeared disposed to contract closer relations with the United States, he had induced them to send a naval officer, Amin Bey, to the United States. Should Amin's inspection tour of navy yards, docks, and warships prove successful, much might be accomplished. Believing that the plan would commend itself to the government, Marsh had called upon Lieutenant David D. Porter, the son of the Commodore, to embark the envoy and John Porter Brown in the U.S.S. *Erie* for passage to America.[41]

In September 1850 *Erie* delivered the Ottoman representative at New York. Although shortly to become the victim of a newspaper quarrel and to find himself attacked as an imposter, Amin received a warm welcome. Webster's letter to Hülseman had not yet issued, but hostility to Austrian tyranny was strong and the Sultan's popularity correspondingly high. Despite the lack of prior consultation and the political overtones of Marsh's dispatch, the State Department had given the enterprise wholehearted approval. Cordial attention was attracted by "the first Turk of importance that has visited our shores," the "worthy representative of a humane and magnanimous sovereign." Amin was taken to hear Jenny Lind, the mayor called upon him at the Astor House, and on Sunday, "there being no Mosque in New York," he was given a dinner at the Mansion House and a visit to the Croton waterworks. Proceeding to Washington with his suite, the visitor was tendered a brilliant reception, serenaded by the Marine Band, and presented to the President. The sum of ten thousand dollars was voted by the Congress to defray his expenses and a general order was issued providing that he should receive a thirteen-gun salute and see anything he wished when visiting military establishments.

Then came the grand tour. At Boston, which now effectively monopolized the Turkey trade, the guest was subjected to a series of dinners, was taken to visit the public schools, to Bunker Hill, and to Marshfield to call upon Webster. An inspection of textile factories elicited the observation that "the harems of Lowell are much too large." Then westward from Boston, traveling on passes provided

[41] Despatches, Turkey: Brown to Sec. of State, 7 February 1846, 27 May 1846; Marsh to Sec. of State, 14 March 1850, 20 May 1850. Squadron Letters: Long to Sec. of Navy, 10 March 1850, 12 March 1850.

by railroad and steamship companies and sustained by the hospitality of civic groups, the party proceeded to Cincinnati, Detroit, and Chicago; down the river to New Orleans; east to Pensacola, and back to the capital by way of Charleston, Norfolk, and Annapolis. At Washington, while Congress debated the invitation to Kossuth and Brown urged action on the State Department, Amin attended a fancy-dress ball at which Samuel Colt, ever the salesman, also appeared as a Turk. In April 1851, his introduction to the Republic of the West completed, Amin Bey sailed for home.[42]

While the Turkish officer was touring America, the American minister to the Porte was visiting Egypt. Struck by the similarity between the Nile and America's western waters, Marsh suggested to the Pasha that the Egyptians might profitably send an emissary to study American river steamboats, and American arsenals and dockyards as well. The suggestion was taken up, and in February 1851 the Consul General at Alexandria called upon Commodore Morgan for a warship to transport Admiral Hereddin Pasha to the United States.[43]

This scheme was perforce abandoned when tension developed between Egypt and the Porte. Hereddin never made the voyage. But at Constantinople, if not at Alexandria, Marsh's policy seemed to be bearing fruit. There Brown was reporting repeated thanks from various officers of government for the reception of Amin Bey, and in August 1851 he received in private audience the expression of the Sultan's gratitude for the kindnesses shown his emissary. This cordiality may have eased the final negotiations over the release of Kossuth; on the larger scene Brown saw signs of progress in the evident concern of the British embassy, jealous of the increasingly intimate Turco-American relations and apprehensive for Britain's position as supplier of machinery and mechanics. Further evidence appeared in the Turkish decision to participate in the New York Industrial Exhibition of 1853 and to send, at long last, a minister to the United States.

For the moment, indeed, success seemed to follow success. The

---

[42] Instructions, Turkey: Sec. of State to Marsh, 28 June 1850. Despatches, Turkey: Brown to Sec. of State, 16 September 1850, 29 December 1850, 15 February 1851, 3 March 1851, 16 April 1851. *Congressional Globe*, 31C 1S, pp. 1872-75. Amin's tour is best followed in the files of the *New York Herald*, 13 September 1850-27 March 1851.

[43] Squadron Letters: McCauley to Morgan, 10 February 1851; Morgan to McCauley, 6 March 1851; Morgan to Sec. of Navy, 5 August 1851.

plan to exhibit Turkish products at New York was expanded to include the visit to the United States of an Ottoman steam warship, which would both carry articles for the exhibition and convey the new envoy to his post. An effort by the Americans to secure the Washington appointment for Blacque Bey, son of the French founder of the *Moniteur Ottoman*, the Turkish Empire's first official newspaper, and son-in-law of Dr. Valentine Mott, gained the desired end. In discussion of these plans with Brown, the Minister of Foreign Affairs took pains to expand on the friendly history of Ottoman-American relations, as contrasted with Turkish experience with European governments, and to attribute the difference less to the remoteness of the United States than to its "pacific and just" policy of promoting its own prosperity while refraining from meddling in the affairs of others. But friendship, unfortunately, was not enough. Increasing pressure from Russia, growing Turkish financial embarrassment, and difficulties in Montenegro which imposed new duties upon the Ottoman Navy combined to frustrate the plan. The dispatch of the minister was indefinitely postponed; the warship never sailed. Yet although prevented from exhibiting the products of his empire at New York and from establishing a legation at Washington, the Sultan did appoint a new consul at Boston and presented the government of the United States with a block of Turkish marble for incorporation into the Washington Monument.[44]

A block of marble was something less than Brown and Marsh had hoped for from their effort to develop closer relations. Nor were the immediately ensuing years to prove helpful to their cause. The strains of the Crimean War wholly preoccupied the Turkish government; suspicions of American support of Russia chilled relations; the war and its aftermath imposed upon the Ottoman Empire an increased degree of European tutelage. But this tutelage itself tended to emphasize the virtues of alternative and detached sources of assistance, sources which John Porter Brown did not cease to offer.

With the return of peace these efforts had results. In the autumn of 1857 Marsh's successor, Carroll Spence, advised the State Department of the Sultan's decision to construct a three-decked, screw-

---

[44] Despatches, Turkey: Brown to Sec. of State, 14 June 1851, 24 July 1851, 13 August 1852, 20 November 1852, 11 December 1852, 26 January 1853, 27 April 1853; Brown to the President, 4 August 1851; Spence to Sec. of State, 10 October 1854. Instructions, Turkey: Sec. of State to Brown, 15 February 1853; Sec. of State to Marsh, 5 April 1853; Sec. of State to Spence, 27 July 1854. Squadron Letters: Stringham to Sec. of Navy, 26 December 1852.

propelled ship of the line in the United States, and to send a second and more important Turkish naval person to oversee the work. This decision was the result of prolonged negotiation. In 1856 the Capudan Pasha had approached Brown on the question and for over a year the discussions had continued. These talks had been conducted with the strictest secrecy, in the hope of preventing interference by the British ambassador, Lord Stratford de Redcliffe, who, as Brown observed, was possessed of "English Egotism to no ordinary degree." Models of a screw ship of the line, procured from New York, had convinced the Capudan Pasha; the lack of a diplomatic agent to oversee the construction would be remedied by the dispatch of Vice Admiral Mehmed Pasha, who had commanded the Ottoman flagship in the operations before Sebastopol. Reminding the Department of the secret article in the Treaty of 1830 and of Porter's undertaking which had replaced it, and dwelling on Mehmed's elevated rank, Spence expressed the hope that the visitor would be treated with all consideration.[45]

Accompanied by a naval constructor and an interpreter, the Admiral reached New York in March 1858. Less fortunate than his predecessor in the circumstances of his coming, Mehmed was greeted by a great snowstorm; civic hospitality was tarnished when the New York aldermen overslept the scheduled reception at City Hall; on his arrival at Willard's Hotel in Washington his room was broken into and his luggage ransacked. But New York did give him the freedom of the city and an evening at the theater; in Washington a government distracted by Bleeding Kansas and the Mormon War provided dinner at the White House and an invitation to hunt buffalo on the Red River of the North in company with the Vice President. Among the provincial celebrations which accompanied Mehmed's tour of the navy yards was a great dinner at the Revere House in Boston, at which the principal speaker, Edward Everett, first of the philhellenes and more recently secretary of state, ate his words of thirty years before by unfavorably contrasting the present state of Greece with its condition under Turkish rule.[46]

In May 1858 the Turks expanded their consular representation by the appointment of George A. Porter, another nephew of the Commodore, as consul at Washington. Once again it seemed that rela-

---

[45] Despatches, Turkey: Spence to Sec. of State, 8 November 1857, 16 December 1857; Brown to Sec. of State, 16 December 1857.

[46] *New York Times*, 8-27 March 1858; *New York Herald*, 7-12 March, 27 May 1858. 35C 1S *SR 62*.

tions were drawing closer. But by this time the secret of Mehmed's mission was out and "English Egotism" was making itself felt. In London, British naval constructors brought pressure on the Ottoman ambassador, and a report of their slanders on American ship design and the quality of American naval construction was indignantly communicated to Brown by the Capudan Pasha. Nevertheless, the cordiality shown the Turkish emissary on his American visit had given satisfaction at Constantinople: in his initial audience with the Sultan the new minister, James Williams, affirmed that no similar reception had ever been given the representative of any other country; informed of His Majesty's deep gratification, Williams reported home that judicious measures could greatly improve commercial relations.[47]

Judicious measures were undertaken. Ordered out to take over the Mediterranean Squadron, Flag Officer Élie LaVallette was embarked in the magnificent new steam frigate *Wabash*, 3,200 tons and 40 guns. Instructed to proceed without delay to Constantinople "to enable the Ottoman Government to view one of our finest specimens of Naval architecture," LaVallette reached the capital in October 1858, a month after Mehmed's return. Turkish hospitality to American naval officers had always been generous, but this time the Turks outdid themselves. The Capudan Pasha gave a banquet for officers and diplomats; on the next day all precedent was shattered as the Sultan himself visited *Wabash*. Intended as a mark of respect to President Buchanan in recognition of his kindness in sending the flagship to Constantinople, Abdul Medjid's act so dramatized the presence of the American man-of-war that the European ambassadors protested the visit as a violation of the Treaty of Paris. But the protests were relayed to the American minister with the assurance that *Wabash* could remain as long as was desired.

Both in this European reaction and in the later coolness of certain Turkish officials, Williams thought he detected British handiwork. Observing that this was the first time the presence of an American warship had been protested, he remarked that whatever the reason for closing the straits to the ships of European navies, it could hardly apply to a remote and friendly nation like the United States. In this last comment he was certainly correct, and history gave evidence that Turks as well as Americans considered the United States a

[47] Despatches, Turkey: Brown to Asst. Sec. of State, 22 March 1858, 26 October 1858; Williams to Sec. of State, 14 May 1858, 1 June 1858, 22 September 1858.

quantity apart from Europe. Although the closure of Bosporus and Dardanelles to foreign warships in peacetime was an ancient rule, and one repeatedly reaffirmed in nineteenth-century treaties, Americans believed in the freedom of the seas and American warships had passed the straits on thirteen occasions between the arrival of Commodore Porter and the coming of the Crimean War.[48]

But again the project foundered. Despite Turkish satisfaction with Mehmed's visit and the cooperative attitude of the American government, no screw-propelled three-decker ship of the line was built in America. Perhaps the failure of the scheme represented a victory for "English Egotism," although the financial stringency which beset the Sultan's government and which provided the official reason for abandoning the enterprise was of itself a sufficient cause. Yet while no ship was built, the Turkish envoys had no reason to regret their journeys, and American influence on Ottoman naval policy did not entirely disappear. On his return from the United States, Amin Bey had been placed in charge of the construction of a ship of the line then building at Constantinople; succeeding, in 1863, to the post of capudan pasha, Mehmed would continue to call upon his transatlantic friends for technical information and advice. Nor was this naval influence confined to Turkey. Even before Mehmed's American visit, the magnetism of the United States Navy and of the disengaged position of the United States had reached eastward across the mountains to affect the distant government of Persia.

5. The Persian Treaty

From the time that the Napoleonic wars first brought Persia into the ambit of European diplomacy, that ancient empire had been subjected to pressure from three sides. In the north two wars with Russia had resulted in great losses of territory. To the east there came British penetration of Afghanistan. To the south, with the coming of the steamship and the emerging possibilities of the Euphrates route to India, there developed a British interest in the Persian Gulf. Although the greater menace of Russia had led in 1834 to the arrival of a British military mission and to that expanded British influence so helpful to the missionaries at Urmia, four years later the arrangement was broken off as a result of friction in Af-

---

[48] Confidential Letters: Sec. of Navy to LaVallette, 19 May 1858, 18 November 1858. Squadron Letters: LaVallette to Sec. of Navy, 20 October 1858. Despatches, Turkey: Williams to Sec. of State, 24 October 1858.

ghanistan. Like the Turks after the Battle of Navarino, the Persians at mid-century needed an impartial friend, while the accession in 1848 of Nasir ud Din had provided them with a modernizing ruler on the model of Mahmud.

But outside contacts were historically few. The kings in Persian friezes ride chariots, not ships, and throughout history Persia had been oriented northward, toward the caravan routes of central Asia. The meteorological conditions of the Arabian Sea and Persian Gulf had inhibited the development of maritime commerce, and although Americans had early developed a profitable trade with Muscat, the missionaries reached Persia before the merchants. This lack of commercial interest was reflected in the passivity of the American government, elsewhere so forward: Commodore Porter's early offer to visit Trebizond to investigate the Persian trade had brought no response from Washington, nor did the government evince an interest in 1844 when Dabney Carr, pressed by Rufus Anderson on the issue of missionary protection, raised the question of a Persian treaty.[49]

The project was next put forward by the Persians. In the spring of 1850, while Kossuth was languishing in Anatolia and the mission of Amin Bey was in preparation, George P. Marsh was approached by the Persian chargé at Constantinople on the matter of a treaty. The suggestion was taken up in Washington: the same dispatch that approved the coming of Amin Bey gave Marsh full powers to negotiate, and shortly the Department followed up with queries on the commerce of Trebizond. In due course the Persian chargé got his powers too. Fearing, as had the negotiators of the Turkish treaty, European opposition to this extension of American commercial relations and American influence, Marsh kept the discussions strictly secret. On 9 October 1851 a treaty of friendship, commerce, and navigation was signed.

The Persian negotiator had been instructed to model the arrangement on his country's treaty with Spain. The presence at Constantinople of "Mr. David," interpreter to the Shah and an influential member of the Persian court, enabled Marsh to gain the additional privilege of establishing a consulate at Bushire, principal port of the Persian Gulf coast. But the interpreter's impending departure made the negotiation hasty, and no clause guaranteed to American

[49] Despatches, Turkey: Porter to Sec. of State, 18 June 1832; Carr to Sec. of State, 16 February 1844.

citizens all rights, privileges, and immunities enjoyed by those of other states.

Senate approval was consequently conditioned on the insertion of such a privileges-and-immunities clause. Advised of this requirement in April 1852, the Persian negotiator expressed confidence that the amendment would be accepted. But 1852 was a year of internal stress in Persia. Although in October the Persian chargé reported that approval was imminent, no action was taken and the treaty failed to go into force.[50]

For Persia, the next two years were marked by increasing difficulties with Britain, both in the Gulf and on the eastern frontier, while the advent of the Crimean War complicated affairs to the northward. In the United States a change of administration brought the replacement of Marsh by Carroll Spence. In November 1854, the new minister to Constantinople had just finished a report on the battles of Balaclava and Inkerman when he was approached by the new Persian chargé with a new proposal for a treaty. Failure of the previous attempt was attributed by Spence to imperfect secrecy and British intrigue; the new Persian approach he credited to the Russians, whose influence might prove helpful for the future. Such explanations and such influence had marked the Turkish negotiations, and another reflection of earlier events now developed. The Shah, his Chargé reported, desired to purchase or to have constructed "in the United States several vessels of war and to procure the services of American officers and seamen to navigate them."

Four months later, while this dispatch was still under consideration at Washington, the Shah's interpreter, now described as "General J. David Khan," presented himself to the American minister at Vienna and with many adjurations of secrecy proposed the negotiation of a treaty. Mainly commercial, the project was yet partly political in character, reflecting the tension which existed between Persia and Great Britain and reminiscent of the Turco-American alliance proposed by Pertew following the Battle of Navarino. One article provided that since the Shah lacked a naval force the United States would protect his merchant shipping; a second called for an American promise "to protect the ports and isles which belong to

[50] Miller, *Treaties*, VII, 429-89, deals with the Persian negotiations. Despatches, Turkey: Marsh to Sec. of State, 18 April 1850, 19 August 1850, 20 November 1851, 18 December 1851, 30 April 1852; Brown to Sec. of State, 12 March 1851, 4 October 1852. Instructions, Turkey: Sec. of State to Marsh, 28 June 1850.

Persia from the preponderance of [   ] and from her encroach-
ments and also against the Imaum of Muscat." While these Vienna
conversations were in progress, Spence had reported repeated inquiries from the Persians at Constantinople; a month later he wrote
that the Persian chargé was pressing the treaty project and had asked
for information regarding the construction of warships in the United
States.

In May 1855 a confidential dispatch from Secretary of State Marcy
instructed Spence to proceed with great secrecy in the negotiations,
warned against the inclusion of new principles or unusual provisions, and put forward a draft which omitted all mention of Persian
naval aspirations; at the same time, acting on the Minister's earlier
hint, Marcy moved to gain Russian support. But the Persian chargé
also had his model, from which he did not feel permitted to deviate,
and which required the United States, in exchange for commercial
advantage, to "protect the Persian seas" and Persian shipping, to
permit Persian vessels to fly the Stars and Stripes, to punish the
Imam of Muscat for his aggressions against Persia, and to restore to
the government of the Shah the revolted islands of the Persian Gulf.
Clearly all this was unacceptable, but the Persian would not retreat.
Although November brought another attempt by David Khan to
shift the negotiation to Vienna, there followed a period of inactivity.

By this time the Crimean War was drawing to a close, relations
between Britain and Persia had again been broken, and as the threat
of British pressure grew, so did Persian needs. In May 1856 a special
messenger, a Christian Persian by the name of Malkom Khan,
reached Constantinople with a new plan for an American treaty. But
still the Persians asked too much: the use of the American flag, and
the loan on demand of a force to police the Persian Gulf. To this
proposal Spence replied in a lengthy and eloquent dispatch in which
he emphasized America's traditional avoidance of entangling alliances, her belief in the mutual beneficence of commerce, and the
gains which would accrue to Persia from any substitution of sea for
land carriage: the United States, "possessing now a mercantile tonnage greater than any other power . . . [was] particularly fitted to
destroy that monopoly of the English trade in Persia" so injurious
to that country. But his report to the State Department was pessimistic, and he blamed the invocation of Russian influence for giving the
Persians exaggerated ideas of the importance which the United
States placed upon a treaty.

259

This pessimism proved unwarranted. In September Malkom Khan received new instructions, and a draft treaty with no entanglements was quickly agreed upon. In October Malkom was joined by Far-rukh Khan, most important of Persian diplomats and a special favorite of the Shah, who had been entrusted with the double mission of completing the American treaty and adjusting his country's difficulties with Great Britain. In the first effort he was successful, and on 13 December 1856 the treaty was signed. In the second, however, he was not, and following a British declaration of war a British expedition set forth from Karachi for the conquest of Bushire.[51]

But by now Spence had won the confidence of the Persians, while reported British obstruction of the American negotiations and the overbearing attitude shown by Stratford toward the representative of this weaker nation had gained the Persian envoy the sympathy and support of the American minister. On Spence's advice, Farrukh shifted his discussions with the British from Constantinople to Paris; at Farrukh's request Spence wrote the American ministers at Paris and London to solicit "the bestowal of the same disinterested advice as he had received from me." Advice, in due course, was given and gratefully acknowledged, and by this time the course of events had led Spence beyond traditional American attitudes to the point where he could see political opportunity in the Persian connection. The mission to Persia, he wrote the State Department, "may one day become a most important one for our Country. Our relations with England may one day become hostile." Since friction will always exist between Persia and England, policy suggests that we obtain the friendship "of a power, which in case of a war between us and England, could by a proper use of money, be made. . . . most serviceable to us in annoying a nation, which has never ceased to interfere with our foreign policy. It would at all times be a thorn in the side of England, which could be rendered piercing, whenever we desired it, by the secret pressure which the Russian Government could be induced to bear upon it."

To ensure the safe delivery of the treaty of friendship and commerce, Spence entrusted it to his brother Charles, whom he commissioned a special courier. Unlike Rhind's treaty with Turkey, this one had no separate and secret article, and Persian desires for a naval

[51] Despatches, Turkey: Spence to Sec. of State, 25 November 1854, 14 May 1855, 17 September 1855, 29 January 1856, 16 April 1856, 22 June 1856, 22 December 1856. Instructions, Turkey: Sec. of State to Spence, 11 May 1855. Miller, *Treaties*, VII, 459-79.

force remained unsatisfied. Nor had the Persians succeeded in writing in a promise that the United States would immediately establish a legation at Teheran. As in the Turkish negotiation, however, the Americans had proven individually cooperative. Carroll Spence had already reported the urgent Persian desire for an American legation, as well as a request from Farrukh Khan that the United States, on the occasion of ratification, would send a warship to the Persian Gulf to impress the people of the region with American naval strength. Before leaving Constantinople with the treaty, Charles Spence undertook to ascertain for Farrukh "the prices of firearms and steam vessels, and at what cost they could be delivered, and if it were possible for Persia to obtain a loan in the United States and upon what terms."[52]

This time the Senate did consent. But despite repeated urgings from the American minister at Constantinople and the recommendation of President Buchanan, no appropriation could be secured for the establishment of a legation. In contrast to the earlier situation in Turkey, there was no direct American trade with Persia and no domestic commercial pressure for representation at Teheran; the missionary interest did not command sufficient support; the Congress was not yet thinking in Spence's advanced political terms. Only in 1883 would concern for an expanded missionary effort result in the establishment of an American legation in Persia.

Yet while the Congress was unwilling to appropriate, the executive remained obliging. In April 1857 the Secretary of the Navy instructed the commander of the East India Squadron to order a ship to visit the Persian Gulf region, and in February 1859 the U.S.S. *Minnesota*, Captain Samuel F. DuPont, touched at Muscat. But that was all. Not until 1879 and the Eastern cruise of Commodore Robert W. Shufeldt in *Ticonderoga* did an American warship enter the Persian Gulf, while the establishment of a Persian naval force waited until well into the twentieth century.[53]

[52] Despatches, Turkey: Spence to Sec. of State, 22 December 1856, 27 December 1856; Spence to Sec. of State, 12 March 1857. Miller, *Treaties*, vii, 479-82.

[53] Miller, *Treaties*, vii, 482, 488; Paullin, *Diplomatic Negotiations*, p. 355; Abraham Yeselson, *United States-Persian Diplomatic Relations, 1883-1921* (New Brunswick, 1956), pp. 23-25.

CHAPTER VIII

Leavening the Levant,[1] 1835-1862

1. The Missionary Establishment

DISCOURAGING though it was to lovers of humanity, the failure of the European revolutions of 1848-49 merely bore out the perceptive pessimism of earlier Americans. Barlow and Dwight had been convinced that Europe would be the last of the continents to partake of Columbia's bliss. Writing in 1823, John Quincy Adams had observed that although the Europeans had all caught the infection of constitution-making from America, their efforts led only to civil war, and had predicted that if the great powers ever did succeed in establishing good government, it would not be for more than half a century. So far, except perhaps in Britain, the prediction had stood the test. "Fell Despotism" had triumphed. Yet some still found it possible to hold out hope, if not for Europe at least for the Levant. The Turkish connection remained, and the Sultan, unlike the European despots, was a supporter of religious toleration and a defender of political refugees. A new treaty relationship had been entered into with Persia. And in both these empires the expansion of missionary enterprise continued.[2]

This expansion, indeed, had pretty well kept pace with the growth of American population, of American territory, and of American foreign trade. Although the extraordinary rate of increase of the Jacksonian era was not maintained, the annual income of the American Board nevertheless grew from $250,000 in the forties to $375,000 at the end of the subsequent decade; with Civil War prosperity the figure would pass the half-million mark. Where in the early days the Board had been almost entirely supported by New England and New York, a fifth of its income now came from regions outside the Northeast, and the westward stream of Congregational migration was producing contributions from the upper Mississippi Valley, from Oregon and California, and even from Texas. As in the earlier

---

[1] The chapter title derives from the parable of the leaven (Matthew 13:33; Galatians 5:9), a missionary favorite, by way of J. K. Greene, *Leavening the Levant* (Boston, 1916).

[2] Dwight, *Greenfield Hill*, VII, lines 303-4; Barlow, *Columbiad*, VIII, *passim*. Adams to C. J. Ingersoll, *Writings*, VII, 488.

period, the funds annually budgeted for the Levant grew even faster than total income, doubling from the $75,000 of the forties to $154,000 in 1860 and passing $200,000 in the war years. As had been the case since it had surpassed the Sandwich Island mission in the decade of the thirties, the Near East remained by far the largest field, leading even in rate of growth. While China in 1850 had a budget about a fifth of that of the Levant, the proportion ten years later had declined to about an eighth.[3]

Such generosity on the part of Protestant America was more than amply justified by the consecrated labor of those in the field, labor carried out in the face of hardships not easily comprehensible to the twentieth-century reader. If Fisk and Smith and Dwight remain the most notable explorers of the Levant, the generation of frontier workers that followed equally deserves remembrance. Before the dangers of life in unknown lands could be confronted, the ocean had to be crossed, and this voyage, in ships of less than three hundred tons, was itself sufficient to intimidate the fainthearted. To some, it seemed unlikely that even divine intervention would solve the problem: "A sea life," wrote Josiah Brewer, "under the most favorable circumstances, and even in the approaching millennial days, will be regarded as a necessary evil to be borne for the good of society." After a stormy passage in 1828, Rufus Anderson included in his first letter home some heartfelt practical advice: to limit the impact of seasickness and depression upon the departing missionary, he advised the ample provision of such items as pickled pigs' feet and hard crackers, which "agree with the stomach"; nor was he the last missionary traveler to comment on the ocean's "nauseating power." For those assigned to Constantinople or Beirut the journey ended when the ship dropped anchor, but for others the path led onward to new hazards. Mrs. Perkins barely survived the overland trip from Trebizond to Tabriz; of two couples proceeding to Urmia by way of Aleppo and Mosul in 1841, "that being the more practicable route for females," one man and one woman died on the way.[4]

Journey's end brought not rest but a confrontation of new dangers from climate and disease. Enlistment of missionaries was, as a rule, for the duration, and the duration could be tragically short. Of the ten missionaries and four wives who came out in the twenties, Par-

---

[3] ABCFM *Annual Reports.*

[4] Brewer, *Residence,* p. 22. ABC 16.5, Vol. 1: Anderson to Evarts, 19 December 1828. Hamlin, *Life and Times,* p. 102; Perkins, *Residence,* pp. 139-43; Anderson, *Oriental Churches,* I, 200.

sons, Fisk, Gridley, and Mrs. Temple were dead before the end of the decade. Eli Smith's first wife died in 1836 as a result of exposure suffered when the two were shipwrecked on the coast of Asia Minor. At Smyrna in 1837 Daniel Temple opened the dispatch box from Constantinople to find a note: "You had better smoke the contents of the box before touching them. I have done it already, but you had better do it again. The plague is among us. W. Goodell." This plague cost H.G.O. Dwight his wife and one of his sons. Four years later, reflecting on the remarkable mortality of the Syrian mission, Temple noted that "Death has already cut down eight adults belonging to it . . . and sickness and loss of sight called three more quite away from the field," and hoped these tragedies were not indicative of the Lord's displeasure. The first nine years of the Nestorian mission saw the arrival of ten couples and the deaths of three men and three women. Of five mission children born in the space of two months, all were dead within a year and a half. In his first six years in Persia, Justin Perkins buried all three children born to him. Nevertheless, the volunteers still came.

However praiseworthy the zeal which could withstand such tragedy, the dangers of these distant stations argued strongly for the presence of missionary physicians, and indeed for rudimentary medical training for all. The first American medical missionary had gone out to India in 1819; the first in the Levant, Dr. Asa Dodge, reached Palestine in 1834, to be followed in the next year by Dr. Grant of the Nestorian mission; in Syria, in 1842, Dr. Henry A. DeForest, the novelist's brother, assumed the post. This work, in which the United States came to lead all nations—of a world total of forty medical missionaries in 1849, twenty-six were American—was to prove doubly justified, for the physician, the dispensary, and the hospital opened doors otherwise closed to the gospel, and gave access to all sects and faiths. But the medical missionaries were also vulnerable.[5]

For the workers who survived there remained the prospect of prolonged exile in alien lands amid alien peoples, and the Sisyphean task of altering the deepest beliefs of the contemptuous, the uncomprehending, and the hostile. In such a situation the individual counted for much: more even than the gospel word, it was the wit-

---

[5] Temple, *Life of Temple*, pp. 164-67, 258, 284; Perkins, *Residence*, pp. 368-70, 385-88, 406-7; Anderson, *Oriental Churches*, I, 176-77; Bliss, *Encyclopaedia of Missions*, "Medical Missions."

ness of the missionary lives that was crucial in the foreign field. This witness, be it said, was very impressive, but problems nevertheless arose: over the years a few wrongheaded individuals appeared, unable to cooperate either with colleagues or constituency; at times discipline had to be prayerfully applied; even the problem of Eve presented itself. Among the reasons for Rufus Anderson's first Mediterranean journey had been some difficulties at Malta, where the printer Hallock was taking too much upon himself, and the need to justify to the brethren there the Board's decision to sever connections with Gridley and Brewer owing to doubts about their fiancées. While the visit was in progress, Jonas King's marriage to a Greek girl raised fear of adverse reaction at home; from this event, which indeed remained unique, dated the practice, followed with very few exceptions, of sending only married men to foreign fields. With women, however, the custom was different. By the 1840's the growth of schools and the expansion of women's work had brought the dispatch of numerous unmarried female assistants, most of them products of Mount Holyoke, whose presence also provided a source of replacement wives.[6]

To maintain the necessary standard of performance, the Board exercised great care in the choice of missionaries. Happily, the early years saw a steady surplus of volunteers, while selection was aided by sound advice from the field. Of this advice a notable example was the "Hints and Cautions to Missionaries," a series of letters composed in 1834-35 by Goodell and his colleagues at Constantinople. Read and concurred in by that sturdy realist Commodore Porter and forwarded to Boston for the perusal of new workers, the "Hints" provide an appropriate text for missionaries of every age and clime and whatever persuasion. The need, wrote Goodell, was for common-sense workers, apt to learn as well as teach, patient and adaptable, willing to settle for gradual results and to avoid agitation and meddling. Pity or a patronizing attitude toward the "heathen" should be rigorously avoided. Respect for the intelligence of those with whom the missionary worked was essential, as was a willingness to recognize the local value of customs which at first appeared outlandish. Impetuosity on the part of new recruits was undesirable. He who saw himself accomplishing miracles of conversion and end-

---

[6] ABC 16.5, Vol. 1: Rufus Anderson, "Mediterranean Letters." Phillips, "Pagan World," pp. 308-13. Bliss, *Encyclopaedia of Missions*, 11, 479-523, gives an extended account of the "uprising" of American women on behalf of their downtrodden Oriental sisters.

ing with a martyr's crown was the reverse of useful. What was wanted was not a headful of romantic notions but a willingness to work.[7]

With this philosophy, these people, and these funds the work went on. The termination of the Palestine mission and of the work among the Jews of Constantinople, and the exile of Jonas King from Greece, left but three operating missions: those to the Armenians and Nestorians in the north, and the Syrian mission south of the Taurus Mountains. But all were in a reasonably healthy state, while the withdrawal from other fields was to prove only the prelude to a further expansion.

Of all Near Eastern missions, that to the Armenians, with its headquarters at Constantinople, was most immediately subject to the political vicissitudes of the Ottoman Empire. In 1844 the installation of a new Armenian patriarch, formerly a friend to the evangelists but now, under the pressures of his new office, seemingly resolved to extirpate the Protestant heresy, marked the start of a period of difficulties. A boycott instituted against those Armenians consorting with the missionaries was made the more bitter by the outspoken support of Horatio Southgate, recently returned from Philadelphia after ordination as Episcopal bishop for all the dominions and dependencies of the Turkish sultan. Soon Armenian priests with evangelical leanings were being persecuted by reassignment and banishment; in the provinces, particularly at Erzerum, evangelicals were imprisoned and bastinadoed. With time the Patriarch's spiritual warfare embraced the economic, for given the theocratic structure of the Ottoman Empire, the wholesale excommunications and anathemas that issued forth carried with them such far-reaching temporal penalties as loss of livelihood or dwelling.

For shelter against these storms the missionaries and their charges had to rely principally upon God and Great Britain: although defending the persons of American citizens with vigor, the American ministers carefully refrained from interference in Turkish domestic politics. Not so, however, Stratford de Redcliffe. Already the great Ambassador had secured the abolition of the death penalty for Moslem apostasy; now, with the support of Palmerston, he succeeded in freeing the Protestant Armenians from patriarchal supervision by gaining official recognition of an independent Protestant sect. Frus-

---

[7] ABC 16.5, Vol. 2: W. Goodell, W. G. Schauffler, H.G.O. Dwight, D. Temple, "Hints and Cautions addressed to Missionaries destined to the Mediterranean."

tration thus confronted the hierarchy, while punishment fell upon the persecutors from on high: an Armenian magnate who had procured the imprisonment of an evangelical priest was thrown from his horse and "received a fracture of the skull, from which he died; and his splendid mansion was subsequently consumed by fire." As for Southgate, his efforts accomplished little but ill-feeling, and in 1849 he returned to the United States to resign his post.

Hardly was the threat from within surmounted than there came a threat from without, and the danger that Russian expansion would bring the dominance of the Eastern Church. But salvation came with the Crimean War: the movements of the armies, as the missionary historian observed, were "evidently made subservient . . . to the progress of the Gospel; . . . and the fall of Sebastopol was a more direct benefit to the missions, than it was to the nations that fought against it." Materially, too, the war brought missionary prosperity. In order to provide employment for dispossessed Armenian Protestants during the persecutions of the forties, Cyrus Hamlin had established among other industrial enterprises, a flour mill and a bakery as adjuncts to the Bebek high school. Now, observing the collapse of the British logistic and medical services, Hamlin contracted to supply hospitals and camps with good bread and clean linen, and turned both faculty and students to the task. However hard on education, this humanitarian diversion of effort had resulted by war's end in a profit of $25,000 for the mission treasury, and in the founding in England, under the presidency of the Earl of Shaftesbury, of the Turkish Missions Aid Society, dedicated to providing financial support for the work of the Americans.

So the schemes of both Patriarch and Czar were frustrated. Far from restoring uniformity, persecution had brought the founding of evangelical churches and the creation of an independent Protestant Armenian community, and while this development was very different from the original American purpose of individual regeneration, it had for some time been anticipated as a probable consequence of hierarchical resistance and could be looked upon as a success. Far from winning new rights in Palestine and Turkey, Russian policy had led to defeat in war and to the neutralization of the Black Sea. In Turkey the reformers had returned to power, the influence of the Western allies remained strong, and the peace settlement was accompanied by a new imperial rescript, the Hatt-i Humayun of 1856, which explicitly recognized freedom of religion, the equality of all, and the need to profit from Western arts and science.

All this made the fifties a period of great progress. The Armenian evangelical churches, four of which had been formed in 1846 in consequence of patriarchal anathemas, grew rapidly in number and membership, and outstations multiplied. In the nine years following the occupation of Erzerum in 1839 no new posts had been established, but in 1848 work was begun at Aintab. Four years later Marsovan was occupied, and by 1855 missionaries had taken up residence at Arabkir and Harput in western Armenia, at Caesarea, Tokat, and Sivas in Anatolia, and at Marash and Aleppo south of the Taurus. Retracing in 1860 his journey of thirty years before, H.G.O. Dwight found indifference replaced by sympathy, barbarism giving way to Protestantism, and instead of isolation the telegraph. By this time the Armenian mission numbered thirty-six missionaries, two physicians, forty-one female assistants, and over two hundred native helpers; forty-seven churches had been established, with almost two thousand members; from the press at Constantinople there issued some five million pages a year. With the administrative reorganizations of 1856 and 1869, which divided the field into eastern, western, and central Armenian missions, it could be said that the opening of Armenia to evangelical work had been completed, and that, for the future, development and supervision would be the order of the day.[8]

To the east, beyond the Armenian highlands, the revival of 1846 had marked the start of an auspicious period for the Nestorian mission. Persian favor had been demonstrated and the danger of oppression by local Moslems warded off by the appointment of an Armenian governor for the province of Urmia. By 1848 some six hundred pupils, more than a fifth of them girls, were attending missionary schools, and remarkable advances in female piety and education were in the making under the guidance of the saintly Fidelia Fiske. The creation of a Nestorian literature was proceeding apace. By 1852 Perkins' translation of both New and Old Testaments had been completed and printed in modern Syriac with type made by the printer Breath. There followed editions of *The Dairyman's*

[8] Anderson, *Oriental Churches*, I, 386-426, II, 24-58; Arpee, *Armenian Awakening*, pp. 108-56; Richter, *History of Missions*, pp. 107-18; Hamlin, *Among the Turks*, pp. 132-53; Cameron, "Horatio Southgate"; *Minutes of a Conference of Missionaries held at Constantinople in November 1855* (Boston, 1856).

Daughter, of a church history and a Scripture geography, and of *Pilgrim's Progress*. By 1858 the total output of the Urmia press had reached 68,000 volumes and more than 13,000,000 pages.

Like his Armenian colleague at Constantinople, the Nestorian patriarch had at first been friendly; like him, again, he turned against the missionaries with their increasing success. But although assisted by the "marvelous audacity" of French Jesuits, his efforts in obstruction were of little effect. In 1852 British and American pressure was successfully brought to bear from Constantinople; although some uneasiness developed in the course of both the Crimean War and the Anglo-Persian war that followed, no untoward events took place. Through the decade of the fifties, new arrivals strengthened the mission, and these newcomers, like the pioneers, showed a remarkable facility with languages in their preaching and teaching. Twenty years after its founding, the mission could understandably feel that its influence had become pervasive: the seven missionaries and nine female helpers at Urmia and the outstations were assisted by fifty Nestorian fellow laborers, and the schools were full. Most surprising and gratifying of all, perhaps, was the enthusiasm and liberality of the Nestorian community in supporting the mission with material contributions.

The earlier effort of the Nestorian mission to expand west of the Kurdish mountains and establish a station at Mosul had been broken off in 1844 owing to Anglican interference, the dispersion of the mountain Nestorians, and the death of Dr. Grant. But in 1849 a visit by missionaries from Urmia indicated a receptivity to the gospel among the numerous sects of upper Mesopotamia, and later in the same year a member of the Syrian mission reached Mosul from Aleppo. Soon he was joined by others, approaching from the northward, who floated down the Tigris, through scenery reminiscent of the Hudson River, on rafts supported by inflated goatskins. Printed matter was provided by the press at Constantinople, and translations into Kurdish were at once begun; the services of a medical missionary tamed the hostile Pasha. There were, of course, some intermittent troubles, a few stonings and persecutions, and during the Crimean War some fears of a serious outbreak of Moslem fanaticism. But by 1860, when the Assyria mission was transferred for administrative purposes to Constantinople and lost its separate identity, influential conversions had been made, flourishing evangelical churches had been established, and outstations were in operation at Diarbekir, Mardin, and Bitlis.[9]

With the one great exception of the station at Constantinople, the efforts of the American Board in Ottoman regions were long confined to Syria and to Asiatic Turkey. At mid-century, however, there came a move westward into Rumelia with the establishment of missions to the Jews of Salonica and to the Bulgarians. To Salonica, where the descendants of fifteenth-century Jewish refugees from Spain comprised about half the population, two missionaries were sent in 1849, to be joined subsequently by two more. But language difficulties complicated the work, climate and disease took their usual toll, and the Salonica Jews, although more approachable than their coreligionists of Constantinople, were nevertheless unresponsive. In 1852 the station was relinquished to native helpers, and for a generation, except for intermittent visits of inspection, Salonica remained neglected by the American churches.[10]

To the northward, however, a brighter opportunity beckoned. Between Salonica and the Danube dwelt the Bulgarians, a people of perhaps two million, anciently Christianized by Saints Cyril and Methodius. Subjected in the eighteenth century to the spiritual control of the Greek patriarch at Constantinople, the Bulgarians were now evincing signs of a restive ecclesiastical nationalism. The opportunity which this offered to American evangelists was to be embraced by not one but two missionary groups.

In 1852 the Methodist Episcopal Church (North), whose previous efforts had been concentrated in West Africa, South America, and India, resolved to commence a mission among the Bulgarians. Five years later, a tour of the country by Cyrus Hamlin and a member of the Turkish Missions Aid Society produced flattering reports of the people, their land, and their farming, which seemed to indicate a providential opportunity for the American Board. By agreement the two societies divided up the territory at the Balkan Mountains, with the Methodists establishing themselves at Shumla in the north in 1857 and the American Board to the south at Adrianople in the following year. Discovering, as they thought, a thirst for the gospel and a zeal for education in the new constituency, the Americans

[9] Anderson, *Oriental Churches*, I, 333-61, II, 107-49; Richter, *History of Missions*, pp. 116-17, 298-303; Laurie, *Woman and Her Saviour*; W. S. Tyler, *Memoir of Rev. Henry Lobdell, M.D.* (Boston, 1859).

[10] Anderson, *Oriental Churches*, II, 161-69; Bliss, *Encyclopaedia of Missions*, I, 75-76.

rapidly expanded their efforts. By the early sixties, churches were being formed and a promising future appeared to lie ahead.[11]

South of the Taurus, the struggles of Druses and Maronites had sorely buffeted the Syrian mission, while the paucity of recorded conversions occasioned criticism at home. In 1844, following a visit by Rufus Anderson, the mission press was temporarily suspended and the educational effort diminished in favor of an increased emphasis on evangelical preaching and field work. But in the next year fighting broke out with renewed ferocity, and field work for a time consisted principally of binding up wounds, sheltering refugees, and carrying flags of truce between the contending parties. For once, indeed, it appears that the hazards of missionary life had adverse effects upon recruitment: in 1847, when the Syrian brethren published an earnest and eloquent appeal for additional colleagues, the response was painfully lacking.

Again, however, darkness heralded the dawn. In 1848 a first native church was organized at Beirut, and within four years three more had arisen. Printing was resumed and expanded, the girls' boarding school prospered, and in 1855 another visit from the corresponding secretary did lead to the arrival of new personnel. By the end of the decade it not only seemed possible to see the twenty years of effort as twenty years of progress, but the American Board's Syrian mission had gained a small ally with the arrival of two representatives of the Reformed Presbyterian Church. After a number of false starts these Covenanters settled at Latakia, the seaport of Aleppo, where they ministered to the Nusairiyeh, a remarkable people who were at once Moslem, Trinitarian, and pantheistic.

By this time the American Board was maintaining mission stations at Beirut, at three tributary locations, and at Sidon to the south and Tripoli and Hums to the north. Where there had once been stonings and execrations there was now universal welcome and respect. Even at this distance from Constantinople the Sultan's rescript had opened the way for toleration, and the effect was noted in larger audiences and increased conversions. In the Sabbath Schools the children now "sang the same songs in Arabic, which American chil-

[11] Anderson, *Oriental Churches*, II, 174-90; Richter, *History of Missions*, pp. 167-69; Bliss, *Encyclopaedia of Missions*, I, 77-78, 216-17, II, 76-77; Hamlin, *Among the Turks*, pp. 261-73; Constantine Stephanove, *The Bulgarians and Anglo-Saxondom* (Berne, 1919), pp. 271-72. For the background of American interest, J. F. Clarke, "Bible Societies, American Missionaries, and the National Revival of Bulgaria" (unpublished doctoral dissertation, Harvard University, 1937).

dren love to sing in their own language," and the American educational effort had inspired the emulation of both Greek and papal adversaries. Both in quantity and in quality the output of the press had been impressive, and the publication of the Arabic version of the New Testament, begun by Eli Smith and completed by Dr. Cornelius V. A. Van Dyck, had not only set a new standard for Arabic typography but had resulted in a pocket edition which had "this advantage, that it could be carried and read without attracting notice."[12]

Southward from Syria lay the refractory land of Palestine, and beyond it Egypt and the northern shore of Africa. On the Barbary coast, as Isaac Bird had reported in 1829, the absence of any Christian population inhibited access; although the Coptic Christians formed some 10 percent of the population of Egypt, that country had been passed over by the American Board in favor of work elsewhere. Now, however, this situation was to be rectified with the occupation of the Egyptian field, briefly by the American Missionary Association, a Congregational antislavery offshoot of the American Board, and more importantly by the Associate Reformed Presbyterian Church and its successor, the United Presbyterian Church.

The Associate Reformed Presbyterians had for some years maintained workers in Damascus. In the winter of 1851-52 a visit to Egypt by one of these, the medical missionary Dr. James G. Paulding, led to a proposal for the occupation of this new ground. Inadequate opportunities at Damascus, the needs of the Egyptians, and the presumed favor of the Pasha, as well as the probability that distance would insulate from the effects of the Eastern crisis, led Paulding's colleagues to support the suggestion. In turn, the General Synod at Pittsburgh gave its approval. Late in 1854, with the arrival of one missionary from America and of a second from Damascus, work was begun in "the great and wicked city of Cairo."

In Egypt, the Presbyterians faced the inevitable discouragements of the beginning mission field. Ninety percent of the country was Moslem and inaccessible, and the ancient Coptic Church, mummified by time, was unreceptive. Audiences were negligible, and the missionaries found themselves victimized by their servants and abused on the streets as "Nazarenes, dogs, and pigs." Despite the

[12] Anderson, *Oriental Churches*, I, 362-85, II, 324-45; Richter, *History of Missions*, pp. 194-98; Bliss, *Encyclopaedia of Missions*, II, 187-91, 271-73; Tibawi, *American Interests*, pp. 105-49; J. W. DeForest, *Oriental Acquaintance* (New York, 1856).

cushioning effect of distance, both Crimean War and Indian Mutiny heightened existing tensions between native and foreigner and between Moslem and Christian; in 1860 an influx of refugees from disordered Syria brought added responsibilities; with Civil War in America, financial support diminished. But slowly, as the work went on, the light began to break and congregation and schools began to expand.

In 1857 the Reverend Gulian Lansing, veteran of five years at Damascus, arrived to open a second station at Alexandria and to assume responsibility for a girls' school formerly supported by Scottish Presbyterians. With the purchase of a Nile boat in 1860, the distribution of tracts was extended upstream. One year later the persecution at Asyut of the Syrian convert Faris el Hakim had fortunate issue when intervention by the American consul general gained the imprisonment of the persecutors and increased respect for the mission. In 1862, in response to repeated entreaties, the Pasha presented the missionaries with a house in Cairo; with these new facilities the boys' school expanded rapidly from sixty to two hundred pupils. Shortly the mission found itself able to purchase its own premises in Alexandria.[18]

Predictably enough, these successes generated the hostility of the Coptic hierarchy. But this development was more than offset, and the expansion of the American effort aided, by an extraordinary stroke of fortune. Passing through Egypt, the exiled Christianized heir to the Punjab, His Highness Maharajah Dhulup Singh, visited the mission and confided to the American clergymen his need of a wife. Bamba Muller, the girls' school's first convert, was presented to His Highness; the Maharajah was pleased; after some intensive training in the higher social graces, Bamba was translated from hovel to palace and the mission enriched by an allowance of £1,000 a year from the grateful bridegroom.

So by devoted efforts and in wondrous ways the work began, which by century's end could be described as "the means of saving many souls, gathering many companies of believers, establishing

---

[18] Richter, *History of Missions*, pp. 344-46; Bliss, *Encyclopaedia of Missions*, II, 432-34; Andrew Watson, *The American Mission in Egypt, 1854-1896* (Pittsburg, 1904); Gulian Lansing (ed.), *Religious Toleration in Egypt* (London, 1862); J. P. Thompson, *Photographic Views of Egypt, Past and Present* (Boston and Cleveland, 1854), pp. 140, 331-32; M. J. Wright, "Some Bold Diplomacy in the United States in 1861," *American Historical Association Annual Report*, 1895, 405-10; 37C 2S HED 117.

many schools, diffusing secular as well as religious knowledge far and wide, and aiding in giving the Egyptian nation a start on the road to enlightenment and freedom."[14] With the occupation of Bulgaria and Egypt, the structure of the Near Eastern missionary effort was to all intents and purposes complete. Greatly enlarged in the years since the first small beginnings, the enterprise had also been increasingly rationalized and institutionalized, while the coming of steam and of the telegraph had not only tightened the administrative structure but had notably lessened the isolation of the earlier days.

Yet there still remained, surrounded but untenanted by the organized missionary groups, one obvious and important field. This was the Holy Land.

2. *Going to Jerusalem*

Inevitably, when first it cast its eyes on the Near Eastern field, the American Board had proposed to establish a station at Jerusalem. But the unhealthy climate, the hostility between the various Christian sects, and the disorder that accompanied Greek revolt and Syrian wars had combined to prevent effective work. In 1825 the death of Fisk had been followed by suspension of the effort in Palestine; although reopened in 1834 and persevered in for nine years, the mission was finally discontinued in 1843 and its members assigned elsewhere. Yet while the principal executive agent for American Protestantism in foreign parts had abandoned its effort in the Holy City, the deep and continuing American interest in the cradle of Christianity was in no way diminished. The quarter-century which followed the departure of the Board's missionaries witnessed a curious history of American activity in Palestine.

If, in a sense, it was in the nineteenth century that Western society discovered the Jew, the same years brought a related discovery of Jerusalem. Where Zion and Canaan had earlier been metaphysical concepts, appearing now in England, now in Massachusetts, now in Connecticut, they were so no longer. An age of exploration and travel was fulfilling the prophecy of Daniel 12:4, and as many ran to and fro and knowledge increased, Jerusalem moved from the minds of Mortons and Mathers to assume a fixed geographical location.

[14] Watson, *Mission in Egypt*, pp. 71, 163-72.

In America this shift was first evident in the closing years of the eighteenth century. In literature it could be seen in Timothy Dwight's *Conquest of Canaan.* The eccentric Austin, building his docks and magazines at New Haven to facilitate the embarkation of the Jews, was perhaps the first to act upon it. With the establishment of the American Board, Fisk and Parsons were sent to explore the Holy Land. Over the next fifty years, an increasing flood of missionary letters and memoirs, travelers' writings, and reports of archaeological investigation would keep Palestine plainly before American eyes, while the Jews, the importance of whose conversion and return gave them an unassailable eschatological position, remained objects of peculiar interest.

This interest, in its origins, was a mixture of the theological, the humanitarian, and the patriotic. Although European nationalism and persecution would by the century's end have linked the problem of the Holy Land and the problems of the Jews in an expanding Zionist movement, the early concerns were different. Those who thought of the individual Jew thought of conversion; those thinking in terms of a Jewish refuge thought not of Palestine but of America. In 1816, societies for the promotion of Christianity among the Jews were founded both in Boston and in New York. Three years later a Philadelphian, W. D. Robinson, published a memorial in London inviting the Jews of Europe to emigrate to the United States and proposing their settlement in the territories along the upper Mississippi and Missouri rivers. In the 1820's, the New York Society for Ameliorating the Condition of the Jews suggested the purchase of a large tract in the Genesee country for the use of immigrants from Europe. Most dramatic of all such schemes was the attempt in 1824-25 by Mordecai M. Noah, schoolmate of Stephen Decatur and former consul at Tunis, editor, playwright, and Tammany politician, to establish the "City of Ararat" as a refuge for his coreligionists on Grand Island in the Niagara River. Nothing came of this remarkable mixture of self-promotion and idealism, of land speculation, Zionism, and utopianism, and with the years Noah's thoughts turned eastward. In 1837 and again in 1844 he called for the acquisition of Syria by purchase, and urged the Christian community to cease from proselyting and instead to assist unconverted Jews to regain their homeland.[15]

[15] Milton Plesur, "The American Press and Jewish Restoration during the Nineteenth Century," in I. S. Meyer (ed.), *Early History of Zionism in America* (New

In all except the method of acquiring Palestine, this vision would in time be answered. But if Noah's efforts had any immediate impact, it was in strengthening Christian concern rather than in arousing Jewish interest. Excepting only the activities of Noah himself, the transition from building Jerusalem to going to Jerusalem was made by the evangelical and millenarian Protestants. And while this development resulted in some spectacular demonstrations of eccentricity, it was hardly limited to these. So deeply was the millenarian pattern embedded in the American consciousness that the unpromising land of Palestine, deforested, desiccated, and depopulated, came briefly to be a focus not only of evangelical and humanitarian concern, but also of the commercial interest, naval and scientific activity, and export of modern techniques that characterized American activity overseas.

American concern for the Jews, early evinced by both domestic and foreign missionary groups, was first enunciated by the government in 1840. Moved by persecutions at Damascus and Rhodes, the Van Buren administration instructed the Minister to Turkey and the Consul at Alexandria to do what they could to prevent or mitigate "these horrors." And by this time individual Americans, moved by prophecy, had begun to journey toward Jerusalem. Among the early arrivals was Miss Harriet Livermore, vouched for by the Secretary of State as a "lady of high character, both moral and religious" and as a member of one of New Hampshire's "most respectable" families, who believed herself one of the witnesses mentioned in the eleventh chapter of Revelation and who reached the Holy Land, seeking martyrdom, in 1836. In 1841 a Mormon missionary arrived from Illinois to try his hand at the conversion of the Jews.[16] More important than these was Warder Cresson.

Cresson was a Philadelphia Quaker of respectable and prosperous background, reputed, although he denied the allegations, to have adopted at various times the Shaker, Mormon, Millerite, and Campbellite persuasions. Having sired eight children, he had come to

---

York, 1958), pp. 55-76; B. D. Weinrib, "Noah's Ararat Jewish State," 43 *Publications of the American Jewish Historical Society*, 170-91. *Niles' Register*, 3 April 1823, 24 September 1825, 21 January 1826.

[16] Instructions, Turkey: Sec. of State to Porter, 28 April 1834, 17 August 1840. Stephen Olin, *Travels in Egypt, Arabia Petraea, and the Holy Land* (New York, 1843), II, 318; J. G. Whittier, *Snow-Bound* (Boston and New York, 1892), pp. v-vi, 27-32; E. F. Hoxie, "Harriet Livermore: 'Vixen and Devotee,'" 18 *New England Quarterly*, 39-50; Finnie, *Pioneers East*, pp. 183-86; Perkins, *Residence*, pp. 404-5.

disapprove the commerce between the sexes, particularly within marriage, and had written against it. Under the influence of a distinguished Philadelphia rabbi he had been confirmed in the belief that "salvation was of the Jews," and that God was about to gather His chosen people again. Moved by these views, Cresson in 1844 decided to abandon his family and to devote himself to assisting "the poor oppressed Jews" of the Holy Land; with support from E. Joy Morris, a Philadelphia congressman who had traveled in the East and who would later serve as minister to Turkey, he applied for the post of consul at Jerusalem. Although the application was successful, the commission, issued in May, was canceled a month later when protests reached the State Department. But by that time Cresson had sailed for Palestine, leaving wife and children behind but taking with him his favorite dove.

Establishing himself at Jerusalem in the house recently vacated by the missionaries of the American Board, Cresson informed the local pasha that the European powers and the United States were about to intervene in Syria, and that the Jews would infallibly return. Shortly he began to issue protection papers "to Jews and others, not Citizens of the U.S.," to the consternation of both the Consul at Beirut and the Minister at Constantinople. Increasingly identifying with those he had come to help, Cresson by 1847 was attacking the English Episcopal mission in Jerusalem. On 28 March 1848 he became a Jew, was circumcised, and assumed the name of Michael C. Boaz Israel.[17]

Others had meanwhile developed an interest in Palestine. In May 1847, while Scott's army was fighting its way up to the Mexican plateau, Lieutenant William F. Lynch, U.S.N., feeling there was "nothing left for the Navy to perform," applied to the Secretary of the Navy for permission to circumnavigate and explore the Dead Sea. Although the war continued, naval responsibilities had indeed diminished, ships were available, and Lynch's object—"to promote the cause of science, and advance the character of the Naval service"—commended itself to Secretary Mason. The application was approved in July; in October the Lieutenant was ordered to the command of

[17] Warder Cresson, *Babylon the Great is Falling!* (Philadelphia, 1830), p. 51; A. J. Karp, "The Zionism of Warder Cresson," in Meyer, *Early History of Zionism*, pp. 1-20; H. J. Cadbury, "Hebraica and the Jews in Early Quaker Interest," in H. H. Brinton (ed.), *Children of Light* (New York, 1938), p. 163. Despatches, Turkey: Carr to Sec. of State, 7 December 1844, 5 March 1845.

the storeship *Supply*, and news of the project was communicated by the State Department to Minister Carr at Constantinople. Over the summer Lynch had recruited his exploring party of "young, muscular, native-born Americans," pledged to abstinence from all intoxicating drink. In November, having acquired some "metallic boats," one of copper and the others of galvanized iron, the expedition sailed for Smyrna in the simultaneous pursuit of Christian and scientific truth.

Leaving his ship at Smyrna, Lynch proceeded by steamer to Constantinople to seek the firman which would permit entrance into Syria. As the bearer of a copy of Catlin's works on the American Indian, he was granted an audience with the Sultan; as a visiting naval officer, he was affably received by the Capudan Pasha, whom he presented with a galvanized boat and advised against the proposed purchase of an English steamship. In this pleasant atmosphere the documents were quickly procured. By the end of March, Lynch had engaged a traveling American physician, Dr. Henry I. Anderson, to conduct scientific researches and watch over the health of the expedition, and had landed his boats at Haifa preparatory to moving them overland to the Sea of Galilee. "For the first time, perhaps, without the consular precincts, the American flag has been raised in Palestine. May it be the harbinger of regeneration to a now hapless people!"

At Haifa, Lynch obtained some camels, with whose aid the boats were hauled across the thirty miles of hill country that separate the Mediterranean from Tiberias on the Sea of Galilee. Startled and impressed by the spectacle, and especially by the copper boat, which they took to be made of gold, the natives proved extremely friendly. Doubting, as Lynch reported, the purely scientific purpose of the expedition, knowing of American successes in wars with Britain, and resentful of British support of Ottoman rule, they were gratified by this demonstration of American power; shortly Lynch "entered a league" with the Sherif of Mecca, lineal descendent of the Prophet, whom he persuaded to join him on the journey. On 8 April 1848 the boats were launched, and the American expedition commenced its arduous and dangerous passage down the Jordan.

Here the metallic boats abundantly proved their worth, surviving rocks and rapids which dashed wooden ones to pieces, and the explorers proceeded without loss of a man. Near Jericho they encountered large numbers of bathing pilgrims, including some countrymen "gratified at seeing the stars and stripes floating on the consecrated river, and the boats which bore them ready to rescue, if necessary, a drowning pilgrim." By the end of April, Lynch could write from Engeddi, on the western shore of the Dead Sea, that the expedition had "elicited several facts of interest to the man of science and the Christian," and that the survey would substantiate the scriptural account of the destruction of the Cities of the Plain. By mid-May the circumnavigation had been completed, as had a geological survey; the northeastern bay had been named Mason's Bay in tribute to the Secretary of the Navy, and a float bearing the American flag had been moored in eighty fathoms as a memorial of the visit. July saw the exploring expedition back at Beirut, and by February 1849 Lynch had returned to Washington and had submitted a first brief report.

The longer and more complete *Official Report* which followed three years later was to prove somewhat anticlimactic, for by that time the explorer's popular *Narrative of the United States' Expedition to the River Jordan and the Dead Sea* had run through seven American and two English editions. The employment of modern science in the cause of Scripture appears to have had a wide appeal, as also, perhaps, the author's comments on missionary activity at Damascus and Beirut, his discussion of the market for American cottons, and his expectations with regard to the future of the Holy Land. To Lynch, as at an earlier date to Timothy Dwight, it appeared that Moslem rule was degenerating and that the fall of the Ottoman Empire was imminent; following this event the Jews would be restored to their homeland and the progress of civilization speeded.[18] Interacting over the following decade, these various trains of thought—scriptural, commercial, and eleemosynary—would give rise to an increasing American concern with Palestine.

In the autumn of 1848, while Lynch was voyaging homeward, Warder Cresson, now Michael C. Boaz Israel, returned to Philadelphia. Intending to settle up his affairs before departing permanently for Jerusalem, Cresson found himself subjected to lunacy

[18] Confidential Letters: Sec. of Navy to Lynch, 11 November 1847. Instructions, Turkey: Sec. of State to Carr, 15 October 1847. Expedition to the Dead Sea: Lynch to Sec. of Navy, 27 February 1848, 8 March 1848, 31 March 1848, 7 April 1848, 29 April 1848, 18 May 1848, 3 February 1849 (Naval Records Collection, National Archives). Lynch, *Narrative of the United States' Expedition to the River Jordan and the Dead Sea*; idem, *Official Report of the United States' Expedition to explore the Dead Sea and the River Jordan* (Baltimore, 1852). The short report of 1849 is in 30C 2S *SED* 34.

proceedings by a family covetous of his wordly goods. Acquitted after a sensational trial, he published *The Key of David*, a 344-page mixture of autobiography, prophecy, and polemic, and in the fall of 1852 set sail again. His aims, now matured by experience, centered on the improvement of the condition of the Jews of Palestine by the introduction of a modern agriculture. Never doubting that divine intervention would produce an inevitable return, and looking forward to a restoration in 1856, Cresson nevertheless advocated the use of human means to prepare the way. To prevent conversions to Christianity brought about by want, he proposed the establishment of a soup kitchen for destitute Jews. Imbued with Jeffersonian views on the difference in "the moral and physical health of those educated and brought up in large manufacturing districts and those brought up in agricultural pursuits," he planned to bring about the good society by establishing a model farming community in the valley of Rephaim, on the road from Jerusalem to Bethlehem.

To support his endeavors, Cresson appealed to the Jews for financial aid, to the Sultan for a land grant, and to the government of the United States for protection of the project in its infancy. None of these desiderata materialized, and, like so many utopian projects of the nineteenth century, the plan failed of fruition. But Cresson, or Israel, remained in the Holy Land. Despite his published views on matrimony, he married a Jewess who bore him two more children. In the years that remained to him before his death in 1860, he became a member of the Sephardic community of Jerusalem and served for a time as its head, while devoting his best efforts to the frustration of Christian missionary activity.[19]

Unique though he was in his conversion, Cresson was but one of a number of Americans whose mingled Jeffersonianism and millennialism carried them to Palestine. Inspired with the idea of founding an agricultural academy for the Jews, and perhaps also by Cresson's lunacy suit, a Mrs. Clarinda S. Minor of Philadelphia visited the Holy Land with her son. After returning to America to collect money and implements, this modern Tabitha again emigrated, ac-

---

[19] Warder Cresson, *The Key of David. David the True Messiah, or The Anointed of the God of Jacob. The Two Women who Came to King Solomon Were designed, in the greatest depth of Wisdom, to represent The True and False Churches, and the Living and Dead Child, or Messiah. Also, Reasons for Becoming a Jew; with a Revision of the Late Lawsuit for Lunacy on that Account. Together with An Appendix.* (Philadelphia, 5613 [i.e., 1852]). Karp, "Zionism of Cresson." Despatches, Jerusalem: Page to Sec. of State, 8 November 1860.

companied by some young ladies, and acquired a tract of land near Jaffa. Following a visit to Jerusalem in 1852, a Dr. C. F. Zimpel, a naturalized American of German birth, put forth proposals for the colonization of the Holy Land; in these, despite the opposition of European Jews, he persevered for more than a decade, while devoting his engineering talents to preparing the way by drawing plans for a breakwater at Jaffa and for a railroad to link that port with Jerusalem and Damascus. In July 1852 Philip D. Dickson of Groton, Massachusetts, took ship for Palestine as an independent agricultural missionary. Within the year he was dead, and in October 1853 his widow returned to Boston, only to find that her father-in-law, Walter Dickson, had sailed with his family on the same errand. In 1854, from its headquarters at Westerly, Rhode Island, the Seventh-Day Baptist Missionary Society sent out a Mr. and Mrs. Charles Saunders in the twin hopes of redeeming the Jews and promoting modern agricultural practices. The Society for Ameliorating the Condition of the Jews sent out another New England farmer. There may have been one or two more. By the summer of 1854, when the U.S.S. *Levant* touched at Jaffa, several American families had settled themselves on small farms or plantations and appeared to be succeeding in their efforts to civilize the natives and prepare the way for the millennium. Since this was frontier farming, and since small bands of Bedouin raided the neighborhood from time to time, the commanding officer saw fit to answer the request of one of these families by providing them with a few Hall's carbines and the necessary ammunition.[20]

The attraction of the Holy Land for Americans of mid-century was not, it must be emphasized, confined to such enthusiasts as these. As early as 1816 *Niles' Register* had observed that if the Jews would unite their efforts, they might well overcome the weak and imbecile Ottoman Empire, the degraded East might again become the seat of commerce and the arts, and the desert blossom like the

[20] Herman Melville, *Journal of a Visit to Europe and the Levant*, ed. H. C. Horsford (Princeton, 1955), pp. 130-33, 154-60; N. M. Gelber, "A Pre-Zionist Plan for Colonizing Palestine," 1 *Historia Judaica*, 81-90; "Report on the Jaffa-Jerusalem Railway," *Accounts and Papers*, 1893, Vol. 91; Noel Verney and Georges Dambmann, *Les puissances étrangères dans le Levant, en Syrie et en Palestine* (Paris and Lyons, 1900), pp. 355-56; S. A. Green, "Walter Dickson's Family," 2 *Groton Historical Series*, 238-40; *Seventh Day Baptists in Europe and America* (Plainfield, N.J., 1910), pp. 348-49; W. C. Prime, *Tent Life in the Holy Land* (New York, 1857), pp. 31, 36. Squadron Letters: Stringham to Sec. of Navy, 18 July 1854.

rose. Increasingly, from that time, American travelers had visited the Holy City; inevitably they had published accounts of their experiences, and these artifacts of mixed piety and geography had commanded a ready sale and had brought more travelers. In his early years in the Pacific, Herman Melville had developed a strong distaste for the missionaries

> Who in the name of Christ and Trade. . . .
> Deflower the world's last sylvan glade.

Visiting Jerusalem in 1857, he liked little of what he saw and thought the agricultural missionaries ridiculous, but the experience was a sufficiently moving one to occupy his mind for twenty years.[21]

As well as the travelers and the enthusiasts, the practical men were now beginning to show an interest, stimulated perhaps by the reports of the Dead Sea expedition. In May 1856 the recently organized American Geographical and Statistical Society petitioned the Secretary of the Navy to send forth an expedition which would go beyond the limits that had been imposed on Lynch and explore the Syrian desert. Of the eight signers of the memorial, only Henry V. Poor, the railroad economist, is remembered today, but they formed a most respectable group, including a New York rabbi, a prominent Congregational minister, a naval officer recently returned from the Mediterranean, a philanthropic banker, and the physician and geologist of the Lynch expedition. In the absence of a favorable response from the Secretary, the Society in the next year published a report in amplification of its proposal.

This report, in its own admixture of God and trade, was a sufficiently remarkable document to issue from a learned society. Noting the currently depressed state of business and observing that maritime commerce was the best index of future national greatness, the Society called for rapid action. The hub of future world trade, which some had seen in the United States and others at the Central American isthmus, was now located at the junction of Europe, Africa, and Asia, on the main route to the East; pending the construction of a canal at Suez, the Syrian desert was the most important of the world's thoroughfares and "the link to unite and civilize all mankind by commerce." American trade with the Orient was growing

---

[21] *Niles' Register*, 9 November 1816. Melville, *Journal of a Visit*, pp. 155-60; *idem, Clarel*, ed. W. E. Bezanson (New York, 1960), p. 434. This remarkable poem, the matured fruit of the journey of 1857, was published only in 1876.

rapidly; American river steamers were well suited to the Tigris and the Persian Gulf; the Near East possessed an atmosphere salutory to invalids and favorable to extended life, as well as such valuable resources as pearl banks and a tea plant which promotes "social feelings, serenity of temper, sprightliness, and power of enduring fatigue." The planting of olive trees, irrigation by artesian wells, and the turning of rivers would make the desert blossom. Colonization of the Syrian desert would, it was contended, form an effective barrier between Russia and India. Only by Syrian railroads could "Great Britain, France, the Jews as a people, the United States, the Mohammedans, including Arabs and others, . . . be commercially united," while "Jewish influence brought to bear, by a proper representation, in what is called Syrian Arabia, would most effectually give a new impetus to the commerce of the East, as well as of the world." Leadership in the exploration of Syria, an enterprise beneficial to commerce and tending to the diminution of religious prejudice, is "the true field" of action for the United States Navy. Let America lead and the nations will follow.[22]

In fact, however, other nations were leading, for concern with this pivot of the world's commerce was inevitably international. As far back as the thirties, the British Indian Navy had shown its interest in the Persian Gulf, and the efforts of the British Captain Chesney to launch iron steamers on the Euphrates had drawn skeptical comment from Commodore Porter at Constantinople. Since that time the solicitude of both England and France had grown. Ignorant, perhaps, of this early history, since Chesney's narrative went long unpublished, Lynch in 1847 had fruitlessly bombarded the Secretary with requests for permission to extend his explorations to include a descent of the Euphrates. But by the middle fifties, interest in Syria had become widespread, as French schemes for a canal at Suez stimulated British interest in the Euphrates-Persian Gulf route to the East, and in other alternatives. In *The Dead Sea, A New Route to India*, William Allen, a captain in the Royal Navy and a Fellow of the Royal Geographical Society, argued with much information from Lynch and other explorers for "a noble canal," to be made by cutting in from the Bay of Acre and out at Akabah, and so flooding the entire valley from Tiberias to Mount Hor. Himself interested in the restoration of the Jews, Allen foresaw that England, as the mari-

[22] American Geographical and Statistical Society, *Report and Memorial on Syrian Exploration* (New York, 1857).

time nation in the west described in Isaiah 18:1-2, would be the agent of their return. So, ultimately, it would be. But in the 1850's England was not the only nation that answered this description.[23]

Home again after a period devoted to the exploration of the Guinea coast, Lynch now joined the group pressing for Syrian exploration. In a lecture on "Commerce and the Holy Land," the officer who had earlier displayed the American flag in Palestine as a "harbinger of regeneration" returned to the themes of Barlow and Dwight. Pointing to the awakening of China and to the possibilities inherent in the engrafting of new wants upon that mighty population, Lynch emphasized that the preferred route to the Orient lay through the Mediterranean rather than the Pacific. As well as entering the markets of Asia, the United States should become, as her faster merchant ships fitted her to become, the carrier of Europe. To unite East and West and to fulfill the prophecies of Daniel and Isaiah, the Syrian Desert should be explored and the Jews restored. Those who encouraged such exploration encouraged commerce, civilization, and Christianity. In 1860 this lecture was published, with extended remarks, at the urging of a committee which counted among its members three individuals with family links to the Near Eastern missionary effort, three signers of the Geographical Society's memorial, the political scientist Francis Lieber, the isthmian expert William H. Aspinwall, and Luther Bradish.[24]

Such aspirations were easier to state than to accomplish. The efforts of those who had commenced the task of redemption had not been crowned with success. The younger Dickson had died in 1853 and Mrs. Minor, abandoned by her followers, in 1855. Although the elder Dickson had cultivated some twelve acres with reasonable success, his efforts to prepare the soil both literally and figuratively for the Second Coming by "setting [the Jews] right in their faith and their farming," had come to naught: the Jews, he reported, "are lazy & dont like work." Despite the Hall's carbines left by a protecting Navy, harassment had continued, and after an Arab raid in 1858

---

[23] H. L. Hoskins, *British Routes to India* (Philadelphia, 1928). Despatches, Turkey: Porter to Sec. of State, 1 June 1835, 10 March 1836. Expedition to the Dead Sea: Lynch to Sec. of Navy, 9 February 1848, 17 February 1848, 8 March 1848. Confidential Letters: Sec. of Navy to Lynch, 28 February 1848, 31 March 1848. William Allen, *The Dead Sea* (London, 1855); G. P. Marsh, *Man and Nature* (New York, 1864), pp. 524-25.

[24] W. F. Lynch, *Commerce and the Holy Land* (Philadelphia, 1860). Although in less expansive form, the interest in Palestine exploration was to outlast the Civil War. See, e.g., 43C 1S *HMD* 158; Tibawi, *American Interests*, pp. 230-31.

in which wife and daughter were raped, a son-in-law killed, and he himself wounded, Walter Dickson returned to the United States. Two years later the Seventh-Day Baptists gave up the effort and recalled their people.[25] In happier times, perhaps, the government might have answered the summons of the Geographical Society and sent forth an exploring expedition, but in 1860 other cares took precedence. Shortly the Union would dissolve, and Lynch, far from helping in the fulfillment of prophecy and the spread of freedom through commerce, would find himself a flag officer in the Confederate Navy, defending one kind of freedom against another.

Here one might think the story would have ended, but convictions founded on prophecy die hard. The war came. The last best hope of earth was threatened with extinction. But the war years also brought the mobilization, in the distant state of Maine, of the most considerable of all American efforts to colonize the Holy Land.

3. The Sacred and Secular Arms

The fate which overtook the Dickson family was but one example, if more tragic than most, of a problem with wide ramifications. Even before the arrival of the agricultural colonists, the expansion of Near Eastern missionary activity had exposed increasing numbers of Americans to the hazards of life in Ottoman dominions, had raised puzzling problems for the American government, and had forced the extemporization of a policy. Much as the attacks on American commerce and the incarceration of American citizens had first drawn the Navy to the shores of Barbary, so violence directed against missionaries and missionary property made for involvement farther east. By mid-century, the protection of American missionaries had become an important responsibility of diplomat and naval officer alike.

For the missionaries themselves these troubles had also raised problems of policy, and had forced them to consider just what their relationship to their government might be. Appearing originally as individuals, in areas where their government had no diplomatic or consular representation, the first evangelists had been on their own. As individuals, too, they had shared to the full the American bias in favor of individual rights and against state power: the "Hints and

[25] Green, "Dickson's Family"; *Seventh Day Baptists*, p. 349; Melville, *Journal of a Visit*, pp. 159-60. Despatches, Jerusalem: Gorham to Sec. of State, 19 January 1858, 19 January 1859. Despatches, Turkey: Brown to Sec. of State, 17 February 1858. Despatches, Alexandria: DeLeon to Sec. of State, 29 January 1858, 9 March 1858.

Cautions to Missionaries" had counseled the avoidance of consuls and representatives of their own nation, and Commodore Porter had approved these hints; although willing to preach to the crews of visiting squadron ships, Daniel Temple had made it clear that he was "no friend to national armaments of any kind." But circumstances alter cases. From the shores of the Mediterranean to the interior of Persia the missionaries had profited from the support of British emissaries, representatives of a government lacking the American inhibitions on the use of power. And in time these inhibitions came to be regretted, as the American evangelists, tossed about like Paul between Ananias and Agrippa, came to follow his example: as he "at times fell back on his high position as a Jew and Pharisee," so they found themselves tempted to assert their "privileges of birth and country."[26]

Such assertion, once diplomatic relations had been established, depended largely on the American minister. The attitude of Commodore Porter, of whose salvation the missionaries were repeatedly hopeful but never quite certain, was one of measured support. He enthusiastically encouraged their educational efforts; he assisted their penetration into Anatolia by obtaining vizierial letters of protection. When difficulties developed in Syria during the decade of Egyptian occupation, he managed to secure redress from Alexandria for the Bird outrage of 1833 and arranged for ships of the squadron to visit the Syrian coast. By 1835 his repeated recommendations to Washington had led to the establishment of consulates at Alexandria, Beirut, and Aleppo. But while supporting the missionaries as individuals, Porter firmly disassociated himself from all proselyting, and repeatedly advised his countrymen "to avoid doing anything that will be likely to offend the prejudices of the musselman." In 1841, when trouble came to the Lebanon, this attitude was insufficiently positive for those involved.[27]

Complaints by the Maronite patriarch of missionary interference with his flock had been relayed to Porter by the Ottoman government, accompanied by an expression of hope that the situation would not lead to incivility to the Americans and by a request for their

---

[26] ABC 16.5, Vol. 2: "Hints and Cautions," Goodell to Schauffler, 6 December 1834; Goodell to Anderson, 30 January 1835. ABC 16.9, Vol. 1: Goodell to Anderson, 9 May 1835. Temple, *Life of Temple*, p. 262; Dwight, *Encyclopedia of Missions*, p. 270.

[27] ABC 16.9, Vols. 1, 2; ABC 16.7.1, Vol. 3, *passim*. Despatches, Turkey: Porter to Sec. of State, 22 April 1835 and *passim*.

removal. In reply, Porter pointed out that the trouble originated in the opening of schools by the missionaries, and explained that he had no power to remove his compatriots but could only bring the situation to their attention. In the Syrian mission, where Eli Smith had already written of the need to demonstrate American power, this attitude led to an eruption, and to intimations that complaints would be made in Washington. At Constantinople the missionaries took the extraordinary step of intercepting and returning the Commodore's dispatches, to argue for a change of phraseology. Apprised of the crisis, the American Board formally discussed the relation of the missionary to his own government and concluded that both as individual American citizen and as agent for many others, he deserved the same support in his evangelical profession as did those in any other lawful business. A former governor of Massachusetts was sent to Washington to remonstrate with the State Department, and in February 1842 Daniel Webster advised Porter that the President was "profoundly interested," and instructed him to omit no occasion to extend to the missionaries all proper assistance "in the same manner" as he would in the case of merchants.[28]

Although considered by the missionaries as a milestone, Webster's dispatch was in fact brilliantly vague. In acknowledgment, Porter merely observed that he had protected all Americans in accordance with the treaty and would continue to do so. Nor was the letter followed up by any comprehensive instructions, and their absence, over the years, brought repeated requests for guidance from the legation at Constantinople: in 1843, when the Turks requested the removal from Erzerum of missionaries alleged to be subverting national and religious principles; in 1846, when the Armenian patriarch commenced his persecution; in 1851, when the Porte complained of missionary activity in Kurdestan; in 1853, when letters critical of the legation, written from Urmia and signed by "Persicus," appeared in the American press.[29]

But if the State Department stood mute, the missionaries were in no way backward in asserting their claims. At Constantinople, in 1844, Rufus Anderson raised the question of the protection of the

[28] Despatches, Turkey: Porter to Sec. of State, 16 May 1841, 31 July 1841, 16 October 1841. Instructions, Turkey: Sec. of State to Porter, 2 February 1842. ABC 16.7.1, Vol. 3: Goodell to Anderson, 19 February 1842. *Memorial Volume of ABCFM*, pp. 197-202.

[29] Despatches, Turkey: Porter to Sec. of State, 16 July 1842; Brown to Sec. of State, 7 October 1843, 1 March 1846, 25 March 1853, 2 April 1853.

Urmia missionaries with the American minister, and so stimulated the first suggestion of a Persian treaty. In the next year, while insisting on his right to protection while traveling about the Ottoman Empire, Dwight vigorously denied that the Turks had any right to inquire into his purposes. In 1846 Cyrus Hamlin forcefully if unsuccessfully insisted that the legation protect his Armenian gardener against arrest for nonpayment of debt. These and similar efforts to secure government support gained backing from the adoption by the State and Navy departments of Elliot's *Diplomatic Code*, for Elliot had reprinted the letter, written by Secretary of the Navy Southard in the last days of the administration of John Quincy Adams and carried by warship to the King of the Sandwich Islands, which had expressed the President's belief that the extension of "a knowledge of letters and of the true religion" was "the best and the only means, by which the prosperity and happiness of nations can be advanced and continued," and which bespoke favor for the missionaries who had come to promote "the cause of religion and learning."[30]

As well as by the assertion of rights, the cause of religion and learning could be promoted by the proper selection of diplomatic and consular personnel, and here too the missionaries were active. Although a proposal by Commodore Porter to appoint a missionary to the Jerusalem consulate had been early declined by the Constantinople brethren, in accordance with the views of Goodell's "Hints," in time the suggestion was put forward that the power of appointment to this office and the responsibility for the salary of the incumbent should be vested in the American Board, and that the government should confer only the title. On the death of Porter in 1843, the Constantinople mission wrote home to suggest that the Board attempt to influence the choice of his successor. In 1850 the appointment of Homes as assistant dragoman gave the mission one of its own inside the legation; in 1851 Jonas King became acting consul at Athens; three years later a New Hampshire clergyman was appointed to the Beirut consulate.[31]

The first notable result of these developments appeared in the

[30] Despatches, Turkey: Carr to Sec. of State, 3 February 1844; Brown to Sec. of State, 4 December 1845, 18 April 1846. Phillips, "Pagan World," pp. 105-6, 169; Elliot, *Diplomatic Code*, ii, 679-80.

[31] ABC 16.9, Vol. 1: Goodell to Anderson, 16 September 1835. ABC 16.7.1, Vol. 3: Goodell to Anderson, 15 March 1843. Despatches, Turkey: Marsh to Sec. of State, 24 September 1850. Instructions, Turkey: Sec. of State to Spence, 14 September 1854. Melville, *Journal of a Visit*, p. 161.

forward policy of Dabney Carr. Whatever the reasons for his appointment to the Constantinople legation, Carr proved highly satisfactory to his evangelical compatriots, by whom he was early reported as reading the Bible with much seriousness and in an interesting state of mind. Even more satisfactory, perhaps, was the vigor with which he supported them in their trials, acting on his own responsibility and, perhaps most remarkably, not reporting his actions to the State Department until long after the event.

Writing to the Secretary in November 1848, Carr enclosed copies of some twelve-month-old correspondence by which he had obtained, against the will of the local pasha, the right for Protestants to bury their dead in Trebizond. Gratified and presumably also emboldened, both by Department approval of this action and by a change of administration at home which promised his imminent recall, Carr then reported in February 1849 on his activities during the Armenian persecution of 1846. This correspondence he hoped would be personally perused by the Secretary of State, since it had "made a deep and lasting impression on the Armenian people," and seemed to have "fixed the policy of the Sublime Porte" on the subject of American missionaries.

It could, one might think, have fixed more than this, for the tone was very strong. An attack on the house of a medical missionary at Erzerum had gone unpunished, and there had been reports of further insults to Americans in the interior. Together with the suggestion that these events indicated a concerted effort to drive the Americans from the country, Carr transmitted to the Porte a memorandum from the missionaries which asserted that their work had no sectarian or political color and proposed that John Porter Brown be sent to investigate on the spot. Although the Mexican War was in progress and the Mediterranean Squadron had been withdrawn, the note was sufficiently emphatic: "The Undersigned cannot resist the apprehension that the Sublime Porte has not heretofore, given due consideration to the subject of the American missionaries. . . . It is, indeed, worthy of its gravest consideration. . . . If neglected and the course which has hitherto been pursued towards these American Protestants and their Rayah friends be continued, it will be impossible to preserve the friendly relations of the two countries, which have so long existed."[32]

[32] Despatches, Turkey: Carr to Sec. of State, 21 November 1848, 14 February 1849. Instructions, Turkey: Sec. of State to Carr, 7 December 1848.

Three years after the event there was little the State Department could do about these fighting words, and in any case the missionaries had support at home. To his instructions of May 1850 to the commanding officer of *Cumberland*, ordering him on an Eastern cruise, Commodore Morgan appended a letter to the Syrian missionaries reminiscent of Southard's to the Hawaiian king, informing them that their safety and prosperity were the main concerns of the warship's visit, which he had ordered in view of the deep interest felt by the Secretary and the President in their high vocation. The delivery of this missive called forth warm thanks from the Syrian mission, together with the suggestion that more frequent visits would be desirable and would produce "a far deeper impression of the strength and resources of our country, than it is possible for any description, verbal or written, to give."[33]

So the record stood, and Webster, the friend of missionaries, was again secretary of state, when in 1851 the American Board asked governmental action in support of Jonas King in Greece. After a year in European exile, this combative individual had returned to Athens in June 1848. There followed a period of comparative calm in which the sale of books increased, preaching was resumed, and the principal friction was with the American Baptists. But there also remained a long-standing issue with the government, which had seized a plot of the missionary's land and would neither return it nor give compensation. In 1851, as difficulties again developed, King's status was both strengthened and complicated by his acceptance of appointment as acting consul. An angry crowd having packed one of his meetings and raised such an outcry that "no voice could well be distinctly heard, I was obliged to hoist the American Flag, on seeing which the tumult ceased, and they dispersed." In Greece this new tide of hostility led to another trial for blasphemy and to a sentence of fifteen days' imprisonment followed by exile. In America it brought the intervention of the American Board.[34]

Since no diplomatic representative had as yet been sent to Greece, the Board's call for help raised puzzling problems of procedure. These were met in the summer of 1852 by orders to George P. Marsh to proceed from Constantinople to Athens in the capacity of spe-

[33] Squadron Letters: Morgan to Latimer, 17 May 1850; Morgan to Sec. of Navy, 1 November 1850.
[34] ABC 17.1, Vol. 3: King to Anderson, 25 March 1851, and *passim*. Anderson, *Oriental Churches*, I, 293-303.

cial agent, and to Commodore Stringham to provide a steam frigate as a suitable conveyance. An able lawyer and a distinguished linguist, Marsh as well equipped to undertake the mission, but a month's negotiations with the wily Hellenes was productive only of strong views on Greek lack of good faith, on the arbitrary nature of the Greek government, and on its "slavish submission to an ignorant, bigoted, and corrupt priesthood." Although the forms had been observed, King's trial appeared to have been a travesty of justice; in the question of the missionary's sequestered property, Greek conduct was indefensible.

In Washington, where Edward Everett had succeeded Webster at the State Department, these opinions received acceptance. But while their effect on the Secretary's views of Greece prepared the way for his welcome to Mehmed Pasha, they offered little guidance for future moves at Athens. Since an attempt to disprove the charge of blasphemy would involve the government in undesirable argument about "the greatest niceties of dogmatic theology," the real-estate claim was seized on as a lever. In the spring Marsh was ordered back by warship and instructed, while avoiding "the tone or language of menace," to state the President's low opinion of the trial, to ask a revocation of the sentence of banishment, and to press for settlement of the claim. Language and tone of menace were avoided, but Marsh's arrival with *Cumberland, Levant,* and *St. Louis* constituted the greatest Mediterranean show of force in years. Yet even this was of little avail before the falsehoods and evasions of the Greek foreign minister, and in the end the best that could be obtained was a doubtful promise of monetary redress.

To Marsh the case appeared of great importance to "the friends of civil and religious liberty," and in the interest both of the national character and of the security of Americans abroad he urged further steps to bring the Greeks to book. The effort was complicated by a change of administration at home, but missionary pressure continued. In 1854 the documents in the case were published, and in the next year another special agent, the forceful Roger A. Pryor, was sent forth both to press for settlement of the claim and to gather information on the commerce and condition of Greece. Payment of a small indemnity was obtained; already the sentence of banishment had been revoked; Jonas King stayed on at Athens. But three visits of American agents and two naval demonstrations in support of the

American controversialist had added significantly to the precedents available for consultation when difficulties next arose.[35]

They arose in 1858, with the raid on the Dickson farm at Jaffa. At Constantinople, Carroll Spence had departed, his successor, James Williams, had not arrived, and Brown was again acting minister. Together with a visit to Syria by the Consul General at Alexandria, Brown's vigorous protests to the Porte resulted in some arrests, but trial and punishment were long delayed. Again the Board bestirred itself at Washington, while upon Williams at Constantinople the Syrian missionaries brought heavy pressure. Fearing for the safety of all Christians should the murderers go unpunished, they invoked the honor of the United States, reprobated the American consul at Jerusalem as a useless victim of delirium tremens, and called for a warship. After six months of voluminous and unrewarding correspondence with the Porte, Williams, too, reached the conclusion that the best defense available was "in the frowning guns of our own ships of war." But by this time Flag Officer LaVallette was steaming eastward with orders which required him not only to exhibit *Wabash* at Constantinople, but also to visit the Syrian coast "at as early a period as possible" to inquire into the outrages. This, on leaving the capital, he did; ultimately the guilty received sentences of life imprisonment.

The ending was perhaps satisfactory, but the settlement had been difficult to reach, and in fact it seemed that disorder was spreading throughout the Ottoman Empire. To Williams' suggestion that a small steamer be ordered to Constantinople as station ship came the reply that none was available. But some precautions could be taken, and LaVallette, before departing for the western basin, had ordered *Macedonian* to remain throughout the winter on the Syrian coast. Since *Macedonian* was commanded by Uriah P. Levy, owner of Monticello and admirer of Jefferson, friend of agriculture, and the first Jew to reach flag rank in the United States Navy, the circumstance would surely have delighted Warder Cresson, had he but known.[36]

[35] Instructions, Turkey: Sec. of State to Marsh, 29 April 1852, 5 February 1853; Sec. of State to Pryor, 18 July 1855. Despatches, Turkey: Marsh to Sec. of State, 21 August 1852, 9 October 1852, 27 May 1853, 2 June 1853, 23 June 1853, 29 June 1853, 6 July 1853. Squadron Letters: Stringham to Sec. of Navy, 6 April 1852, 26 May 1853. Anderson, *Oriental Churches*, I, 303-7. Marsh's extensive correspondence in the King case was published as 33C 1S *SED* 67 and 33C 2S *SED* 9.

[36] Despatches, Turkey: Brown to Sec. of State, 17 February 1858, 24 March 1858;

Inland, however, beyond the range of *Macedonian's* guns, lawlessness continued to increase. In the summer of 1859 Williams reported a series of new outrages: the burning of a missionary residence, an assault on an American citizen, the expulsion of a missionary family from Zahleh in the Lebanon and the plundering of its property. Again satisfaction proved difficult to obtain; again Williams returned to the suggestion of a station ship. Feeling also that a showing of the flag on land might be of help, he set out in the autumn on a tour of Syria and Palestine.

At Beirut the Governor proved wholly cooperative and missionary difficulties were discussed at length; while none too optimistic, particularly regarding regions inhabited by difficult Christian populations, the official promised to do his best. On his journey to Damascus, Williams was met and escorted with great military display; the Pasha, both civil governor of the city and military governor of Syria, proved able and affable. Returning to the coast, the Minister was greeted with distinguished receptions wherever he went: at Zahleh, whence the missionary family had but recently been expelled, "the house tops upon the side of the street were covered with the female portion of the population, singing in concert their wild and most peculiar songs of welcome. After the manner of the country, they sprinkled perfumed water upon the procession below, and in various other ways exhibited every mark of respect."

Southward along the coast and then inland to Jerusalem the progress continued. Generous hospitality was provided by the "celebrated chief" who had accompanied the Lynch expedition, and everywhere there were evidences of good feeling. Reinforced by missionary requests from the interior, the experience led Williams to consider a tour through Anatolia, extending perhaps as far as Urmia, to "visit officially some of the more important of the 'American colonies' " and to conciliate the local magnates by the distribution of sets of American pistols.[37]

But Williams' Syrian idyll came just before the storm. In June 1860 bloodshed again swept the Lebanon, and the war of reciprocal

---

Williams to Sec. of State, 16 June 1858, 23 July 1858, 8 September 1858, 4 October 1858, 20 March 1859. Confidential Letters: Sec. of Navy to LaVallette, 19 May 1858, 14 August 1858. Squadron Letters: LaVallette to Sec. of Navy, 2 November 1858, 3 December 1858. Miller, *Treaties*, VIII, 519-32.

[37] Despatches, Turkey: Williams to Sec. of State, 21 June 1859, 30 August 1859, 28 December 1859, 22 September 1860.

massacre and town-burning between Maronites and Druses was followed in July by terrible slaughters at Damascus. At Hasbeiya a thousand Christians were reported slain. At Damascus, whence almost the entire Christian and Jewish population fled, the number reached six to eight thousand. As the smoke of burning towns rose high into the air and as the refugees descended upon the seaports, the American missionaries and their British brethren found themselves faced with the responsibility for the relief of a very large population.

Once more the protection of foreigners in Turkey became a pressing task; once more Williams called upon the Navy. But this time there came no answer. The squadron had been greatly reduced: from May to November only *Iroquois* was on station, and she was occupied elsewhere. Other nations, however, were better off. In August, France received the mandate of the powers to restore order in Syria, and shortly a French expeditionary force set sail.

The Turks, for once, were also acting. As a dominantly Moslem province, Syria, after all, was very different from the Christian and contentious Balkans, and the magnitude of the massacres and the imminence of foreign intervention made deeds necessary. In July the Foreign Minister, Fuad Pasha, was sent to Syria with special powers, and by energetic measures succeeded in restoring order. But as often in such cases, the measures were intermittently excessive. For the Governor of Damascus, who had so cordially received him and whom he thought the best of the provincial pashas, Williams had ordered a pair of ornamented pistols. But by the time the gift arrived the intended recipient had been degraded and executed, in consequence, as Williams thought, of political necessity and European pressure; and the pistols, their inscriptions hastily altered, were presented to Abd el Kader, the exiled Algerine patriot, who had performed great services for the Christians of Damascus.

To most Americans in the Levant the Syrian tragedy seemed less the result of Moslem malevolence than of Ottoman impotence, itself the consequence of European pressure on behalf of Christian sects, which had undercut the power to rule. In any case, there were some consolations: on his arrival in Syria, Fuad had had the imperial firman printed on the mission press at Beirut; "even in the midst of the carnage" Americans had been respected. Alone in an isolated village when it was assaulted by Moslems, a missionary wife had raised the flag over her house; alone of all the village dwellings, hers and its inhabitants had survived. But the main effect of the Syrian warfare was to excite the Hopkinsian imperative to do good. By October an Anglo-American relief committee was feeding more than fifteen thousand displaced persons at Beirut, and Williams, as its vice president, was asking permission to contribute government funds. In America, meanwhile, another humanitarian effort was being mobilized. In November a Navy storeship sailed for the Mediterranean with supplies for the dispossessed of Syria, and this cargo, transshipped to *Susquehanna* at Spezia, was delivered early in the next year.[38]

At Constantinople, too, the summer of 1860 had brought problems. In July the attempted burial of an Armenian Protestant with services by an American clergyman had resulted in a three-day riot and in fears of another major outbreak. This event, the apparent consequence of Russian intermeddling, led to action by the Protestant powers, as the ministers of Great Britain, Holland, Prussia, Sweden, and the United States joined in a memorial to the Grand Vizier on the subject of Protestant safety and Protestant right to burial. From Washington, at least, the response was vigorously negative: roused by this report of collaborative intervention in Turkish internal affairs, the State Department in October delivered a forceful reprimand. But to this Williams replied with a long and spirited defense, claiming that his aim had been primarily the protection of Americans and only secondarily of Protestants, arguing that joint action had been the best available procedure, and contending that his defense of the rights of humanity and religious liberty was consonant with the genius of America. As well as for its vigor, the defense was interesting for its traditional American resort from particular instances to general principles and in its choice of precedent: avoiding all reference to the effort expended on behalf of Jonas King, Williams took his examples from the larger sphere and adverted to such actions in freedom's cause as the provision of a warship to revolutionary Greece, the money and influence employed on behalf

[38] Despatches, Turkey: Williams to Sec. of State, 1 June 1860, 16 June 1860, 27 June 1860, 5 July 1860, 13 July 1860, 19 July 1860, 31 July 1860, 7 August 1860, 26 August 1860, 8 September 1860, 26 September 1860, 26 October 1860. Squadron Letters: Bell to Sec. of Navy, 13 December 1860, 3 January 1861. Anderson, *Oriental Churches*, II, 346-52. The Damascus massacres and their aftermath are dealt with in what is perhaps the only respectable missionary novel: [J. W. DeForest], *Irene the Missionary* (Boston, 1879).

of Hungarian revolutionaries, and the forceful liberation of Martin Koszta.

More important than the lessons of the past was the question of the future, and neither in America nor in Turkey did this seem promising. At home, the Republican victory at the polls had been followed by secession of the sovereign state of South Carolina. In the East, the Turkish government appeared to be collapsing in consequence of internal tensions and external pressures. Although holding to the view that the Turks were more sinned against than sinning and that no European government matched theirs in religious liberty, Williams thought the future dark. The government was bankrupt, the soldiers were unpaid, and while Britain appeared uncertain of her ability to maintain the Sultan, the French were prepared for any emergency and the Russians were "vigorously shaking the tree."[39]

Unquestionably, the continuing pressures from without and the twin forces of nationalism and liberalism within had placed terrible strains upon both Ottoman government and Ottoman society. But the Turks, for the moment, were at least trying to maintain order, as became apparent in their response to the murder of two American missionaries in 1862. In April, Jackson Coffing was ambushed outside Alexandretta, at the instigation, it was thought, of hostile Armenians; apprehended within the month, the murderers were decapitated in October "with unusual solemnity." In July, William W. Meriam of the Bulgarian mission was shot down by brigands on the road to Philippopolis; again the exertion of great efforts brought the capture of the assassins, who were soon hanged, "a form of punishment of which Mussulmen have great abhorrence."

The issue, nevertheless, remained a live one. At Constantinople the new minister, E. Joy Morris, the sometime patron of Warder Cresson, was ably upholding the interests of a country dissolved in civil war. Profiting by the Porte's own lack of sympathy with rebellion, the fruit of long experience, and by the ancient Turco-American friendship, Morris obtained full cooperation on the vital issues of Confederate belligerency and privateering, only to find himself the target of the missionaries. From the first he had experienced difficulties on the general question of the protection of Ottoman

---

[39] Despatches, Turkey: Williams to Sec. of State, 18 July 1860, 20 July 1860, 23 July 1860, 22 August 1860, 12 September 1860, 11 December 1860. Instructions, Turkey: Sec. of State to Williams, 22 October 1860.

subjects who had embraced Protestantism, and particular trouble with Cyrus Hamlin, a man of "very querulous disposition, and a despotism of character," who was feuding with the authorities over the proposed site for a new college. These frictions were exacerbated by incidents of violence which seemed, despite the swift administration of justice in the Coffing and Meriam cases, to threaten the whole missionary position. Complaints issuing from Constantinople, and particularly from the contentious Hamlin, led in America to allegations by the Board of inefficiency in office and other grave charges. There followed such a bombardment of dispatches from Washington as to raise the question of who was persecuting whom. Yet despite these pressures, the new treaty with Turkey which Morris negotiated in 1862 was concerned solely with routine commercial matters. In notable contrast to the American treaties with China, it contained no special provisions in support of missionary interests.[40]

4. The Gifts of the Magi

Exasperating though they were, the intermittently recurring outrages posed no real threat to the missionary establishment, while conversions, the growth of schools, and the expanding output of the press testified to the fact that many among whom the Americans dwelt valued their presence. Nor was it only the invisible exports of America that were welcome in the Levant: shipments of American rum were still gratefully received by the population at large, while American help was still purposefully sought by the governments. Like the enduring naval connection with Turkey, the course of the Persian treaty negotiations underscored the importance, for states attempting to modernize and maintain themselves, of an uncommitted nation with skills to sell.

To the patriot of whatever calling, such evidence of the esteem in which his country was held was gratifying indeed. But there was another consequence of the contact between the Republic of the West and the civilization of the East which went more or less unnoticed. For all the firm belief in the mutual beneficence of commerce, small attention was generally paid the reciprocal consequences of cultural interaction. Truth, to most Americans, traveled

[40] Despatches, Turkey: Morris to Sec. of State, 12 April 1862, 14 April 1862, 26 April 1862, 11 July 1862, 28 August 1862, 18 September 1862, 16 October 1862, 11 December 1862, 8 January 1863. Instructions, Turkey: Sec. of State to Morris, 25 August 1862, 1 September 1862, 6 November 1862. Miller, *Treaties*, viii, 717-52.

a one-way street; the "philanthropic band" was always outward bound. Yet by mid-century, the history of American activity along Europe's Mediterranean frontier had left, in greater or lesser ways, its impress on America.

This impress was not in terms of people: except for the short-lived increase in arrivals from southern Europe which followed the abortive Mazzinian revolutions, immigration from both Mediterranean shores remained negligible until late in the century. But in cultural matters, signs of the Mediterranean involvement can be observed. The impact of the Greek revolt, already noted with regard to literature and names on the land, remained visible in that female posture known as the "Grecian bend." For practitioners of literature and the arts, Italy had exerted a powerful pull, and numerous devotees of the "art life" had left Boston and points west for Florence and Rome. The visit of the Hungarian Washington, immortalized in Kossuth County, Iowa, had domesticated the beard among the younger generation: with the accession in 1861 of its first, if hesitantly, bearded president, the United States would enter a period of half a century in which a sizable proportion of its male citizens would be so adorned. Inevitably, no doubt, the more exotic culture of Moslem lands was less readily assimilable than that of the European shore, but it too had left some traces on the American scene.

The American map memorialized the wars with Barbary in Prebles, Decaturs, and Tripolis; commercial aspirations had given rise to Smyrnas and Odessas; biblical names were plentiful. The uncompleted pyramid on the back of the Great Seal perhaps reflected Egyptian influence; in any case, the interest in things Egyptian, which had stemmed from the discoveries of Napoleon's scientists, had affected American life. Incidental Egyptian artifacts had been brought back from early in the century, and the first mummy to reach America, the gift of a Smyrna merchant with missionary connections, arrived in 1823. The golden plates of the Book of Mormon, recovered by Joseph Smith in 1827, were written in "reformed Egyptian." In 1832 the first important collection of Egyptian antiquities was brought back to Baltimore by Colonel Mendes I. Cohen. Over the next two decades an Egyptian influence became visible in American architecture, while the American lectures and writings of George R. Gliddon, son of the consul at Alexandria, contributed importantly to the concepts of racial distinctness that characterized the so-called "American school" of ethnology.

From Smyrna, throughout these years, there continued to flow a supply of nuts and fruits for the tables of American cities and a sufficiency of opium to make tolerable, through home remedies and patent medicines, the existence of the American housewife. The Turkish bath, an experience missed by no traveler, naval officer, or missionary, had reached America by way of England, and had even entered literature in *The Oriental Bath, a poem, by C. B. Peckham, proprietor of the Oriental baths, Pelham Street, Newport, R.I.*:

> How great the use of bathing to the skin!
> The largest outlet of what's taken in.

Peckham rhymes like a Byron, and his twenty-eight pages of couplets are of interest both to the historian of public health and to the literary critic. But the most purposeful attempt to apply Oriental experience to Occidental problems came not in sanitation but in transportation.[41]

For a generation after the Red River expedition of Major Stephen Long, the Great American Desert had lain upon the maps of the American West, both obstacle and challenge. As early as 1826, an army officer with frontier experience had suggested that the camel might prove the answer to the transportation problems of the arid regions. With the conquest of California the issue assumed immediate importance, and when the suggestion was renewed by Major Henry C. Wayne, fresh from quartermaster duty in Mexico, an interested response developed. In the Senate in 1851, and again in the following year, Jefferson Davis pressed the scheme. The July 1852 issue of the *American Whig Review* carried an unsigned article on "The Desert" by George P. Marsh, minister to Constantinople; Marsh had traveled by camel in the course of his visit to Egypt, and his article contained, together with a lengthy description of the animal and its ways, support for its introduction into the trans-Mississippi West. When the Pierce administration took office in the next year and Jefferson Davis became secretary of war, sectional concern for the control of Pacific communications led him to recur, in his annual reports for 1853 and 1854, to the desirability of importing camels

---

[41] E. H. Clark, Jr., "United States Place Names Honoring the Navy," 74 *U.S. Naval Institute Proceedings*, 453-55; W. B. Dinsmoor, "Early American Studies of Mediterranean Archaeology," 87 *Proceedings of the American Philosophical Society*, 70-104; J. A. Wilson, *Signs and Wonders Upon Pharaoh* (Chicago, 1964), pp. 36-41; Finnie, *Pioneers East*, pp. 164-65; William Stanton, *The Leopard's Spots* (Chicago, 1960); Peckham, *The Oriental Bath* (Providence, 1847).

for employment on the southern route. By this time interest was spreading. The American Camel Company had been chartered in the state of New York; recalled from Constantinople with the change of administration, Marsh in the winter of 1854-55 lectured on the camel at the Smithsonian Institution and commenced a book on the subject; in March of 1855 the Congress appropriated $30,000 for the experiment.

At this point the American fund of Near Eastern experience was drawn upon to implement the scheme. Among the supporters of the proposal was Edward F. Beale, a connection of the Porters, who had served in the Mediterranean Squadron, distinguished himself under Stockton in California, and carried the first nugget of California gold to Washington. Having resigned from the Navy, Beale was now serving as superintendent of Indian affairs for California and Nevada; at his suggestion, his kinsman, Lieutenant David D. Porter, applied for command of the expedition. Detailed to assist him were that Major Wayne who seven years before had urged the scheme upon the War Department and Porter's cousin, Gwinn Harris Heap, who had grown up at Tunis, where his father had served as consul for twenty-four years.

In the more than half a century since Bainbridge had transported the lions and tigers from Algiers to Constantinople, no such cargo had been carried on a Navy ship. But, while Wayne went on ahead to tour the zoos of Europe, the U.S.S. *Supply* was fitted out as a camel transport and in May 1855 sailed for the Mediterranean. There, while the vessel unloaded squadron stores at Spezia, Porter visited Pisa to inspect the celebrated herd with which the Grand Duke of Tuscany worked his estate; rejoined by Wayne, the expedition then sailed for the East. Three camels were embarked at Tunis; a visit to the Crimea provided useful information on the military employment of the animal; the end of November found *Supply* at Alexandria, where six beasts were procured. By the time a stop at Smyrna rounded out the total to thirty-three camels and five native handlers, Porter was waxing enthusiastic over the multipurpose ship of the desert, which yielded milk richer than the cow and wool warmer than the sheep, carried immense loads, and would eat anything. This enthusiasm was reflected in such excellent care that *Supply*, having loaded thirty-three camels in the Mediterranean, was able, despite an eighty-seven-day homeward passage and encounters with heavy storms, to disembark thirty-four at Indianola, Texas, in May 1856.

No sooner was the task completed than Porter was ordered back for more, to return in the following February with forty-one animals and eight handlers. At the year's end, the American consul at Alexandria forwarded to the government a manual on the camel in peace and war, in which the author, Kyan Bey, also a believer in the civilizing effects of commerce, praised the project as one which might transform the warlike hunting tribes of the American West into peaceful camel breeders.

Although the Civil War would disorganize the Camel Corps and disperse its animals, and although all government camels were to be auctioned off by 1866, the experiment seemed for the moment a great success. Lieutenant Beale had been ordered to survey a wagon route west along the 35th parallel; with twenty-five of the animals he left San Antonio in June 1857 for Fort Defiance, New Mexico, whence he marched his beasts westward across the desert, swam them across the Colorado River, and arrived without loss at Los Angeles in November to deliver a glowing report. At Galveston, as enthusiasm spread, the importation of ninety-two camels by a private citizen resulted both in proof of their suitability for agricultural work and in an ordinance forbidding them to be brought, driven, or ridden within the city limits. On the West Coast, the newly organized California and Utah Camel Association brought in fifteen Mongolian animals from the Amur River country. In 1858, and again in 1859 and 1860, the Secretary of War urged the purchase of another thousand for government use. But this acquisition was never made, and the day of the camel was brief. Soon the Great American Desert was to be crossed by the iron horse, and long before the century's end Americans would be exporting locomotives to the Near East.[42]

5. The End of an Era

In the western Mediterranean, the period between the Mexican War and the secession of the southern states ended as it had begun, with war in Italy. Returning in December 1858 from his visit to Constantinople and the Syrian coast, Commodore LaVallette was impressed by the unusual amount of naval activity along both

[42] G. P. Marsh, "The Desert," *American Whig Review* (July, 1852), pp. 39-51; *idem, The Camel; his Organization, Habits, and Uses, Considered with Reference to his Introduction into the United States* (Boston, 1856); L. B. Lesley (ed.), *Uncle Sam's Camels* (Cambridge, 1929); Stephen Bonsal, *Edward Fitzgerald Beale* (New York, 1912). Kyan Bey's manual on camel management is printed, with agreeable illustrations, in 35C 1S *SMD* 271.

Italian coasts. In April 1859 such "squally appearances" as the mobilization of Piedmont and Austria signaled the imminence of war. With the outbreak of fighting came the usual calls for naval support from all the consuls in the area, but by August the issue had been settled. The battles of Magenta and Solferino, in which Philip Kearny, the millionaire American cavalryman, rode in every charge, had forced an Austrian retirement; the Peace of Villafranca had restored an unstable equilibrium. Despite this instability and the likelihood of further attempts at Italian unification, the Mediterranean Squadron was diminished. In October 1859 the recall of *Wabash* left *Macedonian* alone on station. Although *Iroquois* arrived from the United States in February, Levy was shortly ordered home, and American strength in the Mediterranean was again reduced to a single ship.[43]

When *Macedonian* left for the United States in May 1860, the excitement had already begun. In April, distressed by the cession of his natal city to France, Garibaldi had inquired of the American minister to Piedmont whether, if Nice declared its independence and established a free form of government, it could expect the protection of the United States. Soon larger issues arose. In Sicily, in the same month, an abortive rising had been put down, but on 5 May Garibaldi and his Thousand sailed from Genoa for that island, where they effected a landing on the 11th. Throughout the Western world, all eyes were turned upon this most famous of filibustering expeditions. As had been the case with earlier revolutions and uprisings, this effort on behalf of the principles of liberalism and nationality was hailed by meetings and celebrations and speeches in America and assisted by American sympathizers. In New York, throughout the winter, committees organized by General Avezzana and others had been raising money and shipping arms, and the Italian agents had received a present of a hundred repeating carbines from Samuel Colt. But the most important American contribution to the cause was made in the theater of operations, where the movement of Garibaldian reinforcements to Sicily was in large part the work of a citizen of the United States.

This individual was William DeRohan, born a Dahlgren and brother to the distinguished naval officer of that name, who in con-

---

[43] Confidential Letters: Sec. of Navy to LaVallette, 24 September 1859; Sec. of Navy to Levy, 28 March 1860. Squadron Letters: LaVallette to Sec. of Navy, 20 October 1859; Levy to Sec. of Navy, 27 April 1860, 12 July 1860.

sequence of a family quarrel had affected this improvement upon his mother's maiden name of Rowan and who, in the course of a wandering and adventurous life, had become associated with Garibaldi. In the spring of 1860 DeRohan purchased three French steamers at Marseilles. The ships were rechristened *Washington, Franklin,* and *Oregon*; American papers were procured from the Consul at Genoa, who himself came on board to hoist the American flag. On these vessels, and on the American merchant ship *Charles and Jane,* chartered by subterfuge, about 8,000 stand of arms and large quantities of ammunition were loaded; some 3,500 men were embarked, ostensibly for Suez to work on the canal; and on the night of 9 June the flotilla left the Gulf of Genoa for Cagliari in Sardinia. Off Sardinia, in international waters, the *Charles and Jane* was captured by Neapolitan warships and taken into Gaeta, where she was subsequently released in response to the demand of the American minister. But the steamships reached their destination safely, and on 13 June, DeRohan wrote from Cagliari to Commander James S. Palmer, commanding officer of *Iroquois*, asking him to escort the filibustering fleet.[44]

For Palmer the invasion of Sicily had already raised problems. Arriving at Palermo on 22 May, eleven days after the first landings, he had found the harbor crowded with foreign warships; within a week the Garibaldians had taken most of the town. On the 30th, in the course of a parley on board the British flagship between Garibaldi and representatives of the Neapolitan commander, the Italian leader had asked Palmer to provide him with powder. Notwithstanding the allegations of certain European diplomats, it appears that Palmer's response was negative; in any case, despite his own feelings of sympathy and his expectation of strong support for Garibaldi in America, he declined DeRohan's request for escort. But the delicacy of his situation was in no way diminished by the arrival at Palermo, flying the American flag and steaming in formation, of

---

[44] Despatches, Sardinia: Daniel to Sec. of State, 10 April 1860, 10 May 1860, 15 May 1860. Despatches, Two Sicilies: Chandler to Sec. of State, 15 May 1860, 14 June 1860, 23 June 1860, 26 June 1860, 30 June 1860. Commanders' Letters: Palmer to Sec. of Navy, 21 June 1860 (Naval Records Collection, National Archives). Marraro, *American Opinion*, pp. 287-96; Charles Moran, "James Sheddon Palmer," 66 *U.S. Naval Institute Proceedings*, 31-40. There is an unsatisfactory sketch of DeRohan in 5 *National Cyclopedia of Biography*, 24. His subsequent prosecution of claims against the Italian government was productive of an exhausting diplomatic correspondence: Instructions and Despatches, Italy, 1874-81, *passim*.

the ships which all were aware had brought in the reinforcing troops and the desperately needed ammunition.

Other trips would be made by the "soi-disant American steamers" and other ships would be employed, but this first reinforcing movement was of decisive importance: only the ammunition and the troops brought in by DeRohan enabled Garibaldi to continue the campaign and to extend his control over the island and pen the Neapolitans up inside the garrison towns. And even as late as early July, two months after the sailing of the Thousand, more than three-fourths of the reinforcements that had left the mainland for Sicily had been carried by the "American" ships.

In Sicily, by late July, only the royal garrison at Messina still held out. Already the Neapolitan government was collapsing; victory would now follow victory. On 22 August the Garibaldians crossed the straits and invaded the Italian peninsula. American sympathy had by now reached full flood. After carrying diplomatic dispatches to Commander Palmer in June, the young Henry Adams had rejoiced at the spectacle of one more civilized race "forming itself on the ground that we have always stood on." By early September, when the King fled to Gaeta, American volunteers were crossing the Atlantic, while American merchant seamen in Italian ports were leaving their ships to join in. And while the fighting was over before most of the volunteers reached Italy, General Avezzana did arrive from New York in time for the battle of the Volturno, in which the American consul at Messina also fought on the Garibaldian side.

In September, well before this decisive action, the forces of Piedmont had invaded the Papal States. In October they entered Neapolitan territory and joined the Garibaldians, and on 7 November Victor Emmanuel made his triumphal entry into Naples. For the representatives of some governments this victory was perhaps ambiguous, but this was hardly the case for the Americans. Of all the foreign warships that crowded the bay, the only one to salute the auspicious event and to join the Piedmontese squadron gun for gun was the U.S.S. *Iroquois*.[45]

Like the revolutions of 1848, the turmoil of 1860 seemed to re-

---

[45] Moran, "Palmer"; H. G. Elliot, *Some Revolutions and Other Diplomatic Experiences* (New York, 1922), p. 39; G. M. Trevelyan, *Garibaldi and the Thousand* (London, 1912), p. 320; *idem, Garibaldi and the Making of Italy* (London, 1914), pp. 316-19; "Henry Adams and Garibaldi," 25 *American Historical Review*, 253-54; Marraro, *American Opinion*, pp. 285-86.

quire the reinforcement of the Mediterranean Squadron. In November, Flag Officer Charles H. Bell arrived in *Richmond*, to be followed shortly by *Susquehanna* and by the storeship with supplies for the Syrian refugees. In Italy, at least, things were by this time settling down: only in Rome, defended by French forces, and at Gaeta and Messina, where the last Neapolitan garrisons still held out, was the liberal triumph incomplete. In January, Bell took *Richmond* to Messina to watch over the score of American merchant ships in harbor, and for three months, with the help of a single British warship, strove to assist neutrals, delay hostilities, arrange negotiations, and prevent the destruction of the town.

This useful work went on in depressing circumstances. Although Italian unification seemed to constitute a great triumph for liberal principles in Europe, at home the world was collapsing. The flagship had sailed from New York in mid-October; in November had come the election of Lincoln; on 3 December, Bell reported to the Secretary that he had granted permission to return to the United States to a South Carolina lieutenant who desired to resign his commission. The event was followed by others of a like nature, which culminated on 31 December in the departure of Captain Duncan N. Ingraham, commanding officer of the flagship and hero of the Koszta affair.

On 4 May 1861 the uncertainty was ended by the Commodore's receipt of orders to return the squadron to the United States. Encountered the next day, *Susquehanna* was sailed for New York within the space of two hours. Reached by telegram at Malta and recalled to Italy to coal, *Iroquois* departed on the 20th. In the course of the next few days, while tidying up the affairs of his command, Bell warned the Department of reports that rebel privateers were to be fitted out in Spain to cruise against American commerce, and of the exposed position of the squadron stores at Spezia, distant from the town and vulnerable to a descent from the sea by persons recently belonging to the Navy. On 29 May *Richmond* passed Gibraltar; on 3 July, after a coaling stop at Madeira, the flagship reached New York. While at sea, Bell had written a dispatch to offer his services to the Department in any situation that might be deemed useful, and had requested that the Navy Register be changed to show him, not as a citizen of New York, but as a citizen of the United States.[46]

[46] Squadron Letters: Bell to Sec. of Navy, 3 December 1860, 13 December 1860, 31 December 1860, 14 January 1861, 19 May 1861, 20 May 1861, 29 May 1861, 12 June 1861.

CHAPTER IX

After Appomattox, 1865-1876

1. A Newer Order of Ages

FOUR YEARS later the ordeal was over. The Union had been preserved. In Europe, through these four years, American diplomats and consuls had struggled in the face of general official antagonism to maintain the prestige of their divided country; although popular sympathy for the Union cause had afforded some encouragement, only in Turkey and in Russia had official and ruling classes given any support. Through these years the missionaries in the Near East had kept their posts, sustained, despite wartime financial difficulties, by their supporters at home. Not so, however, the squadron, and except for the tardy assignment of the corvette *Constellation* to random Mediterranean cruising, no force had been available for this sea. But at last the Confederacy was subdued and the Union restored. History could begin again.[1]

In point of fact, history now speeded up, and the ensuing years, in Europe and in the Mediterranean, were years of crisis. In Spain, at the Continent's western tip, there came a period of internal chaos, enduring until 1875 and impinging upon the United States through the associated miseries of the Ten Years' War in Cuba. North and east of the Pyrenees there developed a series of conflicts which accomplished the unification of Italy and of Germany and the downfall of Imperial France. Although the Eastern question was temporarily quiescent, the Ottoman Empire remained subject to the strains of internal nationalism, external pressure, and the corrosive effects of modernization; these, all too soon, would pose problems, as increasing disorder stimulated American concern for the missionary establishment and American sympathy for disaffected Christian minorities.

So Spanish revolutions and Bismarckian wars formed but the prelude to the prolonged Near Eastern crisis which began, following

---

[1] That some expected it to begin on much the same plan as before is suggested by Charles Sumner's curious compendium of 1867, "Prophetic Views about America," 20 *Atlantic Magazine*, 275-306, in which the parable of the mustard seed, a favorite missionary metaphor for the coming kingdom, is applied to the United States.

the financial collapse of the Ottoman Empire, with the Balkan insurrections of 1875. The next year brought the murder of European consuls at Salonica and great massacres in Bulgaria, the deposition of two sultans, and a Serbo-Turkish conflict; in April 1877 came war between Russia and Turkey. Three years of acute tension and of recurrent fears of a general European conflagration finally ended with the Berlin Congress of 1878 and a complicated settlement which resulted in British occupation of Cyprus, a redrawn map of the Balkans which incited to further change, and an Ottoman Empire wholly at the mercy of the powers.

With the European holdings of the Ottoman sultan reduced to crumbs for the picking, the focus of European diplomacy shifted to the African shore. There Western penetration proceeded apace, marked by a political and financial rivalry which resulted, in the early eighties, in French seizure of Tunis and British occupation of Egypt. With these events an age had ended. For more than a thousand years the frontier between two civilizations, the Mediterranean was such no longer, and in the years that followed, interest shifted outward to the partition of Africa and to the problems of the Orient.

These changes in Europe and in the Mediterranean were at least matched by developments in America. To the country that had fought its way out of history at Yorktown, history had happened. Even from a consenting government, it had developed, consent could be withheld. The federal bond, once so light, had become galling and had been broken; America, not Europe, had for four years been a vast Aceldama. At immeasurable cost, a very large area and a great number of people had been denied the blessings of self-determination in the name of the higher good of the Union and of the city set on a hill. By these events the world of the American Revolution had been turned upside down: this time the redcoats had defeated the farmers. The exerters of power had prevailed over its resisters, and excepting perhaps the greatest, the heroes in the new pantheon were no more than conquerors.

So great a transformation was inevitably followed by changing ways of thought. Like the victory over Mexico, but in vastly greater degree, the conquest of the Confederacy by the armies of the Union had testified to the enormous power of organized aggregates. Over the next decades and in almost every walk of life the lesson was reflected in the steadily increasing importance of structured groups. As doctrines of natural right gave way to organic and historical views of the state, the concept of mankind was replaced by a concern for nationality and the individual was reimprisoned in the social process. For a time, at least, and in some quarters, the visionary patriotism of the first generation of independence was replaced by new ideals or none; the doctrine of equality came to be looked upon as an inherent absurdity; and the Declaration, to John Quincy Adams the foundation of American institutions, was dismissed as a collection of glittering generalities.

Such changes, and the overpowering fact that freedom had been conferred by force, had their influence on the poets. Through the years the American literary set had continued its quarrel with tyrants and its defense of freedom: Lowell wrote scathingly of Louis Napoleon and Francis Joseph; Dr. Holmes hailed the liberal Czar. But two wars had brought a change of tone and an increasing concern, foreshadowed by the Young Americans after victory over Mexico, with the uses of power.

> United States! The ages plead,—
> Go put your creed into your deed,

Emerson had written in 1857, raising again the problem of the relations between ideal and action and between the new order of ages and the growing power of America. Four years later, one answer to the problem was offered as Julia Ward Howe, wife of the phil-hellene doctor, hymned the terrible swift sword.[2] Although the contrast between Mrs. Howe's fiery gospel and the serenely patriotic poetry of the Revolution was notable, its portent for the future remained obscure. Given the internal preoccupation with the problems of Reconstruction and industrialization and the diminished interest in matters overseas, some time would be required to work the answers out. But if subtly, the ancient attitudes were already shifting.

The effects of these developments were soon enough discernible among both diplomats and missionaries in the Levant. The early confidence in rapid Ottoman progress, so notable in the days of Commodore Porter and of those missionaries who foresaw the evangelization of the world in one generation, was fading; to some the influence of the West now seemed merely destructive. This con-

---

[2] J. R. Lowell, "Ode to France," "Kossuth," "Villa Franca"; O. W. Holmes, "America to Russia," "Welcome to the Grand Duke Alexis"; R. W. Emerson, "Ode, sung in the town hall, Concord, July 4, 1857"; Julia Ward Howe, "Battle Hymn of the Republic."

clusion and the concomitant doubts about the future prospects of
the Ottoman Empire were emphasized both by the expressed discouragement of Turkish reformers and by the visibly increasing
disparity of Western and Moslem civilization. Over the years, the
diplomatic dispatches manifest a diminishing sympathy for the Porte.
No longer does the extra-European situation of Turkey constitute
an obvious bond with the United States; less and less does resentment
of European aggression against the Sultan's dominions appear;
increasingly the Turk himself is seen as the oppressor of subject
Christian minorities. Nor, for that matter, was it only among the
Americans that a change in attitude was evident. On the part of
the Turks, as well, the ancient feelings of trust and friendship suffered some erosion. A developing xenophobia was exacerbated by
American sympathy for rebels against Ottoman rule and by an
American policy which, basing itself on ancient treaties and ancient
attitudes, emphasized the independent status of Tunis, Tripoli, and
Egypt. Recurrent rumors in the European press of an American
intent to intervene in Mediterranean matters and of an imminent
American alliance with Russia did nothing to diminish this alienation.

These were, of course, gradual developments, but if, on the American side, a date were to be chosen to mark the shift from old attitudes to new, that of the death of John Porter Brown in the spring
of 1872 would serve as well as any. Largely responsible for the liberation of Kossuth and primarily for that of Koszta, the persistent
advocate of naval aid to Turkey, Brown had epitomized the ancient
ways both in his vigorous patriotism and in his understanding support of the Turks. His linguistic ability had given him a considerable
reputation as Orientalist and translator; his forty years of service
at Constantinople had provided a stabilizing continuity unequaled
in the American diplomatic service. But with his passing this continuity was broken, and new appointees to the Constantinople legation, arriving with little knowledge of the problems which would
confront them, found themselves largely on their own.[3]

Paralleling these changes in the American outlook were changes
in the American economic system and in its relations with the outer
world. In the United States new forms of energy were revolutionizing manufacturing and transportation, bringing opportunities of

[3] Despatches, Turkey: Boker to Sec. of State, 28 April 1872, 2 May 1872, and
passim. Commercial Relations, 1873, p. 1060.

wealth beyond the dreams of avarice and far beyond those based on the simple physiocratic exchange of goods on which traditional American foreign policy had been founded. Over the years, as opportunity at home replaced opportunity upon the oceans, a new mercantilism developed, the one world of free trade began to separate into a high-tariff world of discrete power centers, and the navy of Jefferson gave way to the navy of Mahan. More and more the trade that counted was that which took place across the North Atlantic with the developed countries of western Europe, and as the production of the new industry and agriculture went up, the importance of exotic and colonial items declined. Less apparent, too, were the wandering mechanics and inventors of earlier days, whose function was increasingly fulfilled by the export of novel finished products, such as the new agricultural machinery in which a considerable trade developed with Turkey and the Crimea. But isolated instances continued to appear, as in the case of the emigrant from the state of Maine who for a time prospered by cooling the champagne of the Pasha of Egypt with the product of ice houses which he had established on the Danube.

Yet despite the growing dominance of manufacturing and large-scale agriculture, American trade with the Near East continued, and indeed increased in value. And as commerce had been the guiding light which from the time of Jefferson's tenure as secretary of state had drawn Americans into the Mediterranean, it was appropriate that the first multilateral international undertaking ever adhered to by the United States was the Convention of 1867 for the erection of a lighthouse on Cape Spartel, at the southern entrance to the Strait of Gibraltar.

Given the vastly greater expansion of other branches of commerce, the postwar rise in dollar value of the Levant trade was perhaps of less importance than the changes in its composition and direction. Although the United States continued to take about half the crop of Turkey opium and a considerable amount of raw wool, the invoice of figs and dates was greatly diminished, and increasingly the bills of lading recorded the emergence of such unromantic commodities as licorice, birdseed, and rags for the manufacture of paper. On the other side of the ledger, the decade of the seventies was notable for the development of a favorable balance in American trade with the Ottoman Empire. Historically the Turkey trade had been an import trade, in which America took some three or four times the value of the goods she sent: in but two years prior to 1870, and then only in the special circumstances of the Crimean War, had exports exceeded imports. But now this situation was radically changed by the large-scale export of two commodities, one new and one old. The first of these was petroleum; the second, arms and ammunition.[4]

For a quarter-century after Titus Drake brought in his well on Oil Creek, Pennsylvania, the United States held an effective world monopoly of petroleum. Not yet the prime strategic commodity that it was later to become, oil found its first great use as an illuminant. But in this field its success was notable: by 1868 illuminating oil had become America's chief export to Syria and Egypt; among American consumer goods imported at Constantinople, it was equaled in value only by rum. Although important petroleum discoveries would soon be made in the Caucasus, much American oil continued to be carried across the Black Sea to Odessa; although the world's largest pools of petroleum underlay the Near East, the American consul at Constantinople could report in 1879 that "even the sacred lamps over the Prophet's tomb at Mecca are fed with oil from Pennsylvania."[5]

In matters of armament the naval link with Turkey still remained, as the appeal of America's disengaged position was reinforced by Civil War experience and technological advance. In 1864 the Capudan Pasha—that Mehmed who had earlier visited the United States—inquired about the possibility of obtaining an American naval constructor to build iron ships and of procuring some of the new large-caliber naval guns. But while disengaged from Europe, the United States of 1864 was preoccupied at home, and all that could be done was to supply him with plans and models of the new warships. With the return of peace, however, the expanded American source of supply was quickly tapped by others. The Italian ironclads which took part in the battle of Lissa in 1866 were American-built; the Sultan of Zanzibar purchased an ex-Confederate raider; in

---

[4] Despatches, Cairo: Beardsley to Sec. of State, 22 March 1875. Verney and Dambmann, *Puissances étrangères*, pp. 464-65, 544-46, 637-80; Gordon, *American Relations with Turkey*, pp. 46-47; Henry Reiff, *The United States and the Treaty Law of the Sea* (Minneapolis, 1959), pp. 75, 93.

[5] *Commercial Relations, passim*, and especially: *1872*, p. 842; *1873*, pp. 1053-69; *1879*, II, 584-85.

311

1867 the Navy Department's offer to sell surplus warships brought interested inquiry from French, Japanese, Greeks, and Turks alike.[6]

Like the American Civil War, however, the European wars of the later nineteenth century were primarily fought on land, and the voracious demands were those of the armies. The result was a great boom in the sale of American military equipment. Looking back on his career in Turkey, the missionary educator Cyrus Hamlin observed that while the East had once led the world in arms, "now it gets its cannon from Krupp in Germany, its Martini-Henry rifles from Providence, Rhode Island, and its ammunition from New Haven, Connecticut!" So it did, and so, indeed, did much of the rest of the globe. Ever since that admirable salesman Samuel Colt had traversed the world, impartially presenting samples of his work to Turkish sultan, British prime minister, and Garibaldian patriot, American small arms had enjoyed a deserved reputation. American successes against Mexico, the mid-century industrial exhibitions, and the Crimean War had stimulated sales; American superiority in manufacturing techniques had brought a profitable trade in machine tools as well as in finished products. When the end of the Civil War left the United States with great excess arms-manufacturing capacity, the unsettled state of Europe acted to absorb the slack, and there followed, in the years from 1867 to 1880, a very considerable export of small arms, ordnance, and ordnance stores. An immense business was done with France during the Franco-Prussian War. The Russians became large purchasers of Smith and Wesson revolvers and Springfield rifles. In addition to the Martini-Henry rifles noted by Hamlin, the Turks contracted for sizable quantities of other material, including 236,000 sabers, 60,000 war-surplus Enfield rifles, and 50,000,000 rifle cartridges.[7]

But whatever went out and whatever came back was increasingly carried by others. New developments in shipbuilding, rising American costs, and the success of Confederate raiders in forcing a flight from the flag had accomplished the collapse of the American merchant marine. In the 1850's the United States had been pressing for leadership in ocean commerce; from 1861 there followed a catastrophic decline. Although the extraordinary development of Amer-

[6] Despatches, Turkey: Brown to Sec. of State, 14 June 1865, 29 November 1865; Morris to Sec. of State, 3 September 1867. J. T. Morse, Jr. (ed.), *Diary of Gideon Welles* (Boston and New York, 1911), III, 91-92, 206-7.

[7] Hamlin, *Among the Turks*, p. 27; F. J. Deyrup, *Arms Makers of the Connecticut Valley* (Northampton, Mass., 1948), pp. 124-212; *Commercial Relations, passim.*

ican agriculture and industry produced a steady postwar rise in exports and imports, the tonnage of United States shipping in foreign trade in the administration of William McKinley was smaller than it had been in the second administration of Jefferson.

This regrettable situation brought frequent comment from both naval officers and consuls. In 1866, after a northern cruise, the commanding officer of *Swatara* reported "the melancholy and notable circumstance" of having met but two American vessels, while at the same time encountering numerous "whitewashed" ships, formerly American but now sailing under foreign flags. In the Levant, in the next year, the only American shipping encountered was at Smyrna. Of 905 ships clearing Odessa in 1869, only one was American. Although large quantities of American muskets, petroleum, and rum reached Constantinople in 1873, only four American merchant vessels entered that port. At Tripoli some years of effort by the American consul to revive the trade, "once so lively," with the United States culminated in 1876 in the arrival of a single sailing ship. All in all, it might have seemed that American participation in the Cape Spartel convention would serve less to facilitate the commerce of the future than to erect a memorial to an age that was past.[8]

Yet for all these differences in the post-Appomattox world, things started out much the same. Times change, but habits and ideas live on and so do people. The Navy returned to cruise the waters of the Old World's frontier. A revolution in Crete brought forth the aging philhellenes and agitated again the ancient questions of intervention, recognition, or sympathetic abstention. In numbers larger than ever before, millennialists traveled to the Promised Land.

2. Echoes of the Past

On 3 June 1865, eight days after the capitulation of the last Confederate armies, the Navy Department established the European Squadron, successor to the Mediterranean Squadron of prewar years. Command of the new force was entrusted to Rear Admiral Louis M. Goldsborough, son of the old chief clerk and senior officer

[8] Hutchins, *American Maritime Industries*, pp. 316-24; *Historical Statistics*, pp. 444-45; *Commercial Relations, 1869*, pp. 293-94; *1873*, pp. 923, 1053-59; Verney and Dambmann, *Puissances étrangères*, pp. 548-49. Despatches, Tripoli: Vidal to Sec. of State, 6 March 1876, 16 March 1876. Letters from the Commanding Officer, European Squadron: Goldsborough to Sec. of Navy, 26 November 1866; Farragut to Sec. of Navy, 1 October 1867 (Naval Records Collection, National Archives).

of the Navy. Sailing promptly in his flagship *Colorado*, Goldsborough reached Holland on 19 July. Relations with Great Britain were still touchy, and the squadron was under orders to avoid British ports and to exchange no courtesies with British warships. But three Confederate raiders remained unaccounted for, so Goldsborough at once spread his six ships to cover the approaches to the British Isles.

This effort at interception was unsuccessful, and with the news that two of the raiders had been interned at Liverpool the search was discontinued. In the absence of any instructions on where to winter his force, Goldsborough had recommended the Mediterranean, and as autumn approached the squadron moved southward to rendezvous at Lisbon. By November the Navy Department had approved the Admiral's proposal, and after an investigation of French and Italian ports Goldsborough settled his ships at Villefranche on the Riviera.[9]

Consistent with the implications of its new name, the original directive to the European Squadron had limited its cruising ground to the Atlantic coast of Europe and the Atlantic islands. Consistent with this intent, new orders received with the new year instructed Goldsborough to shift his base outside the straits. But the new orders also expanded his station to include not only the African coast as far south as St. Paul de Loanda but the entire Mediterranean as well, and directed him to arrange at the earliest possible date for visits by squadron units to all important places trading with the United States. In January 1866, in compliance with these instructions, Goldsborough again moved to Lisbon, and with the coming of spring sent forth his ships to show the flag in upwards of seventy ports, from the Baltic south to Liberia and east to the Levant.[10]

Already the problems of the new age were emerging, as revolution in Spain and the Seven Weeks' War between Prussia and Austria called for the movement of ships to Spanish ports, to the Adriatic, and to the German coast of the North Sea. But despite these and other new developments, echoes of the Civil War persisted. The

---

[9] Letters to Flag Officers and Commandants of Vessels: Sec. of Navy to Goldsborough, 3 June 1865, 30 September 1865 (Naval Records Collection, National Archives). Squadron Letters: Goldsborough to Sec. of Navy, 19 July 1865, 5 August 1865, 10 September 1865, 3 December 1865. The Admiral derived his seniority from the fact of his appointment as midshipman, at the tender age of seven, in 1812.

[10] Letters to Flag Officers: Sec. of Navy to Goldsborough, 28 October 1865, 18 December 1865. Squadron Letters: Goldsborough to Sec. of Navy, 5 January 1866, 24 February 1866.

discovery at Rome of John Surratt, implicated in the assassination of Lincoln, and his subsequent flight into Egypt, required the dispatch of a ship to Alexandria to return him to the United States for trial. A more important event, also an outgrowth of war and assassination, was the mission to Russia of Assistant Secretary of the Navy Gustavus Vasa Fox.

In April 1866 the Czar Alexander II narrowly escaped assassination; in May the Congress, grateful to "the nation that had given us its warmest sympathies in our hour of peril," passed a joint resolution of congratulation on this escape. Appointed to convey the resolution to St. Petersburg, Fox set sail in the double-turreted ironclad monitor *Miantonomah*, with the paddle-steamer *Augusta* in company, reaching Cronstadt in early August. There the reception of the Americans was hospitable in the extreme; only in mid-September, after a six-week visit, did the ships again set sail.

With his mission to Russia completed, Fox turned to his second task. Orders from the Navy Department instructed him to visit "the most important naval installations of Europe" and gain "for national purposes" all possible information on modern warship design and on techniques of building, repairing, and laying up. This task he had already begun by submitting detailed questionnaires through the appropriate American legations to the admiralties of Britain, France, Denmark, and Russia; similar requests were now sent off to Italy, Austria, Spain, and Turkey, and on 2 October the Assistant Secretary debarked at Kiel to commence his European tour.

In its execution, as well as in its original conception, Fox's dual mission reflected the state of American foreign relations in the immediate postwar years. The congressional resolution was indicative of the tradition of amity with Russia and of gratitude for the wartime visits of Russian naval squadrons. That similar feelings did not exist for all the nations of the Old World could be seen in the phrasing of Fox's interrogatories: six of the eight asked for information of value "to a friendly naval power," but in those directed to Britain and France this pleasant phrase did not appear. And the other side of the coin was also visible in the reaction to the arrival from across the ocean of the powerful *Miantonomah*, a ship which, promising as it did to make all previous naval construction obsolete, appeared to British eyes as a wolf among the sheep.[11]

---

[11] J. F. Loubat, *Narrative of the Mission to Russia, in 1866, of the Hon. Gustavus*

Such impressions were not likely to be diminished by the assignment, following their return from the Baltic, of both *Miantonomah* and *Augusta* to Goldsborough's command. The size of this force, comprising as it now did the first-rate *Colorado*, the powerful monitor, three screw and three paddle sloops, and two storeships, offered the Old World powers food for thought. The flag of a reunited and powerful America had returned to European seas. The American squadron had wintered in the Mediterranean and had subsequently been reinforced. To some this raised the possibility that the United States intended to pursue a newly aggressive policy in an area in which it had long been interested.

As the year 1866 drew to a close, Goldsborough moved his strengthened force southward, to Lisbon and Port Mahon, preparatory to wintering again at Villefranche. This, it will be remembered, was the millennial year, which many within the Admiral's lifetime had expected to bring the fall of Pope and Sultan and the commencement of the thousand years of peace. But the calculations, by this time largely forgotten, had proven inexact. Much material progress had been made, but the world had not been evangelized. The Jews had obdurately resisted conversion. Peace had not come. Pope and Sultan still survived. Yet while the full promises of prophecy were not borne out, the year did prove productive of trouble for both Papal States and Ottoman Empire. These events made calls upon the European Squadron.

For the Papacy the latter weeks of 1866 proved, if briefly, a time of crisis, brought about by the withdrawal of protecting French forces from Rome and the attacks of Garibaldian troops. It would, one may guess, hardly have occurred to the millenary enthusiasts of earlier times that in this state of affairs the first reaction of the American secretary of state would be to offer asylum to the incumbent Antichrist, and to suggest that a Pope who two years previously had declared that no pontiff could "reconcile himself to, and agree with, progress, liberalism, and contemporary civilization," should be conveyed to America in a ship of war to be received "as the nation's guest." Opposed by other members of the Cabinet,

---

Vasa Fox (New York, 1873); M. M. Laserson, *The American Impact on Russia—Diplomatic and Ideological—1784-1917* (New York, 1950), pp. 187-95. Miscellaneous Letters Received by the Secretary of the Navy: Fox to Sec. of Navy, 26 December 1866, 27 December 1866 (Naval Records Collection, National Archives). *The Times* (London), 17 July 1866. R. S. West, Jr., *Gideon Welles* (Indianapolis and New York, 1943), pp. 325-26.

the proposal was, however, shortly dropped. But calls to Goldsborough from the American minister at Rome did result in the dispatch of two warships to Civitavecchia for the period of greatest tension.[12]

The difficulties which the year 1866 brought the Sultan, longer lasting than those of the Pope, were also to prove a greater source of complications for American diplomats and naval personnel. When looked at in conjunction with the reinforcement of the European Squadron, moreover, they contributed to the European apprehensions of a new departure in American policy. Nor was this wholly illogical. Had such a policy in fact been contemplated, opportunity now presented itself on the island of Crete, where a rebellion against Turkish rule had begun.

As was the case with so many other peoples with whom they came in contact, the welfare of the Cretans had long engaged the sympathies of individual Americans. Ever since the thirties there had been intermittent proposals to send missionaries to the island. In 1855, as an earlier insurrection was impending, the American consul had reported that the Stars and Stripes were hailed upon their every appearance, and that some vague expectation existed among the islanders that American influence would redeem them from Turkish rule. But serious involvement only developed in 1865, with the appointment to the Cretan consulate of William J. Stillman, painter, critic, journalist, sometime secret agent for Kossuth, and former consul at Rome. In the endemic unrest which prevailed upon the island, Stillman, in predictable contrast to the European consuls, sided with the Greek population against its Turkish overlords; by early 1866 he was warning the State Department of the possibility of revolt. Soon revolution did break out, supported from Greece, and in August the Consul forwarded an appeal from the Cretans to the President of the United States which invoked the memory of Washington and solicited American action in the cause of Cretan independence and union with Greece.[13]

At Constantinople, Minister Morris for the moment confined himself to reporting the facts of revolt, of Greek assistance to the rebels,

---

[12] Morse (ed.), *Diary of Welles*, II, 638-42. Squadron Letters: Goldsborough to Sec. of Navy, 26 November 1866, 2 December 1866, 5 January 1867.

[13] ABC 16.9, Vol. 1: Goodell to Anderson, 8 September 1834. Despatches, Turkey: Spence to Sec. of State, 20 February 1855. W. J. Stillman, *The Autobiography of a Journalist* (Boston and New York, 1901); Marraro, *American Opinion*, p. 212; A. J. May, "Crete and the United States, 1866-1869," 16 *Journal of Modern History*, 286-93.

and of growing tension between Greece and Turkey. Turkish support for the Union cause had predisposed him to sympathy for the troubled Ottoman Empire, and only a few weeks earlier he had gratified the Sultan with an assurance of the support of the American people; in August he found himself preoccupied with the straits question, owing to Turkish refusal to permit *Ticonderoga* to pass the Dardanelles. Shortly, however, this decision was reversed, and in September the warship arrived for an eleven-day visit to the capital. As a "clear infraction" of the Treaties of 1841 and 1856, and the first such infraction since the visit of *Wabash* in 1858, this event created a diplomatic sensation and gave Morris a taste of triumph. But despite this success, the appeal of the Cretan revolutionaries had by this time begun to work upon the Minister's latent philhellenism. Sensible of the selfish nature of European policy and proud that the suffering islanders, like the masses everywhere, turned to the Great Republic in their hour of need, Morris now took it upon himself to urge the British and Russian ambassadors to intervene at the Porte, and to press for a change of Turkish officials in Crete.[14]

The United States of 1866 was not, perhaps, a country in which one would expect to find much sympathy with rebellion, yet as early as September, Secretary of State Seward instructed Morris to do what he could to alleviate the suffering of the Cretans. The motive, presumably, was simple American humanitarianism, but the fact of the message encouraged others to go farther. At Constantinople the news of the dispatch produced excitement and stimulated Morris' spread-eagle pride in America's moral prestige and in her leadership in the cause of humanity. Describing the increasing horrors of the fighting in Crete, and reporting that the Greeks would join the American Union if only they could, the Minister inquired of the State Department whether, assuming Turkish consent, Admiral Goldsborough could not send a ship to evacuate noncombatants. The proposal was approved by the American government, but the likelihood of Turkish consent was greatly diminished by the conduct of the American representative in Crete. Seeing himself as "the recognized official protector of the Cretans," Stillman had remained at his post in the strife-torn island, working to frustrate the government to which he

---

[14] Despatches, Turkey: Morris to Sec. of State, 27 August 1866, 28 August 1866, 7 September 1866, 20 September 1866, 21 September 1866, 29 September 1866, 2 November 1866.

was accredited and writing up the revolution for the *Nation* and the *Atlantic* at home.

There, in the Athens of America, the embers of the ancient phil-hellenism were flickering into flame. Although now well into his sixties, Dr. Samuel Gridley Howe grasped at the new opportunity to assist his beloved Greece, organized a committee, and staged a meeting at which Edward Everett Hale, Dr. Oliver Wendell Holmes, Wendell Phillips, and others "presented the claims of the Cretans to the sympathy of the civilized world." Having raised $37,000, Howe again set out for Greece, accompanied this time by wife and daughters, to supervise the expenditure of the funds. One other American, Major Sydney DeKay, whose father had accompanied Henry Eckford to Constantinople, also sailed to join the struggle, only to find on his arrival in Crete that the amount of actual fighting hardly repaid the effort. But that was all. In press and politics alike the philhellenic reaction was but a pale reflection of earlier times: of all state legislatures, only that of Maine resolved in favor of the Cretan cause, while the best that Congress could do was to express its sympathy with the "present sufferings of this in-teresting people" and its hope that the war would shortly cease.[15]

Slight though it was, this concern for the Cretan revolution, when coupled with the return of the squadron and the Fox mission to Russia, seemed to emphasize the possibility of an American seizure of a Mediterranean foothold. As early as June 1866, General Igna-tiev, the Russian ambassador to the Porte and a "warm friend of the U.S.," had queried Morris about press reports that the United States was negotiating for the purchase of a depot in the Archipelago. Upon the American's dismissal of the rumor as improbable, Ignatiev observed that he hoped that it was true, that the United States should have a foothold in the Levant, and that he knew of an easily ob-tainable site. In the autumn, rumors out of Russia, presumably de-riving from the Fox mission, suggested that the United States had made a demand upon the Porte for a Mediterranean island; follow-ing Fox's visit to Prussia, the British ambassador to that country reported that an "American traveller of distinction," while denying

---

[15] Instructions, Turkey: Sec. of State to Morris, 25 September 1866. Despatches, Turkey: Morris to Sec. of State, 10 November 1866, 15 November 1866, 22 Novem-ber 1866. Stillman, *Autobiography*, pp. 417-18; Julia Ward Howe, *Reminiscences, 1819-1899* (New York, 1899), pp. 312-20; Richards, *Letters of S. G. Howe*, I, 312-13; Harold Schwartz, *Samuel Gridley Howe* (Cambridge, 1956), pp. 281-82; May, "Crete and the United States."

that his country desired a naval port, had conceded that it did seek a coaling station; in November a Greek diplomatic report from Constantinople referred to an American plan for the purchase of Melos. But a new direction was given these rumors by the evident American concern with Crete, and in December the official journal of the Porte voiced fears of American intervention, under humanitarian guise but for commercial and strategic reasons, and observed that it hardly befitted a republican government which professed Monroeism to develop an annexationist policy overseas.[16]

Despite these rumors, and despite the libertarian enthusiasm of diplomatic personnel, the Navy remained, as in the earlier Greek revolt, correctly neutral and unenthusiastic. In Washington, Secretary Welles was highly critical of Morris' actions; in the European Squadron similar views prevailed. Morris might feel it "no more than just that though we are excluded from European politics as such, we should claim especial right of taking the initiative in matters where humanity is in question," but Goldsborough did not. Although showered by messages from the Minister which described in the strongest terms the starvation of the innocent and the "fiendish cruelty" of the Turks, and which urged him in the interest both of American prestige and of the cause of humanity to send a ship to evacuate refugees, the Admiral made no move. As a young man he had served in *Porpoise* against the Greek pirates; in 1853, when commanding one of the ships of the Mediterranean Squadron, he had supported Marsh in his effort to gain justice for Jonas King; for the moment he was preoccupied with the pursuit of John Surratt, and in any case he had no orders. Not until March 1867, when he received copies of the State Department correspondence promising the dispatch of a warship, did the Admiral reluctantly decide to act, and even then his moves were carefully circumscribed. The instructions which ordered *Canandaigua* to the East were drawn up with great care, and while authority was given the commanding officer to transport Cretan refugees to Greece as an act of humanity, it was made very clear that such action could take place only with Turkish consent.

On her arrival in Crete, *Canandaigua* met a somewhat chilly re-

---

[16] Despatches, Turkey: Morris to Sec. of State, 27 June 1866, ? December 1866. "America as a European Power," *Saturday Review* (London), 13 October 1866, reprinted in 91 *Living Age*, 371-73; Driault and Lhéritier, *Histoire diplomatique*, III, 192; Blumenthal, *Franco-American Relations*, p. 70; May, "Crete and the United States."

ception, the result of the tension between Stillman and the Turkish authorities and of a recent delivery by blockade-runners of American supplies for the Cretan rebels. Offers to remove suffering women and children were peremptorily refused, and it proved difficult to verify atrocity stories; what was easily verifiable was that the Consul was on poor terms with the government. Five months later, a somewhat warmer welcome was afforded the captain of *Swatara* by a Turkish flag captain who had visited America with one of the naval missions and who spoke English fluently. While conceding that barbarities had taken place, the Turk argued that both sides were guilty; with this view, after investigation, the American officer concurred. But Stillman's conduct still made for difficulty, while in addition it appeared that Dr. Howe, that "notorious revolutionist and philhellene," had been contemplating an attempt to embroil his country either by blockade-running under the American flag or by providing an American crew to cruise against Turkish commerce under the flag of the Cretan revolutionaries.[17]

The attempt to help the Cretan refugees thus came to nought. Nor, indeed, despite Morris' reiterated concern and despite inquiry from a Cretan leader as to whether, if asked, the United States would extend its protection to the island, did the government take further action. But if this revolution did nothing else, it at least increased the diplomatic ties between the United States and the nations involved. In 1867, at long last, the mission of Blacque Bey was implemented and a Turkish legation established at Washington with the primary aim, at least according to Stillman, of obtaining his and Morris' recall; simultaneously the Greeks dispatched Alexander R. Rangabe, a fiercely expansionist historian, as minister to the United States. In the following year this action was reciprocated when Rangabe's philhellene translator, Charles K. Tuckerman of Boston, was sent out as minister to the Kingdom of Greece. In June 1868 Tuckerman reached the Piraeus in the U.S.S. *Frolic* after a voyage in which he made himself obnoxious to the commanding officer by his insistence on how the "'Friends of Greece' in the U. States" desired "to inaugurate the mission with as much éclat as possible," and by complaints about restrictive regulations on the expenditure of gunpowder in saluting. At Athens, Tuckerman's arrival excited

---

[17] Morse (ed.), *Diary of Welles*, III, 71, 138, 425. Squadron Letters: Goldsborough to Sec. of Navy, 26 November 1866, 2 December 1866, 27 December 1866, 28 February 1867, 14 March 1867, 21 March 1867, 29 August 1867; Farragut to Sec. of Navy, 20 September 1867.

momentary enthusiasm, but a visit from a more important American personage was soon to follow.[18]

In the summer of 1867 Admiral Goldsborough had been relieved of command of the European Squadron by David Glasgow Farragut, son of an immigrant from the island of Minorca, adopted son of David Porter, first admiral of the United States Navy, and the outstanding naval figure of the Civil War. For the new flagship *Franklin*, the period of Farragut's command was one long triumphal tour, with visits along the entire European coastline from Cronstadt to the eastern Mediterranean. After a winter at Villefranche and a second northern cruise, August of 1868 saw Farragut at Constantinople, where special permission was given for *Franklin* to pass the straits and where the Admiral was received both by the Sultan and by the Khedive of Egypt, then visiting the capital of his overlord. Both at Constantinople and subsequently at Athens, Farragut's visits were complicated by the troubles in Crete, which, indeed, were shortly to bring a rupture in relations between Greece and Turkey. While lying in the Golden Horn, *Franklin* was boarded by some Constantinople Greeks who attempted to deliver political addresses; at the Piraeus, Farragut was greeted by masses of Cretan refugees, lined up along the shore to cheer the American flag. Again the rumors ran around Europe as the arrival of an American minister in Greece, the visit of the American admiral, and a new and thorough investigation of the Cretan situation by the commanding officer of *Ticonderoga* caused concern. Talk of American desire for a Mediterranean naval station was revived, and Sir Henry Elliot, the British ambassador to the Porte, ever suspicious of American intrigue, informed his government that the Cretans were about to claim American protection and that Farragut had his eyes on Suda Bay.[19]

Although Tuckerman, whose dispatches reported that the Cretans would happily place themselves under the American flag, may have had such thoughts, Farragut did not: as befitted his Minorcan ancestry, his only contribution to the logistic discussion was a suggestion that the squadron should return to Port Mahon. And in any

[18] Despatches, Turkey: Morris to Sec. of State, 2 January 1867, 9 April 1867, 3 May 1867, 31 July 1867. Squadron Letters: Farragut to Sec. of Navy, 13 July 1868.

[19] J. E. Montgomery, *Our Admiral's Flag Abroad* (New York, 1869). Squadron Letters: Wyman to Farragut, 22 February 1868; Farragut to Sec. of Navy, 5 September 1868, 25 September 1868. Driault and Lhéritier, *Histoire diplomatique*, III, 192, 255.

case the revolution in Crete was now fast dying out. Finding his situation untenable, Stillman abandoned his consulate and departed for the mainland in the fall of 1868. Early in 1869 rumors of improper use of the American flag by Greek vessels brought a second visit by *Ticonderoga* to investigate. But the report proved in error; the rebellion had reached its end. While noting in his report that Tuckerman appeared at one with the Greek war party in his insistence on Greek annexation of Crete and on northward expansion as well, the commanding officer reported that American interests in the area were nil.[20]

In America nobody seemed to care. The great age of revolutions was over and the old philhellenism was dead. Nor, with so many wounds to bind up at home, did Americans seem much interested in appeals from overseas. This disinterest, indeed, extended beyond foreign revolutionaries to include fellow citizens in distress. And a number of Americans were in trouble in the Holy Land.

If the passing of the years and the experience of the Civil War had moderated American philhellenism and American enthusiasm for popular revolutions, other aspects of the past survived. Violent though the impact of the war had been, its effects were nevertheless limited. In the older rural regions, where the forces of change were attenuated by distance, the ancestral ways retained life and vigor. New developments in American Protestant thought had little affected the tradition-bound country churches; in remoter rural New England the millennial views of earlier days retained their appeal.

Early in 1862 a certain George J. Adams had arrived at Jonesport, Maine, where he organized the "Church of the Messiah." As his congregation grew under the impact of his powerful personality and magnetic preaching, Adams also founded a religious monthly, the *Sword of Truth and Harbinger of Peace,* which contained much against the Mother of Harlots and much about the imminent return of the Messiah. Soon the minister organized the Palestine Emigration Association, dedicated to the acquisition of land in that strategic spot in anticipation of the ingathering of the Jews. In 1865 Adams and an associate journeyed, or said they journeyed, like Joshua and Caleb, to spy out the Holy Land, returning with enthusiastic descriptions of a country of multiple crops and magnificent yields, of a climate where the aged renewed their youth, and of a govern-

---

[20] Stillman, *Autobiography*, pp. 450-57. Squadron Letters: Farragut to Sec. of Navy, 9 January 1868; Pennock to Sec. of Navy, 25 January 1869.

ment so desirous of American immigration as to have promised a large grant of land in the Plain of Sharon. At the same time, and with the aid of Senator Lot Morrill of Maine, Adams wrote to Morris at Constantinople to make application to the Sultan for such a grant. In the twenty-two years since his patronage of Warder Cresson, Morris had apparently learned discretion, but his reply, which reported that the proposal would not be entertained, seems not to have reached his correspondent.[21]

For the inhabitants of farther Maine, Adams' appeal was strong. For the devout, principally the women, there was the promise of being on the spot when the Redeemer came to set up his temporal kingdom. For the farmers of that cold and rockbound coast there was the land flowing with milk and honey, a warm and salubrious climate, and three or four crops a year. For Yankee bargainers there was the prospect of successful land speculation, almost a sure thing, one would think, when the Jews came crowding back to Palestine in the free-enterprise millennium. Despite exposure in the press as a former itinerant actor and lecturer, drunkard, temperance campaigner, and Mormon, and despite an arrest for performing marriages without a license, Adams retained his hold upon his flock. In August 1866 the chartered bark *Nellie Chapin* sailed from Jonesport carrying 156 emigrants, their plows and tools, some horses, and building material—bricks and precut and preframed lumber—for the construction of their dwellings. As the *Nellie Chapin* was of but six hundred tons burden, it was a crowded passage.

In September, after a forty-two-day voyage, the emigrant ship reached Jaffa and anchored two miles off. Unloading proved arduous, while to the difficulties of disembarkation was added the shock of discovery that Ottoman law forbade the acquisition of land by aliens and that in fact no land grant had been made. Yet, at least briefly, confidence and enthusiasm prevailed. Early in October, while the emigrants were still camping in improvised shelters along the beach, the U. S. S. *Ticonderoga* reached Jaffa from Constantinople. There, while liberty parties went up to visit the Holy City, the sailing master was ordered to investigate the condition of the colony.

At Constantinople the news of the landing of the Americans had

[21] On the Jaffa colonists: J. A. Johnson, "The Colonization of Palestine," 2 *Century Magazine* (New Series), 293-96; G. W. Chamberlain, "A New England Crusade," 36 *New England Magazine*, 195-207; Harold Davis, "The Jaffa Colonists from Downeast," 3 *American Quarterly*, 344-56. Some of the diplomatic correspondence was printed in 39C 2S *SED* 10.

brought immediate protest from the Ottoman government, but at Jaffa this was not yet known. The emigrants reported they had been cordially received and that the authorities had been helpful; the sailing master opined that the visit of the warship would be useful in perpetuating this attitude. No mention of the problems of land tenure passed Adams' lips: on the contrary, the visitor was told of large and fine tracts in the Plain of Sharon which had been selected for settlement. "In accordance with the usual American go-ahead proclivity, a site for a city has already been chosen ... and laid out in streets and lots, on paper. On the plan of the city may also be seen sites for churches, hotels, two colleges, one for the natives and the other for the colonists; public squares and all the other public localities which are necessary to an American community." Already, indeed, the construction of that railroad to Jerusalem which Dr. Zimpel had planned was under active consideration.

As explained by "President" Adams, the mission of the emigrants was to prepare the way for the Messiah; to the naval officer, however, the religious enthusiasm, concentrated among the female portion of the community, seemed to be combined with "a great deal of shrewd care for their temporal welfare." The building lots, it appeared, had been already paid for by parties confident of a rise in value, and indeed "the expectation of becoming rich, or the prospect of exchanging the cold, wintry climate of Maine and their hard work, for the delightful climate in Palestine and the easy life which some expect to lead; were greater inducements for their emigration than the fulfilling of certain prophecies or revelations...."[22]

Undaunted by the failure of the promised land grant, the Adamsites bought ten acres through a dummy and rented more. With the materials brought out from Maine they erected, in the course of the first year, a meeting house, seventeen homes, and a large hotel; so surprisingly located in this alien setting, these square New England clapboard structures would astonish American visitors for years. But despite the report of the sailing master, and despite these evidences of industry, the enterprise was already dissolving. To difficulties over land tenure were added difficulties with the American consul, whom Adams attempted to browbeat by claiming close acquaintance with the Secretary of State; the "President's" addiction

[22] Despatches, Turkey: Morris to Sec. of State, 31 November 1866. Despatches, Jerusalem: Beauboucher to Sec. of State, 2 October 1866, 23 October 1866. Squadron Letters: Goldsborough to Sec. of Navy, 26 November 1866.

to the bottle was becoming a public scandal; far from renewing youth, the climate was proving deadly to young and old. Within two months of the landing, one settler, having lost both property and health, was calling upon the Vice Consul at Jaffa to send him and his family home, and other such petitions quickly followed. By December, Morris was urging from Constantinople that the colonists sell their effects to defray the costs of a return to America.[23]

Disturbed by reports in the European press that indigent Americans were begging through the streets of Jaffa, Secretary Seward in early 1867 commissioned a traveling American clergyman to look in on the colony. Successfully imposed upon by the ingenious Adams, the visitor rendered a favorable verdict, but the masquerade covered deep dissension and the next naval visit elicited a different story. Arriving in April after his abortive visit to Crete, the commanding officer of *Canandaigua* found the settlement in a deplorable condition and deeply divided, and concluded that the enterprise had been a swindle from the start; on the urgent petition of thirteen colonists he transported them to Alexandria, where, assisted by a subscription from the ship's company, they were bundled aboard a steamer for Liverpool and home. After an investigation made on orders from the State Department, the Consul General at Beirut provided passage for another sixteen or so. In June the survivors published to the world "An Appeal! to Philanthropy and Common Humanity," in which they reported seventeen deaths and fifty-four departures and asked for contributions to pay their way home. But their cry fell upon deaf ears.

In October 1867, when *Swatara* stopped by, the colony was still dispersing and the ship's officers reported "President" Adams to be "no enthusiast but a common swindler. . . . a common fellow, a prototype of the Mormon Elder." Again the bluejackets took up a subscription to send a family home. The fortunate arrival of the steamship *Quaker City*, with its own cargo of innocents abroad, provided another forty penitents with passage to Alexandria, a $1,500 loan from a charitable passenger, and immortality in the pages of Mark Twain. By this time the government at Washington had authorized the expenditure of public funds for the relief of the colonists. In the spring of 1868, when the American consul general at Alexandria visited Jaffa in response to further requests for repatri-

---

[23] Despatches, Jerusalem: Beauboucher to Sec. of State, 2 December 1866. Despatches, Turkey: Morris to Sec. of State, 12 December 1866.

ation, he found that but twenty-six of the original colonists re-mained, that "new and bitter feuds had broken out among the few remaining members," and that the Adamses had quarreled with each other. Shortly the "President" himself reached Alexandria, en route to London to lecture in Exeter Hall, only to return at once to Jaffa in consequence of a message received in a dream.[24]

In due course, however, even the Adamses departed. For the moment Morris' problems with Americans in Syria were limited to the curious case of H. M. Canfield, a former American consul at the Piraeus, who had deserted his post, adopted an alias, and associ-ated himself with some other adventurers in attempted rebellion against the Turkish government. In time most of the lands and buildings at Jaffa were sold off to a group of German Adventists, whose disciplined indifference to land speculation made their agri-cultural efforts more successful than those of their predecessors; in 1875 Charles Dudley Warner reported a mere half dozen of the original 156 Americans remaining. Two of these were destined to achieve a certain success in life, as Cook's Tours representatives and travelers' guides, and in this sense, at least, to prepare the way for later comers to the Holy Land. In 1892 the Jaffa-Jerusalem railway, which Dr. Zimpel had planned so long before, was finally com-pleted, and while its construction was the work of a French com-pany, the carriages were American and the locomotives were built by the Baldwin Works at Philadelphia.[25] Ultimately, of course, the Jews did return to Palestine. But while this ingathering was accom-plished, as Mordecai Noah had hoped, with assistance from Amer-ica, it took place in ways which none of the nineteenth-century millennialists had foreseen.

3. Navy and Naval Base

Except for the revolt in Crete, the period following the American Civil War was, for the Ottoman Empire, one of comparative sta-

[24] Despatches, Turkey: Morris to Sec. of State, 5 April 1867, 3 May 1867, 21 May 1867, 24 May 1867, 3 June 1867, 30 July 1867, 17 October 1867. Despatches, Alex-andria: Hale to Sec. of State, 19 February 1868, 9 May 1868. Squadron Letters: Goldsborough to Sec. of Navy, 29 August 1867; Farragut to Sec. of Navy, 7 Novem-ber 1867. Twain, *Innocents Abroad*, Chap. 30.

[25] Despatches, Turkey: Morris to Sec. of State, 5 March 1868, 27 November 1868, 3 January 1869, 27 January 1869, 17 March 1869. Caspar Morris, *Letters of Travel, 1871-1872* (Philadelphia, 1896), II, 575-80. "Report on the Jaffa-Jerusalem Railway," *Accounts and Papers*, 1893, Vol. 91.

bility. The early years of the reign of Abdul Aziz were good ones, by and large, both for the Turks and for their guests. Although increasingly arbitrary and extravagant, the Sultan was still restrained by able ministers. No serious unrest disturbed the mainland provinces; missionary difficulties were conspicuous by their absence; where an earlier Jaffa outrage had greatly preoccupied both the American minister and American naval officers, the postwar Jaffa problems could be blamed on none but the Americans themselves.

This situation was reflected in the history of the European Squadron. On her arrival in the east in the spring of 1866 the U.S.S. *Ticonderoga* was heartily welcomed both at Constantinople and at Smyrna; two years later Farragut enjoyed a notable reception at the Turkish capital; in the summer of 1871 *Guerrière* was handsomely received in Syrian ports. Visiting the missionary schools at Beirut and venturing inland to Damascus and Baalbek, members of the ship's company were everywhere accorded the greatest civilities, with much saluting and parading of guards of honor, all of which the commanding officer attributed to the prestige which the United States derived from the high character of the American consul general and the influence of the American missionary establishment.[26]

Coinciding as it did with intended American policy, this eastern calm was the more gratifying. The threat of European intervention during the Civil War and the arrival of the French in Mexico had focused attention on the powers of western Europe; the recreated naval force had been given a new name. Now designated the European rather than the Mediterranean Squadron, its cruising grounds were in the first instance restricted to Europe's Atlantic shore and to the Atlantic islands; when this area was expanded, the African coast as well as the Mediterranean was added to Goldsborough's command. Five years later the Atlantic orientation was reemphasized by the creation, if only on paper, of a subordinate Mediterranean Squadron within the European fleet.

This increased preoccupation with western Europe, a response to changing patterns of trade and politics, was reinforced by technological developments. A period of rapid advance in steam propulsion, ordnance, and armor, and of growth of the industrialized establishments required to support a modern fleet, made the navies

---

[26] Squadron Letters: Goldsborough to Sec. of Navy, 26 May 1866; Boggs to Sec. of Navy, 6 June 1871.

of the great powers objects of intense interest. The concern with technological matters, evidenced in the mission of Gustavus Fox, was reflected in the extensive descriptions of British and Continental dockyards, of ships' characteristics, building programs, and new developments which fill the dispatches of Goldsborough and his successors. It was also shared in Washington: in 1869 the squadron commander was ordered to Trieste to observe the demonstrations of the Whitehead locomotive torpedo, and a departmental directive for the first time called for systematic reports on foreign naval forces.[27]

For ten years this new deployment coincided sufficiently well with the course of international affairs: it was in western Europe, not the Levant, that things were happening. In ever-disorderly Spain, outbreaks in the summer of 1866 required the dispatch of a ship; the revolution of September 1868 again sounded the alarm. To the gratification of Farragut, who could not "conceive a worse government than that just overthrown," the Queen was ousted without a shot, but continuing unrest made it necessary to keep squadron units on the Spanish coast. Here, at least, the American flag retained some of its old political magic: at Malaga, when removing American families from harm's way, the officers of *Swatara* were escorted through the town by a large crowd of insurgents cheering for republicanism.[28]

The next crisis, and one of larger dimensions, was provided by the Franco-Prussian War of 1870. Predictably, Americans reacted to this event with hopes for the victory of liberal, Protestant, and parliamentary Prussia over the Catholic emperor who had subverted republicanism in France, sympathized with rebellion in America, and intervened forcefully in Mexico. A similar attitude on the part of the government at Washington was encouraged by the partisan dispatches of the minister to Prussia, the historian and former secretary of the navy George Bancroft, who had taken his doctorate at Göttingen in 1820 and whose relations with Bismarck were close. To the Chancellor, as to the Germans of 1848, it seemed possible that the United States could be helpful in redressing the naval balance. As early as 1867, as tension with France

---

[27] Letters to Flag Officers: Sec. of Navy to Radford, 24 June 1869, 28 September 1869.

[28] Squadron Letters: Goldsborough to Sec. of Navy, 27 June 1866; Farragut to Sec. of Navy, 10 October 1868; Pennock to Sec. of Navy, 15 January 1869.

had begun to mount, he had explored the possibility of purchasing American raiders and of recruiting American officers; in 1870, a week before the opening of hostilities, he again inquired as to the possibility of American naval aid.

In July the French declared war and the United States, at the request of the Prussian government, took over the care of that power's interests in France. This step placed heavy burdens on the American minister, Elihu Washburne, who alone of all the representatives of foreign governments was to remain in Paris through both the siege and the period of the Commune. Other burdens, if of a lesser sort, were imposed upon the European Squadron, but here the response was delayed by smallpox in the flagship and by a summer change of command. In mid-August, however, cabled orders were received to get a ship to the German coast, and before the month was out Commander Stephen B. Luce had reached Helgoland in *Juniata*, only to be held up by the French blockading squadron. But early September brought disaster to the French cause, and on the 11th, with the departure of the French warships, Luce headed into the Elbe and Jade. As the first ship to report the lifting of the blockade, *Juniata* was received with enthusiasm by American merchants, by the German populace, and by the German navy at Wilhelmshaven, and a similar welcome greeted *Plymouth* on her subsequent arrival at Kiel.

Although the great battles were over, the war went on, and Paris lay under siege. In this unpredictable situation the Department bestirred itself to strengthen the squadron, and by year's end the four ships of summer had been increased to eight. Returning from the North Sea, *Juniata* had reached Le Havre in late September to find a beleaguered city. Since the port contained half a dozen American merchantmen and some two million dollars worth of American property, mostly cotton, Luce decided to remain; and so important were these American interests and so pressing the need to support Washburne in Paris that a warship was kept on station at Le Havre until spring. In southern France, as well, duty called, and from late winter until spring one or more squadron units were stationed at Villefranche, in deference to fears of impending revolution entertained by the numerous American invalids residing on the Riviera.

In the upshot, Bismarck was mildly irritated at not having been permitted to outfit ships in American harbors and at the extensive sales of American surplus arms to France. Victor Hugo published a poem attacking Bancroft, and another on the unhelpfulness of the United States toward the country of Lafayette and Rochambeau. In America, German-American societies had busied themselves in collecting money, clothes, and food for the fatherland, and the Congress had authorized the employment of a naval vessel to carry food impartially to both contending countries. With time, American sympathy with the underdog, reinforced by pleasure at the departure of Napoleon III and the reestablishment of a French republic, led to a beginning shift of American attitudes, while in certain French quarters the idea was advanced of gaining American support by giving the United States a Mediterranean naval base.[29]

One diplomatic by-product of the Franco-Prussian conflict, the denunciation by Russia of the neutralization of the Black Sea imposed upon her at the conclusion of the Crimean War, focused attention on the Eastern question and led indirectly to a somewhat farcical flurry in American relations with Turkey. The ancient closure of the Dardanelles and Bosporus to warships, reaffirmed in the European treaties of 1841 and 1856, had historically little affected the United States: although Ottoman control of the straits had always been recognized and firmans obtained before entry, American public ships had frequently visited Constantinople. But by now European hostility to this American practice had come to have effect. Only by admitting the principle of closure by treaty had Morris obtained permission for the visit of Farragut's flagship in 1868, and the Turks, on this occasion, had announced that no future exceptions would be permitted. In this resolve the Porte was no doubt strengthened when Russian denunciation of the Black Sea neutralization was followed by newspaper reports that President Grant had personally congratulated the Czar and had offered to support the

<hr>

[29] Letters to Flag Officers: Sec. of Navy to Glisson, 13 August 1870 (telegram); Sec. of Navy to Boggs, 21 January 1871. Squadron Letters: Glisson to Sec. of Navy, 10 August 1870, 13 September 1870, 22 September 1870, 30 September 1870, 11 November 1870; Boggs to Sec. of Navy, 14 February 1871. Otto zu Stolberg-Wernigerode, *Germany and the United States of America during the Era of Bismarck* (Reading, Pa., 1937), pp. 87-130. H. M. Adams, *Prussian-American Relations, 1775-1871* (Western Reserve, 1960), pp. 93-103; Blumenthal, *Franco-American Relations*, pp. 185-205. Victor Hugo, "Bancroft," "Le message de Grant," in *L'année terrible* (1872).

Russian move by ordering the American fleet to the Mediterranean. In June 1871 a request from *Guerrière* for permission to visit the capital was turned down.[30]

So matters stood when, in the autumn of 1872, anti-Christian riots at Beirut alarmed the missionary community. In October the Navy Department instructed Rear Admiral James Alden to get some ships to the East; in mid-November an impulsive cable ordered him to send two vessels to Constantinople. A telegraphic request from *Congress* for a firman to pass the straits was peremptorily rejected by the Minister of Foreign Affairs, and as alarming rumors ran about Constantinople that an American ironclad squadron was on its way to force the straits, the defenses of the Dardanelles were alerted. Shortly a French mail steamer found herself under fire from the forts on the assumption that she was the U.S.S. *Shenandoah* attempting to force a passage. But by this time the orders from Washington had been countermanded, and calm again descended. When Alden visited Constantinople early in the next year, the only reminder of the episode, if such in fact it was, was the Sultan's expression of a desire to send some officers to America for instruction in techniques of coast defense.[31]

For a year or more Spain had seemed quiescent. But in February 1873, in the crisis which followed the resignation of King Amadeo, the American minister called upon Admiral Alden for ships. Three were sent but nothing happened, so despite repeated appeals from excitable consuls the squadron resumed its dispersed cruising. Although Carlist activity continued in the north, a June report from Captain Wells of *Shenandoah* indicated all calm along the Spanish coast; when the new squadron commander, Rear Admiral A. Ludlow Case, learned in July of spreading unrest and of a naval mutiny at

[30] Despatches, Turkey: Morris to Sec. of State, 24 August 1868, 2 October 1868, 29 October 1868; MacVeagh to Sec. of State, 24 January 1871, 27 March 1871, 15 June 1871. Allan Nevins, *Hamilton Fish* (New York, 1936), p. 507. Standard treatments of the straits question (Coleman Phillipson and Noel Buxton, *The Question of the Bosphorus and Dardanelles* [London, 1917]; Serge Goriainow, *Le Bosphore et les Dardanelles* [Paris, 1910]; H. N. Howard, "The United States and the Problem of the Turkish Straits," 1 *Middle East Journal*, 59-72) overlook the passages of American warships. But see: C. L. Lewis, "The Old Navy at Constantinople," 59 *U.S. Naval Institute Proceedings*, 1442-48.

[31] Letters to Flag Officers: Sec. of Navy to Alden, 8 October 1872 (telegram), 18 November 1872 (telegram), 4 December 1872 (telegram). Squadron Letters: Alden to Sec. of Navy, 24 October 1872, 19 November 1872 (telegram), 7 December 1872, 30 May 1873. Despatches, Turkey: Boker to Sec. of State, 30 November 1872, 6 December 1872, 17 December 1872.

Cartagena, he was inclined to discount the news. But with further alarms from American officials and with the report of a Spanish decree calling upon the warships of all nations to treat the mutinous vessels as pirates, Case ordered *Wachusett* to Spain and himself prepared to follow. On 5 August he left Corfu in the flagship *Wabash*; one day later the government at Washington, responding to requests from the Minister at Madrid, cabled him to keep three ships on the Spanish coast.

Unknown to the Admiral, the previous two weeks had been a busy time. Although subject to the usual orders not to interfere between contending parties, Captain Wells had begun to see opportunities to distinguish himself. On 20 July he left Malaga with the intention of searching out and seizing a rebel steamship reported to be levying tribute on coastal towns. At Cadiz, on the 31st, the entrance of a steamer flying the red flag led him to regret his failure to capture her outside; by the next day his distress had increased, and he was keeping steam up on *Shenandoah* and lying to a single anchor, ready for anything. Soon he was issuing supplies to beleaguered loyal naval officers; by the 5th, despite orders from Case to protect none but Americans, he had the Spanish officers on board.

Startled by all these might-have-beens, of which he learned only after his arrival in mid-August, Admiral Case reproved his ebullient subordinate and informed the Department that the Spanish situation, despite continuing complications, was less important than it seemed to Captain Wells. "Our mission abroad, as I understand it, is one of peace, and our policy is to take no part in any European troubles or complications." All this was true enough, and the explanation for Wells's itch for action, which earned him a departmental reprimand, is perhaps to be found in the fact that he was acting under orders of higher authority: throughout this period, by special permission, he had his wife aboard.[32]

If Spain had nothing that could be called a government, her "everfaithful" isle of Cuba had still less, and in 1868 its mixture of chaos and tyranny had blossomed into civil conflict. Five years later, on 31 October 1873, the steamer *Virginius*, flying the American flag, was captured in international waters by a Spanish gunboat; within

---

[32] Letters to Flag Officers: Sec. of Navy to Alden, 4 February 1873; Sec. of Navy to Wells, 3 August 1873 (telegram); Sec. of Navy to Case, 4 August 1873 (telegram), 6 August 1873 (telegram), 23 September 1873. Squadron Letters: Case to Sec. of Navy, 28 July 1873, 29 July 1873, 5 August 1873, 4 September 1873.

a week, fifty-three of her passengers and crew had been executed without trial and the United States was protesting vigorously to Madrid. There the republican government, although apparently genuinely distressed, was so weak as to be capable only of procrastination; on 14 November the American minister was instructed to present a twelve-day ultimatum and orders went out to Case to start one of his ships for Key West and concentrate the others. On the 23rd the Admiral received instructions to sail the entire squadron, and the Consul at Gibraltar was alerted to prepare for speedy coaling. The response was rapid, and by December, Case had under his command at Key West the united European and North Atlantic squadrons with a total strength of five frigates, fourteen corvettes, six monitors, and some auxiliaries. Not until May 1874 would the United States Navy return a diminished squadron to the European station.

Although the *Virginius* crisis was in time surmounted by American restraint and Spanish promises, the ensuing months saw little improvement in the Cuban situation. In November 1875, seeking to force a solution to an intolerable state of affairs, Secretary of State Fish faced the Spanish government with the possibility of outside intervention. Recognizing the attraction of war for the desperate, the United States accompanied this move by a second naval concentration: in the twenty days between the drafting of Fish's famous dispatch Number 266 and its arrival at Madrid, the European Squadron was concentrated at Villefranche; one day before the note was delivered, *Franklin* and *Alaska* sailed for Lisbon and *Congress* and *Juniata* for Port Royal, South Carolina. But this crisis too blew over, and in 1878 the Ten Years' War in Cuba finally came to an end.[33]

As in antebellum days, the intervals between moments of tension were filled with routine cruising. But the cruising grounds were now enlarged. In the years before the Civil War, American ships had rarely called north of Lisbon; now, however, the units of the European Squadron ranged from the Gulf of Finland to the Gulf of Guinea. Except in times of emergency, a summer cruise to northern Europe was routine; on four occasions in the postwar decade ships were sent south along the West African coast; from time to time

[33] Letters to Flag Officers: Sec. of Navy to Case, 14 November 1873 (telegram), 24 November 1873 (telegram), 14 March 1874. Squadron Letters: Case to Sec. of Navy, 16 November 1873, 23 November 1873, 30 November 1873; Worden to Sec. of Navy, 8 December 1875, 9 December 1875. F. E. Chadwick, *Relations of the United States and Spain: Diplomacy* (New York, 1909), pp. 323-86.

calls were made at the Atlantic islands. In the Azores, where the economy was largely sustained by remittances from emigrants in America, one of these visits touched a sensitive nerve and drew from the Portuguese government a denial of reports that the populace of Fayal had asked the United States to assume a protectorate over them.[34]

For all these voyages to far places, Europe remained the center of things, and there the summer cruises to northern waters gave interesting experience of the lavish glitter of the late-nineteenth-century monarchies. As the ships moved northward, French glamour gave way to English Victorianism, and this to the German emperor's military display and the generous hospitality of Scandinavian kings. Then from Stockholm the course lay eastward, across the Baltic and through the Gulf of Finland, to the domain of the Emperor of Russia, traditional friend of the Great Republic. At Cronstadt salutes and cheers were exchanged with the Russian fleet; when the commanding officer of *Enterprise* asked to inspect such torpedoes as were not considered secret, he was informed that "we have no secrets from America"; briefly, at least, the Russian signal book contained the message, "Let us remember the glorious examples of Farragut and his followers at New Orleans and Mobile." And in a lighter vein, the parties at the Peterhof, with gypsy dances on an island in a lake, provided scenes of "wonderful brilliancy such as is scarcely to be witnessed except in Russia."[35]

Thoughout these cruises the pleasures of European hospitality were enhanced by the gratifying testimony it provided to the prestige of the United States. But it was a new prestige. The revolutionary age was over, the starry flag had acquired new meanings. To the rulers of the Continent, unhelpful during the fraternal fight, it now signified success in war and ever-growing power. To the people of the Old World, the Republic of the West now represented less a political model than an emigrant's goal: in Scandinavian and German ports it was notable how many and how interested were the visitors of the lower orders, to whom ships and crews appeared to represent a kind of concrete embodiment of the "America letters" from their compatriots across the ocean.[36]

---

[34] Despatches, Portugal: Lewis to Sec. of State, 11 March 1874.

[35] Squadron Letters: Farragut to Sec. of Navy, 13 August 1867, 3 September 1867; Worden to Sec. of Navy, 25 July 1875. *Memoirs of Thomas O. Selfridge, Jr.* (New York, 1924), p. 233.

[36] Squadron Letters: Howell to Sec. of Navy, 22 August 1879.

In addition to its principle duty of maintaining an American presence in European waters, showing the flag, and looking out for American interests in troubled regions, other tasks were laid upon the Navy. The great tradition in hydrographic research was continued with the arrival of the U.S.S. *Gettysburg* for a three-year survey of Mediterranean waters. In 1873 American exhibits for the Vienna Exposition were taken out by naval storeship; in similar fashion, three years later, European items for the Centennial Exposition at Philadelphia were brought back. And as in antebellum days, works of art were brought home from Italy and points east.

Writing from Paris in 1780, John Adams had eloquently described the magnificences of that capital, while observing that such were not his country's needs. His grandsons, perhaps, would have the right to study the fine arts, but only if he himself first studied government, politics, and war, and his sons mathematics, navigation, commerce, and agriculture. The vision in large measure had come true: his own successful study of politics and war had been followed by John Quincy's efforts on behalf of commerce; and now that it was time for America to concern herself with the arts, there developed an expanding traffic in antiquities which came to involve the Navy.

This traffic, illustrative of increasing American interest in the past, concerned in one case the Navy's own. In 1871 the anchor of the frigate *Philadelphia*, recovered by the Pasha of Tripoli after sixty-eight years in the harbor mud, was presented to the United States and brought home in *Guerrière*; in 1875 a piece of the ship was grappled and recovered by *Congress*. Five years later the Department was still evincing interest in the acquisition of more fragments, but in the meantime squadron activities had been extended to a wider field. In 1871, on orders from Washington, *Shenandoah* was dispatched to Mersin, seaport of Tarsus, to load a three-ton sarcophagus dug up by the American consular agent and hauled down to the coast by eight buffalo; after Ottoman regulations against the export of antiquities had been circumvented by appeal to the Minister at Constantinople, the sarcophagus was embarked and brought back to New York to decorate the Metropolitan Museum. This institution, indeed, was further aided by the combined efforts of the Navy and of General Luigi Cesnola, an Italian veteran of 1848 and the Crimea, who had emigrated to the United States and married the daughter of the greatest of American privateers. After distinguishing himself in the Civil War, Cesnola was appointed to the consulate in Cyprus, where, as a self-taught archaeologist, he conducted a remarkable series of excavations of ancient burial sites. In 1871 *Guerrière* brought back a box of his curiosities for the Smithsonian Institution; in 1875, on orders from Washington, *Congress* transported the bulk of the finds to New York, where they formed the basis of the collection of the Metropolitan Museum, of which Cesnola himself shortly became director. In 1879, when the Consul General in Egypt successfully completed negotiations on behalf of the city of New York for the acquisition of the obelisk at Alexandria, a naval officer was placed on leave to supervise the difficult task of its lowering, loading, and transportation to the United States.[37]

The necessity for this pillage of the past has been argued. To certain later commentators it appeared that the United States had already all the antiquities it needed, in the Navy of the 1870's with its wooden steam frigates and smoothbore guns. This judgment is perhaps a little pat. In an age of explosive technological advance, the juxtaposed fleets of warring Europe had of necessity to struggle with the uncertainties of the race between ordnance and armor and with the novel problems of fleet tactics under steam. But for the Americans, to whom war remained the exception rather than the rule, the radical diminution in the radius of fleet operations which accompanied the coming of steam increased the virtue of the Atlantic moat. Navies, as Mahan would later observe, were now like land birds, unable to fly far from shore. And since coal capacity was limited and steamships did break down, the other and older aspect of American naval policy, signaled by the reinstitution of distant squadrons, called for emphasis upon endurance and the retention of full sail-power along with steaming ability. Here no easy answer presented itself: each type of motive power interfered with the other; such expedients as the hoisting propeller worked poorly; some ships could neither steam nor sail well. Despite these difficulties, and despite the corruption and inefficiency of the Grant administration, the Navy kept a force in European waters, but both the

[37] Letters to Flag Officers: Sec. of Navy to Boggs, 11 May 1871; Sec. of Navy to Worden, 1 February 1875. Squadron Letters: Boggs to Sec. of Navy, 6 June 1871, 1 July 1871, 30 August 1871; Worden to Sec. of Navy, 13 May 1875, 22 October 1875. Despatches, Tripoli: Vidal to Asst. Sec. of State, 10 April 1871, 26 May 1871. H. H. Gorringe, *Egyptian Obelisks* (New York, 1882).

new fuel problem and the increased maintenance required by the new machinery had their effects. The same pressures that were transforming European naval bases into great industrial enterprises also obliged the Americans to resort increasingly to the hospitality of European navy yards.[38]

One might have thought this growing dependence upon shore establishments would have turned the minds of American naval commanders to the question of an overseas base. The Europeans, as we have seen, had evinced concern in 1866 with the return of the squadron and the Fox mission, and again in 1868 at the time of Farragut's visit to the Levant; in 1871 a French publication revived the rumor of American designs on an island in the Cyclades. This was, of course, a very old story, dating back to the period of the Greek revolt, to the proposals made to Commodore Porter, and to the 1854 suggestion of Edwin DeLeon, the Young American consul at Alexandria. But the earlier suggestions had met with no response, and although in 1866 the Consul at Tunis had raised the possibility of a naval station at Bizerta, no concern for the acquisition of a foothold seems to have existed in postwar naval circles.

Admiral Goldsborough had come out with no instructions in the matter; after receiving permission to seek out a suitable Mediterranean headquarters, he had picked Villefranche. Hardly, however, had he settled his squadron there when the orders of December 1865 expanded his cruising grounds to include the African coast, emphasized the "European" designation of his force, and instructed him to move outside the Mediterranean and base at Lisbon. For three years Lisbon remained the destination for storeships and the squadron rendezvous, but with the inauguration of the Grant administration in 1869 there came instructions to shift, for reasons of economy, from floating support to the use of storehouses ashore. The squadron commander's suggestion of a return to Spezia was approved, but Spezia was now an Italian military port and unavailable, and as between Leghorn and Syracuse, which the Italians did offer, and Villefranche, comfort vanquished strategy. Again the choice fell upon the latter, and early in 1870 the move took place. Some use was made in subsequent years of Port Mahon, where the cooperation of the Governor and what now seemed the ineffable dullness of the town com-

---

[38] Squadron Letters: *passim*. Those skeptical of the virtues of "full sail-power" should read the report of the voyage of *Alaska* from the Gaboon River to Funchal after an engine breakdown: Worden to Sec. of Navy, 1 July 1876.

bined to provide a suitable location for landing force and boat exercises. But this was very intermittent, and for thirteen years the logistic infrastructure of the European Squadron remained, to all intents and purposes, limited to a rented warehouse on the French Riviera.[39]

In the question of a base, as in that of the Cretan revolution, the naval officers remained conservative and the government at home inactive. Such was also the case with American diplomats in Europe, where the proliferation of telegraph lines and the success of the Atlantic cable had diminished opportunities for independent initiative. But no cable yet reached the coast of Barbary, and in the American consul at Tripoli, French by birth, there burned the fire of the Young Americans, an acute consciousness of Anglo-American rivalry, and the antique feelings of American humanitarianism and of America's mission to extend the area of freedom. To Michel Vidal, Louisiana loyalist, newspaper editor, and Reconstruction congressman, the decline of the great powers of western Europe and the high reputation which the United States enjoyed among their people indicated a future of increasing American influence in Europe. In Tripoli the continued existence of the slave trade, flowing from time immemorial from inner Africa to Constantinople, called for action in the name of humanity. Since Great Britain was "the only nation in the world with which the United States will have to contend for that supremacy which is their manifest destiny," and since continuance of this slave trade seemed to depend upon British connivance or negligence at Malta, the problems were linked. A forward policy in the Mediterranean would be helpful in the rivalry with Britain; action against the slave trade would aid the cause of humanity. Quite possibly both aims could be served at once by the American consul at Tripoli.[40]

For two years, while investigating the slave trade, Vidal meditated on the great competition. Increasingly, a Mediterranean naval base seemed a necessity. Before leaving the United States, Vidal had

[39] Albert Dumont, "Souvenir de la Roumélie," *Revue des Deux Mondes*, 1 October 1871. Despatches, Tunis: Perry to Sec. of State, 27 October 1866, 1 November 1866. Despatches, Portugal: Harvey to Sec. of State, 27 January 1867. Letters to Flag Officers: Sec. of Navy to Goldsborough, 18 December 1865; Sec. of Navy to Radford, 22 May 1869, 11 September 1869, 6 January 1870, 10 March 1870. Squadron Letters: Radford to Sec. of Navy, 30 July 1869, 26 November 1869, 14 February 1870.

[40] Despatches, Tripoli: Vidal to Asst. Sec. of State, 6 January 1873. I have dealt with this episode in more detail in "A Scheme in Regard to Cyrenaica," 44 *Mississippi Valley Historical Review*, 445-68.

suggested to the President the acquisition of a Turkish island. But by 1873 this had come to seem impossible, owing to British influence at Constantinople, while a lodgment in the western basin or the acquisition of a Greek island was prevented both by European hostility and by the Monroe Doctrine. With all else eliminated, there remained only Tripoli, located on a continent not subject to the restrictions of Monroe and possessing the longest coastline of any of the regencies. Its eastern province of Cyrenaica, noted for its fertility, for the mildness of the inhabitants, and for its valuable seaports, offered sites "which a powerful Government might perhaps convert into a formidable position." Best of all was Tobruk, "which, according to trusty travellers, is a splendid port, the center of a magnificent country, but without trade of any kind, a sort of San Francisco Bay under the rule of Mexicans." Should the United States desire a footing in the Mediterranean "for military and commercial purposes," on the analogy of Aden or Hong Kong, a vessel should be sent to survey this coast; should a suitable location be discovered, it might be acquired, following the British example at Lagos, as a part of the effort to suppress the African slave trade.[41]

By the autumn of 1873 his success in drying up the slave trade at Tripoli had encouraged the Consul to extend his operations eastward and to plan a visit to Benghazi, capital of the eastern section of the regency and an outlet for slaves from the interior. From Benghazi he proposed to continue on through Cyrenaica to gain reliable intelligence of the region mentioned in his "preceding despatches in connection with a scheme of annexation." In June 1874, despite obstruction from the Tripolitan pasha, Vidal set out on his journey.

At Benghazi, where the plague was raging, the traveler earned the gratitude of all and the thanks of the Ottoman government by his energetic establishment of a quarantine. This humanitarian task completed, he moved on to Derna, where he found some Arabs "still called Americans by their townfolks, on account of their fathers' connection with General Eaton's movements." Proceeding eastward through the Pentapolis and surveying the ports of Bomba and Tobruk, Vidal continued along the coast to the Egyptian frontier, where he arrived weak in body but triumphant in spirit, having accomplished a journey made but twice before by Christians in the twelve centuries since the Moslem conquest.

[41] Despatches, Tripoli: Vidal to Asst. Sec. of State, 6 January 1873, 27 May 1873.

This desert journey had a remarkable sequel. Prevented from advancing further by the Egyptian quarantine and too exhausted to retrace his tracks, the American consul first found himself imprisoned in a fort at Alexandria and then forcibly embarked on an Ottoman trading schooner; only after shipwreck on the coast of Asia Minor, from which he narrowly escaped with his life, did he succeed in returning to his post at Tripoli early in 1875. But despite all troubles his zeal was undiminished, and in June, employing a cipher of his own devising, Vidal forwarded a lengthy dispatch in which he pressed the argument for a naval station, expanded upon the commercial and strategic virtues of Cyrenaica and upon the pleasure with which the Bedouin would welcome the American flag, and outlined a procedure for the seizure of this coastline.[42]

In his concern for a naval base and in his preoccupation with the great competition, the Consul was not alone. In the same month that Vidal set out from Tripoli for Benghazi, the American minister at Constantinople, the Philadelphia poet and playwright George H. Boker, had recommended to the State Department the purchase of Bab el Mandeb at the entrance to the Red Sea. At this strategic spot, within a year of the opening of the Suez Canal, a French company had secured a concession from the local ruler and had surveyed the port, the hinterland, and the resources of the area. But the collapse of France before the Prussian armies had adversely affected the scheme, British pressure had been brought upon the Sultan to undo the purchase, and the company, desirous of saving something of its investment, was looking for another government to which it could sell out. On 28 June 1874 Boker forwarded to Washington a packet containing hydographic and topographic surveys, a plan of the port and the town, and an inventory of local resources. Suggesting that a commissioner be sent to investigate, and volunteering to go himself, Boker expanded on the pleasure it would give him "to be able to assist in planting this thorn in the side of the British lion" and urged that serious thought be given this important project of "establishing a coaling, watering, and provisioning station for our fleets."[43]

But nothing came of it all. The Minister's proposal got no response

---

[42] Despatches, Tripoli: Vidal to Asst. Sec. of State, 6 November 1873, 1 March 1875, 17 April 1875, 22 June 1875. Despatches, Turkey: Maynard to Sec. of State, 6 July 1875.

[43] Despatches, Turkey: Boker to Sec. of State, 28 June 1874.

at Washington; the Consul's scheme had no chance to mature. Before Vidal's cipher dispatch could reach Washington, an incident had taken place and the Navy was on the way. At Tripoli the Consul had become involved in a scuffle with an Ottoman sailor. His protest and his demand for an apology for what he interpreted as an effort to steal his dispatch book were met with equal vigor by the Pasha, supported by the European consuls. As the situation grew increasingly tense, Vidal sent his interpreter to Malta to cable for protection; received in Washington on 10 August 1875, the message was quickly relayed to Rear Admiral John L. Worden, Commander of the European Squadron, at Southampton.

The response of the hero of Hampton Roads was prompt and decisive. *Congress*, then at Corfu, was ordered to Tripoli without delay; cables were sent to Port Said, Palermo, and Messina to intercept and divert *Hartford*, then transiting the Suez Canal on her way home from the Asiatic station; at Southampton, *Alaska* and *Juniata* were ordered to make ready for sea. By the 23rd both *Congress* and *Hartford* were anchored in the harbor of Tripoli with their batteries trained on the fortifications, all business in the town had been suspended, and the Pasha was evincing a willingness to settle.

Settle he did, proceeding in full uniform to the American consulate to apologize for what had taken place. But this famous victory, which to Vidal washed away the stain of Bainbridge's imprisonment, was in fact too good. The Consul's efforts to stem the slave trade, his work against the plague in Cyrenaica, and his vigorous defense of American treaty rights had gained him a considerable notoriety in Mediterranean circles. His discretion in enciphering his dispatch of June 1875 had been undercut by the State Department, which had published without deletion some earlier correspondence hinting at the project of the African naval station. The crisis at Tripoli, with its renewed indication that the United States considered the Pasha to be the head of an independent government, had increased Turkish concern. As Vidal returned to his work, attempting to revive the long-dead American trade with Tripoli, working to check the traffic in slaves, and reporting to his superiors the existence "on this Barbary Coast [of] a whole population, American in feeling and aspirations," the Ottoman government began to press for his recall.[44]

[44] Despatches, Tripoli: Vidal to Sec. of State, 7 August 1875 (telegram); Vidal to Asst. Sec. of State, 21 August 1875, 26 August 1875, 27 August 1875, 6 March 1876.

Much, at this point, could have been said on Vidal's behalf. The extension of the area of freedom, with its implicit limitation on the influence of the great powers of Europe, had been a principal rationale of American territorial growth and of American diplomatic activity in general. The historic rivalry with Britain had received recent emphasis in the diplomacy of the Civil War. The campaign against the slave trade had the sanction of long American tradition, and the Consul's efforts had been approved by his superiors in Washington. The Department had supported him in his contention, based on the Treaty of 1805, that the Pasha was the head of an independent government, and it had undertaken to consider the project of the Cyrenaican naval base.

Had there been any inclination to force the issue with the Turks, either in connection with the status of Tripoli or with the acquisition of a base, a better time than the summer of 1876 could hardly have been imagined. Beset by insurrection and financial collapse, the Sick Man, in Vidal's words, appeared about to "breathe his last"; while for those concerned with the great Anglo-American competition, action appeared the more urgent owing to the probability of British seizure of the Suez Canal. All this was sufficiently apparent to others. In July 1876, as the Eastern crisis approached its climax and dissolution of the Ottoman Empire seemed increasingly imminent, fears of American intervention brought the British and Italian ministers to the State Department to join in protesting the conduct of the American consul in Tripoli.[45]

Revealing though these actions were, they were unnecessary. The decision to recall the Consul had been made. Much had changed as the centenary of American independence approached: the twin impulses of expansion and reform were dead, and policy was for the moment retrograde. The European Squadron had been drastically weakened by the recall of ships to meet the Cuban crisis, and spring of 1876 found Admiral Worden with but a single ship on station. Far from demonstrating an interest in the eastern Mediterranean,

---

Despatches, Turkey: Maynard to Sec. of State, 16 August 1875, 27 September 1875. Notes Received, Turkey: Aristarchi to Sec. of State, 9 December 1875, 30 December 1875. Squadron Letters: Worden to Sec. of Navy, 11 August 1875 (telegram), 18 August 1875, 20 October 1875. *Foreign Relations, 1873*, II, 1167-69; *1874*, pp. 48-49.

[45] Despatches, Tripoli: Vidal to Asst. Sec. of State, 6 March 1876. Despatches, Turkey: Maynard to Sec. of State, 21 March 1876, 30 March 1876, 12 July 1876. Notes Received, Great Britain: Thornton to Sec. of State, 18 July 1876; Italy: Blanc to Sec. of State, 26 July 1876.

the Navy Department was again planning to shift the squadron headquarters to Lisbon, outside the straits, a move from which it was deterred only by a lengthy and urgent appeal from Worden which emphasized how greatly such a move would compromise the support of missionaries in Ottoman regions.[46]

[46] Notes to Foreign Legations, Turkey: Sec. of State to Aristarchi, 3 May 1876, 28 June 1876. Letters to Flag Officers: Sec. of Navy to Worden, 26 February 1877. Squadron Letters: Worden to Sec. of Navy, 17 March 1877.

CHAPTER X

The Pressures of Modernity, 1835-1881

1. Missions and Education

IN NOTABLE CONTRAST to the decline of the once great merchant marine was the vigor of the American missionary effort. With the confidence engendered by the preservation of the Union and the wealth deriving from the new industrialism there came, in the post-war decades, a great expansion of an already impressive structure. Although in rate of growth the Far East now came to take the lead, the transatlantic effort, older and still vastly larger, also continued to expand. New probes of Catholic Europe were attempted, one of them, remarkably enough, by the Presbyterian Church (South), which only two years after Appomattox opened an evangelical school in Italy. Although a foray by the American Board in 1872 was soon abandoned, the Methodist Episcopal Church (North) entered the peninsula in the following year; by 1875 it had established itself at the capital and in four other cities, and had counted up conversions in spite of "Romish violence." In France, where the Baptists had long labored on a small scale and with small effect, and where the Seventh Day Adventists were also at work, some success developed in the late seventies. Even in most Catholic Spain a few precarious footholds were gained. And this same decade saw both Baptists and Presbyterians commence another futile effort in Greece.[1]

Indicative though they were of high morale, these European efforts remained small; although pregnant with significance for the future, the Far Eastern missionary commitment was still secondary. For a generation after the Civil War the redemption of the Christian population of the Levant remained the focus of the American missionary movement and an enterprise of sufficient importance to be a charge upon the government. The Smyrna trade could diminish in significance, the squadron could be rechristened "European," the

---

[1] Richter, *History of Missions*, p. 166; Bliss, *Encyclopaedia of Missions*, I, 43, 54, 57, 80; II, 78, 255, 325. Despatches, Spain: Cushing to Sec. of State, 27 November 1876, 9 January 1877.

Navy Department could issue periodic orders to base outside the straits, but time and again, throughout the latter part of the nineteenth century, the recurrent difficulties of the missionary establishment would recall American warships to the eastern Mediterranean.

These difficulties, however, did not materialize at once. Except for the Coffing and Meriam murders of 1862, the decade of the sixties was generally calm, and in time would be looked back upon as a period of peace, prosperity, and freedom. In such a situation the principal obstacle to missionary success appeared to lie in that French influence, dominant at Constantinople since the Crimean War, which made Jesuit rivalry the more dangerous for the American Protestants.

This threat was ended by the defeat of France in 1871. Again, for the moment, it seemed to the missionaries that the movement of the armies had but served the divine will; in fact, however, the destruction of French influence was followed by the growth of new tensions. Renewed Russian pressure upon Turkey gave rise to a duel between the northern colossus and Great Britain, personified at Constantinople in the struggle of the two ambassadors, General Ignatiev and Sir Henry Elliot. Within the empire, the death of Aali Pasha in 1871 removed the last of the architects of reform, and was followed by unchecked governmental extravagance which led through bankruptcy and rebellion to the tense years of the Eastern crisis.

The problems of this new era were to be faced by new men: the missionary pioneers had gone. Feeling himself too old to learn another language, Daniel Temple had returned to the United States upon the discontinuance of the mission to the Greeks. In 1857, after years of labor which had brought his Arabic version of the Bible close to completion, Eli Smith died at Beirut. Edward Breath, the Persian printer, died in 1861, a victim of the cholera contracted in the performance of a charitable deed. A year later H.G.O. Dwight was killed in a railroad accident while on a speaking tour of the United States. In 1865, after forty-three years in the Turkish Empire, William Goodell returned to America in failing health. In the next year, control changed at home with the retirement of Rufus Anderson, who, as assistant corresponding secretary since 1824 and corresponding secretary since 1832, had directed the overseas deployment of the representatives of the American Board. In 1869 Justin Perkins retired after thirty-six years of work in Persia; in the same year, after forty-six years in service, Jonas King died in Greece. For some time King had been free from all but petty persecution, and with some of the authorities he was on good terms. Yet the story of this sturdy controversialist suggests that the true wisdom of the serpent is to show the harmlessness of the dove: the Episcopalian John Henry Hill, who had reached Athens in the same year as King, had avoided controversy and had limited his work to education; on his death at the age of ninety in 1882 the Greeks gave him a public funeral, with a file of soldiers, a band of music, and a procession almost a mile long.[2]

These pioneers left a notable legacy. Although the world had not been evangelized within a generation, and although 1866 had not brought the commencement of the millennium, Hopkinsian zeal had left its impress on the Levant. As a result of the efforts of the American Board alone, the word of God had been first or newly translated into five important vernaculars: modern Armenian, Armeno-Turkish, Arabic, Bulgarian, and modern Syriac. Paralleling the efforts of translators and printers in making Scripture and tract available to the populations of the Near East had been those of the teachers in making them accessible, while the preaching of the American evangelists had brought the organization of churches and of new Protestant sects. Indeed, there was much truth in the claim that American effort had largely changed the locus of interaction of the cultures of East and West: where fifty years earlier this had been seen in the meeting of camel and ship at Smyrna, now it took place at Constantinople in the confrontation of caliph and gospel preacher.

For by now the capital of the Grand Turk was not only the site of the largest mission of the American Board and the base from which numerous outlying enterprises were directed; it was also the Near Eastern headquarters of the American Bible Society. This organization, which with its British counterpart supported evangelical efforts throughout the globe, had been organized in 1816. It had sent its first agent to the Levant in 1836. But the work was long beset by difficulties, and for twenty years the missionaries had been forced to rely largely on their own efforts and their own press for their supplies of printed materials. In 1857, however, the Bible Society's Near Eastern agency was confided to the Reverend Isaac G. Bliss,

---

[2] Richter, *History of Missions*, pp. 107-8, 196-97, 401-6; biographical sketches in Bliss, *Encyclopaedia of Missions*.

a graduate of Amherst and a former missionary at Erzerum. Under the new management the enterprise was wholly revolutionized, order and system were introduced into its proceedings, and colportage was increased; in the course of two decades, Bible circulation was driven up from 2,500 to more than 50,000 copies a year. In size Bliss's empire exceeded that of the Sultan, running eastward from Greece through the Ottoman dominions to those of the Persian shah. Like the empires of Shah and Sultan, it was also impressively polyglot, requiring a steady supply of scripture in Turkish, printed in three characters; in Armenian, in three characters; and in Greek, in two; in Arabic, Kurdish, Persian, two kinds of Syriac, and Hebrew; in Judeo-Spanish, Bulgarian, Slavic, Rumanian, Croatian, and Russian.

So considerable an enterprise inevitably required a home. With funds that he raised in America, Bliss purchased a site at the capital, and there, between 1867 and 1872 and in the face of determined opposition, erected Constantinople Bible House. On its completion, this building became the general headquarters of the evangelical effort in the Levant, with offices and storerooms for the American Bible Society, the British Bible Society, and the American Board of Commissioners for Foreign Missions, and with printing and binding establishments run by Armenians who had learned their trade in the United States. If Bible House in Constantinople was not, like Bible House in New York, the largest business structure of the metropolis, it was still "universally recognized as the handsomest business building in the city."[3]

So the leavening of the Levant went on. Among the Armenians and Bulgarians the efforts of the American Board had continued through the later Civil War years with only routine troubles in the form of minor outrages, seizures of Bibles, and threats of censorship. Among the Nestorians a great increase in conversions had led to patriarchal opposition, and this in 1862 to the separation of the American-dominated congregations under their own rules of discipline and confession of faith. In Syria, despite recurrent local difficulties and a continuing shortage of personnel, the American Board missionaries continued to maintain their position, while at Latakia

---

[3] Bliss, *Encyclopaedia of Missions*, I, 63, 170, 323, and facsimile verses reproduced in the articles on the various translations; Dwight, *Encyclopedia of Missions*, pp. 84-85; Laurie, *Ely Volume*, pp. 242-50, 498; *Memorial Volume of ABCFM*, pp. 339-44.

the Reformed Presbyterian mission to the Nusairiyeh survived and grew.

In Egypt, meanwhile, the recently inaugurated Presbyterian mission had entered upon its period of expansion. There, during the war years, a first native congregation had been organized, and stations had been established at Asyut and Fayoum to facilitate work in the interior. The hostility of the Coptic patriarch, who "vowed over his cups of Arab whisky" to exterminate Protestantism in Egypt, was frustrated: although the missionaries deplored the passivity of official American policy, designed as it seemed to afford as little protection as possible, the aggressions of the Coptic hierarchy were warded off by British support and by the intervention of the American consul general. In 1865 Asyut College was founded. With the decade of the seventies there came a rapid growth, manifested in church-building and in the establishment of girls' boarding schools and of a theological seminary; attendance at the mission schools passed the 2,000 mark, while church membership increased from a mere 180 to almost 1,000.

Such growth was not limited to Egypt, for the twenty years after 1870 saw an expansion of the Near Eastern missionary effort beyond anything ever previously contemplated. Stabilized in the seventies, the Levantine budget of the American Board increased in the following decade by more than a third, total American missionary expenditure in the Near East went up still faster, and from the mountains of the Balkans eastward to Persia and south to the valley of the Nile there swarmed increasing numbers of missionaries, missionary physicians, and Bible men. With the postwar reunion of Old and New School Presbyterian churches, the Near Eastern field was reorganized and the Persian and Syrian missions transferred from the custody of the American Board to that of the Presbyterians. In Persia, by 1890, this transfer had resulted in a quadrupling of ordained missionaries, a doubling of communicants, and an invasion of new provinces; in Syria missionary resources were multiplied by three. Through these same years the American Board, now wholly Congregational, continued its work in Bulgaria and Asia Minor, while north of the Balkan Mountains the Methodists expanded their own Bulgarian effort.[4]

[4] Despatches, Turkey: *passim.* ABCFM *Annual Reports*; Anderson, *Oriental Churches*; Watson, *American Mission in Egypt*; Verney and Dambmann, *Puissances étrangères*, pp. 63-67; Richter, *History of Missions*, pp. 168-69, 212-22, 302-6, 346-50; Bliss, *Encyclopaedia of Missions*, ii, 377; Tibawi, *American Interests*, pp. 275-77.

Although this increase in resources was accompanied by a division of administrative responsibility, missionary aims remained identical and cooperation intimate. By 1885 the Secretary of the American Board could point out to the President of the United States that the territories of the Sultan contained more than two hundred American citizens engaged in missionary work, and Egypt another thirty-two, and that almost a million dollars had been invested in educational and publishing enterprises. Americans in Ottoman regions administered eight colleges with over a thousand students, some seventy-five secondary schools, and hundreds of elementary institutions; in Egypt there was another college and another network of schools. Ten years later, in an attempt to energize a laggard American minister at Constantinople, the local missionary representatives argued on economic grounds that an investment of some $7,000,000, an annual contribution of $150,000, a book trade with branches in 25 cities, and an educational establishment of 435 schools with almost 20,000 pupils fully warranted the support of the United States government.[5]

This emphasis on education was to the point, for by now the tail was threatening to wag the dog and education to take precedence over the gospel mission. The pioneer venture of Goodell and Bird had cast a long shadow. The clear connection between a literate population and the diffusion of Bible Christianity had brought the creation of schools at every turn: on arrival in Syria, with the first penetration into Greece, with entry into Constantinople, with the occupation of the Persian, Egyptian, and Bulgarian fields. Everywhere these foundations had been welcomed by their beneficiaries, while the national belief in the efficacy of education had commended them to Americans unconnected with the missionary effort. As early as 1835 Commodore Porter had noted as "among the greatest benefits which the Empire has derived from its alliance with the United States is the means she has acquired of giving instruction to the people. . . . The march of intellect which America has everywhere given rise to is a sufficient answer to those who assert that she has done no benefit to mankind. The time may come when as great, and as beneficial a change may be produced by her in Turkey, as she has produced on the minds of the greater part of Europe. A

[5] *Commercial Relations, 1869*, p. 359; *Foreign Relations, 1885*, pp. 857-78; *Foreign Relations, 1895*, pp. 1427-30; E. M. Earle, "American Missions in the Near East," 7 *Foreign Affairs*, 398-417.

reading nation cannot be long in understanding what are its true interests, and when instructed, will not be long in acting on them."[6]

With such sentiments few would have disagreed, yet the burgeoning of the educational structure raised difficult questions concerning the use of means. The creation of primary schools to produce Gospel readers had been followed by the establishment of secondary institutions for the training of preachers. And while the response was gratifying, it was also true that in a period when European penetration of the Near East was placing a premium on the command of Western languages, Levantine eagerness for education was frequently motivated less by piety than by ambition. For a time this situation could be rationalized with the hope that missionary teachers, like missionary physicians, would acquire an influence which might forward the gospel effort, but there remained a real question of where education for Christianity stopped and education in the arts of the West began.

It is the Gospel, not the American gospel, that we are appointed to preach, William Goodell had written, but even he found it difficult to restrict the curriculum to the simple question of literacy. Rejoicing, in the early years, in the receipt of an orrery, and of an electrical machine "worth to us more than its weight in gold," he wrote the Board: "I do love to give a shock to these people, and especially to the great rich bankers; it really seems to move them a step forward toward the millennium." Wholly unselfish, deeply devoted, and increasingly involved with the welfare of those to whom they ministered, Goodell and his fellows accomplished notable things, but the millennium toward which they shocked their neighbors was an American one.

In a sense, the ambiguity had existed from the beginning. The missionary purpose was to evangelize the world; the orders to individual missionaries required them to do good. But this very requirement demonstrated the tension implicit in the Hopkinsian system between individual regeneration and the worldly millennium, while the problems of ends and means were reemphasized by the distance which separated the makers and the executors of policy. In the churches of America, where the plate was passed and the funds collected, the original aims retained their primacy and conversions were the index of success. But as year by passing year the

---

[6] Despatches, Turkey: Porter to Sec. of State, 25 July 1835. Richter, *History of Missions*, pp. 123-24.

reports from overseas dwelt less on souls saved than on services performed, a certain restiveness developed. Reminded, at intervals, of their primary concern, the missionaries would attempt reform; admonished with regard to their peripheral activities, they would express regret; instructed to discontinue printing and teaching in favor of gospel preaching, they would endeavor to comply. But always the needs of their people drew them back to witness less by their preaching than by their lives, and the conflict between those at home and those in the theater of operations remained. Presumably it was ineradicable. A century later it would reappear in striking form in the enlarged and secularized missionary enterprise, in the question of whether aid to backward nations should be made contingent on political tests or should be granted without strings.[7]

This tension between ends and means, evident throughout the missionary movement, was clearly visible at Constantinople. There the developing need for pastors, teachers, and helpers had early called for education beyond the elementary level, and following the establishment by the Syrian mission of a high school at Beirut, the decision had been taken to follow suit at the capital. In 1840 the school was opened at Bebek, five miles from the city, under the direction of the Reverend Cyrus Hamlin, a graduate of Bowdoin College and of the Bangor Theological Seminary and a cousin of Lincoln's first vice president. Greatly gifted, indomitably self-willed, possessed of a fierce energy, and discouraged by nothing, Cyrus Hamlin was an extraordinary example of nineteenth-century American individualism. A shatterer of precedent in all he did, he was the first emissary of the American Board to evade that organization's economical requirement of crossing the Atlantic by sailing ship, a privilege gracefully conceded by Rufus Anderson, "inasmuch as Brother Hamlin has always gone by steam." Always a storm center, but also a great initiator and overcomer, Hamlin left the indelible impress of his personality on the American educational effort in the Near East.

The Bebek seminary opened in 1840 with two pupils; in the next year it was forced to seek quarters for twenty; by 1843 it had forty students and its influence was radiating outward. Although the enrollment was wholly Armenian, the scientific and philosophical

[7] ABC 16.5, Vol. 2: Goodell to Schauffler, 5 December 1834, 6 December 1834; ABC 16.9, Vol. 2: Goodell to Anderson, 31 May 1835; ABC 16.9, Vol. 1: Goodell to Anderson, 17 September 1836.

demonstrations drew visitors of all persuasions and from every walk of life. Soon Hamlin's efforts in the writing and translation of textbooks bore fruit in the adoption, by the Turkish minister of public instruction, of his arithmetic. Shortly, French Jesuits paid the Americans the compliment of founding a competing institution.

Nevertheless there remained great difficulties. The early years of the seminary were the years of persecution by the Armenian patriarch and of anathemas and boycotts directed against the evangelically inclined. In these circumstances it seemed necessary, in order to preserve the school, to provide employment for the pupils, a step which could also be rationalized as teaching the dignity of labor and the need to avoid the vice of idleness. Here the Yankee mechanic in Hamlin proved its worth, with the establishment first of a stove factory, then of a business in the production and sale of Boston rattraps, and finally with the creation of a steam-powered flour mill and a bakery. The opposition of local vested interests to this last enterprise was circumvented by resort to the proviso of the capitulations of 1453, which entitled each foreign community to its own mill and bakery. More serious was the opposition to the entire program of secular employment which arose among the other members of the Constantinople mission and at the Boston headquarters of the American Board. But all troubles were surmounted: when Hamlin's request for a flour mill was turned down by the Board, the desired equipment was contributed by an individual member; a vote by the Constantinople mission station to halt the work program was avoided by subterfuge; a grudging approval of the bakery went unrecorded in the mission records so as to avoid repercussions at home.

The industrial aspects of the Bebek seminary, inaugurated as work relief for the dispossessed Armenian evangelicals, became big business with the Crimean War. The needs of the British commissariat brought about a vast expansion of the bakery, while the uncontrolled filth of the British hospitals led to the establishment of a large laundry. Berating British officers of every grade, exposing grafters in the logistic establishment, and supervising his projects with a furious energy, Hamlin came to embody in his own person the mechanic band of missionaries for which Goodell had earlier hoped. The enterprise was productive both of good and of profit, and at war's end the monetary return was transferred to a church-building fund for the evangelical Armenians. But by this time the industrial plant had almost obliterated the seminary, and the question of what kind of education the missionaries should provide had been raised in exacerbated form.[8]

There was, it should be emphasized, no question of the whole-hearted commitment of the American Board to education. This question, indeed, could hardly be expected to arise among these representatives of the New England Congregationalist tradition, although an occasional eccentric like President Seelye of Amherst could argue on apostolic precedent for no education at all. By 1860 enrollments in the common schools of the Western Asia mission had passed the five-thousand mark, while around the globe the educational expenditures of the American Board exceeded those of Presbyterians, Baptists, and Episcopalians combined. But funds were not unlimited, a case could be made that missionary organizations should not train for secular careers, and opinion differed as to the best means of educating for the Christian ministry. To some, like Cyrus Hamlin, the continued improvement of general education seemed the answer; others, like Rufus Anderson, had reservations.

To Anderson, to whom the gospel message rather than the civilizing mission was of primary concern, the Board's early experience in education had taught two principal related lessons: that the language of instruction should be not English but the vernacular, and that schooling should be carried out not in the United States but in the individual's home country, and there preferably not at the metropolis. In support of these views the Secretary could point to the history of the Cornwall school, and to the experience with the Greek youths who had attended American colleges. Those trained in America had tended to become denationalized, and raised in their own estimation above their countrymen; some had been reluctant to return home; those who had done so had proven demanding and costly to support as workers. Equally persuasive in support of vernacular education were the accomplishments of the distant and isolated Nestorian mission, whose schools, conducted in Syriac, led all the rest in revivals and conversions.

The arguments did Anderson credit, emphasizing as they did his central concern with salvation. Doubtless, as he contended, the vernacular was preferable both for the communication of truth and as the language which would reach the heart; doubtless, too, life at the

---

[8] Anderson, *Oriental Churches*, I, 22, 414-15; II, 214-18; Richter, *History of Missions*, pp. 126-28; Hamlin, *Among the Turks*, pp. 28, 68, 195-203, 213-59; *idem*, *Life and Times*, pp. 207-16, 256-79, 296-312, 326-72.

capital or abroad tended to corrupt the countryman, and to emphasize the value of the English tongue. But the Secretary's position
failed to take account of the rate of change which Western influences, not least the missionaries, had by this time brought about in
the Levant. For the world, like Cyrus Hamlin, was increasingly
propelled by steam, and in a great polyglottery like the Ottoman
Empire all vernaculars were vulnerable.

Rightly or wrongly, Rufus Anderson had his way. Increasingly
confirmed in his opinions, he pressed the causes of vernacular education and of the rural location of schools on a worldwide basis.
In 1846, on his second visit to the Mediterranean, he caused the substitution of Arabic for English as the basic language of the Syrian
seminary's curriculum, and accomplished the removal of that institution from Beirut to the country. On his journey of 1855-56 he
enforced his policy upon mission schools in both India and Turkey;
in 1856 the decision was taken to move the Bebek high school from
the seductions of Constantinople to the Jeffersonian atmosphere of
Anatolia, and to transform it into a theological seminary at
Marsovan.[9]

This decision, so contrary to Hamlin's views, threatened to end
his educational career. But providentially a new opportunity arose.
Although H.G.O. Dwight had been one of those who preferred a
seminary in the interior, two of his sons had interested themselves
in the project of a secular American college at Constantinople and
had approached Christopher R. Robert, a New York merchant, for
support. But this was slow in forthcoming, in part because of the
Panic of 1857, in part perhaps because of the youth of the protago-
nists, and with time Hamlin's insistence that the college should be
"a decided, Christian school from its very commencement" gained
him the favor of the philanthropist. In 1859 Robert offered to support the enterprise if Hamlin would assume control; urged on by
his colleagues in the Constantinople mission and convinced of the
error of Anderson's policy of vernacular education, Hamlin accepted
the charge and resigned his connection with the American Board. In
1862 a site overlooking the Bosporus was purchased. In 1864 Robert
College was incorporated in the state of New York.

Yet the enterprise long hung in the balance. In America the Civil

[9] Anderson, *Oriental Churches*, I, 273; II, 49, 217-20; *Memorial Volume of ABCFM*, pp. 317-20, 323-27, 329-32; Hamlin, *Among the Turks*, pp. 274-86; *idem*, *Life and Times*, pp. 371, 413-14.

War made financial backing doubtful; at Constantinople efforts to build on the new site were frustrated by Turkish procrastination and by Jesuit and Russian intrigue. For six years Hamlin struggled to gain his building permit, an effort in no way simplified by a quarrel with the American minister which made it necessary to conduct all dealings with the legation through intermediaries. Instruction, nevertheless, was begun at Bebek, in the building abandoned by the American Board, and despite intermittent warfare between Hamlin and his faculty, the work moved steadily ahead. From the one American and three English students enrolled in the autumn of 1863, Hamlin by the fifth year had built up to a total of 102, including 14 Armenians, 16 Bulgarians, and 33 Greeks, while again his example had been imitated by the French, whose pressure on the Porte had led to the foundation of the Lycée of Galata Serai. In 1868, after representations by Secretary Seward to the Turkish minister in Washington and by Admiral Farragut in the course of his visit to Constantinople, permission to build was finally received.

With permission at last in hand, Hamlin threw himself wholeheartedly into the task, designing the building, ordering materials from America and arranging for their duty-free admission, and overseeing all details of construction; having fought so long and fiercely to gain his site, he now bled in the erection of his college, losing two fingers to a buzzsaw. On 5 July 1869, the 4th being a Sunday, the cornerstone was laid by the American minister, with whom relations had at last been resumed. On 4 July 1871 the new building was opened with a speech by former Secretary of State Seward.

For Hamlin this moment of triumph was not to be repeated. Recalled to America by the philanthropist, he found himself served, after some years of unsuccessful efforts in fund raising, as he had served the younger Dwights. In 1877 his resignation was forced by his benefactor, Robert, and by his own son-in-law, the Reverend George Washburn, hitherto director of the college and henceforth its second president. But the work went on.[10]

Although Robert College was in large part the outgrowth of Cyrus Hamlin's disagreement with the policies of Rufus Anderson and of

---

[10] Hamlin, *Among the Turks*, pp. 287-301; *idem, Life and Times*, pp. 415-503; *idem,* "The Political Duel between Nicholas, The Czar of Russia, and Lord Stratford de Redcliffe, the Great English Ambassador," 6 *Proceedings of the American Antiquarian Society*, 196-212; George Washburn, *Fifty Years in Constantinople* (Boston and New York, 1911), pp. 1-76, 135, 138; Richter, *History of Missions*, pp. 128-31.

the American Board, it could also be seen as a natural development of the missionary effort. Almost inevitably, in the context of the times, the establishment of lower schools gave rise to calls for higher ones, and the existence of these to a demand for foundations of college grade. Influenced, perhaps, by the contemporary efforts of Hamlin and Robert, the members of the Syrian mission in 1862 proposed to establish a Protestant college at Beirut. Encouraged by the linguistic unity of Arabic-speaking Syria, which made vernacular instruction seem feasible, the American Board approved the enterprise and supported it through its preliminary stages. In the midst of the Civil War, Dr. Daniel Bliss, who had been Washburn's roommate at Amherst, set forth to seek support, and succeeding in raising $100,000 in greenbacks at home and an additional £4,000 in England.

In 1864 the Syrian Protestant College was incorporated in the state of New York by the same act which incorporated Robert College, and two years later it opened its doors. The following year brought the inauguration of the medical school, which, over the years, was to have the greatest importance in introducing the concepts of Western science and in training doctors and nurses for work among the peoples of the Near East; ultimately a theological seminary was also added. For a considerable time Arabic continued as the language of instruction at the Beirut college, but with the passage of years difficulties arose. The linguistic brilliance of the first missionary generation was not duplicated in the second, and the procurement of competent instructors and satisfactory textbooks became increasingly difficult; the growing fame of the institution resulted in an expanded constituency, and in the arrival of Persian, Armenian, and Greek students with little or no competence in Arabic. In the eighties, the replacement of Arabic by English seemed to show that Hamlin had been right and Anderson wrong.[11]

The advances in higher education at Constantinople and Beirut had their parallels in the interior regions to which the American Board had transferred its principal effort. The establishment, in the sixties, of theological seminaries at Aintab, Harput, Marash, and Marsovan testified to the strength of Rufus Anderson's commitment

[11] Anderson, *Oriental Churches*, II, 385-91; Richter, *History of Missions*, pp. 218-20; Laurie, *Ely Volume*, pp. 374-79; Tibawi, *American Interests*, pp. 160-61, 167, 206-8, 244-47; Daniel Bliss, *The Reminiscences of Daniel Bliss* (New York, [1920]), pp. 170-88; S.B.L. Penrose, *That They May Have Life* (New York, 1941); H. H. Jessup, *Fifty-Three Years in Syria* (New York, 1910).

to the cause of evangelical education. But for the Armenians of Anatolia, theology was not enough. A demand arose for a foundation on the model of Robert College, and competition for possession of this institution between the inhabitants of Aintab and Marash resulted in surprising pledges of local financial support. The choice fell on Aintab, whose Central Turkey College, opened in the mid-seventies, proved only the first of a series of new establishments. The same decade saw the creation of Euphrates College at Harput; the eighties brought the opening of Anatolia College at Marsovan and of St. Paul's College at Tarsus; in 1891 International College was founded at Smyrna. All this was but part of a continuing process which involved the creation of new medical departments and hospitals, as at Aintab and Marsovan, and efforts to improve the standards of female education. At Constantinople the Home School for Girls, founded in 1872, soon raised its sights, and in 1890 secured a Massachusetts charter transmuting it into what became, after some further changes of name, Constantinople Woman's College.[12]

The educational system created in these years forms a remarkable monument to American disinterested benevolence and to the American confidence in education as the panacea for the problems of mankind. Much of this work was lasting: although intervening wars and revolutions have destroyed many of the smaller institutions in the interior, the major establishments at Constantinople and Beirut survive today. This survival is remarkable enough; still more so, it would seem, is the very existence of these foundations, which, as the world's history goes, appear so improbable that if they did not exist they could hardly be imagined. The inhabitants of the Turkish Empire were far away, remote from the mainstream of American life. Yet from the beginning, Americans were found who would tax themselves for the support of these colleges and of the underlying structure of primary and secondary schools, and other Americans who would cut themselves off from home to staff these institutions. With all allowance for the human tendency to rationalization and self-deception, this seems a magnificent record, and one for which any historical parallel is difficult to discover.

What the Americans brought the Near East can, of course, hardly be weighed and measured, yet their influence is not subject to doubt. In training up groups of leaders, in inculcating the arts of the West,

[12] Anderson, *Oriental Churches*, II, 455-57; Richter, *History of Missions*, p. 131; Laurie, *Ely Volume*, pp. 384-88, 392-403; Bliss, *Encyclopaedia of Missions*, I, 103-4.

in the teaching of English, the language of commerce and colonization which, as Cyrus Hamlin said, "seems destined to form a band
of sympathy and intercourse among the nations, beyond any other
language," they occupied a position of extraordinary importance.[13]
By the standard which they raised they stimulated a more widespread educational revival, and competition on the part of Greek,
Armenian, Ottoman, and French Jesuit institutions. And for better
or for worse they did still more: debarred from any considerable
influence on the ruling Turkish population, the Americans of necessity had to cater to the subject peoples of the Ottoman Empire. What
the Constantinople mission had early done to stimulate Armenian
nationalism, the Syrian College did for the Arabs, and other institutions for other groups. In the critical state of that fissionable mass
governed by the Turkish sultan the Americans provided a detonator.
Indeed, the claim has been made, and perhaps without too much
exaggeration, that within two decades of its founding Robert College
had made a nation.

2. The Independence of Bulgaria

The process of education, however necessary to modernity, is
frequently unsettling. Such, certainly, was the case in the Near East
with respect to the educational efforts of the American missionaries.
From the time of the establishment of the first schools this work had
formed an important aspect of the larger problem of Westernization,
but along with its constructive consequences there came serious corrosive effects.

For the Turks the modernizing process had not proved easy. Outside the empire, an increasingly vigorous Europe pressed against the
Ottoman frontier. Inside, the two acids of nationalism and liberalism continued to eat away the ancient structure, as subject
nationalities were energized by mission school and mission press
and as the newly developing Turkish elite, product of the reforms
of Mahmud II, became increasingly committed to Western solutions and increasingly at odds with the conservatives.

The lesson, perhaps, was that human nature is more refractory and
culture more resistant than had been suggested by the optimistic
formulations of Barlow and Dwight and assumed by charitable
Americans. In any event, the formulations were changing. The

[13] Hamlin, *Among the Turks*, p. 282.

optimism of the early years, which had led diplomat and missionary alike to hail Ottoman adoption of Western forms, had begun to fade by the time of the Crimean War. In 1854 Carroll Spence reported that a decline in Moslem zeal and "a spirit of reform in trifles dissecting the customs and habits of the people, had left the Turk with many of the vices of the Christian and few of the chevalric and enterprising characteristics of the Saracen." Little more than a year later Spence was anticipating, although for different reasons, that same collapse of the Turkish Empire toward which the early missionaries had confidently looked. The revolutionary aspirations of Greeks, Slavs, and Rumanians had led him to conclude that reform merely weakened the Ottoman Empire, and that if its preservation was desired, the efforts to improve the lot of the subject Christian populations should perhaps be given up. This view was reaffirmed by his successor in 1860, in a dispatch which noted that the principal evil besetting Turkey was that excess of religious liberty, which increased the power of irresponsible priesthoods and diminished that of government.[14]

But the Westernizing process was patently irreversible, and the downward spiral continued. In 1871 the death of the Grand Vizier Aali marked the end of a period of comparative stability; in the years that followed, the growing autocracy and extravagance of the Sultan Abdul Aziz brought a rapid descent into chaos. But the geographical focus of Ottoman troubles had shifted since the days of Mahmud. Although Arab nationalism was beginning to flower, assisted by the American College at Beirut, and although Egypt was once again restive, there were no more Syrian wars. In the new age the difficulties centered in the Balkans, whose Christian nationalities, long subject to the Grand Turk but now beginning to stir, found in Russia to the northward an eager protector.

With these Turkish troubles official American policy was unconcerned. As earlier, at the time of the Greek War for Independence, the United States had correctly abstained from intervention in the Cretan revolution, and this despite the pressures exerted by Consul Stillman and Minister Morris. As had been uniformly the case since the Americans had first reached the Levant, the important activities were those of such unofficial organizations as the missionary

[14] Despatches, Turkey: Spence to Sec. of State, 8 February 1854, 20 June 1855; Williams to Sec. of State, 1 June 1860.

boards, and those of that mixed type, peculiar to the Great Republic, in which officials managed to act in unofficial capacities.

One such case involved the Jews. Humanitarian concern for this subject people, first evidenced by the representations of the Van Buren administration in 1840 on behalf of the Jews of Damascus and Rhodes, now reappeared in response to Rumanian persecutions. Troubles in that country, which still acknowledged a shadowy suzerainty of the Sultan, brought instructions to the American minister at Constantinople to intervene with the Rumanian agent, a step followed by the appointment in 1870 of Benjamin Franklin Peixotto, a San Francisco lawyer and leader of the Jewish community, as consul at Bucharest. As his instructions quite frankly stated, Peixotto's appointment was intended less to benefit the United States than to provide "a missionary work for the benefit of the people he represents." Serving without salary, and with his expenses paid by the subscription of American Jews, the Consul became in short order "the recognized champion of the Hebrews in the East." In his six-year tour of duty at Bucharest, Peixotto is said to have done much to diminish, at least temporarily, the prevalent anti-Semitism of that most anti-Semitic of countries. In his approach to his task Peixotto was typically American, for his principal efforts, over and above remonstrance with the authorities, were concentrated on a missionary effort to modernize, most notably by the organization of schools, his backward coreligionists.[15]

A more important missionary work was that of the Protestants in Bulgaria. There two decades of effort had borne good fruit. Despite the usual discouragement from the nationalism of those they sought to serve and the problems presented by the intimate linkage of Bulgarian patriotism and Bulgarian religion, the American missionaries had made progress both north and south of the Balkans. Schools for both sexes had been well received, and in time the boys' school at Samokov would send a number of its graduates to America; the magazine *Zornitsa* had begun its long and influential career; a scattering of converts had been made. In the late sixties both the American Board and the Methodists sent in reinforcements, while by 1870 the Board's mission had sufficiently matured to be reor-

[15] Despatches, Turkey: Morris to Sec. of State, 31 May 1867, 9 June 1870, 15 July 1870; Boker to Sec. of State, 20 August 1872. Cyrus Adler and A. M. Margolith, *With Firmness in the Right* (New York, 1946), pp. 100-11; *Universal Jewish Encyclopedia* (New York, 1939-43), "Peixotto."

ganized, separated from Constantinople, and reconstituted as the European Turkey mission. The year 1871 brought the publication of a vernacular Bible, the work of the great translator Elias Riggs and of Albert L. Long, one of the Methodist pioneers, and the organization of the first evangelical church in Bulgaria.

All this did not go without remark in Europe. In the autumn of 1871 an article in the *Revue des Deux Mondes*, commenting on the Bible translation and on other missionary contributions to the moral and intellectual needs of the Bulgarians, went on to link the large number of American missionaries in the Near East, the proliferation of American consulates in areas of negligible American commercial interest, the activity of the American consul in the Cretan insurrection, and the rumored American purchase of an island in the Cyclades as evidence of a developing forward policy in the Levant.[16]

Throughout these years of ministry to the Bulgarians, a peculiarly potent influence had been exercised by Robert College. Of the twenty-five individuals who had completed the college course by 1874, all but two were Bulgars; the tone of their education and its implications for their country's future may be indicated by the commencement proceedings of 1875, at which members of the graduating class delivered orations on the freedom of the press, unjust national acquisitions, the instability of human governments, Spartacus, and Toussaint L'Ouverture. By the seventies, indeed, American missionaries and American teachers had become in considerable degree the mediators between Bulgaria and the outer world, and this despite the diligent efforts of Pan-Slav Russians. Owing allegiance to no party, serving no individual, with one group resident in Bulgaria and mingling freely with the people and with another at Constantinople performing a crucial role in education, the strangers from the New World occupied a uniquely influential position.[17]

[16] Anderson, *Oriental Churches*, II, 174-210; Bliss, *Encyclopaedia of Missions*, I, 77-78, 217; II, 76-77; H. M. Field, *The Greek Islands and Turkey after the War* (New York, 1885), pp. 161-63; Dumont, "Souvenir de la Roumélie," *Revue des Deux Mondes*, 1 October 1871; Constantine Stephanove, *The Bulgarians and Anglo-Saxondom*, pp. 272-86. For a surprising suggestion of Egyptian fear of the United States, Georges Douin, *Histoire du règne du Khédive Ismaïl* (Rome and Cairo, 1933-41), II, 582.

[17] Washburn, *Fifty Years*, pp. 48-99; W. S. Monroe, *Bulgaria and Her People* (Boston, 1914), pp. 326-29. Despatches, Turkey: Maynard to Sec. of State, 23 July 1875. Laurie, *Ely Volume*, p. 383, lists a similar group of commencement parts for 1880.

Such was the situation when the trouble came. In Bosnia and Herzegovina the year 1875 brought insurrection against Turkish rule. European diplomatic attempts to damp the crisis by persuading the Turks to measures of reform were still in progress when, in May 1876, the French and German consuls at Salonica were murdered by a mob in the presence of the governor and chief of police. The affair had originated in a dispute between Christians and Moslems over the custody of a young girl who had been sheltered in the home of the American consular agent. Since this individual, Russian by birth, was rumored to be an instigator of Bulgarian sedition, and since relations with Washington were already strained by reports of American-Russian friendship and by the Tripolitan activities of Vidal, the Turks attempted to shift the blame onto the United States. In April, Horace Maynard, who had succeeded Boker as minister in the preceding year, had asked for a station ship at Constantinople; now, as excitement developed throughout Europe, he telegraphed Admiral Worden for naval support.

But events in Cuba and Secretary Fish's Number 266 had made calls upon the European Squadron, and Worden's force was limited to his flagship *Franklin*, then repairing at Villefranche. Cabling the Department for reinforcements, the Admiral hastened his preparations for sea. On 24 May he reached Salonica to discover fourteen warships of various nationalities present, an international commission in charge, and some executions of presumed culprits in progress. On the 29th, in response to a request from Maynard, Worden set out from Salonica for Constantinople; as the flagship was too large to pass the straits under the treaty provisions, he took passage on the mail steamer. One hour before the steamer sailed, a Turkish admiral came aboard to inform him that the Sultan Abdul Aziz had been deposed.

For the Turks a new period of torment had now begun, and another season of carnage and terror had opened at Constantinople. Already there had been riots in the capital. Shortly the deposed Sultan was found dead, possibly by his own hand. In mid-June the Ministers of War and of Foreign Affairs were murdered by a disaffected army officer. Two weeks later Serbia declared war. Mentally unhinged by these events, the new Sultan Murad was in his turn removed in late August and replaced by Abdul Hamid. While these happenings convulsed the capital, and war and insurrection the Balkans, there loomed over all the threat of Austria and Russia from the north. With another Russian war imminent, and with France and Germany antagonized by the Salonica murders, the only Turkish hope lay in British support. But this hope was to be gravely endangered by the course of events in Bulgaria.[18]

There a revolt against Turkish rule, planned for May, had been betrayed to the authorities. With troops in short supply owing to the Serbian crisis, the local authorities mobilized the irregular forces, the bashi-bazouks, provided them with a little artillery support, and turned them loose upon the Bulgarian population. The result was a series of frightful massacres, the destruction of entire villages, and a death toll variously estimated at anywhere between ten and sixty thousand.

For some time the world knew little of these events. A few rumors were briefly noticed in the European press in May, but communications with Bulgaria were poor, the embassies at Constantinople were ill-informed, and in any case the Salonica murders preoccupied the diplomats. The first real information of the massacres came as the Bulgarians turned to their American missionary friends and as these communicated with their colleagues of the Constantinople mission, with President Washburn of Robert College, and with Professor Long, the Bible translator and former missionary in Bulgaria.

Washburn had earlier attempted to prevent the Bulgarian rising. Now, armed with information of the atrocities, he and Long waited upon Sir Henry Elliot, the British ambassador, to ask him to restrain the Turks. But Elliot was distracted by the Constantinople riots and the deposition of the Sultan, and the new Turkish regime denied the stories; while admitting that excesses had perhaps occurred, the Ambassador felt that the missionaries' reports were more excessive still. Finding their efforts fruitless, Washburn and Long took counsel with the more sympathetic British consul general and with Edwin Pears, Constantinople correspondent of the *Daily News*, Britain's chief Liberal organ. An appeal to British public opinion was decided on; a dispatch describing the massacres, prepared by the two Americans, was published in the *News* on 23 June.

With this event the issue was joined in another of those conflicts

---

[18] Despatches, Turkey: Maynard to Sec. of State, 18 April 1876, 12 May 1876, 20 May 1876, 17 June 1876, 1 September 1876. Squadron Letters: Worden to Sec. of Navy, 15 May 1876, 11 June 1876. 44C 1S *HED* 170. Elliot, *Revolutions and Diplomatic Experiences*, pp. 219-23, 232-50; Davison, *Reform in the Ottoman Empire*, pp. 323-59.

between policy and humanity which have so bedeviled the modern world. When the question was raised in Parliament, Washburn's and Long's dispatch was discounted by Disraeli as coffeehouse babble. Two weeks later the *News* printed a second dispatch from the Robert College professors, which replied to the Prime Minister with further detail and which impugned the competence of the British ambassador. In England, as humanitarian concern began to develop, the government instructed Elliot to make the investigation which Washburn had earlier urged. But the junior secretary to whom the task was entrusted was new at his post, and to the worried Americans, it looked like a whitewash.[19]

Enter now two other American citizens. Early in June the prince of American foreign correspondents, Januarius Aloysius MacGahan, had arrived at Constantinople. Handsome, charming, and gifted with boundless energy, MacGahan had enjoyed a remarkable career which in Europe had encompassed the Paris Commune, a winter at St. Petersburg, marriage to a Russian aristocrat, and a campaign with the Russian armies on the Oxus. After leaving Russia he had visited Cuba at the time of the *Virginius* crisis and had explored the Arctic; returning to Europe to cover the Carlist War in Spain, he had heard rumors of the Bulgarian atrocities and had hastened to the Turkish capital.

One month later there arrived from Russia a minor American diplomat, Eugene Schuyler. A graduate of Yale, which had also conferred upon him one of the first doctorates of philosophy granted in America, Schuyler had become a considerable linguist and had translated Turgenev and the *Karevala*; in the course of nearly a decade of service in various posts in Russia he had traveled widely in central Asia, where he had made the acquaintance of MacGahan. Discontented with a world that advanced Civil War heroes and hack politicians to prominence while keeping the learned in inconspicuous positions, Schuyler had at last received his long-sought transfer; appointed consul general and secretary of legation at Constantinople, he reached the capital on 6 July.[20]

[19] Washburn, *Fifty Years*, pp. 100-109; Edwin Pears, *Forty Years in Constantinople* (London, 1916), pp. 13-15; Eugene Schuyler, *Selected Essays, with a Memoir by Evelyn Schuyler Schaeffer* (New York, 1901), pp. 59-62; Dimitri Mishew, *The Bulgarians in the Past* (Lausanne, 1919), pp. 448-50; David Harris, *Britain and the Bulgarian Horrors of 1876* (Chicago, 1939).

[20] Despatches, Turkey: Maynard to Sec. of State, 6 July 1876. F. L. Bullard, *Famous War Correspondents* (Boston, 1914), pp. 116-41; Schuyler, *Selected Essays*, pp. 17-56.

For some at Constantinople these arrivals were opportune. Deeply concerned for their Bulgarian friends, President Washburn and Professor Long felt themselves blocked by Sir Henry Elliot and by the policies of the British government. Stung by the slighting remarks which the first dispatch had elicited in Parliament, the correspondent Pears was also hostile to the policy of the Disraeli ministry and its ambassador. American missionaries and English correspondent alike wanted a thorough investigation of the Bulgarian situation. For such an investigation the presence of these experienced travelers and observers offered possibilities.

While MacGahan, at Pears's request, was taken on by the *News,* Washburn turned for help to the American minister. Having vainly urged Sir Henry Elliot to investigate the reported massacres, and subsequently and equally fruitlessly protested his choice of his most junior secretary as emissary, the president of Robert College now asked Maynard to dispatch the new Consul General, with appropriate interpreters, to make an independent and impartial investigation. To this request Maynard pleaded want of official authority, while undertaking to permit such a step should Washburn succeed in persuading Schuyler to go. Persuasion proved simple, and on 23 July Schuyler and MacGahan left Constantinople, accompanied by a Bulgarian graduate of Robert College who was to serve as interpreter.[21]

The British Embassy was still procrastinating and the British government was still poorly informed when, on 7 August, MacGahan's first telegraphic dispatch was printed in the *News* and the worst rumors confirmed. The results were impressive. An editorial in *The Times* accepted the facts as stated; the Queen was reported to be upset; within two days, mass meetings protesting Turkish policy were being held. On the 16th both *News* and *Times* published letters from MacGahan and Schuyler to the radical reformer Sir Charles Dilke, together with MacGahan's first detailed report from the scene. Steadily the excitement increased, until the appearance on 22 August of MacGahan's celebrated dispatch from Batak— "Since my letter of yesterday," it began, "I have supped full of horrors"—drove public opinion into a frenzy. Although the American correspondent's articles reflected pointedly on both the policy of the

[21] Despatches, Turkey: Maynard to Sec. of State, 23 February 1877. Washburn, *Fifty Years,* pp. 104-9; Pears, *Forty Years,* pp. 16-18; Schuyler, *Selected Essays,* pp. 63-64; Field, *The Greek Islands,* pp. 171-74; Harris, *Britain and the Bulgarian Horrors.*

Disraeli government and the competence of the British ambassador, the agitation in Britain became increasingly nonpartisan and was accompanied by reiterated demands for Elliot's recall.

If, after reading MacGahan's searing reports, any wished further verification, it was soon provided. The fact that he was accompanied by the American consul general had been frequently mentioned in the American correspondent's dispatches, and Schuyler himself had not been idle. On 10 August he had sent Maynard from Philippopolis a nineteen-page account of his findings. Sober, restrained, and objective in style, at least at the start, but with statistics, village by village, of churches burned and of killed, tortured, and mutilated of both sexes and of all ages, Schuyler's report was the ideal complement to the dispatches of the correspondent. Yet it, too, went beyond the facts of the situation to impugn, apparently intentionally, British policy in the defense of the Turks. Somehow the letter leaked, and on 29 August it was published in the *News* as "Mr. Schuyler's Preliminary Report."[22]

Although Gladstone, as leader of the opposition, had spoken briefly against the Turks in the closing days of Parliament, when the House rose in mid-August he put the matter from his mind and retired to the country to concern himself with the question of Future Retribution. But as indignation increased and agitation spread, it dawned upon him that a cause had been born which needed a leader. Abandoning his theological preoccupations, he began to move with the tide and on 28 August commenced work on a pamphlet on the Bulgarian question. As he applied himself to this project with his accustomed energy, the publication of Schuyler's report provided quotable material. On 6 September *The Bulgarian Horrors and the Question of the East*, with its celebrated call upon the Turks to pack up and leave Bulgaria "bag and baggage," burst upon the world.

Like the speeches that followed, in which Gladstone called upon the government to join with Russia in support of the Christian population of the Ottoman Empire, this spectacularly successful pamphlet was consequence rather than cause of the British concern with the Bulgarian horrors. For the cause one had to look to Constanti-

[22] Despatches, Turkey: Maynard to Sec. of State, 21 November 1876. *The Turkish Atrocities in Bulgaria, with Mr. Schuyler's Preliminary Report* (London, 1876); Schuyler, *Selected Essays*, pp. 66-76; Bullard, *War Correspondents*, pp. 141-43; Field, *The Greek Islands*, pp. 174-79; Harris, *Britain and the Bulgarian Horrors*.

nople, and to the decision taken by a handful of friends of Bulgaria to appeal, over the heads of British ambassador and British government, to the conscience of the British public. Rarely, indeed, has such an appeal enjoyed such notable success, for so violent was the resulting outcry that British support of the Turks was for the moment gravely weakened. But only for the moment, and by October the agitation was subsiding and the Russian bogey was again dominant in British minds. There was a singular kind of evenhanded justice at work in this, for the change of opinion was assisted by the publication, in the intervening weeks, of Eugene Schuyler's *Notes of a Journey in Russian Turkistan*, which said much the same kind of thing about the Russian Army as his "Preliminary Report" had said about the Turks.[23]

Despite their troubles in Bulgaria and their double change of sultan, the Turks had won their summer war against the Serbs. But the accounts of the Bulgarian horrors which had shaken Britain's pro-Turkish policy had also inflamed Russian Pan-Slavism and had placed great pressure on the Russian government to intervene. An ultimatum from the Czar forced Turkey to grant the Serbs an armistice, while Russian preparations for war were only headed off by the prospect of a Constantinople conference of British and Russian plenipotentiaries, which it was hoped might plaster over the threatening Balkan situation. If ever there were vicissitudes relating wholly to Europe, and with which America could refuse to interweave her destiny, here was surely a prime example. Yet even here the individualistic and forward Americans were to be found serving the cause of liberty and contributing, in their centennial year, to the new birth of Balkan freedom. The ambassadors' conference was scheduled to commence in mid-December. Well before that time the British had turned to the faculty of Robert College for expert information on Bulgaria, while on 15 November Schuyler wrote his sister: "Just now I am getting up a Constitution for Bulgaria. General Ignatief is to present it at the Conference, and as Russia threatens to fight unless she gets what she wants, I am anxious to make it a good one."

A good one it must have been, for it was adopted by the conference with little change. Those ignorant of the fact that it had been written

---

[23] W. E. Gladstone, *Bulgarian Horrors* (London, 1876); Schuyler, *Selected Essays*, p. 82; *idem, Turkistan. Notes of a Journey in Russian Turkistan, Khokand, Bukhara, and Kuldja* (London, 1876); Pears, *Forty Years*, pp. 18-20; Mishew, *The Bulgarians*, pp. 452-54; Harris, *Britain and the Bulgarian Horrors*.

by the American consul general were astonished at its democratic nature, as were all at the fact of Russian support. After its approval by the conference, the constitution was in due course accepted by a Bulgarian assembly "made up largely of peasants, many of them in their sheepskin clothes," none of whom had any experience in civil government and none of whom "knew anything about parliamentary law except the old students of Robert College, who were in force."[24]

All this did not come to pass without a period of prolonged crisis which brought war between Russia and Turkey and threatened the peace of Europe. Nor were the relations between Turkey and America unaffected, for the tensions in Tripoli and elsewhere, which had been reflected in the effort to blame the Salonica murders on the United States, were exacerbated by Schuyler's activities in Bulgaria.

In late August and early September 1876, while British agitation about the Bulgarian horrors was at its peak, the U.S.S. *Marion* had visited Constantinople. In October, foreseeing the outbreak of war, Admiral Worden emphasized to the Department "the importance of the interests which American Citizens have acquired or rather, created, in Turkey and in Syria:—interests for the protection of which, as well as for their own personal safety, these citizens and their many and influential friends at home have every right to expect prompt and effective measures to be taken." In November he sent one of his two ships to the east, to be followed by a second in January; and from this time on, one was maintained constantly on station at Constantinople. By April 1877, the month in which Russia declared war, Worden's pleas for added strength had been heeded: *Trenton* and *Alliance* had reached the Mediterranean, and the Department had accepted his argument against the transfer of the squadron's base to Lisbon. By June six American warships were in the Mediterranean, squadron headquarters had been temporarily shifted to Smyrna, and while one of Worden's vessels remained at Constantinople, the others were busy showing the flag at Salonica and Beirut. But the situation remained touchy, and reports of the cordial reception of a Russian naval squadron in America brought questions from the Turkish minister of foreign affairs.

[24] Despatches, Turkey: Maynard to Sec. of State, 27 November 1876, 30 January 1877. Schuyler, *Selected Essays*, pp. 85, 91; Washburn, *Fifty Years*, p. 147; Mishew, *The Bulgarians*, p. 459.

For the Americans at Constantinople, above all for those at Robert College with its predominantly Bulgarian student body, the presence of the American station ship was reassuring. Although, as President Washburn later wrote, they could not be as proud of the vessels as they were of the crews, the ships did represent a measure of protection and an emergency refuge. And since the emergency never came, the other dividends were the more appreciated, as when the sailors came up the hill to stage minstrel shows or baseball matches for the edification of the college community.[25]

Through the summer of 1877 the fortunes of war favored the Turks. But with autumn the Russian advance began, and in January 1878 Turkey appealed for an armistice. There followed a dramatic confrontation between the Russian army, occupying lines just outside the capital, and the British fleet, which had been sent up the straits. As the Anglo-Russian tensions increased there occurred a curious incident which showed that the United States could still, as in earlier decades, play the part of a distant source of naval power. Faced with the possibility of a new war, the Russians commenced to plan an offensive against British shipping. In April 1878 three ships were purchased in Philadelphia for conversion into raiders, and by the end of the month Russian officers and crews had reached Southwest Harbor, Maine; in May the construction of a fourth vessel was ordered. But the crisis was of brief duration and the enterprise productive only of newspaper excitement and Turkish irritation; so little were the British affected that in May the Constantinople Embassy requested the American minister to take charge of British interests in the event of war.[26]

The Constantinople Conference had provided for a large Bulgaria; the Treaty of San Stefano provided for an even larger one. But these decisions, gratifying to the Bulgarians, were undone at the Berlin Congress in the summer of 1878. The country was divided, with only Methodist territory, north of the Balkans, gaining autonomy, while to the southward the area of the American Board, rechristened Eastern Rumelia, received lesser concessions. If this was but a half a loaf it still seemed better than none, and to some observers territory

---

[25] Despatches, Turkey: Maynard to Sec. of State, 5 September 1876, 12 September 1876, 5 June 1877. Squadron Letters: Worden to Sec. of Navy, 25 October 1876, 20 January 1877, 12 May 1877, 24 May 1877, 29 June 1877. Washburn, *Fifty Years*, pp. 112-13, 121, 204.

[26] L. I. Strakhovsky, "Russia's Privateering Projects of 1878," 7 *Journal of Modern History*, 22-40. Despatches, Turkey: Maynard to Sec. of State, 11 May 1878.

and population were "quite large enough for the experiment of self-government which they were about to undertake. . . . Who shall say," wrote an American clergyman, "that the world does not move, when out of such materials—a people oppressed and trodden down for four hundred years—there arises a free Christian State?" And in any case the two regions were reunited within a decade, after violent nationalist agitation and a war with Serbia in which, at the great victory of Slivnitza, two Bulgarian regiments were commanded by Robert College graduates of the class of '76.[27]

For the Americans who had worked so wholeheartedly in the Bulgarian cause, the sequel can be quickly told. The sheepskinned peasants who adopted the constitution written by the American consul general also passed resolutions of gratitude to Washburn and Long, and for Robert College the future held a continued connection with the new country. For another decade Bulgarians predominated among its graduates, as did Bulgarian girls at the Home School at Constantinople. Although a number of their compatriots were educated through the missionary connection at institutions in America —Amherst and Hamilton, Harvard, Yale, and Princeton—it was Robert College which, in the words of King Ferdinand, was "the nursery of Bulgarian statesmen." Of this statement, and of the power of the engine which Americans had created on the shore of the Bosporus, sufficient evidence is given by the class of 1871. The graduates totaled five, all of them Bulgars, and together they provided their newly independent country with two mayors, four members of the National Assembly, three ambassadors, three cabinet members, and two prime ministers.[28]

For Eugene Schuyler the years that followed were years of disappointment and frustrated ambition. His activities in Bulgaria, carried out at the request of the president of Robert College, had certainly not been official; more, they had been sheltered by Maynard behind a wall of silence. Not until November 1876 did the American minister report on the Bulgarian atrocities and on Schuyler's investigation and enclose for the edification of the Department a copy of the Consul General's "Preliminary Report" of 10 August, long since published in the British press. For this delay Maynard was reprimanded by Secretary of State Fish, as was Schuyler for having

[27] Field, *The Greek Islands*, p. 165; Washburn, *Fifty Years*, p. 114; W. T. Stead, *The Americanization of the World* (New York, 1902), pp. 189-90.

[28] Washburn, *Fifty Years*, pp. 49, 147, 175; Monroe, *Bulgaria and Her People*, pp. 323-38.

published his report without departmental approval. Subjected to Turkish protests against Schuyler's activity, and against the paper which the Turkish minister described as having done "more to influence England than any other document of the war," Fish could only agree that both propriety and consular regulations had been breached. Hesitating, nevertheless, to recall Schuyler at once, for fear the action would be construed as condonation of the atrocities, the Department delayed his transfer until 1878.

There followed tours of duty in England and in Rome. In 1880 Schuyler became the first American diplomatic representative to Rumania, and in 1882 resident minister and consul general for Greece, Rumania, and Serbia. But the post was abolished by Congress two years later, and with no new employment in sight Schuyler turned to lecturing and writing. Briefly, in 1889, suitable preferment seemed imminent with the offer of the position of assistant secretary of state, but opposition in the Senate caused the nomination to be withdrawn. Three years previously Schuyler had published in book form his lectures on *American Diplomacy and the Furtherance of Commerce*, and it has been suggested that the frankness of his comments on congressional treatment of the diplomatic and consular service was the cause of this opposition. Possibly so, but in any case the whole burden of the work was representative of an America that now seemed out of date, the America of Jefferson and John Quincy Adams. Reflecting its title, the book concerned itself almost wholly with freedom of navigation, neutral rights, and commercial treaties, and its longest single narrative section was that which described the defense of commerce against the Barbary powers.[29]

Important as were the contributions of the diplomat and of the college, it was the reporter who became the Bulgarian folk hero. In February 1877, as war with Russia became imminent, MacGahan left Constantinople for St. Petersburg. With the outbreak of fighting he hastened to join the Russian armies, where he found in General Skobelev, his companion of the Oxus days, the hero of the campaign. His leg twice broken and encased in plaster, his health further undermined by Balkan fever, the American correspondent

[29] Despatches, Turkey: Maynard to Sec. of State: 21 November 1876, 22 December 1876, 21 January 1877, 23 February 1877. Instructions, Turkey: Sec. of State to Maynard, 5 January 1877, 26 January 1877, 1 February 1877, 22 January 1878. Schuyler, *Selected Essays*, pp. 131-83; *idem, American Diplomacy and the Furtherance of Commerce* (New York, 1886), pp. 193-232.

continued with the Russian forces, riding on a gun carriage and filing, through the telegraph at Bucharest, dispatches which gave his English readers prompter information than the Czar himself received. But it was to be his last assignment. At Constantinople, in June 1878, MacGahan died of typhus, contracted while nursing the American military observer with the Russian forces. His funeral at Pera was attended by the American minister and the officers of the station ship *Dispatch*, by General Skobelev and other Russian officers, and by his fellow foreign correspondents.

Briefly, at least, MacGahan had his place in history as the man whose dispatches, echoing throughout Europe, so stimulated the Pan-Slav movement as to force a reluctant Czar to war upon the Turks. "It is not too much to say," wrote Archibald Forbes, the famous British reporter, "that this Ohio boy, who worked on a farm in his youth, and picked up his education anyhow, changed the face of Eastern Europe." Six years after his death, on the initiative of the Ohio legislature, MacGahan's body was brought home on an American warship; in time a monument was raised above his tomb in New Lexington, Ohio. In Bulgaria, at least until the First World War, MacGahan was remembered as "the Liberator," and folksongs and poems circulated about the American champion of Bulgarian freedom. In the United States, for many years, the Bulgarian envoy to Washington made intermittent ceremonial visits to the New Lexington grave. But history continues to move on, and so does the writing of history. The contrast between the aftermaths of two world wars is reflected in that between the books of Mishew and Stephanove, with their emphasis on American missionaries, Robert College, and Eugene Schuyler, and works published after mid-century, which, foregoing mention of the Americans, derive Bulgarian freedom from the innate proletarian and revolutionary tendencies of the Slav.[30]

3. *To the African Shore*

For nations, as for individuals, habits are hard to kill. Despite the impact of the Civil War, and the compelling internal preoccupations of the years that followed, much of the earlier pattern of American activity survived. The American squadron returned to European

---

[30] Bullard, *War Correspondents*, pp. 143-53; Pears, *Forty Years*, p. 24; Field, *The Greek Islands*, pp. 180-81. A good example of the new school is Mercia Macdermott, *A History of Bulgaria* (London, 1962).

waters; the missionary establishment continued to grow; the course of events in Crete, Rumania, and Bulgaria revived the ancient American interest in the liberties of subject peoples and elicited the traditional mixture of passive governmental sympathy and active private concern.

For the United States, nevertheless, the Mediterranean had become an area of diminished interest. The disappearance of the effective commercial pressure groups of earlier years removed the principal spring of overseas diplomacy, and as the tariff rose and the merchant marine declined, the government at Washington, traditionally inactive overseas except with regard to commerce, became still more so. The sorrowful comment of a commander of the European Squadron that "we have almost entirely lost our Eastern trade and American vessels are as rare as black swans" brought no response; the repeated recommendations of American consuls that steamer service be established with the Levant went unheeded. When Turkish closure of the straits to American warships raised old questions of freedom of navigation, the reaction was negligible: questions were asked in Congress and inquiries made by the State Department, but although the matter of right was not conceded, no effort was made to contest the Turkish decision. The expansion of diplomatic and consular relations, so prominent a feature of the earlier commercial diplomacy, gave way in the Grant administration to contraction, as consulates were closed or reduced to consular agencies and as ministers were replaced by chargés d'affaires. In 1883, it is true, repeated recommendations finally led to the appointment of an American minister to Persia. But this was a missionary rather than a commercial matter.[31]

Paralleling this withdrawal on the part of the United States, and indeed perhaps contributing to it, was an increase in European pressure, the consequence of industrialization and nationalization. The half-century since the Greek War for Independence had brought great changes. New collectivities had developed, interposing themselves between the individual and mankind, and as kings, priests, and nobles gave way to nation states, bankers, and industrialists, the Europe with which the individualistic Americans had traditionally

[31] Squadron Letters: Howell to Sec. of Navy, 25 May 1880. *Commercial Relations, 1873*, p. 1089; *1879*, I, 17; II, 585. Instructions, Turkey: Sec. of State to MacVeagh, 5 January 1871. Despatches, Turkey: MacVeagh to Sec. of State, 24 January 1871, 27 March 1871. 41C 3S *SED* 52. Yeselson, *United States-Persian Diplomatic Relations*, pp. 23-25.

seen themselves in competition was replaced by something new. Increasingly, through the years that followed the Civil War, the growing power of this new Europe became visible in the Mediterranean, in the Near East, and on the North African shore.

By the sixties and seventies the industrious and industrializing French had joined the British in the role of accumulators of capital and bankers to the outer world. The tempting availability of ready money in London and Paris had involved the rulers of Turkey and Egypt in indebtedness on a very grand scale. Set against these European loans, the American contributions for relief or for education paled into insignificance, while the continuing importance of the Eastern question made the new problems of international high finance of serious interest to the European statesmen.

To the power of politicized finance was added the power of the new navies. In these same years the new technology was radically altering the nature of the maritime confrontation between East and West, and this beyond the power of future Eckfords or Porters to rectify. However disastrous to the Turks, the Battle of Navarino had been hard-fought, and had cost Codrington's squadron heavy casualties. But a mere quarter of a century later, Russian possession of the new ordnance made the Battle of Sinope an expeditious massacre; and as naval fashion turned increasingly toward the construction of ironclads, the disparity between Europe and the East—as, for the moment, between Europe and the United States—increased.

When to these changes in transatlantic affairs were added the new preoccupations at home, the diminution of American activity in the Mediterranean seems hardly surprising. On the part of the American government, moreover, this tendency toward passivity was effectively implemented by that same advancing technology that was changing the relationships between western Europe and its neighbors. Increasingly the extension of cable and telegraph inhibited local initiative; steadily, for diplomat and naval officer alike, the system came to prevail over the individual. Of that world in which Richard Rush could recognize a government and John Porter Brown could free a Koszta, the activities of Vidal in Tripoli and of Schuyler in Bulgaria were the last echoes.

Yet even the most passive policy may meet with obstacles. If the field of individual activity was now restricted, the organized missionary movement continued to thrive. The evident inclination of the American government to disengage from the Levant was frustrated, in no inconsiderable degree, by "the importance of the interests which American Citizens have acquired or rather, created, in Turkey and in Syria," and by the troubles of the Turkish Empire. Whatever the desires of the government at Washington, these interests and the recurrent calls for "prompt and effective measures for their protection" repeatedly drew the squadron eastward, and when orders were issued in 1877 to close the Villefranche depot and move outside to Lisbon, Admiral Worden's protest carried the day.[32]

With the end of the Russo-Turkish War and the Berlin settlement of the Eastern crisis, disengagement became easier. The advanced base at Smyrna was dissolved. The recall of Eugene Schuyler improved American-Turkish relations, as did also, perhaps, the departure of Horace Maynard in 1880. Briefly the post of minister to Turkey was occupied by General James Longstreet, the reconstructed Confederate; in 1881 Longstreet was succeeded by General Lew Wallace. Wallace's appointment was an unusual one, stemming as it did from President Garfield's desire to give the author of *Ben Hur* a chance to accumulate material for another book. But however capricious the reasons for his selection, Wallace did well, and in his four-year residence at Constantinople developed a friendship with the Sultan Abdul Hamid reminiscent of that between Porter and Mahmud: both on the occasion of his recall and subsequently, the Sultan pressed him to accept employment in the service of Turkey.[33]

In these circumstances, the years that followed the Berlin Congress were generally routine. There were, of course, intermittent offenses against missionaries, most of minor importance. For the rest, the bulk of the diplomatic correspondence is concerned with problems of extraterritoriality, questions relating to the Turkish tariff, the progress of Robert College, the procurement of firmans for an increasing number of American archaeological expeditions, and intermittent Turkish requests for naval aid. Together with the liquidation of diplomatic issues nearer home and with the end of Reconstruction, this diminution of Near Eastern tension opened the way for increased American initiative. With the inauguration of President Hayes and the accession as secretary of state of William

[32] Squadron Letters: Worden to Sec. of Navy, 25 October 1876, 17 March 1877. Letters to Flag Officers: Sec. of Navy to Worden, 26 February 1877 (telegram), 9 April 1877.
[33] D. M. Pletcher, *The Awkward Years* (Columbia, Mo., 1962), p. 19; Lewis Wallace, *Lew Wallace: An Autobiography* (New York, 1906), pp. 963, 967, 976, 996.

M. Evarts, leader of the American bar and leading participant in the *Alabama* arbitration, steps were taken to seize the opportunity.

Inevitably the missionary community rejoiced at the appointment of one whose parents had been married by Timothy Dwight and whose father had preceded Rufus Anderson as corresponding secretary of the American Board. Nor was this rejoicing unwarranted, for Evarts indeed appeared to have inherited something of the world view of his father's generation. Not only was he a firm supporter of missionary rights; seeing in foreign trade a mechanism which would weave "a flowing mantel of peace . . . over the nations," he worked to improve the consular service and the supply of commercial information, and pressed the Navy to prepare the way for an expanded commerce by the widest possible showing of the national flag. During his tenure of office the United States again began to look outward, however tentatively, and to revive, however briefly, its traditional naval and commercial diplomacy.[34]

In the summer of 1877, in a circular note to all legations and consulates outside the Western Hemisphere, Evarts emphasized the importance of increasing trade and instructed all diplomatic and consular officers to keep the Department constantly informed about commercial possibilities. At Constantinople the receipt of this circular brought from Maynard a long description of the state of Ottoman commerce, and led him to plan a voyage of commercial exploration of the Black Sea. Postponed first by the Russo-Turkish War and then by the lack of a suitable vessel, this voyage was finally undertaken in 1879.

While on leave in the United States the Minister had raised the project with the Secretary of the Navy; on his way back to Constantinople he discussed his plans with the commander of the European Squadron; in July 1879 the U. S. S. *Quinnebaug* was placed at his disposal. There followed some difficulties with the Turks, ostensibly owing to the vessel's size but actually, as the Minister believed, arising from European commercial opposition, which prevented the granting of a firman for entry into the Black Sea. But although *Quinnebaug* was excluded, permission was gained for the passage of another vessel. On 9 August the U. S. S. *Wyoming*, 6 guns and 997 tons, got underway from Constantinople carrying as passengers, in

---

[34] Despatches, Turkey: Maynard to Sec. of State, 2 April 1877. Brainerd Dyer, *The Public Career of William M. Evarts* (Berkeley, 1933), pp. 217-18, 234-37; LaFeber, *New Empire*, pp. 39-41.

addition to the American minister, President Washburn and Professor Stephan Panaretoff of Robert College.

With her boilers leaking steam and her guns reputedly incapable of firing, *Wyoming* entered the Black Sea. Heading eastward at about six knots, the best sustained speed of which she was capable, she visited in the course of a three-week cruise four Turkish and seven Russian ports, including Yalta, Sebastopol, and Odessa. At long last the mission of Henry Henry had been accomplished. An American public ship had sailed the Black Sea. But the detailed report which Maynard submitted on this effort on behalf of God and trade, while replete with scenic description and classical allusion, contained little of commercial interest.[35]

In point of fact, of course, the new age was to look outward in other directions: it was in Africa, and above all in the Pacific, rather than in the Levant, that promise seemed to lie. So far as the coast of Africa was concerned, the new orientation had been evident from the immediate postwar period. The shift from a Mediterranean to an Atlantic orientation had been signaled not only by the redesignation of the squadron but by the expansion of Goldsborough's cruising ground to include the African coast as far south as St. Paul de Loanda in Portuguese Angola. For three years, from 1865 to 1868, a depot was maintained at Loanda for the joint use of the European and Brazil Squadrons. Although Lisbon was abandoned in 1870 in favor of Villefranche, the Atlantic and African interest remained, and was responsible for the abortive orders of 1877 to shift the base again outside the straits.

Through these years African concerns brought intermittent calls upon the squadron. *Kearsarge* visited the coast in 1866. In 1867 and again in 1870 the government of Liberia asked American naval assistance in defending the civilized coastal settlements against the tribesmen of the interior. In response to the first request a ship was ordered south to check on the Navy Department's coal piles at Fernando Po and Loanda, to investigate the status of the slave trade, and to ascertain the progress of the Liberian experiment in planting civilization in Africa. Although others were later to have doubts,

---

[35] Instructions, Turkey: Sec. of State to Maynard, 7 August 1877. Despatches, Turkey: Maynard to Sec. of State, 26 November 1877, 5 July 1879, 8 July 1879, 17 July 1879, 5 August 1879, 27 August 1879, 10 September 1879. Squadron Letters: Howell to Sec. of Navy, 8 August 1879, 22 August 1879, 4 October 1879. Log of 3rd Rate *Wyoming*, 9-27 August 1879 (Naval Records Collection, National Archives). Washburn, *Fifty Years*, p. 149.

the commanding officer saw a promising future for the "colony," founded as it was on "Christianizing and moralizing principles," in contrast to the other west coast establishments, all of which were based on gunpowder, muskets, and rum. Through the decade of the seventies requests for naval visits, emanating from American missionaries and American commercial agents, were answered by vessels moving between the European station and the United States; in 1878 a boundary dispute between Liberia and Great Britain brought orders to the European Squadron to detail an officer to arbitrate the issue. For some months the commanding officer of *Marion* was held ready for the task, but the assignment ultimately passed to Commodore Shufeldt, who reached the coast in early 1879 on his way to the Far East.[36]

By this time, indeed, a visible American concern with West Africa was developing. The interest evidenced by Lynch's 1853 survey of the Guinea coast and by the gorilla hunts of Paul du Chaillu had burgeoned, largely as a result of the well-publicized explorations of Henry M. Stanley. But this interest was also gaining a new focus, and although Shufeldt, on his visit, declared Liberia to be "the *objective* point of American trade on this Coast" and "the garden of Africa," it was the Congo effort of the King of the Belgians which developed the greater appeal. With the enlistment of American politicians in Leopold's schemes, vigorous lobbying at Washington would lead to increased naval activity on the African coast. But this was a matter for the decade of the eighties, of a piece with the outburst of European imperialism which brought the speedy partition of the Dark Continent.[37]

Although concern for the new possibilities, Pacific as well as African, was by no means fully-developed, they were far from being ignored in Washington. This, indeed, was sufficiently demonstrated during Evarts' term of office by the Samoan treaty of 1878 and by the world voyage of Commodore Shufeldt, the most ambitious effort in naval commercial diplomacy in many years. In the course of this voyage, in the years 1878-80, Shufeldt attempted the Liberian arbitration, gained the right to establish an American coaling station on Madagascar, and negotiated a commercial treaty with the

[36] Letters to Flag Officers: 1866-75, *passim.* Squadron Letters: 1866-85, *passim.* Paullin, *Diplomatic Negotiations*, pp. 362-63.

[37] Pletcher, *Awkward Years*, pp. 225-33, 308-24; Walter LaFeber, *The New Empire* (Ithaca, 1963), p. 52.

Sultan of Johanna, in the Comoro Islands; continuing on his way, he visited Zanzibar, Muscat, the Persian Gulf and the Euphrates, and Borneo; reaching the Far East, the Commodore commenced the negotiations which in time resulted in the opening of Korea.

But Korea, too, was to be a matter of the eighties, and of the period of increasing European pressure upon the Orient. For the moment, by contrast, Europe's frontier still lay in the Balkans and in the Mediterranean. For centuries, while transatlantic empires rose and fell, this line had remained largely unchanged. But by the early nineteenth century Ottoman decline and the growth of European power had ended this stability, and from the time of the Greek revolt the frontier had been on the move, eastward through the Balkans and southward to the African shore.

The advance into Africa had begun in 1830, with the French occupation of Algiers. Although French control was for some years limited to the seaports, and arduous efforts were required for the conquest of the hinterland, pacification was largely completed in the fifties. Through these years the extension of French dominion was accompanied by a sizable colonizing enterprise. By the seventies Algeria contained a considerable European population, and railroad-building and other measures of development were underway.

Since the Porte, in 1835, had assumed a control over Tripoli that even the United States had finally come to acknowledge, only Tunis, of all the North African regencies, remained effectively independent. But in this country, bordered by French Algeria and separated only by the narrow straits from Sicily and Sardinia, European pressures were becoming serious. By the sixties Tunis found itself threatened by the neighboring French presence, subjected to European economic penetration, weakened by internal financial disorder, and the target of an increasing Italian immigration. Concerned for his future, the Bey was working hard to improve his position by the dispatch of envoys to the capitals of Europe and by various measures of reform, including the promulgation, in 1861, of the first written constitution of any Islamic country. Nor was the United States omitted from the list of hoped-for friends. A mission to study America's "mechanical arts" and "engines of war" was mooted in 1863. In the autumn of 1865 a Tunisian general was dispatched to America, bearing a large portrait of the Bey and accompanied by the American consul, to express His Highness' happiness at Union victory and abolition and his distress at the assassination of Lincoln.

Six years later the defeat of France by Prussia opened the way for increased Italian pressure. Early in 1871, in response to a purported outrage, the Italian consul broke off relations. To the American consul, Gwinn Harris Heap, son of the old doctor, nephew of Commodore Porter, and member of the camel-seeking expedition of 1855, Italian annexationist ambitions seemed clear. Reporting in his dispatches that a crisis appeared unavoidable, that Tunis had no real means of resistance, and that if worst came to worst the Bey would invoke the assistance of the Sultan, Heap also testified to Tunisian appreciation of the American way. He had, he wrote, been approached by a high official with a query as to whether the United States, if asked, would annex and protect the regency; while rejecting this flattering suggestion, he had gone so far as to suggest, like Spence at the time of the Anglo-Persian difficulties, measures that might provide a way out of the imbroglio. And for the moment it seemed that these measures worked.[38]

In North Africa, as elsewhere, the State Department under Evarts displayed a new interest and a new energy. In August 1879, as Shufeldt was moving northward through the Indian Ocean and *Wyoming* cruised the Black Sea, the Department developed a plan for a voyage of commercial exploration on the model of the earlier ventures of Bradish, Hodgson, and Cass. This plan was spelled out in instructions to General Edward F. Noyes, the American minister to France.

In Washington, attention had been aroused by French commercial penetration of North Africa and by related exploring ventures and development schemes. Since American industrial production was now approaching that of France and England, and since the United States, like those countries, was emerging from the Depression of 1873, the question of markets would soon become of great importance. If a share of the commerce of the Mediterranean and of interior Africa was to be gained, action seemed necessary. "The most natural initial step should be to cause American influence to be felt in those Mediterranean countries, if not in the same emphatic manner as in the early part of this century by Preble and Decatur, at

---

[38] Despatches, Tunis: Perry to Sec. of State, 21 February 1863, 17 June 1865, 3 July 1865, 30 August 1865, 23 December 1865, 30 December 1865; Heap to Sec. of State, 14 January 1871, 29 January 1871, 4 February 1871, 20 February 1871. Instructions, Tunis: Sec. of State to Perry, 27 July 1865, 9 May 1866; Sec. of State to Heap, 16 March 1871. Heap was commended by the Department for discouraging Tunisian hopes of annexation, "especially under the circumstances adverted to."

least in a way potential for the material good of commerce and civilization." In pursuit of this Hopkinsian aim the Minister to France, qualified both by ability and by position to make "American influence to be authoritatively felt," was to proceed at the earliest moment on a three or four months' journey, visit all accessible towns and stations on the northern coast of Africa, and penetrate into the interior if necessary. Everywhere he was to confer with American representatives and with the local authorities; if understandings beneficial to American commerce could be gained, he was to reduce them to official form for the subsequent action of the government.

Here, well before the scramble for Africa had begun, was the large vision, and here also, it would seem, the blank check. Between October 1879, when Noyes left France, and February 1880, when he returned to his post, he visited Italy and Greece, Constantinople and Smyrna, Rhodes and Cyprus, Syria and Palestine, Egypt, Malta, Tunis, and Algeria. Everywhere he conferred at length with the representatives of the American government, with private persons and prominent businessmen, and with the responsible authorities. Everywhere he was received with the greatest kindness and courtesy.

Since Noyes's instructions were printed in *Foreign Relations*, his journey did not go unremarked. Indeed, taken in conjunction with American participation in the Madrid conference of 1880 on the Moroccan question, it appears to have caused some concern. In July 1881, more than a year after the Minister's return, a newspaper article on "American Intervention in the Mediterranean," which stated that only the assassination of President Garfield had put off the forward American policy which the Noyes mission had been designed to initiate, stimulated the American minister to Spain to a disavowal of all political aims. But this step was hardly necessary, for the sequel of Noyes's journey was less interesting than either his instructions had seemed to promise or than appears to have been hoped at Washington. Far from making American influence "to be authoritatively felt," Noyes limited his efforts to the submission of a fifty-four-page report which described the absence of American shipping, the need for subsidized steamships, and the excellent work of the American missionaries. But all this information was available, and in vastly greater detail, in consular reports already filed in Washington, and no understandings had been reached with local authorities. Whatever it was that had been wanted had not been gained, and the disappointment of the State Department was evidenced in Evarts' acknowledgment of Noyes's report, couched in a tone of cutting sarcasm rarely found in official correspondence.[39]

However unsuccessful the Noyes mission, there was one part of the North African shore, vastly more important than Tunis or Morocco, where other outsiders had for years been making themselves "authoritatively felt," and in ever-increasing degree. This was Egypt. Subject to the Sultan and so linked to the Eastern question, situated at the bridge between Asia and Africa and influenced by both, historic outpost of French policy but lying athwart the British lifeline to India, Egypt had long vibrated in the winds of international rivalry like an aeolian harp. A great prosperity derived from cotton growing during the American Civil War had made the country a prime target of European financial adventure; in 1869 the completion of the Suez Canal made it the custodian of a new and more important Bosporus. Yet Egypt itself was not a negligible entity, and its ruler, the Khedive Ismail, like his grandfather Mehemet Ali, was a man of force and will. And like both grandfather and grandfather's opponent, the Emperor Mahmud, Ismail was a modernizer, seeking to employ the techniques of the West in the interest of his country.

Modernization is always costly. In Ismail's Egypt it was especially so, as there was added to the expense of great public works—roads, railroads, mills, and canals—the expense of extravagant display: the Suez Canal opening, which cost a reputed ten million dollars, the commissioning of *Aïda*, the support of opera and theater companies "of the most pronounced French type, . . . offensive to the modesty of the more fastidious." Yet for a time all went well. The country's agricultural prosperity provided a sufficient base for these developments. The ready availability of European capital speeded the work and permitted, in addition to investment in development and in ostentation, investment in defense. Briefly Egypt rejoiced in the possession of an impressive purchased ironclad squadron which attracted the attention of American naval officers in the Mediterranean. But there were two problems that money alone could not solve: the problem of Egypt's subordination to the Ottoman Sultan, and the problem of expanding the country to viable size.

[39] Instructions, France: Acting Sec. of State to Noyes, 29 August 1879 (*Foreign Relations, 1879*, pp. 342-44), Sec. of State to Noyes, 10 April 1880. Despatches, France: Noyes to Sec. of State, 11 October 1879, 10 March 1880, 28 April 1880. Despatches, Spain: Fairchild to Sec. of State, 22 July 1881, 24 July 1881.

From the time of his accession in 1863, it seems, the question of independence was never far from Ismail's mind. An Egypt subordinated to Turkey was also an Egypt subordinated to European control. Yet independence, once gained, would have to be maintained, and for this even a modernized Egypt limited to the Nile valley seemed too small. The needs for manpower and resources that had drawn Mehemet Ali into Syria still remained, and with northward expansion forbidden both by the settlement of 1841 and by the attitude of Europe, Ismail of necessity came to look southward. Thus there arose the double problem of Egypt, a country both coveting and coveted. On the one hand it was embarking upon a career of imperialism, attempting to forestall the Europeans in the division of the Ottoman Empire and in expansion into Africa. On the other hand, as site of the Suez Canal and target of financial penetration, Egypt was both strategically and economically of great importance to the powers. When, with the Berlin settlement of 1878, the Eastern question was transferred from the Bosporus to the Nile, the full pressures of European diplomacy were brought to bear.

With this fascinating country Americans had long been intermittently concerned. John Ledyard, the "American traveller," had died there; there General Eaton had mounted his expedition against Tripoli; there George B. English had marched with the army of Mehemet Ali. The secret mission of William Hodgson and subsequent naval and diplomatic visits had looked forward to a possible commercial treaty and had given rise to the plan to send an Egyptian admiral to visit the United States. Entering the country at midcentury, American missionaries had expanded their operations from their Cairo headquarters northward to Alexandria and southward far up the Nile. In still more subtle ways American influence had been apparent: a Boston girl, the wife of a French consul, had been reportedly the only Western female to dent Mehemet Ali's iron reserve; in 1869, seeking to refresh his soul after the turmoil of the Suez opening, the Khedive Ismail retired up the Nile in his houseboat with a California beauty.[40]

Although the treaty of commerce, the basis of all official approaches, was never consummated, the United States nevertheless looked upon Egypt, in the words of the instructions to the first Con-

[40] Schroeder, *Shores of the Mediterranean*, II, 8; *Levant Herald*, 12 January 1870; *New York Daily Tribune*, 21 February 1870; Finnie, *Pioneers East*, pp. 137-66. The more formal aspects of American-Egyptian relations are dealt with in L. C. Wright, "United States Policy toward Egypt" (unpublished doctoral dissertation, Columbia University, 1954).

sul General, as "in point of fact, an Independent Power." The early consuls were accredited directly rather than by way of Constantinople; the additional title of "agent" gave some color of legality to their performance of diplomatic functions; the dispatches from Alexandria were filed with those from the Barbary powers. Nor did the absence of a treaty prevent continued efforts to develop trade: repeatedly the instructions to the consul general adjured him to extend and enlarge commerce, and any progress in this direction met with departmental approbation.

Despite all efforts, commerce remained small. Yet of all the nations of the world, it was Egypt whose economy was most affected by the American Civil War. As southern policy and northern blockade combined to keep American cotton from the textile mills of Europe, world prices rose and with them Egyptian production and prosperity. Anxious to minimize the risk of European intervention to break the blockade, the government of the Union did all it could to assist the expansion of the Egyptian cotton crop, and in other ways kept closely in touch with the situation. In 1862, as the Egyptian viceroy prepared for a journey to England, the American consul general was ordered to go along.

One singular development of the war years raised echoes of the principles of Mr. Monroe, and provided a gloss to his doctrine which may be termed the "Egyptian corollary." Having hitched his wagon temporarily to the star of the Emperor of the French, the Egyptian ruler in early 1863 was prevailed upon to provide a detachment of Sudanese soldiers for service with Bazaine in Mexico. While war in America continued this passed unnoticed, but the report in the summer of 1865 that nine hundred Negroes from upper Egypt were preparing to sail to relieve the original contingent led Seward to lodge protests at Alexandria, Constantinople, and Paris. The situation in Mexico was described as a threat to the "safety of the free Republican institutions of this continent," and the dictum advanced that "in the opinion of the President, negroes, natives of Africa, cannot rightfully be employed as soldiers in any way to subvert established political institutions, or disturb society on the American Continent."[41]

With the withdrawal of the French from Mexico, relations resumed

[41] Instructions, Alexandria: Sec. of State to MacCauley, 23 October 1848; Sec. of State to Jones, 17 January 1853; Sec. of State to Thayer, 8 April 1862, 6 March 1863; Sec. of State to Hale, 21 September 1865, 14 December 1865. Instructions, Turkey: Sec. of State to Morris, 18 December 1865.

their even tenor. The new wealth of Egypt was reflected in the modernizing efforts of Ismail, that of the United States in an expanded tourism. Egyptology had become the rage, and although the visits of the Civil War greats, such as Seward, Sherman, and Grant, were what drew attention, ordinary American tourists already outnumbered all but the British. So numerous were these health and curiosity seekers that a principal duty of the Consul General now became the shipment home of his countrymen's remains, while the demand for curios had resulted in the residence at Luxor on the Nile of "Antiquity" Smith, a Yankee reared in the Connecticut wooden nutmeg tradition, who busied himself in the fabrication of relics for the gullible.[42]

With contact between the two countries largely limited to tourism, little friction developed. The problems of missionary enterprise and of missionary land tenure occasionally arose for adjudication. In the postwar years some tension developed from the impact of Grantism upon the consular service, and the appointment as consul general of George H. Butler, a nephew of the notorious General. But the career of this hard-drinking individual, who quarreled with the missionaries, was accused in the American press of the purchase of slave girls, and became involved in a spectacular shooting brawl, was ended by Egyptian requests for his removal.[43]

In the absence of any important divisive issues, the official attitude toward Egypt was governed by the generalized American approval of progress and the conventional American sympathy for self-determination. Acknowledging, in 1862, a report of a projected rail line from Alexandria to the Red Sea, Secretary Seward drew the analogy of the proposed Pacific railroad and noted that it "ought to be the work of the present generation to remove the obstructions to universal commerce which nature has so long maintained on the two great continents." Five years later, in response to a report of constitutional innovations, he observed that "Europe has been for some time showing that popular government follows in the track of

---

[42] C. D. Warner, *Mummies and Moslems* (Hartford, 1876), pp. 356-57; Morris, *Letters of Travel*, I, 415-18; John R. Young, *Around the World with General Grant* (New York 1879), I, 283; Edwin de Leon, *The Khedive's Egypt* (New York, 1878), p. 427; Wilson, *Signs and Wonders*, pp. 52-57.

[43] Instructions and Despatches, Alexandria: 1870-72, *passim*. Despatches, Turkey: Boker to Sec. of State, 11 July 1872, 13 July 1872, 18 July 1872, 25 July 1872. *The Nation*, 22 June 1871, 28 November 1872. "In some places," it was reported, Butler's "demands even shocked the Egyptian police, who are not purists."

the steam engine and the telegraph; but we were hardly prepared to expect similar demonstrations so soon in Africa." Such demonstrations, nevertheless, were welcomed. An Egyptian reform of weights and measures received praise. The possibility of an American-Egyptian convention for the suppression of the slave trade was mooted. Although opposed by some of the European powers, the projected Egyptian court reforms, intended to limit extraterritorial jurisdiction, were supported by the United States, and in due course American judges were appointed to the mixed courts. As so often before, the possibility of a commercial treaty was taken up.[44]

Yet all this, while pleasant enough, was incidental to the real business of nations, and the true measure of American interest in Egypt is perhaps best seen in two events of 1869. On 10 May the Pacific railroad, for which Americans had long hoped and to which Seward had adverted, was completed. The tracks were joined at Promontory Point; the golden spike was hammered in; the champagne and the whisky were consumed. Six months and six days later, amid still greater festivities, came the official opening of the Suez Canal.

To the Americans the railroad was the triumph. It was, after all, the railroad age, all eyes were focused on internal development, and in the imagination of the citizens of the Western world the locomotive had displaced the clipper ship. To the hopes of those Whitneys and Bentons who for a generation had seen in the transcontinental railroad the gateway to China and the control of the commerce of the Orient, the Union Pacific had promised to provide the answer. But they were wrong, and it was Lynch and his fellows of the American Geographical Society who proved, in the end, to have had the clearer vision. More than any other event since the discovery of America, the cut at Suez remade the geography of the world; far more than the California gold discoveries, it wrenched the commerce of the oceans into a new pattern. With the opening of this short route to the East, the South Atlantic, previously one of the busiest of oceans, rapidly became the loneliest, while the Orient, suddenly deprived of the protection of distance, found itself subject to greatly increased European pressures.

So transcendent an example of "the Application of Physical Sci-

---

[44] Instructions, Alexandria: Sec. of State to Thayer, 2 December 1862; Sec. of State to Hale, 5 January 1867; and *passim*. Despatches, Alexandria and Cairo: *passim*. Wright, "U.S. Policy toward Egypt," pp. 99-107.

ence to Political Economy" would surely have delighted Barlow and Fulton. Here, indeed, was "The Canal" par excellence. But alas for the days of maritime greatness. In anticipation of a possible visit by the President of the United States, Egyptian military bands had been hopefully taught the principal American national airs, but all in vain. The sole American representative at the opening was a delegate from the Boston Board of Trade; no American ship took part in the parade which celebrated the occasion; the European Squadron was on the Riviera and no mention of the occasion appears in the correspondence of its commander. Seven years after its opening the canal had handled 7,584 ships, of which 5,317 were British and only 11 American.[45]

Yet to all this evidence of disinterest and detachment one exception must be made. Although normal American commerce with Egypt remained minimal, consisting primarily of the export of petroleum, the import of rags for paper, and such one-time sales as that of the Pullman palace cars which made up the Khedive's special train, one new trade did become important in the postwar years. This was the trade in arms. Inevitably the Khedive's desire for a free hand in policy-making called for the acquisition of the means of self-determination. Equally inevitably, that American postwar surplus of arms and of arms-manufacturing capacity which had excited the interest of French, Russians, and Turks drew the attention of the Egyptians. By 1870 the Remington Company alone had sold the Khedive 285,000 stand of arms, together with machinery to equip the arsenal at Alexandria.[46]

And, finally, another postwar American surplus became important to the Egyptian ruler. As well as an excess of armaments, the United States had an excess of experienced military men; as well as providing the instruments of defense and expansion to the Egyptians, the United States contributed personnel to supervise their use. Like the earlier assistance afforded the navy of Mahmud's Turkey, this activity was unofficial, or almost so. Nevertheless, in the years that Ismail's experiment lasted, it gave rise to a remarkable history.

---

[45] Despatches, Alexandria: Hale to Sec. of State, 27 November 1869, 23 December 1869; Butler to Sec. of State, 3 June 1870, noted that through the railroad and the canal the two countries had "simultaneously accomplished the greatest triumphs of 19th century civilization." Despatches, Cairo: Farman to Sec. of State, 10 September 1877. Douin, *Règne du Khédive Ismaïl*, ii, 434, 452.

[46] Deyrup, *Arms Makers*, p. 211.

CHAPTER XI

The Khedive's Egypt, 1869-1882

1. Help From Afar

THE travels of Dr. Valentine Mott had lasting influence upon the lives of his children. Revisiting Europe after their father's return to the United States, his sons expressed their American love of freedom by participating in the Old World's revolutions. In 1848, Valentine, Jr., rode with the Sicilian rebels in the dual capacity of surgeon general and colonel of cavalry. His younger brother, Thaddeus Phelps Mott, served as sublieutenant in Italy, and was one of the signers of the Paris letter which urged the American minister at Constantinople to assist the interned Kossuth. But the most important transatlantic link came from the marriage of the doctor's daughter to Blacque Bey, son of the French founder of the *Moniteur Ottoman,* educated in France at the expense of the Sultan, and first Ottoman minister to the United States. It was through this connection that Thaddeus Mott became, in 1869, a major general in the Egyptian Army.

Mott had led a wandering life. Returning to America after the Italian revolutions, he spent some years at sea and in Mexico; in the Civil War he rose to the post of colonel of a regiment of New York cavalry. In 1868, after declining appointment as minister to Costa Rica, he sailed for Constantinople, where he seems to have made the acquaintance of the Khedive Ismail while the latter was visiting the Sultan. In Egypt, in the next summer, Mott was named major general and pasha and ordered to the United States to recruit officers for the Egyptian service.[1]

In that year of the opening of the Suez Canal, Egypt needed help from outside. The ever-difficult tie with Constantinople had been further strained during the period of canal construction, while Is-

[1] Despatches, Alexandria: Hale to Sec. of State, 14 April 1869, 27 January 1870. A. S. Southworth, *Four Thousand Miles of African Travel* (New York and London, 1875), pp. 345-46. Biographical information on Mott and the other Americans from: *Appleton's Cyclopaedia of American Biography*; *National Cyclopaedia of Biography*; G. W. Cullom, *Biographical Register of the Officers and Graduates of the U.S. Military Academy* (Boston and New York, 1891); F. B. Heitman, *Historical Register and Dictionary of the United States Army* (Washington, 1903); U.S. Naval Academy Graduates Association, *Register of Graduates* (Annapolis, 1925).

mail's aspirations for greater independence and for territorial expansion promised to place heavy responsibilities upon his army. In earlier years the Khedive had profited from his connection with Napoleon III, but this historic link was wearing thin. Distance still lent enchantment, and Ismail, distrustful of European assistance, turned to the United States.

Large orders for weapons, ammunition, and manufacturing equipment were placed with the Remington Arms Company, and the recruitment of American personnel was begun. Upon his return to New York in the autumn of 1869, Mott Pasha enlisted the aid of his brother, Henry A. Mott, and of General Fitz-John Porter, nephew of the old Commodore. A score of former Union and Confederate officers were taken into Egyptian service on five-year contracts, with the proviso that they would never have to act against the United States, and in the early months of 1870 the first arrivals reached Alexandria.[2]

This first group was to be followed by others. Over the next three years a dozen more Americans arrived in Egypt, and in 1875 another ten were engaged. As individuals these American officers were of varying quality, some serious professionals, some adventurers, some a little of each. A few became chiefly notable for their demands for promotion while in service or for extra compensation after departure; one, a son-in-law of James G. Blaine, aimed too high, found his proposed rank protested by others, and failed of appointment. Among the more exotic of the recruits was Carroll Tevis, a graduate of West Point who had served in the armies of Persia and Turkey, published a book on minor tactics in Paris, fought for the Union, and held the grade of brigadier general in the French Provisional Army during the Franco-Prussian War; but this spectacular rolling stone remained only briefly before departing to rejoin the Turks.

The majority, nevertheless, was both competent and diligent, and the best were very good indeed. Considered as possible combat officers, whether in a fight for independence from the sovereign across the sea or in an effort to expand the frontiers, these veterans

---

[2] Charles Chaillé-Long, *My Life in Four Continents* (London, 1912), p. 16; W. M. Dye, *Moslem Egypt and Christian Abyssinia* (New York, 1880), pp. 2-3; Fitz-John Porter, *In Memory of Charles Pomeroy Stone* (reprinted from the *Record of the Alumni Association of the Military Academy*, [n.p., n.d.]), p. 20. The most valuable single source for the activities of the Americans in Egypt is Douin's massive *Histoire du règne du Khédive Ismaïl*.

of the American Civil War had unmatched qualifications, while for peacetime duty in the Egypt of the seventies, experience in western exploration and Indian warfare was of the greatest value. In its attempts to develop its national estate and to thrust its frontiers outward through arid and unmapped areas populated by doubtfully disposed aborigines, the Khedive's Egypt had obvious resemblances to an earlier America. The need for improved communications and for the development of natural resources paralleled the situation in the American West a generation before, and the area in question was of comparable size. As camels had once been thought suitable to the navigation of the Great American Desert, so at this later date there existed in Egypt the same engineering requirements which, in the United States, had placed so great a premium on the training of graduates of West Point.

Finally, as the chief among them later wrote, the Americans came not as members of an official mission from a foreign government, but as individuals and members of the Egyptian Army. As individuals they were not subject to divided loyalties; as members of the army they could command as well as instruct; as Americans they were insulated from European pressures and could advise on international politics in an impartial, anti-European way. For some, certainly, it was just a job, but for most, sharing as they did the American preconceptions about self-determination, progress, and the use of science in the cause of man, this "call upon the youngest, freest, and most progressive of great nations, to help lift . . . the most enslaved of peoples" was something more.[3]

The first American contingent included four general officers, among whom Mott held precedence. But he had served his purpose in recruiting the others, and the problem presented by his elevated rank and comparative inexperience was solved by making him aide-de-camp to the Khedive. The post of chief of the Egyptian General Staff went to General Charles P. Stone of Massachusetts, a highly intelligent and cosmopolitan soldier who had distinguished himself in Mexico and had been brutally sacrificed by McClellan and the politicians during the Civil War. William W. Loring, a Floridian who had fought the Seminoles, the Mexicans, the Mormons, and the Union, now found himself brigadier general, detailed first as inspector general of the Egyptian Army and then as commander

---

[3] C. P. Stone, "Military Affairs in Egypt," 5 *Journal of the Military Service Institution,* 167-68; Dye, *Moslem Egypt,* p. v; Douin, *Règne,* II, 550.

of the First Army Corps and of the coast defenses at Alexandria. The fourth member of this group, Henry H. Sibley, who had served twenty-three years in the old Army before resigning to go South, became chief of artillery with headquarters at Rosetta.

In March 1870 Stone reached Cairo and assumed his post. Establishing himself in the Citadel, the great fortress built by Saladin, he found the General Staff in a state of suspended animation. A staff had existed at the time of the Syrian wars, organized by the French Colonel Sève; but Sève, now Suleiman Pasha, had retired to his harem, and only a single French officer remained on active duty. A few years earlier some fifteen Egyptian officers had been sent to study in France; to such of these as were still available Stone added a number of Americans, most important of whom was Colonel Erastus Sparrow Purdy. A veteran of western exploring expeditions who had served with Franklin's corps during the war, Purdy was placed in charge of the Third Section, the geographical bureau of the staff. But although the work of this group in exploration and mapping would ultimately prove to be of great importance, the immediately pressing question was that of defense.

In 1869, as the recruitment of American officers began, the relations between the Khedive and the Sultan had so deteriorated that Ismail was considering a fight for independence. Some at least of the American officers had understood that they were being employed to strike a blow for liberty against the sovereign in Constantinople. Ismail, on the occasion of their arrival, had expressed his confidence that they would faithfully aid him "in the establishment of the independence of Egypt," and although the moment of greatest tension had passed, first priority was still accorded the defense of the Syrian border and the Mediterranean coast. Some of the newcomers, it is true, were assigned to tasks of a logistic nature: a Confederate artillery specialist was placed in charge of the government powder mills near Cairo, and two former Confederate naval officers were given command of khedivial mail steamers on the Alexandria-Constantinople run. But the central problem was reflected in the establishment of a Commission for Frontier and Coast Defense under the Chief of Staff and in the duties assigned the majority of the Americans.

General Loring, who held the principal field command, took three: Colonel Vanderbilt Allen of New York, a nephew of Commodore Vanderbilt who had been twice brevetted for gallantry while serving under Sheridan in the Valley; and Colonels Alexander W. and Frank A. Reynolds, father and son, graduates of West Point and veterans of the Confederate Army. Of two other colonels who had fought for the South, one was given a cavalry command, while Beverley Kennon, whose Louisiana gunboat had distinguished itself against Farragut's squadron in 1862, took charge of the coast artillery, assisted by a former master's mate in the Confederate Navy.[4]

By January 1871 the work of the Commission for Frontier and Coast Defense had borne fruit in a report, submitted by Stone to the Khedive, which stressed the importance of a means of rapid concentration of troops at threatened points. In the long run this need would require construction of a coastal rail line; more immediately it called for topographical information. Since accurate maps were nonexistent, Colonel Purdy was assigned to a survey of possible military routes between Cairo and Suez; this work completed, he embarked upon a detailed reconnaissance of the entire eastern desert from the Nile to the Red Sea and south to Kenneh and Kosseir. Simultaneously another survey was taking place, as Lieutenant Colonel Charles Chaillé Long, a Marylander who had volunteered for Egyptian service as a result of tales spun by his wartime commanding officer, a Hungarian refugee, searched the eastern desert for defensive positions against an invasion from the north. The result of Long's efforts was the construction of earthworks at Tel el Kébir, works destined ultimately to be defended not by khedivial forces against a Turkish onslaught but by Egyptian nationalists resisting a British invasion.

A second point emphasized in Stone's report was the importance of mine warfare for harbor defense. Already orders for underwater ordnance had been placed in England and America; soon there arrived from the United States the engineer and inventor John L. Lay and the former commander of the C.S.S. *Tallahassee*, William H. Ward. In April these commenced a survey of the Nile from Cairo to the sea; this done, Lay was assigned to coastal survey, while Ward was put to development work; in the autumn Stone ordered the

---

[4] Despatches, Alexandria: Butler to Sec. of State, 7 July 1870. Stone, "Military Affairs," pp. 168-69; Porter, *Stone*; Cullom, *Biographical Register*, "Stone"; Dye, *Moslem Egypt*, pp. 56-68, 70, 77; Chaillé-Long, *My Life*, pp. 17, 31-32, 39-40; W. W. Loring, *A Confederate Soldier in Egypt* (New York, 1884), pp. 298-99, 349-54, 361-62; Mohammed Sabry, *L'Empire égyptien sous Ismaïl, et l'ingérence anglo-française, 1863-1879* (Paris, 1933), pp. 384-86.

latter to organize a mine school for Egyptian officers. Continuing its studies at the Citadel, the Commission for Frontier and Coastal Defense had by now submitted two other important papers, one on underwater aspects of harbor defense and one on the use of irrigation canals as defensive positions. But by this time the arrival of the Americans had had diplomatic repercussions and had led to pressure from the great powers upon the Egyptian government.[5]

To the nations of Europe the news of the Remington contract and of the assumption by Americans of positions of responsibility in the Egyptian Army had come as something of a shock. For English and French the presence of each other's nationals in Egyptian or Turkish forces was an accustomed phenomenon, to be dealt with by the normal methods of diplomacy. But the arrival of these outsiders, whose allegiance was apparently to their employer and whose unofficial status protected them from any exertion of pressure by way of Washington, presented a new problem. No time was lost in making plain the resultant concern.

Early in 1870, as the Americans were arriving and taking up their tasks, Nubar Pasha, the Egyptian foreign minister, reached Europe on a diplomatic mission. It proved impossible to limit the topics under discussion. At a reception in London, Nubar was told to advise his master that "the road upon which His Highness seemed to be launched was a bad road," and the warning was officially repeated the next day. In Paris, a few days later, the Duc de Grammont emphasized French hostility to the American dealings, while Émile Ollivier, head of the ministry, told the Egyptian that "these armaments, instead of consolidating the position of His Highness, weaken it." At Constantinople, in the months that followed, European diplomats worked sedulously to revive memories of Mehemet Ali; and as reports of work on the Egyptian coastal defenses came in, Abdul Aziz moved to exert his authority. In April 1871 the Sultan dispatched his grand chamberlain to Cairo to require the "cessation of the building of forts and the preparation of torpedoes for the coast of Egypt and the Suez Canal."

The menace was clear. Ismail felt constrained to obey. Although

---

[5] C. P. Stone, "Le Général E. S. Purdy Pasha," *Bulletin de la Société Khédiviale de Géographie,* 2nd series, pp. 57-64; R. E. Colston, "Stone-Pasha's Work in Geography," 19 *Bulletin of the American Geographical Society,* 48-50; Chaillé-Long, *My Life,* pp. 39-40; Frederico Bonola, *L'Égypte et la géographie* (Cairo, 1889), p. 48; F. J. Cox, "The American Naval Mission to Egypt," 26 *Journal of Modern History,* 173-78.

planning for underwater harbor defense continued, and although another flurry of defensive activity occurred in 1874, Stone's proposals were never fully developed. An American cannon salesman was turned away, work on the coast artillery batteries was stopped, and Kennon was transferred to other duty. The Duc de Grammont had been reported by Nubar as saying that "in the event of trouble America will be far away, and it is not Egypt or the Canal that will suffer, but the Khedive." One might be inclined to credit the Frenchman with second sight. Long before the trouble came, the fall of Sedan had changed things, and Grammont was no longer concerned. But trouble did come, he was right about the Canal, and the only thing wrong with his prophecy was that all Egypt suffered along with the Khedive.[6]

2. Exploration and Expansion

The choice of General Stone as chief of the Egyptian General Staff, whether made as some aver on the recommendation of General Sherman or whether on that of Fitz-John Porter, was a fortunate one. After graduating high in the class of 1845 at West Point, Stone had served in the Mexican War and had subsequently spent two years in Europe, studying the military establishments of the powers. In the course of his travels he had visited the Prussian court and had gained the friendship of the great Humboldt; from Germany he had journeyed eastward to study the organization of the Cossacks; while returning by way of Austria, Italy, and Turkey, he had visited Egypt. To this cosmopolitan experience Stone added a linguistic competence which included French, German, Spanish, and ultimately a little Arabic. His technical training was excellent: in addition to his West Point background he had served as chief of ordnance in the Department of the Pacific; after resigning from the Army in 1856 he had spent three years in engineering work in Sonora and in the construction of a military road in New Mexico. Industrious, tactful, solicitous of local custom, he quickly gained the trust of the Egyptians. "General Stone," the Khedive observed to the secretary of the American Geographical Society in 1872, "is not only capable

[6] Despatches, Alexandria: Butler to Sec. of State, 30 December 1870. Despatches, Cairo: Beardsley to Sec. of State, 15 August 1874. Despatches, Turkey: Morris to Sec. of State, 1 July 1870; MacVeagh to Sec. of State, 15 May 1871. Pierre Crabitès, *Americans in the Egyptian Army* (London, 1939), pp. 44-45; Douin, *Règne*, ii, 558-70.

and thorough as the chief of staff of the Egyptian army, but he is capable to be the chief of staff of any army in the world. He is not only a gentleman and a learned gentleman and a soldier, but he is an honorable gentleman and an honorable soldier."

It was in fact Stone's sense of honor, which had availed him little in his native country when the Radicals were hounding him from the service, that proved the key to his success in Egypt. A foreigner in a xenophobic army, the loyal servant of the Khedive in an atmosphere of slander and intrigue, he taught his subordinates, American and Egyptian alike, his own devotion to duty and the public welfare. As one of his Egyptian colleagues observed after his death, he had an antique feeling for human dignity, esteeming men more for their moral worth than for their wealth or station. The proof may perhaps be seen in the fact that Stone, almost alone of the foreigners holding high place in nineteenth-century Egypt, left the country poorer than when he arrived.[7]

Withal he was a realist, fully aware that reform breeds opposition and that he was faced with formidable problems. The Egyptian Army had for some years suffered from neglect, and the first inspections showed a sorry state of affairs. The coast defenses were inadequate; there was no torpedo school and no signal service; supply depots were short of material. Field artillery pieces were few and of mixed and obsolescent models. Although the infantry had been rearmed with the Remington musket, there were no domestic facilities for ammunition manufacture, and the army remained wholly dependent upon imports. Favoritism in promotion had led to the advancement of uneducated officers and to a corollary contempt for schooling. There was no brigade or divisional organization, no uniformity of drill, no staff corps. Nor did the mechanism for restoring coherence exist. The former French staff had disappeared, and most of the Egyptians trained in the old staff college or in France had left for better jobs.

A report from Stone to the Khedive describing the functions of a general staff and the need for trained staff officers brought orders to revive that institution and to establish a staff college. Both steps were taken, but progress led to new problems. Creation of a self-contained general staff was one thing; but if staff officers were to

---

[7] Obituary notices in *Bulletin de la Société Khédiviale*, 2nd series, *Supplément*, pp. 665-85, 723-25; Southworth, *African Travel*, pp. 345-46; J. M. Morgan, *Recollections of a Rebel Reefer* (Boston and New York, 1917), pp. 300-302.

be posted to the field commands, the commanders had to be educated as to their function, and this, given the friction between staff
and line and Moslem resistance to infidel innovation, was much
more difficult. Something, nevertheless, was accomplished. Entering
upon his duties without fanfare, Stone soon gained the confidence
and support of both Khedive and Minister of War; thus armed, he
managed to overcome in considerable degree the obstructionism of
Ratib Pasha, the general in chief, as well as to deal successfully with
discontent and intrigue among a few of the Americans.

So the work began. The officers' school at Abassieh was reshaped
along the lines of West Point. Drill was standardized by the establishment of a school for noncommissioned officers at Cairo. In 1873
an expanded army was reorganized into five infantry divisions and
three regiments of artillery. By this time a powder mill, a cartridge
factory, and a foundry were in operation, new rifled guns had been
acquired to strengthen the coast defenses, and the mine school had
been established. Some progress had been made in improving the railroad network in lower and middle Egypt, work on the Sudan railway had been begun, and the telegraph was being extended to the
southern frontiers. At the Citadel in Cairo, the General Staff had
itself become a going concern: where the Americans on their arrival
had discovered but three maps and hardly any books, the mid-seventies showed some thousands of maps, a library of six thousand volumes, and a printing office. The staff college was producing a steady
flow of graduates for duty in the bureaus of the staff itself, in exploration, or with Loring's command. Wider employment, unfortunately, could not be gained. The hope had been to provide staffs at all
echelons down to brigade level; but resistance from the pashas, un-
accustomed to the encumbrance of expert advice, led to discrimina-
tion against the graduates of the staff school, and this step did not
prove feasible.

Considerable though they were, these improvements in military
organization were far from the sum of Stone's accomplishments.
Possessed both of the American faith in education and of an intuitive
understanding of the central role of the military in underdeveloped
countries, the Chief of Staff moved to make the army the regenerator
of the nation, in the first instance by an attack on the problem presented by an illiterate soldiery. Appalled by a situation in which a
third of the officers and nine-tenths of the enlisted personnel were
unable to sign their names, Stone obtained the Khedive's approval

for the establishment of regimental schools and for conditioning promotion upon literacy. The reported results were astounding: by 1873, after three years' effort, 75 percent of the enlisted strength could write their own names and fill out routine applications, and the soldiers were bringing their children to school with them. Such a response gained Stone Ismail's support for the establishment, within each division, of a school for soldiers' sons. This experiment in mass education, a step toward doing for the Moslems what the mission schools had long done for the Copts, not only argued well for the future of Egypt but greatly improved the morale of an army in which the tradition of forced service for indeterminate periods had led to frequent cases of self-mutilation.[8]

Such enlarged concepts of policy and the success with which they were greeted gave the Chief of Staff influence well beyond the normal confines of the military. In 1873 the Department of Public Works was transferred to the General Staff, a step which placed Stone in charge of canal construction and harbor improvement. In the same year the Chief of Staff was appointed vice president of the commission established to organize the Egyptian exhibits at the Vienna exposition of that year, at Philadelphia in 1876, and at Paris in 1878. In 1877 he became a member of the Superior Commission of Agriculture, and of a board of generals set up to devise a new conscription law; two years later he was named president of the Société Khédiviale de Géographie. Through his secretary, Charles I. Barnard, a young graduate of the Massachusetts Institute of Technology and of the Harvard Law School who became a member of the Supreme Council of Public Instruction, Stone's influence extended to general educational policy. But his most enduring contribution was in geography, as organizer of the exploring and mapping expeditions which, during his term of service, surveyed vast regions of the expanding Egyptian empire.[9]

Since the time of Claudius Ptolemy, in the second century of the Christian era, the science of geography had largely passed Egypt by. Even in the lower Nile valley, mapping was inadequate, while the traveler who passed the second cataract or left the riverbanks

---

[8] Stone, "Military Affairs," pp. 168-74; Dye, *Moslem Egypt*, pp. 56-74; Loring, *Confederate Soldier*, pp. 349-53, 356-58.

[9] Despatches, Cairo: Beardsley to Sec. of State, 16 November 1873. Stone, "Military Affairs," p. 174; *Bulletin de la Société Khédiviale*, 2nd series, *Supplément*, pp. 665-85; J. H. Gore, *American Members of Foreign Orders* (Washington, 1910), "C. I. Barnard."

quickly entered unknown territory. For Ismail, laboring to project his country into the modern world, the exploitation of his grandfather's annexations in the Sudan depended upon improved communications and on the development of caravan and railroad routes to bypass the great meanders and cataracts of the Nile and to link the river with the Red Sea. Additionally, if Egyptian dependence upon cash-crop agriculture were to be diminished and freedom from the whims of the London and Liverpool markets obtained, an audit of resources was an urgent necessity. The steam navigation of the Nile, an expanded rail network, and efforts at mechanized production all required fuel; since steam engines run poorly on camel dung, the Khedive had promised a title and a fortune to the discoverer of coal within his realm. All these problems had arisen by the time of Ismail's accession, but as the frontier was pushed out to the southwest to include the provinces of Kordofan and Darfur and south toward the Equatorial Lakes they became ever more urgent.

With the shift in emphasis from defense to exploration, it became necessary to reinforce the American contingent. The area to be explored was immense, and the Americans in Egypt were already spread thin. As in the days when Commodore Porter was helping Mahmud's navy, the problem was answered by the unofficial support of the American government, and General Stone obtained most of his reinforcements through the assistance of the General in Chief of the United States Army. While on a visit to Egypt in the autumn of 1872, General Sherman had been received by the Khedive and had discussed Egyptian affairs with Stone; after returning to America he helped in the procurement of technically qualified personnel. Some of these individuals were Union or Confederate officers who had returned to civil life after Appomattox; some, still in active service, were granted leave to serve in Egypt.

Three new officers, variously recruited, had arrived in 1872, and by the next year the results of Sherman's visit were apparent. Colonel Raleigh E. Colston, sometime colleague of Stonewall Jackson at the Virginia Military Institute and brigadier in the Army of Northern Virginia, arrived to teach geology at the military academy and to lead three exploring expeditions. Colonel William M. Dye, a West Point graduate and veteran of the war in the West, was given charge of the section of the General Staff which corresponded to the adjutant general's department. The technically trained contingent was reinforced by Major Henry G. Prout, a Civil War veteran and graduate of the University of Michigan with recent experience on the United States Territorial Survey. In the person of Dr. Edward Warren, a former medical inspector of the Army of Northern Virginia, the General Staff acquired its own surgeon; although a decidedly unpredictable personality whose ultimate departure from the Khedive's employ was somewhat less than creditable, Warren performed good work in cleaning up the venality and corruption of the Egyptian medical service. The year 1874 saw five new arrivals: Wilburn B. Hall, son-in-law of Captain Ingraham of Koszta fame and a former officer in the Confederate Navy; Horatio B. Reed, whose battle experience read like a summary of the war in Virginia, and who since 1870 had been pushing a railroad through the Adirondacks; and three young postwar graduates of West Point on leave from the Army.[10]

With this augmented personnel, Stone so pressed his program of exploration that in the space of eight years the Egyptian General Staff completed the preliminary mapping of a territory the size of western Europe. Detached from the command of one of the khedivial steamers, Colonel Alexander M. Mason, a former Confederate naval officer, had already explored and mapped the Fayoum, southwest of Cairo, and the Oasis of Siwa, site of the temple of Jupiter Ammon, three hundred miles to the west. But the main problem of the early seventies was the survey of possible railroad routes. In September 1873 Colonel Colston led an expedition across the desert from Kenneh on the Nile to the ruins of Berenice on the shore of the Red Sea. There, after three months spent in mapping and in geological investigation, he was joined by a second party under Purdy and Mason which had come down from Suez by sea. After a hydrographic survey of the gulf and harbor of Berenice, the combined expedition headed southward through the Nubian Desert to map the three-hundred-mile route to Berber on the Nile and to investigate the gold mines of Derehib, worked first by the Ptolemies and most recently in the ninth century. This journey completed, the party returned to Cairo by a desert march across the great bend of the Nile from Berber to Korosko. Since the shortcut across the great bend was of extreme importance for the projected Sudan railway, a second expedition was sent out, commanded by another

[10] Despatches, Cairo: Comanos to Sec. of State, 19 September 1874. Chaillé-Long, *My Life*, pp. 17, 39, 58-59, 232; Edward Warren, *A Doctor's Experiences in Three Continents* (Baltimore, 1885).

American, to investigate the alternative route from Assouan to Abou Ahmet and then to continue to Khartoum.[11]

It was not only in the question of communications that the Egyptian situation resembled that of the United States of half a century before. Accompanying the problems of distance and of needed internal improvements were those of the resource-hungry, underdeveloped debtor nation. Since the contrast between the existing and the hoped-for state of affairs was greater in Egypt than it had been in America, the issues were more acute. Since Ismail was both given to oriental extravagance and subject to European political and economic pressures, the costs of borrowing were vastly higher. Irrigation works, sugar mills, and railroads would surely pay off in the end if only the interest charges could be sustained. This, in turn, would be much easier if easily exploitable resources could be found. Coal or oil to diminish the costs of foreign exchange would be extremely helpful; best of all would be the discovery of gold, and of a new Egyptian California.

Included in the intelligence brought back by Colonel Purdy from his survey of the eastern desert had been a report of hieroglyphic inscriptions relating to the ancient gold mines of Hammamat, worked as early as 2700 B.C. This report had prompted the Khedive and General Stone to attempt the reopening of these mines and to plan an expedition under the command of an American with California mining experience. But this individual returned to the United States, the enterprise was delayed until the services of an American geologist could be procured, and not until early 1875 did Professor Lebbeus H. Mitchell set forth on this errand into the wilderness. Thirty days were spent at Hammamat, and the discovery of another gold region in the neighborhood led to further investigation. But all was in vain: although the gold was there, the seams were small, the neighborhood was barren of fuel, and exploitation seemed impossible. Similar conclusions had been reported by Colonel Colston after inspecting the ancient diggings at Derehib, and other expeditions proved equally discouraging. In the summer of 1875 Colonel Ward was sent to survey the silver mines and marble quarries of the Aegean island of Thasos, but his report indicated no great promise. Two years later the British explorer Sir Richard Burton persuaded the Khedive to finance a gold-seeking expedition

[11] *Bulletin de la Société Khédiviale*, 2nd series, pp. 343-52, 431-37, 489-568; 19 *Bulletin of the American Geographical Society*, 48; Douin, *Règne*, III, Part 2, 636-41.

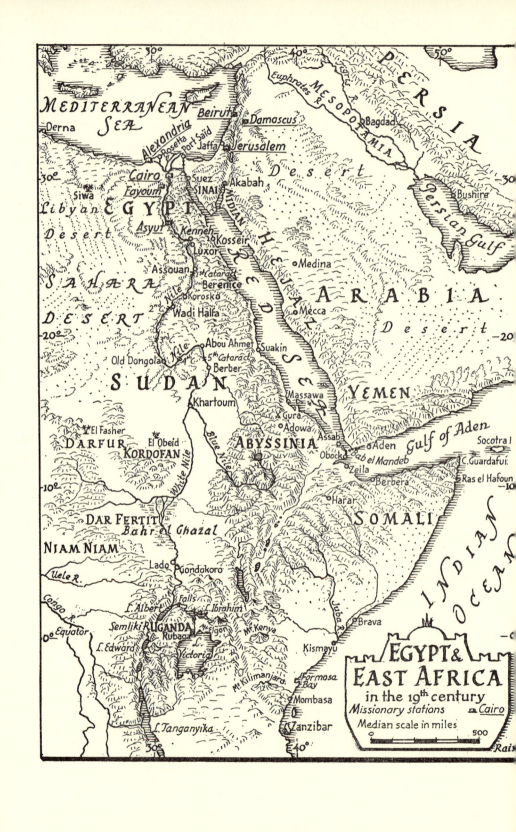

MEDITERRANEAN SEA

Derna

Beirut
Damascus
Alexandria
Rosetta
Port Said
Jaffa
Jerusalem

PERSIA

Euphrates R.
MESOPOTAMIA
Tigris R.
Bagdad

Cairo
Suez
SINAI
Akabah

Desert

Bushire
Persian Gulf

30°

Siwa
Fayoum
EGYPT

Libyan
Desert

Asyut
Kennet
Kosseir
Luxor

Medina

ARABIA

30

SAHARA

Assouan
1st Cataract
Berenice
Koroskó
2nd Cataract
Wadi Halfa

Mecca

Desert

DESERT

Old Dongola
Abou Ahmet
5th Cataract
Berber

Suakin

20

20°

Nile

SUDAN

Khartoum

Massawa
Gura
Adowa
Assab
Obock
Bab el Mandeb
Zeila

YEMEN

Aden

Gulf of Aden

Socotra I.

C. Guardafui

DARFUR
KORDOFAN

El Fasher
El Obeid

White Nile

Blue Nile

ABYSSINIA

Berbera

Ras el Hafoun

10

10°

DAR FERTIT
Bahr el Ghazal

Harar

SOMALI

NIAM NIAM

Uele R.

Lado
Gondokoro

Congo R.

L. Albert
Falls
L. Ibrahim
Semliki
RUGANDA
Rubaga
M. Elgon
Mt Kenya
L. Edward
Equator

Juba R.

Brava

INDIAN OCEAN

0°

L. Victoria

Kismayu

EGYPT & EAST AFRICA
in the 19th century
Missionary stations   Cairo
Median scale in miles

M. Kilimanjaro
Formosa Bay
Mombasa

L. Tanganyika

Zanzibar

0

500

Ras

30°
40°
50°

in Midian, beyond the Sinai Peninsula. Much time and money were expended and twenty tons of minerals brought back to England for analysis, but the results were only smoke.[12]

In Egypt, too, as earlier in America, exploration and expansion went hand in hand. For the revivified, Westernized, and independent Egypt of Ismail's aspirations more territory seemed essential. The reasons which had motivated the Syrian ventures of Mehemet Ali still held good: need for military manpower, need for wood, need for economic diversification. But with the northern road blocked by the settlement forced on Egypt after the second Syrian War, future expansion had perforce to be directed southward into central Africa.

This expansion became Ismail's great task. The administration of the Sudan was reorganized and plans were made to advance the Egyptian frontiers. Yet the situation was a delicate one. Like any power of the second rank that attempts to alter the map, Egypt was subject to pressures from outside, and these in her case were peculiarly acute owing to the strategic importance of her location. French influence, previously supreme, had declined as a result of consular arrogance, the contumacy of the French military mission, and defeat at the hands of Prussia. This decline, and Ismail's turn to America for military assistance, was dramatized in April 1874, when a two-year dispute over canal tolls resulted in permission from Constantinople to force the issue with the French canal company. On Ismail's orders General Stone assembled some pilots, deployed two frigates and three battalions of troops against the canal zone, and himself proceeded to Port Said, prepared to seize and operate the canal. The company gave in.[13]

Such defiance of the previously dominant power was made the easier owing to British concern with the passage to India and British desire for lowered canal tolls. At the same time, however, Britain's interest in the canal, the controlling British position in Zanzibar, and the existence of the British Indian Navy made it painfully evident that southward expansion would depend in large degree upon British complaisance. In the effort to gain such support, Ismail had

---

[12] *Bulletin de la Société Khédiviale*, 1st series, No. 6, pp. 7-10, 15-21; Dye, *Moslem Egypt*, pp. 78-79, 500; Samuel S. de Kusel, *An Englishman's Recollections of Egypt, 1863 to 1887* (London and New York, 1915), p. 107; Bonola, *L'Égypte et la géographie*, pp. 67-68, 71; Douin, *Règne*, III, Part 3, 507-8.

[13] Despatches, Cairo: Beardsley to Sec. of State, 29 April 1874. F. J. Cox, "The Suez Canal Incident of 1874," *Cahiers d'histoire égyptienne*, 4th series, pp. 193-203. The figure of ten thousand troops, given in various older works, is excessive.

assisted Sir Charles Napier's Abyssinian expedition of 1868. In the hope that a British public opinion passionately concerned with the evils of slavery would support the Egyptian civilizing mission, he had emphasized the importance of replacing the slave trade with a modern commerce, and as evidence of his sincerity had appointed Englishmen to the post of governor of the Equatorial Provinces.

The first of these, Sir Samuel Baker, had been appointed in 1869 at the suggestion of the Prince of Wales. Entrusted with supreme power over all territory south of Gondokoro, Baker was assigned the mission of extending Egyptian control into central Africa, opening navigation on the Equatorial Lakes, and suppressing the slave trade. His actions were on the grand scale: leaving Cairo in 1870 with seventeen hundred soldiers, thirty demountable steamboats, and a vast quantity of bone china and vintage wines, Baker also carried with him an oversimplified concept of his function. For a year and a half the expedition was not heard from, and rumors of troubles in the interior led to preparations for a relief effort. But in 1873 Baker returned to Cairo, having spent half a million pounds and having succeeded only in antagonizing the populations of the interior.[14]

His successor was a very different type of individual. Appointed to undo this mischief, Charles George Gordon reached Cairo in February 1874, and after consulting with the Khedive headed for the interior with only a handful of men. From his acquaintance with Ward and Burgevine, the American adventurers with China's Ever-Victorious Army, Gordon seems to have derived a good opinion of the citizens of the Great Republic; over the opposition of the British representative at Cairo he selected Lieutenant Colonel Long as chief of staff and commander of his Egyptian troops. By April, Gordon and Long had traversed twenty-five degrees of latitude and had reached Gondokoro, capital of the Equatorial Provinces, where they encountered envoys from King Mutesa of Uganda. To exploit this evidence of good will and to cement relations with this central African kingdom, Gordon dispatched Long southward on an embassy to Uganda.

Mounted on a horse, armed with a Reilly elephant gun, and

[14] Sabry, *L'Empire égyptien*, pp. 445-60; H. G. Prout, "Where Emin Is," 6 *Scribner's Magazine*, 529-31; Douin, *Règne*, III, Part 2, 1-105. The period of Egyptian southward expansion is well summarized in Richard Hill, *Egypt in the Sudan, 1820-1881* (London, 1959).

accompanied by two servants, a groom, and two Egyptian veterans of the French campaign in Mexico, Long left Gondokoro in late April 1874, and after a fifty-eight-day journey reached Rubaga, the capital of Uganda. His horse, the first ever seen in this domain of the tsetse fly, astonished the Ugandans; his full-dress uniform appealed to their aesthetic sense; so gratified was King Mutesa at this visit from the "Great M'Buguru" or White Prince that he decapitated thirty of his subjects on the spot. Civilization had accompanied Long in the form of a cheval glass, a music box which played Civil War marching songs, and an electric battery which administered powerful jolts to Mutesa and his henchmen. If it did not shock them toward the American millennium, this medicine did at least prove helpful to the American explorer, gaining him a stay of a month to recover from the strains of the journey, an escorted visit to Lake Victoria, and assurances from Mutesa which promised the important consequence of diverting the Uganda ivory trade from Zanzibar on the Indian Ocean to Gondokoro on the Nile.

In mid-July, having completed his month of recuperation, the Great M'Buguru left Rubaga for Urondogani on the Victoria Nile. There, after some trouble with the local chieftain, Long embarked and headed downstream along a stretch of water never before seen by white men. Soon he entered a large lake which he named Ibrahim in honor of the Khedive's father; here he fought his way through a day-long naval battle with four hundred hostile tribesmen. For the rest of the journey the hardships were merely routine, and on 18 October 1874 the party reached Gondokoro, haggard, exhausted, but alive.

As a feat of skill and endurance the journey had been impressive. Equally notable were its contributions to geography, the first actual proof that Lake Victoria fed into the Nile and the discovery of Lake Ibrahim. Its political implications are more difficult to assess. Yet whether Long's treaty with Mutesa provided, as he later claimed, for the "annexation" of Uganda to Egypt, or whether, as indicated in his first reports, it was limited to an agreement that the Uganda ivory export would be shifted to Egypt, is perhaps unimportant. Economic penetration of this sort can have powerful political consequences, and Long's citation for "having successfully accomplished . . . the mission confided to him in Uganda" implies rather more than simple exploration. Some weight, it would seem, should be attached to the Khedive's oft-quoted remark that "that young man has done more with two men and no money than great expeditions with thousands of men and much treasure."

In December, after a period of recuperation at Khartoum, Long headed south again to Lado. Ordered by Gordon to lead an expedition into the Niam-Niam country, he departed in late January 1875 with a party of soldiers armed with Remington rifles. One month later the hostile Yanbari tribe had been dealt with, relations had been cemented with the warlike but friendly Makraka Niam-Niam, "anthropophagic only by reason of the absence of all cattle," and the country had been garrisoned. Reaching the Nile with six hundred tusks and a pygmy he had purchased with a red handkerchief, Long set out for Cairo bearing dispatches from Gordon to the Khedive.[15]

While Gordon and Long were at work in the Equatorial Provinces, the Egyptian frontier had also been pushed out to the westward. In 1874 a resolute governor of the Sudan, employing disciplined troops armed with modern American rifles, had annexed the great province of Darfur, with its central oasis and capital El Fasher. No sooner was the conquest complete than the Governor asked for officers of the General Staff to map the country and for mineralogists to explore its resources. Since the most pressing problems of exploration in Egypt and the Sudan had by this time been dealt with, and since new arrivals had strengthened the American contingent, it proved possible to meet this request. By October General Stone was at work on the organization of two expeditions.

Command of the first of these was entrusted to Colonel Purdy, who with Lieutenant Colonel Mason, a General Staff detachment, and some sixty soldiers was ordered directly to the newly conquered province. Under Colonel Colston the other group, with Lieutenant Colonel Reed as second in command, five Egyptian staff officers, a German naturalist, and about ninety men, was to explore and map the province of Kordofan, west of the White Nile, and then join Purdy in Darfur. The destination of the two groups was a thousand miles from Cairo; it was estimated that their tasks would require two or three years; their combined strength amounted to about a tenth of that which had accompanied Baker. In December 1874

[15] Despatches, Cairo: Beardsley to Sec. of State, 9 March 1874, 12 September 1874, 28 December 1874. Long's reports in: 19 *Proceedings of the Royal Geographical Society*, 107-10; 8 *Bulletin of the American Geographical Society*, 285-304; 19 *ibid.*, 194-98; 36 *ibid.*, 346-52. Douin, *Règne*, III, Part 3, 15-27, 89-105, 145-55; 21 *Petermann's Mittheilungen*, plate 22.

these expeditions, described by an American observer as "a brave overture of civilization to barbarism," set out by boat for Wadi Halfa and thence overland along the Nile. At Old Dongola, where the stream recurves to the north, the Purdy expedition struck out southwestward through unknown country, to reach El Fasher in May 1875, while Colston headed southward for El Obeid, the capital of Kordofan.

But the breakdown of Reed's health forced his evacuation; Colston, too, became critically ill; and Major Prout, who had replaced Purdy as head of the Third Section, was ordered out to relieve them. Reaching Suakin by way of the Red Sea, Prout marched overland to the Nile, surveying a possible rail route from Suakin to Berber, and then onward to Khartoum and El Obeid, where he arrived in June 1875 and assumed command. By the next month he had completed the map of his approach route and was deploying his surveying parties. By March 1876 his people had covered almost four thousand miles, had produced a general map of Kordofan and a number of detailed profiles, and had compiled notes on the land, resources, commerce, and climate in preparation for a comprehensive report which was published in the following year. Pursuant to the original orders to Colston, Prout then headed westward to join Purdy in Darfur, reaching El Fasher in April.

While the Kordofan survey was in progress, Purdy's expedition had been busy in Darfur. There, where only two white men had preceded them, they first surveyed the route into El Fasher and then settled down for a period of work which was to result in a complete report and map of this new Egyptian province. Here, indeed, exploration was contemporary with conquest, for while Purdy's men were making their surveys, the Governor of the Sudan was still moving garrison forces into the country. But by early 1877, when the expedition completed its work, security had been established, travelers and caravans moved undisturbed, and "stations hospitalières" had been established as far as the frontiers of Wadai, six hundred miles west of the Nile, and southward through Dar Fertit.[16]

So Ismail, in the words of his Chief of Staff, "carrying out the policy of his wise and farseeing grandfather, added to the map of

---

[16] Despatches, Cairo: Beardsley to Sec. of State, 1 January 1875, 20 January 1875, 24 March 1875. 21 *Petermann's Mittheilungen*, 353-55; 25 *ibid.*, 361, 26 *ibid.*, 377-81; 11 *Bulletin of the American Geographical Society*, 48, 304; 19 *ibid.*, 48-50; 23 *ibid.*, 574. Dye, *Moslem Egypt*, pp. 84-103; Warner, *Mummies and Moslems*, p. 286; Bonola, *L'Égypte et la géographie*, pp. 54-59; Douin, *Règne*, III, Part 3, 504-45.

Egypt territories sufficient for three empires and populations amounting to probably ten or twelve millions." Not only were the borders pressed southward to the Equatorial Provinces and westward to include Kordofan and Darfur; the Egyptian flag was also advanced to the southeast, down the Red Sea coast to the Gulf of Aden and the shores of the Indian Ocean. With this extension of political control came notable contributions to geographical knowledge, as the reports of the General Staff's exploring parties, which in the years between 1871 and 1878 mapped more unknown African territory "than all the other explorers of the world," were published in the geographical journals of Germany, England, and America. And finally, both conquest and exploration had large cultural implications, not least, as General Stone wrote, in their expansion of facilities for "the great civilizer, commerce."[17]

Understandably enough, the American officers were proud of their work. Others, too, were impressed by the accomplishments of Ismail's Egypt, and by the middle 1870's it appeared probable to many that the Khedive would realize his vision of a great African empire. So, at least, thought Richard Beardsley, the American consul general, when he reported in 1873 that "the Egypt of today bids fair to be swallowed up by the great African Empire of the future." So also thought the secretary of the American Geographical Society, who, peering into the future, foresaw a powerful, prosperous, and independent Egypt which exported bullion to all Europe; which had linked Lake Victoria with the Indian Ocean by the "Sherman Canal," named in grateful recognition of the help afforded by the President of the United States; and where Field Marshal Stone presided over the land forces while Admiral Ward's fleet cruised the Albert Nyanza. If the geography of the Sherman Canal was a little impractical, the vision was still an attractive one for a believer in progress who, sharing the century-old vision of Samuel Hopkins, looked forward to "the day when capital and Anglo-Saxon energy will release the degraded negro peoples from their ages of bondage," and who felt that "in a word, Africa should be Americanized." But none of this came true. Sherman evinced a disinclination to become president; the Great Lakes fell from the Egyptian grasp; and

[17] *15 Bulletin of the American Geographical Society*, 369-70; Loring, *Confederate Soldier*, p. 355.

while the land of Egypt did export money to all Europe, it was in a different context than that which the American had foreseen.[18]

3. The Throw of the Dice

The early explorations of the American members of the General Staff had been directed toward the improvement of Egyptian communications through the survey of strategic routes in the Delta, shortcuts across the bends of the Nile, and potential railroad lines. With the southward expansion of Egypt, the importance of such internal improvements was reemphasized. Immense distances separated Cairo from the outlying provinces: a thousand miles to Khartoum, another thousand to the Equatorial Lakes. Between these regions and the capital, the Nile, long and meandering and with its navigation obstructed by cataracts and dense masses of vegetation, traversed territory totally lacking in steamboat fuel. The projected Sudan railway would reduce both time and distance, but its construction called for great expenditures with no immediate prospect of return, and in any case the fuel problem remained unsolved. If a civilizing commerce and a progressive agriculture were to replace the ivory and slave trades, and if the wealth of the interior was to be opened to exploitation, better transportation was essential. Since the distances from Khartoum to Red Sea ports and from the Equatorial Lakes to the Indian Ocean were respectively about a third and an eighth of those to Cairo, logic suggested the opening of lateral lines of communication which would link the interior with the sea.

To the rulers of Egypt these geographical facts were clear enough. As early as 1846 Mehemet Ali's forces had occupied Massawa on the lower Red Sea; from the outset of his reign Ismail had worked to parallel the move into the interior by a southward expansion along the African coast. A variety of expedients, of which bribery was the chief, had brought firmans from Constantinople extending Egyptian control. By 1875 the ports of Berbera and Zeila had been occupied by the Khedive, a step which promised additional profit from control of the considerable traffic moving by caravan from the African interior and destined for the cities of Arabia.

Nevertheless, the situation remained delicate. British interest in the short route to India had brought the occupation of Aden in

---

[18] *Commercial Relations, 1873,* p. 1088; Southworth, *African Travel,* pp. v, 85-89.

1839 and the subsequent acquisition of other footholds. At Obock, where France held a shore station, French missionaries were urging further intervention upon their government. With completion of the Suez Canal outside pressures increased, and although Boker's proposal of an American enclave at Bab el Mandeb went unheeded, the Italians arrived at Assab. For the moment Italians and French offered little hazard, but the British presence was another matter. In 1865, when the Egyptian steam frigate *Ibramieh* was sent to the Red Sea by way of the Cape of Good Hope, Moslem demonstrations of enthusiasm at the ports visited enroute drew the attention of the British government; in 1870 a visit to Berbera by an Egyptian warship was protested by the British resident at Aden. Although the cut at Suez, linking the two Egyptian coasts, made Egypt the dominant sea power in East Africa, there remained the British Indian Navy.[19]

As well as reemphasizing the importance of communications, the southward advance had given rise to a frontier problem, for the main lines of Egyptian expansion, to the headwaters of the Nile and southward along the coast, were separated by the mountain kingdom of Abyssinia. There, after a period of civil war, the accession of King John had been followed by border raids into the Sudan and against the Egyptian coastal strip. The response to these incursions, as developed by General Stone, involved a reorganization of the administration of the Sudan and the construction of strategic telegraph lines, the establishment of a series of fortified posts to pen up the Abyssinians within their mountains, and reinforcement of the Massawa garrison in anticipation of a move inland. In its turn this Egyptian activity brought cries out of Abyssinia, and the dispatch by John of his English commander in chief, a former steward on the Peninsular and Orient Line, to complain to Queen Victoria of Egyptian aggression. Protestations from the Khedive that his sole concern was the suppression of the slave trade temporarily smoothed the difficulties, but again Egyptian expansion had been called to the attention of the European powers.[20]

Such was the situation when the Egyptian advance to the Equatorial Lakes posed in acute form the question of an outlet to the Indian Ocean. This question, indeed, had arisen earlier when the

[19] Despatches, Cairo: Beardsley to Sec. of State, 17 July 1875. Douin, *Règne*, III, Part 1, 233-88; III, Part 2, 227-36, 266-79. Sabry, *L'Empire égyptien*, pp. 384-86.
[20] Dye, *Moslem Egypt*, pp. 120-27; Douin, *Règne*, III, Part 2, 321-433.

prolonged silence that followed Baker's disappearance into the interior had suggested the need for a relief expedition. A staff study of November 1872 had led Stone to propose an expedition which would land at Mombasa, below the equator, and advance inland to Lake Victoria; the proposal had been accepted by the Khedive, and Colonel Purdy had been chosen to command the enterprise. Purdy's instructions from the Chief of Staff were far-reaching, calling as they did for the establishment of permanent posts and authorizing him to take Baker prisoner should such a step seem necessary to conciliate the local inhabitants and prove the good intentions of Egypt. As the planning proceeded, the effort was enlarged, the officer complement was doubled, and equipment for a two-year expedition was assembled together with a careful selection of presents for King Mutesa. But just as Purdy was about to sail came the news of Baker's return, and the enterprise was canceled.[21]

So the great leap southward failed to take place. But Egyptian consolidation of the Red Sea and Somali coasts continued, and in 1874 Colonel Long reached Uganda by way of the Nile. Far in the interior, Gordon had also seen the facts of geography, and among the dispatches which Long brought to Cairo in May 1875 was one which urged the Khedive to send an expedition to Formosa Bay, just north of Mombasa, and thence inland, to open a line of communication which would bypass the Nile valley route. This proposal found ready response at Cairo. Recalled from leave in Paris by urgent messages from Stone, Long reached Egypt in early September. There he found preparations almost complete for an expedition to the Indian Ocean headed by McKillop Pasha, an ex-captain in the Royal Navy, in which Long himself would command the troops.

Such a venture involved a possible clash with Sultan Barghash of Zanzibar, a British protégé who claimed title to the coast as far north as Ras el Hafoun. No such claim was substantiated by existing maps, but some did show the territories of Zanzibar extending north of the equator and so encompassing the Egyptian objective. The problem had been considered at the time of the projected Baker relief expedition, and Purdy's orders had instructed him to call upon the Sultan and explain the nonpolitical nature of his mission. But this time no such precautions were taken. The objective, the Juba

---

[21] Despatches, Alexandria: Beardsley to Sec. of State, 5 March 1873. *Bulletin de la Société Khédiviale*, 2nd series, pp. 57-64; Dye, *Moslem Egypt*, p. 81; Chaillé-Long, *My Life*, p. 54; Sabry, *L'Empire égyptien*, p. 396; Douin, *Règne*, III, Part 2, 88-96.

River, lay on the equator, somewhat to the north of Formosa Bay and in a region to which Egypt had some color of claim. For the rest, Ismail perhaps relied upon the English aspect of an expedition proposed by Gordon and commanded by McKillop.

At this very moment, by ironic chance, the Sultan of Zanzibar was visiting Egypt. Returning from a journey to London, where he had been praised for his "desire to further the political interests of England" and urged to foster humanitarian methods in elephant hunting, Barghash reached Cairo in August 1875. While the Sultan was being entertained by the Khedive, the orders to McKillop were issued; on the same day that Barghash sailed for home, Long sailed with two Egyptian transports bearing three companies of troops. At Berbera, where this force rendezvoused with McKillop and the warships *Latif* and *Mehemet Ali*, two more infantry companies and one of artillery were embarked. On 30 September the expedition sortied for the Indian Ocean.

Four days later McKillop's flotilla rounded Cape Guardafui; on 5 October, while stopping to water in the bay at Ras el Hafoun, the expedition took possession of the adjacent Somali country in exchange for a red flannel gown and twenty Maria Theresa dollars. On the 15th a force was put ashore at Brava and the Zanzibar garrison obliged to capitulate. When landing conditions off the mouth of the Juba proved difficult, the ships continued to Kismayu, where Long effected a night landing and took the town from the rear in a dawn attack. While McKillop assumed command of the coast from Berbera to Kismayu, Long marched his thirteen hundred men and seventy-five camels inland, established a fortified camp overlooking the Juba, and settled down to await news from Gordon.

One month later the steamer *Mahallah* reached Kismayu, bringing reinforcements for Long, a hydrographic party under Colonel Ward, and orders for McKillop to advance the Egyptian frontier another two hundred miles by taking possession of Formosa Bay. While the naval officer was absent on this errand, Long explored 150 miles of the Juba by steam launch: the inhabitants were friendly, but the river's northward course made it useless as an avenue to the Great Lakes. Although this fact and the inactivity of Gordon in the interior rendered the future of the original plan obscure, at Kismayu the Egyptian civilizing mission was underway. A quay was under construction and McKillop was planning a waterworks, local potentates were making their submissions to the Khedive, commerce was developing, and requests had been sent to Cairo for doctors, engineers, and artisans.

But by now political repercussions had developed in the larger sphere. Apprised of the Juba River expedition, British agents had at first made no objection. But at Zanzibar, following the arrival of one of McKillop's ships for coal, the British consul had appealed to the Foreign Office to support the Sultan. Shortly orders from London instructed the British agent in Cairo to ask the recall of the Egyptian expedition. And by this time the Khedive was faced with other difficulties stemming from increased Abyssinian raiding activity.[22]

So persistent, indeed, had these incursions into the Sudan become, that Ismail had already ordered a punitive expedition against King John. In September 1875, on the very day that orders were issued for the McKillop-Long expedition, a second force was organized with instructions to proceed to Massawa and march inland against the Abyssinians. Command of this force was entrusted to a Colonel Arendrup, a former Danish lieutenant of artillery, while Major James A. Denison, a recently arrived graduate of West Point, was given charge of the engineering detachment. Early progress was complicated by European intrigue, as British journalists passed the Egyptian lines with information for King John and as ammunition was brought in to Abyssinia under escort of the French vice consul. But worse was to come. In mid-November, while fording a river to attack the enemy in his camp, the inexperienced Arendrup was caught with his forces dispersed by a host of seventy thousand Abyssinians. Of fifteen Egyptian companies engaged, only one escaped death or capture. On receipt of news of the battle, Denison's rear guard refused orders to advance. Only with the greatest difficulty did he succeed in maintaining order during the retreat to Massawa.

One week later the report of this defeat reached Cairo. Reinforcements were at once dispatched to Massawa, while to the Governor of the Eastern Sudan, then on a mission to the interior, went a message reporting the defeat and urging prudence. But the effort was in vain: one day before Arendrup's defeat the Governor's force had itself been attacked, and he and most of his men killed.

[22] Despatches, Cairo: Beardsley to Sec. of State, 31 August 1875, 29 September 1875. 19 *Proceedings of the Royal Geographical Society*, 194-98; E. A. Stanton, "Secret Letters from the Khedive," 34 *Journal of the African Society*, 269-82. Chaillé-Long, *My Life*, pp. 146-95; Sabry, *L'Empire égyptien*, pp. 397-98; Douin, *Règne*, III, Part 3, 133-36, 246-56, 629-70.

News of this second tragedy reached Cairo just as British pressure against the Juba River expedition was beginning to make itself felt. These developments brought a complete change in policy. The project of linking the Equatorial Lakes with the Indian Ocean was put aside, the McKillop-Long expedition was ordered home, and preparations were begun to send a really serious punitive force against Abyssinia.[23]

Such an expedition would require management, and by good fortune an increased number of American officers was now on hand. The military duties which had been laid upon the staff together with the responsibility for the survey and development of vast regions of the interior had threatened to overwhelm Stone's group, weakened as it was by the departure of a number of its original members. The Chief of Staff had consequently called upon General Sherman for additional personnel, and in midsummer of 1875 a final contingent of ten Americans reached Alexandria. Senior officer of the group was Colonel Charles W. Field of Virginia, graduate of West Point and brigadier in the Army of Northern Virginia, who had commanded Lee's last remaining effectives on the morning of Appomattox. In addition to Major Denison, the group included three other engineering officers: Colonel Samuel H. Lockett of Alabama, sometime chief engineer of the Confederate forces at Shiloh and Corinth, who was placed in charge of the Third Section of the General Staff; Colonel Clarence Derrick, another West Pointer who had gone South; and Colonel Charles I. Graves, graduate of Annapolis and former lieutenant in the Confederate Navy. There were two more doctors, William H. Wilson and Thomas D. Johnson, the one an army surgeon on leave, the other a son of the former congressman and postmaster general Cave Johnson. Two officers, Major Charles F. Loshe and Captain Henry A. Irgens, came on leave from the Army, while an echo of earlier times was raised by the arrival of Captain David Essex Porter, son of the Civil War admiral, grandson of the Commodore, and namesake of the frigate of 1812.[24]

The two defeats already suffered at the hands of the Abyssinians had emphasized the problem of command. But here nationalism and

[23] Despatches, Cairo: Beardsley to Sec. of State, 1 December 1875; Comanos to Sec. of State, 18 February 1876. Dye, *Moslem Egypt*, pp. 128-46; Loring, *Confederate Soldier*, pp. 300-305, 329-30; Sabry, *L'Empire égyptien*, pp. 469-70; Douin, *Règne*, III, Part 3, 671-72, 687-89, 724-812; 22 *Petermann's Mittheilungen*, 77, 107-8.

[24] Biographical sources in note 1, above. Dye, *Moslem Egypt*, pp. 499-500; Loring, *Confederate Soldier*, pp. 359, 363-66.

competence came in conflict, and Arendrup's failure had not increased the prestige of foreigners. Wary of friction, Colonel Dye declined to serve as chief of staff to an Egyptian commander. A decision to entrust the expedition to General Loring was first taken and then countermanded. Ultimately the responsibility was assigned to the Egyptian general in chief, Ratib Pasha, small and "shriveled with lechery," who had been "educated in the salons of the demimonde" of Paris, and Loring was detailed as chief of staff.

Since speed was essential if the expedition was to accomplish its mission before the spring rains, General Stone provided the inexperienced Ratib with a considerable staff. Colonel Dye, next senior to Loring, was made chief of the first section and Colonel Field inspector general. Colonel Derrick was named chief of engineers, assisted by Major Denison, Captain Irgens, and two Egyptian graduates of the staff college. Major Loshe became staff quartermaster and commissary, assisted by Captain Porter; Dr. Wilson was named staff surgeon, assisted by Dr. Johnson; the operation of the port of Massawa was confided to Colonel Graves. With the help of these officers Stone managed, in the space of a couple of weeks, to assemble four triangular infantry regiments armed with Remington rifles, a regiment of cavalry, two Krupp field batteries, two batteries of mountain artillery, and five companies of engineers, a total of perhaps fourteen thousand men. Hastily embarked, the expedition sailed from Suez, to reach Massawa in late December.[25]

At Massawa, efforts to organize the move inland met with difficulties. Egyptian xenophobia had been already felt in the revocation of Loring's appointment to command. Now, with the support of the Khedive and the Chief of Staff attenuated by distance, the Americans found their troubles increased. The staff labored under the double burden of being not only foreign but a staff, while the pashas, accustomed to self-sufficiency at whatever level of command, looked upon the Americans as Loring's personal assistants and considered the General's position purely advisory. Communication between Ratib and Loring presented a problem, since the former knew no English and Loring's French was weak; the arrival of Prince Hussein, favorite son of the Khedive, recently returned from Oxford and now minister of war, further distracted the commanding general. To these

[25] Dye, *Moslem Egypt*, pp. 151-61, 172-73; Loring, *Confederate Soldier*, pp. 329-38, 359-60; "Americans in Egypt," *New York Tribune*, 26 February 1876; Douin, *Règne*, III, Part 3, 813-33.

complications was added the conflict between Turkish or Circassian commanders and Egyptian field grade officers: to some of the latter it seemed that the pashas were procrastinating in the hope of recall and that Ratib was defeatist from the start. Nor was the morale of the enlisted soldiery improved by the arrival of thirty-seven members of the Arendrup expedition who had managed to survive both their battle and their subsequent castration by the Abyssinians.

As always, logistics were governing, and here the difficulties were great. Although hard work by the staff got a quarter of the army on the move by mid-January 1876, there followed a complete breakdown of the transport service. After two Egyptian officers had been relieved, Major Loshe was transferred to the post of chief of transport, in which capacity he succeeded, despite the greatest frustrations, in moving a second echelon inland by the end of the month.

Things began to look brighter as the troops advanced out of the burning coastal desert into the Abyssinian hills. To the older Americans, veterans of the expedition to Mexico City, and to Egyptians who had served with Bazaine, the country looked familiar, reminding them of the road up from Vera Cruz. To the rear, in the meantime, a series of reorganizations of supply caravans and the abandonment of much unessential gear enabled the transport force to at least come close to meeting its responsibilities. On 30 January, after an eighty-mile march inland, the army reached Kaya Khor Pass, and after leaving a detachment to guard the defile, advanced its main strength into the Plain of Gura.

There, under the direction of Colonel Derrick, the engineering troops threw up Fort Gura, and while the army was entrenching, the staff labored to improve the line of communications. Great efforts were expended in road-building, in linking Gura and Massawa by telegraph, and in bringing up the artillery. But the situation remained touch and go: by late February mishandling had caused the loss of a third of the six thousand available camels, while Ratib, over the protests of the staff, had ordered up the reserve before its support could be assured. To recover this critical situation, Field and Denison were placed in charge of the supply line and sent back to Bahr Reza, halfway to the sea, where by prodigious effort and with the help of Loshe at Massawa they managed to maintain at least an adequate supply of essential matériel.[26]

[26] Dye, *Moslem Egypt*, pp. 169-71, 174-80, 186-200, 214-79; Loring, *Confederate Soldier*, pp. 339-46, 366-85; "The Egyptian Campaign in Abyssinia," 112 *Blackwood's*

But by this time the Abyssinian hordes were gathering, and the forces of King John, advancing northward from Adowa, were variously reported at between 100,000 and 400,000 men, women, and children. As this human sea flowed northward, passing the Egyptians on the west and recurving eastward to threaten the line of communications, the American staff redoubled its activity. A series of reconnaissances produced a steady flow of information; a cavalry demonstration led by Irgens had encouraging results. On receipt of information that John intended to attack from the north, Loring and the staff developed a battle plan and urged Ratib to concentrate at Kaya Khor Pass, to take the Abyssinians in the flank as they entered the plain. But Ratib had grown increasingly irresolute, and a council of war resulted only in a welter of ambiguities. No plan emerged, the Egyptian forces remained divided, and only tardily were orders dispatched to Field at Bahr Reza to bring up the remainder of the army by forced marches.

On the morning of 7 March, with the dust clouds raised by the advancing Abyssinians clearly visible, Ratib suddenly ordered two-thirds of his force to leave the fort and move toward the pass. But this step, long urged upon him by the staff, now promised only an attack in the open, and as the improvised movement continued and the commander in chief became increasingly confused, control was progressively lost.

Some fifty thousand Abyssinians were now within the valley. A charge directed at the Egyptian right reached within twenty-five yards of the guns. Attempts by the staff to reinforce the crucial point were countermanded by Ratib, and as the enemy circled into the hills to take the Egyptians from the rear, the commander was seen riding off in the direction of the fort. As word of this development spread, regiment after regiment drifted off after their leader, and despite the efforts of the staff to rally and hold, the movement degenerated into flight. Notable work on the part of a few checked the Abyssinians long enough to permit the retreating troops to escape, but here again there was mismanagement and the unguided force wandered into a cul-de-sac, where much of it was overrun. Nor was there any coordination of the supporting arms: no artillery fire was forthcoming from Fort Gura, and the force at Kaya Khor made no attempt to engage. By afternoon the Egyptians had been

Edinburgh Magazine, 28-29; Douin, *Règne*, III, Part 3, 836-87. The Prince, Ismail's second and favorite son, was the future (1914-17) Sultan of Egypt.

defeated in detail. Of some five thousand troops that had marched forth that morning, more than half were casualties or prisoners; most of the survivors were either wounded or weaponless; the bravest of the Egyptian brigade commanders was dead, while among the staff, Dye and Dr. Wilson had been wounded and Dr. Johnson captured.

The action of 7 March served only to increase the passivity of the Egyptian command. Marching their reinforcements to the sound of the guns, Field, Denison, and Loshe reached Kaya Khor late in the day, but no arguments could induce the Egyptian commander to attack. In the fort on Gura Plain, Loring's attempts to bring the camels inside the works, to succor the wounded outside, and to mount a dawn attack on the Abyssinian camp were blocked by Ratib: hiding behind bags of hard bread, the "cowardly Circassian" forbade anyone to leave the fort and refused to order the advance. There followed two days of sporadic Abyssinian attacks, but the Egyptians, knowing they could expect no quarter, held firm, while their modern Remington rifles and Krupp guns told against their adversaries. On the 10th, after eating all the food for miles around and amusing themselves by a massacre of prisoners, the Abyssinians marched away.

In the sequel, Prince Hussein attributed the defeat at Gura to the cowardice of the Egyptian troops. Ratib blamed it all on Loring; Loring and the other Americans blamed Ratib; an Egyptian officer of the transport service, Ahmed Arabi, blamed both Loring and Ratib. Certainly the major problems had been those of command. The skills of the American staff had made the advance to Gura possible, the activity of the staff had provided a steady flow of intelligence, and Ratib had been presented with a sound battle plan. But all broke down in the area of communication and persuasion, advice was not transmuted into action, and the failure of implementation at Gura Plain constitutes an early but classic example of the difficulties which confront the military advisory group operating in an alien environment.[27]

Egyptian errors had been many, and the Egyptian army had been very roughly handled. But however discouraging, the outcome of this fight against odds of perhaps ten to one was very far from a

[27] Dye, *Moslem Egypt*, pp. 280-398; Loring, *Confederate Soldier*, pp. 393-433; "The Egyptian Campaign," pp. 30-32; Sabry, *L'Empire égyptien*, pp. 324-25; Douin, *Règne*, III, Part 3, 893-954, 992-93.

defeat of the sort that the Abyssinians would later inflict upon the Italians at Adowa or the Mahdi upon Hicks Pasha in the Sudan. Abyssinian casualties had also been very heavy, and desertion had halved John's force. No territory had been abandoned, the Egyptians still held Fort Gura and the line of communications from Massawa, and reinforcements were on the way. The situation was still retrievable.

So, presumably, it seemed to the Abyssinians, for two days after their retirement there came a messenger from King John to protest the Egyptian invasion and to ask for peace. Soon the courier was followed by an envoy, and the lapse of military operations which accompanied the commencement of negotiations afforded opportunity to improve the Egyptian position. While Colonel Derrick threw up a fort at Addi Rasso, and Denison and Irgens worked to strengthen the position at Bahr Reza, Colonel Lockett, recently sent down from Cairo to take charge of surveying and fortification, busied himself with the improvement of the works at Kaya Khor. In anticipation of a permanent Egyptian occupation, Derrick next commenced a survey for a rail line between Massawa and Bahr Reza, while Field led an expedition inland to map a strategic wagon road from Massawa to Sanheet. Late in April the Americans were heartened by the return of Dr. Johnson after a forty-five day captivity, during which the hardships of being marched stripped and bound about the countryside had been somewhat alleviated by the women accompanying John's army, who, according to their custom, had been kind.[28]

Against all this, however, had to be set serious problems of morale and prestige, for the battle on Gura Plain had repercussions both within the army and at Cairo. Ratib had never been sanguine about the enterprise, and his pessimism now showed itself in negotiations with the enemy and in his messages to the Khedive. Soon there appeared evidence of spreading discouragement, as officers of higher grades engineered their recalls and as desertion among the rank and file increased. Shortly, the tension between Moslem line and infidel staff brought the transfer of the Americans to other duties, a step which produced a melancholy testimonial to their earlier effectiveness in the many deaths, largely from thirst, which the army suffered in its unopposed retreat to the sea.

[28] Dye, *Moslem Europe*, pp. 399-422, 431-81; Loring, *Confederate Soldier*, pp. 428-30, 437-38, 443-46; Douin, *Règne*, III, Part 3, 971-91, 994-1028.

At Cairo, where the first reports of the battle arrived at a moment of financial crisis, European handling of the news gave the impression that disaster had been complete. The effects on Egyptian prestige were catastrophic; for the moment, at least, Ismail found himself blocked in all directions. All hope of either punishing John or holding the country back of Massawa had to be abandoned. Before the year was out, the army had been recalled to Cairo.[29]

4. Collapse

The year 1875, which saw the surveys of Kordofan and Darfur and Ward's venture to the island of Thasos, the Indian Ocean expedition and the war with Abyssinia, saw also a great triumph of Egyptian reforming statesmanship. After prolonged effort, the consent of the powers was secured for the ending of unlimited consular jurisdiction over resident foreigners and for its replacement by a system of mixed courts with European, American, and Egyptian judges. Opposed at the start by Britain and to the last by France, this reform had been supported by American consuls and ministers as a legitimate national aspiration; to the optimistic its accomplishment promised well for Egypt's future.[30]

But the same year also marked the beginning of the end. The expedition to the Indian Ocean and the first efforts against Abyssinia, no less than the court reform, had shown the vigor of Ismail's aspiration; what was shortly to be clear was the weakness of the foundation upon which his ambitions were based. The financial structure erected with the pressing cooperation of European moneylenders was beginning to totter, and in November 1875 the Khedive, heavily pressed, sold his shares in the Suez Canal Company. The news of their purchase by Disraeli, which added to Britain's paramount interest in the canal the influence of the largest stockholder, led the American consul general to foresee the establishment of a British

---

[29] Despatches, Cairo: Farman to Sec. of State, 1 June 1876. "The War in Abyssinia," *New York Tribune*, 14 March 1876, 21 June 1876, 13 October 1876; 23 *Petermann's Mittheilungen*, 157-58; Douin, *Règne*, III, Part 3, 1041-94.

[30] The question of the proposed court reforms recurs frequently in the diplomatic correspondence with Alexandria, Cairo, and Constantinople, 1868-75. See also: De Leon, *The Khedive's Egypt*, pp. 297-311; E. E. Farman, *Egypt and its Betrayal* (New York, 1908), pp. 292-300; J. M. Howell, *Egypt's Past, Present, and Future* (Dayton, Ohio, 1929), pp. 281-92; J. Y. Brinton, *The Mixed Courts of Egypt* (New Haven, 1930), pp. 9-40; Sabry, *L'Empire égyptien*, pp. 209-48; Wright, "United States Policy toward Egypt," pp. 98-107.

protectorate; more immediately it brought the arrival of a British mission to investigate Egyptian finances. The mission's report, completed early in 1876, was a reasoned and moderate document which compared Egyptian troubles with those of such other developing countries as the United States and Canada, observed that Egyptian extravagance in no way matched that of the early English railway builders, and pointed out that the country had made great progress under Ismail and had resources sufficient to meet its liabilities. But its content bore little relation to its effect.

March of 1876 brought both defeat in Abyssinia and the destruction of Egyptian credit on the playing fields of European high finance. In England the publication of the financial report was so managed as to bring the collapse of Egyptian securities on European exchanges. In April, as pressure for intervention on behalf of the creditors increased and as news of the check at Gura Plain began to leak, interest payments on the debt were postponed.[31]

Nor were Egyptian troubles limited to the financial field: at the moment of announcing his annexation of central Africa, Ismail found himself undercut by his chief agent and opposed by the powers of Europe. Deep in the interior, Gordon had abandoned both his planned advance to the Indian Ocean and his effort to strengthen Egyptian control in Uganda. In the Congo the King of the Belgians was readying his own move toward the control of central Africa; to the south British missionaries were advancing from Zanzibar toward Lake Victoria; in England, in the year of the Bulgarian horrors, the conflict between Egypt and Abyssinia was seen as a war of Crescent against Cross and Egyptian expansion toward the equator as a Moslem plot to close central Africa to Christianity.

The threat that these developments posed to the Egyptian position on the Equatorial Lakes was pointed out by General Stone in a sober and detailed memorandum of 21 October. If Lake Victoria was to become Egyptian it was now or never; the danger of British control was clear. "In my view," the General wrote, "a strong nation controlling the sources of the Nile will always hold the key to lower Egypt." To keep this key, he urged the immediate dispatch of reinforcements, so that Gordon could consolidate the newly

---

[31] Despatches, Cairo: Beardsley to Sec. of State, 1 December 1875, 11 December 1875; Comanos to Sec. of State, 21 April 1876. Vidal in Tripoli also expected British seizure of the canal: Despatches, Tripoli, 6 March 1876. W. L. Langer, *European Alliances and Alignments* (New York, 1950), pp. 253-58; J. C. McCoan, *Egypt as It Is* (New York, 1877), p. 135, Appendix; Sabry, *L'Empire égyptien*, pp. 166-74.

conquered territories, occupy the country of Mutesa, and inaugurate Egyptian-flag navigation of Lake Victoria.[32]

The appreciation was sound, but the remedy was impossible: within the month, the installation at Cairo of British and French financial controllers proclaimed the commencement of alien rule. With replacement of the absolutism of the Khedive by that of the bondholders, there began that transfer to European pockets of the earnings of the fellaheen which Loring was later to describe as "a crime against humanity which no words can properly stigmatize." All funds were henceforth earmarked for the service of the debt. None would be forthcoming for imperial ventures. These ventures, for the future, were to be reserved to the nations of Europe.

So Egypt, as Turkey earlier, became a part of Europe. And again as in Turkey, European dominance was followed by a decline in American activity. A few more tasks were performed. In December 1876, his work in Darfur completed, Colonel Prout moved on to the Equatorial Provinces, where he served first as Gordon's deputy and then as governor. Early 1877 brought an echo of the Abyssinian campaign when the civilian geologist Mitchell was captured by a raiding party, marched to Adowa, and finally, after a harrowing six-weeks' captivity, sent naked back into Massawa. On a mapping expedition in the same year, Colonel Mason made the first circumnavigation of Lake Albert and discovered the Semliki River which feeds it from the south. In 1878 Colonel Graves surveyed the region of Cape Guardafui to select a site for a lighthouse. But these efforts, and Mitchell's final fruitless search for coal deposits, were last gasps. The Americans were drifting home.[33]

In 1877 the Egyptian sea of troubles rose still higher. Failure of the Nile to reach normal flood led to near-famine conditions; an epidemic of rinderpest, apparently brought back from Abyssinia, had catastrophic effects upon the livestock population. Under British pressure two onerous conventions were accepted limiting Egyptian rights and Egyptian revenues on the Red Sea coast. With the out-

[32] Stone's estimate of the situation is printed in Sabry, *L'Empire égyptien*, pp. 497-99, and in Douin, *Règne*, III, Part 3, 339-41.

[33] Despatches, Cairo: Farman to Sec. of State, 27 March 1877, 11 April 1877, 25 May 1878. *Bulletin de la Société Khédiviale*, 1st series, No. 5, pp. 5-11; No. 9-10, pp. 29-42; 2nd series, p. 350. Dye, *Moslem Egypt*, pp. 79, 98-103; Loring, *Confederate Soldier*, pp. 174, 365-66; 19 *Bulletin of the American Geographical Society*, 48-50; *New York Tribune*, 19 March 1897. Bonola, *L'Égypte et la géographie*, pp. 71-72, 80; Crabitès, *Egyptian Army*, pp. 201-12, 215-27, 229-39.

break of the Russo-Turkish War, the requirements of financial and troop support of the Sultan imposed an added strain.

In this situation the control of Egyptian finances, now in the hands of Europeans, was administered on the basis of paying the debt first and everything else last. Army and navy budgets were cut in half. The staff college and the army schools for soldiers' sons were abolished, and expenditures for general education drastically cut down. Except for Stone and Mason, all the remaining Americans were discharged in the summer of 1878, while at the same time a swarm of European functionaries arrived to assist in spoiling the Egyptians. "In fact," wrote Elbert Farman, the American consul general, a year and a half later, "it is, today, as if the whole country was owned by a company of Paris and London bankers, and the people were either their slaves or serfs, attached to the soil." Indeed, he added, "an examination of the detailed statements of the items of the budget reveals some curious facts. In a population of 5,000,000 $200,000 are appropriated for schools. The same amount is paid as salaries of twelve European Controllers and Commissioners, whose principal, and in some cases sole, business is to watch native officials."[34]

Not all of this was new, of course, for through most of recorded history Egypt had been the prey of foreigners. But this time there was a difference. No longer was it a simple matter of two classes, alien oppressors and indigenous oppressed, in which a little vigorous bloodletting would guarantee pacification. Such, indeed, had been the case upon the arrival of Mehemet Ali seventy years before, but by the time of Ismail the Egyptians were awakening to a new spirit. The discoveries of the Egyptologists provided a heartening sense of a great past. The replacement of Turkish by Arabic stimulated nationalism. At home and abroad, doctors, teachers, and soldiers had been trained in Western ways; the reforms of Mehemet Ali and the modernizing efforts of Ismail had speeded the formation of a middle class; the emphasis placed on education by such diverse individuals as the Khedive, the American missionaries, and General Stone had encouraged the ferment.

By the middle seventies these developments had produced a budding nationalist movement with multiple and at times conflicting aims: for constitutional government and against the absolutism of

[34] Despatches, Cairo: Farman to Sec. of State, 28 December 1876, 30 May 1877, 3 July 1878, 9 July 1878, 18 March 1879, 24 April 1879, 14 February 1880. Farman, *Egypt and its Betrayal*, p. 280.

the Khedive; for Egyptian control of Egypt and against both Turco-Circassian dominance and European exploitation; for and against the past. In the army, where Turco-Circassian control had prevented any Egyptian from rising above the rank of colonel, the new movement was powerful. Shortly the army would provide a leader.

In the course of the Abyssinian campaign there had briefly presided over the collapsing transport service an obscure lieutenant colonel named Ahmed Arabi. Reserved and serious, distrusting Ratib and the Circassians on the one hand and Loring and the Americans on the other, Arabi returned from the campaign to assume a leading part in an army movement dedicated to the proposition that Egypt was for the Egyptians.

Purposely, as Stone thought, but unwisely, the foreign controllers had reduced the size of the army and had let its pay fall into arrears. But this effort to disarm Egypt while at the same time reducing expenditures succeeded only in mobilizing the active opposition of the one organized Egyptian nationalist force. In February 1879 a demonstration by unpaid army officers toppled the alien-dominated ministry. Although Ismail brought the military under control and rallied his country behind him by ousting the foreign controllers, these events were but the prelude to his further humiliation by what Loring, the Floridian, referred to as "that oligarchy of carpetbaggers." On the argument that Europe lacked confidence in him, the British and French consuls put great pressure upon the Khedive to abdicate in favor of his more tractable son. This failing, the powers turned to work through Constantinople. In June 1879 Ismail was deposed by the Sultan and Tewfik, a man "with the soul of a slave," reigned in his stead.[35]

It was a great fall. Of all foreign representatives in Egypt, only the Consul General of the United States called upon Ismail in the interval between his deposition and his departure into exile. But the Americans had always admired the modernizing Khedive, and no less at the end when his dignity and self-control elicited the admiration of all. On his departure large crowds gathered along the road to show their sympathy; he had not been greatly loved during his reign, but that was past and now "the feeling was only that of a

---

[35] Despatches, Cairo: Farman to Sec. of State, 22 February 1879, 14 April 1879, 24 April 1879, 20 June 1879, 27 June 1879. Despatches, Turkey: Maynard to Sec. of State, 28 June 1879, 11 July 1879. Stone, "Military Affairs in Egypt," pp. 176-80; Loring, *Confederate Soldier*, p. 178; Farman, *Egypt and its Betrayal*, pp. 245-63; Sabry, *L'Empire égyptien*, pp. 315-25; Douin, *Règne*, III, Part 3, 867-69.

conquered people parting with their sovereign at the dictation of hated foreigners." We may leave him with a final word from Loring: "though I had been desirous for more than a year to return to my own country, having made all my arrangements to do so, I should not had left had I known the troubles which beset this extraordinary man, and which resulted most unjustly in his abdication. In his exile he has my sympathies, and he will always find at least one who honors him."[36]

General Stone had promised Ismail that he would stand by his son, and for three and a half years the Chief of Staff remained. Through these years he watched the steady undoing of his earlier accomplishments, as Egypt fell increasingly under the control of outsiders and as unrest among the military increased. As was true of most of the Americans, Stone's sympathy was with the Egyptians, but as one dedicated to loyalty and discipline he regretted the increasing insurbordination of the army. Yet none of the Egyptian staff officers whom he had trained ever wavered in loyalty to the Khedive, and from this at least he could derive some satisfaction.[37]

Throughout these years of increasing European pressure, the American government maintained its habitual political aloofness. This was not, perhaps, from lack of opportunity. Insofar as there existed any general Egyptian attitude toward America, it was a friendly one—"There is scarcely a native but knows from his Arabic paper that the United States are their friend, that we are not here to plunder and oppress but to aid and encourage"—and this feeling was reflected by the country's rulers. Despite opposition from European residents, the coveted obelisk had been presented to the city of New York by Ismail and its removal approved by Tewfik, while the latter, shortly after his accession, had asked the acting American consul general "to encourage the United States to take part in the solution of the difficulties which surround the Egyptian government."[38]

[36] Despatches, Cairo: Farman to Sec. of State, 1 July 1879. Farman, *Egypt and its Betrayal*, pp. 268-71; Loring, *Confederate Soldier*, p. 450.

[37] Stone, "Military Affairs," pp. 180-82; *Bulletin de la Société Khédiviale*, 2nd series, p. 413; *Supplément*, pp. 682, 725.

[38] Despatches, Cairo: Comanos to Sec. of State, 1 September 1879; Wolf to Sec. of State, 21 March 1882. On the obelisk: Instructions, Cairo: Sec. of State to Farman, 19 October 1877, 13 June 1879, 1 August 1879, 11 February 1881. Despatches, Cairo: Farman to Sec. of State, 24 November 1877, 4 March 1878, 19 May 1879 - 12 June 1880, *passim*. Farman, *Egypt and its Betrayal*, pp. 142-71. H. H. Gorringe, *Egyptian Obelisks*.

Briefly, it seemed that the United States might prove responsive. An Egyptian proposal for the establishment of an international commission to supervise the liquidation of the debt, received at the State Department while the instructions for General Noyes's African journey were in preparation, brought a cabled request from Evarts for American representation. But second thoughts soon prevailed in Washington, and although Noyes's arrival in Egypt did stir some rumors of imminent American moves, Tewfik's hopes were not answered.

If this was disappointing, the Egyptians nevertheless continued to enjoy a generalized American sympathy and support. So anti-European in tone were the consular dispatches from Cairo that extensive deletions were necessary before they could be printed in *Foreign Relations*. Early in 1878 Consul General Farman had suggested that his government intervene to reduce the interest on the Egyptian debt; subsequently he advanced Madisonian views, arguing that interest should be paid only on the amounts actually loaned to Egypt; in 1880 he urged the State Department to "have no part" in a European proposal for debt liquidation which promised to impose still heavier burdens upon the Egyptians. The government at Washington, for its part, had supported the plan for judicial reform and had appointed American judges to the mixed courts. In negotiations on commercial questions and on the slave trade the State Department had upheld, at least by implication, the view that Egypt was competent to engage in treaty relations with other powers. The War Department had assisted Egyptian arms procurement; the General in Chief had helped in the recruitment of officers; the Department of Agriculture had supplied advice on the control of the rinderpest. To these evidences of support there was added, in 1880, a dramatic instance of fair dealing when the United States minister at Constantinople, ordered to Cairo to try an American for murder, sentenced him, to the astonishment of all, to hang.[39]

As well as serving as a source of incidental help and sympathy, the United States remained important in Egyptian eyes as the outstanding example of a successfully developed backward country. Repeatedly, in interviews with American travelers, Tewfik expressed his admiration for American institutions, above all for America's

[39] Instructions, Cairo: *passim*. Despatches, Cairo: Farman to Sec. of State, 18 February 1878, 24 April 1879, 3 July 1879, 14 February 1880, 8 March 1880, 2 June 1880, 12 July 1880; Comanos to Sec. of State, 1 September 1879.

school system. His aims, he said, were to model Egypt on the United States; although this would take time, a start had to be made, and "the foundation of that commencement lies in founding public schools." These views were echoed by a new American consul general after an investigation of the American missionary establishment: "My pride, as an American, was greatly aroused when I saw our country in counterdistinction to others, dealing out elements of culture, instruction and civilization . . . anxious and ready to spread the light of truth and knowledge. We must war in the East not with cannon and shot but with schoolbooks, bibles, and constitutions."[40]

The writer of these words, Simon Wolf, a leader of the American Jewish community and the individual chiefly responsible for the appointment of Peixotto to Bucharest, had been named consul general in 1881. His arrival in Egypt in September had coincided with a new army rising led by Colonel Arabi; his first official act had been to cable for American warships. For the rest of the month Wolf's dispatches reflected opposition to the colonels and support of the Khedive, but by early October he was writing with increasing sympathy of the officers' desire for a constitution and of the spreading national support for the movement "to put an end to what they called the pacific conquest of Egypt by Europe."

The September crisis had brought new rumors of American intervention. A New York newspaper story, picked up and reprinted by the Egyptian press, argued from the visit of General Noyes, the arrival of the new American consul general, and unspecified American plans, that the United States intended to defend the integrity of Egypt and that Wolf, Stone, and Farman, the last now a judge on the mixed court, were to work together toward that end. With regard to Wolf, at least, the dispatch was prescient: hoping in the Egyptian interest to moderate the tension between Khedive and army, the Consul General on his own initiative arranged a meeting with Arabi, and the ensuing dialogue between American Jew and Arab nationalist has an interest which time has in no way diminished.[41]

---

[40] Despatches, Cairo: Wolf to Sec. of State, 7 February 1882, 2 March 1882, 25 March 1882.

[41] Despatches, Cairo: Wolf to Sec. of State, 11 September 1881 (telegram), 12 September 1881, 15 September 1881, 5 October 1881, 8 October 1881, 17 October 1881. M. J. Kohler, "Simon Wolf," 29 *Publications of the American Jewish Historical Society*, 195-206; Warren, *A Doctor's Experiences*, pp. 568-69.

Although General Stone had stood with the Khedive against the army agitators, he had retained the confidence of all, and the interview took place at his home with Edward A. Van Dyck, consular clerk and son of the Syrian missionary, acting as interpreter. Disclaiming all American involvement in European or Levantine politics, Wolf informed Arabi that his request for a meeting was wholly unofficial, and sprang only from his "deep and generous sympathy for their national aspirations. As an Israelite, a brother of the Arab branch of the human family, I fully appreciated all they longed for. I felt grateful to Mohammedans for the shelter and protection and freedom my brethren had enjoyed for years in moslem countries." As the free citizen of a free country, where liberty had triumphed over tyranny only by strenuous and continued effort, he could only sympathize with the goal of Egypt for the Egyptians, but in view of the danger of European intervention he urged upon Arabi the need for moderation, loyalty to the Khedive, and the avoidance of hasty steps.

In reply Arabi observed that in recent centuries the inhabitants of the East had "lost the learning and science that they possessed of old," and that the capture and development of this science by Europeans was the source of Europe's strength. Nevertheless, Egypt should control her own destiny, even though the lack of qualified Egyptians at times made it necessary to seek outside help, and "here he mentions as examples, the case of General Ch. P. Stone, who had served Egypt by actually creating the General Staff of the Army. . . . Such men, said he, served Egypt for Egypt's good, and should be well remunerated."

Whatever the effects of Wolf's counsels of moderation, and he thought there were some, his intervention seems to have been appreciated by all. General Stone at once reported the conversation to Tewfik, who twice thanked Wolf for having met with Arabi. In February 1882, when the nationalists forced in a new government, the Prime Minister and Arabi, now minister of war, waited together on the American to assure him that their determination to control internal affairs implied no disturbance of external obligations. Reiterating his American sympathy for those who sought self-government, Wolf praised the wisdom and moderation of the reformers' program, again urged caution, and concluded by presenting the Egyptians with a biography of the martyred President Garfield, together with the suggestion that it be translated into Arabic and distributed to Egyptian schoolboys for inspirational purposes. This Arabi promised would be done.[42]

Within the month these friendly relations were reemphasized at a grand Washington's birthday celebration. The Prime Minister took Mrs. Stone in to dinner, Arabi escorted the wife of the Vice Consul, and while the Khedive's band played American airs under the windows, the speeches concerned themselves with liberty, the freedom of the press, and good wishes for Egyptian progress. The guests, in addition to the chief officers of government, the consular staff, and the Stones, included the American minister to Vienna, a traveling United States senator, the officers of the visiting U.S.S. *Quinnebaug*, a number of Egyptian politicians, and some foreign consuls. But the absentees were also important, for the consuls general of England, France, and Italy had all declined their invitations.

Wolf's health had for some time been precarious; soon, after a new setback, he left Egypt. In his farewell interviews with the Khedive, the Prime Minister, and Arabi he again voiced the best wishes of the United States; again he was thanked for his sympathy, advice, and calm judgment. To the departing Consul General these talks seemed reassuring. Taken together with evidence of increasing European sympathy for the Egyptian nationalist government, they led him to look optimistically to the future. But his hopes were not to be fulfilled.[43]

In late May 1882, as tensions between the nationalists and Tewfik increased, British and French ironclad squadrons were sent to Alexandria. Under this European pressure the Arabi government was first forced out and then, in the absence of any alternative, recalled to power. To the British and French this mortifying outcome seemed to call for further action; to the Egyptians the presence of the squadrons appeared to threaten the fate of Tunis, where European financial control had led, only a few months earlier, to French occupation. Concerned by the increasing likelihood of European military action, General Stone had already ordered more underwater ordnance from America. Now Arabi's government set to work to improve the fortifications of Alexandria, while simultaneously issuing renewed guarantees of the preservation of order and security.

[42] Despatches, Cairo: Wolf to Sec. of State, 10 November 1881, 7 February 1882, 27 February 1882.

[43] Despatches, Cairo: Wolf to Sec. of State, 25 February 1882, 25 March 1882. H. M. Field, *On the Desert* (New York, 1883), p. 15.

So critical had the situation seemed, when seen from Constantinople, that the American minister had cabled Washington for warships. All appeared quiet at Alexandria on the arrival of the U.S.S. *Galena* in early June, but on the 11th an outbreak of rioting led to the deaths of some fifty Europeans. Some suspected that the violence had been fomented by Tewfik to force an intervention on his behalf; some blamed it on the nationalists; Commander Batcheller of *Galena* thought it accidental; Judge Farman suspected British intrigue. Whatever its origins, the outbreak was soon magnified into an anti-Christian massacre. As Europeans began to flee Egypt by the thousands and the powers began to work for Turkish intervention, Rear Admiral James Nicholson, the commander of the European Squadron, was ordered to get his entire force to Alexandria.[44]

While Nicholson steamed eastward in his flagship *Lancaster*, the flight out of Egypt continued. With *Galena* crowded with half a hundred American refugees and with more expected, Commander Batcheller felt forced to charter a merchant ship; with these two vessels he managed ultimately to accommodate some two hundred and fifty individuals, including the acting Consul General, the members of the missionary community, and a number of foreigners whose governments had not provided for their protection. But this was as nothing to the more than twenty thousand Europeans who had fled the country by the end of June. Since the acting American consular agent at Alexandria was one of these, a replacement was necessary and was found in the person of Colonel Charles Chaillé Long, recently returned to Egypt to practice law before the mixed tribunals.

In marked contrast to the panic of the foreigners was the orderly behavior of the Egyptian populace. From Cairo, where the American consulate alone remained in operation, General Stone reported total calm. At Alexandria, too, although rumor continued rife, the surface was peaceful, and on 3 July, the Sultan's birthday, all men-of-war in harbor dressed ship. Since a more important anniversary was to occur the following day, Admiral Nicholson invited the

[44] Despatches, Cairo: Comanos to Sec. of State, 21 May 1882, 27 May 1882, 30 May 1882, 12 June 1882, 13 June 1882, 19 June 1882. Instructions, Cairo: Sec. of State to Comanos, 8 June 1882. Despatches, Turkey: Wallace to Sec. of State, 25 May 1882, 26 May 1882. Letters to Flag Officers: Sec. of Navy to Nicholson, 26 May 1882 (telegram), 13 June 1882, 5 July 1882. Squadron Letters: Nicholson to Sec. of Navy, 29 May 1882, 16 June 1882. De Kusel, *Recollections*, pp. 179-83; Edward Malet, *Egypt, 1879-1883* (London, 1909), pp. 165-70; Farman, *Egypt and its Betrayal*, pp. 303-12.

Egyptian authorities and the foreign naval commanders to join him in its observance. With all forty warships in harbor beautifully dressed and flying the American flag at the main, and with all the larger vessels firing a national salute at noon, the Admiral could proudly report "that never before in our Country's history, has so grand as well as beautiful a Celebration been seen afloat." But the next firing was to be of a different sort, and with little to do with the idea of national independence.[45]

While time stood still at Alexandria, where the European ironclads confronted the Egyptian forts, the efforts of the powers to master the situation by way of Constantinople had involved the United States. Pressed by an ambassadorial conference for a solution to the Egyptian problem, alarmed by the apparent imminence of hostilities, and concerned for his rights as suzerain, the Sultan Abdul Hamid summoned the American minister and on 4 July inquired whether his country, as the only country not seeking territory or money, would employ its good offices to settle the dispute between Egypt and Britain. Apprised of this move by cable from General Wallace, the State Department at once raised the question with the British and cabled the Minister for an estimate of the likelihood of successful mediation. To this inquiry Wallace responded energetically: on the 8th and 9th he met with both Sultan and British ambassador, and his optimistic report was relayed by the Department to the Foreign Office with the statement that good offices would be proffered if acceptable to Great Britain.

Apparently they were not. On the 10th Wallace's hopes were dashed by the statement of the British ambassador that the squadron would open fire in the morning. Further last-minute efforts served only to convince the American minister that the ambassadors' conference was but a mask for far-ranging British plans, and that the Sultan could not have averted the bombardment without giving *"the English government a quit claim deed for the Canal and Egypt."*[46]

Already, at Alexandria, the rumor that Britain intended the

[45] Squadron Letters: Nicholson to Sec. of Navy, 30 June 1882, 5 July 1882, 15 July 1882. Despatches, Cairo: Comanos to Sec. of State, 15 June 1882. Chaillé-Long, *My Life*, pp. 245-47.

[46] Despatches, Turkey: Wallace to Sec. of State, 5 July 1882 (telegram), 9 July 1882 (telegram), 10 July 1882 (telegram), 20 July 1882. Instructions, Turkey: Sec. of State to Wallace, 7 July 1882 (telegram), 10 July 1882 (unsent telegram), 21 July 1882, 30 August 1882.

seizure of the canal had caused panic; already the British admiral had received orders to prevent all further work on the Alexandria fortifications. On 10 July, after foreign consuls and naval officers had been warned of possible hostilities, an ultimatum was served upon the military governor demanding that he permit his forts to be disarmed. The Egyptian declined to comply, the Admiral refused a compromise offer, and on the next day the squadron bombarded the works and the town.

By afternoon of the 11th the forts were no longer resisting. On the 12th Arabi's forces withdrew from Alexandria, leaving the city undefended and burning. Surprisingly, considering the vigor of his previous actions, the British admiral appeared reluctant to put a force ashore. Equally surprising, if in a way appropriate, was another development: the first foreigners to enter the city from which General Eaton had so long ago set forth for Tripoli were United States Marines.

The 12th had been spent in waiting. On the 13th Colonel Long was twice blocked in attempts to reopen the American consulate by crowds of looters and incendiaries. Not until evening did small British patrols take up positions outside the city walls. On the 14th Admiral Nicholson brought his ships back in across the bar, informed the Khedive that he desired to reopen the consulate, and asked permission to land a force to guard it. Requested by Tewfik to assist in fire fighting and in reestablishing order, Nicholson sent a party of a hundred men into the city, where they performed important work in extinguishing fires and preventing looting. On the 15th a sufficient British force at last entered the city and assumed control.[47]

Arabi, in the meantime, had retired eastward toward Suez. But the militarily logical step of seizing the canal was not attempted, in part perhaps because of De Lesseps' promise that it would remain neutralized, in part because of pressure from General Stone, who emphasized how certainly this move would ensure further foreign intervention. But while Arabi, dismissed by Tewfik for not resisting enough, prepared for further resistance, the British were bring-

[47] Squadron Letters: Nicholson to Sec. of Navy, 14 July 1882, 15 July 1882. Despatches, Cairo: Comanos to Sec. of State, 18 July 1882; Long to 3rd Asst. Sec. of State, 17 August 1882. C. F. Goodrich, *Report of the British Naval and Military Operations in Egypt, 1882* (Washington, 1883), pp. 9-11, 18-36, 80-82; Farman, *Egypt and its Betrayal*, pp. 314-22; De Kusel, *Recollections*, p. 208; Chaillé-Long, *My Life*, pp. 250-72; C. P. Stone, letter of 4 April 1884, 28 *Century Magazine*, 288.

ing in troops from India by way of Suez and the Khedive was co-operating with the invader. This situation placed an agonizing strain upon the loyalties of the Egyptian military. For the members of the General Staff whom Stone had trained, the dilemma was solved, if painfully, by following the example of their American chief and supporting the Khedive. And shortly, and in considerable degree as a result of their efforts, the situation was resolved. In September, with the aid of intelligence on Arabi's plans secretly transmitted by loyal staff officers in Cairo to General Stone at Alexandria, the British routed the Egyptian forces at Tel el Kébir.[48]

So the process of foreign interference reached its logical end. Egypt was occupied, the nationalists were broken, Arabi was a prisoner. Ended also was the greater Egypt of Ismail's imperial vision: the Sudan was in revolt, and the Egyptian garrisons were retiring before the forces of the Mahdi of Allah. As a last service to the dynasty which he had served for twelve years, Stone drew up a plan for the reconquest of the Sudan, an operation which he estimated would require a force of 27,000 men. The British administration refused the money and disbanded the army. In the next year Stone's estimate was borne out when a 10,000-man expedition under Hicks Pasha was annihilated at the battle of El Obeid.

Well before this tragic confirmation of his military judgment, it had become apparent that the new dispensation held no place for an American chief of staff. In December 1882 Stone resigned his post and early in the next year sailed for home, stopping off at Paris to call on Ismail, his old employer, whom he considered even in failure to have been one of the great modernizing rulers of the century. Once more in his native land, Stone found employment as supervising engineer charged with the construction of the foundations for the Statue of Liberty. The symbolism was wholly appropriate; the lesson, that it is easier to underpin the statue than the concept, to work with bricks and mortar than with refractory humanity, was only too true.

Of all the Americans, only Mason Bey remained. After duty with the cadastral survey he became for a time governor of Massawa and

---

[48] Despatches, Cairo: Comanos to Sec. of State, 25 July 1882, 3 August 1882, 21 August 1882, 13 September 1882. Stone, "Military Affairs," 5 *Journal of the Military Service Institution*, 181-82; "Stone-Pacha and the Secret Despatch," 8 *ibid.*, 94-95; "Diary of an American Girl in Cairo, During the War of 1882," 28 *Century Magazine*, 288-302; Farman, *Egypt and its Betrayal*, pp. 331-33; Chaillé-Long, *My Life*, p. 272.

in 1884 Egyptian plenipotentiary on a mission to Abyssinia; at his death in 1897 he was still in Egyptian service. But the continued presence of a single individual from the Western world served only to emphasize the changes that had taken place. The period in which Egypt had attempted to revolutionize her own way of life with the help of freely chosen outsiders was over, and Egypt was henceforth to be governed in the interest of others.

To the Egyptians, of course, this was no matter of indifference. Such friction as had existed with the Americans was quickly forgotten, and the resignation of the Chief of Staff was seized on by his former colleagues for the opportunity it gave them to express their deeper feelings. A banquet was tendered Stone, attended by both past and present presidents of the Council of Ministers, by the Ministers of Justice and of the Interior, by his friends of the Société Khédiviale de Géographie, and by the graduates of the staff school. His works were detailed and praised; as the former president of the Council remarked, if some of his efforts had not been crowned with success, the fault was hardly the General's but was owing to "the instability of things in this life." Still more touching was the memorial meeting of the Société Khédiviale which followed Stone's death in 1887. In an emotional speech, the most distinguished of the staff school graduates praised the departed American and described his fatherly interest in his officers, his generosity in time of crisis in pledging his personal credit to ensure that his subordinates were paid, his devotion to the highest forms of duty. "Yes, he has gone, the man of battle, the prince of mathematicians, the protector of science and the champion of civilization. Stone! Stone! My distress is inconsolable; my tears will not cease." But Stone was dead, and dead also was the Egypt he had worked to create.[49]

That the British governed well even the Americans recognized, but they governed in the imperial interest. Logical and inevitable this might be, but to those who held to the old-fashioned principles of the Declaration of Independence it could not seem right. Law and order there were, and some slight development of resources, but little heed was given the continuing transitional problems of Egyptian civilization. Whatever his errors, Ismail had surely been correct

[49] Despatches, Cairo: Pomeroy to Sec. of State, 4 January 1883. Farman, *Egypt and its Betrayal*, p. 272; R. E. Colston, "The British Campaign in the Soudan," 17 *Bulletin of the American Geographical Society*, 161-62; *New York Tribune*, 25 January 1887, 19 March 1897; *Bulletin de la Société Khédiviale*, 2nd series, pp. 411-14; *Supplément*, pp. 665-85, 723-25.

in his emphasis on capital investment and education, but now service of the debt took precedence over all else. Although the virtue of imitating "Robert's Training College" at Constantinople was realized by the British, the financial situation seemed to forbid; equally, the need for economy was used to justify a rapid shrinkage of Egyptian territory.

In 1884 the Sudan was abandoned, along with the coast of the Gulf of Aden and the lower half of the Red Sea. From Harar, where a thriving settlement had been established, 14,500 Egyptians were brought back. At Assab and Massawa the Italians established their colony of Eritrea. The French and British divided up Somaliland. Ten years after the Indian Ocean expedition and the campaign in Abyssinia, the frontier was back at Wadi Halfa and the powers of Europe controlled the Red Sea. In still other ways the map was changed, and Lake Ibrahim, discovered by Colonel Long, now became Lake Kioga. With the rise of a new school of historiography dedicated to downgrading Ismail and the native effort, the Americans were all but forgotten. South of the Sahara the scramble for Africa was underway. Again, as in Roman times, the Mediterranean had become a European lake. No longer traversing the sea that washed the Continent's southern shore, the frontier of Europe now had to be sought for in the Far East.

CHAPTER XII

Epilogue

1. The Past in Limbo

IN JANUARY 1853 Miss Harriet Preble went to church in Pittsburgh to pray for the conversion of the world. Saddened that she could do so little in so great a cause and troubled that the Kingdom of God did not come faster upon earth, she consoled herself by reflecting in her journal on the progress of Christianity over the past four centuries. The New World had become the refuge of Christian nations. India, in British hands, was ripe for mission work. The Pacific had heard of the Redeemer, and in sleeping China five ports had been opened to the importation of the pearl of great price. But of the gospel effort in the eastern Mediterranean, the niece of the great Commodore and daughter of the merchant who had hoped to become the first American consul at Constantinople made no mention.[1]

Miss Preble was perhaps a little premature in her preoccupation with further Asia and her neglect of the Levant. There were, after all, only five Chinese treaty ports, and Commodore Perry, persuaded with difficulty to renounce his claims to command the Mediterranean Squadron, had sailed on his errand to Japan a mere five weeks before. But the future was on her side, and as history moved on and historical writing changed, the long years of American activity in the Mediterranean and Near East came to be forgotten.

This development stemmed in no small degree from the expanded efforts of those intent upon the world's conversion. Although closely linked in its early years with commercial and maritime interests, the missionary effort had in time become self-sustaining, and had survived the Civil War destruction of the merchant marine without a check. By 1890 American expenditures on foreign missions exceeded even those of England and quadrupled those of the next nation, Germany. Through the years since Miss Preble's prayer the emphasis on the Orient had steadily increased. In the decade of the fifties the Chinese expenditures of the American Board, the oldest and still perhaps the most important missionary organization,

[1] R. H. Lee, *Memoir of the Life of Harriet Preble* (New York, 1856), p. 378.

436

amounted to but a sixth of those in the Levant. Soon, however, the Far East became the faster growing field, with all the attractions normally possessed by an expanding enterprise. In the seventies the growth of the Chinese effort and the commencement of work in Japan raised the Board's expenditure in the Far East to half of that in the Levant. By 1890 the two fields were running even, and together accounted for more than half of a total budget of almost a million dollars a year. By this time, too, the Presbyterians and Methodists had arrived in force, with the result that ordained American missionaries in China, Japan, and Korea outnumbered those in the Levant by more than three to one.[2]

This shift in the geographical focus of the missionary movement found parallels in the activities of other Americans and of the American government. Throughout the nineteenth century, as the Mediterranean was being Europeanized, the Pacific was being opened up. In the Pacific, as earlier along Europe's southern shore, the development of American trade was followed by the arrival of the United States Navy for its protection and of naval officers and diplomats to negotiate for its increase. In the post-Civil War years the pace of activity was accelerated: Alaska was purchased from the liberal Czar, the connection with Hawaii grew closer, interest in a steamship connection with the Antipodes brought a lasting involvement in Samoa, and the Navy accomplished its final opening of a closed civilization. The voyage on which Commodore Shufeldt sailed in 1879, and which led him first to Liberia and then to the Persian Gulf, resulted, in the year of the bombardment of Alexandria, in the conclusion of the first Western treaty with the Kingdom of Korea.

Yet the novelty of these developments should not be overemphasized. Concerned as they were with the expansion and protection of commerce, the extension of the benefits of Western civilization, and the carrying of the gospel to those who dwelt in darkness, these Pacific ventures were sufficiently traditional in nature. Equally, the unity of the open maritime world of the nineteenth century could be seen in the commercial and cultural ties between Mediterranean and Pacific and in the linking activities of both institutions and individuals. The same Navy that had chastised Barbary pirates

[2] ABCFM *Annual Reports*; Bliss, *Encyclopaedia of Missions*, II, 606-34. Turn-of-the-century missionary statistics are available in quantity in J. S. Dennis, *Centennial Survey of Foreign Missions* (New York and Chicago, 1902).

dealt also with those in China seas; naval ships and naval personnel served interchangeably in Mediterranean and Pacific; the same missionary organizations that worked to leaven the Levant also deployed their workers to Hawaii, the Isles of the Sea, and the countries of eastern Asia. Turkey opium, at an early date, had been an important ingredient in the development of the China trade; at the century's end the Ottoman sultan would employ his influence as caliph to encourage "harmonious relations" between the Sultan of Sulu and the Americans in the Philippines. Commodore Porter, commander of the first American warship to enter the Pacific and first American to propose the opening of Japan and Korea, later became the first American representative at Constantinople. John O. Dominis, son of a Mahonese seaman who had signed on an American ship in the Mediterranean trade, in time became governor of Oahu and, through marriage to Princess Liliuokalani, prince consort of the Hawaiian Kingdom. Following the British occupation of Egypt, both Colonel Dye and Colonel Long appeared in Korea, the former as military adviser to the Korean king and the latter as American consul.

So far, in whatever ocean, the overseas activities of American citizens and of their government remained much as before, and so also did much American thinking concerning the nature and meaning of these activities. Writing in 1878, Commodore Shufeldt argued the national importance of a revived merchant marine and of the Navy as "the pioneer of commerce." Eight years later, the publication of Eugene Schuyler's lectures showed that to some, at least, the promotion of commerce was still the principal purpose of American diplomacy. If these works tended to the specific, and confined themselves to the functions of the government agencies concerned, the tendency to generalize on these matters also survived, as in the writings of the historian John Fiske.

Fiske's choice of title for the lecture series which he delivered in 1880 and published in 1885—*American Political Ideas Viewed from the Standpoint of Universal History*—would have commended itself to Barlow, Dwight, and Humphreys, as would the content of the book. His attack, in the new protectionist age, on the "shameful" American tariff harked back to earlier times. His praise of the federal principle, as the mechanism for the extension of English liberties from New England township to areas of continental size, merely confirmed the hopes of the first generation of independence. In his final lecture, on "Manifest Destiny," Fiske looked to the future, and after a brief offhand reference to the millennium proceeded to the argument, hardly new in American life, that progress consisted in the triumph of dollar-hunter over scalp-hunter. His conclusion, that industrial civilization was winning out over military civilization, that "the wretched business of warfare" was becoming obsolete, and that history was working through the federalization of mankind toward a "sabbath of perpetual peace" echoed the antique American aspirations of *The Vision of Columbus*.[3]

Yet while ideas about America's role in "universal history" were little changed, the same could not be said about America itself. The extraordinary vigor of its development had brought the United States, in the century that followed the Declaration of Independence, to a position of great potential power. The scattered coastal settlements of the revolutionary period had expanded to form a continental nation. In population, between 1850 and 1880, America successively overtook Great Britain, Austria-Hungary, France, and Germany. In the same years there developed a colossal agricultural export; from the mid-seventies the country enjoyed a favorable balance of trade; by 1890 it led the world in production of iron and steel, and by 1900 in that of coal. These facts, with all their implications, strained the ancient theoretical constructs and gave urgency to the difficult problem of how to marry America's new power to her ancient mission—of how, in Emerson's words, to put her creed into her deed. This was to be the question of the second century of independence.

Inevitably the answers were worked out over time, and less on the basis of books read by the few than of traditions and experiences shared by the many. In considerable degree these answers were themselves the product of America's astounding economic growth. The country that had produced John Adams and Pliny Fisk and David Porter had been a poor country: in Paris the first of these had confronted a civilization immeasurably richer than his own; in the Mediterranean the others had encountered cultures which, while exotic enough, were not, when measured on the economic scale, of a wholly inferior order. But by the end of the nineteenth century the

[3] R. W. Shufeldt, *The Relation of the Navy to the Commerce of the United States* (Washington, 1878), p. 6; Schuyler, *American Diplomacy*; John Fiske, *American Political Ideas* (New York, 1885); *idem, The Destiny of Man* (Boston and New York, 1884). Frederick Merk, *Manifest Destiny and Mission in American History* (New York, 1963), pp. 238-39.

situation had changed, and the new wealth had produced a discernible temptation to Americans abroad to adopt a new tone, to resort to new means of persuasion, and to slide, at times, from righteousness into self-righteousness.

Upon the shape of the government that presided, somewhat absently, over the American cornucopia, the new economic developments also had their impact. The increase in American exports, up some 200 per cent in the decade of the seventies, was relevant not only to the missions of General Noyes and Commodore Shufeldt, but also to President Hayes's call for naval expansion. Such expansion could be paid for with the new wealth, yet with this wealth there had also developed unprecedented packages of power which, being privately controlled, were unsusceptible to the primitive American remedy of neutralization through constitutional forms. And as these possibilities and problems became apparent, it also began to appear that the experiences of Civil War and Reconstruction and the subsequent cries of farmers and reformers had made morality, once the private responsibility of the Hopkinsian individual, a matter of governmental concern.

Of these linked private and public developments some literary traces can be found, for again in these years America had a poet in politics. A friend of Lincoln as Humphreys had been the "Friend of Washington," John Hay, in the years after Appomattox, held a succession of diplomatic posts much in the fashion of Humphreys and Barlow. But while the Wits had looked forward to a new order where "reason triumphs o'er the pride of power," Hay's muse bore witness that the greatest event of the poet's lifetime had been the conferring of freedom by force of arms:

> Wherever man oppresses man
> Beneath thy liberal sun,
> Oh Lord, be there Thine arm made bare,
> Thy righteous will be done!

he wrote in 1891. The adjective "liberal" survived from the age that was past, but the poem's celebration of the headsman's ax as instrument of the divine will was a far cry from the "influence mild" that Humphreys had thought would accompany the spread of Christianity.[4]

[4] Hay, "Thy Will Be Done," 83 *Harper's Magazine*, 674; *idem*, "God's Vengeance," *Poems by John Hay* (Boston and New York, 1897), pp. 201-2; Tyler Dennett, *John Hay* (New York, 1933), pp. 75-76.

To some extent, both at home and abroad, the bare-armed Lord came to influence the actions of America. Once equipped in the cause of righteousness, whether externally by the new Navy or internally by new laws and regulatory commissions, the government which had freed the slaves found itself impelled to free the Cubans and to war both with Spain and with the trusts. So the summer of 1898 brought a new departure. The onset of a war to free Cuba was followed by the Battle of Manila Bay, and the country which had shown no interest in the purchase of Aegean isles, or in a naval base in Cyrenaica or at Bab el Mandeb, found itself seized of an archipelago off the eastern shores of Asia. Since the aim of Dewey's attack on the Philippines was merely to provide additional leverage to get Spain out of Cuba, it might be argued that the state of affairs that resulted was an historical accident, as much the consequence of British failure to retain these islands after the Seven Years' War as of conscious American purpose. But however accidental the situation, it did in fact exist, and the questions that it posed were argued out in the old American way and within the old American assumptions.

Whether the United States should act as exemplar only, or should participate actively in the struggle for freedom elsewhere, had been debated at the time of the French Revolution, during the Latin American revolutions, and during the Greek War for Independence; the question had recurred in 1848, during the visit of Kossuth, and with the rise of Young America. Now, in the case of Cuba, the country had indeed "put a weight into the balance," and had given more than "a salaam to oppressed humanity." And while this time the dispute was more over the consequences of intervention and the question of Philippine annexation than over the decision to intervene, the premises were largely unchanged. The night thoughts of President McKinley, with their emphasis on national pride, on commerce, and on disinterested benevolence, came straight from the end of the eighteenth century, and so did the arguments of his anti-imperialist opponents.

But however traditional the rhetoric, the conditions which called it forth were new. The triumphs of "America's favorite Navy" had restored that service to a popularity approaching that of the years after the War of 1812, and had directed attention to the oceans and what lay beyond them. With the flag planted in Hawaii and the Philippines, the changed American map pointed dramatically to eastern Asia as the new field for the American mission, whether conceived

441

in the sacred terms of the evangelization of the world or in the secular ones of Open Door and maintenance of the integrity of China. Almost as important as the new activism of the government and the new departure in the annexation of overseas territory was the new nationalistic context in which these events were seen. For this new context, which drew a curtain over a hundred years of history, two new historians appear to have been largely responsible.

A decade and a half before the war with Spain, an American naval officer, Captain Alfred Thayer Mahan, had begun to read and think about his trade. The results were revolutionary. Brought up in the single-cruiser, commerce-destroying, anti-imperialist tradition, Mahan now turned his back upon the service in which he had spent his life. Drawing upon the history of eighteenth-century Europe, the "vast Aceldama" from which his ancestors had won their freedom, he provided the theoretical foundations for the navies of the new mercantilism. On the world scene, his writings proved the influence of history upon sea power and made him the most influential of American thinkers. At home, although his shadow was somewhat less, his focus on the command rather than the freedom of the seas, reinforced by the eclipse of the merchant marine, the new technology and the new tariff, and the victories of 1898, made the activities of the Old Navy all but incomprehensible.[5]

In the same years that saw the metamorphosis of the world's navies from guardians of commerce into instruments of national power, the history of the United States was acquiring a new emphasis. In 1893 a Wisconsin historian, resentful of the slighting of the forests of his native state in favor of those of an earlier Germany, placed himself in his imagination at Cumberland Gap. Observing the passage of the American procession—Indian, trapper, cattleman, and farmer—he derived much of the American character from the action of the frontier. Had Frederick Jackson Turner stood instead at Gibraltar, he could have watched an equally distinguished procession—Barlow and Preble, David Offley and William Goodell, David Porter, Cyrus Hamlin, Charles P. Stone—but the lessons of their lives were for the moment out of fashion.[6]

[5] Compare, in this context, the Mahanist approach of H. and M. Sprout, *Rise of American Naval Power* (Princeton, 1939) with the authors' matured views as expressed in the introduction to the 1966 edition.

[6] By a curious irony, the presidential address at the famous 1893 meeting of the American Historical Association dealt with "The Inadequate Recognition of Diplo-

As it was, these new historical approaches combined with the evidence of the new map to prove again the westward course of empire. The John Quincy Adams who had seen in the Preamble to the Treaty of Amity and Commerce with France the cornerstone of American foreign policy, and who had worked tirelessly for the expansion of commerce, gave way to a more modern Adams, negotiator of the Transcontinental Treaty and author of the Monroe Doctrine. Hawaii and the Philippines came to seem logical consequences of Texas and California, and few remembered that ships of the United States Navy had operated in both Indian Ocean and Mediterranean long before the first American frigate rounded Cape Horn, that the missionaries had reached further Asia before the Austins entered Texas, that Perry and Shufeldt alike had voyaged to the Far East by way of the Cape of Good Hope, or that, in the late nineteenth and early twentieth centuries, vessels of the Asiatic Squadron habitually proceeded to and from their duty station by way of Suez.

This last fact, paradoxically, had its own importance in furthering the new habits of mind. The annexation of the Philippines and the problem of China reemphasized the need for a less vulnerable passage to Asia; once the new isthmian canal was in prospect, a secure and stable Caribbean became a necessity. The effects of this strategic imperative upon the refurbishing of the Monroe Doctrine, together with the limited range of the new steam navies, reinforced the idea that the Atlantic was, ought to be, and so had always been a barrier. With the elevation of the Monroe Doctrine to a position of primacy in American foreign policy, and with the growing activism of the government, there developed a school of diplomatic history, wholly at variance with that of Theodore Lyman and Eugene Schuyler, which increasingly overlooked the healing ministrations of commerce and the action of the individual to focus on the doings of the state. The further emphasis on the mechanics of diplomacy which followed from the catastrophe of 1914 merely strengthened this preexisting tendency.

When to all this was added the development of a relativism which saw all religions as culturally determined and possessed of equal validity and which made the missionary a figure of fun, it is not hard to see how the early history of individual commercial enterprise, of

---

matists by Historians." Its author, President James B. Angell of the University of Michigan and former minister to China, was later to serve as minister to Turkey.

the police-force Navy, and of the gospel effort in the Levant came to be almost totally forgotten. Like Miss Preble, the nation turned its back upon its past.

2. *The Past Continued*

There was, of course, real justification for the new emphasis upon the Pacific, for among the most notable developments of the later nineteenth century was the rise of the Far East to world importance. Through the outlet from the Atlantic world created by the canal at Suez the European powers descended upon the Orient. Increasingly, the ancient Chinese Empire and its dependent kingdoms found themselves pressed between the maritime states of Europe and the eastward-moving Russian frontier. Shortly a third factor was added, as the Japanese, succeeding where Mahmud and Ismail had failed, assimilated their ancient culture to the arts of the West, and by creating a second extra-European center of maritime power brought about a strategic revolution analogous to that which had earlier followed the winning of American independence. Soon the United States found itself deeply entangled in the area. To the importance of these events the history of the twentieth century would bear eloquent witness.

Yet while East Asia was becoming an area of world concern, the shape of history was changing in other ways. No longer were the restless Europeans and their American cousins engaged in the exploration and settlement of empty space. The temperate grasslands of the world which had lain open to the age of discovery were now full, and their exploitation by an advanced agriculture and a modern transportation, together with the coming of steam-powered industry, had redirected the stream of population movement. No longer oriented to the frontiers, the Western nations were now becoming urbanized, with the consequence that their push into the Pacific and Far East was very different in nature from their earlier expansion into the western hemisphere. The main thrust of history now concerned the industrialization of the region between the Mississippi and the Urals, and when the cut at Suez let the Europeans through, their concern was no longer the colonization of areas which were in any case well populated, but involved the search for markets, for investment opportunity, and for strategic bases.

So, in a sense, the drama of Pacific history tended to obscure the facts. Despite the notable developments in eastern Asia, the North Atlantic remained the pivot of the world. From its two shores there continued to issue forth the new inventions and techniques which shaped and reshaped human society; across it there moved the greater part of the world's trade; and as the countries around its rim became more closely intertwined, the independence of 1776 began to give way to the interdependence of the twentieth century. In social structure the maturing United States gave momentary signs of approximating European patterns, while the liberalized and industrialized Europeans equally reflected American influence. Politically, despite the obeisance paid the Monroe Doctrine, American assimilation to the Atlantic community could be detected in the administrations of Grover Cleveland and Theodore Roosevelt. Culturally, this development was manifested in the transatlantic marriages of American heiresses, the transatlantic novels of Howells and James, the development of Anglo-American friendship, and in what the British journalist W. T. Stead could describe, as early as 1901, as *The Americanization of the World*.

Nor, for that matter, however clean it swept the history books, could America's new Oriental involvement eliminate in other areas the concrete legacies of her past. However Europeanized, however overshadowed by new Asiatic ventures, Mediterranean history did not stop. An American commerce continued with the Levant, and an American squadron still cruised the inland sea. The Near Eastern missionary establishment remained active, and the educational institutions supported by American philanthropy continued to prosper. And as the years went by and the internal condition of the Ottoman Empire continued to degenerate, these enterprises remained hostages to fortune.

So they proved when tragedy came to Armenia, long the center of missionary effort and the area of the evangelists' greatest Near Eastern successes. In 1894-95 the Sultan's exaggerated fears of conspiracy among his Armenian subjects led to massacres which made the Bulgarian horrors seem of small account, and which involved large losses of mission property. But in contrast to the Bulgarian episode, this bloodshed, although productive of indignation in the West, was not followed by European intervention, while a proposal of cooperative Anglo-American action, provisionally accepted by the Cleveland administration, equally failed to materialize. What did materialize, however, were some difficult negotiations with the

Turks, who at first refused compensation for the destruction of missionary property. Only in 1898 did the Sultan accept responsibility for the payment of damages.

Hardly had this agreement been reached when an American missionary, Miss Ellen Stone, was kidnapped by Macedonian brigands and held captive for five months, while a large ransom was raised in America and negotiations for her release were carried on both by the government and by President Washburn of Robert College. In the next year tension between the American minister and the Porte came close to causing a break in relations, while in 1903 and 1904 further missionary difficulties and renewed outbreaks of violence required visits of squadron units to Beirut. Since the latter year also witnessed, at the opposite end of the Mediterranean, the kidnapping of Perdicaris by the bandit Raisuli and the dispatch of warships to Tangier, there seemed reason enough to wonder whether disengagement from the Mediterranean would prove feasible, however great the attractions of China.[7]

These calls upon the European Squadron served to reemphasize the close connection, existing since the Syrian Wars, between the two most visible Near Eastern manifestations of the American republic, the missionary establishment and the Navy. The aftermath of the Armenian massacres brought further testimonial to this relationship, as well as evidence of changing times, in events which seemed to parody the early activities of Goodell, Eckford, and Porter at the Constantinople of Mahmud. Reluctant at first to accept the missionary claims, Abdul Hamid finally proposed that the payments be disguised by inclusion in the price of a cruiser which he contemplated having built in the United States. This curious mixture of sacred and secular finance was accepted by the Americans, and the contract for the warship was signed with the Cramp Company

---

[7] Verney and Dambmann, *Puissances étrangères*, pp. 59-62; A.L.P. Dennis, *Adventures in American Diplomacy, 1896-1906* (New York, 1928), pp. 443-45, 447-71; E. R. May, *Imperial Democracy* (New York, 1961), pp. 25-60; E. M. Earle, "American Missions in the Near East," 7 *Foreign Affairs*, 398-417; J. A. DeNovo, *American Interests and Policies in the Middle East, 1900-1939* (Minneapolis, 1963), pp. 1-45. In 1899, in *Captain Brassbound's Conversion*, George Bernard Shaw sent an American cruiser to Morocco. Of the ship's archetypally American commanding officer, Captain Hamlin Kearney, the author observed that "the world, pondering on the great part of its own future which is in his hands, contemplates him with wonder as to what the devil he will evolve into in another century or two." Shaw's own hypothesis was presumably implicit in the officer's name, evocative of both the missionary and the naval traditions.

of Philadelphia, perhaps appropriately, on Christmas morning, 1900. Early in 1904 the cruiser *Medjidie* reached the Golden Horn under the command of Captain Ransford D. Bucknam of the building firm, and so greatly did Bucknam's "bluff personality" commend him to the Sultan that he was retained as naval adviser, admiral, and pasha, in which capacities he served until his death in 1915.[8]

As well as the link between missions and Navy, there remained that between the Navy and commerce. But commerce, in the new age, was assuming new forms. In command of the battleship *Kentucky* in Turkish waters at the time the missionary claims were being pressed was Captain Colby M. Chester. Summoned to Constantinople and there feted, like so many of his predecessors, by the Sultan, Chester derived from his visit a vision of the economic possibilities of the Ottoman Empire. In 1908, following his retirement, he returned to the capital as the representative of a number of American commercial groups. The result of a second cordial reception was the organization of the Ottoman-American Development Company and the projection of a grandiose scheme which envisaged linking the Black Sea, the Mediterranean, and the Persian border by a thousand miles of Anatolian railroad and the exploitation of mineral deposits along the right-of-way. At the outset the same old considerations of American distance, impartiality, and skill, and the possibility of playing the United States off against the powers of Europe, made for a favorable Turkish attitude, and there followed some years of negotiation for formal approval. But despite a remarkable degree of State Department support for an effort in dollar diplomacy which lacked either the strategic rationale of Caribbean episodes or the concern, evident in Chinese ventures, for the integrity of the country involved, the concession never finally materialized.[9]

Along with the ancient triad of American activities—commerce, missions, and Navy—there survived the old American attitudes. The traditional belief in limited government showed itself in 1909 in presidential eulogy of Ottoman and Persian constitutionalism.

[8] *New York Tribune*, 2 May 1904, 30 May 1915; Pears, *Forty Years*, pp. 171-72; Dennis, *Adventures in Diplomacy*, pp. 450-52. Despite his rank and station, Bucknam was no Porter, and his contributions to the Turkish Navy were of small importance. But the cruiser had a long life: mined and sunk, salvaged by the Russians, recaptured by the Austro-German armies and returned to the Turks, *Medjidie* survived the First World War and at the time of the Second was still in use as a training ship.

[9] DeNovo, *American Interests*, pp. 58-87, 210-28.

Sympathy for oppressed nationalities continued to be manifested in connection with the Armenians, Jews, and Arabs of the Turkish Empire. The willingness to assist, when opportunity offered, in providing techniques that would make both progress and self-determination possible, also remained.

As to this last, the expanding sway of Europe had pretty well eliminated Mediterranean opportunities, but in 1886 the Persians, pressed between Russia and British India and alarmed by the British occupation of Egypt, opened negotiations. Hoping to ward off the threat to independence posed by European economic exploitation, the country which thirty years earlier had sought American naval aid now offered "industrial and commercial ascendancy" in exchange for American technical assistance. Once again nothing came of the talks that followed, but the missionary connection remained, to provide both bond and possibility of trouble. The trouble came first, in 1904, with the murder of a missionary by Kurdish tribesmen; the bond appeared five years later, in the course of civil war between constitutionalist and royalist factions, when Howard Baskerville, a young Princeton graduate and teacher at a missionary school, was killed leading a constitutionalist charge. That the need for outside help, preferably American, also persisted was shown by the Persian requests for financial advice which resulted in the Shuster mission of 1911 and the Millspaugh mission of 1922-27.[10]

These American continuities, and still more the history of the entire Near East, were powerfully affected by the First World War. With the entrance of Turkey into the conflict, the need to protect the American missionary establishment and educational system again made for calls upon the Navy. For the teachers and missionaries in Turkey, life was made difficult from the start by wartime shortages and tensions and by outbreaks of typhus and smallpox, while in Persia as well the missionary stations suffered from the backwash of the struggle. But shortages and epidemics were as nothing to the disaster which impended, for in 1915 there took place the greatest of Armenian massacres, an effort at genocide which brought tragedy to the missionary community, public outrage in America, and protest from the American government, and which led to the founding of Near East Relief, a philanthropic endeavor which in

[10] Merle Curti and Kendall Birr, *Prelude to Point Four* (Madison, Wis., 1954), pp. 72-74; DeNovo, *American Interests*, pp. 46-47; Yeselson, *United States-Persian Diplomatic Relations*.

the next fifteen years was to raise more than one hundred million dollars.

If unprecedented in magnitude, this response was traditional in form, repeating as it did that of the 1820's to the war in Greece and that of 1860 to the massacres in the Lebanon, and tradition continued to influence events even after the United States had joined in the war against Germany. Although diplomatic relations were severed by Turkey, neither country declared war, while with Bulgaria relations were not even broken, and throughout the conflict the Bulgarian minister, the former Professor Panaretoff of Robert College, remained at his Washington post. In the aftermath, again, there were echoes of earlier times, as the United States once more found itself represented at Constantinople by a naval officer of great distinction in the person of Rear Admiral Mark L. Bristol, high commissioner from 1919 to 1927.[11]

The defeat of the Central Powers gave history another chance, or so at least it seemed. Armed like the early commissioners with "Innocence and the Olive Branch," Woodrow Wilson voyaged to Europe to attempt the remaking of the world. With him as model he carried the history of the American past, in the emphasis of the Fourteen Points on the freedom of the seas, the elimination of artificial economic barriers, and the self-determination of peoples, and in the eighteenth-century panacea of a general association of nations which would guarantee the political independence and territorial integrity of great and small alike. Less obvious, perhaps, but just as important as the promise of these principles for European nationalisms, were the opportunities they offered in territories ruled formerly by the Ottoman sultans.[12]

The collapse of the Ottoman Empire left a very large vacuum. To the crossroads of three continents, to the birthplace of three great religions, and to countries of ancient civilization now beginning to approach modernity came the chance to make all new. And to many, as it turned out, the preferred means of accomplishing this renovation was the replacement of the House of Othman by the President of the United States. Such a succession, however surpris-

---

[11] ABCFM *Annual Reports*; 13 *Near East Colleges News Letter*, 1; Earle, "American Missions"; J. L. Barton, *The Story of Near East Relief* (New York, 1930); DeNovo, *American Interests.*

[12] Gilbert, "New Diplomacy," 4 *World Politics*, 37-38. Wilson's Twelfth Point called for autonomy for the subject nationalities of the Ottoman Empire and for permanent opening of the Dardanelles to the ships and commerce of all nations.

ing, had been earlier anticipated: in his turn-of-the-century vision of the coming American Æra, W. T. Stead had predicted that another missionary murder would bring Dewey and Sampson to the Dardanelles. Then the "Stars and Stripes would soon fly over the waters of the Sea of Marmora, and the thunder of American guns would sound the death-knell of the Ottoman dynasty"; in the interest of order the Americans would occupy Constantinople, and the "great Republic of the West [would] become the agent for restoring prosperity and peace to the desolated East." No such events in fact ensued, but with war's end the opportunity to help rather than to punish presented itself.[13]

By January 1919, Wilson's calls for the impartial adjustment of colonial claims and for opportunity of unmolested autonomous development for the peoples of the former Ottoman Empire had led to Allied acceptance of the mandate system. Moved by the historic American connection with the Levant, the President then secured the establishment of an international commission to ascertain, in this connection, the condition and wishes of the subject peoples of the Near East. But Allied appointments to the commission failed to materialize, and in June the American members, President Henry C. King of Oberlin College and Charles R. Crane, a retired Chicago manufacturer, set forth on their own to investigate the territories explored by Fisk and Parsons a century before.

After a six-week tour of Syria and Palestine, during which more than four hundred delegations and nearly two thousand petitions were received, the King-Crane commission drew up its report. Recommending that Syria, Mesopotamia, Armenia, Anatolia, and Constantinople be provisionally recognized as independent states, subject to the assistance and supervision of a mandatory power, the commission reported that everywhere popular opinion favored the United States as holder of the mandate. In two of these areas there were serious obstacles to such a solution: Mesopotamia seemed too remote, while with regard to Syria the Balfour Declaration, the existence of an influential Jewish community in the United States, and the feeling of the commission that a Jewish Palestine would violate the principle of self-determination promised future embarrassment. But for the other three regions—Constantinople, Anatolia,

---

[13] Stead, *Americanization of the World*, pp. 195-96. For a much earlier British vision of America as the rejuvenator of Turkey, see Richard Cobden, *Political Writings* (London, 1903), I, 19-20.

and Armenia—it seemed clear that a single mandatory power was essential and that the wishes of the people and the convictions, faith, and record of the United States pointed to American assumption of this responsibility.[14]

Except for a brief visit to Constantinople, the King-Crane commission had confined its investigations to the area south of the Taurus. So to conduct the necessary researches in Armenia, President Wilson in September dispatched an American military mission headed by Major General James G. Harbord to the area anciently explored by Smith and Dwight. After traversing all Asia Minor and Transcaucasia, the Harbord group submitted a report which urged the assignment of Constantinople with its European hinterland, together with Armenia, Anatolia, and Transcaucasia, to a single mandatory power, and which reported that a plebiscite fairly taken in these areas would in all probability opt for the United States. "Without visiting the Near East," the military mission noted, "it is not possible for an American to realize even faintly the respect, faith, and affection with which our country is regarded throughout that region. . . .[It] is the one faith which is held alike by Christian and Moslem, by Jew and Gentile, by prince and peasant."

Whether the faith of the Armenians and Turks was sufficient reason for the United States to undertake a task that would require the long-term commitment of a couple of divisions of troops and the expenditure, over the first five years, of three-quarters of a billion dollars, was another question. So the soldiers then proceeded, in military fashion, to list the reasons for and against the undertaking of so great and novel a responsibility. The conclusion, transcending practical considerations and more American than military, was that there existed a moral imperative to assume the burden in the interest of the populations involved, and that the United States could not give the answer of Cain.[15]

To this point the trail blazed by colonial shipmasters and followed by the Navy and the missionaries had led: not merely poets but representatives of government now called upon America to "lead whole nations in the walks of truth." But such devotion to "humanity's extended cause" had always been the property of a minority, in the world and also in the United States. A task of this sort, if not

---

[14] 55 *Editor and Publisher*, i-xxviii; *FR 1919: PPC*, xii, 749-86; DeNovo, *American Interests*, pp. 119-24.

[15] *FR 1919*, ii, 841-89; DeNovo, *American Interests*, pp. 122-24.

of this size, could be accepted by individuals or groups, but for the government it was another matter: such a politicizing of disinterested benevolence required a larger consensus than was yet available. At Paris, as King and Crane set forth on their errand, cynicism was already affecting the peacemakers; in America, after the reports were in, the President could propose but Congress in the end disposed. In September 1919 a joint resolution authorizing the employment of American forces to maintain order in Armenia was buried in committee. In May 1920, when Wilson reported the tender of the Armenian mandate to the United States and urged, in eighteenth-century phraseology, the virtue of the "appearance on the scene of a Power emancipated from the prepossessions of the old World," it took Congress only ten days to decline the offer.[16]

So other dispositions were made of the former Ottoman territories, some determined by the British and French, some self-determined by the inhabitants of the region themselves. Unwilling to undertake political commitments, the United States returned to Washington's Great Rule, limiting its efforts to the traditional protection of American citizens and American property and to a policy "purely commercial." No more than in the earlier time, however, could this amount to total withdrawal. Many continued to run to and fro, and American philanthropic, business, and technical contacts with the Near East suffered no diminution; knowledge continued to increase, and the period between the wars became, among other things, a golden age of American Near Eastern archaeology.

Through the interwar years much of the American contact with the Levant remained traditional in form, although affected in greater or lesser degree by the emergent nationalisms to which the works of earlier generations had so effectively contributed. But two notable changes did take place, as the Zionist movement began to gain a degree of support which would come to influence policy, and as the ancient invoice of figs and opium came to be outweighed by a modern exploitation of petroleum. With this development the stream of oil was reversed, and where once the lamps in the Prophet's temple had been lit by Pennsylvania kerosene, now pipelines and tankers brought this most strategic of commodities from the cradle of civilization to fuel the mechanized societies of the West. By the thirties the diplomacy of petroleum and the problems presented by

---

[16] *Congressional Record*, 66C, 2S, p. 7533; DeNovo, *American Interests*, p. 126.

a developing Zionism had become principal determinants of American Near Eastern policy.

The Second World War and its aftermath clarified the underlying shape of things. In American strategy, Europe and the Mediterranean took precedence over the Pacific, while Atlantic Charter and North Atlantic Pact evidenced the recognition that an Atlantic community had replaced the Atlantic moat. A century and a half of spreading technological development and of ideas of popular government had changed the ancient formulations. Even in Europe, Columbia's bliss had sprung, and while the newly powerful United States puzzled over the problem of how to employ state power in the service of an antistatist ideology, the maritime nations of the Old World had become liberalized. Paralleling these developments and aided by the same technology had come an inland displacement of the tyrant, as George III and Napoleon were replaced by the Kaiser's and Hitler's Germany and by Stalin's Russia. Now the "great fallen pow'rs" lived to the eastward, and since power had always been the enemy, it was possible—indeed perhaps necessary—to see Atlantic Europe as friend. So an America whose early bias had been anti-European, and most of all anti-British and anti-French, found herself leagued with those ancient states.

With the entrance of the United States into the conflict, American moves along the new frontier of power repeated, in surprising degree, the earlier moves along the old. As the Barbary wars had been followed up by support for the Greek revolt and been capitalized on in the negotiations for the Turkish treaty, so the strategic gains of the landings in North Africa were consolidated by the Truman Doctrine's aid to Greece and Turkey. With the coming of the cold war, the sea first cruised by Dale and Preble came to be patrolled by the United States Sixth Fleet, while within the NATO structure there developed an international naval force of the sort first urged by Jefferson.

Yet what was at least as notable, in the years after 1945, as the echoes of a distant past, was the contrast with events of a quarter-century before. This time there was no relapse, and pursuit of the basic ends of policy continued after victory had been won. A generation after Wilson's failure it proved possible to accept membership in the new international organization, and to take at least a step toward the uniting of the nations and the federalizing of mankind. The rise of a new center of unbridled power and the dangers which this presented brought a rapid response in the support of threatened friendly governments and in a far-ranging network of military arrangements.

But alliances and armaments were not all. Along with strategy and policy, humanity was also attended to, and here the American continuities were marked. Still impelled by the old Hopkinsian morality, the citizens of the United States continued to perform functions which elsewhere, if they were attended to at all, were left to the attention of the state, while their government, having assumed with their approval large responsibilities for the human race, set itself to tasks no other government had ever contemplated.

Again, as after the preceding war, massive aid was sent forth as the Americans taxed themselves both publicly and privately in the interest of distant peoples. In addition to the vast governmental expenditures for relief, for economic reconstruction, and for development there continued a large-scale private philanthropy of religious and eleemosynary groups. In Palestine, whither the Jews at last returned, there arose a newly independent state, largely financed by American private citizens. To assist in the defense of freedom, as Porters and Stones had earlier done, military advisory groups proliferated around the world. Again, as in the early years of the republic, there came a systematic effort to reduce the barriers to international trade. Under the auspices of Point Four and the Peace Corps, the "philanthropic band" again set forth, to teach a progressive agriculture and industry and to spread the gospel of education. In a world where much was changing almost beyond recognition, one thing remained curiously the same. As the second centenary of their independence approached, the citizens of the United States continued still the creatures of the American Enlightenment: friends of humanity, believers in rational solutions, and hopers for the millennium.

A Note on Source Materials

In the footnotes I have attempted to provide a sufficient indication of the sources on which any given passage is based, without, it is to be hoped, overloading the text or exhausting the reader. Here a few additional comments may prove useful in suggesting lines of approach to any who may be interested in pursuing these matters further.

Archival Sources

Although published works have been of the greatest importance in fleshing out the story, it seems proper to say that the chronological structure of the narrative derives almost wholly from the archival sources, with their unmatched continuities. I have relied heavily upon the records of the Department of State (primarily the Diplomatic and Consular Instructions and Despatches; to a lesser degree the Notes to Foreign Legations and the records of Special Agents); on those of the Navy Department (Commanders', Captains', and Squadron Letters; the Area 4 File; certain categories of outgoing correspondence); and on the archives of the American Board of Commissioners for Foreign Missions. State and Navy department records are located in the National Archives, Washington, D.C.; the papers of the American Board are deposited in the Houghton Library, Harvard University.

These are extremely rich collections: the diplomatic and consular correspondence is highly productive, and the naval and missionary archives only slightly less so. Yet while the utility of this material goes far beyond the history of purely American activity, its employment for other purposes has historically been very limited, apparently owing to the belief in American absence (or abstinence) from the nineteenth-century world. More than a generation ago, when discussing the sources for his *Americans in Eastern Asia* (New York, 1922), Tyler Dennett observed that the American diplomatic correspondence had been "uniformly ignored" by historians of other nations. Whatever the situation in Far Eastern studies today, the comment holds generally good for the areas along the frontier of Europe. The meridian of partition still divides the historical profession.

Much of the governmental material, it should be noted, is in fact available in one or another published form. Of the greatest importance here is the program, instituted by the National Archives in 1940, of making available at reasonable cost microfilm copies of the records of the State and Navy departments, a service for which conventional expressions of appreciation seem inadequate. But the United States has always been the least secretive of nations, and there is also a good deal of official material in print. For the period 1789 to 1828, the *American State Papers*—six volumes on *Foreign Relations*, four on *Naval Affairs*, and two on *Commerce and Navigation*—are extremely useful. The publication by the Navy Department of two collections assembled under the supervision of the late Commodore Dudley W. Knox, U.S.N., the seven-volume *Naval Documents Related to the Quasi-War Between the United States and France* (Washington, 1935-38) and the six-volume *Naval Documents Related to the United States Wars with the Barbary Powers* (Washington, 1939-44), made it for the first time easy to go beyond the traditional emphasis on cutlasses and roundshot for the period 1785-1807. A large amount of useful material for the years from 1828 to 1861 can be located in the Congressional Documents series by way of the indispensable A. R. Hasse, *Index to United States Documents Relating to Foreign Affairs, 1828–1861* (Washington, 1914-21). For the years after 1861, extensive excerpts from the diplomatic correspondence and quantities of commercial information are accessible in the annual volumes of *Foreign Relations* and *Commercial Relations*. On treaty negotiations, the admirable David Hunter Miller, *Treaties and Other International Acts of the United States of America* (Washington, 1931-37) is of the greatest value.

Published Works: General

As regards the question of published books, it seems fair to say that the principal subjects dealt with in this study have been somewhat neglected in recent decades, and that our ancestors knew more about, and were more concerned with, the merchant marine, the peacetime employment of the Navy, and the missionary effort than we. Something of this contrast can be seen by comparing the contents of *Appleton's Cyclopaedia of American Biography* (New York, 1887-1900) with that of the *Dictionary of American Biography* (New York, 1928-36). Of squadron or ship commanders mentioned in the text of this book, Bell, Breese, Engle, English, Glisson, Lavalette, Leroy, and Morgan are sketched in *Appleton* but omitted from the later work; although the missionaries come out better, the older compilation provides data on Josiah Brewer, Daniel Temple, and (most importantly) Rufus Anderson, while the newer one does not. For historical writing in general, the situation is much the same. Outdated though they are in various ways, the old books are frequently better than the new ones, and in some cases the old books are all there are.

To these general statements, however, certain exceptions must be made. The first stems from the expansion of the historical profession and of historical writing and from the consequent search for new subjects of investigation. These developments have brought a number of special studies, both published and unpublished, of American relations with various countries (including those of Europe, Africa, and the Near East), of the American response to specific events (such as the revolutions of 1848), and of the lives of various individuals (such as Samuel Gridley Howe and George Perkins Marsh) who were active overseas. Secondly, the growing interest of recent years in the development of backward regions has focused attention on the Ottoman and Egyptian experiences in the nineteenth century (and on those of China and Japan as well) and on the American contribution to the "third world" of the traditional societies. To this interest in modernization we owe such works as H.A.R. Gibb and Harold Bowen, *Islamic Society and the West* (London and New York, 1950-57), Bernard Lewis, *The Emergence of Modern Turkey* (London, 1961) and *The Middle East and the West* (Bloomington, Indiana, 1964), and R. H. Davison, *Reform in the Ottoman Empire, 1856–1876* (Princeton, 1963); the concern with America's part in the process has produced Merle Curti and Kendall Birr, *Prelude to Point Four: American Technical Missions Overseas, 1838–1938* (Madison, Wisconsin, 1954) and Merle Curti, *American Philanthropy Abroad: A History* (New Brunswick, N.J., 1963). Finally, note must be taken of the recent appearance of two studies of American activity in the Levant, John A. DeNovo, *American Interests and Policies in the Middle East, 1900–1939* (Minneapolis, 1963), and David H. Finnie, *Pioneers East: The Early American Experience in the Middle East* (Cambridge, 1967). The first of these works is a solid and comprehensive study of the years from the turn of the century to the outbreak of the Second World War, with an introductory chapter on what preceded. The second deals with the period before 1850, with emphasis on the second quarter of the century.

Since Finnie modeled his discussion on the travel books of John L. Stephens, the treatment is episodic and the continuities are sometimes difficult to pin down, but the book is based on an extensive acquaintance with the contemporary literature and includes a useful bibliography.

The Poets of the Enlightenment

The Hartford or Connecticut Wits have been hardly treated by the posterity for which they hoped so much; more hardly, it seems to me, than they deserve. Neither Barrett Wendell nor Vernon Parrington could find much good to say about them, and such has been the antihistorical bias of recent literary study that one can now find teachers of American literature who do not recognize their names. Although their works have never been reprinted *in extenso*, and although those who wish the full flavor must read them in the original editions, short snippets (usually Dwight's "Columbia" and Barlow's "Hasty Pudding") appear in most anthologies of American literature. Somewhat longer selections are available in V. L. Parrington (ed.), *The Connecticut Wits* (New York, 1926; reprinted, Hamden, Connecticut, 1963), but the editor's introduction suggests that he read little of what he anthologized. Fortunately, however, one scholar has indeed read the corpus, and Leon Howard, *The Connecticut Wits* (Chicago, 1943) is a solid, workmanlike, and sympathetic study. For the persistence of Enlightenment ideals in a very different context, see the first chapter and last word of Gunnar Myrdal, *An American Dilemma* (New York, 1944).

Foreign Commerce and Merchant Marine

If the professors of literature ignore the Wits, the writers of books on diplomatic and economic history tend to skip lightly over questions of trade and shipping. The standard general treatment remains the aging and inadequate E. R. Johnson et al., *History of Domestic and Foreign Commerce of the United States* (Washington, 1915). Although three volumes of the *Economic History of the United States*—C. P. Nettels, *The Emergence of a National Economy, 1775–1815* (New York, 1962), G. R. Taylor, *The Transportation Revolution, 1815–1860* (New York, 1951), and E. C. Kirkland, *Industry Comes of Age, 1860–1897* (New York, 1961)—provide useful discussions of maritime commerce, it remains true, as Taylor observes, that "surprisingly little careful analytical work has been done on the general history of foreign trade." For detailed statistics on what came in and what went out, resort must still be had to the government documents. For the early period, however, Timothy Pitkin, *Statistical View of the Commerce of the United States* (New Haven, 1835), and J. Smith Homans, Jr., *An Historical and Statistical Account of the Foreign Commerce of the United States* (New York, 1857) will generally suffice. On the theoretical level, those who prefer to derive their ideas about the virtues of maritime trade and the commercial nature of American diplomacy from prose sources rather than from poetry should consult Theodore Lyman, Jr., *The Diplomacy of the United States* (Boston, 1826), the first historical treatment of its subject, and Jonathan Elliot, *The American Diplomatic Code* (Washington, 1834); of secondary publications in this area, Joseph Dorfman, *The Economic Mind in American Civilization* (New York, 1946-49), is preeminent.

Although the quantity of published material on the American merchant marine greatly exceeds its utility, two books and one article deserve mention as touching on the subject of the present work. S. E. Morison, *The Maritime History of Massachusetts, 1783–1860* (Boston, 1921) is a classic which unfortunately has no parallels dealing with the other seaboard states. J.G.B. Hutchins, *The American Maritime Industries and Public Policy, 1789–1914* (Cambridge, 1941) is a study of great value with an extremely useful bibliography. On the importance of the merchant marine to the well-being of the entire American economy, see C. J. Bullock et al., "The Balance of Trade of the United States," 1 *Review of Economic Statistics,* 215-66. For some indication of how maritime commerce has in fact worked to unite, or at least to link, the nations, see Henry Reiff, *The United States and the Treaty Law of the Sea* (Minneapolis, 1959).

The Navy

Here the essential guide to the extensive nineteenth-century literature is R. W. Neeser, *Statistical and Chronological History of the United States Navy, 1775–1907* (New York, 1909): Volume 1 contains an inventory of government archival material and a bibliography of 9,284 published items; Volume 2 provides an extensive chronology of naval events with references to both archival and published sources. The collections of documents on the difficulties with France and Barbary, edited under the supervision of Commodore D. W. Knox, have already been mentioned. Knox's own *History of the United States Navy* (New York, 1936; revised edition, 1948) has some useful chapters on the relation of the Old Navy to the support and expansion of ocean commerce. In this same context, C. O. Paullin, *Diplomatic Negotiations of American Naval Officers* (Baltimore, 1912) remains the standard treatment of its subject. Until the publication of Harold and Margaret Sprout, *The Rise of American Naval Power, 1776–1918* (Princeton, 1939), naval policy, as opposed to naval warfare, had been pretty much neglected; for the early period, the Sprouts' work has now been supplemented by Marshall Smelser, *The Congress Founds the Navy, 1787–1798* (Notre Dame, 1959). Despite their great utility, both of these works seem to me to overemphasize the Federalist-Republican and North-South cleavages, a tendency for which J. H. Macleod, "Jefferson and the Navy: A Defense," 8 *Huntington Library Quarterly*, 153-84 provides a partial corrective.

For the activities of the various squadrons, the archival records can be helpfully supplemented by the cruise journals, memoirs, and biographies which exist in considerable quantity, especially for the period before the Civil War, and which can be tracked down through Neeser's bibliography. Those that I have found most directly useful are cited in the footnotes. In some cases the authors of these books are interesting, quite apart from their published works, as exemplifications of the various aspects of American overseas activity. One may instance the Reverend Walter Colton, author of *Ship and Shore: or, Leaves from the Journal of a Cruise to the Levant* (New York, 1835) and of *A Visit to Constantinople and Athens* (New York, 1836). A graduate of Yale and of the Andover seminary and a onetime worker for the American Board, Colton served for almost two decades as naval chaplain, at home, in the Mediterranean, and in the Pacific; assisting, in 1846, in the extension of the area of freedom to the American West Coast, he found himself first the appointed, and then the elected, alcalde of Monterey, and is said to have been the author of the first report of California gold published in the Eastern press.

One wholly neglected aspect of naval history, so far as I am aware, is that of the logistic support of the cruising squadrons, and the role, in this connection, of Navy Agent and Naval Storekeeper. Except for a brief mention of domestic Navy Agents in *The Jeffersonians*

(New York, 1951), L. D. White's volumes on administrative history ignore these functionaries, yet by the 1840's Navy Agents or Naval Storekeepers were permanently stationed at London, Marseilles, Port Mahon, Porto Praya, St. Thomas, Rio de Janeiro, Lima, the Sandwich Islands, and Hong Kong. Some interesting questions about the Anglo-American connection and the strategic freedom of American naval units in European waters are suggested by the importance of the London Agency, long held by the British firm of Baring Brothers (and briefly by the Rothschilds), through which all squadron funds were channeled; R. W. Hidy, *The House of Baring in American Trade and Finance* (Cambridge, 1949) is the authority here. A somewhat similar vulnerability developed in the post-Civil War years, especially after the coming of the Atlantic cable, when all communications with the European Squadron (as with continental legations and consulates) were handled by way of the Government Despatch Agent in London.

Foreign Missions

For the remarkable worldwide growth of Christianity in the nineteenth century, see K. S. Latourette, *History of the Expansion of Christianity* (New York, 1937-45); Volumes 4 and 6 of this magisterial work contain material touching on the present study. As good a way as any to get the feel of the missionary movement is to spend some time with E. M. Bliss (ed.), *The Encyclopaedia of Missions* (New York, 1891), a much more compendious work than either its predecessor, Harvey Newcomb, *Cyclopedia of Missions* (New York, 1855) or the single-volume revision and condensation of 1904 edited by H. O. Dwight, H. A. Tupper, Jr., and Bliss. The edition of 1891 provides the student with histories of missionary boards, missionary societies, missionary fields, and missionary stations; with descriptions and facsimile verses of Bible translations; with biographical sketches of missionaries and with excellent maps of missionary lands. As appendices it includes statistical and other tables, a list of Bible translations, and a bibliography of more than five thousand titles dealing with missionary work, missionary workers, and missionary lands.

Sixty years ago F. H. Foster, *Genetic History of the New England Religion* (Chicago, 1907) made the connection between the Awakening, the Edwardeans, and the movement to evangelize the world,

461

but the subject has drawn little subsequent attention. The only published study of the origins of the American missionary effort is O. W. Elsbree, *The Rise of the Missionary Spirit in America, 1790–1815* (Williamsport, Pennsylvania, 1928). Alan Heimert, *Religion and the American Mind from the Great Awakening to the Revolution* (Cambridge, 1966), which in fact pursues its subject into the nineteenth century, is wholly domestic in orientation, makes no mention of the missionary impulse, and is hard on Samuel Hopkins, but its insights into the Awakening and the significance of the millennial hope suggest answers to questions Elsbree never thought to ask. By far the best work on the origins and growth of the movement is C. J. Phillips' regrettably unpublished Harvard dissertation, "Protestant America and the Pagan World: The First Half-Century of the American Board of Commissioners for Foreign Missions, 1810-1860."

On the gospel effort in the Levant, four historical treatments deserve attention: Rufus Anderson, *History of the Missions of the American Board of Commissioners for Foreign Missions to the Oriental Churches* (Boston, 1872) provides a detailed narrative, written by the foreign secretary of the Board from the correspondence from the field; Julius Richter, *A History of Protestant Missions in the Near East* (New York and Chicago, 1910) takes in the activities of other missionary societies and serves to emphasize how largely the Near Eastern field was an American monopoly; Leon Arpee, *The Armenian Awakening: A History of the Armenian Church, 1820–1860* (Chicago and London, 1909), P. E. Shaw, *American Contacts with the Eastern Churches, 1820–1870* (Chicago, 1937), and A. L. Tibawi, *American Interests in Syria, 1800–1901* (Oxford, 1966) are useful. Thomas Laurie, *The Ely Volume* (Boston, 1881), not confined to the Near East, is important for its suggestions regarding cultural interaction. Many of the missionary biographies are arid enough, but some are of great interest; anyone wishing to sample the field might begin with William Goodell, *The Old and the New; or, The Changes of Thirty Years in the East* (New York, 1853), with E.D.G. Prime's biography of Goodell, *Forty Years in the Turkish Empire* (New York, 1876), and with two books by Cyrus Hamlin, *Among the Turks* (New York, 1878) and *My Life and Times* (Boston and Chicago, 1893).

Like the naval presence in the Mediterranean, the missionary effort in the Near East raises interesting questions in the sphere of

462

Anglo-American relations: in the first efforts at cooperation, in the support provided by British consuls and diplomats, in rivalry and competition with the emissaries of the Church of England, in the financial assistance provided by the Turkish Missions' Aid Society and the contributors to the founding of the Syrian Protestant College. But this is an aspect of the generalized reforming effort which Frank Thistlethwaite, *The Anglo-American Connection in the Early Nineteenth Century* (Philadelphia, 1959) does not touch on. It is perhaps worth noting incidentally that overseas transfers of funds for the American Board, as for the Navy and State departments, were handled by Baring Brothers.

Relations with Particular Countries

The literature of this more conventionally diplomatic aspect of foreign relations is covered, for works published up to 1933, in S. F. Bemis and G. G. Griffin, *Guide to the Diplomatic History of the United States, 1775–1921* (Washington, 1933). Henry Blumenthal, *A Reappraisal of Franco-American Relations, 1830–1871* (Chapel Hill, N.C., 1959) is thorough and useful; H. M. Adams, *Prussian-American Relations, 1775–1871* (Western Reserve, 1960) is much slighter, although helpful on the American side of the story. Although French E. Chadwick, author of *The Relations of the United States and Spain: Diplomacy* (New York, 1909), was a retired rear admiral, he makes no mention of Mediterranean relations, the Mediterranean Squadron, or the history of the base facilities at Port Mahon; nor, for that matter, does anybody else. On Italian affairs, the works of H. R. Marraro, *American Opinion on the Unification of Italy, 1846–1861* (New York, 1932) and *Diplomatic Relations Between the United States and the Kingdom of the Two Sicilies, 1816–1861* (New York, 1951), are helpful. On Greece, the pioneer articles of E. M. Earle are still basic; the most recent and most compendious treatment is S. A. Larrabee, *Hellas Observed: The American Experience of Greece, 1775–1865* (New York, 1957). As indicated in the footnotes, interest in American-Bulgarian relations had a brief flurry in the second decade of this century, stimulated on the Bulgarian side by worries about the postwar settlement. For the Ottoman Empire, W. L. Wright's unpublished Princeton dissertation on "American Relations with Turkey to 1831" is detailed and meticulous; L. J. Gordon, *American Relations with Turkey, 1830–*

1930: An Economic Interpretation (Philadelphia, 1932) is a useful work which, however, never quite lives up to either title or subtitle. For Syria, there is little beyond the missionary literature and the book by A. L. Tibawi noted above. On American-Egyptian relations, L. C. Wright's unpublished Columbia dissertation, "United States Policy toward Egypt, 1830-1914" is an adequate survey and guide to the material.

Of two published works on the American contingent in Egypt, Pierre Crabitès, *Americans in the Egyptian Army* (London, 1938), the work of an American judge on the Cairo mixed court, is the better; W. B. Hesseltine and H. C. Wolf, *The Blue and the Gray on the Nile* (Chicago, 1961) contains a deal of personal information about the Americans but shows little understanding of the situation in Egypt. By far the most voluminous and useful source on the Egyptian Army in this period and on the work of its American officers is Georges Douin's monumental *Histoire du règne du Khédive Ismaïl* (Rome and Cairo, 1933-41). Of the writings by American participants in these events, the book of E. E. Farman, consul and judge, *Egypt and its Betrayal* (New York, 1908) and that of W. M. Dye, the soldier, *Moslem Egypt and Christian Abyssinia* (New York, 1880) are perhaps the most valuable. General Loring's *A Confederate Soldier in Egypt* (New York, 1884) is half travel book and half personal experience, the latter half being the more interesting. Charles Chaillé-Long (C. C. Long to his comrades in arms, but more elegantly hyphenated in his literary manifestations and in later life) described his trip upstream in *Central Africa: Naked Truths of Naked People* (London, 1876); Gordon, Arabi Pasha, and the Mahdi in *The Three Prophets* (New York, 1884); and everything in *My Life in Four Continents* (London, 1912). Since the publication of Lytton Strachey's *Eminent Victorians*, Long's veracity has come under heavy fire from the Gordon brigade; my own impression is that while his stories tended to improve with the passage of time, on the whole he checks out pretty well.

Books of Travel and Description

Increased literacy, increased wealth and leisure, and improved modes of transport made the nineteenth century notable for travel and exploration and for writing and publishing on strange lands and far places. As the prophet Daniel had foreseen, many ran to and fro and knowledge was greatly increased, and Americans participated vigorously in both activities. The naval and missionary memoirs, noted above, are of course specialized types of travel books, but there also exists an extensive literature outside these categories, a considerable sampling of which can be found in any large library. Most famous of all American contributions to the genre are the works of John L. Stephens, "the American traveller," whose *Incidents of Travel in Egypt, Arabia Petraea, and the Holy Land* (New York, 1837) and *Incidents of Travel in Greece, Turkey, Russia, and Poland* (New York, 1838) preceded his better-known descriptions of Central America and Yucatan. But there are a good many others of comparable merit, and in any case if Stephens sold well, he was far outsold by W. M. Thomson, one of the missionaries of the American Board, whose *The Land and the Book* (New York, 1859) was one of the most successful works of description of all time. Finnie, *Pioneers East*, has an eight-page appendix which lists American writing "relating to American activities in the Middle East before 1850." Bliss, *Encyclopaedia of Missions*, offers a still more extensive listing of books of travel, covering the entire missionary world and complete to 1890, which includes French, German, and Italian, as well as English-language works. In conclusion, it seems appropriate to cite the book (not noted in either of the above listings) in which I first encountered the Sultan's American naval constructor: Henry Wikoff, *The Reminiscences of an Idler* (New York, 1880), an entertaining autobiographical fragment by an amiable American scoundrel whose mid-century difficulties with his ex-fiancée got him time in the Genoa jail and space in the diplomatic correspondence with Piedmont.

INDEX